(Continued on back endsheets)

Dictionary of Literary Biography® • Volume One Hundred Forty-Nine

Late Nineteenth- and Early Twentieth-Century British Literary Biographers

Dictionary of Literary Biography® • Volume One Hundred Forty-Nine

Late Nineteenth- and Early Twentieth-Century British Literary Biographers

Edited by
Steven Serafin
Hunter College of the City University of New York

A Bruccoli Clark Layman Book
Gale Research Inc.
Detroit, Washington, D.C., London

Printed in the United States of America

Published simultaneously in the United Kingdom
by Gale Research International Limited
(An affiliated company of Gale Research Inc.)

The paper used in this publication meets the minimum requirements
of American National Standard for Information Sciences–Permanence
Paper for Printed Library Materials, ANSI Z39.48-1984. ∞ ™

Library of Congress Cataloging-in-Publication Data
Late nineteenth- and early twentieth-century British literary biographers / edited by Steven Serafin.
    p. cm. – (Dictionary of literary biography; v. 149)
"A Bruccoli Clark Layman book."
Includes bibliographical references and index.
ISBN 0-8103-5710-0 (alk. paper)
    1. Biography as a literary form – Bio-bibliography. 2. English prose literature – 19th century – Bio-bibliography. 3. English prose literature – 20th century – Bio-bibliography. 4. English prose literature – 19th century – Dictionaries. 5. English prose literature – 20th century – Dictionaries. 6. Biographers – Great Britain – Biography – Dictionaries. 7. Biography as a literary form – Dictionaries. I. Serafin, Steven. II. Title: Late 19th and early 20th-century British literary biographers. III. Series.
PR756.B56L38   1995
820.9'492'09034 – dc20   95-3288
                                                                                      CIP

10 9 8 7 6 5 4 3 2 1

Contents

Plan of the Series

. . . Almost the most prodigious asset of a country, and perhaps its most precious possession, is its native literary product — when that product is fine and noble and enduring.

Mark Twain*

The advisory board, the editors, and the publisher of the *Dictionary of Literary Biography* are joined in endorsing Mark Twain's declaration. The literature of a nation provides an inexhaustible resource of permanent worth. We intend to make literature and its creators better understood and more accessible to students and the reading public, while satisfying the standards of teachers and scholars.

To meet these requirements, *literary biography* has been construed in terms of the author's achievement. The most important thing about a writer is his writing. Accordingly, the entries in *DLB* are career biographies, tracing the development of the author's canon and the evolution of his reputation.

The purpose of *DLB* is not only to provide reliable information in a convenient format but also to place the figures in the larger perspective of literary history and to offer appraisals of their accomplishments by qualified scholars.

The publication plan for *DLB* resulted from two years of preparation. The project was proposed to Bruccoli Clark by Frederick C. Ruffner, president of the Gale Research Company, in November 1975. After specimen entries were prepared and typeset, an advisory board was formed to refine the entry format and develop the series rationale. In meetings held during 1976, the publisher, series editors, and advisory board approved the scheme for a comprehensive biographical dictionary of persons who contributed to North American literature. Editorial work on the first volume began in January 1977, and it was published in 1978. In order to make *DLB* more than a reference tool and to compile volumes that individually have claim to status as literary history, it was decided to organize vol-

From an unpublished section of Mark Twain's autobiography, copyright by the Mark Twain Company

umes by topic, period, or genre. Each of these free-standing volumes provides a biographical-bibliographical guide and overview for a particular area of literature. We are convinced that this organization — as opposed to a single alphabet method — constitutes a valuable innovation in the presentation of reference material. The volume plan necessarily requires many decisions for the placement and treatment of authors who might properly be included in two or three volumes. In some instances a major figure will be included in separate volumes, but with different entries emphasizing the aspect of his career appropriate to each volume. Ernest Hemingway, for example, is represented in *American Writers in Paris, 1920–1939* by an entry focusing on his expatriate apprenticeship; he is also in *American Novelists, 1910–1945* with an entry surveying his entire career. Each volume includes a cumulative index of the subject authors and articles. Comprehensive indexes to the entire series are planned.

With volume ten in 1982 it was decided to enlarge the scope of *DLB*. By the end of 1986 twenty-one volumes treating British literature had been published, and volumes for Commonwealth and Modern European literature were in progress. The series has been further augmented by the *DLB Yearbooks* (since 1981) which update published entries and add new entries to keep the *DLB* current with contemporary activity. There have also been *DLB Documentary Series* volumes which provide biographical and critical source materials for figures whose work is judged to have particular interest for students. One of these companion volumes is entirely devoted to Tennessee Williams.

We define literature as the *intellectual commerce of a nation:* not merely as belles lettres but as that ample and complex process by which ideas are generated, shaped, and transmitted. *DLB* entries are not limited to "creative writers" but extend to other figures who in their time and in their way influenced the mind of a people. Thus the series encompasses historians, journalists, publishers, and screenwriters. By this means readers of *DLB* may be aided to perceive literature not as cult scripture in the keeping of intellectual high priests but firmly positioned at the center of a nation's life.

DLB includes the major writers appropriate to each volume and those standing in the ranks immediately behind them. Scholarly and critical counsel has been sought in deciding which minor figures to include and how full their entries should be. Wherever possible, useful references are made to figures who do not warrant separate entries.

Each DLB volume has a volume editor responsible for planning the volume, selecting the figures for inclusion, and assigning the entries. Volume editors are also responsible for preparing, where appropriate, appendices surveying the major periodicals and literary and intellectual movements for their volumes, as well as lists of further readings. Work on the series as a whole is coordinated at the Bruccoli Clark Layman editorial center in Columbia, South Carolina, where the editorial staff is responsible for accuracy of the published volumes.

One feature that distinguishes DLB is the illustration policy — its concern with the iconography of literature. Just as an author is influenced by his surroundings, so is the reader's understanding of the author enhanced by a knowledge of his environment. Therefore DLB volumes include not only drawings, paintings, and photographs of authors, often depicting them at various stages in their careers, but also illustrations of their families and places where they lived. Title pages are regularly reproduced in facsimile along with dust jackets for modern authors. The dust jackets are a special feature of DLB because they often document better than anything else the way in which an author's work was perceived in its own time. Specimens of the writers' manuscripts are included when feasible.

Samuel Johnson rightly decreed that "The chief glory of every people arises from its authors." The purpose of the *Dictionary of Literary Biography* is to compile literary history in the surest way available to us — by accurate and comprehensive treatment of the lives and work of those who contributed to it.

The *DLB* Advisory Board

Introduction

Acknowledging the utilitarian nature of biography as a means to satisfy the commemorative instinct, Harold Nicolson writes in *The Development of English Biography* (1927) that the "slow and somewhat confused" evolution of the genre has been determined by what he concludes to be a series of advances and regressions. Referring to the sensitivity of biography to "the spirit of the age," Nicolson posits that the development of biography is primarily the development of the taste for biography. As noted by Nicolson, "over no form of literary composition have the requirements of the reading public exercised so marked and immediate an influence." This is exemplified by the unprecedented interest in literary figures in the wake of Samuel Johnson and James Boswell that increased the popularity of the genre in the eighteenth century. In contrast, the impact of "moral earnestness" on Victorian biography illustrates the extent to which applied orthodoxy can regulate if not stultify artistic merit as well as growth. For Nicolson the late nineteenth century initiated a revival of British literary biography, notably with the publication of James Anthony Froude's life of Thomas Carlyle (1882–1884). "With Froude," Nicolson says, "we return to biography in its purest form. Froude was not an earnest-minded man: as an historian he reacted against the scientific method in favour of the picturesque; as a biographer he reacted against the commemorative method in favour of truth."

Prior to the revival attributed to Froude, Richard D. Altick observes in *Lives and Letters: A History of Literary Biography in England and America* (1965), "there was no lack of theoretical belief in the historian's — and, by extension, the biographer's – obligation to scrutinize every piece of data before admitting it to his pages as established fact. A small handful of British literary biographers had applied the acid of critical intelligence to the error-encrusted mass of received information. But most biographers were content to print their data without worrying too much about its absolute accuracy. If they offered their readers information previously unknown, the novelty of these supposed facts tended to still any doubt of their truth; and if they drew their data from preceding biographies, they implicitly assumed that prior existence in print was warrant enough of reliability." Altick concludes that truth was not "the supreme strength" of nineteenth-century biographical writing: "The diverse forces that made biography what it was in the age combined to suppress, distort, and otherwise render mistaken, inaccurate, or incomplete the record of a life and character as mediated by a biographer from the documentary sources." Yet it is also true, Altick observes, "that a tradition of severe and exhaustive biographical scholarship persisted throughout the century, producing books which, though themselves superseded in time, laid the indispensible foundation for further inquiry."

The biographical methodology forged early in the nineteenth century by authors such as Robert Southey, Thomas Moore, Carlyle, and John Gibson Lockhart was later enhanced by Lucy Aikin, Elizabeth Cleghorn Gaskell, George Henry Lewes, and David Masson, among others, anticipating both the contribution of Froude and the emergence in the second half of the century of the professional biographer as "a writer of integrity and discipline." According to Ira Bruce Nadel in *Biography: Fiction, Fact and Form* (1984), the professional biographers combined the didactic with the ethical and then the psychological to shape a modern approach in biography. As demonstrated by John Forster and later by John Morley, Leslie Stephen, Edmund Gosse, and Hesketh Pearson, the professional biographer employed scholarly objectivity as well as critical analysis to produce an accurate description of the subject's life that simultaneously "redefined the role of the biographer from casual historian to reliable narrator." As readers came to appreciate and to expect biography of cohesiveness, authenticity, and authority, the role of the professional biographer became increasingly more solidified within the context of the genre; nonetheless, biography continued to be practiced by authors drawn to the genre for a personal or occasional purpose.

The late nineteenth and early twentieth century is noteworthy both for the unprecedented quantity of biographical works produced during the period and for the historical range of literary figures treated as subjects, extending from William Shakespeare and his contemporaries to the contemporaries of the biographers themselves. In addition, there was an increased demand for various lives of a single subject. Dissatisfaction with previous biographical treatments, often of controversial subjects, supplemented by the discovery of information offering new insight or perception into the life and work of an author accentuated the need for reassessment. Numerous authors received multiple biographical treatments: Samuel Pepys, Sir Walter Scott, William Wordsworth, Percy Bysshe Shelley, John Keats, Matthew Arnold, John Ruskin, and Charles Dickens, among others. Illustrative of the prominence afforded literary subjects by the reading public, Shakespeare, for example, was treated by Edward Dowden (1875), Frederick S. Boas (1896), Sir Sidney Lee (1898; revised and enlarged, 1915), Charles Harold Herford (1912), John Drinkwater (1933), and Pearson (1942); Robert Browning by G. K. Chesterton (1903), Dowden (1904; revised and enlarged, 1915), and Herford (1905); William Blake by Arthur Symons (1907), Chesterton (1910), Mona Wilson (1927), and John Middleton Murry (1933). As a genre, Nadel writes, "biography continually unsettles the past, maintaining its vitality through its continual correction, revision and interpretation of individual lives. Each new life is a provocation to reassess all past lives of the subject. Versions of a life are necessary stages in the evolution of the genre as well as in the understanding of the subject."

The history of literary biography, Altick writes, "records the process by which readers from era to era turn an object of literary interest — the received image of a poet, or his work itself — this way and that, each generation adopting the perspective and concentrating on the facets that are selected by its characteristic set of literary, intellectual, and ethical values." Biography, Altick adds, "affords a means of enlarging the experience which literature itself affords," illustrated in the late nineteenth century by works such as Dowden's *The Life of Percy Bysshe Shelley* (1886), George A. Aitken's *The Life of Richard Steele* (1889), W. C. Collingwood's *The Life and Work of John Ruskin* (1893), Boas's *Shakspere and his Predecessors* (1896), and Lee's *The Life of William Shakespeare* (1898). As the nineteenth-century fear of objectifying impulses was replaced by the twentieth-century belief that the disclosure of the self is a moral good, Nadel observes, biography "responded to this social and moral change by becoming, itself, more intimate, both in revealing more personal details and in presenting those details more creatively." This is evident early in the twentieth century by works such as E. V. Lucas's *The Life of Charles Lamb* (1905), Percy Lubbock's *Elizabeth Barrett Browning in her Letters* (1906), George Paston's *Mr. Pope, His Life and Times* (1909), Edward Tyas Cook's *The Life of John Ruskin* (1911), and Sir Sidney Colvin's *John Keats: His Life and Poetry* (1917). Without ques-

tion, however, the most significant event that would alter the course of biographical writing in the early twentieth century was the publication in 1918 of Lytton Strachey's *Eminent Victorians*.

"The art of literary biography," Strachey writes in the preface to *Eminent Victorians,* "seems to have fallen on evil times in England." Acknowledging the importance of the "few masterpieces" produced by British biographers, Strachey laments the absence of a biographical tradition or artistic merit. "With us," Strachey adds, "the most delicate and humane of all the branches of the art of writing has been relegated to the journeymen of letters; we do not reflect that it is perhaps as difficult to write a good life as to live one." The publication of *Eminent Victorians* generated unparalleled debate concerning the genre, but most critics agree with Altick, who stated: "After *Eminent Victorians,* biography could never be the same." As noted by Altick, *Eminent Victorians* "not only acclimatized biography to the twentieth century but — equally important — finally vindicated biography's claim to be considered an art."

In *Eminent Victorians,* Nicolson writes, Strachey "attacked the complacent credulity of the nineteenth century, and had exposed the several legends with which that objective age had flattered its own self-esteem." Nicolson is clear, however, in pointing out that Strachey's criticism was not intended to be "merely destructive." "Everybody was delighted and amused," Nicolson observes, "but when they had recovered from their amusement they realised that behind it all lay something far more serious and important — a fervent belief, for instance, in intellectual honesty; an almost revivalist dislike of the second-hand, the complacent, or the conventional; a derisive contempt for emotional opinions; a calm conviction that thought and reason are in fact the most important elements in human nature; a respect, ultimately, for man's unconquerable mind."

The new age of biography advocated by Strachey clearly resulted in a renewed emphasis on the part of the biographer with design and presentation. According to Nadel, experiment with structure, time, and point of view in biography signaled "a new biographical consciousness responsive to changes in the novel and non-fiction writing." As biography acknowledges its duality of record and narration, he adds, "it becomes a more vigorous and self-conscious literary form. But part of this consciousness is its understanding the fundamental paradox of biography, that it can gain completeness only by selectivity. Consequently, biography has displayed an increased awareness of narrative strategies and plot structures that enhance the meaning of the life to the reader."

This is exemplified by such diverse works as P. P. Howe's *The Life of William Hazlitt* (1922), Nicolson's *Byron: The Last Journey* (1924), Geoffrey Scott's *The Portrait of Zélide* (1925), Herbert Read's *Wordsworth* (1930), and A. J. A. Symons's *The Quest for Corvo* (1934).

The challenge of biography, Nadel writes, "is, how, given the tool of language on one hand and the data of a person's life on the other, the biographer can create a work of truth and pleasure." *Late Nineteenth- and Early Twentieth-Century British Literary Biographers* is designed to introduce the lives and works of those individuals who influenced the development of the genre in accepting this proposition. Merging scholarship with creativity, biography became solidified as a literary art. As noted by Altick, literary biography shapes our understanding of a writer's character and influences "the popular attitude toward literary people in general. It helps determine how, in any era, the public will look upon literary artists as a class of people, and even, to some extent, how the public will regard literature itself."

– *Steven Serafin*

Acknowledgments

This book was produced by Bruccoli Clark Layman, Inc. Karen L. Rood is the senior editor for the *Dictionary of Literary Biography* series. James W. Hipp was the in-house editor.

Production coordinator is James W. Hipp. Photography editor is Bruce Andrew Bowlin. Photographic copy work was performed by Joseph M. Bruccoli. Layout and graphics supervisor is Penney L. Haughton. Copyediting supervisor is Denise W. Edwards. Typesetting supervisor is Kathleen M. Flanagan. Systems manager is George F. Dodge. Julie E. Frick and Laura S. Pleicones are editorial associates. The production staff includes Phyllis A. Avant, Ann M. Cheschi, Melody W. Clegg, Patricia Coate, Brigitte B. de Guzman, Joyce Fowler, Laurel M. Gladden, Stephanie C. Hatchell, Kathy Lawler Merlette, Jeff Miller, Pamela D. Norton, Delores I. Plastow, Patricia F. Salisbury, and William L. Thomas, Jr.

Walter W. Ross and Robert S. McConnell did library research. They were assisted by the following librarians at the Thomas Cooper Library of the University of South Carolina: Linda Holderfield and the interlibrary-loan staff; reference-department head Virginia Weathers; reference librarians Marilee Birchfield, Stefanie Buck, Cathy Eckman, Rebecca Feind, Jill Holman, Karen Joseph, Jean Rhyne, Kwamine Washington, and Connie Widney; circulation-department head Caroline Taylor; and acquisitions-searching supervisor David Haggard.

Dictionary of Literary Biography® • Volume One Hundred Forty-Nine

Late Nineteenth- and Early Twentieth-Century British Literary Biographers

Dictionary of Literary Biography

George A. Aitken
(19 March 1860 – 16 November 1917)

Michael Mandelkern
Graduate Center of the City University of New York

BOOKS: *The Life of Richard Steele,* 2 volumes (London: Isbister, 1889; New York: Houghton, Mifflin, 1889);

The Life and Works of John Arbuthnot (Oxford: Clarendon Press, 1892);

Matthew Prior (London: Society of Archives, 1897);

Notes on the Bibliography of Pope (London: Blades, East & Blades, 1914);

Notes on the Bibliography of Matthew Prior (London: Blades, East & Blades, 1919).

OTHER: *Satires of Andrew Marvell,* edited by Aitken (London: Lawrence & Bullen, 1892; New York: Scribners, 1892);

Robert Burns, *Poetical Works,* edited by Aitken (London & New York: Bell, 1893);

Sir Richard Steele, *Richard Steele,* edited by Aitken (London: Unwin, 1894; New York: Scribners, 1894);

Poetical Works of Thomas Parnell, edited by Aitken (London & New York: Bell, 1894);

Daniel Defoe, *Due Preparations for the Plague, as well for Soul as Body,* edited by Aitken (London: Dent, 1895);

Richard Brinsley Sheridan, *The Critic: or, A Tragedy Rehearsed,* edited by Aitken (London: Dent, 1897);

Andrew Marvel, *The Poems of Andrew Marvel,* edited by Aitken (London: Lawrence & Bullen, 1898; New York: Scribners, 1898);

Daniel Defoe, *Romances and Narratives of Daniel Defoe,* edited by Aitken (London: Dent, 1898; New York: Croscup & Sterling, 1898);

Joseph Addison and others, *The Spectator,* 8 volumes, edited, with an introduction and notes, by Aitken (London: Longmans, Green, 1898);

Steele and others, *The Tatler,* 4 volumes, edited by Aitken (London: Duckworth, 1898–1899);

Jonathan Swift, *The Journal to Stella,* edited, with an introduction and notes, by Aitken (London: Methuen, 1901);

Later Stuart Tracts, edited, with an introduction, by Aitken (Westminster: Constable, 1903);

Sheridan, *The School for Scandal,* edited, with preface and notes, by Aitken (London: Dent, 1911).

A Victorian public servant and man of letters, George A. Aitken was an expert on the Queen Anne period of English literature, although he also did much scholarly work involving the literature of the Restoration. He was the author of *The Life of Richard Steele* (1889), *The Life and Works of John Arbuthnot* (1892), and forty-six entries in the *Dictionary of National Biography* (*DNB*), which were written between 1892 and 1901, and the editor of works of numerous authors, among them Andrew Marvell, Robert Burns, Thomas Parnell, Richard Brinsley Sheridan, Daniel Defoe, and Jonathan Swift.

George Atherton Aitken was born in Barkingside, Essex, on 19 March 1860 and was the only son of John Aitken and Mary Ann Elizabeth Salmon. He attended King's College School and University College, London, from 1879 to 1880 and 1882 to 1883, respectively. He won numerous awards while a student there, including the junior- and senior-class prizes. In 1888 he entered the secretary's office of the General Post Office. The following year he published the biographical work for which he is probably best known, his *Life of Richard Steele.* It is a detailed, leisurely (some critics would say tediously) written work, executed in a manner similar to that which James Boswell employed in the *Life of Samuel*

Johnson, LL.D. (1791). Whenever Aitken can use actual documents in relating the story of Steele's life, he does, and he supplies the connecting portions on his own. The documents to which he had recourse were the product of the exhaustive nature of his research. The *DNB* comments that Aitken's biography is "a work, of extraordinary patience in research, which practically exhausts the facts of the subject."

Steele was one of the most famous men of the Queen Anne era, a gentleman noted as much for his personal weaknesses as for his excellencies of character. Steele and Joseph Addison perfected the periodical essay, a literary form the influence of which upon the British reading public — not to mention future authors such as Samuel Johnson, whose essays in *The Rambler* and *The Idler* were heavily indebted to Steele and Addison — was incalculable. Aitken included the history of Steele's parents (Aitken shared the English fascination with genealogy and went into Steele's in considerable detail); Steele's life from his birth in March 1672 to his early education, attained through the aid of his uncle Henry Gascoigne, at the Charterhouse where he met Addison; the career of the two friends at Oxford; Steele's abandonment of Oxford for the army; his career as a writer, ranging from his early publication of *The Christian Hero* (1701) to his career as a playwright (Aitken dwells at length upon Steele's largely successful efforts to "clean up" the stage, which, in the era of Charles II, had been primarily renowned for its bawdiness) and, most notably, his foray into the world of the periodical essay; his complex political career; his two marriages; and, finally, his frequent acquisition of debts, which, along with his ailing health, caused his removal to Wales, where he died on 1 September 1729.

A high point of the narrative is the series of letters which Steele wrote to his second wife, "Prue," letters which, in their intensity of feeling, show Steele to have been a man of remarkable depth of sentiment and, as such, a true precursor of the eighteenth-century "Man of Feeling," a character personified later in the century by figures such as Boswell and Jean-Jacques Rousseau, as well as numerous characters found in literature, including, for example, the hero of Johann Wolfgang von Goethe's *The Sorrows of Young Werther* (1774). In a typical letter Steele writes: "The Vainest Woman upon Earth never saw in her Glasse half the attractions which I veiw in you, your Air, y^r Shape, Your Every glance Motion and Gesture have such peculiar Graces that you possesse my whole Soul and I know no life but in the hopes of your approbation . . .

I love y^u with the Sincerest passion that ever enter'd the Heart of Man." Indeed, in their reverence for a woman of exemplary moral virtue, the letters depict just the kind of edifying instruction at which Steele aimed, and which he often accomplished, in his periodical essays, such as those in *The Tatler,* in which he tried to improve the morals and manners of his readers.

Assessing Steele's literary accomplishment, Aitken writes, "Steele's literary fame rests chiefly upon his essays." He adds, "His plays are full of excellent humour, but we cannot help feeling that there is a certain weakness in them all as plays, due sometimes to an over-didactic strain, and sometimes to the improbability of the plot." Aitken writes that Steele was also not at his best as either a poet or as a political pamphleteer, although he was not without talent at either. Finally, he writes, perhaps describing the exact nature of Steele's contribution to literature better than anyone else has: "What he wrote is always of interest, and often exercises a fascination over us through the earnest manner in which he speaks from the heart of the questions that most concern mankind; we feel the author to be a friend, for he describes the actual life that he saw around him, and the whole is told with a kindly humour and genuine pathos easily distinguishable by their large-heartedness and truth."

Assessing his character, Aitken writes, "He was thriftless and often in debt." However, Aitken finds ample grounds upon which to pardon Steele. He writes, "His income . . . was for the most part fluctuating and uncertain, and until he had reached the prime of life he was decidedly poor." Aitken is also quick to add, "His difficulties, too, were due much more to his open-handed generosity than to prodigality." As for Steele's drinking — an aspect of his character for which he was often criticized — Aitken writes, "It must be borne in mind that the general practice as to drinking was at that time very different from what it is now." Commenting further on the tendency toward licentiousness which Steele occasionally evinced and which seems out of keeping with his character, Aitken writes, "The inconsistency which was so often evident between [Steele's] private life and his published writings arose from a certain weakness of character; his purpose was consistently good, but he had not always sufficient strength of will to enable him to carry it out." Aitken concludes — thinking of Steele's open-heartedness, a characteristic which his letters to his second wife alone are enough to prove — "Many of those who expressed contempt or pity for Steele would have been truer and better men if they had possessed

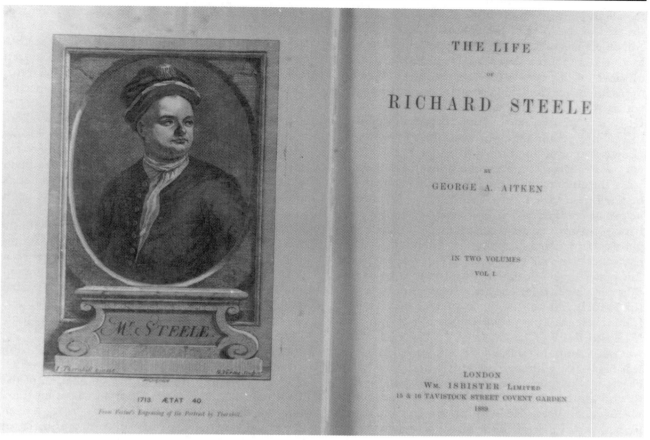

Title page and frontispiece for Aitken's biography of the eighteenth-century playwright and essayist

more of the noble and charming traits which stand out so clearly in his character."

In 1890 Aitken became private secretary to Sir Arthur Blackwood, K.C.B., the permanent secretary of the General Post Office. Later that year he transferred to the Home Office, an organization which was entrusted with supervising child welfare. During this time, however, he was not idle in his literary pursuits. In 1892 he published *The Life and Works of John Arbuthnot*. About a third of the work consists of Aitken's life of the early-eighteenth-century physician and wit, the other two-thirds being devoted to Arbuthnot's works. Aitken had to exercise judgment, as he later would in editing *Romances and Narratives of Daniel Defoe* (1898), in selecting from Arbuthnot's works. Although not nearly as prolific as Defoe — few writers have been — Arbuthnot, a self-effacing and generous man, not only contributed much to works by his friends without taking credit, but he even wrote entire works himself without affixing his name to them.

Like *The Life of Richard Steele*, the biographical portion of *The Life and Works of John Arbuthnot* relies heavily upon actual documents, some of which are among the most entertaining portions of the work. Jonathan Swift, for example, frequently mentions Arbuthnot in his *Journal to Stella* (1766), from which Aitken quotes. He also reprints many of the letters which Arbuthnot exchanged with Alexander Pope and Swift, among others, testifying to the close friendships which Arbuthnot had with them. Another highlight is the description of Arbuthnot which Aitken reprints from a letter by Lord Chesterfield, another Arbuthnot friend and correspondent, although, unlike Arbuthnot, he was not a pious Christian.

Combining the documents with his own narration — as he did in his *Life of Richard Steele* — Aitken tells the story of Arbuthnot's life, including his attendance upon Queen Anne and Prince George (later George I). Aitken is careful to intersperse the narrative with frequent historical references. He also has much to say about Arbuthnot's literary works, or rather, those works which have been attributed to him. In particular, Aitken discusses the *John Bull* pamphlets (1712), a satirical allegory written about political events in England which came at the end of the War of the Spanish Succession. As Aitken explains, "The object of these pamphlets was to give a humourous account, from the Tory point of view, of the events leading up to the negotiations for peace, and to recommend the proposals which were ultimately embodied in the Treaty of Utrecht." Arbuthnot uses comic names in referring to real-life personages, substituting, for example, "Lewis Baboon" for Louis XIV, the French king who was descended from the house of Bourbon. Since the authorship of the John Bull pamphlets can be attributed to Arbuthnot with relative certainty, he can be credited with inventing the term *John Bull,* which has become a synonym for the English people. Aitken writes, "Arbuthnot . . . drew the character, which has ever since been accepted as a type, of this honest, plain-dealing fellow, choleric, bold, and of a very inconstant temper. He was not afraid of the French; but he was apt to quarrel with his best friends, especially if they pretended to govern him. If he was flattered he could be led like a lamb. He was quick, and understood his business well; but he was careless with his accounts, and was often cheated by partners and servants. He loved his bottle and his diversion, and no man spent his money more generously. He was generally ruddy and plump, with a pair of cheeks like a trumpeter."

Arbuthnot was a member of the Martin Scriblerus Club, the group of wits which included Pope and Swift and whose goal, when its task was completed, was, in Pope's words, "to have ridiculed all the false tastes in learning, under the character of a man of capacity enough, that had dipped into every art and science, but injudiciously in each." Aitken discusses the *Memoirs of Martin Scriblerus* (1741), which he attributes to Arbuthnot. He expresses some appreciation for the work, writing, "The *Memoirs* are excellent in their kind, and the mock gravity is admirably maintained." He does not agree, however, with the high position which some have accorded the work, and he writes, "the *Memoirs* . . . do not seem to me more interesting than the *History of John Bull,* and they are marred by coarse touches not usually found in Arbuthnot's writings, though common enough in those of some of his friends." (Objecting to a work because of its "coarseness" was rather a constant preoccupation with Aitken.) Furthermore, in according the memoirs a low status, Aitken, as he mentions, is concurring with Johnson, who, in his *Life of Pope* (1781), argues "that the want of more of the *Memoirs* need not be lamented" (only the first book was completed or, in any event, published). Johnson's criticism was

twofold: "the follies ridiculed were hardly practised, and the satire could only be understood by the learned." For Johnson, however, both of these criticisms were one in the end: the memoirs "has been little read," he wrote, "or when read has been forgotten, as no man could be wiser, better, or merrier by remembering it."

Another work to which Aitken devotes attention, logically enough, is Pope's *Epistle to Dr. Arbuthnot* (1735). Pope's epistle, a poem which was addressed to Arbuthnot, who was on his deathbed when it was written, and in which Pope defends himself against attacks which had been made upon him by Lady Mary Wortley Montagu and Lord Hervey, is perhaps the work with which Arbuthnot's name is most closely identified. Aitken writes that the poem "is in the form of a dialogue between Pope and his friend, though very few words are put into Arbuthnot's mouth." It has often been asserted that Arbuthnot's reputation for honesty and integrity provided Pope with credibility in fending off his attackers.

In the conclusion of the biographical portion Aitken makes the commendatory remarks which one would expect to find in the summation of the life of one of the best-loved individuals of his time, and then concludes that Arbuthnot's "story — even if we had not the lives of Addison, of Steele, of [George] Berkeley, and of others of less note — ought to show how many reservations must be made when we speak of the materialism and hardness of the eighteenth century." Apparently Aitken saw Arbuthnot's intelligence and nobleness of spirit — qualities which endeared him to later English writers such as Johnson and William Makepeace Thackeray — as representative of his era, contrary to type.

Between 1892 and 1901, a time during which he became secretary to the Reformatory and Industrial Schools Departmental Committee and the Inebriate Reformatories Committee (in 1898) and served as private secretary to the permanent undersecretary of state, Sir Kenelm Digby, K.C.B. (from 1896 to 1901), Aitken wrote numerous entries for the *Dictionary of National Biography.* Several of them have to do with literary figures, including the playwright William Wycherley, author of *The Country Wife* (1675), which Aitken calls "the most brilliant but the most indecent of Wycherley's works." Speaking of the play's licentiousness, Aitken refers to Steele, who in *The Tatler* "said that the character of the profligate Horner was a good representation of the age in which the comedy was written, when gallantry in the pursuit of women was the best recommendation at court," and then cannot forbear adding himself, "A man of probity in such manners would have been a monster." Aitken also discusses Wycherley's friendships with John Dryden and Pope, and he asserts that several lines in Pope's *Essay on Criticism* refer to Wycherley.

Aitken writes, "It is Wycherley's serious intentness that at once marks him off from the brilliance of [William] Congreve, the boisterousness and humour of [Sir John] Vanbrugh, and the pleasing good fellowship of [George] Farquhar. As [William] Hazlitt says, in Congreve the workmanship is more striking than the material, but in Wycherley's plays we remember the characters more than what they say." Returning to the subject that was evidently most troubling to him, Aitken writes, "In Wycherley's plays the immorality is more realistic, and therefore more harmful, than in other Restoration dramas." He adds, however, referring to the aspect of Wycherley's art which was praised by Hazlitt, "his vigour and clearness of delineation are his greatest merits."

Aitken was also the author of the *DNB* entry on Thomas Shadwell, the Restoration playwright and poet laureate most remembered for his quarrel with Dryden, about whom the latter wrote his masterful satiric poem *MacFlecknoe, or a Satire on the True Blue Protestant Poet, T.S.* (1682). Aitken narrates the history of the dispute between the two in objective, dispassionate terms; he is careful not to take sides. Later he writes, "Estimates of Shadwell's literary powers differ widely. . . . His comedies are useful for the vivid account they give of the life of his time. Although no poet, he was, as [Sir Walter] Scott says, an acute observer of nature, and he showed considerable skill in invention." Returning to the bawdiness of Restoration drama — a characteristic not only of the plays but of the period — by which Aitken was evidently disgusted, he concludes, "[Shadwell] seems to have been naturally coarse, and was grossly indecent without designing to corrupt." The final comment seems to be the nicest thing Aitken could say about him.

Another minor literary figure best remembered today for her connection with Dryden, whose entry Aitken wrote in the *DNB,* is the poet Anne Killigrew. Killigrew, who died young, also had the serendipity of being immortalized in Dryden's ode *To the Pious Memory of the Accomplished Young Lady, Mrs. Anne Killigrew* (1686), about which Aitken writes, "Johnson considered this ode to be the noblest in our language — a judgment then bold and now scarcely intelligible." Aitken's statement in itself is rather bold, considering the high reputation which

the poem enjoys today. Of interest is the fact that Aitken was also the author of the *DNB* entry on Anne Killigrew's father, Henry, a clergyman and occasional poet and playwright.

An interesting personage who may not be a literary figure himself but was the basis for one of the most famous characters in literature — a character who, indeed, is more famous than he is — and whom Aitken memorialized in the *DNB* is Alexander Selkirk, whose life was the basis for Defoe's *Robinson Crusoe* (1719). Aitken may have been led to write about Selkirk because of his connection with Steele; the two men knew each other. Steele wrote about Selkirk in a number of *The Englishman* (1713), a fact of which Defoe — Steele's chief competitor in the field of the periodical essay — no doubt was aware. Aitken writes, "Steele describes [Selkirk] as a man of good sense, with a strong and serious but cheerful disposition." Steele's description is especially important because Aitken maintains that "despite some apocryphal stories, there is nothing to show that Defoe knew anything of Selkirk beyond what had been published by [Woodes] Rogers, [Edward] Cooke, and Steele." Rogers and Cooke were ship's captains whose published accounts of their travels mentioned Selkirk. In spite of the lack of firsthand experience which Aitken asserts that Defoe had with Selkirk, Aitken concludes that *Robinson Crusoe* is one of the "best memorials" to Selkirk's life.

Yet another literary figure about whom Aitken wrote for the *DNB* is the poet Thomas Parnell, who was also a member of the Martin Scriblerus Club. Parnell's contribution to the club was minimal, owing to the indolence of his disposition; Aitken writes, "Swift complained that Parnell was too idle to contribute much to the Scriblerus scheme." Instead of focusing on the club, Aitken's entry focuses, logically enough, on the relationship which Parnell had with Pope exclusive of it. Pope rewrote some of Parnell's poems, which he published after Parnell's death. However, given Pope's superiority as a poet, Parnell is more likely to be remembered not for the contributions which Pope made to his work but for the contributions which he made to Pope's (an able classical scholar, Parnell helped him with his translation [1715–1720] of the *Iliad*).

Aitken quotes Oliver Goldsmith's line in reference to Parnell's character, stating that he "was the most capable man in the world to make the happiness of those he conversed with, and the least able to secure his own." Aitken writes, continuing the assessment, "[Parnell's] company was much sought by men of both parties, for he was agreeable, generous, and sincere. When he had a fit of spleen he withdrew to a remote part of the country, that he might not annoy others." Interestingly, Aitken mentions and pardons Parnell's drinking, as he does with Steele, writing that "Pope ascribes the intemperance to dejection occasioned by the death of Parnell's wife." He adds, in further extenuation of Parnell's conduct, "the vice was apparently neither gross nor notorious." Referring to his poetic achievement, Aitken writes, "Parnell's work is marked by sweetness, refined sensibility, musical and fluent versification, and high moral tone. There are many faulty lines and awkward expressions, and there would have been more had not Pope revised the more important pieces."

While Aitken cannot be said to have broken any new ground in terms of the methodological approach to biography, he was nevertheless an important contributor to the field in terms of his research. There is no doubt he added immeasurably to our knowledge of figures such as Steele and Arbuthnot. Furthermore, in his editions he presented works which were not then widely available, some of which have not reappeared in more modern editions, and, hence, are still used today.

In 1902 Aitken was appointed life governor of University College, and in the following year he married Emma Cawthorne. In 1905 he returned to the Home Office, serving on the Committee on Grants to Reformatory and Industrial Schools. He also served as British delegate at the International Conference at Paris on White Slave Traffic in 1910. In 1911 he became a member of the Royal Victorian Order. That same year he again served as British delegate, this time at the International Congress of Brussels on the Protection of Child Life, and returned to the Home Office, as head of the organization. In 1914 he became chairman of the Committee on Superannuation of Officers of Reformatory and Industrial Schools. During this time he continued to pursue his literary interests and published *Notes on the Bibliography of Pope* (1914) and *Notes on the Bibliography of Matthew Prior* (1919). He died in London on 16 November 1917.

Richard Aldington
(8 July 1892 – 27 July 1962)

Marcy L. Tanter

University of Massachusetts – Amherst

See also the Aldington entries in *DLB 20: British Poets, 1914–1945; DLB 36: British Novelists, 1890–1929: Modernists;* and *DLB 100: Modern British Essayists, Second Series.*

BOOKS: *Images (1910–1915)* (London: Poetry Bookshop, 1915); revised and enlarged as *Images Old and New* (Boston: Four Seas, 1916); enlarged again as *Images* (London: Egoist Press, 1919);

Reverie: A Little Book of Poems for H. D. (Cleveland: Clerk's Press, 1917);

The Love Poems of Myrrhine and Konallis, A Cycle of Prose Poems Written after the Greek Manner (Cleveland: Clerk's Press, 1917); enlarged as *The Love of Myrrhine and Konallis and Other Prose Poems* (Chicago: Covici, 1926);

Images of War: A Book of Poems (Westminster: C. W. Beaumont, 1919; enlarged edition, London: Allen & Unwin, 1919; Boston: Four Seas, 1920); enlarged as *War and Love (1915–1918)* (Boston: Four Seas, 1921);

Images of Desire (London: Elkin Mathews, 1919);

Exile and Other Poems (London: Allen & Unwin, 1923; Boston: Four Seas, 1924);

Literary Studies and Reviews (London: Allen & Unwin, 1924; New York: MacVeagh/Dial, 1924);

A Fool i' the Forest: A Phantasmagoria (London: Allen & Unwin, 1925; New York: MacVeagh/Dial, 1925);

Voltaire (London: Routledge, 1925; London: Routledge / New York: Dutton, 1925);

French Studies and Reviews (London: Allen & Unwin, 1926; New York: MacVeagh/Dial, 1926);

D. H. Lawrence: An Indiscretion (Seattle: University of Washington Book Store, 1927); republished as *D. H. Lawrence* (London: Chatto & Windus, 1930); revised and enlarged as *D. H. Lawrence: An Appreciation* (Harmondsworth, U.K.: Penguin, 1950);

Remy de Gourmont: A Modern Man of Letters (Seattle: University of Washington Book Store, 1928);

Collected Poems (New York: Covici-Friede, 1928; London: Allen & Unwin, 1929);

Death of a Hero: A Novel (New York: Covici-Friede, 1929; London: Chatto & Windus, 1929); unexpurgated edition, 2 volumes (Paris: Babou & Kahane, 1930);

The Eaten Heart (Chapelle-Reanville: Hours Press, 1929; enlarged edition, London: Chatto & Windus, 1933);

At All Costs (London: Heinemann, 1930);

Last Straws (Paris: Hours Press, 1930);

Two Stories (London: Elkin Mathews & Marrot, 1930);

Love and the Luxembourg (New York: Covici-Friede, 1930); republished as *A Dream in the Luxembourg* (London: Chatto & Windus, 1930);

Roads to Glory (London: Chatto & Windus, 1930; Garden City, N.Y.: Doubleday, Doran, 1931);

The Colonel's Daughter: A Novel (London: Chatto & Windus, 1931; Garden City, N.Y.: Doubleday, Doran, 1931);

Stepping Heavenward: A Record (Florence: Orioli, 1931; London: Chatto & Windus, 1931; Garden City, N.Y.: Doubleday, Doran, 1932);

Soft Answers: Five Stories (London: Chatto & Windus, 1932; Garden City, N.Y.: Doubleday, Doran, 1932);

All Men Are Enemies: A Romance (London: Chatto & Windus, 1933; Garden City, N.Y.: Doubleday, Doran, 1933);

The Poems of Richard Aldington (Garden City, N.Y.: Doubleday, Doran, 1934);

Women Must Work: A Novel (London: Chatto & Windus, 1934; Garden City, N.Y.: Doubleday, Doran, 1934);

D. H. Lawrence: A Complete List of His Works, Together with a Critical Appreciation (London: Heinemann, 1935);

Artifex: Sketches and Ideas (London: Chatto & Windus, 1935; Garden City, N.Y.: Doubleday, Doran, 1936);

Richard Aldington

Life Quest (London: Chatto & Windus, 1935; Garden City, N.Y.: Doubleday, Doran, 1935);

Life of a Lady: A Play, by Aldington and Derek Patmore (Garden City, N.Y.: Doubleday, Doran, 1936; London: Putnam, 1936);

The Crystal World (London: Heinemann, 1937; Garden City, N.Y.: Doubleday, Doran, 1938);

Very Heaven (London & Toronto: Heinemann, 1937; Garden City, N.Y.: Doubleday, Doran, 1937);

Seven Against Reeves: A Comedy-Farce (London & Toronto: Heinemann, 1938; Garden City, N.Y.: Doubleday, Doran, 1938);

Rejected Guest: A Novel (New York: Viking, 1939; London & Toronto: Heinemann, 1939);

W. Somerset Maugham: An Appreciation (Garden City, N.Y.: Doubleday, Doran, 1939);

Life for Life's Sake: A Book of Reminiscences (New York: Viking, 1941; London: Cassell, 1968);

The Duke: Being an Account of the Life & Achievements of Arthur Wellesley, 1st Duke of Wellington (New York: Viking, 1943); republished as *Wellington: Being an Account of the Life & Achievements of Arthur Wellesley, 1st Duke of Wellington* (London & Toronto: Heinemann, 1946);

The Romance of Casanova: A Novel (New York: Duell, Sloan & Pearce, 1946; London & Toronto: Heinemann, 1947);

Four English Portraits, 1801–1851 (London: Evans, 1948);

The Complete Poems of Richard Aldington (London: Wingate, 1948);

Jane Austen (Pasadena: Ampersand Press, 1948);

The Strange Life of Charles Waterton, 1782–1865 (London: Evans, 1949; New York: Duell, Sloan & Pearce, 1949);

Portrait of a Genius But . . . The Life of D. H. Lawrence, 1885–1930 (London: Heinemann, 1950); republished as *D. H. Lawrence: Portrait of a Genius But . . .* (New York: Duell, Sloan & Pearce, 1950);

Aldington, second from right, at a house party in 1914, with, from left, Victor Plarr, Sturge Moore, W. B. Yeats, Wilfred Scawen Blunt, Ezra Pound, and F. S. Flint (Fitzwilliam Museum)

Pinorman: Personal Recollections of Norman Douglas, Pino Orioli, and Charles Prentice (London: Heinemann, 1954);

Ezra Pound and T. S. Eliot: A Lecture (Hurst, Berkshire: Peacocks Press, 1954);

Lawrence of Arabia: A Biographical Enquiry (London: Collins, 1955; Chicago: Regnery, 1955);

A. E. Housman and W. B. Yeats: Two Lectures (Hurst, Berkshire: Peacocks Press, 1955);

Introduction to Mistral (London: Heinemann, 1956; Carbondale: Southern Illinois University Press, 1960);

Frauds (London: Heinemann, 1957);

Portrait of a Rebel: The Life and Works of Robert Louis Stevenson (London: Evans, 1957);

Richard Aldington: Selected Critical Writings, 1928–1960, edited by Alister Kershaw (Carbondale: Southern Illinois University Press, 1970).

OTHER: *Letters of Madame De Sévigné to Her Daughter and Her Friends,* selected, with an introductory essay, by Aldington (London: Routledge, 1927; New York: Brentano, 1927);

D. H. Lawrence, *Last Poems,* edited by Aldington and G. Orioli (New York: Viking, 1933; London: Secker, 1933);

D. H. Lawrence: Selected Poems, edited by Aldington (London: Secker, 1934);

The Spirit of Place: An Anthology Compiled from the Prose of D. H. Lawrence, edited, with an introduction, by Aldington (London: Heinemann, 1935);

The Viking Book of Poetry of the English-Speaking World, edited by Aldington (New York: Viking, 1941); republished as *Poetry of the English Speaking World* (London: Heinemann, 1947);

The Portable Oscar Wilde, edited by Aldington (New York: Viking, 1946); republished as *Oscar Wilde: Selected Works* (London: Heinemann, 1946);

Walter Pater: Selected Works, edited by Aldington (London: Heinemann, 1948; New York: Duell, Sloan & Pearce, 1948).

TRANSLATIONS: *The Poems of Anyte of Tegea* (London: Egoist Press, 1915; Cleveland: Clerk's Press, 1917);

Feodor Sogolub (Feodor Teternikov), *The Little Demon,* translated by Aldington and John Cournos (New York: Knopf, 1916);

Greek Songs in the Manner of Anacreon (London: Egoist Press, 1919);

Medallions in Clay (New York: Knopf, 1921); republished as *Medallions from Anyte of Tegea, Meleager of Gadara, the Anacreontea: Latin Poets of the Renaissance* (London: Chatto & Windus, 1930);

French Comedies of the XVIIIth Century (London: Routledge, 1923; London: Routledge / New York: Dutton, 1923);

Cyrano de Bergerac, *Voyages to the Moon and the Sun* (London: Routledge / New York: Dutton, 1923; London: Routledge, 1927);

Pierre Choderlos de Laclos, *Dangerous Acquaintances (Les Liaisons Dangereuses)* (London: Routledge, 1924; London: Routledge / New York: Dutton, 1924);

The Mystery of the Nativity, Translated from the Liégeois of the XVth Century (London: Allen & Unwin, 1924);

Pierre Custot, *Sturly* (London: Cape, 1924; Boston: Houghton Mifflin, 1924);

The Fifteen Joys of Marriage, Ascribed to Antoine De La Sale, c.1388–c.1462 (London: Routledge, 1926; London: Routledge / New York: Dutton, 1926);

Voltaire, *Candide and Other Romances* (London: Routledge, 1927; London: Routledge / New York: Dutton, 1927);

Letters of Voltaire and Frederick the Great (London: Routledge, 1927; New York: Brentano, 1927);

Remy de Gourmont: Selections from All His Works (Chicago: Covici, 1928; London: Chatto & Windus, 1932);

Julien Benda, *The Treason of the Intellectuals (La Trahison des clercs)* (New York: Morrow, 1928);

Euripides, *Alcestis* (London: Chatto & Windus, 1930);

The Decameron of Giovanni Boccaccio (New York: Covici-Friede, 1930; London: Putnam, 1930);

Larousse Encyclopedia of Mythology, translated by Aldington and Delano Ames (New York: Prometheus Press, 1959).

During his lifetime Richard Aldington was praised for his poetry, novels, biographies, criticism, translations, and essays. He is also credited with being one of the founders of the Imagist movement in poetry, which began in 1912. Each of his eleven biographies reflects not only Aldington's dedication to his writing but also his intense interest in his subjects. Several of the biographies, especially those on D. H. Lawrence and Voltaire, remain important. Just prior to his death in 1962, Aldington's popularity waned; the 1980s saw the beginning of a reappraisal of his work that has continued into the 1990s.

Edward Godfrey Aldington (he adopted the name Richard during his boyhood) was born in Portsmouth, England, on 8 July 1892. He was the first of four children born to Albert Edward Aldington, a solicitor, and Jessie May Godfrey Aldington, later an amateur novelist. He was exposed to literature early through books in his father's library, which inspired him, at age fifteen, to begin to write his own. Aldington was raised in Dover, and the family moved to London when he was seventeen. He entered University College, London, in 1910 but had to leave after a year when his father's finances suffered several blows. Although the circumstances left Aldington somewhat impoverished, he was made to fend for himself and discovered that he could earn a living by his pen.

In 1911 Aldington met Ezra Pound, of whom he later said in his autobiography *Life for Life's Sake: A Book of Reminiscences* (1941), "Ezra was the first poet I met on equal terms." During the spring of 1912 Aldington met with Pound and Hilda Doolittle (H. D.) on a regular basis to share and discuss poetry; it was during one of these meetings that the Imagist movement was born. He later claimed that his part in the movement was minimal and that H. D.'s poetry was the true Imagist poetry. Aldington and H. D. were married on 18 October 1913.

Aldington's literary pursuits continued, and he became the assistant editor of the *Egoist* (originally the *New Freewoman*) when Rebecca West resigned the post in October 1913. As he began his work for the *Egoist,* Aldington was developing a friendship with F. S. Flint, who encouraged Aldington, Pound, and H. D. to read contemporary French poetry. At this time Aldington translated some prose by the poet Remy de Gourmont, with whom he had established a correspondence.

Until June 1916 Aldington devoted much of his time to his job and to reading French literature, to translating French and Latin poetry, and to writing his own poetry. He entered the army with a book of poetry in print – *Images (1910–1915),* published in 1915. During his service as a British soldier in World War I, Aldington continued to write both poetry and prose. When he was discharged at

Aldington in 1932

the end of the war, he went to work as the French-literature critic for the *Times Literary Supplement,* where he later helped T. S. Eliot find work.

His marriage to H. D. had been deteriorating for some years, and they separated by 1919, although they did not divorce until 1938 and remained friends until her death in 1961. After the divorce he married Netta Patmore, and their daughter, Catherine, was born in 1938. They separated in 1950 and ultimately divorced, although they maintained close contact.

The 1920s were a characteristically prolific period for Aldington. Aside from his work for the *Times Literary Supplement,* he wrote many reviews and articles for other publications, translated several French and Italian works, brought out books of poems such as *Exile and Other Poems* (1923) and *A Fool i' the Forest: A Phantasmagoria* (1925), and wrote his first biographies: *Voltaire* (1925), *D. H. Lawrence: An Indiscretion* (1927),

and *Remy de Gourmont: A Modern Man of Letters* (1928).

Voltaire is written to "provide a guide-book to the continent of Voltaire." Aldington's approach is to make the "philosophe" accessible; he states in the introduction that the volume is meant to condense the density of information on Voltaire for the reader who has neither the time nor the inclination to make a "close study" of the writer and his work. The biography is divided into two parts: life, which traces Voltaire's relationships with the "enlightened despots" of his time; and works, in which Aldington states that "his fertility alone is a problem of great interest" and proceeds to delineate skillfully Voltaire's worth as a great writer. Throughout, Aldington presents Voltaire as a man possessed of a great mind and adroitly seeks to dispel the "legende" that precludes many readers from enjoying *Candide;* perhaps the focus is weighed too heavily in favor of Voltaire's

13

greatness, but Aldington's admiration for his subject does not cloud his argument that "the extinction of a flaming spirit like his . . . is a painful thought to entertain."

Aldington's next two biographies were written for the University of Washington's series of chapbooks. Because he knew Lawrence as a friend, *D. H. Lawrence: An Indiscretion* is an intensely personal appraisal of the man and his works, written "entirely from my own feelings and [I] allowed my words to flow spontaneously." He offers a brutally honest assessment of his friend's character, calling him a heretic, "a true Anarchist," and then announcing, "he is rude, cantankerous, vain, presumptuous, pigheaded, satirical, but he is a man, a savage defender of his own liberty; and I love him for it." Aldington's praise of Lawrence may be exaggerated somewhat, but he equates Lawrence's greatness as a writer with his ability to characterize himself candidly in his novels. He makes no apologies for highlighting Lawrence's "positive qualities," declaring that they are the very thing that "make Lawrence's books a genuine contribution to literature." As with Voltaire, Aldington speaks of Lawrence as a philosopher and details the assertion with examples from his novels coupled with a defense of the author against people who fail to acknowledge him as a genius, who "cannot believe that one of the gods is moving among *them*." In his autobiography Aldington notes Lawrence's approval of this short pamphlet, although Lawrence wrote to Aldington that it was more about the author than his subject. Aldington was inclined to agree. In his essay "Richard Aldington and D. H. Lawrence," Norman T. Gates sees in this precursor to Aldington's more substantial work on Lawrence "one of the best general critical assessments of Lawrence's writing."

The brief biography of Gourmont is written from a more critical perspective. Although he and Aldington corresponded for some years prior to Gourmont's death, the two never met; Aldington admired Gourmont as "one of France's most able and industrious journeymen of letters." From the start of the pamphlet Aldington admits that Gourmont "will never be a subject for the novelist-critics," but he sees worth in Gourmont as a philosopher — not in the sense that he sees Voltaire and Lawrence as philosophers, but in the sense that Gourmont was, for Aldington, a sort of French Everyman who "tried to unite in the flow of one personality the various streams of French intellectual and artistic life." Aldington sees Gourmont as becoming a mature artist late in life, which relegates him to "journeyman" status, although he goes to great pains to stress that,

had Gourmont found his genius earlier, he might have been a great artist. The influences upon him that Aldington notes, such as Villers de Lisle Adam, Herbert Spencer, and Stéphane Mallarmé, appear as more of a defense of Gourmont's genius than as his touchstones. This is perhaps the least interesting of Aldington's early biographies, as it lacks the charm and accessibility of the Voltaire and the Lawrence. Aldington's small book on Gourmont was not so well received as his Gourmont translations that followed in 1928, although Harry T. Moore has called it a "valuable introduction" to Gourmont's work.

By 1928 Aldington felt that England was no longer a country in which he wanted to live and decided to take "the long-meditated but grave step of quitting England 'for ever.' " He moved to Paris and, while still writing reviews for the London *Times,* published his first novel, *Death of a Hero,* in 1929. From 1929 until 1939 Aldington's focus as a writer was on the novel, while he continued to work in other genres. His novels satirize the English society he had rejected in favor of a life on the Continent and, when that became tedious for him in 1935, in the United States. He gave up novel writing in September 1939, as he felt that on the brink of war "it would be absurd to denounce calamity; ignoble to satirize people fighting for their existence." He did publish *The Romance of Casanova,* a historical novel, in 1946, but it was not successful.

In 1941 Aldington published his autobiography, *Life for Life's Sake;* it is an engaging book, though he steers away from discussing personal details such as his failed marriage to H. D. The style and tone of the autobiography are characteristic of those found in his early and late biographies; Aldington strives to engage the reader with anecdotes and analyses of historical details while creating an honest understanding of the man or woman he is discussing. Despite being autobiography, *Life for Life's Sake* is a more modest account of Aldington's life than he believed it was. In the dedication he claims that "an autobiography is a license to be egotistical," but throughout the book it is Aldington's friends who are warmly praised, not his own accomplishments. The autobiography reflects a recognition of his talents as a writer yet acknowledges the help and encouragement of many friends, editors, and colleagues such as Pound, H. D., Herbert Read, and Eliot. The book ends with Aldington's claim that "I have not yet succeeded in writing either a poem or prose book which satisfied me entirely, but it is fun to go on trying." At the end of 1941 Aldington became interested in writing a biography of the duke of Wellington, which he hoped would help

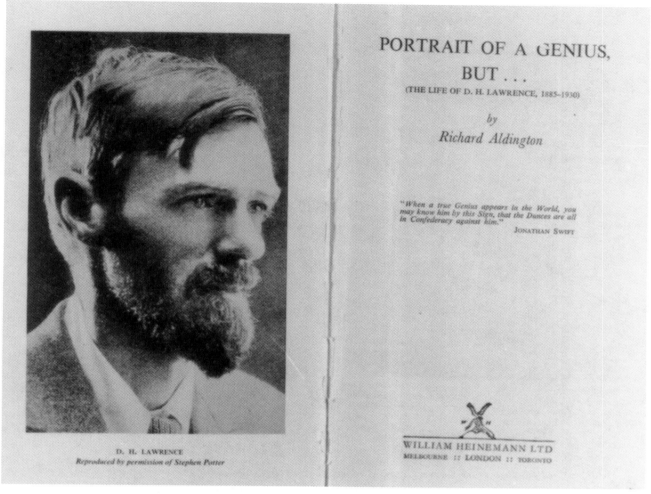

D. H. LAWRENCE
Reproduced by permission of Stephen Potter

PORTRAIT OF A GENIUS,
BUT . . .
(THE LIFE OF D. H. LAWRENCE, 1885-1930)

by

Richard Aldington

*"When a true Genius appears in the World, you
may know him by this Sign, that the Dunces are all
in Confederacy against him."*

JONATHAN SWIFT

WILLIAM HEINEMANN LTD
MELBOURNE :: LONDON :: TORONTO

Frontispiece and title page for the first edition of Aldington's second biographical work on Lawrence

the Americans sympathize with the plight of the Allies in Europe.

October 1943 saw the publication of *The Duke: Being an Account of the Life & Achievements of Arthur Wellesley, 1st Duke of Wellington,* republished in 1946 as *Wellington: Being an Account of the Life & Achievements of Arthur Wellesley, 1st Duke of Wellington.* Nine thousand copies were sold within three weeks, and the book was in its third printing by mid November, proving its success. Aldington's purpose in writing about Wellington, so the introduction explains, is to dispel the legend of the national hero and to uncover the man who became a national hero. He begins with a sympathetic account of Wellington's early years, during which his family showed little interest in his desire to follow a financial career at a time when the family found itself in debt. Young Arthur was sent to a military school, and then, rather than direct him

into a career that might be of interest to him, his elder brother managed to have him "gazetted" (his appointment announced in a periodical) into a regiment of the army which was on its way to India. From this point Wellington's career is of paramount concern. From a few years in India to the brilliant campaigns he led against Napoleon to his eventual political career, the duke is shown to be human, faults and all. While abandoning the details of his own marriage in his autobiography, Aldington treats the duke's marriage and infidelities carefully, suggesting that his betrothal to Catherine Pakenham was due to "the ethics of sentiment as understood in Sir Arthur's age and social class" and that his later extramarital dalliances were the result of a loveless union. Throughout the biography Aldington's insights into Wellington's motives and decisions are well informed; he brings the hero to life, making him out to be a man worthy of admira-

LAWRENCE
OF
ARABIA

A Biographical Enquiry
by
RICHARD ALDINGTON

Untruthful! My nephew Algernon?
Impossible! He is an Oxonian.
OSCAR WILDE

HENRY REGNERY COMPANY
CHICAGO 1955

Frontispiece and title page for the American edition of Aldington's biography of the soldier and author he calls "a half-fraud"

tion. In 1947 Aldington received the James Tait Black Memorial Prize for *Wellington*.

Aldington moved his family back to France in 1946 and set about publishing a short book, *Four English Portraits, 1801–1851* (1948). Each short sketch is "designed as an introduction or supplement to more serious studies of nineteenth-century history and biography." He begins at the top of the social ladder with "The Grand World of 'Prinney,' " in which King George IV appears as an intelligent, educated man who preferred the company of writers such as Sir Walter Scott and politicians such as Wellington, and the pomp and circumstance of his office rather than the tact and decorum expected of him. "The Lustrous World of Young Disraeli" shows the "literary adventurer" who traveled widely, was influenced by George Gordon, Lord Byron's poems, and used his genius to overcome prejudice against his Judaism to become prime minister. "The Strange World of Squire Waterton" depicts a true eccentric, as "true to himself as the disci-

ples of Polonius never are," a breed, Aldington tells us, that no longer exists. Finally, "The Underworld of Young Dickens," which is more of an annotated chronology of his work than a biographical sketch of the novelist, shows that it is London, and its influence upon him, that makes Dickens the great novelist. The four portraits form a coherent whole in that they make plain the common influence of the first half of the nineteenth century on the lives of four very different men. Despite initially slow sales, *Four English Portraits* became a commercial success in England, selling more than ten thousand copies. The book failed to find an audience in the United States.

A similar success occurred the following year, when Aldington published a book-length study of *The Strange Life of Charles Waterton, 1782–1865*. He had been intrigued by Waterton for some years and expanded his sketch from *Four English Portraits* into a lively account of the man Aldington calls "a character so artless, a career so grotesque, an eccentric so unique." Aldington presents Waterton as a man truly shaped by his education and experience; the Jesuits under whom he studied encouraged his interests in biology and natural history. This, coupled with his love of travel, became the foundation of his life's work as a naturalist and writer. Aldington acknowledges the flaws that the Squire (as he was known) developed in his personality, such as extreme bigotry and a habit for making unqualified judgments. These flaws make him appear an unsuitable subject for Aldington's claim that "none comes to know the Squire without learning to love him," but other aspects of his character, such as his defense of "unpopular causes," his respect for nature, and his tenacity, make him fascinating. While Waterton appears as an obscure figure in the catalogue of Aldington's biographies, he is also one of the most colorful. Charles Doyle suggests that the British fondness for eccentrics such as Waterton is lacking in the United States, hence the U.S. disinterest in this biography.

Aldington was publishing other works at the end of the 1940s: *The Complete Poems of Richard Aldington, Walter Pater: Selected Works,* and *Jane Austen,* an introduction to the novels of Jane Austen, all appeared in 1948. However, his most important work at that time may well have been the biography of Lawrence he began writing in 1949. Aldington had been collecting material for a biography of his friend for several years, and March 1950 saw the publication of *Portrait of a Genius But . . . The Life of D. H. Lawrence, 1885–1930.* A more sophisticated work than *D. H. Lawrence: An Indiscretion,* this is Aldington's endeavor to write a general biography in which he defines Lawrence's genius. He undertook the task, as he says in the author's note, because critics would judge that "of course, Lawrence was a genius, but . . . ," as if stressing something other than his genius. As Gates carefully chronicles, Aldington had long published articles and essays in which his admiration and respect for Lawrence's work are apparent and "wrote the first important biography," although Moore gives barely a nod to *Portrait of a Genius But . . .* in his biography of Lawrence. Both faults and admirable qualities are surveyed throughout an empathetic search of Lawrence's life. Aldington explores the complex psychology and motives behind Lawrence's works, his marriage, and his relationships, and he even defends *Lady Chatterley's Lover* (1925) as "the expression of his latest thought." He reaches an understanding of Lawrence's genius through Richard Wagner's *Art-Work of the Future,* which Lawrence may or may not have read, in which art "is not a product

of the mind alone . . . but of 'the deeper impulses of the Unconscious.' " Aldington sees Lawrence's genius to be the product of his unconscious coupled with his belief that he was "part of the living, incarnate cosmos," despite having lived for many years with the knowledge that he was dying of tuberculosis. Aldington's biography is successful in its portrait of Lawrence; it received much approbation from reviewers and Lawrence's widow, Frieda, and remains an important work.

After the publication of the Lawrence biography, Aldington began work on a short biography intended to focus on the friendship of three men: Norman Douglas, Pino Orioli, and Charles Prentice. Douglas, the central figure of the biography, was a minor but popular British author who chose to live mainly in Florence, Italy, and was known for his travel books and for his novels set in exotic locales. His close friend, Orioli, was an Italian publisher and antiquarian bookseller. Prentice, who is featured to a lesser extent than Orioli, was an editor at Chatto and Windus with whom Aldington maintained a long friendship. The book was published in 1954, two years after Douglas's death. The title, *Pinorman,* "is a portmanteau word used by themselves and friends for Pino . . . and Norman." Having known the three men well, Aldington draws from personal recollection and letters to portray the friendships they shared. The roles Orioli and Prentice are given in the book are somewhat peripheral to the focus on Douglas, with Orioli playing an active part in Douglas's life and Prentice being the catalyst who brought Aldington and Douglas together. As this book is intended to provide notes for "future biographers of Norman Douglas," *Pinorman* is not full of the detail and interpretation that characterize Aldington's previous biographies. While none of his biographies is meant to be definitive, *Wellington, The Strange Life of Charles Waterton,* and *Portrait of a Genius But . . .* do attempt to follow their respective subjects from birth to death; *Pinorman* is uncharacteristic in that its concern is with Douglas as an adult and his relationships with other adults. The treatment of Douglas's gastronomic tastes, his pederasty, his "control" over Orioli, and other "flaws" Aldington discusses displeased many of Douglas's friends, although he does praise Douglas as an author and admires his independent spirit. *Pinorman* was not a great success and caused quite a furor, but the biggest controversy of Aldington's career was to occur following the publication of his next biography, a life of T. E. Lawrence.

In 1950, at the suggestion of his friend Alister Kershaw, Aldington began making notes for a biog-

Richard Aldington, Lawrence Durrell, Henry Miller, and Jacques Temple, 1959

raphy of Thomas Edward Lawrence, known popularly as Lawrence of Arabia. Four years later, just prior to its publication in 1955, *Lawrence of Arabia: A Biographical Enquiry* raised a stir from which its author never quite recovered. In the course of his research Aldington discovered that Lawrence tended toward a "systematic falsification and over-valuing of himself and his achievements . . . from a very early date." Aldington sets out to tear down the legend of Lawrence, whom he calls a "half fraud," and to replace it with several stark truths which he realized during the course of his research. As the basis for Lawrence's tendency to overexaggerate, Aldington reveals that he was the illegitimate son of Sir Thomas Chapman and the governess with whom Chapman fathered five sons. It is this family history which Aldington feels produced Lawrence's "habits of dissimulation," though he does allow that his subject had "his own remarkable gifts." Lawrence's loyal followers, "the Lawrence Bureau" as Aldington named them, took exception to Aldington's work and began a campaign against him that included a petition to the queen, asking her to stop publication of the book. Aldington's "enquiry" into Lawrence's life consistently refutes the legend with careful documentation, often proved by

Lawrence's own letters to various correspondents. Fred D. Crawford rightly points out that the evidence uncovered by Aldington has become important in the studies of Lawrence subsequent to *Lawrence of Arabia,* but the evidence is not presented with the objectivity expected of a biographer. While Aldington can sympathetically view Lawrence as "an unhappy, wistful, tortured, hag-ridden self," in the same breath he condemns him as "a glib showman untroubled by the majesty of truth"; he rejects the built-up legend of the great soldier conquering evil forces much as he rejected the hypocrisy of British society in 1928 and as he portrayed it in his novels. Despite excellent sales of the book in England and France, reviews tended toward a hostility Aldington took personally. His reputation was damaged by the controversy surrounding the biography, but the significance of the work outweighed the damage it caused.

Just prior to the publication of *Lawrence of Arabia,* Aldington was contracted to write a short biography of French poet Frédéric Mistral. Despite the problems he was facing in 1955, he decided to continue work on Mistral and produced *Introduction to Mistral* in 1956. Although Aldington again makes the disclaimer that the biography is "a very informal book," it is carefully written and is set up to prove that "his memory and his writings are to be loved and revered." There is no reason to disbelieve Aldington's sincerity in making such a claim, but it should be pointed out that the reverential tone of *Mistral* sharply contrasts the accusatory tone of *Lawrence of Arabia,* perhaps a conscious choice by the author to try to repair some of the damage done to his character.

Aldington admits to having known little about Mistral before gathering material for his book and expresses surprise that a poet who was awarded half a Nobel Prize in 1904 (the committee may have had trouble with the Provençal language) was "forgotten" by British and U.S. readers. The biography becomes a respectful discussion of Mistral's life and works, designed to encourage the reader to pursue Mistral on his or her own. Aldington's Mistral is a kind and generous genius, loyal to the region and language of his birth; Aldington also praises the Provençal language and its appropriateness as a poetic vehicle. Unlike his previous biographies, Aldington's "discovery" of his subject is subdued and is not marked by an examination of any complexities or motives behind Mistral's life and work. The book was reviewed fairly well, and sales were moderate. In 1959 he was awarded the Prix de Gratitude Mistrallien for *Mistral.* The award renewed interest in the book in Great Britain and the United States.

From 1954 to 1957 Aldington found himself in serious financial trouble. Sales of all his books were down, and the royalties were not enough to cover his debts, which included alimony to Netta and months of back rent. When his standing with the British and U.S. public was at its lowest, his spirits were buoyed somewhat by an invitation from the Soviet Writers Union to visit the Soviet Union at their expense. Ill health prevented the visit, which he eventually made in 1962, but the invitation reflected the popularity of Aldington's work in the Soviet Union. Mikhail Urnov states that "at the end of the thirties [he] became almost the most popular English writer in this country [the Soviet Union]," and his works are still published and sold in Russia today. While this attention from an unexpected public did not solve Aldington's financial crisis, it is indicative of a slight improvement of his circumstances as reprints of some of his early work in England brought in a small income.

Aldington published a small book in early 1957: *Frauds,* "a miscellany that presents some of the most celebrated frauds and impostors who have gained notoriety in England since the late fifteenth century." The title provoked interest in the book, but the subject matter did not appeal to a specific audience, and sales do not appear to have been good.

On 9 September 1957 the last of Aldington's biographies was published. Research for *Portrait of a Rebel: The Life and Works of Robert Louis Stevenson* had begun just after the *Lawrence of Arabia* fiasco and was a tedious book for Aldington to write. He did not enjoy his subject, but eventually he was able to write an engaging, readable biography. Stevenson is portrayed as a gifted writer whose craft was shaped by the love of his doting parents and nanny; the inherited ill health which plagued him from age two; the rebellion against his father's Scottish Presbyterianism; his reading; and his traveling. Although Doyle states that Aldington did not like Stevenson's wife Fanny, she appears as a loyal woman whose chief concern was for her husband's well-being. Omitting any serious discussion of Stevenson's flaws, perhaps out of respect for his physical condition, this is the most impartial of Aldington's biographies. Aldington sets out simply to relate the life of the writer while admiring his "indomitable spirit" and noting that he accepted "the medical restrictions and periods of rest imposed upon him" rather than working himself to the grave. These statements are compassionate but not piteous; the strength of this biography lies in its portrayal of Stevenson as a man who succeeded in his struggle to live his life as he wished, until his body could no longer fight its disease. Despite the gentle nature of the book, sales were not as high as expected. *Portrait of a Rebel* was the last piece of substantial writing Aldington produced; other short pieces and reprints appeared in English and Russian before his death, but it is ironic that his last book was written in the genre through which his reputation was ruined.

Richard Aldington remains an important figure in the literary history of the twentieth century. His was a versatile career that spanned several decades and offers honest, personal responses to the complex world of which he was a part. The current revival of interest in Aldington's work is long overdue and will allow an appraisal of his work that was denied during his lifetime.

Letters:

A Passionate Prodigality: Letters to Alan Bird from Richard Aldington, 1949–1962, edited by Miriam J. Benkovitz (New York: New York Public Library, 1975);

Literary Lifelines: The Richard Aldington–Lawrence Durrell Correspondence, edited by Ian S. McNiven and Harry T. Moore (New York: Viking, 1981);

Bubb Booklets: Letters of Richard Aldington to Charles Clinch Bubb, edited by Dean H. Keller (Francestown, N.H.: Typographeum, 1988).

Bibliographies:

Alister Kershaw, *A Bibliography of the Works of Richard Aldington from 1915 to 1948* (London: Quadrant Press, 1950; Burlingame, Cal.: Wredon, 1950);

Paul Schlueter, "A Chronological List of the Books by Richard Aldington," in *Richard Aldington: An Intimate Portrait,* edited by F. J. Temple and Kershaw (Carbondale: Southern Illinois University Press, 1965);

Norman T. Gates, "The Richard Aldington Collection at the Morris Library," *ICarbS,* 3 (1976): 61–68;

Gates, *A Checklist of the Letters of Richard Aldington* (Carbondale: Southern Illinois University Press, 1977).

Biography:

Charles Doyle, *Richard Aldington: A Biography* (Carbondale: Southern Illinois University Press, 1989).

References:

Fred D. Crawford, "Richard Aldington's Biography of Lawrence of Arabia," in *Richard Aldington: Reappraisals,* edited by Charles Doyle, ELS Monograph Series, 49 (1990): 60–80;

Norman T. Gates, "Richard Aldington and D. H. Lawrence," in *Richard Aldington: Reappraisals,* pp. 45–59;

Harry T. Moore, *The Priest of Love, A Life of D. H. Lawrence* (New York: Penguin, 1981);

Richard Eugene Smith, *Richard Aldington* (Boston: Twayne, 1977);

Mikhail Urnov, "A Note on Richard Aldington Yesterday and Today in Russia," in *Richard Aldington: Reappraisals,* pp. 81–85.

Papers:

The largest collection of Aldington's papers is at Southern Illinois University at Carbondale. Other important collections of letters are at Harvard University, Yale University, the University of California at Los Angeles, and the University of Texas.

Frederick S. Boas
(24 July 1862 – 1 September 1957)

R. S. White
University of Western Australia

BOOKS: *Shakspere and his Predecessors* (London: John Murray, 1896; New York: Scribners, 1896);

Shakespeare and the Universities (Oxford: Basil Blackwell, 1923; New York: Appleton, 1923);

University Drama in the Tudor Age (Oxford: Clarendon Press, 1914);

Songs of Ulster and Balliol (London: Constable, 1917);

An Introduction to the Reading of Shakespeare (London: Duckworth, 1920);

Marlowe and his Circle: A Biographical Survey (Oxford: Clarendon Press, 1929);

An Introduction to Tudor Drama (Oxford: Clarendon Press, 1933);

From Richardson to Pinero: Some Innovators and Idealists (London: John Murray, 1936; New York: Columbia University Press, 1937);

Queen Elizabeth, the Revels Office and Edmund Tilney (London: Oxford University Press, 1938);

Christopher Marlowe: A Biographical and Critical Study (Oxford: Clarendon Press, 1940);

Aspects of Classical Legend and History in Shakespeare (London: British Academy Proceedings, 1943);

An Introduction to Stuart Drama (London and New York: Oxford University Press, 1946);

Ovid and the Elizabethans (London: English Association, 1947);

Queen Elizabeth in Drama and Related Studies (London: Allen & Unwin, 1949);

The Player's Library: The Catalogue of the Library of the British Drama League (London: Library, 1950);

Thomas Heywood (London: Williams & Norgate, 1950);

An Introduction to Eighteenth-Century Drama, 1700–1780 (Oxford: Clarendon Press, 1952);

Sir Philip Sidney: Representative Elizabethan: His Life and Writings (New York: Russell & Russell, 1956).

OTHER: *The Works of Thomas Kyd,* edited by Boas (Oxford: Clarendon Press, 1901);

George Chapman, *Bussy D'Ambois* and *The Revenge of Bussy,* edited by Boas (Boston & London: D. C. Heath, 1905);

William Shakespeare, *The Taming of a Shrew,* edited by Boas (New York: Duffield, 1908; London: Chatto & Windus, 1908);

The Poems of Giles and Phineas Fletcher: Poetical Works, edited by Boas (Cambridge: Cambridge University Press, 1908–1909);

Caesar and Pompey. The Tragedy of Caesar's Revenge, edited by Boas (London: Oxford University Press, 1911);

Francis Beaumont and John Fletcher, *Philaster; or, Love lies a-bleeding,* edited by Boas (London & Toronto: J. M. Dent, 1915);

Shakespeare, *The Tempest,* edited by Boas (Boston & New York: D. C. Heath, 1916);

The Christmas Prince, edited by Boas (Oxford: Clarendon Press, 1923);

Fulgens and Lucres, edited by Boas with A. W. Reed (Oxford: Clarendon Press, 1926);

Elizabethan and Other Essays by Sir Sidney Lee, edited by Boas (Oxford: Clarendon Press, 1929);

Christopher Marlowe, *The Tragical History of Dr. Faustus,* edited by Boas (New York: Dial, 1932);

Five Pre-Shakespearean Comedies, edited by Boas (London: Oxford University Press, 1934);

The Diary of Thomas Crosfield, edited by Boas (London: Oxford University Press, 1935);

Songs and Lyrics from the English Playbooks, edited by Boas (London: Cresset Press, 1945);

Songs and Lyrics from the English Masques and Light Operas, edited by Boas (London: Harrap, 1948);

Hon. Edward Howard's The Change of Crownes, edited by Boas (London: Oxford University Press, 1949).

SELECTED PERIODICAL PUBLICATIONS-UNCOLLECTED: "Coming of Age," (London) *Times,* 28 April 1927, pp. 15–16;

Frederick S. Boas

"Some Oxford Memories, 1881–1886," *Essays and Studies,* 9 (1956): 113–121.

To generations of students from 1900 at least up to the 1960s, the name Frederick S. Boas was synonymous with the study of Renaissance dramatists and particularly Shakespeare. While his reputation was overshadowed by those of E. K. Chambers as a biographer and W. W. Greg as a textual editor, Boas shared their dedicated, professional approach to scholarship. He was also committed to taking Shakespeare into schools and making Renaissance drama accessible to the general reading public.

Frederick Samuel Boas, eldest son of Hermann, was born into a Jewish family on 24 July 1862. He went to Clifton School, the first public school to make special provision for Jewish boys by dedicating a house specially for them. He entered Balliol College, Oxford, as an exhibitioner and distinguished himself there with a first in Classical Moderations in 1882, a first in *Literae Humaniores* in 1885, and a first in History in 1886. About the time

of his marriage to Henrietta O'Brien Owen, daughter of Sidney J. Owen, reader in Indian History at Oxford, he was baptized into the Church of England. From 1887 to 1901 he was a Lecturer to the Oxford University Extension Delegacy, the context in which his first and still best-known book, *Shakspere and his Predecessors* (1896), was published. The Balliol connection helped, as the writers for the University Extension Manuals series were almost all Scotsmen, many with Balliol in their background. He became a fellow of the Royal University of Ireland in 1901 and was a Professor of History and English Literature at Queen's College, Belfast, from 1901 to 1905. Between 1903 and 1905 he was College Librarian. In the year he left Belfast he delivered a commemorative address in the Theatre Royal to recognize the Belfast Shakespeare Festival. In 1904 he delivered the Clark lectures in English Literature at Trinity College, Cambridge. In 1905 he returned to England (where he lived permanently except for an appointment as visiting professor at Columbia University in New York in 1934–

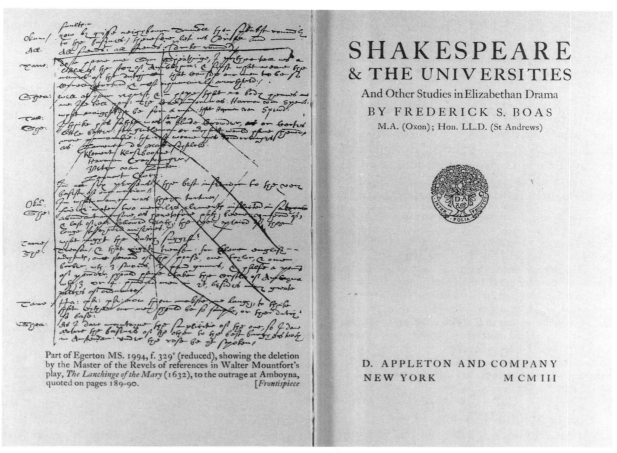

Part of Egerton MS. 1994, f. 329ᵛ (reduced), showing the deletion by the Master of the Revels of references in Walter Mountfort's play, *The Lanchinge of the Mary* (1632), to the outrage at Amboyna, quoted on pages 189-90. [*Frontispiece*]

SHAKESPEARE
& THE UNIVERSITIES
And Other Studies in Elizabethan Drama
BY FREDERICK S. BOAS
M.A. (Oxon); Hon. LL.D. (St Andrews)

D. APPLETON AND COMPANY
NEW YORK   MCMIII

Frontispiece and title page for the first American edition (with misdated title page) of Boas's volume of essays on Elizabethan drama

1935) as inspector in English literature and history for the London County Council, a post he held until 1927. As a member of the Departmental Committee on English between 1919 and 1921 he helped shape the syllabus for schools, and he published many reports and papers in this role. He was for a time examiner in English to Edinburgh University and special lecturer in English at University College, London.

It seems extraordinary that Boas's life in professional employment was really only the prelude to his academic career. Although he edited many Elizabethan texts up to (and after) 1927, the bulk of his writing was published after he retired, and he came to wield enormous influence in the world of English studies by editing *The Year's Work in English Studies* for the period from 1922 to 1955 and by being the first, and an immensely energetic, Honorary General Secretary to the English Association, in which capacity he wrote an article on the work of the English Association subtitled "Coming of Age" for the

(London) *Times*, 28 April 1927. He recruited a thousand members to the association and contributed to its growing prestige and influence. He was president of the association in 1944. The volume of *Essays and Studies* for 1956, a year before his death, is dedicated to "A Half-Century of the English Association" and contains Boas's reminiscences, "Some Oxford Memories 1881–1886," as well as a photograph showing him in snowy and venerable old age. It was recalled in his obituary for the (London) *Times* (2 September 1957) that "a few weeks before his ninety-third birthday, at the annual luncheon of the English Association he delighted the company with an admirable 10 minutes' speech, which was the more remarkable as at extremely short notice he had taken the place of Lord Samuel, who had been prevented by illness from attending." Among his many honors were a Fellowship of the Royal Society for Literature, of which he became vice-president and from which he received on his ninetieth birthday the A. C. Benson Silver Medal; honorary degrees from St.

Andrews and Belfast Universities; and an Order of the British Empire (1953). This was the year his wife died. She was herself a prolific writer, and her books introduced English classics to young readers. Their only son, Guy, also lectured in English literature, and he wrote for *Punch*.

H. F. Rubinstein, paying tribute after Boas's death, pointed out in the *Times* obituary that he "ruled" with great distinction the library committee of the British Drama League from its formation in 1925 until he was in his nineties, editing and publishing its voluminous catalogue in 1950. Rubinstein offers the following comments on Boas's personality:

> He was a great scholar, but the "absent-minded professor" was no relation of his. Business-like, meticulous or firm if the circumstances demanded, but never less than kind and considerate, in his grave courtesy. I can recall, after serving under him for more than twenty-five years, no remark or gesture which could conceivably have caused anyone present to feel either foolish or uncomfortable — or indeed, other than "at home" in the company of a man both gracious and grand. But it is of qualities transcending such personal associations that one is most conscious at the news of his passing. It is as if the pillar of a Temple had fallen.

Most of Boas's original books went into several reprints, but none so many as *Shakspere and his Predecessors,* the book which made his name and remains his best known. It was published under the imprint of the University Extension Manuals, a series of commissioned textbooks suitable for advanced study and also for reading by a general audience, intended to unite "simplicity with thoroughness." Boas covers an enormous range, and the book could be judged independently as biography, literary criticism, and literary history. His own claim to its unique contribution was in its linking of Shakespeare's plays with those of his earlier contemporaries and medieval predecessors. As a biographer of Shakespeare, Boas claims no special originality or archival research, and he seeks only to present the evidence soberly and straightforwardly. He is consistently cautious and even skeptical when dealing with more speculative biographies, although he tacitly accepts, for example, the idea current in the late nineteenth century that Shakespeare underwent some personal turbulence, perhaps a breakdown, which caused him to turn from comedy to tragedy. It was Boas in this book who coined the phrase "problem-plays," taken from the fashion of Henrik Ibsen, Anton Chekhov, and Bernard Shaw in his own day, to describe *All's Well that Ends Well, Measure for Measure,* and *Troilus and Cressida,* and he

includes *Hamlet* in the group. By and large, Boas sees Shakespeare as a paradox, embodying medieval respect for custom with Renaissance "ardours," practical success with spiritual depths:

> . . . however complex during the last years of Elizabeth's reign the inner life of Shakspere may have been, with its loves and jealousies, its crises of mind and heart, his outward success was uninterrupted, and he adhered steadfastly to his purpose of returning to Stratford as a man of property.

University drama in the Renaissance was next to absorb Boas's scholarly attention, and, although not primarily works of biography, his two books on the subject involve exhaustive examination of contemporary records and pen sketches of relevant figures. His interest focused on Christopher Marlowe, the greatest of the university dramatists.

Marlowe and his Circle: A Biographical Survey (1929), although a shorter book (137 pages as opposed to 539 for *Shakspere and his Predecessors*), is more genuinely an original contribution. The book relates the significance of materials known, but not considered relevant, by earlier biographers, in particular letters by Thomas Kyd (whose works Boas had edited) and letters concerning the Italian musician Alfonso Ferrabosco, an agent of Elizabeth's government. The book examines in minute detail the circumstances of Marlowe's death as recorded in state papers and other recorded testimony. Boas is at his most impressive in dealing, with the finesse and firmness of an expert advocate, with the varying reliability of those involved, especially the plausible rogue Robert Poley, "a past master in all the arts of equivocation," whose voice carried most weight with the coroner's jury. The jury concluded that Ingram Frizer slew Marlowe in self-defense in a quarrel over a tavern bill: " . . . it was mainly the evidence of Poley that got Frizer off and branded Marlowe as the criminal." The book reads like a scholarly detective story, arriving at no clear-cut verdict but giving ample reason to suspect a political cover-up which will forever obscure the truth, "and that Marlowe, instead of being the aggressor in the affray, was the victim of a deliberately planned political murder." The sinister and ubiquitous Poley emerges as no less colorful than Marlowe himself. Boas has deep admiration for Marlowe, qualified by the fastidiousness of a convert to Christianity:

> Marlowe does not appear as an "atheist" in the modern sense. Of the workings of the speculative faculty dealing with the fundamental principles of religion or of ethics there is little trace in his reported sayings. We see in-

Engraving prefixed to "The Seraphim," Book I of *The Hierarchy of the Blessed Angels*, with Delphi and Jerusalem in the background.

Thomas Heywood

by

FREDERICK S. BOAS
LL.D., D.LITT., F.R.S.L.

WILLIAMS & NORGATE, LTD.
36 GT. RUSSELL ST., LONDON, W.C. 1

Frontispiece and title page for Boas's biographical and source study of the Elizabethan playwright

stead a rationalist intelligence blasting its destructive way through all that was held in reverential awe by its contemporaries and ruthlessly desecrating the Holy of Holies. The supernatural is laughed out of court . . . But Marlowe was not a philosopher conducting an antireligious campaign by elaborate treatises. His method was the more formidable one of sap and mime. Wherever he went, in table-talk and otherwise, he let loose his mordant wit upon sacred subjects.

Christopher Marlowe: A Biographical and Critical Study (1940) is more ambitious and arguably Boas's most successful exercise in the genre of literary biography. It incorporates *Marlowe and his Circle* but is in itself a much more comprehensive study of the enigmatic Renaissance playwright and poet. Exhaustive examination of Marlowe's bills during his six years at Cambridge is made to yield a surprisingly large amount of information about his activities, both public and clandestine. A key to Marlowe's character, Boas believes, lies in his embodiment of almost conflicting Renaissance impulses, "soaring aspiration after power and knowledge and beauty in their ideal" and "the critical, analytic impulse which led to the questioning of orthodox

creeds and standards of conduct." He draws evidence equally from the plays and from what was known of Marlowe's shadowy involvement in the politics and intrigue of his time. Ironically, the aspect of the biography on which Boas most prided himself for its originality is also the part which is least to modern taste. He seems to have checked line by line Marlowe's translations, for example of Ovid, and he draws conclusions not only about Marlowe's classical learning but more generally about his indebtedness to sources. A valuable lesson emerges — that Marlowe was not quite so original or radical as had been supposed — and Boas's learned task could be said to be a valuable service, but it is debatable whether the results fully justified his labors. Another asset which Boas brought to the task and which is not always a biographer's forte was his expertise in the fine detail of Elizabethan texts. He derived this knowledge from his editing and transcriptions of many plays, some for the important Malone Society Reprints series. This experience stood him in good stead in analyzing the tangled textual details of *Doctor Faustus*, such as they were known in the 1940s. On this play especially, Boas uses detail from Marlowe's life in tandem with close study of his sources to make both critical and biographical advances. Boas's tentative conclusions about Marlowe's life story are whimsical: "Thus viewed his life-record forms a drama as absorbing as any of his own tragedies but with the strange inconsequence of one of those modern Russian plays where characters wander in and out without any apparent relevance to the action." It may seem incongruous that such a cautious "pillar of a Temple" as Boas should be so imaginatively fired by the tantalizing glimpses of a subversive dramatist who was not a pattern of "scrupulous rectitude," but nonetheless the work on Marlowe is his most valuable contribution to biography.

The Diary of Thomas Crosfield (1935) aims to extend "tardy justice" to a diarist whom Boas rates as "of permanent interest." Crosfield was Fellow of Queen's College, Oxford, from 1618 to about 1640, and Rector of Spennithorne, Yorkshire, from 1649 to 1663. His diary covers the period 1626 to 1640 and then February 1652 to February 1654 — self-evidently interesting dates, before and after the Civil War. Boas's task in presenting the diaries is made more painstaking by their being bilingual, English and Latin. He opens with a biography, and then transcribes the diaries. *Thomas Heywood* (1950) is a brief book with introductory biographical material but mainly a source study and a critical introduction to Heywood's plays.

Clearly, to one so concerned with placing Renaissance texts in their contemporary settings, Boas's many scholarly editions displayed not only industry in transcription but also an indefatigable effort at presenting biographical evidence of the writers, often obscure and little documented. His contributions in this field are learned and unobtrusive, and if anybody should trouble to collect them together they would add up to a significant documentation of many minor and major figures of the period.

Sir Philip Sidney: Representative Elizabethan: His Life and Writings, published in 1956, ninety-four years after Boas's birth and one before his death, was his last book. Taking into account his age the book is impressive enough, but it could conceivably have come at any time of his writing career since it manifests his lifelong commitment to values of exactitude, sobriety, and a reluctance to make leaps of the imagination or sweeping generalizations. It also follows what by now in his career had become

something of a formulaic pattern of "life and works." Although there is a lot of paraphrase of *The Old Arcadia* (probably justified, given the fact of the neglect that had fallen like a shroud over Sidney's work by the 1950s), there is also much solid information about Sidney and a shrewd insight into the political intrigues represented in his romance: "For a time the *Arcadia* turns from a romance into a political treatise on that perennial Elizabethan bogy, the difficulties and dangers of a disputed succession to the throne."

If Boas still has claims to a central position in English studies it would not be as a biographer, since he worked entirely from published records, synthesized the work of others, and never produced a work which redefines his subject matter. His own self-estimate seems to place him among scholars of classical sources for Renaissance texts. As a literary historian he shows rich scope in the Tudor and Stuart periods. He was an indefatigable editor of plays popular and obscure, and he treated with equal seriousness a variety of dramatists ranging from Kyd, Heywood, Beaumont and Fletcher, to Marlowe and Shakespeare. In some ways it is not inappropriate to claim him as a forerunner of New Historicists, since for him the life, circumstances, and political ideologies of his subjects were immediate context for interpretation rather than mere colorful background. As a critic he is undistinguished but thorough. His real importance lies in his massive, if largely unacknowledged, influence on the rise of English studies, not only in his various introductory studies of drama in different periods but more especially in his various activities for the English Association, *The Year's Work in English Studies,* and his work in curriculum development in schools. Nowadays it is fashionable to decry the conservatism of the English institution in the twentieth century, but it is undeniable that the institution has made a powerful cultural impact on Great Britain and the United States in an area which had previously been the domain of belletrists and marginalized eccentrics. It is people like Boas, perhaps more in the roles of eminences grises than self-publicists, who have enabled English literature to matter, at least to the extent that debates can now be conducted between its various factions taking for granted and building upon a fundamental, disciplinary foundation. Boas was a professional, in the best sense of the word, and he helped to professionalize English studies and literary biography as a branch of them.

Arthur Bryant
(18 February 1899 – 22 January 1985)

P. E. Hewison
University of Aberdeen

BOOKS: *Rupert Buxton — A Memoir* (Cambridge: Cambridge University Press, 1926);

The Spirit of Conservatism (London: Methuen, 1929);

King Charles II (London: Longmans, 1931; revised edition, London: Collins, 1955);

Macaulay (London: Peter Davies, 1932; New York: Appleton, 1933; revised edition, London: Weidenfeld & Nicolson, 1979);

Samuel Pepys: The Man in the Making (Cambridge: Cambridge University Press, 1934; revised edition, London: Collins, 1947);

The National Character (London: Longmans, 1934);

The England of Charles II (London: Longmans, 1934); republished as *Restoration England* (London: Collins, 1960);

Samuel Pepys: The Years of Peril (Cambridge: Cambridge University Press, 1935; revised edition, London: Collins, 1948);

The Letters, Speeches and Declarations of Charles II (London: Cassell, 1935);

Postman's Horn (London: Longmans, 1936; revised edition, London: Home & Von Thal, 1946);

The American Ideal (London: Longmans, 1936);

George V (London: Peter Davies, 1936);

Stanley Baldwin (London: Hamish Hamilton, 1937; New York: Coward-McCann, 1937);

Samuel Pepys: The Saviour of the Navy (Cambridge: Cambridge University Press, 1938; revised edition, London: Collins, 1949);

Humanity in Politics (London: Hutchinson, 1938);

In Search of Peace. Speeches of Neville Chamberlain (London: Hutchinson, 1939); revised and enlarged as *The Struggle for Peace* (London: Hutchinson, 1939);

Unfinished Victory (London: Macmillan, 1940);

Britain Awake (London: Collins, 1940);

English Saga (London: Collins, 1940); republished as *Pageant of England* (New York: Harper, 1941);

The Years of Endurance (London: Collins, 1942; New York: Harper, 1942);

The Summer of Dunkirk (London: Kemsley Press, 1943);

The Battle of Britain (London: Kemsley Press, 1944);

Trafalgar and Alamein (London: Kemsley Press, 1944);

Years of Victory (London: Collins, 1944; New York: Harper, 1945);

The Art of Writing History (Oxford: Oxford University Press, 1946);

Historian's Holiday (London: Dropmore Press, 1946; revised edition, London: Collins, 1951);

A Historian's View of the War (London: RUSI, 1947);

The Age of Elegance (London: Collins, 1950; New York: Harper, 1950);

The Story of England: Makers of the Realm (London: Collins, 1953; Boston: Houghton Mifflin, 1954);

The Turn of the Tide (London: Collins, 1957);

Triumph in the West (London: Collins, 1959);

Jimmy, The Dog in My Life (London: Lutterworth Press, 1960);

A Choice for Destiny (London: Collins, 1962);

The Memoirs of James II (London: Chatto & Windus, 1962);

The Age of Chivalry (London: Collins, 1963);

Only Yesterday (London: Collins, 1965);

The Fire and The Rose (London: Collins, 1965; revised edition, London: Fontana, 1972);

The Medieval Foundation (London: Collins, 1966);

Protestant Island (London: Collins, 1967);

The Lion and the Unicorn (London: Collins, 1969);

Nelson (London: Collins, 1970);

The Great Duke (London: Collins, 1971);

Jackets of Green (London: Collins, 1972);

A Thousand Years of British Monarchy (London: Collins, 1975);

Pepys and the Revolution (London: Collins, 1979);

The Elizabethan Deliverance (London: Collins, 1980; New York: St. Martin's Press, 1982);

Spirit of England (London: Collins, 1982; New York: Parkwest Publications, 1985);

Arthur Bryant (AP/Wide World Photos)

Set in a Silver Sea (London: Collins, 1984; New York: Morrow, 1984);

Freedom's Own Island (London: Collins, 1986; New York: Morrow, 1986);

The Search for Justice (London: Collins, 1990).

Arthur Bryant's biographical works are both an integral part and a reflection of his overall achievement as a historian. In subject matter there is an emphasis on the seventeenth century, the Napoleonic period, and military history. In approach there is a determination to combine scholarship and readability with a strongly moral attitude founded on traditional Christian values and firm patriotism. This has made him seem old-fashioned and the victim of some condescension from modern academic historians; but this is to ignore his enormous popularity among the reading public and his major achievement in explaining the importance of otherwise neglected or misunderstood personalities, notably King Charles II, Samuel Pepys, and Field Marshal Alanbrooke.

Arthur Wynne Morgan Bryant was born on 18 February 1899 in a house on the royal estate of Sandringham. His father, Sir Francis Morgan Bryant, was chief clerk to the Prince of Wales, and when the prince was crowned King Edward VII in 1901, he accompanied Edward to Buckingham Palace, where he was given an official residence in Lower Grosvenor Place beside the Royal Mews. This close association with the historic British monarchy, and the Edwardian splendor and ceremony then surrounding it, was a major influence on the young boy. His mother, May Edmunds Bryant, described by him as "a poet and a dreamer," clearly provided another influence, although as usual in this period he was effectively brought up by his nurse. In fact this arrangement worked well for four years, Bryant an only child under the care of a devoted nurse called Other Nan. The arrival of a younger brother, Philip, and the departure of Other Nan to be replaced by her sister wrecked his happy existence. Philip was not in the end a problem; Bryant described him as "a saint," and he went on to be ordained and a well-loved chaplain of Harrow school for many years. The problem was the nurse, who for some reason seems to have hated Bryant. Nor did Bryant enjoy the mixed kindergarten of the

Bryant at his home, October 1934

Francis Holland School for Girls on Graham Street. Four years of this were brought to an end by a new nurse and brief attendance at the fashionable avant-garde Gibbs' School on Sloane Street. His ninth year, however, brought for Bryant the ultimate, inevitable horror: preparatory school. So miserable was he at Pelham House, Sandgate, that he would seriously consider throwing himself over the banisters.

What is important about all these miseries is how Bryant responded to them. Like so many children in a similar situation he retreated into the personal world of his imagination. In his particular world only two things mattered: books and soldiers. The one good thing about Pelham House was that it was only a mile away from Shorncliffe Camp, birthplace of the Rifle Brigade. Here the fascination with things military, already aroused by the glittering lancers who escorted the king, was strengthened. "I always wanted to be a soldier," he later told his secretary. He was to be, briefly; but it was the combination of soldiers and books which would make him a military historian, one of whose finest achievements was the biography of that same Rifle Brigade.

The books too were prophetic: in his father's vast library the favorite reading was history, notably Sir William Napier's *War in the Peninsula* (1828–1840), and also bound volumes of the *Illustrated London News,* to which he would be a regular contributor for nearly fifty years.

Bryant's next school was Harrow. His four and a half years there were different from those at Pelham House but ambiguous. He seems to have been unhappy, certainly bored, but in later years he expressed great pride in, even love for, the place. Perhaps what Harrow symbolized, rather than what it was, is important here. Writing about it in the *Illustrated London News* on 12 June 1943, it is the fact that it produced Winston Churchill and Field Marshal Harold Alexander that he stresses. In any event his rather undistinguished school career was transformed when he began to be taught by the senior history master, George Townsend Warner, who had also taught G. M. Trevelyan. Under his influence, in 1916 he altered his original intention of proceeding via Sandhurst into the army, to trying for a scholarship at Cambridge and then joining the Royal Flying Corps (RFC). This way in fact he would get into World War I sooner (it might soon be over), and the RFC was still part of the army. Although Warner died in the interim, by the summer of 1917 Bryant had gained an exhibition at Pembroke College, Cambridge, and was in the RFC.

He proceeded through the RFC Depot at Farnborough, Officer Training Corps at Hursley, and School of Military Aeronautics at Oxford to his first solo flight. Here, while looping the loop, Bryant made two discoveries: first, that during this maneuver all the dust from the bottom of the cockpit hits you in the face; and second, that it is important to strap yourself in. Not having done so, he clung to the sides of the fuselage, with no control over the airplane, until he managed to lunge forward and switch off the engine, thus coming out of the loop and being able to land. His instructor's comments were memorable. Bryant was no natural pilot: he was in fact totally unmechanical and prone to dizziness while flying. Despite crashing several machines, he did gain his wings; but by then the war was nearly over, and he was in the Royal Air Force — no longer a soldier. Nevertheless even just a few months on the western front left an impression. Bryant's account of his response to the war, written for Armistice Day 1936 in the *Illustrated London News* (14 November 1936), is revealing. For him, the front in 1918 represented "the quintessence of annihilation . . . horror had become static. . . . Before me was the place of Golgotha and dead men's skulls"; but he also saw that "History was in it" and turned to the war poets for a fuller explanation, that this war was part of "another war, an eternal one, which is waged in every human soul between the powers of good and evil, between man's strength and man's weakness. They bear witness that . . . he has it in him to rise above his doom and his own weakness." Bryant's response is vivid and sensitive, but it is also rooted, through history and literature, in firm moral values. His particular experience of the Great War is at one with the vision which underlies all his writing.

Having left the RAF abandoning any idea of a military career, Bryant did not go to Cambridge; instead he went to Oxford. It seems likely that he had been under pressure from Warner, a Cambridge man; but now having saved enough from his service pay to make the exhibition unnecessary, he was free to go up to Queen's College, Oxford, where three members of his mother's family had preceded him. Bryant loved Oxford but stayed only five terms, taking the Shortened Honours Course for Ex-Servicemen. Classes were not awarded, but Bryant's tutor, R. H. Hodgkin, the Anglo-Saxon his-

torian and later provost of Queen's, afterward told him that his papers suggested that if he had taken full honors he would have gained a First.

In now deciding on a career, Bryant, like many others, was influenced by his encounter with the less privileged during war service. He took up a teaching post at Holloway, a London County council school. From here, he attracted the attention of Henry Morris, director of education for Cambridgeshire, who appointed him principal of the Cambridge School of Arts, Crafts and Technology. Between 1923 and 1925 Bryant succeeded in transforming an old-fashioned art school into the leading technical college in East Anglia. It was the finest educational achievement of a man with a lifelong passionate commitment to the value of education. In 1924 he married Sylvia Mary Shakerley, daughter of Sir Walter Shakerley of Somerford Park in Cheshire. Both families disapproved of the match, and they were right: the marriage was dissolved in 1939; there were no children. A more positive result of the meeting was Bryant's discovery of the Shakerley manuscripts at Somerford, some of them later printed in *Postman's Horn* in 1936, which aroused or rearoused in him an interest in the scholarship of history and in particular the value of letters for the historian, the use of which is a major factor in his early biographies. It was also his diligence in editing these letters which so impressed a friend, a reader for Longmans, that he suggested to the firm that they might ask Bryant to write a new life of Charles II, instead of reprinting Osmund Airy's thirty-year-old biography. Since 1925 Bryant had been a lecturer for the Oxford University Extension Delegacy, as well as reading for the bar and producing historical pageants. His thirtieth year was his year of decision. At this point his options seemed to be four: law, politics, theater, or education. Instead he responded to Longmans by offering to write a specimen chapter on the escape of Charles II after the battle of Worcester.

Longmans received it in November 1929 and at once put Bryant to work. Two years later the completed manuscript was offered for criticism to Wallace Notestein, professor of history at Yale. He produced the radical suggestion that the book should actually begin with the dramatic chapter on the flight from Worcester, with the nine chapters dealing with Charles's earlier life reincorporated into the text. After a brief five-page vignette of Charles's childhood, this is exactly what Bryant did. So Bryant's first great biography opens: "As the last streaks of daylight, September 3rd, 1651, fell on the Worcestershire landscape, a tall fugitive

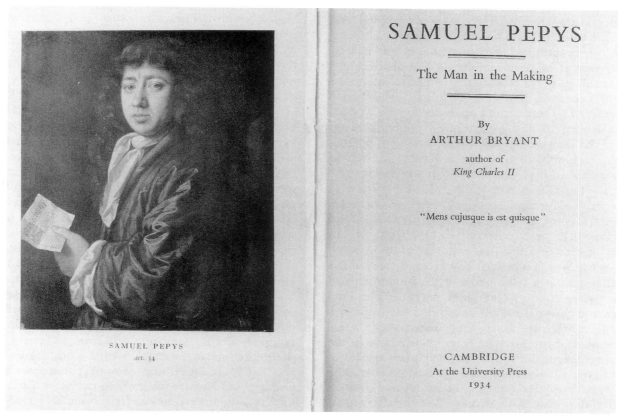

SAMUEL PEPYS

The Man in the Making

By
ARTHUR BRYANT

author of
King Charles II

"*Mens cujusque is est quisque*"

CAMBRIDGE
At the University Press
1934

Frontispiece and title page for the first volume of Bryant's four-volume biography of the seventeenth-century British diarist; John Kenyon called the four volumes "one of the great historical biographies in the language."

drew in his horse on a lonely heath. About him clustered some sixty lords and officers, whose looks told a tale of peril and defeat." Here at once is one of Bryant's major contributions to the writing of biography: he made history exciting. The essence of his approach is readability: lucidity, strong narrative drive, and a sense of drama. The qualities are there throughout this book but perhaps seen at their best in that opening chapter and in those titled "Sword, Pestilence and Fire" and "The Popish Terror." Bryant had already stated in his preface: "A simple narrative is the historical method best suited to our English genius." This may be so; but of course, his narrative is not simple. It appears simple but is in fact masterly contrived, especially in its sense of pace, and it is also buttressed by the massive scholarship tucked away in the notes.

This leads to the book's next important achievement, a massive reinterpretation of a key historical figure and period. The picture of a witty womanizer living in a frivolous but really quite jolly age of English history was swept away forever. Instead we have a shrewd and successful politician amid times of peril, terror, and turmoil. The dual fact that the book was so scholarly and that it was so readable, as illustrated by its enormous unexpected popularity and adoption as a Book Society Choice, increased its impact in changing basic historical perceptions. For Bryant, not for the last time, was out to diminish the Whigs, or at least the Whig historians. In the same year as *Charles II* was published, 1931, Philip Guedalla, in his biography of the duke of Wellington, noted: "By a peculiar division of labour British history, quite considerable parts of which have been made by Tories, has been very largely written by Whigs; and Whig historians are a little apt to dispose summarily of Tory reputations." Bryant was going to change all that.

His dislike of the Whig historians makes his next choice of biographical subject quite extraordinary. The year 1932 saw the publication of his book *Macaulay*. Not surprising, it is something of a puzzle. Its origins seem to lie in the offer from Trevelyan, Macaulay's great-nephew, of the use of his unpublished diaries in Trinity College, Cambridge, and Bryant dutifully plods through the life with these by his side. The narrative is of course clear, but the writer is clearly not happy with his subject. The first chapter notes Thomas Macaulay's bookishness, asexuality, and arrogance; the second desperately argues he was a moderate liberal; the third takes refuge in his relationship with his sisters; the fourth tries to be nice about his *Critical and Historical Essays* (1848), "not history so much as popular commentary on history." Fortunately the book wakes up in the next chapter, about the writing of history, where the subject is as much Bryant himself as Macaulay. In commending Macaulay for his "feeling for the nation as a whole," for his powers of imaginative description and, above all, for his readability, Bryant is clearly revealing his own values. Having thus been generous to Macaulay, he can then proceed to a merciless exposure of the depth of his Whig bias. To be fair, however, the remainder of the book is a celebration of the human side of Macaulay, vivid and at times moving. The final page is archetypal Bryant biography: his subject remains central but is seen against a wider background, and the power of the writing lasts to the final sentences: "They found him sitting upright in his chair, with a book still open at his side. The heart had stopped, and the historian had become part of that which he had made it his business to record."

The next project saw Bryant back on home ground. Cambridge University Press, on the advice of Keith Feiling, asked him to write a definitive life of Samuel Pepys. This not only took him back to the age of Charles II but to a similar task: to change the popular perception of a man chiefly famous for pursuing the ladies into an appreciation of his statesmanlike qualities. In addition, Bryant intended to turn attention to the later, nondiary years, and to reveal Pepys's crucial importance to the naval and imperial history of his country. He originally planned two volumes, but this expanded to four. The first, *The Man in the Making* (1934; revised, 1947), covers the period of the diary but links it to other sources. The second, *The Years of Peril* (1935; revised, 1948), places Pepys firmly in the intrigues of the court. The third, *The Saviour of the Navy* (1938; revised, 1949), concentrates on Pepys as the architect of British naval supremacy. All three share what were becoming the Bryant hallmarks: massive scholarship, even more so than with *Charles II*, combined with vivid readability, the second volume being especially difficult to put down. There is also that sense of the country as a whole which Bryant had praised in Macaulay, seen notably in the openings of the first two volumes. Also,

as in the Macaulay book, the subject is vividly portrayed but always in a larger historical, even moral, perspective, a process again seen in an opening chapter, that of the third volume. World War II interrupted the fourth volume; but the three books written between 1932 and 1938 established Bryant as a historian and biographer of the highest rank.

Pepys was not Bryant's sole preoccupation in these years. In 1936 there was the small business of his succeeding G. K. Chesterton as the weekly writer of "Our Notebook" in the *Illustrated London News*. Over a period of forty-nine years Bryant would contribute material of an estimated, in the *Dictionary of National Biography*, 2,738,000 words. There were also two short biographies. The first was *George V*, published in February 1936, one month after its subject's death; as Bryant admitted, it was written "on the spur of the moment." It suffers from this, not only because it cannot anticipate the abdication crisis, but also because it is written too quickly and, consequently, is repetitious and overly bland. Basically Bryant concedes the king's failings — such as being no intellectual, as seen in his preference for one-syllable words — but argues he was "at least something" compared to previous Georges and stresses his sense of duty and his practicality, suggesting they sprang from his naval career. He summarizes: "Without any outstanding gifts of mind or body, the King possessed a remarkable simplicity and balance of character." This is fair, but it still leaves much unsaid. Perhaps the most valuable parts of the book are the general chapter titled "The English Monarchy" and a typically lyrical final chapter, "Music at the Close." The vivid style is also much in evidence, as when the Agadir incident is resolved "after much heart-burning, and even more burning of naval coal," or again when the tensions in Ireland from 1910 to 1914 were also resolved: "The god duly descended from the machine, but it was from a chariot of fire," meaning, of course, Sarajevo.

The other biography suffers from much the same faults, only more so. *Stanley Baldwin* (1937) was written too soon and too quickly at the close of Baldwin's political career, which ended in 1937. The blandness topples over into special pleading, especially on Baldwin's behavior with regard to rearmament, appeasement, and the abdication, where Bryant actually says "it is too early to comment" and leaves it. To follow this on the very next page with "There remained a feeling now universal that he would go down in history as one of the great Prime Ministers of all time" is just asking too much. The overall interpretation of Baldwin as "honest to

Bryant delivering a wartime radio address on BBC radio (AP/Wide World Photos)

the verge of simplicity" is too naive to convince. Yet Bryant does succeed in making Baldwin more attractive than one might have thought possible. This is mainly achieved by the sympathetic treatment of his childhood, significantly similar to Bryant's own, especially in his love of books; and by justifying a somewhat romantic view of him with the trump card of his mother, one of the famous Macdonald sisters. There is also the familiar Bryant ability to place his subject in a larger context, seen especially in chapter 2, and the Bryant style, as in his view of 1919: "the glittering hour, purchased by a million British dead, when all the greatest statesmen were departing with their costly entourages for Versailles to refashion a broken world in a hall of mirrors."

By the end of the 1930s Bryant's life was not particularly happy. His marriage was finally dissolved in 1939. In 1941 he was to marry again, this time to Anne Elaine Brooke, daughter of Bertram Brooke, Her Highness Tuan Muda of Sarawak. This was also dissolved, in 1976, and again there were no children: according to his secretary, Bryant did not want any. Meanwhile, in his own words he was "almost in disgrace" over his attitude to appeasement. Briefly Bryant agreed with Neville Chamberlain's two basic perceptions that another world war would ruin the British Empire and that to go to war in 1938 would result in total catastrophe, especially in the air. This was not understood then, as it has not been understood since. Bryant tried to make things clear in *Unfinished Victory* (1940), a deeply unpopular book, although it is noteworthy that it was produced not by any of his normal publishers but by Macmillan, and Harold Macmillan was a firm supporter of Winston Churchill.

All this was changed by four major books published during the 1940s – *English Saga* (1940), *The*

Years of Endurance (1942), *Years of Victory* (1944), and *The Age of Elegance* (1950) – in effect a panorama of British history from 1793 to 1940. They represent Bryant at the height of his narrative powers, at his most patriotic and his most popular, and are generally sniffed at by modern academic historians. During the war Bryant was deeply committed to Forces Education, and after the war he pinned his hopes on the Ashridge Bonar Law College as a center for nonpartisan adult education. These hopes were dashed in a bitter argument, eventually lost, with the Conservative Party, which ultimately controlled the college. Bryant returned to his books. These books were now mainly concerned with the broad sweep of medieval history, a period which Bryant considered neglected both by him and by general readers. He dedicated almost twenty years from 1950 onward to putting this right. There was an exception, however, and it is one of his most important biographies, that of Field Marshal Alanbrooke.

In 1954, the year in which he was knighted, Bryant began work on the private diaries Alanbrooke had kept throughout the war. Bryant's aim was to demonstrate Alanbrooke's crucial role in the Allied victory in World War II, especially as chief of the Imperial General Staff. He feared a "false legend" about the war was growing, such as the case with Douglas Haig and World War I, and wished Alanbrooke to be given his due. In his two books *The Turn of the Tide* (1957) and *Triumph in the West* (1959) he succeeded in this; but he also achieved much more. He certainly demonstrates Alanbrooke's strategic vision and the central importance of his relationship with Churchill to the war effort; but what also emerges is a remarkable portrait of an extraordinarily sensitive man, frequently worried and often lonely, who hid all this under an iron-hard exterior, which no one ever penetrated. Bryant keeps a balance between the public and the private man with considerable skill, displaying once again his ability to show an individual in a context. This context is also lucidly presented: Bryant's own summaries of the strategic situation at various points in the narrative are admirably concise and authoritative.

In a sense this is not just a biography but the Bryant history of World War II. As such, it is interesting to see how often he makes sense of events other military historians still puzzle over. To take just one detailed example, there is his explanation of the "miracle of Dunkirk." Bryant makes clear how the counterattack by British armor at Arras on 21 May 1940 not only terrified the Germans witless

about their communications but revealed that British tanks were actually superior, especially in terms of protection. The Germans were already convinced a major tank battle would be a necessary prelude to the destruction of the British Expeditionary Force (BEF), but now the experience of Arras suggested that in such a battle the panzers would suffer severely; yet these panzers were vital to ensure the defeat of the large French armies still in the field. It was this perception, as much as Hermann Goering's ambition, which left the destruction of the BEF to the Luftwaffe. Such clarity of argument, with the books' other qualities, saw them hailed over and over again as "military classics." There was initially some controversy over the treatment of Churchill, but this faded. The most positive verdict on them came from Clement Richard Attlee, who called them "the most important publication on the Second World War."

In 1960 a very different type of biography appeared: the short, affectionate, and often moving *Jimmy, The Dog in My Life*. The rest of the decade saw Bryant as the medieval historian, the London clubman, the (not too successful) farmer, and the companion of honour (1967), with honorary degrees from Edinburgh University, Saint Andrews University, and New Brunswick University. Then in 1970 appeared *Nelson*. This is probably Bryant's most disappointing book. It is not a fully original work but a compilation and expansion of material from his books on the Napoleonic period. The basic problem is that the background provided in the earlier books is here assumed, so that the reader without it is confused, while the informed reader finds things rather elementary, partly because the book is too short. More important, Bryant's usual narrative gift has mysteriously disappeared, and the book is often muddled, containing useless maps that do not help. A final weakness, actually quite common in Bryant, is the neglect of foreign sources. For this reason, for example, the account of Lord Nelson's last battle has been completely superseded by Alan Schom's excellent *Trafalgar* (1990).

All is happily restored to normal in the next two books. Bryant's vast knowledge of the Napoleonic period is put to much better use in *The Great Duke* (1971), a purely military biography intended to complement the other writing on Wellington being produced at the time. There are many similarities to the Alanbrooke volumes, not just in the actual character of the subject, another soldier of firmly concealed emotions, but in the techniques of letting the man speak for himself through extensive quotation from his own writings and of placing him in the wider context of a world war. Other familiar elements are the energetic drive of the narrative, the strong patriotism, and the respect for the military virtues. Also notable is the mastery of telling detail: only Bryant would interrupt his account of the battle of Vimiero to point out that it was being watched through a telescope from a ship off the coast by one of Jane Austen's brothers. Interesting for the student of Wellington is the importance Bryant places on his experience in India: an acute analysis of the Seringapatam incident – the only time when Wellington ever lost his nerve – and a brilliant account of the battle of Assaye are particularly valuable here. More-recent research may challenge some of Bryant's attitudes, such as his lack of sympathy for Kitty Pakenham or his contempt for the Spanish armies. Yet these matters remain controversial; what can never be superseded is the verve and conviction of the writing. All this is exemplified in the final chapter, a fifty-page account of the Waterloo campaign which is vintage Bryant: lucid, incisive, and extremely exciting.

The next year saw the equally masterly *Jackets of Green*, a biography not of one man but of a regiment, the Rifle Brigade, and the men who served in it from its foundation in 1800. It shows Bryant the military historian at his very best, covering a vast panorama of events and personalities with both lucidity and a great love of his subject. As well as a firm grip of tactical and strategic issues, there are the familiar detailed touches, from Harry Smith and his future wife at Badajoz to Geoffrey Keyes, V.C. in the Western Desert, "with a hawk, a hooded hawk, upon his wrist." It is a fitting climax to Bryant's career as a biographer, a fine book about a fine regiment.

In 1977 Bryant fell seriously ill, and cancer was diagnosed. He survived two operations to live another eight years. His last major achievement was the three-volume History of Britain and the British People, which includes *Set in a Silver Sea* (1984), *Freedom's Own Island* (1986), and *The Search for Justice* (1990), in effect a summary of all his work as a historian. At least that is how it appeared to those familiar with his writings; to those not so familiar, it was an awe-inspiring revelation. Bryant retained his gifts, especially his narrative gifts, right to the end. He also worked right to the end. Bryant died at his home in Salisbury Cathedral on 22 January 1985. His last contribution to the *Illustrated London News* was his monthly column appearing in the issue of February 1985.

Tributes paid to him after his death rightly stressed his narrative skill, his lucidity, his readability, and his learning. In an age with which he came to have less and less sympathy it is perhaps not surprising that little was said about his strong moral values. Yet they should not be overlooked. Like Edward Gibbon and Macaulay, or Livy and Thucydides for that matter, Bryant believed that it was the historian's duty to draw moral conclusions from the story he told. What those values and conclusions were is quite clear. As Bryant said in an *Illustrated London News* article (8 November 1969): "There are only two things that matter in this world. They are love and courage."

Biography:

Pamela Street, *Arthur Bryant: Portrait of a Historian* (London: Collins, 1979).

G. K. Chesterton

(29 May 1874 – 14 June 1936)

W. P. Kenney
Manhattan College

See also the Chesterton entries in *DLB 10: Modern British Dramatists, 1900–1945; DLB 19: British Poets, 1880–1914; DLB 34: British Novelists, 1890–1929: Traditionalists; DLB 70: British Mystery Writers, 1860–1919;* and *DLB 98: Modern British Essayists,* First Series.

BOOKS: *Greybeards at Play: Literature and Art for Old Gentlemen. Rhymes and Sketches* (London: Johnson, 1900);

The Wild Knight and Other Poems (London: Richards, 1900; revised edition, London: Dent / New York: Dutton, 1914);

The Defendant (London: Johnson, 1901; New York: Dodd, Mead, 1902; enlarged edition, London: Dent, 1903);

Twelve Types (London: Humphreys, 1902); enlarged as *Varied Types* (New York: Dodd, Mead, 1903); abridged as *Five Types* (London: Humphreys, 1910; New York: Holt, 1911); also abridged as *Simplicity and Tolstoy* (London: Humphreys, 1912);

Robert Browning (New York & London: Macmillan, 1903);

G. F. Watts (London: Duckworth / New York: Dutton, 1904);

The Napoleon of Notting Hill (London & New York: Lane, 1904);

Heretics (London & New York: Lane, 1905);

Charles Dickens (London: Methuen, 1906; New York: Dodd, Mead, 1906);

The Man Who Was Thursday (Bristol: Arrowsmith / London: Simkin, Marshall, Hamilton, Kent, 1908; New York: Dodd, Mead, 1908);

Orthodoxy (New York: Lane, 1908);

All Things Considered (London: Methuen, 1908; New York: Lane, 1908);

The Ball and the Cross (New York: Lane, 1909; London: Gardner, Darton, 1910);

Tremendous Trifles (London: Methuen, 1909; New York: Dodd, Mead, 1909);

George Bernard Shaw (London: Lane, Bodley Head / New York: Lane, 1910; enlarged, 1935);

What's Wrong with the World (London & New York: Cassell, 1910);

Alarms and Discursions (London: Methuen, 1910; enlarged edition, New York: Dodd, Mead, 1911);

William Blake (London: Duckworth / New York: Dutton, 1910);

Appreciations and Criticisms of the Works of Charles Dickens (London: Dent / New York: Dutton, 1911);

The Innocence of Father Brown (London & New York: Cassell, 1911);

The Ballad of the White Horse (London: Methuen, 1911; New York: Lane, 1911);

Manalive (London & New York: Nelson, 1912);

A Miscellany of Men (London: Methuen, 1912; enlarged edition, New York: Dodd, Mead, 1912);

The Victorian Age in Literature (London: Williams & Norgate, 1913; New York: Holt, 1913);

Magic: A Fantastic Comedy (London: Secker, 1913; New York & London: Putnam, 1913);

The Flying Inn (London: Methuen, 1914; New York: Lane, 1914); enlarged as *Wine, Water, and Song* (London: Methuen, 1915);

The Wisdom of Father Brown (London & New York: Cassell, 1914);

The Barbarism of Berlin (London & New York: Cassell, 1914); republished in *The Appetite of Tyranny, Including Letters to an Old Garibaldian* (New York: Dodd, Mead, 1915);

Letters to an Old Garibaldian (London: Methuen, 1915); republished in *The Appetite of Tyranny, Including Letters to an Old Garibaldian* (New York: Dodd, Mead, 1915);

Poems (London: Burns & Oates, 1915; New York: Lane, 1915);

The Crimes of England (London: Palmer & Hayward, 1915; New York: Lane, 1916);

A Short History of England (London: Chatto & Windus, 1917; New York: Lane, 1917);

G. K. Chesterton

Utopia of Usurers (New York: Boni & Liveright, 1917);

Irish Impressions (London: Collins, 1919; New York: Lane, 1920);

The Superstition of Divorce (London: Chatto & Windus, 1920; New York: Lane, 1920);

The Uses of Diversity (London: Methuen, 1920; New York: Dodd, Mead, 1921);

The New Jerusalem (London: Hodder & Stoughton, 1920; New York: Doran, 1921);

Eugenics and Other Evils (London & New York: Cassell, 1922);

What I Saw in America (London: Hodder & Stoughton, 1922; New York: Dodd, Mead, 1922);

The Ballad of St. Barbara and Other Verses (London: Palmer, 1922; New York & London: Putnam, 1923);

The Man Who Knew Too Much and Other Stories (London & New York: Cassell, 1922; abridged edition, New York & London: Harper, 1922);

Fancies Versus Fads (London: Methuen, 1923; New York: Dodd, Mead, 1923);

St. Francis of Assisi (London: Hodder & Stoughton, 1923; New York: Doran, 1924);

The End of the Roman Road (London: Classic, 1924);

Tales of the Long Bow (London & New York: Cassell, 1925);

The Everlasting Man (London: Hodder & Stoughton, 1925; New York: Dodd, Mead, 1925);

William Cobbett (London: Hodder & Stoughton, 1925; New York: Dodd, Mead, 1926);

The Incredulity of Father Brown (London & New York: Cassell, 1926);

The Outline of Sanity (London: Methuen, 1926; New York: Dodd, Mead, 1927);

The Queen of Seven Swords (London: Sheed & Ward, 1926; London & New York: Sheed & Ward, 1933);

The Catholic Church and Conversion (New York: Macmillan, 1926; London: Burns, Oates & Washbourne, 1926 [i. e., 1927]);

The Return of Don Quixote (London: Chatto & Windus, 1927; New York: Dodd, Mead, 1927);

The Collected Poems of G. K. Chesterton (London: Palmer, 1927; New York: Dodd, Mead, 1932);

The Secret of Father Brown (London: Cassell, 1927; New York & London: Harper, 1927);

The Judgement of Dr. Johnson: A Comedy in Three Acts (London: Sheed & Ward, 1927; New York & London: Putnam, 1928);

Robert Louis Stevenson (London: Hodder & Stoughton, 1927; New York: Dodd, Mead, 1928);

Generally Speaking: A Book of Essays (London: Methuen, 1928; New York: Dodd, Mead, 1929);

The Moderate Murderer, and the Honest Quack (New York: Dodd, Mead, 1929);

The Poet and the Lunatics: Episodes in the Life of Gabriel Gale (London: Cassell, 1929; New York: Dodd, Mead, 1929);

The Thing (London: Sheed & Ward, 1929); republished as *The Thing: Why I Am a Catholic* (New York: Dodd, Mead, 1930);

G. K. C. as M. C., edited by J. P. de Fonseka (London: Methuen, 1929);

Four Faultless Felons (London & Toronto: Cassell, 1930; New York: Dodd, Mead, 1930);

The Resurrection of Rome (London: Hodder & Stoughton, 1930; New York: Dodd, Mead, 1930);

Come to Think of It . . . (London: Methuen, 1930; New York: Dodd, Mead, 1931);

The Ecstatic Thief (New York: Dodd, Mead, 1930);

All Is Grist: A Book of Essays (London: Methuen, 1931; New York: Dodd, Mead, 1932);

Chaucer (London: Faber & Faber, 1932; New York: Farrar & Rinehart, 1932);

Christendom in Dublin (London: Sheed & Ward, 1932; London & New York: Sheed & Ward, 1933);

Sidelights on New London and Newer York and Other Essays (London: Sheed & Ward, 1932; New York: Dodd, Mead, 1932);

All I Survey: A Book of Essays (London: Methuen, 1933; New York: Dodd, Mead, 1933);

St. Thomas Aquinas (London: Hodder & Stoughton, 1933; New York: Sheed & Ward, 1933);

Avowals and Denials: A Book of Essays (London: Methuen, 1934; New York: Dodd, Mead, 1935);

The Scandal of Father Brown (London: Cassell, 1935; New York: Dodd, Mead, 1935);

The Well and the Shallows (London: Sheed & Ward, 1935; New York: Sheed & Ward, 1935);

As I Was Saying (London: Methuen, 1936; New York: Dodd, Mead, 1936);

Autobiography (London: Methuen, 1936; New York: Sheed & Ward, 1936);

The Paradoxes of Mr. Pond (London: Cassell, 1937; New York: Dodd, Mead, 1937);

The Coloured Lands (London: Sheed & Ward, 1938; New York: Sheed & Ward, 1938);

The End of the Armistice (London: Sheed & Ward, 1940; New York: Sheed & Ward, 1940);

The Common Man (London: Sheed & Ward, 1950; New York: Sheed & Ward, 1950);

The Surprise (London & New York: Sheed & Ward, 1952);

A Handful of Authors, edited by Dorothy Collins (London & New York: Sheed & Ward, 1953);

The Glass Walking-Stick and Other Essays, from the Illustrated London News, 1905–1936, edited by Collins (London: Methuen, 1955);

Lunacy and Letters, edited by Collins (London & New York: Sheed & Ward, 1958);

Where All Roads Lead (London: Catholic Truth Society, 1961);

The Man Who Was Orthodox: A Selection from the Uncollected Writings of G. K. Chesterton, edited by A. L. Maycock (London: Dobson, 1963);

The Spice of Life and Other Essays, edited by Collins (Beaconsfield, U.K.: Finlayson, 1964; Philadelphia: Dufour, 1966);

The Apostle and the Wild Ducks, and Other Essays, edited by Collins (London: Elek, 1975);

G. K.'s Weekly: A Sampler, edited by Lyle W. Dorsett (Chicago: Loyola University Press, 1986);

Daylight and Nightmare: Uncollected Stories and Fables of G. K. Chesterton, selected and arranged by Marie Smith (London: Xanadu, 1986; New York: Dodd, Mead, 1986).

Collection: *The Collected Works of G. K. Chesterton,* 21 volumes to date (San Francisco: Ignatius Press, 1986–   ).

G. K. Chesterton, one of the most versatile men of letters of his generation — he distinguished himself, to a greater or lesser degree, as essayist, poet, novelist, playwright, detective story writer, polemicist, art critic, literary critic, Christian apologist — gives a clue to his attitude toward the biographer's art in his *Autobiography,* published posthumously in 1936 and composed during the last years of his life. He warns readers of *Robert Browning* (1903), the first of his biographies, that they will find in the book few biographical facts, and these nearly all wrong. The old man is, of course, having a bit of fun, but it remains true that Chesterton's approach to biography was scarcely orthodox, whatever his other orthodoxies. His work in this genre is best appreciated as the work of an amateur; its con-

Chesterton, 1925

tinuing value, which is considerable, is of the sort that can arise when the amateur is also a man of genius.

Gilbert Keith Chesterton was born on 29 May 1874 in London to Edward Chesterton and Marie Louise Grosjean Chesterton. He was the second of three children. A sister, five years older than Gilbert, died at the age of eight. A brother, Cecil, five years younger than Gilbert, remained his close companion and debating partner throughout Cecil's life. Chesterton would look back on his childhood as a time of almost unshadowed happiness. Especially strong and positive memories focused on a toy theater he was given by his father. The unapologetic artifice of the theater, the hard-edged clarity of its figures, and the worlds of romance, adventure, and fundamental moral conflict that could be represented there may have shaped some of Chesterton's lasting views on the powers and functions of art.

Chesterton enjoyed a largely undistinguished academic career, first at Saint Paul's School and later at University College, London, where from 1893 to 1895 he attended classes in English, French, Latin, and fine arts, without ever sitting an examination or taking a degree. His fine arts classes were conducted at the Slade School of Art, then entering one of its great periods; Chesterton was asked to leave after a year. His study of art, though quickly terminated, confirmed in him a distaste for the aestheticism and impressionism that he saw as dominating the art world of the time. He viewed aestheticism as related to a severing of the ties between art and the ordinary world; impressionism, to a drift toward solipsism, which seemed to him the great philosophical temptation of the age, a temptation he found especially repugnant because he himself felt some of its attraction.

After leaving University College in 1895, Chesterton found work at Redway's, a small publishing house; within months he moved to T. Fisher Unwin, a larger house, with whom he would stay until 1901. During this period he was regularly contributing articles and reviews to periodicals. The novelist E. C. Bentley, a lifelong friend Chesterton first met at Saint Paul's, claimed that the true beginning of Chesterton's literary career was marked by the publication of an unsigned review of the *Ruskin Reader* that appeared in the *Academy* in June 1895.

In 1901 Chesterton, already embarked on a career in journalism and letters and able to see the possibility of supporting a wife on his income, married Frances Blogg, whom he had met in 1896. Frances was a devout Anglo-Catholic, and Chesterton, raised in an atmosphere of liberalism and Unitarianism, moved quickly in that direction. Neither could have seen how far this spiritual journey was to take them.

Chesterton published two books of verse, *Greybeards at Play* and *The Wild Knight,* in 1900 and *The Defendant,* a selection from his periodical articles, in 1901. In 1902 he began writing a weekly column for the *Daily News;* the column, which continued uninterrupted until 1913, established Chesterton's reputation. The freedom he enjoyed in choice of subject matter encouraged a readiness to assertion on virtually any topic, in the spirit of the amateur. The free-form weekly column may also have stimulated Chesterton to the development of his distinctive prose style.

Chesterton's growing reputation — a second gathering of essays, *Twelve Types,* had been well received upon its publication in 1902 — led Macmillan to invite him to contribute a volume on Robert Browning to their English Men of Letters series. Upon receipt of the manuscript, the publishers were appalled. Chesterton's reliance on a memory that, while prodigious, was not infallible, had resulted in a quantity of inaccuracies that far exceeded the publisher's level of tolerance. Disgrace was feared.

In any event the book, published in 1903, enjoyed a considerable success. Favorably reviewed on the whole, it was reprinted annually for three years after its first publication and at intervals for many years more. Chesterton thus was given little incentive to change his research practices. It is doubtful that he would have, anyway.

Chesterton found in Browning someone who shared his own middle-class origins and values. And he found in Browning's poetry a reflection of the political liberalism that the poet embraced and with which the Chesterton of that period strongly

identified. The dramatic monologue itself, Browning's preferred form, seemed to Chesterton imbued with the spirit of liberalism, as each character is allowed to speak for himself.

Robert Browning is the most conventional of Chesterton's biographies. It is clearly organized around a handful of issues, of which the most important is whether Browning is to be regarded as a thinker, as many of his admirers would have claimed in 1903, or as a poet. Chesterton's position is typically clear and his expression of it characteristically emphatic: no poet was ever more a poet, and a Romantic poet at that, than Browning. He defends the poet against the charges of obscurity and of excessive indulgence in the grotesque. Browning's occasional obscurity dramatizes the struggle of language to grasp external reality and our experience of that reality; the grotesque, by making the world stand on its head, demands that we see the world with a proper sense of wonder. That there is a truly existing, truly experienced world and that no language can comprehensively grasp it would become a recurring theme in Chesterton's works. The same complex theme can be seen as a justification for Chesterton's own exploitation of paradox and the unexpected analogy. For Chesterton, the language in which texts are written is a limited instrument, but he is no precursor of deconstruction: there is, for him, an "outside-the-text."

Ultimately, the Browning of Chesterton's biography is very much Chesterton's Browning in his character and his concerns. Yet so great is Chesterton's sympathetic understanding of his subject that his assimilation of the poet to his own agenda hardly entails any significant distortion; rather, it often promotes insight and illumination. A contemporary reviewer observed that Chesterton had made the "true Browning fully visible." He had at least significantly raised the appreciation of Browning as a poet.

Chesterton's second biography, *G. F. Watts,* published in 1904 as part of the Popular Library of Art, is of only marginal relevance to this discussion, since it cannot even under a liberal definition be classified as a literary biography. Its subject, moreover, is largely forgotten today, at least by the general public, and the decline of Watts's reputation had in fact already begun when Chesterton wrote, even though the artist himself was still alive. But Chesterton found Watts, a prominent Victorian portraitist — his subjects included Matthew Arnold, Thomas Carlyle, and John Stuart Mill — and allegorical painter, an attractive alternative to aestheticism and impressionism. The decline of Watts's reputation he attributes to a decline of interest in allegorical painting, and that decline, Chesterton argues, is based on a misunderstanding. Allegorical painting is too often dismissed as an imitation of literature by painting. But it is more accurate to say that an authentic allegorical painting is an utterance in the language of painting, a language of line and color, rather than an attempt to imitate something better said in verbal language. Of Watts's painting entitled *Hope* Chesterton says: "The picture is inadequate; the word 'hope' is inadequate, but between them . . . they almost locate a mystery." The theme of the limitations of verbal language, and of the reality of the mystery that language must struggle to locate, here offered as demanding nonverbal languages like painting, had, we recall, informed Chesterton's reading of Browning.

Chesterton's second literary biography, and his most admired accomplishment in the genre, *Charles Dickens,* was published in 1906. Once again, Chesterton's reliance on memory and his generally casual habits as a researcher led to many inaccuracies. The most important, since it compromised a substantial part of Chesterton's portrayal of the emotional life of his subject, involved his claim that Dickens had fallen in love with all of the Hogarth sisters and married the wrong one. A letter from Dickens's daughter, pointing out that the ages of the sisters at the time of Dickens's courtship of her mother invalidated Chesterton's interpretation, chastened him to the point that he offered to make the appropriate changes in later editions. In fact, he never made any changes; nor did he alter his practices as a researcher.

Most of what Chesterton has to say about Dickens remains unaffected by his occasional factual inaccuracy. Chesterton's Dickens, like his Browning, embodies the liberal spirit, combined with a sentimental Christianity to which Chesterton at this point can still respond uncritically. The later Chesterton might have been more inclined to raise, for instance, the troubling matter of Original Sin.

As a critic Chesterton responds most strongly to the earlier Dickens, especially the Dickens of *The Pickwick Papers* (1836–1837). It is in this Dickens that the gifts for caricature, and for exaggeration generally, are given freest play. Dickens had been attacked for his tendency toward exaggeration, but Chesterton argues that exaggeration is the essence of art. Exaggeration here joins the allegory Chesterton championed in *G. F. Watts,* and the obscurity and indulgence in the grotesque he defended in *Robert Browning,* as an emblem of the compulsion of both verbal and nonverbal languages to push be-

yond the limits of the literal and direct in the attempt to come to terms adequately with the wonder that is reality itself.

For many the book's great strength lies not in the distinctions it draws, for instance between early Dickens and late Dickens, but in the enthusiasms it expresses. Chesterton's power as an appreciative critic is nowhere more dazzlingly on display. Specific critical observations permanently influence one's reading of the novels. The commentaries on individual characters have the mark of genuine insight: they astonish by showing just what it is that has been seen but, until then, unrealized. And it seems unlikely that anyone will surpass Chesterton's summation, in reference to Dickens but with potentially wider application, of what distinguishes the authentic popular artist from the commercial hack: "Dickens did not write what the people wanted; Dickens wanted what the people wanted."

The book was enthusiastically received from the first. Bernard Shaw, a self-styled "supersaturated Dickensite," wrote Chesterton that he had read it "right slap through." William James, Algernon Charles Swinburne, and Theodore Roosevelt were among the book's early admirers. André Maurois later called Chesterton's *Charles Dickens* one of the best biographies ever written, in part because it is not a biography. And T. S. Eliot declared Chesterton the finest living critic of Dickens.

To be sure Dickens provided Chesterton with the opportunity once again to examine some of his own central concerns. But this hardly seems an important objection to what Chesterton achieved. For Chesterton in 1906 was a crucial participant in the establishment of a reputation that had previously been by no means secure. In that sense at least he was creating Dickens for the twentieth-century reader. There is thus little point to skepticism about whether Chesterton's Dickens corresponds to the real man. For those of us who have come after, the real Dickens is, at least in part, Chesterton's portrait of him.

Chesterton's willingness to declare himself boldly and wittily on whatever was on his mind laid him open to challenges from all comers, challenges that he met gleefully. In fact, one of his most important books, *Orthodoxy,* was published in 1908 in response to a challenge, on the occasion of the publication of *Heretics* in 1905, that he declare his own beliefs as well as criticizing those of others. In meeting the many challenges he received, Chesterton developed into one of the most effective debaters and polemical writers of his generation.

ENGLISH MEN OF LETTERS

ROBERT BROWNING

BY

G. K. CHESTERTON

LONDON: MACMILLAN & CO., LIMITED
NINETEEN HUNDRED AND THREE

Title page for Chesterton's biography of the Victorian poet.
Chesterton sees Browning's poetry as a product of the poet's
middle-class origins and his political liberalism.

Of all Chesterton's debating partners the one with whom his name will always be most closely associated is Shaw. Chesterton's book *George Bernard Shaw,* published in 1910, is scarcely a biography. It is rather a critical sketch of a man Chesterton came to value highly as an ideological foe and a personal friend. The focus of Chesterton's criticism is on what he calls Shaw's puritanism, manifested in the triumph of intellect, not merely over emotion but over humanity itself. In thus directing his attack against puritanism, Chesterton assumes definitively the role of champion of Catholic Christianity. Puritanism, intellectually in the vanguard of the Protestant Reformation, has come to represent for Chesterton Christianity's wrong turn, and Shaw is made to represent the still-pernicious consequences of puritanism in Chesterton's own day.

In 1909 Chesterton, at the urging of his wife, had moved to Beaconsfield, twenty-five miles west of London, thus for the first time in his adult creative life putting a significant distance between himself and Fleet Street where, as a practicing journalist, he had established himself as a familiar jovial figure, known for his black cape, his sword cane, and his inexhaustible conviviality as well as for his talents. For some, the move contributed to a lessening of Chesterton's creative energy, as distinguished from quantity of output. But there was still important work to come.

Since *William Blake* (1910) is a volume in the Popular Library of Art, the emphasis naturally falls on Blake the visual artist more than on Blake the poet. It is in fact Blake the mystic, revealed both in the visual art and the poetry, that constitutes

Chesterton's subject. His approach to the life is sketchy and anecdotal. He emphasizes those episodes that bear most strongly on the Blake he has in mind, without feeling bound to incorporate these within a coherent narrative.

The book suffers from certain unresolved tensions in Chesterton's view of Blake. He wants Blake to stand as a positive contrast to an oriental mysticism that here joins aestheticism, impressionism, and solipsism on Chesterton's enemies' list. This false mysticism amounts to an insane simplicity, a vapid denial of complexity, as all is absorbed into the one. Insofar as Chesterton can perceive a hard-edged clarity in the style of the artist and a powerful strain of the practical and rational in the man, Blake looks like Chesterton's sort of mystic. But Chesterton is ultimately defeated by Blake's intransigent and resolutely Protestant individualism, an individualism that motivates Blake's withdrawal into the labyrinths of a private symbolism. One is not surprised that Chesterton prefers the *Songs of Innocence* (1789) and *Songs of Experience* (1794) to the prophetic works. In Blake's songs symbols, embodied in forms that are artfully naive, point the ordinary reader toward a reality they do not claim to comprehend: the questions in "The Tyger" are real questions, conveying real urgency. In the prophetic works, at least in Chesterton's reading, the implicit claim, finally a mad one, is of a vision of truth that is fully incarnated in the poet's private symbolic system.

Although not without its admirers, Chesterton's *William Blake* has been widely regarded as one of his less successful efforts. It must certainly be admitted that Chesterton may here be using Blake, rather than encountering him. Yet the tension between recalcitrant subject and importunate author at moments becomes a vital one. If nothing else it forces Chesterton to articulate a view of mysticism that will prove a driving force in his triumphant life of Saint Francis of Assisi.

Between *William Blake* and *St. Francis of Assisi* (1923) thirteen years passed. During these years Chesterton survived a severe breakdown in health and endured the death of his beloved brother Cecil. He committed himself to editing a weekly journal, work for which he was not temperamentally suited but which would absorb significant energies for the rest of his life. His written work during these years included *The Ballad of the White Horse* (1911), probably his finest poem, and stories featuring the priest-detective Father Brown, his most memorable fictional character and one of the greatest fictional detectives.

In 1922 Chesterton was received into the Roman Catholic church. The structured authority of the church, it seems, provided Chesterton with a transcendent perspective that finally and securely grounded the reality that no one human point of view could comprehend. In his acceptance of such an authority, external to the self and to the individual conscience, Chesterton had found the most powerful counterforce to the solipsism that had been the great intellectual and spiritual temptation of his youth.

St. Francis of Assisi appeared soon after Chesterton's decision to join the Catholic church. The basic episodes of Francis's life are here, but Chesterton is, again, not interested in merely getting the facts straight. Although he defines his position as that of the "modern ordinary outsider and inquirer," it seems rather that he finds in Francis an intimate spiritual companion.

What Francis represents above all for Chesterton is the celebration of existence, based on the recognition that nothing, including ourselves, need have existed. For Chesterton, and for Chesterton's Francis, the world exists not merely as the result of an initiating act by a distant creator but through an act of creation that never ceases. Francis is also the poet whose great Canticle, composed over the course of his adult life, announces that celebration. He is a poet as well in his embodiment and transcendence of the spirit of the Troubadours as he courts his Lady Poverty. But he combines with the spirit of the Troubadour that of the *Jongleur de Dieu* (the transcendent tumbler) — a version of the fool in medieval legend.

Of course, Francis is also a mystic, in what for Chesterton is the healthy tradition of Christian mysticism, a mystic who is not infatuated with mystery for its own sake, and a more satisfactory example of what Chesterton means by mysticism than Blake could ever have been. And Francis is a saint, "one for whom God illustrates and illuminates all things." Chesterton gives a portrait of the saint, but he also gives a glimpse of what the saint can mean to a highly intelligent and deeply individual believer. He may also provide a hint of what the saint might mean, after all, to the modern outsider and inquirer. The book has been enduringly and deservedly popular.

If Chesterton's Catholicism drives his life of Saint Francis, his distributism, the social theory he had come to espouse, motivates his *William Cobbett*, which appeared in 1925. For some little more than nostalgia for a world that never was, Distributism called for redistribution of land among the people, a

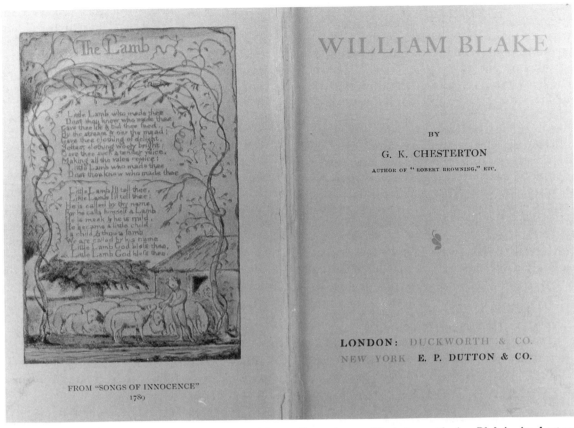

FROM "SONGS OF INNOCENCE"
1789

WILLIAM BLAKE

BY

G. K. CHESTERTON
AUTHOR OF "ROBERT BROWNING," ETC.

LONDON: DUCKWORTH & CO.
NEW YORK E. P. DUTTON & CO.

Frontispiece and title page for Chesterton's biography of the pre-Romantic poet. Chesterton emphasizes Blake's visual art over his poetry.

reaffirmation of craftsmanship over industrial mass production, a general movement toward smallness and decentralization, and a return to a vital sense of community as antidotes to the demoralization industrialism has engendered. Chesterton treats Cobbett as a Distributist *avant la lettre*. This co-optation of Cobbett, while obvious, falls far short of being outrageous. Up to a point, at least, the parallels are there. From a Distributist point of view, Cobbett, active in the early nineteenth century, was angry at the right things and made the right enemies. A true maverick, superficially radical and profoundly conservative, Cobbett sought to break the power of a selfish oligarchy, to restore an earlier, better England that probably had no more basis in reality than the England of the Distributists' imaginations. He despised political parties and industrialism. He championed an ideal of the peasantry and the common people. And, whatever his blind spots and ideological extravagances, he was incorruptible. He was also a vigorous and individual prose stylist, both in his journalism and in *Rural Rides* (1830), the book generally considered his masterpiece.

Cobbett held yet another attraction for Chesterton. Although Cobbett was of Protestant stock, his view of the Protestant Reformation in England was close to Chesterton's own. For Cobbett, the Protestant Reformation was, in its most striking aspect, a land grab. Aside from the theological issues involved, a crime had been committed and not merely a crime against property. England had been robbed of its popular life and of the religious life that had been the heart of it. The churches, still standing though now too grand for the villages that contain them, testify to what has been lost. As Chesterton sums it up, in the Protestant Reformation, "England had been secretly slain." And it is finally to Chesterton's summation that we turn. For, although one would hesitate to quarrel with Chesterton's view that Cobbett saw more clearly than did many of his contemporaries, some of the particulars of what Cobbett is supposed to have seen undeniably reflect the focus of his biographer's attention.

When Chesterton's next biography, *Robert Louis Stevenson*, appeared in 1927, Edmund Gosse, a distinguished critic and a personal friend of Stevenson, commended Chesterton for his restoration of Stevenson to his rightful place in British letters. The Stevenson we find here is an essentially and assertively healthy spirit, who had to struggle to overcome the distorting effects of the puritanism in which he had been raised. Chesterton offers next to nothing in the way of empirical evidence for his interpretation. He merely attributes to Stevenson in a very general way certain psychological and ethical problems and then dilates upon the theme that these are exactly the sorts of problems that might be expected of a young man raised in puritan Edinburgh. At such moments one can only wish that Chesterton had been more willing to expose his version of the truth to the resistance of the fact.

But the Stevenson who really interests Chesterton is not the victim of a puritan upbringing but the spiritually energetic man who refused to be a victim either of psychological distortion or of physical deterioration. Again, Chesterton writes as an appreciative critic, one of his most attractive roles. Noting that Stevenson, like Chesterton himself, spent hours as a boy absorbed in his toy theater, Chesterton argues that this experience encouraged in Stevenson a bias toward the hard, clear edge, which would be the basis of much of his best writing.

Chesterton finds much of this best in Stevenson's adventure stories. Nor does he simply note, as many readers might, that Stevenson happens to be very good at adventure stories. Chesterton finds significant value in the adventure story itself. Its great action motif — a good thing has been endangered and can be saved only by risk — is for Chesterton a metaphor for deep spiritual truths, and Chesterton the critic will always value the metaphorical over the metonymic. Thus that the adventure story develops its motif in terms of romance rather than of realism is for Chesterton no barrier to serious appreciation. Romance is one of those broadly metaphorical approaches to reality, an approach by analogy, that Chesterton prefers.

Responses to *Robert Louis Stevenson* have been mixed. Maisie Ward, Chesterton's friend, publisher, and biographer, regards it as the best of his literary studies. Eliot, while approving of parts of the book, finds Chesterton's style exasperating. Christopher Hollis numbers the book among Chesterton's failures. It may be noted that while he was writing *Robert Louis Stevenson,* Chesterton was also at work on his *Autobiography.* This may have contributed to a domination of subject by biographer that seems extreme even by Chesterton's usual standards in these matters.

At the time of the publication of *Robert Louis Stevenson,* Chesterton announced that biographies of Savonarola and Napoleon were in preparation. Neither was ever published, and there is no manuscript evidence that either was ever begun. His next biography, *Chaucer,* appeared in 1932. The skimpiness of factual knowledge of Chaucer might have proved an obstacle for many biographers; for Chesterton, of course, it was no such thing. His course, as in the past, is to pursue the man behind the work and the world behind the man and to be ready always to address the larger issues that arise from one's reading of the author's symbols.

In this case the world behind the man is medieval England, in fact the very England that Chesterton had said in *William Cobbett* was secretly slain by the Protestant Reformation. Part of Chesterton's effort here is to bring that world to life. Chaucer, he says, is the most English of poets; certainly, in Chesterton's view, he was the greatest of England's poets when England was most truly England. Chesterton praises Chaucer as a novelist before there were novels, and as a poet at once simple and sophisticated, a possibility in a culture in which intellectuals and ordinary people still lived in a vital relationship with one another. His work manifests everywhere a complexity of subject and attitude: a complexity missed by modern readers who are naive enough to confuse Chaucer's criticism of his church with heresy, or modern enough to lack that medieval Catholic sense of balance that can appreciate the Chaucerian palinode, the poet's dismissal of his art viewed in the light of the eternal.

It is the meaning of Chaucer, says Chesterton, that whenever medievalism found its center of gravity that center was always a center of gaiety. The subject of Chesterton's last biography, published in 1933, was the medieval world's great seeker of the center, Saint Thomas Aquinas.

Chesterton could claim no special credentials for this undertaking. Not a trained philosopher, he had not even made a systematic study of the philosophy of Aquinas. Ward has recorded the fears she felt, as Chesterton's American publisher, upon hearing of the project: fears that Chesterton was attempting something beyond his abilities. And her fears, she admits, would have been even more intense had she been aware of his methods of composition, which consisted of dictating to his secretary at irregular intervals, consulting neither notes nor books. When, about halfway through the project, Chesterton decided that he did need some books, he admitted cheerfully that he had no idea just what books he needed.

Chesterton, left, Maurice Baring, standing, and Hilaire Belloc
(painting by Sir James Gunn, National Portrait Gallery)

St. Thomas Aquinas purports to offer a popular sketch of a great historical character. That Chesterton's is one of the more valuable popular studies of Aquinas has been recognized since its original publication. But what he in fact achieved amounts to a good deal more than that. Dom Etienne Gilson, one of the most respected Thomists of his generation, declared Chesterton's the best book ever written on the subject, not finding it necessary to qualify his judgment with words like *popular*.

Since the life of Aquinas was lived mainly in the mind and spirit, it offers few dramatic events to the biographer. One of these, the attempted abduction of Aquinas by relatives in an apparent effort to prevent him from becoming a poor friar – seeing in Thomas the makings of a powerful abbot – Chesterton treats with humorous detachment. As for Aquinas's late perception that all he had done was straw, leading him to abandon his intellectual work, Chesterton seems to feel it would be irreverent to probe; many, of course, would argue that probing

of that sort is precisely the biographer's job. Chesterton also sketches in some of the salient features of the world behind Aquinas, the Holy Roman Empire in the thirteenth century. Yet one may suppose that Chesterton is at least as concerned with Aquinas's relation to the world of the twentieth century.

In his approach to Aquinas, Chesterton radiates all the assurance of the pre–Vatican II Catholic. He sees in the theology of the Protestant Reformation – a theology that, in Chesterton's view, has little meaning in the twentieth century – a resurgence of the old Augustinian pessimism, but now incarnated in that central figure of modernity, the "personality": most impressively, in Martin Luther. Within the Catholic tradition, Augustinian pessimism is part of a complex balance. Cut loose from that tradition, it becomes heresy. Aquinas, according to Chesterton, was one of those who provided a balance to the Augustinian tendency, thus reestablishing the center of gravity. Aquinas also absorbed the challenge to orthodoxy represented by the Aristotelian revolution: the impact, felt throughout Christendom, of the rediscovery of the great Greek philosopher. Aquinas's triumph was, as Chesterton sees it, not to reconcile Christ to Aristotle, but to reconcile Aristotle to Christ.

For Chesterton Aquinas is above all the philosopher of common sense. From an initial trust in the ordinary world as we know it, we proceed to the establishment of a rational foundation for faith in God. Not everyone would follow Aquinas all the way, even assuming one is ready to accept his starting point; but Chesterton finds most congenial the notion that a joyous acceptance of existence, one of his own great themes, leads to an affirmation of God. And there must have been a shock of recognition at Aquinas's declaration that we speak of God and of God's attributes by analogy. It is certainly not the case that Chesterton based the view of language traced throughout the present discussion on a reading of Aquinas, but it was no doubt a source of profound emotional and spiritual satisfaction that a view of language originally meant to suggest the relation between self and external reality could now be seen as of the essence of the relation between the self and ultimate reality.

Aquinas the thinker is of course also Aquinas the writer. Apart perhaps from a Latin poem or two sung in Catholic churches until the advent of the vernacular mass (and, even today, sung in translation), Aquinas's works may deceive us into thinking they are not written at all. In their austerity they seem to proceed directly from a disembodied intellect. But Aquinas was a poet, and Chesterton is not the only critic to note that the *Summa Theologiae* and the other philosophical and theological writings are masterpieces of composition, remarkable for their clarity, range, and balance. Chesterton especially appreciates Aquinas's practice of anticipating and stating — immediately, clearly, and forcefully — the salient objections to each position he takes. He is hectoring himself, and Chesterton, the old debater, is delighted.

Chesterton finds in Aquinas an author whose thought speaks directly to Chesterton's own mature temperament. If the Roman Catholic church gave Chesterton the structure he had been seeking in his spiritual quest, Aquinas provided him with the philosophical-intellectual correlative to the faith in which he had come to rest. Apart from its genuine value as a popular introduction to a great thinker, then, Chesterton's *St. Thomas Aquinas* allows us to observe the engagement of a great philosopher and theologian

by one of the liveliest *English* intellects of the twentieth century.

As Chesterton's remarks on his life of Browning suggest, his values were never those of the biographer by vocation. Biography gave him the opportunity to explore his own intellectual, ethical, and religious interests through the lives and works of artists, writers, and saints. When his imaginative sympathy with his subject was sufficiently strong, as in his books on Browning and Dickens, the result could be an illuminating portrait. When his interests and those of his subject touched only incidentally, as in the life of Blake, the result could, at least as portrait, be less satisfactory. Chesterton would, no doubt, be a more satisfactory biographer had he shown a greater dedication to the factual. There may be no such thing as an objective biography; great biographies are written out of intensely felt relationships between the subject of the biography and the biographer. But the resistance of the fact can provide the tension that leads from felt relationship to fully achieved work of the biographer's art. That tension may be too seldom felt in the biographical writings — "biographical sketches," he often called them — of Chesterton. But much of Chesterton's biographical work provides at the very least valuable perspectives of his subjects, and every biography by Chesterton reaffirms the quality of the mind at play. Chesterton's biographies may be read as parts of an ultimately coherent body of work, and they are perhaps best appreciated within that context. Chesterton's fame has never been eclipsed; he continues to find enthusiastic new readers; he holds the admiration of a critically demanding minority; and a "Chesterton revival" has come to seem almost a biennial event. The biographies play no inconsiderable part in the dynamics of his critical reputation. Chesterton has not yet "outlived his century," but the prospects of his earning a permanent, if not primary, place in our literary and cultural tradition look excellent.

Bibliographies:

John Sullivan, *G. K. Chesterton: A Bibliography* (London: University of London Press, 1958);

Sullivan, *Chesterton Continued: A Bibliographical Supplement* (London: University of London Press, 1968).

Biographies:

W. R. Titterton, *G. K. Chesterton: A Portrait* (London: Organ, 1936);

Maisie Ward, *Gilbert Keith Chesterton* (New York: Sheed & Ward, 1943);

Dudley Barker, *G. K. Chesterton: A Biography* (New York: Stein & Day, 1973);

Alzina Stone Dale, *The Outline of Sanity: A Life of G. K. Chesterton* (Grand Rapids, Mich.: Eerdmans, 1982);

Michael Ffinch, *G. K. Chesterton* (San Francisco: Harper & Row, 1986);

Michael Coren, *Gilbert: The Man Who Was G. K. Chesterton* (New York: Paragon House, 1990).

References:

W. H. Auden, ed., Introduction to *G. K. Chesterton: A Selection from His Non-fictional Prose* (London: Faber & Faber, 1970);

Hilaire Belloc, *The Place of G. K. Chesterton in English Letters* (London & New York: Sheed & Ward, 1940);

Anthony Mattheus Adrianus Bogaerts, *Chesterton and the Victorian Age* (Hilversum, Netherlands: Rozenbeek en Venemans, 1940);

Ian Boyd, *The Novels of G. K. Chesterton: A Study in Art and Propaganda* (New York: Barnes & Noble, 1975);

Emile Cammaerts, *The Laughing Prophet: The Seven Virtues and G. K. Chesterton* (London: Methuen, 1937);

Margaret Canovan, *G. K. Chesterton: Radical Populist* (New York & London: Harcourt Brace Jovanovich, 1977);

D. J. Conlon, ed., *G. K. Chesterton: A Half Century of Views* (Oxford & New York: Oxford University Press, 1987);

Conlon, ed., *G. K. Chesterton: The Critical Judgments, Part I: 1900–1937* (Antwerp: Antwerp Studies in English Literature, 1976);

Alzina Stone Dale, *The Art of G. K. Chesterton* (Chicago: Loyola University Press, 1985);

T. S. Eliot, Obituary for Chesterton, *Tablet,* 20 June 1936, p. 785;

Maurice Evans, *G. K. Chesterton* (Cambridge: Cambridge University Press, 1939);

Jeffrey Hart, "In Praise of Chesterton," *Yale Review,* 53 (1963): 49–60;

Christopher Hollis, *The Mind of Chesterton* (London: Hollis & Carter, 1970);

Lynette Hunter, *G. K. Chesterton: Explorations in Allegory* (London: Macmillan, 1979);

Hugh Kenner, *Paradox in Chesterton* (London: Sheed & Ward, 1948);

Elizabeth Sewell, "G. K. Chesterton: the Giant Upside-Down," *Thought,* 30 (1955–1956): 555–576;

Maisie Ward, *Return to Chesterton* (London & New York: Sheed & Ward, 1952);

Garry Wills, *Chesterton: Man & Mask* (New York: Sheed & Ward, 1961).

Papers:

The largest collection of Chesterton's papers is held in the Robert John Bayer Memorial Chesterton Collection at the John Carroll University Library, Cleveland, Ohio. Other materials are held at Columbia University, Marquette University, and the British Library.

W. G. Collingwood

(6 August 1854 – 1 October 1932)

Phillip Mallett
University of Saint Andrews

BOOKS: *The Philosophy of Ornament* (Orpington, Kent: George Allen, 1883);

The Limestone Alps of Savoy: A Study in Physical Geology (Orpington, Kent: George Allen, 1884);

A Book of Verses (Orpington, Kent: George Allen, 1885);

Astrology in the Apocalypse, an Essay on Biblical Allusions to Chaldean Science (Orpington, Kent: George Allen, 1886);

John Ruskin. A Biographical Outline (London: J. S. Virtue, 1889);

The Art of Teaching of John Ruskin (London: Percival, 1891; New York: Putnam, 1891);

The Life and Work of John Ruskin, 2 volumes (London: Methuen, 1893; Boston: Houghton Mifflin, 1893; revised second edition, London: Methuen, 1900; Boston & New York: Houghton, Mifflin, 1909);

Thorstein of the Mere: A Saga of the Northmen in Lakeland (London: Edward Arnold, 1895; revised edition, Kendal: Titus Wilson, 1909);

The Bondwoman: A Story of the Northmen in Lakeland (London: Edward Arnold, 1896); republished as *The Bondwoman: A Saga of Langland* (London: Heinemann, 1932);

Coniston Tales. Told by W. G. C. (Ulverston: William Holmes, 1899);

A Pilgrimage to the Saga-Steads of Iceland, by Collingwood and Jon Stefansson (Ulverston: William Holmes, 1899);

The Lake Counties (London: Dent's County Guides, 1902; new and revised edition, London & New York: Frederick Warne, 1932);

Ruskin Relics (London: Isbister, 1903; New York: Crowell, 1904);

The Fésole Club Papers, being Lessons in Sketching for Home-Learners (Ulverston: William Holmes, 1906);

Dutch Agnes, her Valentine, being the Journal of the Curate of Coniston, 1616–1623 (Kendal: Titus Wilson, 1910; London: Heinemann, 1931);

The Likeness of King Elfwald: A Story of Northumberland and Iona at the Beginning of the Viking Age (Kendal: Titus Wilson, 1917);

Angles, Danes, and Norse in the District of Huddersfield (Huddersfield: Tolson Memorial Museum Publications, 1921);

Lake District History (Kendal: Titus Wilson & Son, 1925);

Northumbrian Crosses of the Pre-Norman Age (London: Faber & Gwyer, 1927).

OTHER: *The Economist of Xenophon,* translated by Collingwood and A. D. O. Wedderburn (London: Ellis & White, 1876);

The Poems of John Ruskin, edited by Collingwood (Orpington, Kent: George Allen, 1891; New York: Merrill, 1891);

John Ruskin, *Verona: and Other Lectures,* edited, with an introduction, by Collingwood (Orpington, Kent: George Allen, 1894);

The Ruskin Reader, edited by Collingwood (Orpington, Kent: George Allen, 1895);

William S. Calverley, *Notes on the Early Sculptured Crosses, Shrines and Monuments in the Present Diocese of Carlisle,* edited by Collingwood (Cumberland and Westmoreland Antiquarian and Archaeological Society, Extra Series, Volume 11, 1899);

Ruskin Exhibition, Coniston, from July 21 to September 8, 1900. A Catalogue, prepared by Collingwood (Ulverston: William Holmes, 1900);

Transactions of the Cumberland and Westmoreland Antiquarian and Archaeological Society, 32 volumes, edited by Collingwood (Kendal: Titus Wilson, 1900–1932);

The Life and Death of Cormac the Skald, translated by Collingwood and Jon Stefansson (Ulverston: William Holmes, 1902);

Chrétien de Troyes, *King William the Wanderer,* translated by Collingwood (London: S. C. Brown, Langham, 1904).

49

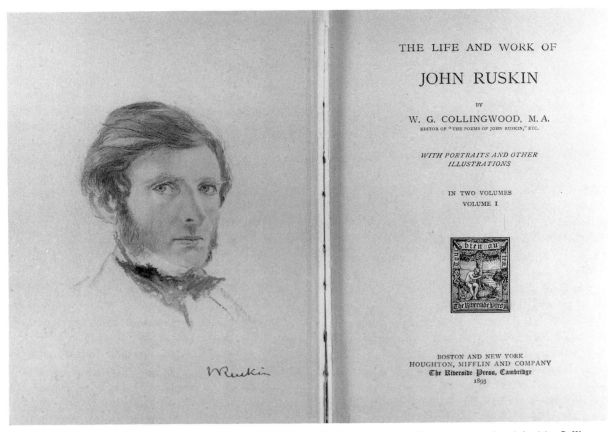

Frontispiece and title page for the American edition of Collingwood's biography of the Victorian art and social critic; Collingwood treats Ruskin's flaws and eccentrities with sympathetic candor

W. G. Collingwood was a man of many talents and interests: a geologist, an antiquarian, an artist as well as a critic and historian of art, a novelist, a translator, and a scholar of Icelandic history and literature. He achieved distinction in all these fields, but he is now best remembered in connection with John Ruskin. In the 1840s and 1850s Ruskin had established himself as the foremost art critic of the age with a series of major books, notably *Modern Painters* (1843–1860), *The Seven Lamps of Architecture* (1849), and *The Stones of Venice* (1851–1853). But his belief that any work of art, good or bad, was necessarily the exponent of the political and spiritual values of the society in which it was produced had driven him to write a series of essays in social criticism, furiously attacking the liberal ideology of the nineteenth century, and to support his written arguments by a range of increasingly desperate attempts to reform English society. By 1872, when Collingwood arrived in Oxford, Ruskin was deeply in need of just such a friend, a younger and a happier man, who would serve him loyally and generously as disciple, secretary, and biographer.

William Gershom Collingwood was born in Liverpool on 6 August 1854, the eldest child of the landscape painter William Collingwood and his Swiss wife, Marie Imhoff. From early childhood he was a regular visitor to the Lake District, in which he was later to make his home and which was the subject of much of his work as art historian and antiquarian. He studied at Liverpool College before going to University College, Oxford, in 1872, where his tutor was Bernard Bosanquet. While in Oxford he attached himself to the idealist school led by T. H. Green but still more deeply to Ruskin, then Slade Professor of Art. Ruskin's lectures at Oxford were only one element of a passionate attempt to renew the spiritual and cultural health of the nation, and he was already engaged in various philanthropic schemes, some quixotic, some profoundly influential. Collingwood soon attracted Ruskin's attention and at his request collaborated with a fellow disciple, Alexander Wedderburn (later, with E. T. Cook, the editor of the thirty-nine-volume Library Edition of Ruskin's *Works*), on a translation of *The Economist of Xenophon,* which Ruskin greatly valued as a treatise on the wise management of a nation's resources. Collingwood recounts that when the work was issued in July 1876 Ruskin gave his translators the profits: "It will keep you in raspberry jam," he said, "and I have had a postal order for my share regularly these nearly thirty years."

In addition to this work, Collingwood distinguished himself by winning the Lothian Prize for an essay on "The Institution and Purposes of Knighthood," a thoroughly Ruskinian topic. After graduating with a First in Greats in 1876, he went on to study under Alphonse Legros at the Slade School of Art, exhibiting at the Royal Academy for the first time in 1880. In 1882 he joined Ruskin on a European tour, sketching French and Italian sculpture for him, and simultaneously gathering material for a geologic and topographical study titled *The Limestone Alps of Savoy: A Study in Physical Geology* (1884), which was conceived as a supplement to Ruskin's own *Deucalion* (1875–1883). In 1883 he married Edith Mary Isaac, daughter of Thomas Isaac, and moved to Gillhead in the Lake District, where he assisted Ruskin as his secretary. He wryly recorded that his duties were hardly so clearly defined as the title suggests, since he "did everything but write, and sometimes was packing parcels or sweeping leaves while the valet was copying lectures on Greek art." "Doing everything but write" included stranger activities than packing and sweeping. On one occasion, while out on the moors, he caught a viper in his bare hands (Ruskin kept and studied the viper and in 1880 gave a lecture at the London Institution called "A Caution to Snakes," later printed in *Deucalion*). On another occasion he built at Ruskin's request a large, hollow astronomical globe, which was set up in the playground at the nearby Coniston school.

Ruskin was at this time living at Brantwood in the Lake District; his mental instability, following his first prolonged breakdown in 1878, was by now all too obvious, and Collingwood learned to understand his sufferings by nursing them. Whatever personal hopes he had of a career were sacrificed to the need to help Ruskin through these last terrible years, and in 1891 the Collingwoods, now with four young children, moved to Lanehead, Coniston, to be nearer at hand. Collingwood continued to paint, but from 1887 he increasingly gave his time to the work of the Cumberland and Westmoreland Antiquarian and Archaeological Society, of which he became president in 1920, a post he held until shortly before his death, when his son, R. G. Collingwood, was elected to succeed him. His antiquarian studies were scrupulously pursued, and he brought a close

attention to bear on the *Transactions* of the society, of which thirty-two volumes were either edited by him or produced under his guidance. He was, in addition, a regular contributor, writing on a huge range of subjects – place names, pre-Norman artifacts, Bronze Age interments, Elizabeth mining – as well as taking charge of a number of excavations. But he also experimented with historical fiction, trying to unite in one work "the outline fact, the shading inference, and the colouring imagination." In 1895 he published his first novel, or rather hybrid of saga and novel, *Thorstein of the Mere: A Saga of the Northmen in Lakeland,* which achieved a moderate success. He followed this in 1896 with *The Bondwoman: A Story of the Northmen in Lakeland,* a re-creation of Langdale in Anglo-Saxon times. To his dismay, he fell foul of various critics who were already agitated by the "new woman" fiction of the time, including Thomas Hardy's *Jude the Obscure* (1895), and found himself attacked for representing a tenth-century slave as her master's unwilling concubine. Like Hardy, he took the attacks to heart, and for the next thirty years he allowed only local Lake District publishers to bring out his books.

He had already begun to write about Ruskin, editing *The Poems of John Ruskin* in 1891 and *The Ruskin Reader,* concentrating on Ruskin's earlier writings on art and architecture, in 1895. These were followed in 1896 by an abridged edition of *Fors Clavigera* (1871–1884), cut down to four volumes by the omission of the letters Ruskin had included from his correspondents, and of various appendices and other additional material. Useful as all these volumes were, Collingwood's most valuable contributions to Ruskin studies were two other books published in the same decade: *The Art of Teaching of John Ruskin* (1891), an intelligent and sympathetic exposition of Ruskin's ideas, and then a two-volume biography, *The Life and Work of John Ruskin* (1893). Ruskin had by this time acquired a large and varied following, not least among working-class readers, and Collingwood's *The Life and Work of John Ruskin* became a widely read book, popular enough to persuade Methuen to bring out an abridged one-volume version in their Shilling Books series in 1911.

Collingwood had also become acquainted with members of the William Morris circle, in particular with Eirikr Magnusson and Jon Stefansson, and they had aroused his interest in Viking art. In 1897 he traveled with Stefansson to Iceland and collaborated with him in a record of their journey, *A Pilgrimage to the Saga-Steads of Iceland* (1899). Soon afterward, in January 1900, after a decade of mostly sorrowful silence, came the death of Ruskin; the cross which stands over his grave was designed by Collingwood. No longer tied to the Lake District, he took up the post of professor of fine art at University College, Reading, while continuing to pursue his studies of pre-Norman sculpture in Yorkshire and elsewhere and to play a leading part in the researches of the Cumberland and Westmoreland Antiquarian and Archaeological Society. Each volume of the Society's *Transactions* carries on its cover a design drawn by Collingwood himself, representing a young man uncovering with his spade an altar on which is inscribed the word *DISCIPULINAE,* and a young woman in classical costume, presumably a votaress of Clio, who is recording his find. The design symbolizes an ideal which Ruskin would have endorsed: the mutual cooperation of physical labor, artwork, and fidelity to the traditions of history.

In 1902 Collingwood published a study of *The Lake Counties* for Dent's County Guides series; the last piece he was to write for publication was a preface for the revised and enlarged edition which appeared in 1932. He also returned to novel writing with *Dutch Agnes, her Valentine, being the Journal of the Curate of Coniston, 1616–1623,* published in 1910; a fourth novel, *The Likeness of King Elfwald,* set in Northumbria and Iona at the beginning of the Viking age, appeared in 1917. But by this time World War I had broken out, and Collingwood was working in London with the Admiralty Intelligence Division. In the spirit of his hero, the presents he had received from Ruskin were sold to raise funds for the Red Cross.

Entering his sixty-fifth year as the war ended, Collingwood returned to the Lake District with his health impaired but his will to work as strong as ever and his enthusiasm as a walker and climber undiminished. In 1925 he published his *Lake District History,* which was quickly accepted as the standard work, but his main effort of these years was the preparation of his monumental study of *Northumbrian Crosses of the Pre-Norman Age,* published in 1927 and marking the culmination of his work on a subject he had been making his own for more than thirty years. But in the same year he suffered the first of a series of strokes. His wife died in 1928, and he himself on 1 October 1932. He left a son and three daughters.

Collingwood was not a professional biographer. He wrote *The Life and Work of John Ruskin* because he knew the man and loved him only just this side of idolatry. His work shows all the strengths and virtually none of the weaknesses one might expect of a book written from this position. Ruskin's private life has frequently drawn attention away from his writings: the annulment of his marriage to Euphemia Chalmers Gray (usually known as Effie) and her subsequent marriage to the Pre-Raphaelite painter John Everett Millais, whose work Ruskin had championed; his infatuation with Rose La Touche, only ten years old when he met her and thirty years his junior; the periods of mental illness, vividly if not precisely diagnosed as "brain fever" — all these have invited the efforts of biographers. Collingwood treats the two first briefly but with a degree of candor, and so far as the brevity allows with sympathy for all those involved: recognizing in Effie, for example, "the disappointment and disillusioning of a young girl who found herself married, by parental arrangement, to a man with whom she had nothing in common." Collingwood's openness is all the more commendable because he was writing while his subject was still alive. His hand was no doubt strengthened by the fact that Ruskin himself had vigorously defended James Anthony Froude's biography (1882–1884) of Thomas Carlyle against those such as Charles Eliot Norton who were indignant at its lack of discretion. But there would in any event have been little point in trying to conceal the long-drawn-out relationship with Rose, since Ruskin had so often referred to it in his own writings, most recently in the autobiographical *Praeterita* (1889). He had also written openly of his mental breakdown in 1878. Collingwood's account of a similar period of illness is eloquent: "all that I now remember of many a weary night and day is the vision of a great soul in torment, and through purgatorial fires the ineffable tenderness of the real man emerging, with his passionate appeal to justice and baffled desire for truth. . . . Some, in those trials, learnt as they could not otherwise have learnt to know him, and to love him as never before."

Ruskin was the greatest writer of nonfiction prose in the nineteenth century and one of the greatest in the language; those who write about him need to look to their own prose. Collingwood writes with an ease and lucidity which no later biographer has been able to surpass, and with an instinctive sympathy. He is, for example, shrewd, in Ruskin's own manner, about Ruskin's first love affair, a hopeless infatuation with the devoutly Catholic daughter of his father's business partner: "he tried to amuse her, but he tried too seriously." The sympathy with which he writes about Ruskin's family life must owe a good deal to conversations with Ruskin. His "gradual estrangement" from his parents was, Collingwood suggests, still more harmful than a sudden breach would have been, since it did not seem to invite "reconciliation on a new basis."

This allowed the pain to linger on, as he seemed to them to drift away from their track, and they saw, or thought they saw, "their work being gradually undone, their cherished hopes frustrated, their intentions unfulfilled." Later biographers have as a rule been less understanding, particularly when writing of Ruskin's father.

Collingwood is also an intelligent commentator on Ruskin's own prose, particularly when writing of *Fors Clavigera*. At a time when many even of Ruskin's friends longed to be given more fine writing, Collingwood recognized a new "unity of style" in *Fors Clavigera*, unlike the style of earlier works "where flowery rhetorical passages are tagged to less interesting chapters." *Fors Clavigera*, Collingwood noted, was not all rhapsodic and elegiac; there was too a continuous play of wit, a "sustained vivacity" challenging the prevailing gloom. But Ruskin's mingling of jest and earnest was often misunderstood. Matthew Arnold, for example, writing on "The Literary Influence of Academies" in *Essays in Criticism* (1865), instanced Ruskin's prose as evidence of the provincialism, the want of urbanity, in English writing. But what Arnold saw as a lack of restraint Collingwood identified as the inevitable urgency of integrity: "He forswore levity, but soon relapsed into the old style, out of sheer sincerity: for he was too much in earnest not to be himself all over in his utterances, without writing up to, or down to, any other person's standard." This is well said, and the emphasis on sincerity is in keeping with the spirit of Ruskin's own criticism.

Most of Ruskin's biographers have shown little interest in Ruskin's poetry, and Collingwood is among the few to have written helpfully about it, rightly noting that his repeated efforts to win the Newdigate prize at Oxford served only to undermine the individuality of his writing. Ruskin's first journey abroad without his parents, made in 1845, released "new and deeper feelings" and "new resources of diction," but by that time the habit of writing to order had eroded his enthusiasm for poetic composition, and he soon abandoned it altogether. As Collingwood puts it, "he was never so near being a poet as when he gave up writing verse."

Collingwood was also a gifted expositor of Ruskin's ideas. It was not his purpose, in writing the biography, to examine the detail of Ruskin's arguments so much as to set out as clearly as possible their main lines and their logical force. Summarizing the famous chapter on "The Nature of Gothic,"

from the second volume of *The Stones of Venice* (1851–1853), Collingwood focuses on "the great doctrine that art cannot be produced except by artists; that architecture, insofar as it is an art, does not mean the mechanical execution, by unintelligent workmen, of vapid working-drawings from an architect's office; that, just as Socrates postponed the day of justice until philosophers should be kings and kings philosophers, so Ruskin postponed the day of art until workmen should be artists, and artists workmen." However, "if the workman must be made an artist he must have the experience, the feelings of an artist, as well as the skill: and that involves every circumstance of education and opportunity which may make for his truest well-being." It follows that an adequate theory of art will have to consider "the fundamental principles of human intercourse and social economy" which shape those circumstances. Ruskin's social essays, then, are not a distraction, but the necessary complement of his work as a critic of art.

The argument outlined here may be right or wrong, but these are clearly the terms in which Ruskin himself saw the development of his life's work. One of the strengths of Collingwood's various books on Ruskin is that he was among the first to recognize in his writings what J. H. Buckley, in a chapter on "The Moral Aesthetic," was to describe as a "deep if chaotic coherence." "The careful student," wrote Collingwood, "should be able to trace [Ruskin's] genius, down to the end, in continuous and rational progression." It was one of the deficiencies of Victorian scholarship in the first half of the twentieth century that so few writers tried seriously to test the validity of Collingwood's claim.

Derrick Leon's biography, *Ruskin: The Great Victorian*, published in 1949, opened a significant new phase in Ruskin scholarship, and since then the research of other scholars — including Helen Gill Viljoen, Mary Lutyens, James Dearden, and Van Akin Burd — have added greatly to a contemporary understanding of Ruskin. But the intimacy of Collingwood's knowledge of Ruskin's later life and the sympathy with his mind that developed over more than twenty years make his biography indispensable to the Ruskin scholar. It was his belief that Ruskin was essentially a good man that led Collingwood to become a disciple and a biographer. A rare and unaffected love of goodness marks almost every page of *The Life and Work of John Ruskin*. It is a testimony to the author as well as to the writer it celebrates.

Sir Sidney Colvin
(18 June 1845 – 11 May 1927)

R. S. White
University of Western Australia

BOOKS: *Children in Italian and English Design* (London: Seeley, Jackson & Halliday, 1872);

A Selection from Occasional Writings on Fine Art (London: Privately printed, 1873);

Albrecht Durer, His Teachers, His Rivals, and His Scholars (London: Seeley, Jackson & Halliday, 1877);

Landor (London: Macmillan, 1881; New York: Harper, n.d.);

Keats (London: Macmillan, 1887; New York: Harper, 1887; revised edition, London: Macmillan, 1918);

Selected Drawings from Old Masters in the University Galleries and in the Library at Christ Church, Oxford, 3 volumes (Oxford: Clarendon Press / London: Henry Frowde, 1903–1907);

On Concentration and Suggestion in Poetry (Oxford: Oxford University Press, 1915);

John Keats: His Life and Poetry, His Friends, Critics, and After-Fame (London: Macmillan, 1917; New York: Scribners, 1917);

Memories and Notes of Persons and Places 1852–1912 (London: Edward Arnold, 1921; New York: Scribners, 1921).

OTHER: *Selections from Landor,* collected by Colvin (London: Macmillan, 1882);

Scientific Papers of Fleeming Jenkin, collected by Colvin and J. A. Ewing (London & New York: Longmans, Green, 1887);

Vailima Letters; Being Correspondence Addressed by Robert Louis Stevenson to Sidney Colvin, November, 1890–October, 1894, collected by Colvin (Chicago: Stone & Kimball, 1895);

The Letters of Robert Louis Stevenson to His Family and Friends, edited by Colvin (New York: Scribners, 1907).

The career of Sir Sidney Colvin appears to be that of a professional art historian and curator who dabbled in literary affairs as something of an amateur hobby. The impression is, however, misleading. Colvin saw his real calling as that of literary biographer and as annalist of great men of letters of his day whom he met and befriended. In this he was right. He is remembered not as Slade Professor of Art at Cambridge, director of the Fitzwilliam Museum, nor as keeper of the Department of Prints and Drawings in the British Museum, but chiefly as the writer of the first academic biography of John Keats and as the faithful chronicler of his close friend Robert Louis Stevenson.

Colvin was born on 18 June 1845 at Norwood in London. He was the third son of Bazett David Colvin, an East Indian merchant who owned The Grove, Little Bealings, Suffolk, where Sidney spent his boyhood, and Mary Steuart Bayley, daughter of William Butterworth Bayley. Like so many from privileged families in Victorian England, both parents had maintained trading and business interests with India for several generations. Colvin was educated at home in Suffolk because, he said later, his mother had a horror of schools. His elderly recollections in *Memories and Notes of Persons and Places 1852–1912* (1921) reveal that in his childhood and boyhood he was encouraged by his mother to read voraciously and that he played on the village cricket team, ran with the local harriers, and wandered happily about the five-hundred-acre grounds of the handsome country house set in quiet lowland landscape. His elderly tutor, a man with "dyed whiskers and corpulent figure and choleric temper," prepared him well in the classics, although the man was "neither by age nor disposition . . . any sort of friend or companion."

From his early years his family visited the Ruskins on Denmark Hill, and Ruskin was an ex-

Sir Sidney Colvin

tremely important influence and something of an idol to Colvin until later a rift developed. Colvin entered Trinity College, Cambridge, in 1863. He was third in his class in the classical tripos and won the Chancellor's Gold Medal for a poem on Florence; he was elected to a fellowship at the college in 1868. However, after he graduated in 1867 he appears to have spent most of his time in London, devoting himself to the study of the fine arts and contributing reviews to the *Pall Mall Gazette* and the *Globe* and, from 1871, articles to the *Portfolio,* an art periodical founded in 1869 by Philip Gilbert Hamerton. He became a member of the New Club, later to be named the Savile Club, in the rooms of which his portrait painted by Theodore Roussel in 1908 still hangs. This gave him an entrée into the London intelligentsia. His growing connections in the literary and artistic communities gained him election in 1871 to the Society of Dilettanti, of which he was to be honorary secretary from 1891 to 1896.

This was "a small private society of gentlemen" founded in the 1730s and loosely dedicated to influencing public taste in the fine arts in England.

Colvin's reputation as an art critic, based on his occasional reviews, essays, and contributions to books, rose so quickly that in 1873 he was elected as the Slade Professor of Fine Arts at Cambridge, which he was to hold through several renewals until 1885. It was over his appointment that relations between Colvin and his hero, the holder of the corresponding chair at Oxford, John Ruskin, soured in a way which could never be recovered. Colvin seems to have solicited Ruskin's support, which was decidedly not given. In a frank letter implicitly accusing Colvin of being young, impudent, and presumptuous, Ruskin ruled out of the running for such a post one who was not a proven "draughtsman" and advised Colvin to spend at least ten years teaching art "in any general sense" before having the temerity to seek such a position.

After the appointment Ruskin tried to impose on Colvin his own dogmatic views on art, but by this stage the scales had fallen from the younger man's eyes. Nowadays it would be inconceivable for someone of Colvin's academic inexperience to be appointed to such a chair, but it must also be said that the "job" was rather different then. Since there was no degree course in fine arts, the professor's students came on an informal and voluntary basis. There was no lecture room, no "teaching aids," and all that the position seemed to require was generally stimulating the taste of the university community through public lectures, in reality delivered to, as Martin Conway told E. V. Lucas, "daughters of professors, a lot of junior dons, girls from Newnham and Girton, and a sprinkling of high-brow undergraduates." Conway, later Lord Conway, also said that Colvin reacted against not only the nature sentiment of Ruskin but the rising aesthetic movement. "He made no attempt at eloquence; he had no impassioned peroration; he did not try to move our emotions. He just gave us facts and left it at that." Throughout his career in fine arts, Colvin revealed a deeply conservative taste, and his speech of retirement from the British Museum on 1 November 1912 runs true to form in dismissing the products of postimpressionism, cubism, and futurism as "objects of mere derision and disgust," using terms such as "this self-imposed crudity and barbarity and puerility of pattern in line and colour . . . indistinguishable from the daubings of incompetence or imposture." Nonetheless, and in spite of his evident misreading of contemporary art history, Colvin was respected in his specialist field of the Italian Renaissance, and he carried out solid work in building up and cataloguing the various collections he curated during his career. From his appointment (held alongside the Slade chair) in 1876 as director of the Fitzwilliam Museum until he resigned on 12 October 1883, he founded a collection of casts of Greek sculpture. In his post of keeper of the Department of Prints and Drawings in the British Museum from 1884 to 1912 (retiring from the Slade professorship in 1885) he acquired several fine collections, raised the standard of scholarship expected in the staff, and generally brought a spirit of administrative professionalism and genuine enthusiasm into the museum, which grew in national importance. At the same time he acquired few works of art for himself, and it could fairly be said that he spent more time acquiring literary friends than paintings.

Conway recalled that Colvin "often said to me that Art was not his chief interest; that was litera-ture," and that while "Art provided his bread and butter" he already looked forward to the day when he could retire and write the life of Keats. This was confirmed in Colvin's retirement speech from the British Museum so many years later when with manifest relief evidenced in moments of rare levity he threw off the shackles of employment: "I am what is called a free man, and I hope to devote the rest of my days to the pursuit of literature, from which destiny drew, or pushed, me away nigh on forty years ago."

Colvin's first foray into literary biography came with *Landor* (1881), his volume on Victorian poet and essayist Walter Savage Landor. John Morley, editor of the English Men of Letters series published by Macmillan, and formerly editor of the *Pall Mall Gazette,* to which Colvin had contributed, invited Colvin in 1879 to write a volume for the series, leaving the choice of subject up to him. Colvin's nomination of Landor seems slightly curious in light of the book as he wrote it, since he seems to have had only qualified admiration and less affection for his subject. Generally speaking, Landor emerges as pampered, cantankerous, hopeless at domestic relations, a minor poet at best, often in Colvin's word "monotonous," and more comfortable writing in Latin than in English. He was antisocial and eccentric in not particularly endearing ways, totally lacking in artistic discrimination and a bit dimwitted. On the other hand, Landor seems to have lived by convictions, since he was consistently republican even through times in England when it was dangerous to be so, and given to impetuous political action such as going to Spain to fight against France, even equipping at his own cost a thousand volunteers with whom he marched to join the Spanish army. Very often he displayed implacable resistance to authority, but not on any identifiably political ground, rather because he had an "inflammable" and "volcanic temperament" and expected to get his own way. The perhaps apocryphal story of how he threw his cook out of the window and instantly thrust out his own head exclaiming "Good God, I forgot the violets" seems to convey something of his respective attitudes to humanity and nature. He was inclined to vent his spleen most often in savage Latin lampoons directed at his indignant and usually innocent victims. Colvin openly acknowledges Landor's faults and tries (with only limited success) to convince the reader of compensating qualities such as generosity, kindness, and loyalty, as well as deep classical learning, "habitual

Colvin and his wife, Frances Fethersonhaugh Sitwell Colvin, whom he married in 1903

moods of lofty thought and tender feeling," and other qualities obtained "at the price of a certain immobility."

Colvin bases Landor's claim to be "a great artist in English letters" on his prose style, in which, he claims, Landor ranks as highly as Milton in poetry or Handel in music. There seems to be some discrepancy, for although Colvin says that "simplicity, parsimony, and the severest accuracy in speech" mark the prose, in the same breath he describes Landor as "at times a magniloquent and even pompous writer," obscure, and unable to sustain the sequence of incidents in a narrative. The works which Colvin celebrates are Landor's sequence of *Imaginary Conversations* (1824–1829) which came out in regular batches after the first volume gained some celebrity. These conversations can certainly be said to emanate from a conception that is original to the point of quirkiness. They are Landor's attempts to construct, on the deliberate policy of doing no historical research whatsoever, conver-

sations between figures such as Lady Godiva and her husband Leofric, Henry VIII and Anne Boleyn, Dante and Beatrice, Diogenes and Epictetus, Plato and Diogenes, the two Ciceros, and so on, almost endlessly. When his much-loved mother heard of the project, she warned Landor, "For God's sake do not hurt your eyes, nor rack your brains too much, to amuse the world by writing. But take care of your health, which will be of greater use to your family." After the publication of the first two volumes and estranged from his family and living in Italy, Landor was sought out by visiting literati (often to their discomfiture), and his celebrity was assured. He became more leonine in every way as he moved into an old age as tempestuous as his youth.

It should be said that the bewilderingly contradictory (rather than complex) impression of the Landor who emerges from Colvin's writing was deliberately constructed by the biographer, who, when he came to prepare *Selections from Landor*

(1882), wrote that "Landor had two personalities, an inner one, so to speak, disguised by an outer; the inner one being that of a stately and benign philosopher, the outer that of a passionate and rebellious schoolboy." Colvin makes the point that previous commentators had stressed one or other "personality" while he tries to do justice to both. For this insight, and for his consequent steady practice of refusing to be swayed toward either whitewashing or blackening the reputation of his subject, Colvin can in fact be claimed as a precursor of the twentieth-century biographer's even-handed attitude to the craft of biography. Landor is a fine, short biography which at the time, judging from their letters, aroused in correspondents such as W. E. Henley, Coventry Patmore, and George Moore the slightly disturbing response of encountering through Colvin a disconcerting, flawed, but intriguing Landor.

The volume was praised highly enough for Colvin to be entrusted with the monograph on Keats for the same English Men of Letters series. It appeared in 1887 and elicited enthusiastic letters from such writers as Patmore, Robert Browning, Matthew Arnold, and others. Arnold made an interesting comment that may have been stimulated by Colvin's account: "If Keats could have lived he might have done anything; but he *could not have lived,* his not living, we must consider, was more than an accident."

Discussion of Colvin as biographer of Keats should center not on the monograph but on his greatest work, *John Keats: His Life and Poetry, His Friends, Critics, and After-Fame,* published in 1917. Colvin had staked his claim to a book on Keats long before, and besides, this one was timed to be published a century after Keats's first volume, so the Great War of 1914–1918 did not influence his choice. However, in general terms the intense revival of Keats before and during World War I is of more general interest. Wilfred Owen's early poetry is saturated with Keats, and his mature work shows its more sublimated influence. Colvin mentions that Edward Thomas's last work before he died in the war was a short "masterly epitome" on Keats. He also mentions another "younger soldier-poet, so far happily unhurt" (Lieutenant Geoffrey Dearmer), who in the tense moments before battle found "thronging before his mind's eye . . . images from the poetry of the self-same Keats, visions of the wrathful Hyperion, and of the groups carved upon the Grecian Urn, and of La Belle Dame sans Merci and Cortez staring on the Pacific." In contemplating the horrors of war, Colvin intuited that Keats, like

Mnemosyme, had seen and suffered all before. It seems certain that for Colvin the conflict influenced to some extent his actual treatment. Speaking of the book in the preface he writes, "Once released from official duties, I began to prepare for the task, and through the last soul-shaking years, being over age for any effectual war-service, have found solace and occupation in carrying it through." "Solace" may be the crucial word, for of all the different facets of Keats's work that have over the years been brought into the foreground, it was the presentation of the poet as healer in *Hyperion: A Fragment* (1820) that seemed to offer consolation to a generation, and Colvin obliquely mentions the importance of Keats when he was himself nursing his ailing wife.

In an extraordinary section at the end of his book, Colvin describes the war experience, how much it includes "of the ghastly and revolting, of the direfully grotesque and *macabre,* and even of mere dead-stale tedium," suggesting that poetry must relinquish "the direct and conscious search for beauty as its primary aim and impulse" and instead concentrate on achieving "true imaginative intensity allied with sheer unflinching veracity and frankness." These qualities he finds in the "new poetry," but their source in Colvin's mind lies in poems such as the *Hyperion* fragments, "On sitting down to read King Lear once again," "To Autumn," and the rest of the later Keats. Along the same lines he stresses the breach with history that the war represents, the knowledge that the future will hold disturbing memories of endurance, suffering, and horror, of "hellishness and heroism, beside which all the dreams of bygone romance must forever seem tame and vapid" as well as forecasting a "future of peace and justice such as mankind has not known before." Again, the late Keats is the poet for such a moment.

Colvin's biography of Keats is a masterly example of the medium. Given the wealth of letters and the attractions of the poetry, one would think it impossible *not* to write well on Keats, but there are in fact dangers which Colvin largely avoids. He does not gush in the Victorian manner but proceeds true to his form as the lecturer who gives "facts," usually quoting long sections without intrusive commentary. Although he does allow himself the indulgence of some speculation, he does so far less often than others of the time, and he sternly admonishes other writers on many occasions for going beyond the evidence. As always, Colvin writes with a dignified grace, and his literary criticism, while betraying its post-Arnoldian time, is generally discreet and restrained. It also should not be forgotten

MEMORIES & NOTES

OF

PERSONS & PLACES

1852-1912

BY

SIR SIDNEY COLVIN

LONDON
EDWARD ARNOLD & CO.
1921
[All rights reserved]

Frontispiece and title page for Colvin's book of impressions and portraits of his acquaintances

in the context of the many fine, scholarly biographies of Keats in the twentieth century that Colvin's was the first of any substance. Richard Monckton Milnes's (Lord Houghton's) two-volume book in 1848 was not scholarly but rather recollective, compiled as it was from memories of people who had known Keats and were ignorant of many of the letters. Colvin pays handsome tribute, as must all Keats scholars, to the work of Harry Buxton Forman, the most thorough and painstaking collector of variant poetic readings and, more significantly, of the letters of Keats. Without his work Colvin could not have maintained his steady factuality. He also refers admiringly to the "elaborate and monumental *Concordance* to his poems lately issued from Cornell University," a hint that already serious Keats scholarship together with the original documents were being transported to North America at a great rate. It is telling that the ambitious and distin-

guished biographies which steadily overtook Colvin's came from Americans – Amy Lowell (1925), C. D. Thorpe (1926), C. L. Finney (1936), and W. J. Bate (1963) – just as the great editors of this century, Hyder E. Rollins and Jack Stillinger, are also Americans. Robert Gittings stands almost alone as a worthy biographer of Keats from Britain. In a field which is now a heavyweight, academic industry, Colvin's "after-fame" flickers only dimly. But if the activity of scholarship involves standing on the shoulders of others to reach higher, then his shoulders are the broadest of all, for he laid down the foundations of a method and a model of Keats's intellectual and poetic development which, it is no exaggeration to say, is followed by all those who have come after.

The one contemporary writer whose biography we might expect Colvin to have written was Robert Louis Stevenson, since he probably knew the Scottish author better than anybody and admired his works and his personality. That he did not do so (other than in short essays) is probably a measure of his valuing of biography as a medium requiring considerable detachment, and he may have felt too close to Stevenson to exercise cool judiciousness. He did, however, pay homage by contributing introductions to some of Stevenson's novels and an epilogue to the posthumous *Weir of Hermiston* (1896), by editing a sizable selection of Stevenson's letters in the 1890s, and by authorizing publication of more letters from Stevenson and Mrs. Stevenson to himself and his wife, which was duly executed by E. V. Lucas in *The Colvins and Their Friends,* published in 1928 after Colvin's death. Colvin also wrote extensively on Stevenson in *Memories and Notes of Persons and Places 1852–1912.* Through Colvin's writings Stevenson emerges as pathetically invalid, somewhat childlike, but an indomitable presence all the same, and Colvin tries to capture something of his essence: "imagine this attenuated but extraordinarily vivid and vital presence, with something about it that at first struck you as freakish, rare, fantastic, a touch of the elfin and unearthly, a sprite, an Ariel." As one of the most photographed writers from the period, Stevenson's image still conveys something of the spirit of this description. Stevenson invited criticism from Colvin as a trusted friend, and it may be a little ungrateful of him in a letter to Henry James to describe Colvin as having a quality of "the stern parent about him."

Memories and Notes of Persons and Places 1852–1912 was Colvin's last publication, and it is the book in which, through biography, he comes closest to writing autobiography. Generally speaking it gives brief and vivid pen portraits of some of Colvin's famous acquaintances. He works here through lively impressions rather than facts. Browning is full of "cordiality"; Dante Gabriel Rossetti is "darkly passionate and mystical"; we are discreetly informed of Colvin's change from idolatry to "reserve and critical afterthought" about Ruskin, which he publicly explains as a gathering skepticism about Ruskin's political enthusiasms. George Meredith is presented not as the unsparing persona of *Modern Love* (1862) but as a man of enormous "exuberance," his behavior marked by "brusque transitions from grave wisdom to riotous, hyperbolical laughter." The reminiscences of Victor Hugo, whom Colvin with reverence met when Hugo was very old, reveals Colvin's deep regret at the anti-Romantic movement in the late nineteenth century: "The progress of lethal invention in the last fifty years has so far outstripped the dream of poet-prophet as to make his imagined expedient sound primitive and futile enough. . . ."

Colvin says of himself that he cultivated "the habit of privacy . . . concerning my own affairs," and publicly he seems to have lived and revealed himself through those others on whom he wrote rather than in his own person. In this sense biography can be seen as a kind of transferred autobiography of the writer's own soul. We do, however, get glimpses of his personal life directly. His most intimate female confidante was Frances Fethersonhaugh Sitwell, widow of the Reverend Albert Hurt Sitwell and daughter of Cuthbert Fethersonhaugh. After close companionship carried over some thirty years they married in 1903. The long delay is explained by Lucas as a reflection of Colvin's precarious financial situation rather than any coyness. They had no children, and their marriage seems to have been the happiest period of Colvin's life. As Lady Colvin, his wife seems to have been the more outgoing partner, introducing new, younger friends into their household and maintaining faithful correspondence with, among others, the Stevensons. Reading the letters as a whole, it seems clear that an unusually close intimacy developed between the foursome, with ever-shifting emotional nuances reticently revealed. Colvin's financial problems stemmed from family claims which Lucas says Colvin felt "bound to honour." He confessed that "I am going out of the world a poorer man in money than I came into it." His wife's death in 1924 was a devastating blow and precipitated a rapid decline into aimless loneliness. To one who, as indicated in his biographical profession, found people's voices to be important (an essay is called "Famous Voices I Have Heard") it was crippling to be inflicted by deafness, for which he refused to try any improving device. A limp which had developed after suffering a broken leg must also have caused increasing pain, but he insisted on walking each day to the florist's to buy flowers for the table beside his late wife's chair in which he allowed nobody to sit. He considered collecting some of his old articles for publication in book form but found he could not concentrate for long enough periods to do the necessary work. He became more prone to sudden collapses. Knighted in 1911, Colvin died in Kensington on 11 May 1927, one month before his eighty-second birthday.

It is idle to claim that Sir Sidney Colvin's works attract much attention now, although admittedly there does seem to be a small surge of interest in North America in Landor's works and commentators have dusted off and praised his monograph. It is fair to say that, although his biography of Keats has fallen into such neglect that the most recent chronicler, Robert Gittings, does not even mention it, Colvin's was the first of the line of distinguished biographies of Keats in this century. Furthermore, his style of biography can be said to be in essence less like Victorian hero worship than we might expect from one of his generation and more like a twentieth-century sobriety. It is tempting to conclude that he would be happier to be remembered through his portraits of others more famous than himself, people such as Stevenson, Henry James, Meredith, George Eliot, J. M. Barrie, Hugo, William Gladstone, Edward John Trelawny, Edward Burne-Jones, and Rossetti, among many others. But the following anecdote, in which Colvin would appear to be insensitive to an uncommenting Lucas,

shows in him a glimmer of hope, apparently dashed even as it is shyly expressed, that he might be remembered for his own sake. On 29 January 1925 Colvin received a letter from a five-hundred-strong group of young women and men training for business at a local senior high school, saying they had chosen him as a wise "guardian" whose advice and inspiration might help them to be better citizens. Lucas writes: "On my next visit to Colvin I found him in a state of delight at the honour thus paid him; and handing me his letter in answer, he asked if I thought that it would do. When I said that I had received the same appeal he was visibly depressed and withdrew his reply."

Reference:

E. V. Lucas, *The Colvins and Their Friends* (London: Methuen, 1928).

Edward Tyas Cook

(12 May 1857 – 30 September 1919)

Carolyn Lengel
Graduate Center of the City University of New York

BOOKS: *Studies in Ruskin: Some Aspects of the Work and Teaching of John Ruskin* (London: Allen, 1890);

Half-Holidays at the National Gallery (London: Pall Mall Gazette, 1890);

A Popular Handbook to the Tate Gallery (London: Macmillan, 1898);

The Passing of Gladstone (London: Simkin, Marshall, 1898);

Rights and Wrongs of the Transvaal War (London: Arnold, 1901);

Edmund Garrett: A Memoir (London: Arnold, 1909; New York: Macmillan, 1909);

The Life of John Ruskin, 2 volumes (London: Allen, 1911; New York: Macmillan, 1911);

The Homes and Haunts of John Ruskin (London: Allen, 1912; New York: Macmillan, 1912);

The Life of Florence Nightingale, 2 volumes (London: Macmillan, 1913; New York: Macmillan, 1942); abridged and revised by Rosalind Nash (London: Macmillan, 1925);

How Britain Strove For Peace: A Record of Anglo-German Relations, 1898–1914 (London: Macmillan, 1914);

Britain and Turkey (London: Macmillan, 1914);

Why Britain is at War (London: Macmillan, 1914);

Britain and the Small Nations (London: Wyman & Sons, 1914);

Delane of the Times (London: Constable, 1915; New York: Holt, 1916);

Britain's Part in the War (London: Wyman & Sons, 1916); revised and rewritten with the Dowager Countess of Jersey (London: Wyman & Sons, 1917);

Literary Recreations (London: Macmillan, 1918);

More Literary Recreations (London: Macmillan, 1919);

The Press in Wartime (London: Macmillan, 1920).

OTHER: *A Popular Handbook to the National Gallery,* compiled by Cook (London & New York: Macmillan, 1888); revised and enlarged (London & New York: Macmillan, 1890); revised and enlarged again (London & New York: Macmillan, 1893); revised and enlarged again (London & New York: Macmillan, 1901);

Emily C. Cook, *London and Environs,* with chapters on the British Museum, the National Gallery, and South Kensington by E. T. Cook (London: Darlington's Handbooks, 1897);

John Ruskin, *Ruskin on Pictures,* 2 volumes, edited by Cook (London: Allen, 1902);

A Popular Handbook to the Greek and Roman Antiquities in the British Museum, compiled by Cook (London & New York: Macmillan, 1903);

Ruskin, *The Works of John Ruskin,* 39 volumes, edited by Cook and Alexander Wedderburn, with biographical notes by Cook (London: Allen, 1903–1912; New York: Longmans, Green, 1903–1912);

Dulwich College Catalogue of Pictures, revised and compiled by Cook (London: Darling & Son, 1914);

Charles Morley, *Travels in London,* with recollections by Cook (London: Smith, Elder, 1916).

SELECTED PERIODICAL PUBLICATIONS – UNCOLLECTED: "The Connection Between Poetry and Painting," *Temple Bar Magazine* (July 1880): 351–361;

"Ruskin as Artist and Art Critic," *International Studio,* 10 (April 1900): 77–92;

"Ruskin and the New Liberalism," *New Liberal Review* (February 1901): 18–25;

"Ruskin and His Books: An Interview with His Publisher," *Strand Magazine* (December 1902): 709–719;

Edward Tyas Cook (photograph by Reginald Haines)

"Buried Turners: Selected Treasures at the National Gallery," *Pall Mall Magazine* (May 1905): 515–528;

"Book Wars: Ruskin as the Father of the Net System," *Book Monthly* (May 1907): 553–556;

"The Story of a Great Literary Undertaking: The Editing of Works, Life and Letters of J. Ruskin," *Pall Mall Magazine* (October 1909): 517–531.

In his lifetime Edward Tyas Cook was known for his work in journalism and as the editor of three major London daily newspapers, the *Pall Mall Gazette,* the *Westminster Gazette,* and the *Daily News.* He also published several biographical studies of major public figures of his time. The best known of these is his two-volume *The Life of John Ruskin,* published in 1911 and considered to be one of the standard

early biographies of the nineteenth-century writer and thinker. Cook's journalistic temperament is indicated by the many works he published on current events, but his writings on other biographers' works, on painting, and on literature both classical and contemporary prove that he was equally at ease with literary and artistic topics. He wrote knowledgeably and with evident enjoyment about many artists and writers, but throughout his life his interests centered firmly on Ruskin, whose complete works were edited by Cook and Alexander Wedderburn.

Edward Tyas Cook was born on 12 May 1857 in Brighton, England. He was the youngest son of Silas Kemball Cook, secretary of the Seamen's Hospital at Greenwich, and Emily Archer Cook. Cook entered Winchester College in 1869 and was elected a scholar of the school in 1870. He distinguished himself in sports but gave up football "that he might have more time for reading Ruskin," as his school-mate Sir L. A. Selby-Bigge recalled. Cook's interest in Ruskin, although particularly intense for that of a boy his age, was not unusual for those years: Ruskin was well respected by intellectuals, serious readers, and political and social reformers by 1860. The three volumes of lectures and descriptive works published in 1875 – *Sesame and Lilies, The Crown of Wild Olive,* and *Frondes Agrestes* – made him one of Britain's most popular writers. Cook was fascinated with politics, even as a schoolboy. He delighted in political argument and won praise for his talent as a member of Winchester's debating society. He worked his way up to the position of editor of the Winchester College magazine, the *Wykehamist,* and won school medals and prizes for essays on literary, political, and historical subjects.

After leaving Winchester in 1876, Cook continued his education at New College, Oxford. His growing interest in literary criticism led him to contribute a lengthy piece to Oxford's *Temple Bar Magazine* in July 1880 on "The Connection Between Poetry and Painting." He was active in the Oxford Union, where he debated regularly and skillfully on political subjects of the day; he became its president in 1879. During the Michaelmas term of 1877 Ruskin was serving as the first Slade Professor of Fine Arts. Cook's youthful admiration for the writer had not abated: Ruskin's reputation as the "prophet of a new social consciousness" appealed to the young student, who was increasingly inclined to ally himself with Liberal Party politics. Cook attended Ruskin's lecture series that term and kept careful notes. "Mr. Ruskin's . . . lectures had much solid stuff in them, but no lecturer knew better than he how to relieve the strain by supplying . . . those pleasant digressions which are the salt of oral discourse," he wrote. "It was the frequent digressions in the form of self-deprecatory egoism that gave a peculiar charm to Mr. Ruskin's lectures, by investing them with . . . the personal note of familiar conversation."

Cook left Oxford in 1881, having received first classes in Classical Moderations and in *literae humaniores.* His success with school publications led him to consider writing for a living after a hoped-for fellowship at New College failed to materialize, and through Oxford friends he was able to get an introduction to another alumnus, John Morley, who was editor of the *Pall Mall Gazette* in London. Cook's first contribution to that newspaper was printed on 6 December 1881.

Other freelance contributions followed, but Cook could not yet support himself financially by writing. He served from 1881 to 1885 as secretary of the London Society for Extension of University Teaching, a position which allowed him the free time to work on his edition of Aristotle's *Poetics,* which was never completed. During this period he also considered a career in English literature seriously enough to apply for a professorship at Nottingham.

On 14 August 1883 Cook received a letter from the *Pall Mall Gazette* simultaneously rejecting his latest piece – "there is a squash just now of literary articles," the assistant editor observed – and offering him a salaried position at that newspaper. Cook accepted the offer, beginning a full-time career in journalism that he was to continue for most of the remainder of his life.

The following year Cook married. He had been engaged in 1880 to Mary Vincent, whose brother later married Cook's sister, but the engagement was broken off. However, Cook's relationship with Emily Constance Baird of Northumberland resulted in marriage in 1884. The couple remained childless but collaborated on a popular guide to London in 1897. They lived together, by all accounts happily, until Emily's death in 1903.

After returning to Oxford to attend Ruskin's lectures on "The Art of England" and "The Pleasures of England," Cook summarized them in the *Pall Mall Gazette* at the request of William Thomas Stead, the editor who had replaced Morley in 1883. Although these lectures had been published from Ruskin's manuscript notes, Cook's series of articles showed that "the published lectures . . . often differed greatly from the lectures as actually delivered." Cook noted that "[o]ften . . . the lecturer would lay aside his manuscript at some important point, and giving free play to his feelings, drive it home in burning passages of extempore irony."

In November 1885 Stead was jailed for three months in connection with an investigative article. Cook, who had by this time risen to the position of assistant editor, was left in charge. His skillful handling of the newspaper ensured that he was allowed a fairly free rein upon Stead's return. Cook conceived of and edited a number of "extras" for the newspaper on political (*Guide to the House of Commons*) and artistic subjects (*Art Extra*). In 1886 he organized a literary symposium for which he solicited lists of "The Best Hundred Books" from eminent people; the resulting letters and lists formed the basis for another series of articles.

Meanwhile, the articles on Ruskin's Oxford lectures had attracted Ruskin's attention. "You have a man on your staff who knows more about my works than I do myself," he wrote to Stead, and he asked to be introduced. On 28 October 1887 Cook went to interview Ruskin at his London hotel. In this meeting Cook asked Ruskin for permission for the *Pall Mall Gazette* to publish his old letters. "All the world may read any letters I ever wrote," Ruskin responded. He went on to complain to Cook about the "terrible ugliness of London" and to discuss his autobiography, *Praeterita* (1885–1889), which was never completed. Ruskin spoke candidly to Cook about his periodic mental breakdowns and was pleased to learn of ongoing public disagreement over his works because, he said, "I've thought no one cared even to abuse me now."

Cook saw Ruskin twice more in London over the next few months. On 9 December 1887 Ruskin sent for Cook to vent his anger at the *Pall Mall Gazette*, which had not published two letters Ruskin had sent – because, Cook said, the paper had not known they were meant for publication. On 19 April 1888 Cook and Ruskin met to discuss *A Popular Handbook to the National Gallery* (1888), which Cook had edited and compiled; it included a preface written by Ruskin and notes collected from his works. The April meeting was apparently their last: Cook attempted to visit Ruskin at his Brantwood home the following year but was informed by Joan Severn, Ruskin's literary executrix, cousin, and heir, that Ruskin was suffering one of his recurring illnesses and could not see him. Cook made no other mention of contact with Ruskin, who spent most of the last decade of his life seriously mentally ill and unable to recognize most visitors.

In 1890 Cook's first book on Ruskin reached print. *Studies in Ruskin: Some Aspects of the Work and Teaching of John Ruskin* is called by George Allan Cate "a clear and winsome set of essays" written with a pupil's enthusiasm and zeal. An essay titled "The Gospel According to Ruskin," reprinted from a series in the *Pall Mall Gazette* on great writers and thinkers, details Ruskin's philosophy of art – including his "somewhat wilful paradoxes" – and its application to daily life, which reveal "the teacher of Art [to be] necessarily also a social reformer." Several shorter pieces are gathered under the heading "Some Aspects of Mr. Ruskin's Work." Some provide information about Ruskin's Oxford years, discussing his professorship, the Working Men's College, and the Ruskin Drawing School. Cook

also included an essay on Ruskin's ill-fated social experiment, the Saint George's Guild, which Cook admitted had "produced very little except a plentiful crop of disappointments," adding a note of unrealistic hope "that past failures will lead to future successes." An appendix contained Cook's notes from the 1877 Ruskin lectures at Oxford.

On 1 January 1890 Cook became editor of the *Pall Mall Gazette*. He held this position until 7 October 1892, when the owner sold the newspaper to William Waldorf Astor. Cook and his political staff then resigned; the paper's status as a supporter of Liberal Party causes was no longer guaranteed, and Cook "would accept no contract which did not secure him complete liberty and independence of opinion."

On 8 October 1892, the day after the resignations, Sir George Newnes proposed a meeting with Cook. He hoped to found a new London newspaper "on the old lines of the *P.M.G.*" On 31 January 1893 Cook was at the helm of the first edition of the *Westminster Gazette*. He remained editor there for exactly three years, after which he left to become the editor of the London *Daily News*.

Cook's work at his new post went smoothly for four years. But when the Boer War broke out in South Africa in 1900, his public and personal position as a staunch defender of the war brought him into conflict with much of the Liberal Party. The *Daily News* was sold abruptly in January 1901 to new owners who wanted a decidedly different editorial policy. Instead of agreeing to compromise his opinions and allow the newspaper to present a more neutral view of political events, Cook left the *Daily News*.

Financial necessity, however, ensured his return to journalism. By the spring of 1901 he was writing leader articles for London's *Daily Chronicle* and *Sunday Sun*, which Cook called "a very easy way of making one's living." He added, "[W]hen I am lazy I rejoice in the leisure and absence of all worry and responsibility. At other times I pine for opportunities."

Two years passed before offers came from other newspapers in England and South Africa, and when they did come, Cook rejected them. "I am not sure that I should care to take the editorship of an evening paper again. I am at present very busy with other things," he wrote on 4 March 1903 in response to an offer from the *Pall Mall Gazette*, once again under new ownership. Foremost among these "other things" was the massive Library Edition of Ruskin's works, which he had begun to edit with his friend Wedderburn. Wedderburn had already ed-

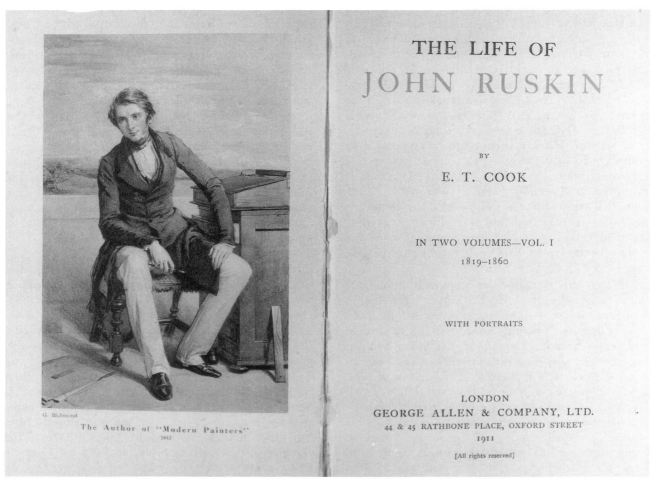

THE LIFE OF

JOHN RUSKIN

BY

E. T. COOK

IN TWO VOLUMES—VOL. I
1819–1860

WITH PORTRAITS

G. Richmond
The Author of "Modern Painters"
1843

LONDON
GEORGE ALLEN & COMPANY, LTD.
44 & 45 RATHBONE PLACE, OXFORD STREET
1911

Frontispiece and title page for volume one of Cook's biography of the British art and social critic; Cook concentrates on Ruskin's character and personality rather than historical events.

ited and indexed some of Ruskin's writings. The edition was supposed to contain "every word ever written by John Ruskin, who . . . wrote more than any three leading British thinkers put together."

Cook was able to devote hours each day to the huge task of the Ruskin edition before reporting to the newspaper in the evening. "Pegging away at Ruskin," he noted again and again in his diary. Cook and Wedderburn devoted ten years to the project, tracking down Ruskin's allusions – Cook checked over ten thousand volumes in the British Museum in search of the sources of these numerous quotations – and indexing the writings of an author who "wrote about everything." Cook recorded in his diary that a week's labor was required to index the single word "colour."

The first volumes of the enormous collection were published in 1903, and the last in 1912. There were thirty-nine volumes in all – an edition Cook called "formidable, even as a piece of furniture." By the time the work was completed, Ruskin had been dead for twelve years, and his reputation, once towering, had begun to decline. The edition was described as "a monument indeed, but one under which Ruskin is buried."

Cook and Wedderburn, of course, were not to blame for the lack of public interest in Ruskin's writings. As Sir Kenneth Clark has observed, "a popular edition of favorite works, which appeared at the same time, was equally unread, and is still in print; and some of the volumes in the London Library set, which was bought on publication, are still uncut." The complexities of Ruskin's prose, his digressions, and a rather Victorian striving for moral uplift all contributed to his falling out of fashion. Few readers still believed, with Cook, that Ruskin had "never written anything worthless or unimportant."

Yet most modern Ruskin scholars acknowledge the contribution made by Cook and Wedderburn. Clark praises their "incredible industry and . . . noble devotion to truth." The thirty-nine volume set is generally considered to be "the starting point for any serious work on Ruskin," as it contains his public writings with "assiduously gathered" footnotes and textual revisions.

Later-twentieth-century Ruskin scholars have pointed out that the editors did not succeed in their stated ambition to include every word that Ruskin wrote: his love letters to Rose La Touche were destroyed after Ruskin's death by well-wishers who were, according to Joan Abse, "even more zealous in the protection of his private life than he himself had been," and Cook and Wedderburn left out, apparently deliberately, letters to a young woman named Kathleen Olander to whom Ruskin had proposed late in life. These notable omissions were due in part to the editors' reluctance to discuss peculiarities of Ruskin's personal life; in this reluctance Cook and Wedderburn were wholeheartedly supported by Severn, who had overseen the letter burning. Cook commented, "Communicative, expansive, un-reticent though Ruskin was, his literary executors felt that these [love] letters [to La Touche], though perhaps the most beautiful things that Ruskin ever wrote, were too sacred for publicity." Cook, himself a reticent man, was probably in agreement with the executors. Although an admirer of Ruskin's prose style, he believed that Ruskin's chief importance lay in his ideas – in his public writings, rather than his private ones.

Each of the Library Edition's volumes contained a biographical introduction written by Cook. In 1911 he expanded these beginnings into *The Life of John Ruskin*. Mindful of Ruskin's complaint that biographies of famous people often "tell us at last little more than what sort of people they dealt with, and of pens they wrote with," Cook proposed to write "the account, mainly, of a character, a temperament, an influence, and seldom of events on the stage of public action," a method he admitted was simplified by his view that "Ruskin's dealings with persons were of comparatively little moment."

This study extends to well over a thousand pages in its two volumes. The first volume covers Ruskin's life and work from his birth in 1819 up to the publication in 1860 of the final volume of *Modern Painters*, the years of his great successes as a critic of art and architecture; the second volume begins with the 1860 publication of *Unto This Last*, the

"turning-point in his literary life," after which he wrote chiefly on political economy and social reforms, and continues to his death in 1900. Though essentially chronological, the volumes depart from strict order to separate Ruskin the artist and art critic from Ruskin the sociopolitical thinker. Thus, Cook includes Ruskin's efforts as an executor of the painter J. M. W. Turner's will in volume one, even though he continued doing this work until 1881. Cook also interrupts the life story periodically to analyze Ruskin's literary, artistic, and political works and ideas. He does so enthusiastically, including critiques of Ruskin – such as the accusation "that he judged art from a purely literary standard" – only to defend him. After Cook's death, J. A. Spender observed in the *Westminster Gazette* (2 October 1919): "[Ruskin] prided himself that he had the most analytical mind in Europe, but . . . he had his equal in Cook, who analyzed the analyst in a manner that would surely have given him exquisite pleasure, could he have watched it."

The book was considered "the standard biography of Ruskin," or at least on a par with *The Life and Work of John Ruskin,* published in 1893 by Ruskin's secretary W. G. Collingwood. Modern scholars agree that Cook's "knowledgeable treatment of [his] subject has always been obviously valuable" and that he knew the works thoroughly and was "an excellent Ruskinian."

The Life of John Ruskin earned the full approval of Severn, so it is not surprising that Cook concentrated in it on the aspects of Ruskin with which both he and Severn felt most comfortable. Cook did not confine his opinions solely to expressions of agreement with Ruskin, but the biography shows a very flattering portrait of its subject. A contemporary reviewer praised Cook's "tact and judgment" and approved his "tone of deferent, and kindly humorous, impartiality."

Today, however, writers on Ruskin disagree with Cook's assumption that the peculiarities of his subject's private life were not fit material for a biographer. The details of Ruskin's unconsummated marriage, attachment to La Touche, and episodes of madness are now considered "very important for an understanding of the man." Cook exhibited a Victorian delicacy in his treatment of these potentially embarrassing matters: he gave only the necessary, and already public, facts about Ruskin's marriage, engagement, and what Cook euphemistically called the "brain fever" his subject suffered in the last decade of his life. Cook admired Ruskin enough to put events in the best possible light, even finding evidence of Ruskin's "approachableness and his good nature" in what modern readers recognize to be his "passion for little girls." As in the Library Edition, he struggled to keep the focus of Ruskin's life on his works, accomplishments, and the tremendous influence he had on his peers, rather than on such personal – and, to Cook, sordid – details.

During this ten-year period devoted to Ruskin, Cook continued to work as a newspaper leader writer and to contribute articles to numerous magazines. These occasionally covered literary topics but were more often on the contemporary political scene. He also found time to lecture frequently on "literary and artistic, mainly Ruskinian, subjects." In 1909 Cook published a "tribute to friendship," a memoir of his friend and former assistant editor at the *Pall Mall Gazette,* Edmund Garrett, fondly recalling the "labour, zeal, and enthusiasm of the newspaper's idealistic staff."

On 30 December 1911 Cook was dismissed from the *Daily Chronicle,* probably because of "differences of opinion" with his employers. It was to be his last job as a journalist. He retired to tributes from well-placed friends and several newspapers, and on 1 July 1912 he received a knighthood.

After the Ruskin biography, Cook wrote two other biographical works. The first, *The Life of Florence Nightingale* (1913), was the only official biography of Nightingale, drawing on family documents and published, like the Ruskin biography, with the blessings of surviving family members. The Nightingale biography consists of two large volumes, chronologically detailing the achievements of its subject's life. Cook's insistence that "[Nightingale's] relations, her friends, her acquaintances, her correspondents only concern us here in so far as their dealings with her affected her work, or illustrate her character" also recalls his treatment of Ruskin. Nightingale was arguably the most famous woman in England during Cook's lifetime. Instead of merely "supplementing [the] popular legend" of Nightingale as saintly nurse, he expressed great admiration for her as "a pioneer . . . in the emancipation of women," as a brilliant administrator, and as "more of a logician than a sentimentalist." Cook followed this work with his 1915 biography of the editor John Delane, *Delane of the Times,* which Spender called "the best book ever written about a journalist." Written as part of the publisher's Makers of the Nineteenth Century series, *Delane of the Times* was not, Cook said, "in the ordinary sense a biography." The book takes only a cursory look at the devel-

opment of the man and at his life outside journalism; instead, it discusses Delane in depth in his capacity as editor of the London *Times* for nearly forty years – an era which had ended in 1879, shortly before Cook began his career in journalism.

In June of 1915 Cook became manager of the Press Bureau – the government office for newspaper censorship during World War I – which had been deemed necessary since the outbreak of the war. In the course of this work, he discovered that his attempts to "reconcile the higher national interest . . . with an insatiable thirst for news on the part of the newspapers" resulted in worry and sleeplessness and gradually in the decline of his health. He was honored with the Knights of the British Empire award in 1917 for his service to the bureau, which he continued to manage until it closed down in 1919.

Cook found time during the war years to publish two volumes of essays, *Literary Recreations* (1918) and *More Literary Recreations* (1919). These volumes include discussions of "The Art of Indexing" and "The Art of Editing," which detail the philosophy behind Cook's "most methodical habit of indexing papers and keeping references." *Literary Recreations* contains an essay on Ruskin's writing, demonstrating the way his style changed (for the better, Cook believed) as he grew older, and a paper read at Oxford on "The Art of Biography." Here Cook wrote, "The great biographies may reveal the hero's faults, but they do so frankly, and the predominant note is sympathy." *More Literary Recreations* was devoted mainly to discussions of Cook's other early literary loves, classical literature and poetry.

In 1919, after the Press Bureau had closed, Cook worked on what was to be his last book. *The Press in Wartime* (1920) describes the principles behind wartime press censorship and defends the necessity of the Press Bureau. Cook submitted the manuscript for official scrutiny in August and lived to learn that it had been approved for publication. Unfortunately, his health had deteriorated greatly; he died on 30 September 1919, before he could revise the proofs or see the work in print.

Cook was memorialized by J. Saxon Mills as "one of the most influential of London journalists in the last fifteen years of the nineteenth and first ten years of the twentieth century" and by Spender as "a man of deadly accuracy and precision . . . with a precise knowledge of public affairs." Cook's reputation at the time of his death was based on the ephemeral work of daily newspaper journalism, and his literary and biographical efforts were relegated to a footnote to his career. He might not be remembered at all today were it not for the revival of interest in Ruskin in recent years; it is as the careful guardian of Ruskin's reputation that Cook seems to have made his most lasting contribution to literature.

Of the censored British press of World War I Cook wrote, "On the whole, [it] did excellent service . . . in the publication of facts upon which an intelligent judgment could be formed, in the exercise of fearless criticism, and in presenting . . . a faithful picture of [British] . . . spirit." Cook's biographical and editorial works on Ruskin might be said to attempt the same services toward their subject, and with the same result: the omission of information once thought damaging that later readers deem necessary for an understanding of the complete picture.

Biography:

J. Saxon Mills, *Sir Edward Cook, K. B. E.* (New York: Dutton, 1921).

References:

Joan Abse, *John Ruskin: The Passionate Moralist* (London: Quartet, 1980);

George Allan Cate, *Ruskin: A Reference Guide* (Boston: G. K. Hall, 1988);

Sir Kenneth Clark, editor, *Ruskin Today* (New York: Holt, Rinehart & Winston, 1964);

Tim Hilton, *John Ruskin: The Early Years* (New Haven: Yale University Press, 1985);

Basil de Selincourt, "Ruskin," *Living Age,* 272 (17 February 1912): 413;

Gary Wihl, *Ruskin and the Rhetoric of Infallibility* (New Haven: Yale University Press, 1985).

Edward Dowden

(3 May 1843 – 4 April 1913)

A. R. Jones
University of Wales

See also the Dowden entry in *DLB 35: Victorian Poets After 1850.*

BOOKS: *Shakspere: A Critical Study of His Mind and Art* (London: King, 1875; New York: Harper, 1880);

Poems (London: King, 1876; enlarged edition, London & Toronto: Dent, 1914);

Shakspere (London: Macmillan, 1877; New York: Appleton, 1878);

Studies in Literature 1789–1877 (London: Kegan Paul, 1878);

Southey (London: Macmillan, 1879; New York: Harper, 1880);

Spenser, the Poet and Teacher, volume 1 of *The Complete Works of Edmund Spenser,* edited by A. B. Grosart (London & Aylesbury: Privately printed, 1882);

The Life of Percy Bysshe Shelley, 2 volumes (London: Kegan Paul, Trench, 1886; Philadelphia: Lippincott, 1892);

Transcripts and Studies (London: Kegan Paul, Trench & Trübner, 1888);

New Studies in Literature (London: Kegan Paul, Trench & Trübner, 1895; Boston: Houghton Mifflin, 1895);

The French Revolution and English Literature (London: Kegan Paul, 1897; New York: Scribners, 1897);

A History of French Literature (New York: Appleton, 1897; London: Heinemann, 1899);

Puritan and Anglican: Studies in Literature (London: Kegan Paul, Trench & Trübner, 1900; New York: Holt, 1900);

Robert Browning (London: Dent / New York: Dutton, 1904); republished as *The Life of Robert Browning* (London & Toronto: Dent / New York: Dutton, 1915);

Michel de Montaigne (Philadelphia & London: Lippincott, 1905);

Essays Modern and Elizabethan (London: Dent, 1910; New York: Dutton, 1910);

A Woman's Reliquary (Dundrum: Cualo Press, 1913; London: Dent, 1914).

Edward Dowden was a poet, scholar, and critic whose work helped to shape the artistic and intellectual life of his time. His position as a critic was well defined by Maurice Alfred Gerothwohl: "But if Dowden was not so *great* a critic as a [Algernon Charles] Swinburne or a [George] Meredith; if he were less brilliant than a Matthew Arnold, he was undoubtedly the best, the finest English critic of his day, and the most representative." Moreover, though Professor of English Literature at Trinity College, Dublin, for well over forty years, his interests were by no means confined to English and included French, German, Italian, and American thought and literature. Indeed, William Kirkpatrick Magee asserted that "Dowden's mind was probably the first point touched by anything new in the world of ideas outside Ireland." As a critic, poet, and editor he showed himself to be sensitive to the movement of European ideas, and his work gained him an international reputation. According to Magee, Dowden "left directions that no life of him should be written," but no literary history of the late nineteenth and early twentieth century would be complete without an assessment of his achievements.

He was born on 3 May 1843 at Mentenotte, a suburb of Cork, in Ireland, the fourth child of John Wheeler Dowden, a merchant and landowner, and Alicia Bennett, described as "grave, noble, God-fearing parents, Spartan in their stern strict simplicity of life. . . . Edward, the youngest, being delicate, was much under his mother's care. Three years his senior was John, the only living brother. There were two sisters: Margaret, six years older than Edward and Anna the eldest of the family." His uncle Richard, at one time mayor of Cork and city librarian, was the author of a book on Irish flowers and an active nationalist who once sat on the same platform as Daniel O'Connell, the Irish political leader known as the Liberator.

Edward Dowden

Edward was described by Thomas W. Lyster as "an extraordinarily mature child. He inherited from his father a steadfast accuracy in financial affairs as in all other matters of life. . . . He was a boy of genius, reared in a home of culture, and educated in early life by his intimacy with the old Cork public library. He was educated privately and for a year attended classes in Greek and Latin as a nonmatriculated student in Queen's College, Cork. At the age of sixteen he entered Trinity College, Dublin, under the tutorship of his cousin Dr. George Salmon, who later became Provost of the College. He shared rooms with his brother, John – who in 1886 became Bishop of Edinburgh – on the ground floor of number 17 in Botany Bay.

According to John Butler Yeats, who was a friend and contemporary at Trinity College, "the two Dowdens shone the brightest stars in the undergraduate sky." At Trinity College he studied philosophy and won the Wray Prize in metaphysical stud-

ies and the Vice-Chancellor's Prizes for both English Verse and Prose Composition. He was president of the undergraduates' Philosophical Society and graduated with a first-class Moderatorship in Logic and Ethics in 1863 at the age of twenty and received his M.A. in 1867. He also went through the divinity school but did not take orders.

On 23 October 1866 he married Mary Clerke. The Dowdens had four children, of whom a son and two daughters survived. According to Lyster, "despairing of getting work in Ireland, he went to live in Exeter with his wife. While looking for work a remarkable thing occurred. He obeyed a letter from the late Dr. Ingram to come back to Dublin and try for a professorship that had just been vacated at Trinity." In 1867 he was appointed Professor of Oratory and English Literature at the University of Dublin. He lectured at Alexandra College, and in the spring his academic reputation was acknowledged when he gave one of the Dublin afternoon lectures on "Mr. Tennyson and Mr. Browning" in the theater of the Royal College of Science. Dowden was appointed to the Chair of Oratory and English in Trinity College, Dublin, in 1867 and remained Professor of English Literature at Trinity College until his death, despite offers from other universities.

But despite what on the face of it seemed to be a fortunate chance, there were those who saw his situation as being unhappy and precarious: "And so an early and romantic marriage was followed by an early and ill-paid professorship, to supplement which it became incumbent upon Dowden to undertake all kinds of literary and examination work — the latter, as he was wont to say, soul-killing." There were those who regarded him as being primarily a poet who feared that academic life would stifle his inspiration. There "were in him the makings of a poet of high lineage," Gerothwohl believed, "the moral earnestness and depth, the imaginative flights, more than a nice feeling for true artistry. And he became, no doubt, something better than a merely graceful verseman, — a thoughtful, sensitive, melodious singer." According to William Butler Yeats, his father, John Butler Yeats, "would sometimes say that he had wanted Dowden when they were young to give himself to creative art, and would talk of what he considered Dowden's failures in life. . . . 'He will not trust his nature,' he would say." John Butler Yeats tended to blame Dowden's early marriage for his failure to commit himself to poetry: "young poets should not follow the example of doctors and marry early. . . . Dowden married early and henceforth had an eye too much for moral and abstract beauty; while towards sensuous beauty he was stony-hearted. George Eliot, whose admirer he was, completed the mischief. This woman author, with her chilly east wind of science and agnosticism, was a wintry frost to all of us, in those faraway days." Yet he nonetheless continued to write poetry off and on throughout his life. In 1876 he published his *Poems,* which were reprinted by his second wife in 1914 with considerable additions.

Dowden's reputation as one of the foremost scholars of his age was firmly established with the publication of his first book, *Shakspere: A Critical Study of His Mind and Art* (1875), and confirmed by his two-volume biography of Percy Bysshe Shelley published in 1886.

Dowden's study of Shakespeare was a pioneering one, the first to "endeavour to pass through the creation of the artist to the mind of the creator." There can be no doubt that his work was a landmark in Shakespearian criticism and established him in the front rank of Shakespearian critics. For many years it was the most widely read appreciation of Shakespeare. Nonetheless, he concludes that Dowden's "virtues are his own — his faults those of his time"; undoubtedly "moral and religious ideas predominate in the criticism of the age." Such content is certainly not to the modern taste, but Dowden deserves to be judged by the standards of the age in which he lived, and by these standards he cannot be denied his stature. His influence on modern Shakespearian criticism has been widespread and pervasive and should not by any means be overlooked.

Aubrey de Vere wrote to Dowden on 17 March 1875 to express his admiration: "I do not exaggerate in saying that it seems to me the best book I have ever read on Shakespeare." A. C. Bradley does not hesitate to recommend that "anyone entering on the study of Shakespeare, and unable or unwilling to read much criticism, would do best to take Prof. Dowden for his guide."

In writing his book Dowden was much influenced by Frederick James Furnivall, who founded the New Shakspere Society in 1873 with the object of studying "the growth, the oneness of Shakspere." Furnivall pursued this end by studying the changes in the verse, through which establishing the order of the plays and the division of Shakespeare's writing career into four periods. Dowden's study is in many ways the work that Furnivall thought was needed, a book which deals with Shakespeare as a whole. Georg Gottfried Gervinus, a Heidelberg professor, had written such a study in four volumes in German in 1849–1850, which was translated into English as *Shakespeare Commentaries* (1863). By means of studying the verse, Gervinus divided the work of Shakespeare into three periods and was the first critic to trace the development of his art. While Dowden is indebted to Gervinus, his interpretation is the first attempt in English to trace the growth of Shakespeare's intellect and character from youth to full maturity, that is, through the four periods established by Furnivall.

In 1943 H. M. O. White summarized Dowden's achievement and put it into perspective:

The roots of Dowden's approach to Shakespeare are really to be found in the pages of Coleridge. Basing his work on the chronological sequence of the plays derived from Furnivall, he attempted to evolve a spiritual and psychological biography of the dramatist . . . he is interested more in the mind than in the art of the dramatist. He shows little concern for the form of the plays. . . . His method is . . . the careful analysis of single characters,

THE LIFE

OF

PERCY BYSSHE SHELLEY

BY

EDWARD DOWDEN, LL.D.

PROFESSOR OF ENGLISH LITERATURE IN THE UNIVERSITY OF DUBLIN

IN TWO VOLUMES
VOL. II.

LONDON
KEGAN PAUL, TRENCH & CO., 1, PATERNOSTER SQUARE
1886

Frontispiece and title page for the second volume of Dowden's biography of the Romantic poet. Dowden reported that his work on the book had caused him to like Shelley and his poetry less.

and, by setting them in the order of their creation, to penetrate behind them to the inner life of their creator.

Despite the objection that Dowden confined Shakespeare too exclusively to "the ivory tower of artistic isolation, forgetting the cares of the box-office, and the hurly-burly of actor-manager in which he undoubtedly lived," his work "remains, and must remain, a remarkable attempt to reconstruct from the plays the living growing soul of the man who shaped them . . . no critic had given us, as Dowden did, an interpretation, still in essentials valid, of his fundamental attitude towards men and women and the great moral realities. The conception of Shakespeare, which many of us still carry in our hearts, follows, despite more recent qualifications, the main lines of Dowden's delineation. . . . That fact alone is the measure of the greatness of his achievement."

In 1877 Dowden published his *Shakspere* in J. R. Green's series of Literature Primers. It became extremely popular: Dowden reported that it "has succeeded better than Macmillan had hoped. I say

10,000 have sold, only on guess, but it is I have no doubt, a well-founded guess for a reprint is about to be made." Almost seventy years later White described it as "invaluable . . . for long the standard summary of Shakespearean scholarship." Dowden followed this with editions of the sonnets, *The Sonnets of William Shakspere* (1881) and *The Passionate Pilgrim* (1883), and several plays, including *Hamlet* (1899), *Romeo and Juliet* (1900), and *Cymbeline* (1903). His *Spenser the Poet and Teacher* (1882) was intended as a corrective to J. R. Lowell's celebrated essay on Spenser (1875) as a poet of beauty and delight and stressed the "sage and serious" poet.

It had been Sir Percy and Lady Shelley's hope that Richard Garnett, an intimate friend of the family, would undertake the authoritative life of Percy Bysshe Shelley, but the pressure of Garnett's official work at the British Museum was so great that the idea was finally abandoned. Garnett recruited Dowden to write the biography and retained a kind of watching brief, helping and advising Dowden and intervening with Sir Percy and Lady Shelley when necessary.

Dowden, recommended by William Michael Rossetti to Garnett as a "Whitman enthusiast," was invited through the intermediary of Sir Henry Taylor to undertake the biography; Dowden recounted that "nothing in all my life came to me more unexpectedly." He immediately abandoned his work on Johann Wolfgang von Goethe.

Dowden was given privileged access to the private collection of Shelley material assembled by Shelley's son and daughter-in-law and kept at their home in Boscombe. There is little doubt that Sir Percy and Lady Shelley tried to influence his biography. They both worked hard to have Shelley and his wife Mary "seen not only as 'great' but as 'good' in the strict Victorian sense," although Dowden insisted that "their responsibility was limited to the choice of a competent biographer and to his using documents with fidelity." When he had nearly finished his book, Dowden reported to Garnett that the Shelleys were unhappy with what he had done: "Two things seem to be unsatisfactory to them. First my treatment of the separation from Harriet. . . . I have also pained them by certain half-satirical references to Godwin as the 'Sage' and the 'philosopher.'" After Garnett intervened, Dowden agreed to amend his "mode of expressions," rephrasing his description of William Godwin and several other matters, though he still could not bring himself to like Godwin. Nonetheless, Dowden realized that in some things he had to choose between pleasing the Shelleys and strict veracity. This was particularly the case in the matter of the poet's separation from his first wife, where the problem was to be fair to both Harriet and to Mary, for whom Shelley left Harriet. Nonetheless, with tact Dowden managed to satisfy both the Shelleys and the Esdailes (Charles E. J. Esdaile and the Reverend W. Esdaile, Shelley's grandsons by his first marriage) in his presentation of this crucial episode. He was acutely aware of the possible charge that since he was working for the Shelleys he would therefore sanitize his depiction of the poet: "I should like nothing worse than that it should be supposed that I had in the slightest degree forfeited my independence." Dowden published the biography in two volumes in 1886. Despite their earlier disagreements, Sir Percy and Lady Shelley were quick to congratulate him on his book which would, they felt, "take its place among the most famous of biographies." William Butler Yeats recalled that "Once after breakfast Dowden read us some chapters of his unpublished *Life of Shelley,* and I who had made the *Prometheus Unbound* my sacred book was delighted with all he read. I was chilled, however, when he explained that he had lost his liking

for Shelley and would not have written it but for an old promise to the Shelley family . . . it was only when he urged me to read George Eliot that I became angry and disillusioned and worked myself into a quarrel or half-quarrel." There is no evidence apart from Yeats's comment that writing the biography ever became a burden to Dowden, but there is good evidence that after his early enthusiasm Yeats became disillusioned with Dowden when Dowden showed himself less than enthusiastic about the Irish literary revival that Yeats was stage-managing.

The biography was widely and, on the whole, well reviewed, though too many of the reviews depended not on the merits of Dowden's work but on the reviewer's attitude toward Shelley. The anonymous reviewer in the *Athenaeum* (11 December 1886) described the separation from his first wife as "this *crux* of Shelleyan biography" and said that Dowden threw more light on the subject than previous accounts had. He praises Dowden for "his essential, though sympathetic moderation of tone [which is] matched by his equability of language: he avoids controversy as far as possible, and is never overheated." Dowden's biography is a tribute to his impartial handling of the facts and to his diplomacy. In this respect, the reviewer with some justice regretted the fact that Dowden had avoided giving "a general estimate and summary either of Shelley's character and course of action or of his standing as poet and thinker."

It was left to T. Hall Caine in his review in the *Academy* (4 December 1886) to criticize Dowden for the way he had dealt with the separation between Shelley and Harriet. First, he praised the biography fulsomely: "This is a book meant to last, and beyond question it will endure and be final. Such an authentic record, such exhaustiveness of enquiry, such fullness of detail, seem to leave nothing to desire, and little to expect. The story is told with admirable impartiality, coupled with wise and inspiring enthusiasm. The style is excellent throughout . . . some of the passages of Mr. Dowden's narrative reach a very high point of excellence." Yet Dowden, he asserted, blames Harriet without cause, for there is no evidence of her infidelity nor any evidence to suggest that Shelley himself believed it. Caine accused Dowden of failing to clarify the fact that Shelley "was deficient in the moral sense. . . . The man who is now revealed to us from top to toe may have been a great poet, but he was not a great man." It was the immorality of Shelley, demonstrated particularly in the way he treated his first wife, that most concerned the Victorian reader. Dowden's evenhandedness in handling this part of his biography

The frontispiece and title page for Dowden's biography of the Victorian poet. The Times Literary Supplement *described the book as "sober (perhaps almost too sober)."*

was widely interpreted as condoning Shelley's subversion of marriage and all family virtues. He was given little credit for the scrupulous way he had examined and presented the facts of the case or the way he had refused to lay the blame on either party. Indeed, he was condemned most strongly for his failure to make such moral judgments on his subject.

Dowden was a self-conscious biographer and well aware of the method he had adopted in writing his biography:

> When I say "Portrait-painter" I express my aim. I avoid with horror, argument and purpose and polemics, and delight in getting down a stroke or a bit of colour as an end in itself. The result is that at present I write much of my narrative without comment, with a slight strain of irony throughout — irony being a form of self-restraint like the censure of the press, and forcing one to say things in the most dextrous way; and at rare intervals I lift up the story out of the irony of my manner of telling it, by a quickly repressed outbreak of enthusiasm.

Matthew Arnold in his review expressed the anxieties of the age, condemning Shelley both as man and poet and his biographer for revealing the sordid facts of his life in such detail and at such length. He was highly disturbed by Dowden's acceptance of the "irregularities" of Shelley's life. He also mocked Dowden's style, expressing the wish that he had "kept his poetic quality of fervour and picturesqueness more under control." "Professor Dowden was too much for my patience," he had written to Lady de Rothschild on 4 January 1888. Arnold repeated his famous description of Shelley as "a beautiful and *ineffectual* angel" from his essay on Byron (1881), which became a blight upon Shelley studies for decades.

George Saintsbury described Arnold's essay with admiration as "a blend of quiet contempt with perfect good-humour and perfect good breeding . . . one of Arnold's demolitions of humourless pedantry." It is hard, nonetheless, to resist the impression that behind Arnold's article was the memory of Dowden's savage review of *Last Essays on Church and*

Religion (1877) and that Arnold enjoyed taking his revenge.

Mark Twain's attack on Dowden in his "In Defense of Harriet Shelley" in the July, August, and September 1894 issues of the *North American Review* was ill-advised; Garnett described it as an "astounding impertinence." Lytton Strachey's attack on Dowden, first published in 1917, was too obviously partisan to be damaging. Beginning from the dubious conviction that biographers of poets are mostly "highly respectable old gentlemen" whereas poets are "apt to be young, and not apt to be highly respectable," Strachey criticized Dowden for being too sympathetic in his treatment of his subject and asserted that Arnold's "distressed self-righteousness," because its bias is so obvious, is to be preferred: "through two fat volumes, Shelley's fire and air have been transmuted into Professor Dowden's cotton-wool and rose-water . . . a subtler revenge of the world's upon the most radiant of its enemies."

Despite the acclaim with which, generally speaking, it was greeted and the controversy it had aroused, two years after its publication only two thousand copies had been sold: "not very many, but quite as many as I expected," Dowden commented in a 2 July 1888 letter to Garnett, though he had every right to expect a far greater sale. Nonetheless, his biography remains the first scholarly biography of the poet and is a monument to Dowden's scrupulous respect for veracity and his ability to deal with the tangled lives involved with objectivity and compassion.

Dowden's biography of Robert Southey, published in 1879, is an admirable and charming study of the man and the writer. There can be no doubt that Dowden was sincere in his assertion that "I did my little Southey book with true love for the man." As a devoted family man and an unusually hard-working writer, Dowden identified closely with his subject.

> Southey never laid hold of me until I began to write his life: I think because his works are so much accumulated materials, well disposed, while I wanted some spiritual light shining through materials. This I found in Wordsworth. But now arrived at these years of middle life and being able to estimate the worth of high industry in literature, and also able to value the good of home-virtues, and steadfastness in the conduct of life, I find an extraordinary degree and an extraordinary QUALITY of what is admirable in Southey's work and life.

Kenneth Curry's assessment of the biography was judicious: "Dowden's portrait of Southey softens the harsh side of his personality and presents him as happy in his family and friends, deeply en-

grossed in the writing of his books and articles. . . . Highest praise is reserved for Southey's biographies. . . . Dowden's partiality for Southey results in a portrait that is almost saintly." Yet Clement Shorter expressed a general view when he said that "His 'Life of Southey' . . . is perhaps the most brilliant book he has yet written, but I am not quite sure that it was worth while writing a brilliant book about Southey." William Kirkpatrick Magee recalled Yeats making a similar judgment when he summed Dowden up as a "man born into the world to write a life of Southey." Both comments demonstrate an attitude toward Southey that is both patronizing and demeaning.

Dowden's biography of Robert Browning (1904), when reviewed in the *Times Literary Supplement* of 15 April 1904, was characterized as "sober (perhaps almost too sober), studious, and mature critical scholarship. . . . Nothing can be more fully informed and accurately stated, or conceived with better taste and feeling, than those parts of Dowden's volume which narrate the external facts and circumstances of the poet's life." As a critic his "method is to converse with his reader, as with almost an equal in knowledge and judgment." The reviewer seemed to believe that Browning is a most obscure poet and that the reader therefore needs a great deal more explication of the poems than Dowden gives in order to understand the poems.

Dowden deserves recognition for his partisan discussion of Whitman's poetic achievements contained in his essay "The Poetry of Democracy: Walt Whitman," published in *Westminster Review* (July 1871), which probably did as much as any other work to establish the currency of Whitman's reputation in Great Britain at a time when his poetry was meeting either ridicule or neglect. Dowden's second wife says that for "Walt Whitman, with whom a personal friendship, strong on both sides was formed, he felt the cordial reverence due to the giver of what he reckoned as a gift of immense value. While condemning whatever was unreticent in *Leaves of Grass,* he at the same time saw there the great flood of spirituality available as a force for emancipation of our hearts from pressures of sordidness in the world." This friendship was conducted entirely by letters and through intermediaries for "they never met in the flesh." Gerothwohl describes how when Dowden "presented the College library with that poet's *Leaves of Grass,* the gift was returned to him as unfit reading for students."

Yet Mahaffy clearly saw his appreciation of Whitman's achievement as a sign of psychological weakness: "Walt Whitman – a writer in whom brute physical force is so prominent that we might have expected so pure and delicate an intellect as Dowden's to recoil from such poetry with disgust. He suggested that Dowden's liking for Whitman was due to his excessive admiration for strong animal vigor since he himself had been a delicate child with a weak chest. Nonetheless, T. W. Rolleston recalled Dowden's "uncompromising championship of Walt Whitman, at a time when to champion Whitman was a very serious thing. As a matter of fact, it was within an ace of leading to Dowden's resignation of his post." His regard for Whitman as a man and his faith in his poetry were unwavering at a time when the man was derided and the poetry mocked.

Dowden's interest in French literature culminated in the publication of *A History of French Literature* (1897) and his *Michel de Montaigne* (1905). His work on German literature and particularly on Goethe was outstanding enough for him to be elected as Chairman of the English Goethe Society.

His interests and scholarship ranged over the whole of English literature from the Elizabethan to the contemporary and also included the literatures of France, Germany, and the United States. From time to time he collected a selection of his numerous published articles and lectures in a series of books, beginning with *Studies in Literature 1789–1877* (1878) and continuing at intervals with *Transcripts and Studies* (1888), *New Studies in Literature* (1895), *Puritan and Anglican: Studies in Literature* (1900), and *Essays Modern and Elizabethan* (1910), which among many other topics contained articles on the French Revolution and literature; the transcendental movement; the scientific movement; William Wordsworth; Walter Savage Landor; Alfred, Lord Tennyson and Robert Browning; George Eliot; Victor Hugo; Whitman; Thomas Carlyle; Shelley; Victorian literature; Edmund Spenser; Shakespeare; Christopher Marlowe; John Milton; George Meredith; John Donne; Arthur Clough; Goethe; Samuel Taylor Coleridge; Edward Scherer; Thomas Browne; John Bunyan; Samuel Butler; William Cowper; George Herbert; Walter Pater; Henrik Ibsen; Heinrich Heine; and Elizabethan masque and romance.

Apart from his editions of Shakespeare, he was extremely prolific as an editor and produced, among much else, scholarly editions and selections of Wordsworth, Southey, Goethe, Carlyle, Coleridge, Shelley, Browning, and Henry Taylor. He was chosen as the first Taylorian lecturer, delivering his lecture at Oxford on 20 November 1889,

and Clark Lecturer in English Literature at Cambridge University, 1893–1896. He was awarded the honorary degrees of LL.D. by the University of Edinburgh and by Princeton University, D.C.L. by Oxford University, and D.Litt. by Cambridge University.

He was widely honored and was president of the English Goethe Society from 1888 to 1911, trustee of the Irish National Library, commissioner of Education, secretary of the Irish Liberal Union, and vice-president of the Irish Unionist Alliance.

Although he enjoyed close friendships with leaders of the Irish nationalist movement – particularly Samuel Ferguson, Aubrey de Vere, and John Todhunter – his reputation undoubtedly suffered in Ireland because of his unwillingness to support the nationalists. William Butler Yeats was particularly upset by what he considered to be his indifference to the movement he endorsed: "Prof Dowden expressed scorn for The Irish Lit movement and Irish lit generally, from which he has been catching it from all the Dublin papers – even the Irish Times which had a leader on him." Yet Dowden stood for a wider allegiance altogether. Ernest Augustus Boyd thought he was without a sense of national identity and says, "In Ireland he was not an Irishman, in any national sense, and in England he was not altogether an Englishman." T. W. Rolleston understood his position more clearly: "The truth is Dowden never had any consciousness of Ireland as a separate national entity, or of himself as specially belonging to it. The root of his spiritual nature was in England or in Germany or France, wherever human nature was at home. He was an apostle of culture. But he loved Ireland enough to spend his whole life there, in spite of the attractive offers he received to transfer his fame and his abilities to other universities." Dowden described his own sense of nationality in a way that was altogether more profound than the narrow political dogmas on which his critics too often took their stand: "If national character be really strong and vivid it will show itself, although we do not strive to be national with malice prepense; it will show itself, whether we occupy ourselves with an edition of Sophocles or of Cicero, or with a song of the deeds of Cuchullain or the love and sorrow of Deirdre." Nonetheless, he actively supported the union and fought strenuously and publicly against the nationalists and the home-rule movement.

His life was dedicated to his work; he was so immensely conscientious and hardworking that Magee described him as "a saint of culture; a saint, however, not lost to humanity." "Busy years, un-

Drawing of Dowden by John Butler Yeats

eventful outwardly, followed in succession. . . . Occasionally came brief excursions of travel abroad or in the British Isles; and occasionally in the midst of toiling days of work, a holiday in the fresh fields or at sea would break the monotony." However, on 21 October 1892 "the happiness of his home was broken by the death of a beloved wife and mother. His sorrow, bravely borne, was deep."

Dowden was remarried on 12 December 1895 to Elizabeth Dickinson West, daughter of the Very Reverend John West, dean of Saint Patrick's, "a woman of remarkable character and culture." She had been a friend for many years and was described as a principal influence in his life. Dowden's collection of poems, a sequence of 101 love lyrics for his second wife, *A Woman's Reliquary,* was published in 1913 in an edition of three hundred copies. The "Editor's Note" is signed "Edward Dowden" and maintains that "the writer and the person addressed are both dead," but the fiction is a transparent one and is in any case exposed by a "Publisher's note"

stating that "If readers desire to attribute authorship of this book to the editor, no wrong is done to anyone." In an enthusiastic review of the poems in the *Nation* (25 March 1915), Martin W. Sampson found a "rare quality" evident on every page and described them as "a shrine, a chapel whose privacy is not disturbed by the wide-open door, for those who enter will be pilgrims to whom the secret gift is precious." His second marriage relieved him to a large extent of anxiety concerning money, and they enjoyed holidays for two months every summer in Cornwall, Wales, western Ireland, and elsewhere.

However, it is clear that he had been suffering severe bronchial trouble for some years, and when lecturing to the students at the University College of North Wales he reported that he had suffered a "little bleeding from my chest following an address I gave the Students at Bangor," when the principal and his wife had to put him to bed in their house. Again, in 1899 he had mentioned the possibility of "getting an assistant-lecturer to be paid out of my salary; possibly resignation." Insomnia caused him much distress and yet the last year of Dowden's life, according to his wife, "had the great gain of a remarkable revival of health and spirits. From midsummer 1912 sleep returned and . . . that restoration remained up to the end."

Dowden died on 4 April 1913 in Dublin, where he was mourned and missed as a person and teacher as well as a scholar and critic whose reputation was international. Yet of all the many obituaries announcing his loss, those written by his friends, students, and fellow Dubliners carry the greatest conviction. D. J. O'Donoghue spoke for the city when he wrote, "The death of Professor Dowden leaves a great blank in the literary life of Dublin." He was recalled as a friend and as a respected and familiar figure: "one caught a glimpse of him in the Dublin thoroughfares placidly reading on the top of a tramcar or hurrying homeward with an armful of books, and noticed how the Dublin citizen turned to look after his picturesque figure."

Rolleston's "Recollections of Dowden" was first read as a paper before a large gathering of students and friends to commemorate his memory, and, as if to bring home the intimacy of the occasion, it was reported that there was only one "person present who could answer off-hand a question once set by Dowden in an examination paper: 'What were the last words of Caliban?'"

Rolleston recalled the teacher and the man:

I came to know Dowden as a student in T.C.D. when, soon after entering, I began to attend his lectures on English literature. These were a surprising experience — epoch making in many a young man's life. For Dowden was able to charm, to stimulate, and evoke that which is one of the most beautiful and touching things in the world, the reverence of young men for those who offer them the priceless treasures of knowledge and thought. Everything about him was impressive. His voice was like no other man's voice, it was neither noticeably deep nor high, but pitched upon a middle note of which he alone had the secret — it was sympathetic, yet it seemed to come from some place remote from common life. . . . He was fairly tall, somewhat high shouldered, with the stoop of the scholar, his complexion brown, eyes and hair brown, his expression calm, yet the look of the man testified to capacity for passion. It was often said that the grave dignity of the oval face, with its short pointed beard, reminded one of the portraits of some of the famous Elizabethans.

Dowden described his recreation as book collecting, and he built up a fine collection of over twenty-four thousand volumes. However, despite pleas that his books, particularly his unique Shakespeare collection, should be kept together in Dublin, his library was sold at auction by Hodgson of Chancery Lane beginning on 5 November 1913 (his unique Shakespeare collection sold for £250) and his collection of autograph letters, manuscripts, and broadsides on 9 June 1914.

John Butler Yeats paid his own tribute to their long friendship: "He was all his life an extremely handsome man. . . . He looked the poet and primarily was the poet. . . . To enter Dowden's house — even to meet him by chance on the roadside — was a touch to recover one's crumbling self-esteem: I have talked with his friends on this subject, and we have all agreed that after meeting Edward Dowden peace would fall on the troubled spirit."

Dowden's influence had been absorbed not only by his contemporaries but also by the younger generation. James Joyce thought that no account of Dublin in 1904 would be complete without the inclusion of Dowden. Dowden found another kind of immortality, in fiction, by being included in *Ulysses* (1922). In episode 9, Scylla and Charybdis, set in the National Library, Stephen outlines his theory of *Hamlet* and the character's relationship with his author. Among others, both Magee and Lyster, Dowden's friends, are present: thus a group of historical characters gather to listen to a fictional character, Stephen Dedalus, discuss Hamlet, another fictional character. Dowden, whose address is given as Highfield House, is alluded to by Buck Mulligan, who says that when he "asked him what he thought of the charge of pederasty brought against the bard, he lifted his hands and said: *All we can say is that life ran very high in those days.*" Also in the same discussion there is a reference to Dowden's view of *Hamlet:* "Dowden believes there is some mystery in *Hamlet* but will say no more." However ironic these allusions may be, they are also respectful, and the whole discussion is indebted to Dowden's search for Shakespeare the man among the plays and poems for, as Magee says, "Shakespeare was to him primarily a person," as, indeed, he was to Stephen. Moreover, Joyce recalls not only the critic and lecturer but Dowden the public figure who lived and worked in Dublin and became part of the soul and fabric of the city.

Letters:

Elizabeth D. and Hilda M. Dowden, *Letters of Edward Dowden and His Correspondents* (London: Dent, 1914; New York: Dutton, 1914);

Elizabeth D. Dowden, *Fragments from Old Letters E.D. to E.D.W. 1869–1892.* (London: Dent, 1914; New York: Dutton, 1914);

Dowden, *Fragments from Old Letters E.D. to E.D.W. 1869–1892 Second Series* (London: Dent, 1914; New York: Dutton, 1914);

R. S. Garnett, *Letters About Shelley, Interchanged by Three Friends — Edward Dowden Richard Garnett and Wm. Michael Rossetti* (London & New York: Hodder & Stoughton, 1917).

References:

E. A. Boyd, "A Lonely Irishman: Edward Dowden," *Appreciations and Depreciations, Irish Literary Studies* (London: Fisher Unwin, 1917), pp. 141–162;

H. S. Fiske, "Recollections of Edward Dowden," *Nation,* 96, 2499, 22 May 1913: 520–521;

M. A. Gerothwohl, "Edward Dowden," *Fortnightly Review,* DLXX, N.S. June 1914: 1009–1021;

William Kirkpatrick Magee, *Irish Literary Portraits* (London: Macmillan, 1935);

Obituary, *Irish Book Lover,* IV, 10 May 1913: 167–169;

T. W. Rolleston, "Recollections of Dowden," *Irish Book Lover,* V, 9, April 1914: 153–155;

Martin W. Sampson, "The Poetry of Edward Dowden," *Nation,* C. 2595, 25 March 1915: 324–325;

C. K. Shorter, *English Illustrated Magazine,* XXIX (February 1903): 204–206;

H. M. O. White, *Edward Dowden 1843–1913. An Address Delivered in the Chapel of Trinity College Dublin, on Trinity Monday. 1943* (Dublin: Dublin University Press, 1943);

J. B.Yeats, "Edward Dowden," *Nation,* XCVI, 2495, 2495, 24 April 1913: 413–414.

Papers:
There are collections of manuscripts at the Huntington Library, San Marino, California, and at Trinity College, Dublin.

John Drinkwater

(1 June 1882 – 25 March 1937)

Steven H. Gale
Kentucky State University

See also the Drinkwater entries in *DLB 10, Modern British Dramatists, 1900–1945,* and *DLB 19, British Poets, 1880–1914.*

BOOKS: *Poems* (Birmingham, U.K.: C. Combridge, 1903);

The Death of Leander and Other Poems (Birmingham, U.K.: Cornish, 1906);

Lyrical and Other Poems (Cranleigh: Samurai Press, 1908);

Poems of Men and Hours (London: Nutt, 1911);

An English Medley (Birmingham, U.K.: Privately printed, 1911);

Puss in Boots: A Play in Five Scenes (London: Nutt, 1911);

Cophetua: A Play in One Act (London: Nutt, 1911);

The Pied Piper (Birmingham, U.K.: Privately printed, 1912);

Poems of Love and Earth (London: Nutt, 1912);

William Morris: A Critical Study (London: Secker, 1912; New York: Kennerly, 1912);

Cromwell and Other Poems (London: Nutt, 1913);

The Only Legend (Birmingham, U.K.: Privately printed, 1913);

Swinburne: An Estimate (London & Toronto: Dent / New York: Dutton, 1913);

Rebellion: A Play in Three Acts (London: Nutt, 1914);

Robin Hood and the Pedlar (Birmingham, U.K.: Privately printed, 1914);

The Storm (Birmingham, U.K.: Privately printed, 1915);

Swords and Ploughshares (London: Sidgwick & Jackson, 1915);

The Lyric (London: Secker, 1915; New York: Doran, 1916);

The God of Quiet (Birmingham, U.K.: Privately printed, 1916);

Olton Pools (London: Sidgwick & Jackson, 1916);

Poems 1908–1914 (London: Sidgwick & Jackson, 1917; New York: Dodd, Mead, 1918);

Prose Papers (London: Elkin Mathews, 1917);

Tides: A Book of Poems (London: Sidgwick & Jackson, 1917);

Pawns: Three Poetic Plays (London: Sidgwick & Jackson, 1917) – includes *The Storm, The God of Quiet,* and *X=0;*

X=0: A Night of the Trojan War (Birmingham, U.K.: Privately printed, 1917);

Abraham Lincoln (London: Sidgwick & Jackson, 1918; Boston & New York: Houghton Mifflin, 1919);

Loyalties: A Book of Poems (London: Beaumont, 1918; enlarged edition, London: Sidgwick & Jackson, 1919);

Poems 1908–1919 (Boston & New York: Houghton Mifflin, 1919);

Lincoln: The World Emancipator, introduction by Arnold Bennett (Boston & New York: Houghton Mifflin, 1920);

Pawns: Four Poetic Plays (Boston & New York: Houghton Mifflin, 1920) – includes *The Storm, The God of Quiet, X=0,* and *Cophetua;* republished as *Pawns and Cophetua* (London: Sidgwick & Jackson, 1922);

Persuasion: Twelve Sonnets (London: Privately printed, 1921);

Seeds of Time (London: Sidgwick & Jackson, 1921; Boston & New York: Houghton Mifflin, 1922);

Oliver Cromwell (London: Sidgwick & Jackson, 1921; Boston & New York: Houghton Mifflin, 1921);

Mary Stuart (London: Sidgwick & Jackson, 1921; Boston & New York: Houghton Mifflin, 1921; revised edition, London: Sidgwick & Jackson, 1922; Boston & New York: Houghton Mifflin, 1924);

Cotswold Characters (New Haven: Yale University Press, 1921);

Preludes 1921–1922 (London: Sidgwick & Jackson, 1922; Boston & New York: Houghton Mifflin, 1923);

John Drinkwater (Hulton Deutsch)

Some Contributions to the English Anthology (With Special Reference to the Seventeenth Century) (London: Oxford University Press, 1922);

The Collected Poems, 1908–1917 (London: Sidgwick & Jackson, 1923);

The Collected Poems, 1917–1922 (London: Sidgwick & Jackson, 1923);

Robert E. Lee (London: Sidgwick & Jackson, 1923; Boston & New York: Houghton Mifflin, 1923);

Victorian Poetry (London: Hodder & Stoughton, 1923; New York: Doran, 1924);

From an Unknown Isle (London: Sidgwick & Jackson, 1924);

Patriotism in Literature (London: Williams & Norgate, 1924; New York: Holt, 1924);

The Collected Plays of John Drinkwater, 2 volumes (London: Sidgwick & Jackson, 1925);

New Poems (Boston & New York: Houghton Mifflin, 1925);

Robert Burns (London: Sidgwick & Jackson, 1925; Boston & New York: Houghton Mifflin, 1925);

The Muse in Council (London: Sidgwick & Jackson, 1925; Boston & New York: Houghton Mifflin, 1925);

The Pilgrim of Eternity: Byron — A Conflict (London: Hodder & Stoughton, 1925; New York: Doran, 1925);

Persephone (New York: Rudge, 1926);

Mr. Charles, King of England (London: Hodder & Stoughton, 1926; New York: Doran, 1926);

Bird in Hand (London: Sidgwick & Jackson, 1927; Boston & New York: Houghton Mifflin, 1927);

Cromwell: A Character Study (London: Hodder & Stoughton, 1927); republished as *Oliver Cromwell: A Character Study* (New York: Doubleday, Doran, 1927);

The Gentle Art of Theatre-Going (London: Holden, 1927); republished as *The Art of Theatre-Going* (Boston & New York: Houghton Mifflin, 1927);

All About Me: Poems for a Child (London: Collins, 1928; Boston & New York: Houghton Mifflin, 1928);

John Bull Calling: A Political Parable in One Act (London: Sidgwick & Jackson, 1928);

Charles James Fox (London: Benn, 1928; New York: Cosmopolitan Book Corporation, 1928);

The World's Lincoln (New York: Bowling Green Press, 1928);

More About Me: Poems for a Child (London: Collins, 1929; Boston & New York: Houghton Mifflin, 1930);

Pepys, His Life and Character (London: Heinemann, 1930; Garden City, N.Y: Doubleday, Doran, 1930);

American Vignettes, 1860–1865 (Boston & New York: Houghton Mifflin, 1931);

The Life and Adventures of Carl Laemmle (New York & London: Putnam, 1931; London: Heinemann, 1931);

Inheritance: Being the First Book of An Autobiography (London: Benn, 1931; New York: Holt, 1931);

Discovery: Being the Second Book of An Autobiography, 1897–1913 (London: Benn, 1932; Boston & New York: Houghton Mifflin, 1933);

Napoleon: The Hundred Days, adapted from the Italian play by Benito Mussolini and Giovacchino Forzano (London: Sidgwick & Jackson, 1932);

Midsummer Eve (London: Sidgwick & Jackson, 1932);

Summer Harvest: Poems 1924–1933 (London: Sidgwick & Jackson, 1933);

Laying the Devil (London: Sidgwick & Jackson, 1933);

Shakespeare (London: Duckworth, 1933; New York: Macmillan, 1933);

This Troubled World (New York: Columbia University Press, 1933; London: Oxford University Press, 1933);

John Hampden's England (London: Butterworth, 1933);

A Man's House (London: Sidgwick & Jackson, 1934; New York & London: French, 1935);

Garibaldi: A Chronicle Play of Italian Freedom in Ten Scenes (London: Sidgwick & Jackson, 1936);

Robinson of England (London: Methuen, 1937; New York: Macmillan, 1937);

The Collected Poems, 1923–1937 (London: Sidgwick & Jackson, 1937);

English Poetry: An Unfinished History (London: Methuen, 1938).

PLAY PRODUCTIONS: *Ser Taldo's Bride,* by Drinkwater and Barry Jackson, Birmingham, U.K., Assembly Rooms, January 1911;

Cophetua, Assembly Rooms, 18 November 1911, Edgbaston; Birmingham, U.K., Birmingham Repertory Theatre, 27 October 1917;

An English Medley, music by Rutland Boughton, Birmingham, U.K., Cadbury Works Summer Party, 1911;

Puss in Boots, Birmingham, U.K., Pilgrim Players, 1911; revised version, London, Apollo Theatre, 27 December 1926;

The Pied Piper, music by F. W. Sylvester, Birmingham, U.K., Cadbury Works Summer Party, 1912;

The Only Legend, Bournville, Birmingham, U.K., Cadbury Works Summer Party, 10 July 1913;

Rebellion, Birmingham, U.K., Birmingham Repertory Theatre, 2 May 1914;

Robin Hood and the Pedlar, music by J. Brier, Bournville, Birmingham, U.K., Cadbury Works Summer Party, 25 June 1914;

The Storm, Birmingham, U.K., Birmingham Repertory Theatre, 8 May 1915;

The God of Quiet, Birmingham, U.K., Birmingham Repertory Theatre, 7 October 1916;

The Wounded, Birmingham, U.K., Birmingham Repertory Theatre, 3 March 1917;

X=o: A Night of the Trojan War, Birmingham, U.K., Birmingham Repertory Theatre, 14 April 1917; London, New Theatre, 8 December 1919;

Abraham Lincoln, Birmingham, U.K., Birmingham Repertory Theatre, 12 October 1918; London, Lyric Opera House, Hammersmith, 19 February 1919;

Oliver Cromwell, Brighton, Theatre Royal, 19 February 1921; London, His Majesty's Theatre, 29 May 1923;

Mary Stuart, New York, Ritz Theatre, 21 March 1921; London, Everyman Theatre, 25 September 1922;

Robert E. Lee, London, Regent Theatre, 20 June 1923;

The Mayor of Casterbridge, adapted from Thomas Hardy's novel, Barnes, Theatre Royal, 8 September 1926;

Bird in Hand, Birmingham, U.K., Birmingham Repertory Theatre, 3 September 1927; London, Royalty Theatre, 18 April 1928;

John Bull Calling: A Political Parable in One Act, London, Coliseum Theatre, 12 November 1928;

Napoleon: The Hundred Days, adapted from Benito Mussolini and Giovacchino Forzano's play in Italian, London, New Theatre, 18 April 1932;

Laying the Devil, Liverpool, Playhouse, 2 May 1933;

A Man's House, London, Malvern, Malvern Festival, 23 July 1934; New Theatre, 12 September 1934.

MOTION PICTURES: *Sally Bishop,* screenplay by Drinkwater, British Lion, 1932;

The King's Reign, screenplay by Drinkwater, Movietone News, 1935;

I Pagliacci, screenplay by Drinkwater, United Artists, 1937;

The King's People, screenplay by Drinkwater, Warner Bros., 1937;

The Mill on the Floss, screenplay by Drinkwater, British Lion, 1937.

RADIO: *Midsummer Eve,* BBC, London, 20 June 1932.

OTHER: *The Poems, Letters and Prose Fragments of Kirke White,* edited, with an introduction, by Drinkwater (London: Routledge, 1907; New York: Dutton, 1907);

The Poems of Sir Philip Sidney, edited, with an introduction, by Drinkwater (London: Routledge, 1910);

The Dramatic Works of St. John E. C. Hankin, introduction by Drinkwater (London: Secker, 1912);

The Outline of Literature, 2 volumes, edited by Drinkwater (London: Newnes, 1923–1924; New York: Putnam, 1923–1924);

A Book for Bookmen: Being Edited Manuscripts & Marginalia with Essays on Several Occasions, edited, with essays, by Drinkwater (London: Dulay, 1926).

Although best known for his work in the theater, John Drinkwater would probably have defined himself as a poet. He was also active in the field of biography, and in fact his most successful play, *Abraham Lincoln* (1918), was the first of his historical prose dramas. As might be expected, Drinkwater's approach to biography clearly grew out of his educational background and personal experiences.

Born 1 June 1882 at Dorset Villa, Leytonstone, Essex, Drinkwater was the son of Albert Edwin Drinkwater and Annie Beck Brown Drinkwater. Albert Drinkwater was the headmaster of Coburn Foundation School at Bow in East London when John was born. As a youth John attended a dame school run by a Mrs. Zinck in Ladbroke Grove.

By 1886 Albert Drinkwater had abandoned his career in education to become a professional actor, playwright, and manager in the theater. John occasionally accompanied his father on tour. The younger Drinkwater's interest in the theater was piqued when he substituted for an actor in the performance of his father's play *A Golden Sorrow.* The next day he wrote "Sorrow Turned Into Joy," a

seven-minute-long, eleven-act playlet; some twenty years later John Drinkwater was to follow his father into the theater, where he, too, performed as an actor, playwright, and manager.

When Drinkwater was nine years old and his mother was about to die, he was sent to live with his maternal grandfather, John Beck Brown, an ironmonger whose home was on Winchester Road in Cornmarket, near Oxford. Drinkwater attended Oxford High School, where he was influenced by one of his teachers, H. G. Belcher, and another student, the son of lexicographer Sir James Murray, who taught him astronomy. Drinkwater won a chemistry prize, but he was more adept at sports, receiving his cricket and football colors as the youngest member of his team. In 1896 he broke the long-jump record for boys under fourteen when he jumped fifteen feet, eight inches.

When released from school on Sunday afternoons and holidays, Drinkwater stayed with his grandfather at Broceliande, the Oxfordshire farm owned by the Brown family. This experience was to be reflected in his later poems such as "History," published in *Loyalties* (1918). Similar experiences at Cousin Arthur's Boarstall Village farm two miles south of Piddington and at his Great Uncle Thomas's farm near Bicester also appear in his poetry. Indeed, Drinkwater's first poem, which won a bronze medal from *Little Folks* magazine, was written at his grandfather's house at this time.

Drinkwater's grandfather died in 1895, and John went to live in the home of the Reverend H. R. Hall on Banbury Road. In February 1897 the fact that he was a better athlete than student led him to leave school to go to work for the Northern Assurance Company at 15 Victoria Street in Nottingham. His annual salary as a junior clerk was twenty pounds. Drinkwater moved up to the level of bookkeeper within a year. Despite having the ambition to take evening classes and learn shorthand and typing in order to qualify to be a guarantee clerk, he considered his three years in Nottingham a period of boredom and privation. He described the company office as a "barren wilderness," and he characterized his profession as having "as much emotion as a stone." Although he described his life throughout this period as having "no landscape, no perspective, no associations," it was at this time that he discovered poetry in the form of the works of George Gordon, Lord Byron, and he performed onstage as Squire Copse in *Sophia* (a play based on Henry Fielding's *Tom Jones* [1774]) in 1900. During his time in Nottingham Drinkwater began his writing

Drinkwater, circa 1910

career with an article that appeared in 1900 in the *Ilkeston News.* In this piece he describes an evening during which Drinkwater and his companions attacked the home of a pro-Boer. This action was to have an impact on the rest of his life. According to Drinkwater, "we trampled on his flowers, and took the paint off his front door and broke his windows, and we dared him to come out and show his ugly face." In retrospect the incident caused the writer to espouse a "lifelong intolerance of intolerance."

In 1901 Drinkwater transferred to the Northern Assurance Company's branch office in Birmingham and his annual salary rose to sixty pounds. He still had not determined his avocation, however. During the four years that he lived at Edgbaston in King's Heath in Birmingham, he moved up to the position of junior inspector, and he spent his free time playing cricket and football. "As for the muses," he later claimed, "I didn't know them from the marsupials, of whom I learnt with the advent of the crossword puzzle."

In January 1903 Drinkwater experienced some sort of epiphany which resulted in his writing sixty lines of poetry one evening. He began an intensive reading program and later that year paid C. Combridge, a local bookseller, to print his first book, *Poems.* In looking back, Drinkwater later was to claim that the volume was "devoid of promise." Early the following year a friend, Herbert ("Bertie") Stowell Milligan, took Drinkwater to the Grange, where he met Barry Jackson and C. R. ("Tim") Dawes, who staged dramas at the palatial Jackson home. Drinkwater was assigned a part in William Shakespeare's *Twelfth Night;* his association with Jackson's group continued for twelve years.

Northern Assurance sent Drinkwater to Manchester in 1905, but the move proved to be "the most melancholy" period of his life; he missed Birmingham, where he had "first begun to form some clear imaginative purpose," and the friends that he had made there. His great success at selling life insurance was offset by the frugal meal that he ate at

Parker's in Saint Anne's Square each day. He continued to write poetry at his lodgings on Cheetham Hill, and in 1906 he published another volume of poems, *The Death of Leander and Other Poems*. In that same year Drinkwater married Kathleen Walpole, who, under the stage name Cathleen Orford, was an actress with Jackson's Birmingham Repertory Company. The marriage lasted until 1924, when they divorced. He married Daisy Kennedy, a successful violinist, the same year that he divorced Kathleen. One daughter, Penelope, was born to John and Daisy in 1929.

In order to return to Birmingham, Drinkwater took a position with the Liverpool, London and Globe Company in March 1906, but the assignment — which should have been divided among four men — proved to be more than he could handle, and he was fired on 2 October 1907. He returned to Birmingham in 1907, the year that Jackson's company became the Pilgrim Players.

Over the next few years Drinkwater was engaged in several different positions, including a surveyorship for London and Lancashire Fire Offices, Birmingham Branch, and the *Birmingham University Mining and Engineering Journal*, but it was clear that his interests lay in the theater. In 1909 he was put on salary by Jackson's acting company. From 1907 to 1918 Drinkwater acted for Jackson under the stage name John Darnley. He played at least forty parts and directed productions of some sixty plays by thirty-five different authors. This experience turned out to be valuable and important for him, and in November 1911 his first serious play, *Cophetua*, was staged by the Pilgrim Players. The one-act, rhymed-verse play was a critical failure largely due to the playwright's excessive sentimentality. In all, Drinkwater published twenty-three plays, the majority of which were produced onstage.

For many years Drinkwater also was active in writing articles and book reviews, as well as being engaged in editing. As he became more involved in the life of belles lettres, he became acquainted with a wide variety of contemporary poets. For example, he produced some of William Butler Yeats's plays, met T. S. Eliot and John Maysfield, and helped produce John Galsworthy's *The Silver Box* (1906). (In 1922 John Middleton Murry claimed that only Maysfield rivaled Drinkwater in popularity.) Galsworthy nominated Drinkwater to the Square Club in December 1911, and there he met Edward Thomas and Conal O'Riordan, among others. The literary, artistic, and musical circles in which he was involved included Ernest de Selincourt, Alfred Hayes,

Charles Gore (the bishop of Birmingham), Joseph Southall, Arthur Gaskin, Rutledge Boughton, Granville Bantock, and Alfred Noyes.

Drinkwater's first literary commission was an edition of the poetry of Henry Kirke White for the Routledge Muses' Library. The same year that he joined the Square Club, Drinkwater became president of the Birmingham Dramatic and Literary Club, and he was commissioned by Martin Secker to write a book on William Morse. The following year he signed a contract with Dent to write a book on Algernon Charles Swinburne. Over the next few years Drinkwater's circle of literary acquaintances widened as he met or corresponded with Middleton Murry and Katherine Mansfield (editors of the journal *Rhythm*) as well as Anderson Graham (of *Country Life*). Arthur Quiller-Couch reprinted one of Drinkwater's poems in his *Oxford Book of Victorian Verse* (1912). Other acquaintances included Stopford Brooke, Edmond Gosse, Laurence Binyon, and Sturge Moore, in addition to Wilfrid Wilson Gibson, Rupert Brooke, and Lascelles Abercrombie, who together with Drinkwater became known as the Georgian Poets. Harold Monro asked him to contribute to the *Poetry Review,* and a meeting with Edward Marsh led to the biennial publication of an anthology, *Georgian Poetry,* which ran from 1912 to 1922.

Interestingly, besides his poetry and dramaturgy, Drinkwater was a prolific writer of prose too, with didacticism being a common thread in both his verse and prose. *The Lyric* was published in 1915; *Prose Papers,* a collection of essays and lectures, appeared in 1917; *The Muse in Council* appeared in 1925; and *The Gentle Art of Theatre-Going,* which was well received, was published in 1927. He also continued to publish volumes of poetry, his efforts culminating in the printing of *The Collected Poems* in 1923. Additional evidence of the writer's versatility is seen in his decision to adapt from the Italian Benito Mussolini and Giovacchino Forzano's play *Napoleon: The Hundred Days.* Drinkwater's version was produced and published in 1932.

Drinkwater's two primary interests, biography and drama, come together nicely. Drinkwater wrote studies of political figures (Abraham Lincoln, Oliver Cromwell, Mary Stuart, Napoleon I, Giuseppe Garibaldi) and military (Robert E. Lee) and literary subjects (William Shakespeare, Robert Burns); he also created dramatic versions of most of these. Indeed, his most popular dramatic works were the historical plays.

Drinkwater's first prose drama, *Abraham Lincoln,* is considered his best play. It was also his most popularly accepted play. In fact, this work, with choric verse links between the dramatic tableaux, established Drinkwater as a playwright and was translated into Japanese and German. Drinkwater wrote *Abraham Lincoln* in a rented cottage in the Cotswolds, and the drama premiered at the Birmingham Repertory Theatre on 12 October 1918. The play's success led to its being moved to London, where it opened at the Lyric Opera House, Hammersmith, on 19 February 1919 for a run of four hundred performances.

This chronicle of Lincoln's life, from his nomination to his assassination, along with two of Drinkwater's other plays of the period, *Oliver Cromwell* (1921) and *Robert E. Lee* (1923), was part of the author's effort to dramatize what he considered the elements of leadership. "The leader inspired by a great moral idea to the vindication of the system, the leader inspired by a great moral idea to the overthrow of the system, and the leader for whom a system became a great moral idea in itself" constituted Drinkwater's concept of the role of the ideal leader. Through a series of episodes the playwright traces the development of the protagonist and his character.

The dramatist's note to the published version of *Abraham Lincoln* sets the tone for his later biographies. Besides admitting that he made no attempt to "achieve a 'local color' of which I have no experience, or to speak in an idiom to which I have not been bred," he states that "my purpose is that not of the historian but of the dramatist." This disclaimer is followed by the explanation that he is indebted to Lord Charnwood for his volume ("a model of what the historian's work should be") on Lincoln, but he admits that he has "freely telescoped [the events of history], and imposed invention upon its movement, in such ways as I needed to shape the dramatic significance of my subject." As a matter of fact, "the fictitious Burnet Hook is admitted to the historical company of Lincoln's Cabinet for the purpose of embodying certain forces that were antagonistic to the President." The rationale for his alteration in history is, Drinkwater reiterates, that his purpose is "that of a dramatist, not that of the political philosopher." Thus his "concern is with the profoundly dramatic interest of [Lincoln's] character, and . . . inspiring example."

In the introductory note to the published version, Arnold Bennett attributes the success of the play to William J. Rea, the Irish actor who portrayed Lincoln, along with the playwright's "deep, practical knowledge of the stage [and] because he [Drinkwater] disdained all stage tricks . . . had the

wit to select for his hero one of the world's greatest and finest characters . . . had the audacity to select a gigantic theme and to handle it with simplicity [and] . . . had the courage of all of his artistic and moral convictions." The result, according to Gerald H. Strauss, was that historical plays and poetic dramas gained a larger audience than they otherwise would have had, thus encouraging other dramatists to write in these genres. Allardyce Nicoll placed *Abraham Lincoln* "at the head of a lengthy line of historical-biographical plays, the number and success of which were so characteristic a feature of the theatre in the [nineteen-]twenties."

The timing of the presentation of *Abraham Lincoln* following World War I was fortunate in light of a newfound British interest in American history. When the play was mounted in New York, American audiences appreciated the patriotic theme and found parallels between Lincoln and President Woodrow Wilson. Drinkwater, on his first trip to the United States, took the part of one of the chroniclers in the production. For a modern audience the play might seem more a melodrama than a tragedy, as does Drinkwater's first dramatic effort. Still, *Abraham Lincoln* brought fame to Drinkwater, who was awarded an honorary M.A. by the University of Birmingham in 1919, and he made several lecture tours throughout the United States. Coincidentally, it was on the voyage home from his second visit to the United States in 1921 that Drinkwater met Daisy Kennedy and initiated the affair which led to the breakup both of his first marriage and Kennedy's marriage to Benno Moiseiwitsh, a Russian pianist.

Drinkwater had a long-standing interest in Cromwell, and the historical figure first appears in the writer's canon as the subject of an epic poem included in *Cromwell and Other Poems* (1913). The drama *Oliver Cromwell* premiered at the Theatre Royal in Brighton on 19 February 1921 (a published version of the drama appeared the same year).

Oliver Cromwell was similar to *Abraham Lincoln,* though considerably less popular. The play begins in 1639 and ends in 1654. Following the pattern established in *Abraham Lincoln,* Drinkwater traces the development of Cromwell's character from an incipient rebel to the position of lord protector. While critics note that the "terse dialogue, realistic domestic scenes, and political confrontations" are effective, the contemporary relevance that had contributed to the success of the earlier drama was lacking, and *Oliver Cromwell* ran for only seventy-one performances after it was transferred to His Majesty's Theatre in London on 29 May 1923.

Drinkwater and Daisy Kennedy, whom he married in 1924

As was his practice, Drinkwater wrote both prose and dramatic versions of his study. In a prefatory note Drinkwater opens his 252-page prose volume, *Cromwell: A Character Study* (1927), with the redundant statement, considering his title, that "This is, specifically, a character study, not a history." Given this, Drinkwater's reliance on and reference to previous biographers of Cromwell is confirmatory. Except in his "Note," Drinkwater does not often cite sources. He does indicate a debt to Cromwell's letters and speeches, "as edited in Carlyle," along with Lord Nugent's *Memorials of John Hampden* (1832); George Trevelyan; the fourth volume of the Cambridge Modern History (1926); Edward Hyde, Earl of Clarendon; Francois Guizot; Gilbert Burnet; John Evelyn; and Samuel Pepys, as well as the "indifferent historians" James Heath and Mark Noble, and those of the "reformed model," such as Charles A. Firth and Samuel Rawson Gardiner. In the text, though they are seldom quoted, Thomas Carlyle and one or two others are mentioned in passing, or in refutation — the latter especially in connection with Heath's *Flagellum: or The Life and Death, Birth and Burial of Oliver Cromwell the*

Late Usurper (1663), although neither the arguments of the "censor" Heath nor Drinkwater's own rebuttals are developed fully. Firth's *Oliver Cromwell and the Rule of the Puritans in England* (1900) is generally considered the "best and the fairest" of Cromwell's biographies. Guizot's volume, *Oliver Cromwell and the English Republic* (1854), was written from the point of view of a distinguished French statesman. Among the more modern critics who wrote about Cromwell and whose works would have been available to Drinkwater but whom he does not cite were two other statesmen of stature: the American Theodore Roosevelt and the Englishman John Morley, both of whose volumes were titled *Oliver Cromwell* and were published in 1900. Drinkwater does not recognize that critical opinion of Cromwell's character changed over the years. In the seventeenth century studies reflected their authors' contempt; in the eighteenth century Cromwell was dismissed as hypocritical; in the nineteenth century Carlyle and others saw him as a constitutional reformer.

Despite his attestation to the contrary, and in spite of his attempts to persuade the reader that he is merely drawing a portrait of Cromwell, Drinkwater has indeed written a history of the period, ultimately, perhaps, even more than he has portrayed his subject. This is in part necessary, as he explains the background of abuses in politics (King Charles I, the duke of Buckingham) and religion (Archbishop Laud) that must be known in order to place Cromwell in a context so that the reader can understand and appreciate the man's nature. Structurally, the civil war comes at the midpoint of the volume, with events leading up to that action comprising the first half of the book and those that follow making up the last third.

As with his other prose biographies, the author's own personal biases would be clear throughout this volume even if he had not inserted his caveat in the opening note. This study is not, then, a model for modern biography. Drinkwater's sympathetic attitude toward his subject is plainly stated and otherwise evident, and the work abounds with general, opinionated statements that are left undocumented. In addition, there are minor factual discrepancies (Cromwell's mother's age at her death). Still, the rambling, conversational tone of the biography along with the writer's observations on Cromwell and his time, together with the fact that the lord protector and his period are intrinsically interesting, result in a book that is easy to read and extremely engaging.

Mary Stuart (1921), Drinkwater's third history play, opened at the Ritz Theatre in New York on 21 March 1921; it ran for forty performances. On 25 September 1922 it moved to the Everyman Theatre in London. The title character in this drama embodies a strength that may reflect Drinkwater's sympathy with the women's movement, although contemporary critics saw the character as being egotistic. Again Drinkwater followed the pattern of publishing a prose version of the study in London and New York in the same year that the play was produced.

The play begins with an introduction set in twentieth-century Edinburgh. An old Scotsman named Boyd attempts to help a young man who is complaining about the fact that his wife seems to love another as well as himself. Boyd uses a portrait of Mary to suggest a metaphoric parallel between the young man's troubles and the life of Mary, Queen of Scots. At this point there is a shift to sixteenth-century Edinburgh, and the play details the queen's relationship with her lovers Darnley, Riccio, and Bothwell. Although less episodic than Drinkwater's earlier history plays and more sophisticated in form and content, *Mary Stuart* once again reveals the author's didactic bent, and the London production ran for only seventy performances.

On 20 June 1923 *Robert E. Lee* opened at the Regent Theatre in London. It ran for 109 performances. Critics claimed that because Lee lacks the historic stature of Lincoln and Cromwell, the "episodic structure and moralizing, common to all three plays, become cumbersome" as Drinkwater presents a series of nine scenes depicting General Lee in political, military, and private moments between 1861 and 1865.

Robert Burns (1925) is a musical drama about the eighteenth-century Scottish poet. The play is filled with Burns's poetry, set to music by Frederick Austin, and throughout the drama the characters sing these poem-songs with great gusto. The play presents only the roughest sketch of Burns's life, beginning approximately in 1784 when the writer is twenty-four or twenty-five years old. When the play ends with Burns's death at the age of thirty-seven in 1796, no great feeling of loss at the passing of a still-young, talented man is engendered.

While Drinkwater touches on the young poet's difficulties with the father of his wife-to-be, James Armour, a glimpse is given of Burns's religious and political beliefs only by inference, and there is but a bare hint at his influence on Sir Walter Scott. The drama lacks breadth and depth. It is limited in details about Burns's background, his companions, and the poet himself, though there is some feeling for the man. Burns, according to the picture that Drinkwater offers, was self-deprecating, a man who loved deeply, and a man who liked drink and the camaraderie of the pub; he was a financial dunce, yet his poetic output garnered the greatest respect from his literary contemporaries, especially those from London.

Composed of six scenes, the drama is typical of late-nineteenth- and early-twentieth-century theater. It is simple and straightforward, and there is nothing special in either the language or the theme. Actually, Burns's poetry comprises a major portion of the dialogue, and there are virtually no images, few similes or metaphors, and nothing of symbolic value original to Drinkwater in the entire piece. The ending is predictably maudlin. Thus even though the dramatist's attempt to tell Burns's life story by using his subject's own words is admirable and potentially intriguing, there is nothing in the play that recommends it to a modern reader. We see only the surfaces of Burns's life. Although it was never performed, the play was published in 1925.

After *Robert Burns*, Drinkwater produced little of note in any of the genres in which he wrote. He enjoyed modest success with the play *Bird in Hand*

(1927), which he directed in its first production at the Birmingham Repertory Theatre. Among the acting company were Dame Peggy Ashcroft and Sir Laurence Olivier in the roles of the young lovers. In the main, however, Drinkwater's later plays were lambasted for being verbose, boring, and lacking in significance. His best poetry was behind him, and the only important writing that he did in the last decade of his life consisted of *Inheritance* (1931) and *Discovery* (1932). Entertaining social narrative, these two autobiographical volumes contain an account of English coaching and farming imbued with a sense of history, and they chronicle the development of the Pilgrim Players.

In many ways *Shakespeare* is representative of Drinkwater's biographies. Published in 1933 as the first in a series of at least twenty-seven volumes in the Macmillan Great Lives series, the book is only half as long as *Oliver Cromwell* — perhaps because not much is known about Shakespeare and his life. From the beginning Drinkwater makes his stance clear: "This brief study of Shakespeare makes no profession of scholarship. . . . It is not even informed by any exhaustive knowledge of all that such scholarship has achieved." He recognizes that he "can admire such exploits with gratitude, but . . . cannot emulate them." With such limitations it is no wonder that he also admits that he is "but an indifferent seeker after truth." He further admits that there is much in Shakespeare's work that he does not understand and many questions about the dramatist's life that he cannot answer. Furthermore, he does not think that questions about the exact order of the plays, for instance, will ever be answered or that knowledge of the poet's life can be expanded in "any fundamental respect."

Why, then, would Drinkwater undertake to write a biography of the world's greatest dramatist? He had shown an interest in the seventeenth century — Shakespeare, Cromwell, Charles I — and he indicates that "If we amplify [what is already known about his subject's genius and 'its spiritual occasion'] with some knowledge of the political and social conditions that he knew, we can further visualize the environment of his genius without much difficulty." Drinkwater continues:

> This book, then, makes no contribution to Shakespearean scholarship, nor will it be much concerned with the problems to which that scholarship is directed. It is written for those people who, liking Shakespeare, may derive some satisfaction from hearing one who shares their liking discuss his reasons for it. I have made but little preparation for the occasion. Of the vast literature known as Shakespeareana I can claim no intensive

knowledge, and I have now no inclination to repair the defect. I have from time to time read a few of the more important works on the subject, and consulted others as necessity arose; but I should be ploughed in any recondite test.

What qualifies him to write this text, he claims, is his thirty-year habit of reading English poetry, including Shakespeare (though he admits his reading has not been structured), and the fact that he has staged and acted in perhaps a dozen of the author's plays at Jackson's Repertory Theatre in Birmingham.

Shakespeare includes eight chapters: "Prologue"; "Who was Shakespeare?"; "Shakespeare"; "Reputation"; "Shakespeare's Stage"; "His Mind"; and "Epilogue." Early on Drinkwater dismisses the question of the true identity of the author of the plays. He is satisfied that it is indeed Shakespeare. He then proceeds to expound on his two main themes, that the playwright was a genius who "swept up and embodied the extraordinary vigor of Elizabethan England" and that the dramatist "was the poet for whom an age already accustomed to heroic action and heroic verse had been waiting." Shakespeare was, Drinkwater contends, a man who "had a job to do in the theatre, and he did it." The reason that he did it so well is that he drew upon the spirit and thought and idiom of his age with an "unfailing veracity" in his plays.

One of the sections of the biography most full of insight, obviously growing out of Drinkwater's own theatrical experiences, relates to Shakespeare's stage. The biographer notes that it "necessitated the closest possible intimacy of contact between the players and the audience," it "encouraged a multiplicity of scenes," and it "facilitated a swift continuity of stage action." At the same time, in evaluating Shakespeare's art, Drinkwater concludes that "His purpose was to tell tales that any lackey could understand, in terms of poetry that would storm Olympus," and it was in his poetry that his "essential greatness lies." Unfortunately, Drinkwater provides little analysis of the poet's writing to prove his argument.

Drinkwater admits that Shakespeare had faults, and he examines the characters of Lear and Shylock to demonstrate. He also wonders what happened to the dramatist after he retired and returned to Stratford in 1611. Perhaps Shakespeare continued to write and the works have not yet been discovered, the biographer posits — a thesis based purely on his own intuition.

The study concludes with a reaffirmation that Shakespeare was a "practical playwright, intent, and

Drinkwater at his home, 9 The Grove, Highgate Village, September 1933

very successfully intent, on providing entertainment for an audience in the theatre," thereby providing for "millions of his countrymen in the course of time [to] have delightedly watched the pageant of his plays, to be influenced and enlightened quite above their reckoning." "An intimacy with this poet's theatre is in itself a liberal enfranchisement of the mind," Drinkwater determines.

Drinkwater died at his London home on 25 March 1937. Drinkwater also wrote children's verse, critical studies of William Morris and Algernon Charles Swinburne, numerous essays, and a novel. He edited literary anthologies and wrote introductions to many books, as well, and he contributed to the emerging popular art form of the twentieth century by penning lyrics for the film musical *Blossom Time* (1934) and the screenplays for five films which were released between 1932 and 1937.

Drinkwater's lack of formal education, and the consequent absence of training in critical scholarship, marks his biographical writing in two ways:

it may be responsible for the easy, familiar style which made his work popular during his lifetime, and it was responsible for the fact that his biographies are not considered major works in the field. As demonstrated in his autobiographical volumes, Drinkwater had a fondness and an appreciation for history — this is seen even in his characterization of Thomas Greenleaf in *Bird in Hand*. That he was more romantic than scholarly in his approach to writing biographies is illustrated by his living in Pepys's house in Brampton near Huntington while he wrote his prose study *Pepys, His Life and Character* (1930).

Drinkwater's two major faults as a biographer are his didacticism and his inability to be completely objective. These two traits certainly grow out of his attitude toward the past, together with his attitude about writing biographies. For Drinkwater a sense of the past gave meaning to the present. In *Inheritance* he says, "It is an emotion that has little if anything to do with pride of family. It arises from a remote, almost imperceptible sense that this frame of ours, with its faculties, intimations, desires, fortitudes, perplexities, is in some sure though incalculable way stabilized by the undefeated courage of many generations." History, says Drinkwater in speaking of historical people and facts, "may be eloquent in a thumbprint on the margin of a nursery rhyme.... Although but the ghost of a ghost, articulated in the echo of an echo, each of these figures has become familiar to me." The connection between Drinkwater's interest in his own family history and the lives of great personages is embodied in these lines from *Abraham Lincoln*:

> When the high heart we magnify,
> And the sure vision celebrate,
> And worship greatness passing by,
> Ourselves are great.

In essence John Drinkwater's performance as a biographer can be summed up by seeing how well his assessment of his subject in *Shakespeare* applies to himself: "His delight, his passion, was to understand the world, not to pass judgment on it." As a biographer Drinkwater studiously intended not to be particularly inquisitive beyond the superficial, or to be scholarly, or to uncover new information about his subject; what he sought was to be a popularizer.

Bibliographies:

Michael Pearce, *John Drinkwater: A Comprehensive Bibliography of His Works* (New York: Garland, 1977);

Peter Berven, "John Drinkwater: An Annotated Bibliography of Writings About Him," *English Literature in Transition 1880–1920*, 21 (1978): 9–66.

References:

Lascelles Abercrombie, "The Drama of John Drinkwater," *Four Decades of Poetry 1890–1930*, 1 (1977): 271–281;

Cyril Clemens, "John Drinkwater: The Poet of Highgate," *Sewanee Review*, 40 (October–December 1932): 422–445;

John W. Cunliffe, *Modern English Playwrights: A Short History of the English Drama from 1825* (New York & London: Harper, 1927), pp. 187–196;

H. H. Anniah Gowda, *The Revival of English Poetic Drama* (Bombay: Orient Longman, 1972), pp. 180–219;

"Historic Figures on the Stage," *Theatre Magazine*, 33 (June 1921): 394, 448;

Mark Twain Quarterly: Drinkwater Memorial Number, 1 (Summer 1937): 1–5, 8, 15, 24;

Godfrey William Mathews, *The Poetry of John Drinkwater* (Liverpool: Bryant, 1925);

A. E. Morgan, *Tendencies of Modern English Drama* (London: Constable, 1924; New York: Scribners, 1924), pp. 257, 277–290, 301;

William Rothenstein, *Men and Memories, 1922–1938*, volume 3 (London: Faber & Faber, 1939), pp. 1, 2, 240, 268, 269;

Laura Sherry, "Drinkwater as Poet and Playwright," *Poetry Review*, 19 (November 1921): 94–99;

Graham Sutton, *Some Contemporary Dramatists* (London: Parsons, 1924; New York: Doran, 1925), pp. 53–72;

Priscilla Thouless, *Modern Poetic Drama* (Oxford: Blackwell, 1934; Freeport, N.Y.: Books for Libraries Press, 1968), pp. 52–65;

Fredrick T. Wood, "On the Poetry of John Drinkwater," *Poetry Review*, 24 (January–February 1933): 27–51.

Papers:

The Beinecke Rare Books and Manuscript Library at Yale University has a collection of approximately thirteen hundred letters written to Drinkwater, mostly between 1910 and 1930; the library at Marquette University has a collection of Drinkwater correspondence; the Brotherton Library, the University of Leeds, has a collection of Drinkwater's books, pamphlets, and press notices.

Charles Harold Herford
(18 February 1853 – 25 April 1931)

William Over
Saint John's University

BOOKS: *Essential Characteristics of the Romantic and Classical Styles: With Illustrations From English Literature* (Cambridge: Deighton, Bell, 1880);

The First Quarto Edition of Hamlet; Two Essays to Which the Harness Prize Was Awarded, 1880 (London: Smith, Elder, 1880);

A Sketch of the History of the English Drama, In Its Social Aspects; Being the Essay Which Obtained the LeBas Prize, 1880 (Cambridge: Johnson, 1881);

Studies in the Literary Relations of England and Germany in the Sixteenth Century (Cambridge: Cambridge University Press, 1886);

The Age of Wordsworth (London: Bell, 1897);

Robert Browning (Edinburgh: Blackwood, 1905);

The Bearing of English Studies Upon the National Life (Oxford: Hart, 1910);

Shakespeare (London: T. C. & E. C. Jack, 1912);

Goethe (London: T. C. & E. C. Jack, 1913);

The Normality of Shakespeare Illustrated in His Treatment of Love and Marriage (Oxford: Oxford University Press, 1920);

Shakespeare's Treatment of Love and Marriage, and Other Essays (London: Unwin, 1921);

A Sketch of Recent Shakespearean Investigation, 1893–1923 (London: Blackie, 1923);

Dante and Milton (Manchester: Manchester University Press, 1924);

A Russian Shakespearean, A Centenery Study (Manchester: Manchester University Press, 1925);

English Literature (London: Benn, 1927);

The Post-War Mind of Germany and Other European Studies (Oxford: Clarendon Press, 1927);

Wordsworth (London: Routledge, 1930);

Philip Henry Wicksteed, His Life and Work (London: Dent, 1931).

OTHER: Henrik Ibsen, *Love's Comedy*, translated, with introduction and notes, by Herford (Chicago: Sergel, 1900);

The Works of Shakespeare, 10 volumes, edited, with introduction and notes, by Herford (London: Macmillan, 1901–1914);

Ibsen, *Brand: A Dramatic Poem in Five Acts*, translated, with an introduction and notes, by Herford (London: Heinemann, 1904);

The Aldus Shakespeare, 40 volumes, edited, with notes and comments, by Herford and others (New York: Bigelow, Smith, 1909);

"Shelley," in *The Cambridge History of English Literature* (Cambridge: Cambridge University Press, 1916), XII: 63–86;

"Keats," in *The Cambridge History of English Literature* (Cambridge: Cambridge University Press, 1916), XII: 87–103;

The Man and His Work, Ben Jonson, 11 volumes, edited by Herford and Percy Simpson (Oxford: Clarendon Press, 1925–1952);

Hans Fingeller, *The Case of German South Tyrol Against Italy*, translated and edited, with preface and introduction, by Herford (London: Allen & Unwin, 1927);

Joseph Estlin Carpenter; A Memorial Volume, edited, with a memoir, by Herford (Oxford: Clarendon Press, 1929).

SELECTED PERIODICAL PUBLICATIONS – UNCOLLECTED: "A Few Suggestions on Greene's Romances and Shakespeare," *New Shakespeare Society*, 12 (1888), II: 181–190;

"Goethe's Italian Journey," *Studies in European Literature* (1900): 273–312;

"National and International Ideals in the English Poets," *John Rylands Library Bulletin*, 3 (1916): 382–403;

"Norse Myth in English Poetry," *John Rylands Library Bulletin*, 5 (1918): 75–101;

"Is There a Poetic View of the World?," *Proceedings of the British Academy*, 7 (1919): 423–454;

"Romanticism in the Modern World," *Essays and Studies by Members of the English Association*, 8 (1922): 109–134;

"Lessing," *John Rylands Library Bulletin*, 7 (1922–1923): 211–232;

"William Blake," *John Rylands Library Bulletin*, 12 (1928): 31–46.

For thirty years C. H. Herford worked diligently and broadly in Continental as well as English literature, earning a reputation for his discernment and breadth of knowledge. His longtime collaborator on *The Man and His Work, Ben Jonson* (1925–1952), Percy Simpson, observed that Herford's "critical range was marvellous: he knew all the literature of Europe. He was a scholar to the finger-tips. . . . To accuracy and knowledge he added fine and farsighted appreciation and the 'wide and luminous view.' " Herford's major biographical achievements were *The Age of Wordsworth* (1897); the life and critical introductions contained in the first two volumes of the Oxford *Ben Jonson;* two short biographies, *Robert Browning* (1905) and *Wordsworth* (1930); and entries for John Keats and Percy Bysshe Shelley in *The Cambridge History of English Literature* (1916). His early commitment to literary history motivated his first major work, *Studies in the Literary Relations of England and Germany in the Sixteenth Century* (1886). Although his early historical research involved the Shakespearean influence on Continental and Russian literature, Herford's interest in literary biography remained central to his scholarly trajectories, evident in shorter pieces such as "Goethe's Italian Journey" (1900), the Taylorian lecture at Oxford. Herford helped found the Goethe Society (1885–1886), and he often focused on a comprehensive view of what Johann Wolfgang von Goethe termed *Weltliteratur,* while at the same time attending to the social and political dimensions of literary movements. His friend Lascelles Abercrombie has commented on Herford's particularly broad understanding: "The wonder comes to be . . . that any European literature should be absent from the list of his familiar studies."

Although Herford's essays and lectures were for him a more congenial medium than books, as a lecturer "he had not the advantage of an easy delivery," according to his colleague J. G. Robertson, "a certain shyness of manner prevented . . . the impression of intimate personal conviction." Nevertheless, Herford was highly regarded as a teacher and mentor for young scholars, remaining active after retirement, and his efforts as a literary reviewer for the *Manchester Guardian* and as general contributor to *Nation, Contemporary Review, Neue Freie Presse,* and other publications often produced constructive criticism for young writers. His most ambitious scholarly achievement, a collection of the works of Jonson, had only two volumes published at the time of

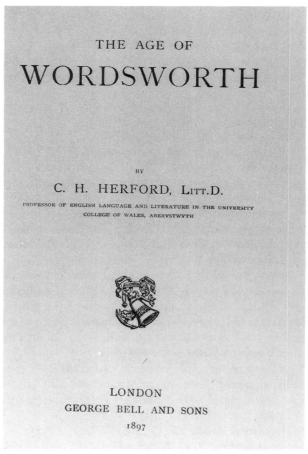

THE AGE OF
WORDSWORTH

BY

C. H. HERFORD, Litt.D.

PROFESSOR OF ENGLISH LANGUAGE AND LITERATURE IN THE UNIVERSITY
COLLEGE OF WALES, ABERYSTWYTH

LONDON
GEORGE BELL AND SONS
1897

Title page for Herford's study of Romanticism in Great Britain and Europe, the book that established Herford's reputation as a critic

his death, but these tomes comprised the most important research of the eleven-volume effort and became his consummate work in the field of Elizabethan and Jacobean literature. Simpson, as the *Ben Jonson* coeditor, observed that Herford's goal in this long labor was "to understand Jonson's aims; then, and only then, to sum up Jonson's achievement and to depict the man as he lived and moved in contemporary London." In this way Herford as biographer attempted an interior understanding of Jonson. Herford believed that much of his subject's inner life could be gleaned from a careful study of his literary efforts. Hence the working method used for both his Wordsworth biography and the life in *Ben Jonson* included the assumption that "each individual work of [the author] should come to mean more to us when we can see it in its place in the order of his lifework." Furthermore, Herford assumed throughout his career that literature included a significant social import. Abercrombie has commented, "it did not seem to him worthwhile to discuss literature except for the purpose . . . of estimating its value."

Charles Harold Herford was born on 18 February 1853 in Manchester, the eldest son of Charles James Herford, a prominent wine merchant, and Mary Jane Robberds, the daughter of a Unitarian minister. He was sent to a private boarding school, Castle Howell School, in Lancaster, in 1861. Learning German at the age of eight, Herford later commented on this early enthusiasm: "In me . . . a germ struck root which held latent within it much of whatever harvest of achievement and happiness it was to be mine to reap." Because of financial shortcomings, Herford could not attend Oxford, opting instead for Owens College (1867–1869), where he came under the influence of James Drummond, a leading Unitarian minister. Herford's talent for drawing led him to accept a position with a prominent Manchester architect, but he soon resigned due to lack of interest. Continuing his study of German, he took night courses at Owens College, where his first published work, an essay on Gotthold Lessing, appeared in the college magazine. He also translated Friedrich Schiller's *Wilhelm Tell* (1804) and Goethe's *Faust* (1808).

Finally securing small grants from relatives, Herford entered Trinity College, Cambridge, in 1875. He early revealed his characteristic critical style – concise, penetrating – when he won four prizes for scholarly essays: "Essential Characteristics of the Romantic and Classical Styles" (Members' Prize Essay, 1880); "The First Quarto Edition of Hamlet" (Harness Prize Essay, London, 1880); "A Sketch of the History of the English Drama, In Its Social Aspects" (LeBas Prize Essay, Cambridge, 1881); and "The Influence of the Teaching of Stoicism on the Civilization of the Early Roman Empire" (Hare Prize Essay, Cambridge, 1882). In 1880 Herford entered the literary world of Bloomsbury, London, where he met several leading English positivists and scholars. With the Berkeley Fellowship from Owens College he attended the University of Berlin in 1882, where he produced *Studies in the Literary Relations of England and Germany in the Sixteenth Century*.

Although Herford met his wife, Marie Betge, daughter of the chief postmaster of Bremen, Germany, before entering Cambridge, they were not married until 1888, after Herford obtained the security of a professorship in English language and literature at University College of Wales, Aberystwyth. They had one daughter and a son, who was killed in World War I. His wife died in 1930. His career at Aberystwyth enlarged his reputation as a teacher and literary critic. His American reputation grew as well when Johns Hopkins University offered him the position of Percy Turnbull Lecturer in 1900. The following year he was made first holder of the independent chair of English literature at his former college, now Victoria University of Manchester, where he retired in 1921. He served as honorary professor until 1927. He subsequently settled at Headington, Oxford, with his daughter. He died on 25 April 1931.

The Age of Wordsworth established Herford's reputation as a literary critic of broad concerns. Its comprehensive analysis primarily involved what Herford described as the "organizing conception" of Romanticism both in England and on the Continent. J. G. Robertson comments on its "undiminished freshness and vigour, its clear insight into men and movements, and its catholic fairness of criticism and appreciation." Herford's wide knowledge of Continental literature contributed to the work's insightful overview of early nineteenth century social and political movements. The distinction drawn between literary history and biography in the preface expresses the author's concern with the relationship between the text and the writer. It also reveals his interest in the microhistory of an individual's life within the wider context of historical progression:

> To the literary historian, as such, the facts of a man's life are of primary concern only in so far as they serve to explain his work. Hence many events which loom large in the general conception of, say, Coleridge or Shelley, and properly occupy much space in the admirable critical biographies which abound for this period, are here on principle ignored. On the other hand, I have everywhere striven to bring out the literary bearing of whatever biographical detail I admitted at all.

In the early chapters of *The Age of Wordsworth*, Herford gives a succinct evaluation of the works of several influential literary scholars offered as representatives of the age of Romanticism. The ability to situate a personality within his historical context is evident in Herford's brief entry for Henry Hallam, an historian and antiquarian with political interests:

> Hallam's critical instinct in literature, though wide and various, had rigid limits in the direction of passion and romance, and without these no man may describe the poetry of the sixteenth century. Hallam represents . . . the English intellect of the epoch in which the eighteenth century was passing into the nineteenth, when the age of "commonsense" was discredited but not extinct, and Romanticism was in the air, but not in the blood.

For the major poets of the era, Herford devotes much longer entries. His analyses of the important figures use skillful comparisons among them to explore each author's contribution to literary thought and sensibility. Thus, Charles Lamb's literary personality is described by a penetrating analysis, contrasting it with the mystical orientation of Samuel Taylor Coleridge. Herford comments, "The sensible world in which [Lamb] lived and loved, and the imaginative world in which his mind was steeped, were two incommensurable regions which he had no metaphysics to bring into accord." Herford's comparisons of Coleridge with Wordsworth, and of Shelley with Wordsworth show similar discernment.

Originally planned in 1905 as a "handbook" for an educated but broad readership, *Robert Browning* became a medium-length biography. Herford intended to include for the most part only salient material from his subject's most important productive period, 1846–1869. Thus, in the preface he acknowledges that Browning's central poetic phase is treated in an "inordinately generous scale." Throughout the biography, however, Herford gives considerable attention to understanding the demands and sensibilities of Browning's reading public. The general failure of Browning's *Sordello* with his reading audience in 1840, coming soon after the great publishing success of *Paracelsus* (1835), Herford describes with characteristic insight, wit, and economy:

> It was the day of the gentle literary public which had a few years before recoiled from *Sartor Resartus,* and which found in the difficulty of a book the strongest presumption against it. A later generation, leavened by Carlyle, came near to regarding difficulty as a resumption in its favour, and this more strenuous and athletic attitude towards literature was among the favouring conditions which brought Browning at length into vogue.

For Herford, Browning was uniquely positioned as the only major English poet who was, by "temperament and genius," a Romantic realist, allied with his contemporary prose writers Charles Dickens, Thomas Carlyle, and Honoré de Balzac.

Elizabeth Barrett Browning's enjoyment of the masculine humor in her husband's dramatic pieces is documented by Herford, who credits her with a disposition for a form of humor which, he observed, contradicts her "fragile" reputation. The couple's blissful years together in Italy and during the revolution of 1848 are examined through Browning's fitful allusions and sardonic humor. Although taken at the time by the revolution in Italy, Browning,

and his "poetic mission," did not sing its sorrows, for, according to Herford, "Nationality was not an effectual motive for him."

Browning's poetic approach to nature through love is brilliantly contrasted to Wordsworth's interests in nature:

> [Browning's] larger command of soul-life embraces just those moods of spiritual passion which beget the irradiated and transfigured Nature for which, since Wordsworth, poetry has continually striven to find expression. Browning's subtler feeling for Nature sprang from his profounder insight into love. Love was his way of approach, as it was eminently not Wordsworth's, to the transfigured Nature which Wordsworth first disclosed.

Furthermore, Herford observes a unique quality of "eerie playfulness" in Browning's approach to Nature: "the uncanny playfulness of a wild creature of boundless might only half intelligible to man, which man contemplates with mingled joy, wonder, and fear."

The "culminating achievement" of Browning's lifework, according to Herford, was in many respects *The Ring and the Book* (1868–1869), which represented a brighter vision beyond Browning's period of "desolate widowhood." Its story produces a "subtle hallowing association" with the most spiritual aspects of his earlier poetry. Herford's analysis of the reading audience for this work clearly illustrates his characteristic method of comparison and contrast to achieve subtle description. Remarking on the fact that the audiences who welcomed Algernon Charles Swinburne's poetry and Browning's *The Ring and the Book* were essentially the same, Herford contrasts the popularity of both poets with that of Tennyson: "the fame of both marked a wave of reaction from the austere simplicity and attenuated sentiment of the later *Idylls of the King.*" Mid-Victorian readers "turned with relish to Browning's Italian murder-story, with its sensational crime, its mysterious elopement, its problem interest, its engaging actuality."

Herford's critical ability is perhaps best demonstrated through his general analysis of Browning's poetic achievement in the chapter "Joy in Form." Exploring his observation that Browning's "isolating self-consciousness" engaged his creative imagination, he concludes that the poet's persistent use of the dramatic monologue device and the prevailing sense of loneliness within his poetry reflected deep strains in his character.

In chapter 10, "The Interpreter of Life," Herford situates his subject in the philosophic thought of his time, which Herford perceives as a tensive holdout between scientific materialism on the one side and a revitalized Romantic spirituality on the other. The former disposition encompasses a mechanistic interpretation of human action, represented by the continued tradition of the British school—David Hume, Jeremy Bentham, Edmund Burke, and Coleridge—while the latter attitude was influenced by German thinking, chiefly Georg Wilhelm Friedrich Hegel and Johann Gottlieb Fichte in philosophy and Goethe in literature. As Herford keenly observes, Browning was very much in conflict between these two distant intellectual poles. Desiring absoluteness in life, he upheld the "infinity" of both God and the human soul, while banishing all the "finiteness" of the sensate world to the limbo of mere illusion. However, as a poet and lover, Browning was inclined elsewhere: "His most intense consciousness, his most definite grip upon reality, was too closely bound up with the collisions and jostlings, the limits and angularities, of the world of the senses." Here again, Herford draws a brilliant contrast with Wordsworth. While the latter turned to childhood for the "intimations of immortality" that so preoccupied him, Browning discovered such intimations in the slings and arrows of everyday human existence. Herford responds pithily, "Body and time had too strong a grip upon him to be resolved into illusion."

Noting that the struggle between the infinite and finite in life preoccupied Browning, Herford comments, "His was one of the rare natures in which revolutionary liberalism and spiritual reaction, encountered in nearly equal strength, seem to have divided their principles and united their forces." However, Herford is reminded of the social and political dimensions of the struggle: "Sociologically, the one stood for individualism" – revolutionary liberalism, positivism, the finite – "the other for solidarity" – idealism, the infinite, the divine. "In their political ideals, the one strove for progress and for freedom . . . the other for order, and for active legal intervention as its safeguard." Thus, Herford remained wholly aware that the thought and productivity of the most individual of geniuses had economic and social dimensions.

The short entries on Keats and Shelley for *The Cambridge History of English Literature* are impressive in both their conciseness and elucidation. Herford draws heavily upon Keats's famous letters for certain biographical details and to interpret the inner life of his subject. The assessment of Keats is indicative of Herford's balanced approach, which first lays out a critique of Keats's mind and poetry, then follows it with an acknowledgment of the limitless

potential of the young poet. Herford's critical style remained masterful:

> *Endymion* . . . has the invertebrate structure, the insecure style, the weakness in narrative and the luxuriance of colour and music, natural to one who still lived more in sensation than in thought; but, also, the enchanted atmosphere and scenery, and the sudden reaches of vision, possible only to one whose senses were irradiated by imagination, and "half created," "half perceived."

Especially illuminating is Herford's analysis of the influence of Wordsworth and Milton upon *Hyperion* (1820), which he considers Keats's greatest poem. Also illuminating in the Keats entry is the rhetorical technique of presenting dualities, then reversing them to comprehend both in a single literary notion, which appeared in the Keats entry: "[Keats's] whole imaginative and emotional life was permeated by his eager and acute sensations; while his senses – it is but the other side of the same fact – were transfigured by imagination and emotion."

Comparing Shelley, in that poet's entry, to Wordsworth and Coleridge, Herford finds the former more intellectual, his sense of beauty more metaphysical and wide-ranging. Emphasizing Shelley's ideological mentors, Herford considers the social critic William Godwin and the philosophers Plato, Baruch Spinoza, and George Berkeley most formative. The famous Oxford expulsion Herford abruptly dismisses with the comment that the incident "need not be recalled here." Herford interprets Cythna in *The Cenci* (1819) as a modern woman seeking intellectual liberation for her sex, as Shelley's wife, daughter of Mary Wollstonecraft, had done.

Herford felt *Prometheus Unbound* (1820) was heavily influenced by Godwin, but not positively. The exuberant optimism of the young Shelley raced beyond his adopted ideology. Nevertheless, the piece succeeded in spite of Godwin's uncompromising materialistic interpretation of history:

> Shelley's ardour, fortified and misled by the cold extravagances of Godwin, hurried him over the slow course of social evolution. . . . But the ideal of love and endurance . . . stands on a different plane; it is rooted in existing human nature, and expresses a state towards which all genuine human progress must advance.

Herford's summation of Shelley's character depends once more upon a comparison, this time with Wordsworth's disposition. The institutions and traditions of his age left Shelley unmoved; he could not find his "home" in these realms, as could

Wordsworth. "For Shelley, society was rather the ground from which (like his *Skylark*) he soared to a heaven far remote."

The short biographical study *Wordsworth* depends partially upon *Wordsworth's Life, Work and Influence* (1916), a comprehensive work by J. M. Harper, and upon the important critical edition of Wordsworth's *The Prelude* (1926), by E. de Selincourt, whose textual research Herford found greatly illuminating. Herford relies heavily at times upon autobiographical commentary from the latter work for both the external events and the inner life of his subject. Thus, Wordsworth's thoughts on his experiences at Cambridge University are taken directly from *The Prelude,* section III. Of the poet's first years at Cambridge, Herford concludes that they were "an early example of Wordsworth's characteristic power of evoking spiritual strength from remembered experience," further observing that Wordsworth would later explain poetry itself as recollected experience.

Herford attempts similar connections between Wordsworth's work and his life when he relies upon *The Prelude,* section VI to describe Wordsworth's feelings of companionship with his sister Dorothy and Mary Hutchinson, his future wife. Wordsworth's notion that human memory spiritualizes the present is applied by the biographer to those moments the three spent together near Penrith Beacon in what was accurately described as the glory of their youth and first love. Herford's comment is penetrating: "Hence the memory of that moment spiritualized the gladness of the lover by fortifying the poet. This, once more, was what Wordsworth meant when he affirmed the power of those 'spots of time' in the past to uplift and rebuild."

Wordsworth's political views, though described as "democratic" in 1792, when he was influenced by his companion Michel Beaupuy, Herford admits cannot be precisely determined, but the biographer relies upon A. V. Dicey's *The Statesmanship of Wordsworth* (1916), wherein the early Wordsworth was regarded as a sort of socialistic reformer. Of Beaupuy, Herford observes that he was not doctrinaire but empathetic, an analysis that leaves much unanswered, although this stage of Wordsworth's political thinking was perhaps ambivalent and immature, hence hard to perceive. Likewise, Wordsworth's important visions of August and September 1793 are faithfully recounted by Herford but left largely without critical comment and analysis, Herford remarking cryptically that they produced much "Guilt and Sorrow."

Herford gives much attention to the influence of Godwin on Wordsworth's poetry; Godwin's radical views of social transformation necessitated by the misery of the poor were first presented to the poet by Beaupuy. In a similar way, the important influence of David Hartley's *Observations on Man* (1749) brought about, the biographer believes, by Coleridge, is given major focus. Wordsworth, according to Herford, "was fascinated by a theory which, linking the man with the child, satisfied not only his mystic reverence for childhood but also his profound demand for continuity; for a link binding all the seasons together 'in natural piety.'" Hence the quintessential Wordsworthian affirmation, "The child is father of the man," was traced to its source and thereby given a wider perspective.

The year 1802 Herford regards as a turning point for Wordsworth. The peace in Europe, followed by the poet's visit to Calais, then the continuation of the war "enlarged the horizon and disturbed the plans of the recluse," although, "The stubborn stuff of Wordsworth's nature yielded its habits gradually, or bit by bit." At the same time, Wordsworth rediscovered John Milton, which Herford judges in relation to the evolving style and orientation of Wordsworth's verse. The poet's trip to Calais, undertaken in August 1802 to feel the magnitude of the threat to England from Napoleon, "lifted into view a more patriotic strain on behalf of freedom over tyranny." A decidedly heroic element pervaded Wordsworth's poetry during this period; however, Herford finds that his subject's heroism found most attractive those historical figures who failed after great struggle — leaders such as Toussaint-Louverture and Andreas Hofer. Secondary sources from C. E. Vaughan and Dicey help refine Herford's judgment of Wordsworth's complex response to the French Revolution, although Herford carefully defines the limitations of each scholar's viewpoint. Herford uses his characteristic method of comparison between authors to further illuminate this important period of creativity; Wordsworth is compared to both Shelley and George Gordon, Lord Byron, as regards the French Revolution, with Wordsworth keeping the sanest attitude, according to Herford.

Herford also carefully develops the backgrounds for Wordsworth's uncharacteristically strong advocacy of the Peninsula Campaign in Spain against Napoleon's forces there and the poet's early support for Guiseppe Mazzini in Italy. But Herford keeps primary focus on his subject's creative production during this period, devoting a whole chapter to his long poem *The Excursion,* composed in 1795 and published in 1814. This was an ambitious project, and Wordsworth invoked both Dante and Milton in his "Prospectus" to the poem. Herford's assessment is balanced and discriminating. Pointing out that Wordsworth himself had been disappointed with the final form of the poem, Herford agrees that it failed not only in substance, but also in style and structure as well. Herford's observation that the poem's value nevertheless remains as a documentation of the transitional phase of a great mind seems strikingly contemporary as scholarship. With conciseness of style, he essentializes this period of his subject's life. Wordsworth's creativity, "if already hardening towards the dogmatisms of old age ... could still interpose splendid bursts of imagination among reaches of dignified eloquence, light up bald argument with felicities of phrase, and expound a social philosophy not yet warped by political and theological prejudice."

Of Wordsworth's recalcitrance in later years; his upholding of strict Anglicanism against the removal of social restrictions for Roman Catholics in England; his defense of capital punishment not as a deterrence to crime, but on moral grounds; and his opposition to the Voting Reform Act are all given a balanced treatment by the biographer, who argues that the poet in fact possessed a more understanding temperament during those years. As evidence he offers the visit of John Stuart Mill to Grasmere in 1831, an event which Mill admitted ultimately modified his own view of utilitarianism. In letters to radical friends Mill gives the highest praise for Wordsworth's comprehensive knowledge and critical faculties. Herford selects an illuminating line from Mill's correspondence: Wordsworth seemed "to know the pros and cons of every question, and when you think he strikes the balance wrong, it is only because you think he estimates wrongly some matter of fact." Furthermore, "He talks on no subject more instructively than on states of society and forms of government."

Although managing to retain a devoted following of friends with radical beliefs, Wordsworth nevertheless remained generally embittered and conservative, a "reactionary Tory." Of this seeming contradiction, Herford remarks, "Wordsworth's talk had the qualities and defects of those whose faith in themselves and their significance is of adamantine security." Herford wisely chooses to offer a full display of opinion about this elusive period of his subject's life rather than to attempt descriptive precision in his own words. Wordsworth's movement towards Chartism late in his life Herford regards as his return to the more open, liberal, even radical sentiments of his youth, when universal education and progress for the poor were among his aims. Perhaps belaboring the point, Herford concludes that the poet's "ruling conceptions of politics ... retained their grandeur.... Where his later mind failed was ... in logical co-ordination with them of the concrete details." On the other hand, Herford seems more certain in his evaluation of the 1839 revision of *The Prelude,* which he finds has more disadvantages than advantages over earlier versions. Disappointed, he finds its tone changed from the youthful openness characteristic of the early Wordsworth to a more circumscribed orthodoxy.

In a final chapter Herford reflects generally on the poet's closing years, which he finds provided Wordsworth with delightful interludes rather than transforming experiences. Herford depends partially on close readings of the poetry, partially on the opinions of the poet's friends and visitors. To assess the claim of Wordsworth as the quintessential "Nature poet," the biographer draws upon his now-familiar method of comparison, this time of his subject with Shelley, Virgil, Lucretius, Thomas Carlyle, and other agrarian and nature writers, who were often of a more scientific bent than Wordsworth. Herford's descriptive assessment proves elucidating, and his final judgment of the "Nature poet" is thoughtfully qualified.

Herford's critical estimate of Ben Jonson is the consummation of his work in the field of Elizabethan literature. The sixty-page introduction to Jonson in the first volume of his edition of the complete works deftly presented the personality of the playwright through a thoughtful analysis of the few biographical facts known but also by an incisive penetration of his literary efforts. Throughout, however, Herford reveals some ambivalence toward Jonson's assertive authorial voice. *Cynthia's Revels* (1600), for example, he found of value only for the student of Jonson's mind and art, commenting, "At no moment of [Jonson's] career did he write with a more profound disdain for any other standard of merit than that supplied by his own intellect." In the introduction Herford remains somewhat uneasy with his subject's keen satiric temperament.

Jonson's numerous interpersonal conflicts are well handled, and the careful observations on the famous conversations between Jonson and William Drummond are aptly compared to the more famous relationship between Samuel Johnson and James Boswell. Moreover, Herford emphasizes the popular trends of the theater audiences and readership during Jonson's most productive period, tracing their possible influences on the writer, who both satirized such trends and followed them. Wisely choosing the masterpiece *Bartholomew Fair* (1614) for illustration, Herford interprets Jonson's character as a writer, not entirely favorably, but certainly formidably. Jonson's correspondence and other autobiographical records proved fertile ground for the biographer, particularly in the clarification of Jonson's complex relations with the aristocracy. Herford shows high regard for his subject's democratic disposition, commenting suggestively, "He writes to his correspondents of every rank with the freedom of an honored friend, familiar but never vulgar, delicately playful, easily well-bred."

Herford's comprehensive understanding of European literature – coupled with a vigorous interest in the interplay of ideas from philosophy, political ideology, and theories of art and literature – was well applied to his biographical efforts, which always set his subjects within a revealing social and intellectual environment. He was particularly involved with the moral and intellectual development of his subjects and how their particular ideas and attitudes modified the more general notions of their times. In the preface to *Shakespeare's Treatment of Love and Marriage, and Other Essays* (1921) Herford asks, "What terms does poetry make with philosophy, or religion, or patriotism, or politics, or love, when one of these is urgent, also, in the mind of the poet?" His lifelong aim became the exploration of what he called "the psychology of poetic experi-ence." His overriding interest, according to Robertson, lay "in the ideas, the men, the peoples behind the books; poetry was but the mirror in which he sought a larger humanity." Similarly, Abercrombie comments, "it did not seem to him worthwhile to discuss literature except for the purpose . . . of estimating its value." Herford's comprehensive approach finally pushed his investigations toward the history of ideas. An observation in his article "Shakespeare and Descartes" (1925) revealed this movement: "how in the age of Wordsworth and Coleridge, Hegel and Fichte, English poetry and German philosophy, though almost unconscious of one another, worked with the same prepossession, the sublime faith in the potency of the human mind."

References:

Lascelles Abercrombie, "Herford and International Literature," *John Rylands Library Bulletin,* 19 (1935): 216–229;

Edmund Garratt Gardner, *Professor Herford as an Italian Scholar* (Oxford: Blackwell, 1932);

J. G. Robertson, "Charles Harold Herford, 1853–1931," in *Proceedings of the British Academy* (London: Oxford University Press, 1931), XVII: 401–413;

Percy Simpson, "In Memoriam: Charles Harold Herford," in *Ben Jonson* (Oxford: Clarendon Press, 1932), IV: xi–xiii.

Percival Presland Howe
(29 July 1886 – 19 March 1944)

A. R. Jones
University of Wales

BOOKS: *The Repertory Theatre: A Record & A Criticism* (London: Secker, 1910);

J. M. Synge: A Critical Study (London: Secker, 1912);

Dramatic Portraits (London: Secker, 1913);

Malthus and the Publishing Trade (London: Secker, 1913);

Bernard Shaw: A Critical Study (London: Secker, 1915);

Criticism (London: Secker, 1915);

The Life of William Hazlitt (London: Secker, 1922; revised edition, London: Secker, 1928); republished, with introduction and memoir of Howe by Frank Swinnerton (Harmondsworth, U.K.: Penguin, 1949).

OTHER: *The Best of Hazlitt,* edited by Howe (London: Methuen, 1923);

The Letters of Thomas Manning to Charles Lamb, edited by Howe and Gertrude Alison Anderson (London: Secker, 1925);

New Writings by William Hazlitt, edited by Howe (London: Secker, 1925; New York: Dial, 1925);

New Writings by William Hazlitt: Second Series, edited by Howe (London: Secker, 1927; New York: Dial, 1927);

William Hazlitt, The Plain Speaker, edited by A. R. Waller and Arnold Glover, introduction by Howe (London: Dent, 1928);

The Complete Works of William Hazlitt: After the Edition of A. R. Waller and Arnold Glover, 21 volumes, edited by Howe (London: Dent, 1930–1934).

SELECTED PERIODICAL PUBLICATIONS –
UNCOLLECTED: "The Theatre: Folly Enthroned," *Outlook* (6 January 1912): 16–17;

"The Theatre: A Palimpsest," *Outlook* (16 March 1912): 403–404;

"The Theatre: The Fourth Wall," *Outlook* (30 March 1912): 479;

"The Playboy in the Theatre," *Oxford and Cambridge Review,* 21 (July 1912): 37–51;

Percival Presland Howe (The Illustrated London News Picture Library)

"Malthus and the Publishing Trade," *English Review* (November 1912): 577–591;

"St. John Hankin, and his Comedy of Recognition," *Fortnightly Review* (January 1913): 165–175;

"Shaw on Laughter," *New York Times,* 19 January 1913, p. 24;

"The Dramatic Craftsmanship of Mr. Bernard Shaw," *Fortnightly Review* (13 July 1913): 132–142;

"England's New Dramatists," *North American Review,* 198 (August 1913): 218–226;

"The Plays of Granville Barker," *Fortnightly Review* (September 1913): 476–487;

"Mr. Galsworthy as Dramatist," *Fortnightly Review* (October 1913): 739–752;

"Hazlitt and *Liber Amoris*," *Fortnightly Review* (February 1916): 300–310;

"Hazlitt's Second Marriage," *Fortnightly Review* (August 1916): 263–273;

"Fiction and Perpetual Life," *Athenæum* (6 June 1919): 422–423;

"Unpublished Letters of William Hazlitt," *Athenæum,* (8 August 1919): 711–713; (15 August 1919): 742–744;

"Hazlitt and Blackwood's," *Fortnightly Review* (October 1919): 603–615;

"Drama: A Play from a Novel," *Athenæum* (21 November 1919): 1234;

"Hazlitt's Patron," *Times Literary Supplement* (19 October 1922): 666;

"William Hazlitt," *Notes and Queries,* 12 (1922): 70–77;

"New Hazlitt Letters," *London Mercury,* 7 (March 1923): 494–498;

"Hazlitt and Landor," *Times Literary Supplement* (20 March 1924): 176;

"Hazlitt Letters: An Addition," *London Mercury,* 10 (May 1924): 73–74;

"The Modern *Gradus Ad Parnassum* by William Hazlitt," *London Mercury,* 10 (July 1924): 273–277;

"Hazlitt and Jeffrey: A New Letter," *London Mercury,* 12 (August 1924): 411–412;

"Hazlitt's Second Marriage," *Times* (London), 30 September 1930, p. 8;

"Lucius and Caius," *Times Literary Supplement* (6 October 1932): 711;

"Lamb and Hazlitt," *Times Literary Supplement* (26 September 1935): 596;

"Three Hazlitt Letters," *Times Literary Supplement* (21 March 1936): 244.

P. P. Howe is inextricably linked in the mind of all those interested in the English Romantic movement with William Hazlitt, whose biography he wrote and whose complete works he edited. Without Howe's work it is unlikely that Hazlitt would fill such a prominent position in the landscape of English Romanticism since few would be willing to lavish the scholarship and devotion that he gave to his subject and fewer still would be capable of redeeming Hazlitt from the calumnies and neglect into which his reputation had fallen.

Percival Presland Howe was born in Lewisham, South London, on 29 July 1886. He was brought up in a large, cultured, middle-class family by refined and gifted parents. His father was devoutly religious, a confirmed liberal, and a supporter of good causes. He had his own ship-broking firm. He also had a love of literature, especially the poetry of William Blake and Robert Browning. Howe was the third of seven sons: Arthur, the eldest son, went into his father's business; Garfield worked for J. M. Dent, the publisher, on the Temple Classics series; Charles, a gifted painter, and Arnold, who went into business, were both killed in World War I; Harold became the headmaster of Keswick School; and Eric became a distinguished psychiatrist. There was one sister. Frank Swinnerton, who described Howe as "my closest friend for more than forty years," described Howe's father as "a man of great longevity and endearing personality . . . with strong religious and social convictions and considerable depth and variety of reading." Swinnerton writes that the "brothers had been habituated to think before they spoke and think carefully again before they acted . . . they were methodical, logical and educated. They were open-minded." From the ages of fifteen to eighteen Howe attended University College School when it was still adjacent to University College. Swinnerton says that he was first introduced to Howe and his brother Garfield by a reference to the amateur journal they ran called the *Scribbler,* which they produced monthly with Howe as the chief contributor and Garfield as the editor. Howe was still a day boy at University College School while Garfield had started work at Dent, the publisher where he managed to get Swinnerton a job and thus launch his career. Together with his brother and Swinnerton, Howe went frequently to the theater in London and developed wide though severe tastes in the arts. Swinnerton considered Howe's enthusiasm for the theater characteristic of his generation: "Besides discovering and exulting in the plays of [Bernard] Shaw, [J. M.] Barrie, [John] Galsworthy, and [Harley] Granville-Barker, and translations of [Henrik] Ibsen, [Gerhart] Hauptmann, and [Hermann] Suderman, we became acquainted, through performances given at the Court Theatre in Sloane Square, with the Irish plays originally produced at the Abbey Theatre in Dublin. The plays offered brilliant miniatures of peasant life to which in England there was no parallel; the acting of Sara Allgood, Maire O'Neill, Arthur Sinclair, and indeed the whole cast was magnificent; we were caught by both tragedy and antic comedy which in retrospect was the fantastic interest of a marionette show. We learned Irish idioms, adopted Irish accents, hurried again and again to hear *The Playboy of the Western World,* without at least understanding what the play meant to the Irish audiences . . . to P. P., drawn by enthusiasm for Synge into the orbit of Irish theatre, they were a part of enchantment. He became more Irish than we did; and we were all, of course, more Irish than the Irish themselves." They also frequented lecture halls to hear Shaw, G. K. Chesterton, and Hilaire Belloc debate and lecture. On weekends they went out into the Kent countryside and talked and argued among themselves in a happy, good-natured way. While Garfield was given to dogmatic rationalism and Swinnerton to effervescent loquaciousness, Howe often reserved his judgment and kept silent until he was sure of his ground.

When Howe left school he tried working in the City in London as a ship broker but decided against a business career, so he, like his brother and Swinnerton, turned to publishing. He took a subeditorial post in the publishing firm of Eveleigh Nash working on the then recently launched *Nash's Magazine*. Martin Secker had joined Nash in 1908 as a reader in the firm, and in 1910 he started his own publishing house, where he published the early work of Compton Mackenzie, Hugh Walpole, and Francis Brett Young. He had the rare gift of discovering young authors destined to be famous and published the works of D. H. Lawrence between 1921 and his death in 1930.

At that prewar period the London stage was undergoing a revival. Shaw, Barrie, Galsworthy, and Granville-Barker were bringing a renewed seriousness to the theater. Howe, who was regularly writing drama criticism for a small-circulation Socialist weekly periodical, wrote a book titled *The Repertory Theatre* (1910) on the Barker-Frohman Repertory Theatre, which was published by Martin Secker. Therefore, at the age of twenty-four he found himself an accepted dramatic critic. His book was reviewed respectfully in *Outlook* on 19 November 1910 as "the full record and grateful criticism of a significant chapter in the history of that movement . . . he has done for that enterprise what Mr. Desmond MacCarthy has done for an earlier and not less significant chapter, the Vedrenne-Barker management at the Court Theatre; and he has done more." A few weeks later, on 24 December 1910, he reviewed Maurice Maeterlinck's play *The Blue Bird* at the Haymarket for *Outlook* and quickly established himself as the journal's regular dramatic critic. In 1912 he published *J. M. Synge: A Critical Study,* two years after his subject's death. He followed this in 1915 with *Bernard Shaw: A Critical Study*. In his study of Synge, as in his drama criticism, he showed himself generally to be a sensitive and receptive critic fully aware of the historical framework of his subject, well-read, and deeply

versed in the technicalities of theater as well as in its creativity. He was particularly appreciative of originality and good writing and found both in abundance in the works of Synge and Shaw. He identified closely with Synge, even adopting from time to time his prose rhythms in his own writing. The first half of his book deals with Synge's plays considered individually, and the remainder discusses his prose and his poetry as source materials for his plays. He argues that the dramatic intensity of the plays comes from their craftsmanship and the fact that they are so firmly rooted in reality. He deals particularly with Synge's heroines, especially Pegeen Mike, and maintains that *The Playboy of the Western World* (1907) confirmed Synge's place "amongst the masters." He draws attention particularly to Christy's increasingly poetic nature, the beauty of the love passages, and the skillful blending of the tragic and comic elements. He suggests that the difficulties Synge experienced in the reception of his poetic diction was comparable to those problems faced by the author of *Lyrical Ballads* (1798) a century earlier. It was his language that so distinguished him. He "brought the theatre back to its first concern, with *words;* and he made it plain that there can be no fine drama without an unfailing care for *form*." He reiterated this assessment in an article he later wrote for the *North American Review* (August 1913), where he praises Synge for his insistence that drama must give joy as well as reality and describes him as the "one writer of our time who, treading no path but his own, yet points more clearly than any other to a future for the English drama."

While he was not able to identify with Shaw to anything like the same extent, Howe is nonetheless sympathetic to his aims and appreciative of his considerable impact on the contemporary theater. He does argue that the prefaces are much more impressive than the plays and in many ways make the plays unnecessary. Thus the prefaces became longer and longer once Shaw got his plays established on the stage. His novels show little technique but the manipulation of ideas, and it is the message of the plays, not the plays themselves, which catch the social conscience. He sees drama primarily as discussion, the aim of which is to change public attitudes. He often achieves in his plays lively and engaging dialogue but is unable to construct his plays so that they develop to achieve dramatic resolution. *The Doctor's Dilemma* (1906), for instance, is not tragic because it is concerned with the medical profession rather than Dubedat, the doctor. His characters are therefore mostly talkers, mere mouthpieces for the author, though some are more specifically personalized. He considered that technically Shaw had not developed since *Arms and the Man* in 1894. Like many critics before and since, he was not able to take Shaw with that degree of seriousness with which Shaw regarded himself and his own achievements. Yet Howe's study is an intelligent response to its subject as thinker and social reformer, however backhanded the admiration may be. He is amplifying his view of Shaw expressed earlier in *Repertory Theatre,* where he describes Shaw as the "symbol of much of the revolt" of the new theater through a whole school of drama in himself, a playwright who has adopted the traditional practices of the theater in order to expound his particular philosophy. He provided the theater with much-needed "intellectual vivacity" but had not affected it greatly because he has not "profoundly mastered it." Indeed, both books are early and valuable responses to two of the most dominant and diverse voices of the pre-1914 theater. What Howe's books may lack in analytic intellection they more than compensate for by the honesty and directness of his reactions, the clarity and vigor of his writing, and the freshness of his judgments. Evidence of his enjoyment of the theater is everywhere in his books as in his weekly column for *Outlook.* He wrote for theatergoers and not for critics or historians.

In 1913 he published a short pamphlet titled *Malthus and the Publishing Trade,* which was the first of Martin Secker's series called the John Street Booklets. This had already appeared as an article in the *English Review* in November 1912. In not too serious a manner Howe redirects the main thesis of Thomas Malthus's famous work *An Essay on the Principle of Population* (1798) to publishing and to the ever-increasing number of "ordinary books" printed annually. He strongly indicates the need for publishers to practice self-denying restraints in the face of this tide of books in order to ensure the continued survival of good books. Also in 1913 Howe published his *Dramatic Portraits,* which contained essays on nine dramatists: Arthur Pinero, Henry Arthur Jones, Oscar Wilde, Barrie, Shaw, Saint John Hankin, Granville-Barker, Hubert Henry Davies, and Galsworthy. Four of the chapters, on Hankin, Shaw, Granville-Barker, and Galsworthy, had, as he points out in a prefatory note, been published in the *Fortnightly Review* (January 1913–October 1913), but the other five chapters appear to have been written especially for the book. Intended as a serious introduction to the work of the leading Edwardian dramatists, the book is a sympathetic, if rather indulgent, assessment of their works, aims, and

achievements. Like so much of Howe's dramatic criticism, the volume's tone is more that of an appreciation than a critique. Nonetheless, it remains a valuable introduction to its subjects' works and demonstrates Howe's attempt to educate his public's taste toward the better dramatists.

The same year that he published *Dramatic Portraits* he married and moved out of London to a small house near Lewes on the Sussex downs. Through his work as a publisher, as a dramatic critic, and as an author, he had achieved financial and professional security. In 1915 he published in Martin Secker's The Art and Craft of Letters series a sixty-two page booklet titled *Criticism,* in which he discusses the procedures and responsibilities of the drama critic as he sees and practices the craft. He sees the critic as "the middleman in the industry of the arts," whose function is to move the appreciation of art from where it is less capable to where it is more capable of satisfying human wants. He rejects the idea that the critic is a creative artist in his own right and argues that although the artist and the critic are both engaged in the act of "imaginative reflexion, the passing of material through the medium of personality" the difference in materials is radical. The function of the one is primary; of the other, secondary — the critic's craft is not creative but "distributive." He quotes Hazlitt to support his view that "the critic is the ideal spectator who has by an accident become vocal; the accident may be, as in the case of Hazlitt, or Charles Lamb, the accident of genius, albeit of a secondary kind." Criticism, he feels, demands self-sacrifice while holding fast to a sense of values. Again he uses Hazlitt as his example: "What Hazlitt had was exquisite sensibility, and unconquerable *sense.*" The critic's task, nonetheless, he says, is with "judicious enquiry," not with "judicial inquiry." He considers artists to be, on the whole, partial and inadequate critics: "There comes a point in the career of the creative artist when he can read with patience no books but his own . . . the subjective consideration of art is the artist's [proper concern], the objective the critic's." This is "part of what Matthew Arnold meant when he said that at all costs criticism must keep itself free of the practical spirit."

It quickly becomes clear he believes Hazlitt not only exemplifies the best virtues of criticism but that in his writings he laid down the guidelines for the proper practice of the critic's craft. He does not doubt that Hazlitt is a better critic than Lamb or Samuel Taylor Coleridge or Leigh Hunt. "What Hazlitt did," he asserts, "was for twenty-five years to speak the truth about the things of art as he saw

THE LIFE OF
WILLIAM HAZLITT

BY
P. P. HOWE

A man in himself is always the same, though he may
not always appear to be so.
Eloquence of the British Senate.

LONDON
MARTIN SECKER
NUMBER FIVE JOHN STREET ADELPHI

*Hazlitt as a Young Man.
From an oil painting by John Hazlitt
in the Maidstone Museum*

*Frontispiece and title page for Howe's biography of the nineteenth-century essayist, which was a popular as well as
critical success*

them." "He was merely exceptionally free from all cants which cloud the judgment; from the cant of the Time Spirit, for example. His own instinctive and disciplined judgment was enough for him, that is all." He defends Hazlitt against the attacks of those such as Augustine Birrell, who in his "timid and cautionary little book," *William Hazlitt* (1902), "takes Hazlitt to task for speaking the truth about Coleridge and Wordsworth." In his own day he singles out Chesterton, "a natural critic"; Arthur Bingham Walkley, "the great exponent in the theatre; and Max Beerbohm, of whom we are "surest." Nevertheless, it is to the example of Hazlitt that he returns, "the true critic . . . we shall not have a better."

Swinnerton succinctly summarized what he saw to be Howe's position as a literary figure at that time: "His first book about the Barker-Frohman Repertory Theatre of 1910, received much praise. His second, on Synge, was naturally scorned by the Irish; his third, on Bernard Shaw, provoked the

Master to a reference in *The New Statesman* to 'Pretentious Pigmies' . . . Not one of these three books established P. P. Howe definitely as a writer. They were superior to many; they did not add up to that mysterious something which is called, by literary astrologers, "promise." World War I put an end to his literary activities for its duration, and he found himself in the army in France serving in the Royal Artillery. He did, somehow or other, manage to continue his research into Hazlitt and published two articles, on *Liber Amoris* (1823) and on Hazlitt's second marriage, in the *Fortnightly Review* in 1916. At least some of his Hazlitt library must have accompanied him to France. Nevertheless, he hated the war and afterward refused to talk about his experiences on the western front. He was profoundly disturbed by the death of his artist brother Charles, to whom he was particularly close; he never ceased to miss him. At the end of the war Secker applied for Howe's release from the army on the grounds that he needed Howe as a partner in his firm. This was an ideal position so far as Howe was concerned, and he gratefully accepted. He moved back to London and took up residence at 21 Primrose Mansions, Battersea Park, where he was still living when World War II broke out. He stayed with Martin Secker until the firm broke up in 1935 and became Martin Secker and Warburg, though in 1937 Secker had no more to do with it. In 1937 the Bodley Head Press was found to be insolvent on the death of John Lane, and the assets of the firm were bought by the publisher Stanley Unwin with the help of two fellow publishers. Unwin records that "When we first took over the business we appointed Percy Howe (the authority on Hazlitt) to manage it. He had been a director of Martin Secker Ltd., and with the failure of that business, and the sale of its assets to Mr. F. J. Warburg, was immediately available." Unwin also records that Howe was succeeded in May 1939 by C. J. Greenwood after Howe became a director of Hamish Hamilton Ltd. At about the same time as he joined Martin Secker, Swinnerton handed over to him the post of drama critic for *Truth*. In Swinnerton's view, "With the maturing of his mind, and I suppose that instinctive wisdom which appears suddenly although it has been long preparing, P. P. Howe found some time in 1912 his true theme. Forsaking criticism, he set himself the task of writing the life of William Hazlitt. He lived Hazlitt, dreamed Hazlitt, and knew the very words of Hazlitt, who had foreseen and settled every moral or aesthetic problem ever raised in conversation." In 1912 in his book on Synge he quotes Hazlitt in a way that suggests he already had a detailed knowledge of his work: "As Hazlitt remarked, when it was said that Gay took from Tibullus one of the prettiest of his songs in The Beggar's Opera, there is nothing about Convent Garden in Tibullus." By the time he came to write his study of Shaw he had found an apposite quotation from Hazlitt to express his feelings about Shaw and his plays: "A person who talked with equal vivacity on every subject excites no interest in any. Repose is as necessary in conversation as in a picture." It seems likely that he was inspired to write his article "Malthus and the Publishing Trade," which he subsequently issued as a pamphlet, by Hazlitt's famous *A Reply to the Essay on Population, by the Rev. T. R. Malthus* (1807), though it would seem to owe little to him otherwise. Certainly, he became obsessed with Hazlitt when he returned home after the war. Between 1919 and 1922, the year he published his biography, he printed several scholarly articles demonstrating the extent to which he had immersed himself in his subject and was making important and primary discoveries of

new Hazlitt materials. Howe developed an interest in Hazlitt – his life and his writings – that amounted to something like a consuming passion. He studied him with great diligence and in considerable detail. He collected his books, searched out his papers and manuscripts, and read everything by his contemporaries and successors that had a bearing on his life and reputation.

His biography, *The Life of William Hazlitt*, demonstrates the extent to which he had mastered his subject. He had gained access to the Hazlitt family papers and acknowledges the cooperation of "Miss Hazlitt, great-grand-daughter of my subject, who by freely and generously throwing open to me all the works of her father, the late Mr William Carew Hazlitt . . . has rendered me assistance with which I could not possibly have dispensed." Howe was, therefore, able to build on, extend, and complete (and also, in some respects, correct) the two-volume *Memoirs* of Hazlitt that his grandson had published in 1867. Howe chose to present his subject in such a way as to ensure that the narrative of his life was shown so far as possible in the words of those contemporaries who witnessed it and of Hazlitt himself. "To the forty-odd examples of his correspondence which have been hitherto known (excluding the somewhat specialised *Liber Amoris* group), I have succeeded in adding eighteen. With the exception of the group mentioned . . . every letter will be found, or will be found quoted, in the course of this book." In this way Howe attempted to get as close as possible to his subject and bring the reader into equally intimate contact, without obtruding himself so far as that was possible. He explains this in his preface: "I have thought it better not to recast the narrative in my own words, but to present it as far as possible in those of the various witnesses. If this method has drawbacks, of which I am conscious, it will be found also, I hope, to have certain advantages, not the least of which is that everything which appears in this book bears its own authority, good or less good, on its face." In addition he says he has aimed at clarity of outline, with reasonable attention to detail, in the presentation of a life hitherto imperfectly known, in the hope of rendering it a little less imperfectly known. His claims on his own behalf are excessively modest, for he was able to add a great deal more by way of fact and information about Hazlitt than was hitherto known and also managed to relieve him of many of the rumors and false reports that had tarnished Hazlitt's name and reputation. He rescues his subject from the prejudices that threatened at various periods of his life to overwhelm him and at that same time builds up a solid, well-documented, and convincing picture of the times in which he lived. The biography shows Howe to be completely immersed in his subject and to a large extent to have identified with him. Whatever the loss of perspective involved in this, there are undoubted advantages insofar as the subject of the biography is brought as close as possible to the reader. There is little direct comment from the biographer, who tends to see people and events from his subject's point of view. Thus, for example, he comments that "It was soon to be Hazlitt's charge against [William] Wordsworth, not entirely without justification, that he himself wrote as though he had never heard of the French Revolution." Howe's "not entirely without justification" demonstrates how far he had adopted Hazlitt's radical attitudes. Wordsworth welcomed the French Revolution, but his hopes were disillusioned at the time of the Reign of Terror, and thereafter he recognized the dangers inherent in social upheaval. Hazlitt never lost his faith in the principles on which the French Revolution was first founded. His consistency in this and in his defense of the socially exploited and deprived was a reflection of those principles. He vilified Coleridge and Robert Southey for betraying, as he saw it, their early political faith and their allegiance to the forces of the establishment which were responsible, in his view, for reaction and repression. Whatever Hazlitt's viewpoint, however, Wordsworth, Coleridge, and Southey were representative of the age that experienced the French Revolution and were chastened by that experience. Indeed, Wordsworth experienced the revolution at close quarters, and, far from forgetting the manner in which hope and happiness turned to disenchantment and terror, his thinking was ever afterward conditioned by it. Only by accepting Hazlitt's rather narrow, personal political standpoint, is it possible to accuse Wordsworth of apostasy. Nonetheless, Howe, by adopting Hazlitt's valuation of the actions of others, was able to demonstrate that Hazlitt acted from consistent and benevolent principles rather than from malicious animosity and personal spite, motives of which he was too often accused by his enemies. Howe's biography was warmly received by the public and praised uniformly by the reviewers. The *Times Literary Supplement* (14 September 1922), for example, reviewed the book in a leader article and commented on the method he had adopted in presenting his subject: "Howe gives us little criticism or comment of any kind. His book consists, as far as possible, of documents upon which the reader may base his own opinion of Hazlitt; and, since he has

collected facts industriously and stated them concisely, it is a useful work, though he might, we think, have sifted his facts a little more. But that, as he modestly says, he leaves to other writers. . . . Mr Howe, for all his documentary method, is always on Hazlitt's side, when he can be. . . . We'd rather have William Hazlitt wrong than, say, William Wilberforce right. And it is the merit of Mr Howe's book that, by the presentment of all the facts he can discover, he works us into this state of mind about his hero. We seem to understand all and so pardon all."

Although it is undoubtedly a scholarly work, scrupulously researched, it also achieved popular success and was issued as a paperback in 1949. However, despite its documentary method, Howe omits any formal system of references, although in a appendix he gives a "List of Principal Printed Authorities for the Life of Hazlitt." He was anxious to avoid pedantry at all costs and determined to write for the common reader while satisfying the exacting standards imposed by traditional scholarship. It was generally agreed that he had succeeded brilliantly on both counts.

In 1925 Howe published *New Writings by William Hazlitt,* which contained thirty-three uncollected essays, nineteen of which he authenticated. These are additional to Hazlitt's known writings published over a period of rather less than two years at the end of his life. Although, as he describes them, they may well be seen as "crumbs from a rich man's table," they nonetheless represent a significant addition to the canon. Two years later he published an additional volume of uncollected work, *New Writings by William Hazlitt: Second Series,* which he describes as "thirty-nine pieces of various lengths," thirty-six of which had not been printed previously which Hazlitt wrote between 1808 and 1828. Both of these collections consist largely of pieces which had been overlooked by A. R. Waller and Arnold Glover and do not appear in their *Collected Works of William Hazlitt* of 1902–1906. In addition, they did not appear in Jules Douady's bibliography, *Liste chronologique des oeuvres de William Hazlitt,* published in Paris in 1906.

Howe's standing as the authority on William Hazlitt was confirmed when he was invited to produce an edition of his complete works to celebrate the centenary of Hazlitt's death. He based his edition on that edited by Waller and Glover. He included all that was contained in his two volumes of *New Writings by William Hazlitt,* as well as the *Life of Napoleon* (1828–1830) and *A New and Improved Grammar of the English Tongue* (1810) that Waller and Glover had omitted. He also rearranged the Hazlitt canon into chronological sequence. He corrected, where necessary, the notes to the previous edition; "added to them, and subtracted from them, without in any way altering the fact that the major proprietorship in them is not my own." *The Complete Works of William Hazlitt: After the Edition of A. R. Waller and Arnold Glover* was published between 1930 and 1934 in twenty-one volumes. It is a memorial not only to Hazlitt but to the scholarship, love, and devotion that Howe lavished on Hazlitt and his achievements. It remains the standard, authoritative edition of his works. Moreover, it includes one of the most complete indexes ever devoted to a writer's work.

At the outbreak of World War II Howe was living with his wife and four children at his eldest son's farm north of Guildford in Surrey. He managed the publishing house of Hamish Hamilton, who was serving in the forces, and traveled back and forth to London taking his share of London fire watching. When he fell ill he was admitted to a hospital for an operation on his lung, and, although he was thought to be making a good recovery, he relapsed and died at Ockham, Surrey, on 19 March 1944.

A short obituary notice in the *Times Literary Supplement* on 1 April 1944 spoke not only of his "admirably proportioned Life of Hazlitt, a standard work" and his complete edition of his writings but also drew attention to his contribution to literature as the publisher of some of the most outstanding authors of his time. The *Times* noticed his work as a dramatic critic for the *Globe* and the *Outlook* as well as his authoritative contribution to Hazlitt studies. Also included was a personal tribute from Hamish Hamilton in which he mentions Howe's work as a literary publisher, his discovery of new authors whom he bound by ties of friendship and respect, his "mature judgment, based on wide reading, his patience and readiness to take infinite pains with the work of others, his integrity of character . . . his great courage and sensitiveness, a discerning wit and a quiet unassuming manner under which lay reserves of intellectual power." Hamilton did not doubt that the world of books, which Howe had always loved and to which he contributed so much, was the poorer for his passing.

However, so far as his devotion to Hazlitt is concerned, the tribute that would most have pleased Howe is that by C. M. Maclean, whose biography of Hazlitt, *Born Under Saturn,* was published in 1943. "The deepest debt of which I am conscious, now that this biography of Hazlitt is about to be published, is to the work on Hazlitt, both biographical and editorial, of Mr. P. P. Howe. I acknowledge this debt most gratefully, and I desire at the same time to pay the work the tribute of my profound respect and grateful admiration." Since that time, students of Hazlitt everywhere have had good cause to echo her gratitude, her respect, and her admiration.

References:

Frank Swinnerton, *Background with Chorus* (London: Hutchinson, 1956);

Swinnerton, *Swinnerton: An Autobiography* (London: Hutchinson, 1937);

Stanley Unwin, *The Truth About a Publisher: An Autobiographical Record* (London: Allen & Unwin, 1960).

Hugh Kingsmill
(Hugh Kingsmill Lunn)
(21 November 1889 – 15 May 1949)

Charles Calder
University of Aberdeen

BOOKS: *The Will to Love,* as Hugh Lunn (London: Chapman & Hall, 1919);

Blondel (London: Benn, 1927);

Matthew Arnold (London: Duckworth, 1928; New York: Dial, 1928);

After Puritanism, 1850–1900 (London: Duckworth, 1929);

The Return of William Shakespeare (London: Duckworth, 1929; Indianapolis: Bobbs-Merrill, 1929);

Behind Both Lines (London: Morley & Kennerley, 1930);

Frank Harris: A Biography (London: Cape, 1932; New York: Farrar & Rinehart, 1932);

The Table of Truth (London: Jarrolds, 1933);

Samuel Johnson (London: Barker, 1933; New York: Viking, 1934);

The Casanova Fable: A Satirical Revaluation, by Kingsmill and William Gerhardi (London: Jarrolds, 1934);

The Sentimental Journey: A Life of Charles Dickens (London: Wishart, 1934; New York: Morrow, 1935);

Brave Old World, by Kingsmill and Malcolm Muggeridge (London: Eyre & Spottiswoode, 1936);

Skye High: The Record of a Tour through Scotland in the Wake of Samuel Johnson and James Boswell, by Kingsmill and Hesketh Pearson (London: Hamish Hamilton, 1937; New York: Oxford University Press, 1938);

Next Year's News, by Kingsmill and Muggeridge (London: Eyre & Spottiswoode, 1938);

D. H. Lawrence (London: Methuen, 1938); published as *The Life of D. H. Lawrence* (New York: Dodge, 1938);

The Fall (London: Methuen, 1940);

The Blessed Plot, by Kingsmill and Pearson (London: Methuen, 1942);

The Poisoned Crown (London: Eyre & Spottiswoode, 1944);

Talking of Dick Whittington, by Kingsmill and Pearson (London: Eyre & Spottiswoode, 1947);

The Dawn's Delay (London: Eyre & Spottiswoode, 1948);

The Progress of a Biographer (London: Methuen, 1949).

OTHER: *An Anthology of Invective and Abuse,* edited by Kingsmill (London: Eyre & Spottiswoode, 1929; New York: Dial, 1929);

More Invective, edited by Kingsmill (London: Eyre & Spottiswoode, 1930; New York: Dial, 1930);

The Worst of Love, edited by Kingsmill (London: Eyre & Spottiswoode, 1931; New York: Holt, 1932);

What They Said at the Time, edited by Kingsmill (London: Wishart, 1935);

Parents & Children, edited by Kingsmill (London: Cressent, 1936);

The English Genius, edited, with an introduction, by Kingsmill (London: Eyre & Spottiswoode, 1938);

Made on Earth: A Panorama of Marriage, edited by Kingsmill (New York & London: Harper, 1938);

Courage: An Anthology, edited by Kingsmill (London: Bles, 1939);

Johnson Without Boswell, edited by Kingsmill (London: Methuen, 1940; New York: Knopf, 1941);

Leonard George Dobbs, *Shakespeare Revealed,* edited by Kingsmill (London: Skeffington, 1948);

Hugh Kingsmill

The High Hill of the Muses, edited by Kingsmill (London: Eyre & Spottiswoode, 1955).

Hugh Kingsmill was a biographer, critic, anthologist, and lover of English literature whose personality is enshrined in his own works and in the recollections of his friends Hesketh Pearson and Malcolm Muggeridge. Both men testified to the impact made upon them by Kingsmill, his robustness, wit, and humor, as well as his impatience with cant and affectation. These are precisely the qualities which animate Kingsmill's works. Michael Holroyd remarked that "behind the big names of twentieth-century literature there stands a shadow cabinet of writers waiting to take over once the Wind of Change has blown. My own vote goes to Hugh Kingsmill as leader of this opposition."

Hugh Kingsmill Lunn was born in London on 21 November 1889. He was the second son of Sir Henry Lunn, founder of the Lunn travel agency. Kingsmill did not enjoy his school days at Harrow; nor did he derive conspicuous benefit from his undergraduate studies at Oxford. He enlisted at the outbreak of World War I, being commissioned in the Royal Naval Volunteer Reserve. He spent fourteen months as a prisoner of war in Karlsruhe: during his confinement he wrote a novel titled *The Will to Love,* published by Chapman and Hall in 1919 under the author's given name of Hugh Lunn. Thereafter he wrote as Hugh Kingsmill: the abandonment of his surname may have been an indication, as Holroyd suggests, of "growing estrangement with the Lunn family, and with his father in particular."

Kingsmill's first marriage, to Eileen Turpin, was already in difficulties before he met Gladys Runican in 1927. At this time he was attempting to finish his biography on Matthew Arnold. Something of Kingsmill's state of mind can be glimpsed from a letter to Pearson dated 23 April 1927: "I wonder if I shall go completely to pieces . . . perhaps you won't mind a restrained extract from my *Calvary at the Cross,* or *Through Gehenna on a Push-Bike* . . . or *Hell and How to Heat It.*" Following the collapse of the marriage, Runican was forbidden by her family to see Kingsmill again.

Matthew Arnold was published in 1928 by Duckworth. Academic reviewers disliked the book; they were especially irritated by Kingsmill's insistence that the "Marguerite" of Arnold's poems had been a real person (his intuition was confirmed five years later). As Muggeridge noted, Kingsmill seldom received credit for his brilliant perceptions. The following year there appeared *After Puritanism, 1850–1900,* a collection of essays on Dean Farrar, Samuel Butler, Frank Harris, and W. T. Stead. The format suited Kingsmill well. The essay on Harris is a delightful piece of work; it whets our appetite for the biography which Kingsmill produced in 1932 (a sixty-page essay is insufficient to do justice to the inexhaustible fascination of Harris's "life and lies"). Kingsmill had briefly come under the spell of Harris after reading *The Man Shakespeare* (1909): "His praise of sensuality . . . sounded melodiously in the ear of youth, and I hastened to sit at the feet of a master whose message agreed so well with what I desired from life." The experience of working with Harris on a journal for women called *Hearth and Home* cured Kingsmill of his infatuation; but, to a biographer who relished human oddity, the challenge of Harris was irresistible.

Frank Harris: A Biography remains a classic of English biography. The subject allows scope for Kingsmill's characteristic gifts of humor, urbanity, and curiosity. The tone never falters. "On what foundation of actual fact Harris has erected the superstructure of his youthful triumphs, even the most indulgent reader of his autobiography [*My Life and Loves,* 1922–1927] will pause to wonder. At the age of thirteen he was already in the school cricket eleven; he had learnt *Paradise Lost* [1667] by heart in a week . . . he had made love to a girl of his own age in church, and had come within measurable distance of overpowering a French governess in a rustic summer-house; he had rejected the supernatural element in religion . . . and he had thrashed the school bully, a boy of seventeen or eighteen, the captain of the cricket eleven." Kingsmill notes in

Harris an abiding sense of estrangement from his fellows: "he was born uneasy; the elements of his nature were ill-mixed and his life was the expression of this inherent disharmony." The evidence of his career bears this out. Kingsmill's concern is to strip away the fictional superstructure and reveal Harris; and this naturally involves the demolition of so many spurious claims made in *My Life and Loves.*

But Kingsmill's enterprise is not a work of destruction or debunking. The book is not disfigured by that pervasive and irritating sense of superiority which distinguishes the Lytton Strachey mode of biographical enquiry. Kingsmill's purpose is not to denigrate his subject but to disentangle Harris from the Harris myth. In his estimate of Harris as critic, Kingsmill is conspicuously fair-minded. He notes the indebtedness of Harris to Georg Brandes, whose *William Shakespeare* had appeared in 1896; and he registers the "hasty" and "impressionistic" quality of the Harris portrayal of Shakespeare. Harris "writes as the passing mood prompts, alternating without any uneasiness between envious depreciation and melting worship." Kingsmill also shows that many of the characteristics Harris attributes to Shakespeare are derived from his conception of Oscar Wilde. Thus Shakespeare is presented as "gentle and witty, gay and sweet-mannered, studious and fair of mind; but physically weak and irresolute, ill-endowed in the virile virtues and vices." But when all is said and all reservations are made, "*The Man Shakespeare* is alive. To many of the 'professors' . . . Shakespeare was a substitute for experience. They came to him to learn about life, and did not venture to question his conclusions . . . Harris, hastily scanning a play between an afternoon in the city and an evening with a girl, had none of this cloistered diffidence." In passages such as these, Kingsmill demonstrates his own critical judiciousness. He is equally concerned to write justly about Harris's fiction. He reminds us that the short stories received extravagant acclaim when they appeared; and it is interesting to the student of literary reputations to reflect upon the praise that was accorded by contemporary critics to the collections entitled *Elder Conklin* (1894) and *Montes the Matador* (1900). Kingsmill concludes that the least ambitious pieces, *Eatin' Crow* and *The Best Man in Garotte,* contain fine narrative work and retain some freshness but that in general Harris's stories, so greatly suited to the taste of the day, lack the quality which keeps authentic work alive after literary fashion has changed.

Kingsmill writes from his own knowledge about Harris's last years. A keen sense of Harris's personality is gained from such chapters as "*Hearth*

Kingsmill, left, as a prisoner of war in Karlsruhe, Germany, in 1916 with Lieutenant Garray, center, and John Holms

and Home and Brixton Jail." Bernard Shaw declared once that Harris was "neither first-rate nor second-rate nor tenth-rate. He is just his horrible unique self." The unappealing side of Harris certainly emerges from Kingsmill's treatment; but Kingsmill shows us, too, the remarkable gusto, energy, and literary enthusiasm of his subject.

In evaluating *My Life and Loves* Kingsmill once again demonstrates his fairness: "The torrent of obscenity . . . has generally been attributed to Harris's desire to make money out of pornography . . . there can be no doubt that money was one of his objects. But he desired also, and far more intensely, to forget his loss of virility in memories enriched by invention, and to soothe his vanity, wounded at every point in life, by recording his youthful triumphs over women." Kingsmill also writes well about Harris's five volumes of *Contemporary Portraits* (1915–1924). There are, as he notes, three categories of subject: those whom Harris knew fairly intimately (such as Wilde); those whom he knew only superficially (such as Robert Browning); and those whom he probably never met (notably Richard Wagner).

Lord Rosebery, chronicler of Napoleon's last days, lamented that "there seems to have been something in the air at St. Helena that blighted exact truth." Given the miasma of untruthfulness that enveloped Harris and his doings, it is an achievement on the part of Kingsmill to have produced such a credible and convincing account. One admires the technical skill which enables the author to blend, unobtrusively, narrative and assessment.

Samuel Johnson (1933) exhibits the familiar Kingsmill virtues: sympathy between biographer and subject, evenness of tone, the easy integration of illustrative material, and the deliberate but undogmatic style of expression. Kingsmill brings to Johnson qualities of affection and insight. He recreates the personality of Johnson and deftly portrays the literary and social world which Johnson inhabited. Kingsmill is an economical writer, and he possesses the virtue of literary tact. He does not adopt a tone of lofty superiority, nor does he attempt tedious, tendentious, and ill-founded psychological analysis. Instead he maintains a firm narrative progression while accommodating anecdotes, reported conversations, and recollections which shed light on character. It is Kingsmill's preference not to gild refined gold and paint the lily but to allow this material to speak largely for itself.

To Kingsmill every aspect of Johnson was appealing. He had no such natural predisposition toward Dickens. *The Sentimental Journey: A Life of Charles Dickens* (1934) contains some mordant observations on Dickens's character. Kingsmill recognizes the "superb comic power" which Dickens the artist commanded, but he finds the personality of Dickens the man strangely marred by an intense egotism. In Kingsmill's view, "the world, as distinguished from his own private emotions, was a play to Dickens, and there was no mean for him between watching the play and taking a leading part in it. He could not mingle in the general life of men like Shakespeare."

Kingsmill's friends and collaborators Hesketh Pearson and Malcolm Muggeridge, May 1950
(photograph by Margaret Ryder)

Some of Kingsmill's shrewdest criticism can be found in *The Sentimental Journey*. He makes telling use of evidence drawn from the fiction and autobiographical writings; it is particularly interesting to note his citing of the little-known *George Silverman's Explanation* (1868). Kingsmill believed that Dickens failed to harmonize his comic genius and his emotions. "The opposition between them was innate and irreconcilable, with the two-fold result that his emotions were unpurged by his humour, and his humour, except in occasional sudden flashes, was unenriched by his emotions." In dealing with the autobiographical writings, Kingsmill identifies the note of self-absorption and self-pity which runs through these Dickensian evocations. He comments on the wounded self-love which animates the childhood recollections. Kingsmill takes pains to do justice to the novelist's mother. As he shows, Mrs. Dickens's life was neither easy nor enviable; and one can fairly assume that she was doing her best to give attention to her family and to cope with financial difficulties that were not of her own making.

The last of the biographies was *D. H. Lawrence* (1938). One may conjecture an imperfect sympathy between biographer and subject. For Kingsmill the essential conflict within Lawrence was between heart and will. On one side, Lawrence loved life; on the other, he strove to reattain the dark "otherness" of the prenatal state. The result was a ceaseless battle, a never-to-be-fulfilled quest in search of an absolute to which Lawrence could attach himself.

The biographies represent only a fraction of Kingsmill's output. He was a prolific writer of essays and reviews. Some of his best and most succinct pieces are contained in the collection titled *The Progress of a Biographer* (1949). This volume provides a pleasing supplement to the biographical studies. Kingsmill, as always, writes as an observer and connoisseur, not as a prophet or pundit. But in these articles one is consistently aware of a keen intellect, a Johnsonian ability to get to the heart of the matter by the most direct means. Like Johnson, Kingsmill clears away cant; and like Johnson, he keeps his eye on the essentials of life.

Holroyd conveys the essential virtues of Kingsmill when he writes that "Kingsmill . . . belonged to no school of critics. . . . No one had a sharper eye than he for detecting humbug. The truth he searched for was the truth we live, not speak." *The Poisoned Crown* (1944) contains Kingsmill's own summation of his creed; it can be taken, as Holroyd notes, as a fine epitaph. "What is divine in man is elusive and impalpable, and he is easily tempted to embody it in a concrete form — a church, a country, a social system, a leader — so that he may realize it with less effort and serve it with more profit. Yet . . . the attempt to externalize the kingdom of heaven in a temporal shape must end in disaster. It cannot be created by charters and constitutions nor established by arms. Those who set out for it alone will reach it together, and those who seek it in company will perish by themselves." Kingsmill's independence of mind, his distrust of utopianism and all collectivist solutions, may well, as Muggeridge surmised, have cost Kingsmill the modest popular success he hoped to enjoy; but it is precisely this honorable independence which confers such lasting validity on his work.

Pearson and Kingsmill collaborated on three "talk and travel" books: *Skye High* (1937), *The Blessed Plot* (1942), and *Talking of Dick Whittington* (1947). The relaxed conversational format was the perfect medium for the talents of the two men; one reviewer commented that Kingsmill and Pearson had "invented the conversation-travel book as a new art form." In addition, Kingsmill compiled several anthologies such as *The English Genius* (1938), *Courage* (1939), and *The High Hill of the Muses* (published posthumously in 1955). Muggeridge paid tribute to Kingsmill's encompassing knowledge of English literature. In conversation he commanded a wealth of quotations and references: he could prepare an anthology in as little as ten days. Kingsmill also composed parodies; as all A. E. Housman enthusiasts know, "What, still alive at twenty-two" is the most elegant burlesque of the Shropshire Lad style that has ever been produced. With Muggeridge, Kingsmill published newspaper parodies under the titles *Brave Old World* (1936) and *Next Year's News* (1938).

Kingsmill combined these activities with editing and contributing to the *New English Review Magazine*. For Kingsmill a literary supplement was precisely that, a collection of articles written by individuals. He protested trenchantly against the contemporary notion that a literary supplement comprised "a co-ordinated series of reviews planned to reinforce such political opinions as are expressed in the main body of the paper." The quotation comes from the opening of the essay in which Kingsmill demolishes the Orwellian claim that a coherent philosophy of "Neo-Toryism" linked together such diverse writers as himself, Muggeridge, T. S. Eliot, Evelyn Waugh, F. A. Voigt, and Wyndham Lewis.

Kingsmill in 1948

After Kingsmill's death Pearson and Muggeridge set down their recollections in *About Kingsmill* (1951). And elsewhere Muggeridge paid affectionate tribute to his friend. "It is difficult to convey the delight, the variety, the sparkle and the immense verve of Kingsmill's talk. . . . No one was ever less oracular than he, or more ready to listen and be amused. He made one feel mentally alive as no one else I have ever met has. He raised one up to his own level. To this day there is not one book I spoke with Kingsmill about whose pages do not still glow with his memory." For Muggeridge, Kingsmill was a man who lived in the imagination; this was the source of his serenity, a serenity which was proof against the frequently atrocious circumstances of his daily life. "The imagination generated love, serenity, literature, faith, laughter, understanding; the will, their opposites — in the individual, appetite for sensual satisfaction, and in the collectivity, for power."

Kingsmill became ill in March 1948, when he suffered a serious hemorrhage. Thereafter he was never wholly well; a further hemorrhage occurred in February 1949. He died in the Royal Sussex Hospital on 15 May 1949. He maintained his courage and spirit to the last. Pearson and Muggeridge visited him separately. "The last time I saw him," Muggeridge recalled, "he was very weak, and held my hand – an unusual thing for him who was, by temperament, undemonstrative. He had, he said, some good news to impart; something wonderful which had come to him about our human situation. He never did manage to get it out, but nonetheless, unspoken, it has often comforted me."

The creative influence of Kingsmill on his two friends is readily apparent. Ian Hunter calls Kingsmill "the tutor Pearson never had"; and indeed Kingsmill must have been the most stimulating, least pontifical of tutors. There is little doubt that as a result of Kingsmill's influence and example Pearson's biographical style became, in Hunter's words, "more balanced, mature and objective." There is an even and tempered quality in Kingsmill's work, a classical temper, which lends his biographies and critical studies an enduring charm. But,

as Hunter shows, Pearson gave Kingsmill practical help (particularly in the writing of *Frank Harris: A Biography*) and general encouragement. Their collaborations delightfully illustrate the qualities of humor, shrewd observation, and companionship which both men possessed in abundance. Kingsmill shows that scholarship need not be laborious and that learning merits all the more respect for being lightly worn.

Biography:

Michael Holroyd, *Hugh Kingsmill: A Critical Biography* (London: Unicorn Press, 1964).

References:

Ian Hunter, *Nothing to Repent: The Life of Hesketh Pearson* (London: Hamilton, 1987);

Hesketh Pearson and Malcolm Muggeridge, *About Kingsmill* (London: Methuen, 1951).

Sir Sidney Lee

(5 December 1859 – 3 March 1926)

D. Mori Thomas
Bilkent University

BOOKS: *Stratford-on-Avon: From the Earliest Times to the Death of William Shakespeare* (London: Seeley, 1885); republished as *Stratford-on-Avon: From the Earliest Times to the Death of Shakespeare* (London: Seeley, 1890; New York: Macmillan, 1890); republished as *Stratford-on-Avon from the Earliest Times to the Death of Shakespeare* (Philadelphia: Lippincott, 1904); revised and enlarged as *Stratford-on-Avon from the Earliest Times to the Death of Shakespeare* (Philadelphia: Lippincott, 1907; London: Seeley, 1907);

The Topical Side of the Elizabethan Drama [London, 1886];

Elizabethan England and the Jews [London, 1888];

Lee Versus Gibbings [London: Spottiswoode, 1892];

The Study of English Literature: An Address Delivered at the Inaugural Meeting of the Toynbee Literary Association at Toynbee Hall, on Tuesday, February 7, 1893 ([London]: Printed for private circulation, 1893);

National Biography: A Lecture Delivered at the Royal Institution on the Evening of Friday, Jan. 31, 1896 [London: Spottiswoode, 1896];

Shakespeare and the Earl of Pembroke (n.p., 1898?);

A Life of William Shakespeare (London: Smith, Elder, 1898); reprinted as *A Life of William Shakespeare* (London: Smith, Elder, 1898; New York: Macmillan, 1898; London: Macmillan & Co., 1898); republished as *A Life of William Shakespeare, with Portraits and Facsimiles* (London: Smith, Elder, 1899; New York: Macmillan, 1901); revised as *A Life of William Shakespeare* (London: Smith, Elder, 1904); republished as *A Life of William Shakespear* (London: Smith, Elder, 1908); revised as *A Life of William Shakespeare, with Portraits and Facsimiles,* with new preface by Lee (New York: Macmillan, 1909); republished as *A Life of William Shakespeare* (New York: Macmillan, 1912); rewritten and enlarged as *A Life of William Shakespere, with Portraits and Facsimiles* (London: Smith, Elder, 1915); republished as *A Life of William Shakespeare, with Portraits and Facsimiles* (London: Murray, 1916); republished as *A Life of William Shakespere, with Portraits and Facsimiles* (New York: Macmillan, 1916); republished as *A Life of William Shakespeare, with Portraits and Facsimiles* (London: Murray, 1922); republished as *A Life of William Shakespeare* (New York: Macmillan, 1924); republished as *A Life of William Shakespeare, with Portraits and Facsimiles* (New York: Macmillan, 1927); republished as *A Life of William Shakespeare* (London: Miller; New York: Macmillan, [1931]);

A Catalogue of Shakespeareana, with preface by Lee (London: Chiswick Press, 1899);

The Shakespeare First Folio: Some Notes and a Discovery [London: Smith, Elder, 1899]; republished as *The Shakespeare First Folio: Some Notes and a Discovery* (New York & London: Macmillan, 1899);

Shakespeare's Handwriting: Facsimiles of the Five Authentic Autograph Signatures of the Poet (London: Smith, Elder, 1899);

Shakespeare's Henry V: An Account and an Estimate (London: Smith, Elder, 1900);

Shakespeare's Life and Work: Being an Abridgment, Chiefly for the Use of Students, of a Life of William Shakespeare (London: Smith, Elder; New York: Macmillan; London: Macmillan, 1900); reprinted as *Shakespeare's Life and Work: Being an Abridgment, Chiefly for the Use of Students, of a Life of Wm. Shakespeare* (New York: Macmillan; London: Macmillan, 1904); revised as *Shakespeare's Life and Work: Being an Abridgment, Chiefly for the Use of Students, of a Life of William Shakespeare* (London: Smith, Elder, 1907);

English Literature: William Shakespeare (Philadelphia: Lippincott, 1901);

Queen Victoria: A Biography (London: Smith, Elder, 1902); republished as *Queen Victoria: A Biography, with Portraits, Facsimile, and Map* (New

Sir Sidney Lee

York: Macmillan, 1903); revised as *Queen Victoria: A Biography* (London: Smith, Elder; London: Murray, 1904);

Shakespeare in Oral Tradition [New York: Scott; London: Sampson Low, Marston, 1902];

A Census of Extant Copies of the First Folio (Oxford, 1902);

The Alleged Vandalism at Stratford-on-Avon (Westminster: Constable, 1903);

Great Englishmen of the Sixteenth Century (New York: Scribners; London: Constable, 1904); republished as *Great Englishmen of the Sixteenth Century* (London: Harrap, [1925]);

The Supremacy of Petrarch (n.p., 1904);

Notes & Additions to the Census of Copies of the Shakespeare First Folio, by Sidney Lee (London: Frowde, 1906);

Pepys and Shakespeare: A Paper Read at the Sixth Meeting of the Samuel Pepys Club, on Thursday, November 30, 1905 ([London: Bedford Press], 1906);

Shakespeare and the Modern Stage, with Other Essays (London: J. Murray, 1906); republished as *Shakespeare and the Modern Stage, with Other Essays* (New York: Scribners, 1906);

The Seigneurs and Sovereigns of Mediaeval Exeter; Also an Account of the Sieges of the City, anonymous, with preface signed "Docendo Discimus" (Exeter: A. Wheaton, Paternoster Press, [1908?]);

The Impersonal Aspect of Shakespeare's Art (Folcraft, PA.: Folcraft Press, [1909]); republished as *The Impersonal Aspect of Shakespeare's Art* ([Oxford: H. Hart, at the University Press], 1909);

A Shakespeare Reference Library ([Oxford: Hart], 1909); revised and republished as *A Shakespeare Reference Library and Sir Edmund Chambers* ([London: Oxford University Press], 1925);

The French Renaissance in England: An Account of the Literary Relations of England and France in the Sixteenth Century (New York: Scribners, 1910); republished as *The French Renaissance in England: An Account of the Literary Relations of England and*

France in the Sixteenth Century (Oxford: Clarendon Press, 1910);

Principles of Biography: The Leslie Stephen Lecture Delivered in the Senate House, Cambridge, on 13 May 1911 (Cambridge: Cambridge University Press, 1911);

The Place of English Literature in the Modern University: An Inaugural Lecture Delivered at East London College on October 2, 1913 (London: Smith, Elder, 1913);

Shakespeare and the Italian Renaissance (London: Milford, Oxford University Press; New York: Oxford University Press, [1915]); republished as *Shakespeare and the Italian Renaissance* [New York: Haskell House, n.d.];

A Catalogue of the Shakespeare Exhibition Held in the Bodleian Library to Commemorate the Death of Shakespeare, April 23, 1616 (Oxford: Hall, 1916);

Shakespeare and the Red Cross: An Address Delivered at the Opening of the Shakespeare Exhibition at the Grafton Galleries on 19 January 1917 (London: Chiswick Press, 1917);

The Perspective of Biography, by Sir Sidney Lee ([Oxford: Oxford University Press], 1918);

Modern Language Research; Inaugural Address, October 19, 1918 (Cambridge: Deighton, Bell, 1919);

King Edward VII; A Biography, 2 volumes (New York: Macmillan, 1925–1927);

Elizabethan and Other Essays, edited by Frederick S. Boas (Oxford: Clarendon Press, 1929).

OTHER: Huon de Bordeaux, *The Boke of Duke Huon of Burdeux, Done into English by Sir John Bourchier, Lord Berners, and Printed by Wynken de Worde about 1534 A.D.*, edited with introduction by Lee (London: Trubner, 1882–1887);

The Dictionary of National Biography, volumes 22 through 26 edited by Leslie Stephen and Lee, volumes 27 through 63 and *Supplement*, volumes 1 through 3, edited by Lee (London: Smith, Elder; New York: Macmillan, 1885–1901); revised and reissued in 22 volumes, volumes 1 through 9 edited by Leslie Stephen and Lee, volumes 10 through 22 edited by Lee (London: Smith, Elder, 1908–1909); republished as *The Dictionary of National Biography, Founded in 1882 by George Smith, Edited by Sir Leslie Stephen and Sir Sidney Lee, from the Earliest Times to 1900*, 22 volumes (London: Oxford University Press, [1921–1922]);

Baron Edward Herbert, *The Autobiography of Edward, Lord Herbert of Cherbury, with Introduction, Notes, Appendices, and a Continuation of the Life*, by Sidney

L. Lee (London: J. C. Nimmo, 1886); republished as *Autobiography of Edward, Lord Herbert of Cherbury, with Introduction, Notes, Appendices, and a Continuation of the Life*, by S. L. Lee (New York: Scribner & Welford, 1886); republished as *Autobiography of Edward, Lord Herbert of Cherbury, with Notes, Appendices, & Continuation of the Life* by S. L. Lee (London: Gibbings, 1892); revised as *The Autobiography of Edward, Lord Herbert of Cherbury, with Introduction, Notes, Appendices, and a Continuation of the Life*, by Sidney Lee (London: Routledge; New York: E. P. Dutton, [1906]);

Marsden J. Perry, *A Catalogue of Shakespeareana*, preface by Lee (London: Chiswick Press, 1899);

"Memoir of George Smith," in *The Dictionary of National Biography, Supplement*, volume 1, edited by Lee (London: Smith, Elder, 1901), pp. xxi–lxi;

William Shakespeare, *Shakespeare's Comedies, Histories, & Tragedies: Being a Reproduction in Facsimile of the First Folio Edition, 1623, from the Chatsworth Copy in the Possession of the Duke of Devonshire, K. G., with Introduction and Census of Copies by Sidney Lee* (Oxford: Clarendon Press, 1902);

The Dictionary of National Biography: Index and Epitome, edited by Lee (London: Smith, Elder, 1903);

The Dictionary of National Biography: Errata, edited by Lee (London: Smith, Elder; New York: Macmillan, 1904);

Elizabethan Sonnets, Newly Arranged and Indexed, edited, with an introduction by Lee (Westminster: Constable, 1904), republished as *An English Garner: Elizabethan Sonnets, Newly Arranged and Edited, with an Introduction by Sidney Lee*, 2 volumes (New York: Dutton, 1904);

"The Last Years of Elizabeth," in *The Cambridge Modern History, Planned by the Late Lord Acton: The Wars of Religion*, volume 3, edited by A. W. Ward, G. W. Prothero, and Stanley Leathes (Cambridge: University Press, 1904), pp. 328–363;

"The Elizabethan Age of English Literature," in *The Cambridge Modern History, Planned by the Late Lord Action: The Wars of Religion*, volume 3, edited by A. W. Ward, G. W. Prothero, and Stanley Leathes (Cambridge: University Press, 1904), pp. 364–382;

William Shakespeare, *Shakespeare's Lucrece, Being a Reproduction in Facsimile of the First Edition, 1594, from the Copy in the Malone Collection in the Bodleian Library*, introduction and bibliography by Lee (Oxford: Clarendon Press, 1905);

William Shakespeare, *Shakespeare's Pericles, Being a Reproduction in Facsimile of the First Edition, 1609, from the Copy in the Malone Collection in the Bodleian Library,* introduction and bibliography by Lee (Oxford: Clarendon Press, 1905);

William Shakespeare, *Shakespeare's Sonnets, Being a Reproduction in Facsimile of the First Edition, 1609, from the Copy in the Malone Collection in the Bodleian Library,* introduction and bibliography by Lee (Oxford: Clarendon Press, 1905);

William Shakespeare, *Shakespeare's Venus and Adonis, Being a Reproduction in Facsimile of the First Edition, 1593, from the Unique Copy in the Malone Collection in the Bodleian Library,* introduction and bibliography by Lee (Oxford: Clarendon Press, 1905);

William Shakespeare, *The Passionate Pilgrim, Being a Reproduction in Facsimile of the First Edition, 1599, from the Copy in the Christie Miller Library at Britwell,* introduction and bibliography by Lee (Oxford: Clarendon Press, 1905);

William Shakespeare, *The Complete Works of William Shakespeare, with Annotations and a General Introduction by Sidney Lee,* 20 volumes (Boston: Jefferson Press; New York: Harper, [1906–1908]); republished as *Complete Works, with Annotations and a General Introduction by Sidney Lee,* 40 volumes (New York: Sproul, 1906–1909); republished as *The Caxton Edition of the Complete Works of William Shakespeare, with Annotations and a General Introduction by Sidney Lee,* 20 volumes (London: Caxton Publishing Company, 1910);

William Shakespeare, *Four Quarto Editions of Plays by Shakespeare, the Property of the Trustees and Guardians of Shakespeare's Birthplace,* preface by Lee (Stratford-upon-Avon: The Trustees and Guardians of Shakespeare's Birthplace, 1908);

King Leir, *The Chronicle History of King Leir: The Original of Shakespeare's "King Lear,"* edited by Lee (London: Chatto & Windus, 1909);

"The Elizabethan Sonnet," in *The Cambridge History of English Literature,* volume 3, edited by A. W. Ward and A. R. Weller (New York & London: Putnam; Cambridge: University Press, 1911), pp. 281–310;

The Dictionary of National Biography: Second Supplement, 3 volumes, edited by Lee (London: Smith, Elder, 1912);

The Dictionary of National Biography: Second Supplement, Index and Epitome, edited by Lee (London: Smith, Elder, 1913);

Shakespeare's England: An Account of the Life & Manners of His Age, 2 volumes, edited by Lee and

Charles Talbot Onions (Oxford: Clarendon Press, 1916);

Stratford-upon-Avon: Shakespeare's Birthplace, tercentenary commemoration exhibition catalogue compiled by Frederick C. Wellstood, with preface by Lee (Stratford-upon-Avon: E. Fox & Son, 1916);

The Dictionary of National Biography, Founded in 1882 by George Smith: The Concise Dictionary from the Beginnings to 1911, Being an Epitome of the Main Work and Its Supplement, to Which Is Added an Epitome of the Supplement, 1901–1911, edited by Lee ([Oxford]: Oxford University Press, 1920);

The English Association, *The Year's Work in English Studies,* volume 1 edited by Lee, volumes 2 through 4 edited by Lee and F. S. Boas (London: Humphrey Milford, Oxford University Press, 1921–1925);

London Shakespeare League, *Tercentenary of the Publication of the First Folio of Shakespeare's Works, Edited by John Heminge & Henry Condell, 1623,* preface by Lee ([London]: London Shakespeare League, [1923]);

University of London School of Journalism, *The Journalist in the Making: Being Points from Sixty Addresses Delivered to Journalism Diploma Students,* preface by Lee (London: Newspaper World Press, 1925).

SELECTED PERIODICAL PUBLICATIONS – UNCOLLECTED: "The Original of Shylock," *Gentleman's Magazine,* 248 (February 1880): 185–200;

"A New Study of 'Love's Labours Lost,' " *Gentleman's Magazine,* 249 (October 1880): 447–458;

"The Jews in England," *Times* (London), 1 November 1883, p. 1;

"An Elizabethan Bookseller," *Bibliographica,* 1, No. 4 (1895): 474–498;

"The Death of Queen Elizabeth: An Anniversary Study," *Cornhill Magazine,* 75 (3rd series, 2) (March 1897): 291–304;

"London County Council," *Quarterly Review,* 187 (January 1898): 259–275;

"Shakespeare and the Earl of Southampton," *Cornhill Magazine,* 77 (3rd series, 4) (April 1898): 482–495;

"Shakespeare in France," *Nineteenth Century,* 45 (June 1899): 930–937; reprinted in *Living Age,* 222 (19 August 1899): 515–521;

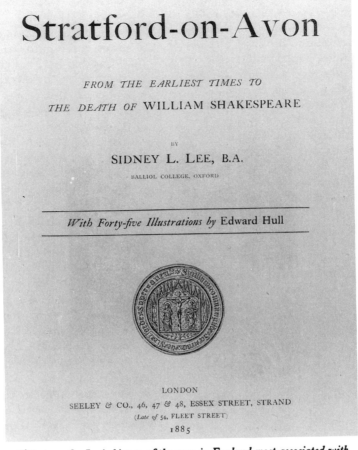

Stratford-on-Avon

FROM THE EARLIEST TIMES TO
THE DEATH OF WILLIAM SHAKESPEARE

BY
SIDNEY L. LEE, B.A.
BALLIOL COLLEGE, OXFORD

With Forty-five Illustrations by Edward Hull

LONDON
SEELEY & CO., 46, 47 & 48, ESSEX STREET, STRAND
(Late of 54, FLEET STREET)
1885

Title page for Lee's history of the area in England most associated with
William Shakespeare

"An Undescribed Copy of the Shakespeare First Folio," *Athenaeum,* 3747 (19 August 1899): 266–268;

" 'Beget' and 'Begetter' in Elizabethan English," *Athenaeum,* 3774 (24 February 1900): 250–251 and 3777 (17 March 1900): 345–346;

"Mr. Benson and Shakespearean Drama," *Cornhill Magazine,* 81 (3rd series, 8) (May 1900): 579–585;

"Shakespeare and Patriotism," *Cornhill Magazine,* 83 (3rd series, 10) (May 1901): 581–592; reprinted in *Critic,* 38 (June 1901): 529–535 and in *Living Age,* 229 (22 June 1901): 763–771;

"The American Method of Appointing University Professors," *Science,* new series, 18 (17 July 1903): 89–90;

"Books in Relation to National Efficiency," *Lamp,* 29 (December 1904): 411–420;

"The Commemoration of Shakespeare," *The Nineteenth Century and After,* 57 (April 1905): 585–600;

"Chapman's Amorous Zodiacke," *Modern Philology,* 3 (October 1905): 143–158;

"The Future of Shakespearian Research," *The Nineteenth Century and After,* 59 (May 1906): 763–768; reprinted in *Living Age,* 249 (23 June 1906): 709–717;

"Charlotte Bronte in London," *Cornhill Magazine,* 99 (3rd series, 26) (March 1909): 390–410; reprinted in *Living Age,* 261 (8 May 1909): 338–352;

"French Culture and Tudor England," *Fortnightly Review,* 91 (June 1909): 1135–1148;

"At a Journey's End," *The Nineteenth Century and After,* 72 (December 1912): 1155–1167; reprinted in *Living Age,* 276 (1 February 1913): 284–294;

"Caliban's Visits to England," *Cornhill Magazine,* 107 (3rd series, 34) (March 1913): 333–345;

"Arctic Exploration in Shakespeare's Era," *The Nineteenth Century and After,* 73 (April 1913): 749–772;

"Shakespeare and Public Affairs," *Contemporary Review,* 104 (August 1913): 173–182 and 104 (September 1913): 340–349; reprinted in *Living Age,* 279 (18 October 1913): 158–166 and 279 (22 November 1913): 479–486;

"Shakespeare Did Not Simply Report His Own Emotions; He Had the Power of Visualizing All from a Hint, and Vitalizing It," *New York Times,* Picture Section, Part 4: Shakespeare Tercentenary Supplement, 9 April 1916, p. [1];

"With the Anzacs in London," *Cornhill Magazine,* 114 (3rd series, 41) (December 1916): 680–691; reprinted in *Living Age,* 292 (20 January 1917): 141–149;

"King Edward and France," *Living Age,* 301 (21 June 1919): 737–746;

"More Doubts about Shakespeare," *Quarterly Review,* 232 (July 1919): 194–206;

"King Edward: New Chapters in His Life – Personal Tie with America. Sir Sidney Lee's Tribute," *Times* (London), 20 July 1921, p. 13;

"King Edward: New Chapters in His Life – Linking India with Britain, The Friend of Ireland," *Times* (London), 21 July 1921, p. 11;

"King Edward: New Chapters in His Life – Friendships with Statesmen, Rebukes for the Kaiser," *Times* (London), 22 July 1921, p. 11;

"Edward VII and the Entente," *Living Age,* 314 (22 July 1922): 193–198.

To the historians, literary scholars, publishers, and journalists who knew Sidney Lee well, he was one of the foremost authorities on Shakespeare and Elizabethan times, a widely known advocate for the preserving of Britain's cultural heritage, and, above all, the archetypal editor. Through his many years as both editor and contributor with the *Dictionary of National Biography (DNB),* as American publisher William Dana Orcutt recalled, Lee "knew everything about everybody" in contemporary British letters, scholarly endeavor, and cultural studies. Yet his geniality, discretion, and tact with others not only ensured the smooth pursuit of their shared interests but also earned Lee himself their respect and friendship.

Orcutt's anecdote of Lee's opposition, for example, to the publisher's intention to invite Alfred Austin, then poet laureate, to write an introductory essay for an important part of Orcutt's Shakespearean edition which Lee was to edit epitomizes Lee's clear expression of his professional judgment tempered by his diplomacy. "The office of Poet Laureate is a curious survival," Lee wrote, obliquely beginning his objection to his publisher.

> The duties consist of composing birthday odes and such trifles. There is no salary, but the poet finds a ready market for his works. He is, besides, I believe, entitled to an annual butt of wine, whether malmsey or not I do not know. . . . When it was suggested in the Commons that, in regard to the office of Poet Laureate, the holder might be held to have retired for good on the demise of a wearer of the Crown, in which case the poet might well be abolished, Lord Salisbury regarded the matter as entirely for the King's decision. The King, who had no great opinion of Mr. Austin, wrote on the point (March 26, 1901):

> "I always thought that Mr. Austin's appointment was not a good one, but as long as he gets no pay it would, I think, be best to renew the appointment in his favor. . . . The appointment was made by the prime minister."

> On 3d November, 1901, the King sent Lord Salisbury some verses by Mr. Austin, and called Lord Salisbury's attention to the "trash which the Poet Laureate writes."

Lee's disapproval of publisher Orcutt's intention, even as expressed in this private communication to him, is unmistakable – yet typically calm in tone, factual in manner. Beginning with an exposition of the historical basis for and the current details about the office of the laureate – all details which Lee felt likely to be unfamiliar to an American publisher – Lee presents his objections in a displaced manner – voicing them through King Edward VII – and in the concise, unemotional, fact-laden style (with dates carefully specified, for example) typical of *DNB* writing. Even in more pleasant situations than this, as one would expect, his characteristic graciousness and geniality were evident to all, both in his private relations and in such esprit de corps-building affairs as the celebratory dinners which he often presided over as editor of the *DNB.* One anonymous writer for the *London Mercury* (April 1926) recalled Lee as "one of the most likeable of men: confident, without parade, within his province, diffident beyond it: utterly free from pomposity and pedantry. . . . [His] personal help was constantly and quietly given to philanthropic and other public causes. . . . His dry humour . . . and great store of memories made him a delightful companion." Such a man made a good editor for the *Dictionary of National Biography* project, and of all Lee's accomplishments, it seems most fitting that that work remains the one which provides on library reference shelves everywhere just the kind of "public memorial" to

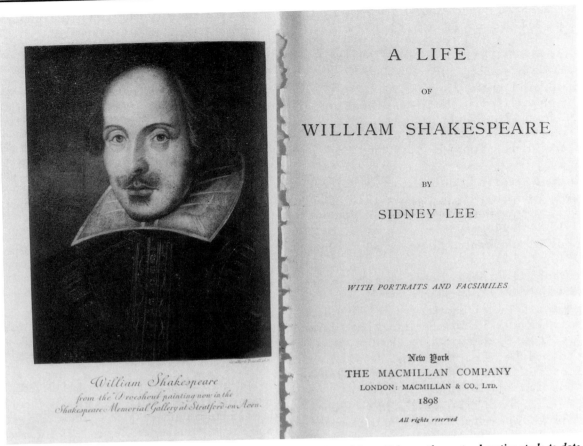

A LIFE

OF

WILLIAM SHAKESPEARE

BY

SIDNEY LEE

WITH PORTRAITS AND FACSIMILES

New York
THE MACMILLAN COMPANY
LONDON: MACMILLAN & CO., LTD.
1898

All rights reserved

William Shakespeare
*from the Droeshout painting now in the
Shakespeare Memorial Gallery at Stratford-on-Avon.*

Frontispiece and title page for Lee's biography of the Elizabethan playwright, which was the most exhaustive study to date

him that he had himself labored to create for others in the *DNB's* biographical entries.

The eldest son of Lazarus Lee and Jessie Davis Lee, a London merchant and his wife residing in Russell Square, Sidney Lee was born Solomon Lazarus Lee on 5 December 1859. The boy was educated under that name at the City of London School in Cheapside, where Dr. Edwin A. Abbott provided him and such Sixth Form classmates as Arthur Henry Bullen and Henry Charles Beeching with both inspiration for English literary study and a model for scholarly work. Dr. Abbott was not only a stimulating teacher who took special interest and enjoyment in Elizabethan literature but also, in another respect, an early model for what Lee would become: a historical scholar and a writer who actively engaged in and encouraged literary disputation.

As a commoner, Lee won an exhibition at Oxford's Balliol College, where he matriculated as Brackenbury history scholar in October 1878. His academic record there was undistinguished: he earned his B.A. in 1882, having achieved a third

class in classical moderations in 1880 and a second class in modern history in his final year. But many friendships he had made by then with such fellow students as Charles Harding Firth and scholarly mentors as J. O. Halliwell-Phillips, F. J. Furnivall, and Benjamin Jowett certainly provided opportunities, and new directions, for the young graduate's personal and professional development.

More than fifty years after Lee's undergraduate days, Orcutt, the American publisher and friend who had arranged for Lee to undertake both editing and American lecture tour ventures, recounted what was supposed to have moved the young graduate ultimately to change his name. Jowett, master of Balliol, is supposed to have advised Lee to divest himself of the potential "handicap" which Jowett foresaw in Lee's given names, "Solomon Lazarus," and to enhance his prospects for professional recognition by adopting the name "Sidney" as an alternative. This change, Orcutt reports Jowett felt, would provide Lee with an identity more amenable, that is, non-Jewish, to British society. Whether or not such a motive underlay the name change, both of the Shakespearean articles which the undergraduate published in the *Gentleman's Magazine* in 1880 are signed simply "S. L. Lee." This is also the case with a later brief piece on "The Jews in England," among the earliest of the innumerable letters Lee would direct to the editor of the London *Times* through the years. In any event, sometime after beginning his editorial work on the *Dictionary of National Biography*, "Solomon Lazarus" or "S. L." Lee did publicly and permanently become "Sidney" Lee.

As the date approached for Lee to complete his B.A., he served briefly as tutor to one of Lord Portsmouth's sons. In May 1882 he was offered, and began to consider accepting, a lectureship in English at a Dutch university in Groningen. But Furnivall, who had been so impressed with the undergraduate's aforementioned Shakespeare articles, arranged for Lee to edit Lord Berners's translation of *The Boke of Duke Huon of Burdeux* (1882–1887) for the Early English Text Society. And when publisher George Smith began seeking an assistant to work on his planned *DNB* under the editorship of Leslie Stephen, Furnivall also strongly recommended Lee for this position. Lee began his subeditorship in March 1883 at an annual salary of three hundred pounds; his work on the *DNB* was to provide both the soil and seeds for the most enduring and important parts of his literary career.

In choosing his assistant for the *DNB,* Stephen could not have made a more serendipitous appointment than that of the twenty-three-year-old Lee, whose abilities, interests, and temperament both reinforced and complemented those of Stephen. The editor had hoped to find an assistant who was, like himself, "a man of knowledge, good at abstracting," but who could also perform what he found less satisfying: the work of an excellent researcher, someone good at "looking up authorities," he wrote, as well as a conscientious editorial administrator, "a considerate autocrat" – "an efficient whip in regard to both printers and contributors." Stephen was a man of letters long used to moving at a pace and in directions prompted by his own will and curiosity, moving amid currents of ideas which surrounded many renowned figures whom he knew and had known personally – Thomas Carlyle; John Ruskin; Alfred, Lord Tennyson; Robert Browning; and other figures of great renown. A widely read, thoughtful man, Stephen possessed greater critical acumen than Lee, but *DNB* staff members insist that what the younger man brought to the editing of such a biographical project was both valuable and even essential.

For such a man as Stephen, the daily stresses and routines of editing the *DNB* soon grew overwhelming. The project, he wrote as early as 1888, was becoming a "damned thing [which] goes on . . . like a diabolical piece of machinery, always gaping for more copy" and threatening ultimately that he himself would "be dragged into it and crushed out into slips." "Much of the work to be done," he recalled in 1898, "was uninteresting, if not absolutely repulsive." But Lee's love of detail, his tireless conduct of historical and bibliographical research following clearly established procedures and formal routines, worked to ensure accuracy and thoroughness of treatment as well as the timely appearance of the *DNB* volumes which, every three months, were published with unbroken regularity. Lee was indeed the "considerate" yet "efficient whip" which Stephen had sought in his assistant.

Lee's scholarly and exact, as well as exacting, approach to the work was incorporated in what his fellow contributor and eventual assistant A. F. Pollard recalls Lee established and enforced among all the *DNB* staff: a set of "draconian rules of attendance and punctuality which were essential to the regular progress and publication of the *D.N.B.*" Assistant editors were expected to spend three hours every morning at work in the British Museum and four every afternoon – without even any standard break for tea – in the Waterloo Place offices of the *DNB,* "except for Saturdays, when the week-end began alternately at 1.30 or 3 p.m." "Detail was more congenial to [Lee] than to his chief [Leslie Stephen]," Pollard concludes, for Lee had a "passion for precision" and thoroughness which drove the assistant editor himself to work sixteen-hour stretches on some Saturdays and Sundays.

Lee, whom Stephen likewise praised for being such a "tireless worker," also differed from his chief by managing to sustain his equanimity in the face of verbose submissions, dilatory contributors, and other problems threatening to undermine the work's production methods, publication schedule, or general standards of quality. In this way, too, Lee proved to be an excellent colleague and lifelong friend to Stephen and the others who comprised what publisher George Smith called the *DNB* "family" of workers. Stephen had as early as 23 December 1882 in an *Athenaeum* article spelled out the focus and basic principles he was to pursue in editing the *DNB*: it would seek to commemorate only British and Commonwealth figures whose lives and achievements promised to fulfill the need of present and future generations to understand and appreciate the historical significance of these in the development of British life and culture. It would exclude from consideration the lives of all still-living figures, and it would necessarily reject any rhetorical or stylistic excesses borne of contributors' verbosity, sentimentality, or just plain bad judgment.

Lee enthusiastically subscribed to his older chief's principles. Indeed, he incorporated and expanded on the rationale for them in several of his own later papers following Stephen's withdrawal as editor and Lee's assumption of all editorial duties in 1891. But while the two men continued their teamwork as editor and assistant on the *DNB* until Stephen's health began to fail late in 1889, they divided editorial duties between them in such ways as to benefit fully from each man's particular strengths. Stephen, who disliked correcting proofs and verifying bibliographical references and did these tasks poorly, concentrated on working with original manuscripts and recruiting contributors. Lee meticulously corrected submissions, verified facts, questioned dubious statements, virtually rewrote some articles, added essential detail to others, and ruthlessly cut redundancies and any rhetorical offenses against that wry editorial precept which came to guide *DNB* contributors: "No flowers by request."

As one of the two editorial overseers of the project, Lee tacitly agreed with what Stephen insisted should be the chief criterion for assessing the value of their biographical dictionary. "The judicious critic is well aware," Stephen wrote in 1898, just before the first edition was to be completed, "that it is not upon the lives of the great men that the value of the book really depends. It is the second-rate people — the people whose lives have to be reconstructed from obituary notices, or from references in memoirs and collections of letters; or sought in prefaces to posthumous works; or sometimes painfully dug out of collections of manuscripts, and who really become generally accessible through the dictionary alone — that provide the really useful reading. There are numbers of such people whom one first discovers to be really interesting when the scattered materials are for the first time pieced together. Nobody need look at Addison or Byron or Milton in a dictionary. He can find fuller and better notices in every library." Only such a work as the *DNB* — "a confidential friend constantly at [one's] elbow, giving . . . a summary of the knowledge of antiquaries, genealogists, bibliographers, as well as historians, upon every collateral point which may happen for the moment to be relevant" to any one of the widest imaginable range of users with their individual interests — might fulfill those users'

needs to know, and to appreciate, the significance of those minor figures' lives within British cultural history.

Reviewers of the *DNB,* when its final volume appeared in 1900, praised it for succeeding in preserving a national record of the lives of just such figures as those Stephen had designated as "second-rate people." The bibliographical citations to its entries lent them an authority which reviewers found lacking in other biographical dictionaries, and the attention given by the *DNB* to information on where portraits of its subjects might be found also earned much approval. The *Athenaeum,* whose quarterly reviews of each new volume had appeared as dependably as the volumes themselves, had long decried many factual errors and omissions it had been finding over the more than fifteen years the work had been progressing. But its final review's summation on 2 May 1903 added to the general chorus of critical approbation: "We can, indeed, conceive no volume of reference more indispensible to the scholar, the literary man, the historian, and the journalist. . . . [T]he aim of the founders has been carried out, and the completed work constitutes a compact and trustworthy guide to the thinkers, rulers, administrators, writers, artists, captains, and experts of ten centuries of national life."

The New York Times likened the quality of many entries and the expertise of many contributors to those of the articles in the *Encyclopaedia Britannica,* and the 4 December 1901 London *Times* published a letter from an agent of the king, who congratulated Lee on completing "this great work" and especially on "the ability and research which have been shown by the writers, as well as by the admirable and careful way in which the work has been edited." Ironically, more than a decade later Lee would write in his controversial article on the king which appeared in the second supplement of the *DNB* that Edward VII "was no reader of books. He could not concentrate his mind on them." But the national euphoria and celebration aroused by the completion in 1901 of such an enormous achievement as the *DNB* either suspended or at least attenuated much serious criticism.

The most interesting and unusual notes of such criticism, however, were sounded in a review by Havelock Ellis, the controversial advocate of scientific social progress. Ellis's perspective of the *DNB,* he claimed, was that of a new class of thinker — one who wished that the *DNB* biographies and its methods had been informed by "scientific modes of thought developed during [the last] century" in such new studies as psychology, anthropology, and

Lee in his study

sociology. Unfortunately, Ellis continued, "when the Dictionary was planned, such methods, as applied in these fields, were less developed and less widely known than they are now beginning to be," and consequently, "though the data with which the national biographers had usually to be content could not satisfy a scientific mind, the recognition of scientific methods would greatly have aided their work."

What Ellis wanted is what biographical writing became more frequently after the publication of Lytton Strachey's *Eminent Victorians* (1918) nearly two decades later. Ellis's review called for more "personal description," and a more complex kind of biographical detail, than the *DNB* afforded: the presentation of psychologically illuminating "personal facts" which show that the biographer has intimately come to know the "exact manner of man that an eminent personage appeared [to be] in the flesh to his contemporaries." Such details alone, he felt, could convey the biographer's understanding of what literary historian Richard D. Altick has since described as "the inner, not the outer, life" of the biographer's subject – those motives, values, temperaments, anxieties, or other characteristic psy-

chological and emotional predispositions which a subject had developed and which necessarily helped explain the complex figure that, throughout a lifetime, his contemporaries had known.

To Lee such biography writing would not have fulfilled the aim of the *DNB* and its staff of national biographers. As he had clearly, repeatedly insisted in his paper (soon afterward republished as a monograph) "National Biography" (1896), their biographies sought to gratify British "commemorative aspirations," rather than to illuminate any individual subject's presumed character or "inner life." Such commemoration necessarily required them, as national biographers, to adopt an extremely concise style and rigorously selective approach, rather than to seek to provide the kind of full, presumably sound psychological characterization of their subjects that Ellis was seeking.

Lee seemed to concede to such criticism as Ellis's in a later paper on "Principles of Biography" (1911), saying that any biography does seek to gratify its reader's "commemorative instinct" through "its power to transmit personality." And in pursuing this aim, the biographer necessarily "proposes to himself to work from without inwards," Lee acknowledged in a final important paper on "The Perspective of Biography" (1918). However, the biographer's work must constitute not an imaginative, interpretive creation but "a compilation, an industriously elaborated composition," and his method of "discovery, not invention." What he offers is not any "nebulous impressionist study" but his carefully induced "conceptions of the truth about the piece of humanity which he is studying."

Even in his last years, Lee continued to express this nineteenth-century scholar's skepticism about the validity and reliability of the interpretations which many contemporary biographers were offering of their subjects and of their subjects' achievements. "National biography is a branch of scholarly literature, and like all scholarly literature, it must be scrupulously exact and definite in statement, with all its references carefully verified," Lee had insisted even in the first of these three major papers he had presented on writing biography: "the more familiar art of individual biography . . . ought to lie within the domain of scholarly literature, though we often observe it stray beyond the fold." The implications of such views help modern readers understand Lee's strengths — and limitations — in the three full-length biographies he wrote, all of which he composed as expanded versions of *DNB* articles he had written. His training as a student of history and of literature, in addition to his apprenticeship as a *DNB* editor and biographer under Leslie Stephen's mentoring, had made him a nineteenth-century scholar: in statements of his principles, Lee was never comfortable with, curious about, or even very sympathetic to interpretations which some assumptions and methods of such new studies as developmental psychology or anthropology might have contributed to his studies of Shakespeare or Queen Victoria.

While Lee's attention had been dominated before 1901 by the demands of editing and writing for the *DNB,* he had managed to pursue some other interests he had held after leaving Oxford in 1882. In 1885 he had published a history of Shakespeare's native environs, *Stratford-on-Avon: From the Earliest Times to the Death of William Shakespeare,* which went through several editions before Lee revised and enlarged it in 1907. *The Topical Side of the Elizabethan Drama* (1886), his first book of literary history, soon followed, and his edition of *The Autobiography of Edward, Lord Herbert of Cherbury* also appeared in the same year with Lee's introductory essay, notes, appendices, and a closing biographical narrative added. Lee revised this edition of the autobiography in 1906, but long before then it had become the

focus of a contention between him and publisher William Gibbings, who had purchased the copyright to the work Lee had initially edited for publisher John C. Nimmo and had republished it in what a perturbed Lee called a "mutilated" edition in 1892. This dispute was conducted both in the courts and in the pages of the *Athenaeum* in 1892, and late that year it was published as *Lee Versus Gibbings.*

Lee's interests in Elizabethan history and literature continued through the end of the 1880s, when Leslie Stephen's illness required Lee's assumption of added editorial responsibilities with the *DNB.* His research on *Elizabethan England and the Jews* (1888) appeared about this time, and in 1890 Lee began serving a thirty-five-year tenure as president of the Elizabethan Literary Society. Frederick Rogers, the social reformer and labor leader whose program organizing for this society had made him the most influential figure in it, had previously drawn Lee into membership as an honorary vice-president. After the society's headquarters moved in 1886 to Toynbee Hall, an early university settlement aimed at bringing extension classes to working-class audiences and expanding social intercourse between them and university men, Lee contributed to the development of the society by involving growing numbers of Elizabethan scholars and men of letters in what had been, largely, a workingman's organization. A frequent lecturer on historical and literary topics before this group, Lee subsequently published one such address on "The Study of English Literature" in 1893, and in 1896 another important address on *National Biography* that he had given before the Royal Institution was published.

The appearance of volume fifty-one of the *DNB* in July 1897 included Lee's most demanding biographical effort, his most sustained research into Elizabethan history and literature. His article on William Shakespeare, a nearly fifty-page contribution which was to be the longest in the entire *DNB,* aroused calls for its expansion into a full-length, authoritative biography and assessment of the poet's work. In November 1898 Lee responded with *A Life of William Shakespeare,* and, like the *DNB* article which had been its precursor, it was enthusiastically received. The book quickly went through four editions in two months and was revised in 1904 and 1909 editions before being enlarged and rewritten in 1915, in anticipation of Shakespearean tercentenary celebrations. In all, the book appeared in fourteen editions, the last being published in 1931 under the auspices of Oxford University's

Board of English Studies, to which Lee had bequeathed the copyright after his death in 1926.

The biography aimed to dismiss the commonplace that very little was known, or was ever likely to be known, about the life of England's greatest dramatist and poet. To compose the definitive biography of Shakespeare, Lee sought "to provide students with a full record of the duly attested facts and dates" of the artist's life and to authorize these by providing "verifiable references to all the original sources of information." These aims echo those Lee had maintained for *DNB* writers, and his fidelity to them in expanding his article into what was to be the standard biography of Shakespeare required him to reassemble all the details he had amassed from his wide reading of other Shakespeareans as well as from his own eighteen years of laborious research into Elizabethan parish records, legal documents, playbill notices, and other resources to ascertain all that might be discovered about such things as the artist's parents and their family backgrounds; Shakespeare's birth, childhood, adolescence, and early marriage; and the unfolding of his associations with the London theatre. But Lee did even more than this.

To these details of Shakespeare's life Lee added his equally impressive knowledge of Elizabethan and Continental literary history in presenting what he had discovered to be the facts of Shakespeare's career as an actor, poet, playwright, and theater manager — a knowledge necessary to provide readers with informed bases for making good readings of Shakespeare's works. Who might have been the likely "Mr. W. H." to whom the publisher of Shakespeare's sonnets dedicated them? Who was the "dark lady" of the sonnets — or was there any real, living source for this figure in the sequence? What features of the Elizabethan stage did Shakespeare have available to establish the physical setting, and modify any corresponding atmosphere, of particular scenes? Such historical questions about textual facts, sources or literary influences, and literary conventions all received in Lee's biography the attention which his fellow *DNB* contributor E. I. Carlyle praised for providing "a reliable basis for sound aesthetic appreciation" of Shakespeare's work, despite Lee's repeated distaste for any "merely aesthetic criticism" which his preface disclaimed any intention to offer.

Lee's respect for the primacy and the authority of historical facts as the basis for any sound understanding and full appreciation of the biographical subject's accomplishments remain at the forefront of his Shakespearean study, as well as of those later biographies he wrote. Many readers and critics less well informed than Lee — like those whose objections to his biography derived from their dedication to such notions as that which held Sir Francis Bacon to be the actual author of Shakespeare's work — tried the temper of such a biographer as Lee, who was always disturbed with those whose conclusions or literary interpretations had no sound historical support or rational basis.

The most approving reviews of the biography were those pleased by Lee's commitment to the discovery and presentation of such historical fact. "[The book] is a marvel of research," concluded one anonymous reviewer for the London *Times* (22 November 1898), which found Lee's study "on the whole, remarkably temperate, judicious, and convincing." "[W]ith regard to . . . the circumstances of [Shakespeare's] external life," agreed another anonymous reviewer in the 21 October 1899 *Living Age,* "Mr. Lee is justified in maintaining that we have very adequate information in the 'mass of details' which modern research has gathered together" and to which Lee himself habitually "appeals to establish the truth . . . of Shakespeare's career, and to refute the legends which have been built up around it." As a result, "If . . . we wish to know how Shakespeare walked the earth, and under what circumstances his transcendent dramas were produced," the reviewer concluded, "we cannot have a better guide than Mr. Lee."

But Havelock Ellis's dismay at the completed biographies of the *DNB* in 1900 was foreshadowed, in a restrained manner, by some readers of the Shakespeare biography who regretted Lee's unwillingness to try to treat either such works as the sonnets or those biographical facts of the artist's life as kinds of textual matter — as material with which a biographer, himself a judicious interpreter of his human subject, might legitimately be expected to construct a "personality" of Shakespeare. Lee's preface had stated that he intended to avoid "merely aesthetic criticism" of Shakespeare's works, for the biographer's assessments of those works were offered "solely to fulfill the obligation that lies on the biographer of indicating succinctly the character of the successive labors which were wrought into the texture of [Shakespeare's] life." As a biographer, Lee adamantly continued to express his belief that the focus of his study of Shakespeare lay on the man himself: the works were of interest chiefly for what an informed awareness of them might contribute to an understanding of the man's life — his relations with patrons, other playwrights, or actors, for instance — and not to any "merely aesthetic" appreciation of their artistry or to any understanding of the artist's personality or psychological profile they might invite one to construct.

Even many who applauded Lee's biography for its marshaling of facts about the life of the poet voiced some reservations about Lee's position, as did the reviewer for *Living Age* in regretting that "in spite of all the research which is summed up in Mr. Lee's pages, it remains true . . . that we know very little of Shakespeare's life" and ironically remain "very far from possessing that intimate knowledge of the poet which a biography should give us" – an intimate knowledge of his character, "a picture of what he was." "We still have the vision of a biography of Shakespeare," the reviewer concluded, "which shall tell us not less of what he did and more of what he was."

This rather impersonal Shakespeare also contributed to the controversy generated by the most innovative proposal Lee offered in his discussions of Shakespeare's literary work. Readers had long assumed that Shakespeare's sonnets, however enigmatic the characters and relationships presented in them, were to be read literally – that is, were to be regarded as autobiographically revealing documents. To Lee, however, they comprised Shakespeare's exercises in a poetic vein which had enjoyed a long history among such Continental poets as Petrarch and his successors and which had become quite fashionable in the 1590s among such Elizabethan poets as Sir Philip Sidney, Samuel Daniel, and Michael Drayton. Ever the historian of literary study, Lee drew on his knowledge of French and Italian Renaissance sonneteers to present an extensive, detailed argument that Shakespeare's sonnets afforded no more personal, biographical revelations about their author than do those of other poets who wrote in this literary convention.

Even following the appearance in 1915 of Lee's rewritten biography, nearly doubled in length after incorporating new findings since the appearance of the first edition in 1898, Lee continued in a 9 April 1916 *New York Times* Shakespeare tercentenary article to dispute what he saw as the misreadings of "the modern impressionist critic" who "claims that well nigh every sentiment and sensation which Shakespeare dramatically feigned is a piece of the poet's private emotion; and that his work finally resolves itself into a massive series of autobiographic revelations or transcripts of personal experience." Not only in dramatic works but also in such lyric poetry as the sonnets, where a poet may appear to be speaking in his own voice, Lee insisted, such works are really giving their

readers only "an illusion of personal confession." Through the calculated, self-dramatizing persona of Shakespeare's sonnets, their "meditative passion . . . seriously qualifies their title to rank with documents of autobiography." The historian's respect for facts and the *DNB* editor's skeptical determination to permit only the most carefully reasoned conclusions from them remained a central principle of Lee's pronouncements on biographical writing.

Years later, another *New York Times* retrospective of "Lee's 'Life' and Shakespeare," which appeared on 5 March 1926, soon after publication of the thirteenth and last edition of the biography to appear in Lee's lifetime, offered this most succinct and equitable estimate of his landmark study:

> Lee carefully sifted fact from tradition and fancy, added results of his own wide researches into Elizabethan biography and records of all sorts, carefully digested and incorporated a rich store of "finds" by others, and presented the whole with a keen eye for perspective, unfailing candor and scholarly acumen. The result is, if not a biography of the first order, yet a work far more valuable than many that are accepted as such.
>
> What it lacks is not so much "the wizardry of words" as the perception of life and character . . . which, in a biographer of Shakespeare, alone make that wizardry possible. . . . Of all this [current biographical writing which proceeds by attempting to merge psychological analyses with chronological, factual narrative] Lee will have nothing.

"Virtually without exception," the review concluded, "competent critics agree . . . that 'there *is* a certain connection between the life and the works of Shakespeare'. . . . Yet the myth-making instinct persists and is not less pernicious for having invaded the field of . . . psychology. Sir Sidney's destructive rage [at the results of such a "myth-making instinct"] is the defect of the quality that placed him, and still maintains him, as the supreme biographer of Shakespeare."

The extensive historical research and study of Elizabethan texts which Lee had done in compiling his original *DNB* article and then expanding it into his full biography of Shakespeare provided a wealth of information which, following publication of the biography in 1898, Lee incorporated in further studies. *Shakespeare and the Earl of Pembroke* had also appeared around 1898, and Lee followed this with *A Catalogue of Shakespeareana, The Shakespeare First Folio: Some Notes and a Discovery,* and *Shakespeare's Handwriting: Facsimiles of the Five Authentic Autograph Signatures of the Poet,* all three published in 1899. A study of *Shakespeare's Henry V* (1900) followed, along with *Shakespeare's Life and Work* (1900), an abridged version of his biography which was intended for student use. This abridgment found an audience wide enough to necessitate its republication in a revised edition in 1907. New academic honors and responsibilities also came to Lee in 1900 when he was awarded an honorary degree from Manchester University and was appointed as the first chairman of the Board of Studies in History at the University of London.

In 1901 growing recognition of Lee's work as editor of the *DNB* and of his contributions, as a man of letters, in literary and historical studies resulted in his election to membership in the Athenaeum Club, a London society of accomplished figures in literature, sciences, and the arts. An article on Shakespeare which Lee had contributed to *Chambers's Encyclopedia of English Literature* was reprinted in America by J. B. Lippincott. In April, however, the sudden death of publisher George Smith, only about six months after the appearance of the sixty-third and final volume of the *DNB,* presented Lee with the responsibility for writing a memoir to be inserted in the first of three *Supplement* volumes of the dictionary then in progress. Elizabeth Smith, the publisher's widow to whom the operations of the *DNB* were bequeathed, provided information, including fragments of autobiographical materials left by her husband, and Lee, who had known the founder-publisher of the *DNB* since the beginning of his editorial assistantship with it, wrote a forty-page "Memoir of George Smith" which was published as a preface to that first volume of the *Supplement* (1901). It was subsequently republished in a collection of other essays compiled by Mrs. Smith and titled *George Smith: A Memoir with Some Pages of Autobiography* (1902). George Smith had headed the Smith, Elder publishing house since 1846 and had published, in addition to *The Cornhill Magazine* and *The Pall Mall Gazette,* the poetry, prose, and fiction of an unusually large number of leading authors, so Lee's memoir recounted Smith's long career as an important chapter in the history of Victorian literature.

Lee had begun to edit, shortly after the final volume of the *DNB* had appeared, its several *Supplement* volumes which were to include articles on people who had been inadvertently omitted from presentation, or who had died during that 1885–1900 period – but after the particular volume in which they would have been included had been published. Only three months before George Smith's death, however, the death of Queen Victoria had ensured that the *Supplement* volumes would include a major

article on a royal figure, and Smith had asked that Lee write this entry. His article on the late queen was completed in time for publication in the final volume of the *Supplement* in October 1901, and, just as his Shakespeare article had aroused interest in having its treatment expanded into a full-length biography, Lee was again called on to rewrite a fully detailed biography of the queen from his article. *Queen Victoria: A Biography* was published in 1902.

He complied, expanding his article with details selected from many kinds of immediately available resources which his Shakespeare study could not have relied on: already-published memoirs and personal reminiscences of ministers and political figures who had known the queen, newspaper articles and periodical notices which recorded important events and dates in her life, and some personal diary excerpts which the queen had herself previously published – as well as many personal letters which she had written to various ministers, relatives, and friends. Not all the queen's personal papers, her letters and diaries, were available so soon after her death. But from the available resources Lee sought, as he stated in the biography's preface, "to let the Queen speak for herself." This, presumably, could allow Lee to characterize her more fully, more personally than he had been able to characterize Shakespeare in his previous biography.

His aims, as his preface indicated, remained loyal to those courtroomlike ones which had guided all his writing for the *DNB*: to record clearly, concisely, and coherently "the main facts known to [him] concerning the Queen's personal history" and throughout the work "to present facts fully, truthfully, and impartially." This was important because, to Victoria herself, "[t]ruth . . . was an enduring passion." But biographer Lee also insisted on the importance of presenting the truths "in a spirit of sympathy as well as in a spirit of justice." Details of the "extended political history" which were commingled with her life were necessary to "touch on," but Lee pledged "to avoid treating such topics in any fuller detail than was needful to make her personal experiences and opinions intelligible." Political matters were largely "the scenery of every sovereign's biography," he acknowledged, but as a biographer his duty was "to subordinate his scenery to the actor who [was] alone his just concern."

While the selection of details in *Queen Victoria: A Biography* does sometimes seem to constitute little more than a recitation of events which might have been scheduled on the queen's daily calendar, Lee's presentation of them does seek to provide more personal characterization of her than had been possible

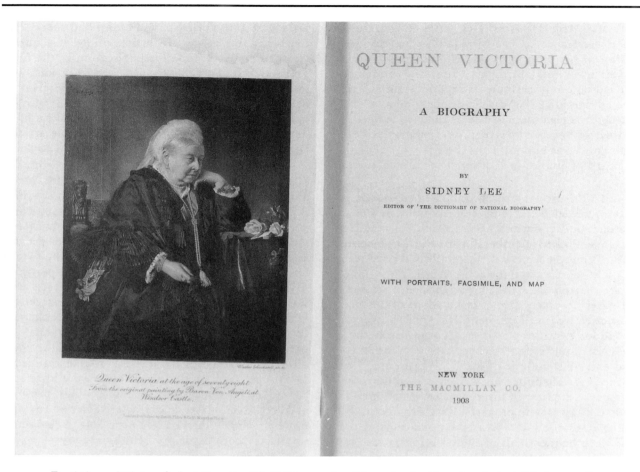

QUEEN VICTORIA

A BIOGRAPHY

BY

SIDNEY LEE

EDITOR OF 'THE DICTIONARY OF NATIONAL BIOGRAPHY'

WITH PORTRAITS, FACSIMILE, AND MAP

NEW YORK
THE MACMILLAN CO.
1903

Frontispiece and title page for Lee's biography of the British monarch, which was based on his work on her in the Dictionary of National Biography

to achieve for Shakespeare in that previous biography. At their best, in his closing chapter on "The Queen's Position and Character," for instance, the details of the narrative have provided bases for making the general assessments which Lee, still writing biography more as a historian than as a psychologist, offers about the woman who had been queen – and about significant political and social changes which had transpired during her reign.

What was so striking to reviewers of *Queen Victoria: A Biography* was Lee's frankness in presenting her character, as well as her very often discordant, stressful relations with those who, as her prime ministers, had increasingly acquired more of the real power in governing nineteenth-century England. Lee candidly acknowledged such personal peccadilloes as the queen's congenital prejudices, her obstinacy, her meager intellect, her unwittingly ironic hostility to and curt dismissal of women's rights issues, or her "morbid" preoccupation with death and its attendant sorrows and suffering. Victoria's death

had raised to new heights the reverence which she had increasingly attracted in the last years of her rule, and such candor as Lee's risked offending those moved by this flood of sympathy which her death had unleashed. In addition, influential members and associates of the royal family might also readily have objected to Lee's violating contemporary canons of appropriateness in composing such a royal biography.

Lee, however, managed to mitigate any offense which his bluntness and honesty might have evoked. He did so, first, by generally immersing his acknowledgment of the queen's weaknesses in that genuinely sympathetic feeling which his preface had promised to adopt as the proper posture for the biographer – and, secondly, by seeking repeatedly to link his acknowledgment of her weaknesses with some strong social values and ideals, or with some often unexpectedly positive consequences. His closing assessment of her unpredictable willfulness, prejudices, and sparse intelligence demonstrates such rhetorical procedures Lee used either to excuse the queen's objectionable features or to ameliorate them, ironically, by associating something admirable with them:

> To the movement for the greater emancipation of women she was thoroughly and almost blindly antipathetic. For women to speak in public or associate themselves with public movements was in her sight almost unpardonable. She never realized that her own position gave the advocates of Women's Rights their strongest argument, and when that point of view was pressed on her attention in conversation, she treated it as an irrelevance. . . . Queen Victoria's whole life and action were, indeed, guided by personal sentiment rather than by reasoned principles. But her personal sentiment, if not altogether removed from the commonplace, nor proof against occasional inconsistencies, bore ample trace of courage, truthfulness, and sympathy with suffering. Far from being an embodiment of selfish whim, the Queen's personal sentiment blended in its main current sincere love of public justice with staunch fidelity to domestic duty. . . . In her capacity alike of monarch and woman, the Queen's personal sentiment proved, on the whole, a safer guide than the best-devised systems of moral or political philosophy.

Modern biographers might condemn this as sophistry, but no contemporary reviews of *Queen Victoria: A Biography* – not even American ones – were disposed to do so.

Lee's assessments of the queen's reign as an era in British political and social history also attracted the attention of many reviewers, nearly all of whom agreed with Lee that, under Victoria, the monarch's power in governing the expanding empire had continued to decay; however much royal influence, as measured by the queen's personal popularity as a figurehead of that imperial power, had increased by the end of her reign. As a historical study of Queen Victoria's times, Lee's biography presents a wealth of detail, notwithstanding his preface's pledge to treat political details as mere "scenery" of the biography. Reviews such as that of the April 1903 *Lamp* were pleased with this: "Mr. Lee has given the royal influence its full value and has portrayed the Queen with a tactful fidelity and a courtesy which would have done credit to Lord Beaconsfield himself," wrote reviewer John Finley, perhaps disingenuously allowing Lord Beaconsfield's reputation as a flattering manipulator to pass without many second thoughts. "Royal *influence* did increase, and that through the force and appeal of her character and homely virtues, but the royal *power* was diminished. This loss is attributed [by Lee's biography] partly to her respect for the consti-

tution, partly to the growth of democratic principles. But, whatever the cause, the Crown in her reign lost its personal authority over the army, its prerogatives of mercy, and much of its old appointive power; and it lost, too, through failure to comply with the old forms [by which the monarch addressed Parliament at its opening session], the 'semblance of hold on the central force of government.' "

Others, such as the anonymous reviewer for the April 1903 *Bookman,* were also grateful for Lee's tracing of these political changes in his book, which was praised for being "more than a mere biography; it has a definite historical value" – particularly for "the light that [Lee] throws upon the Queen's personal characteristics, her temperament, and especially her relation to the inner history of her reign." Even Charles W. Colby, the most reserved American reviewer of the biography, agreed in the July 1903 *American Historical Review* that "The praise which Mr. Lee merits is that . . . of having won the success which is due to honesty, and of having written the best sketch of the Queen's character in relation to her reign." The biography was published in an American edition in 1903 and was revised in yet another edition published in 1904. Subsequent biographies of Queen Victoria, of course, have profited from having access to richer and more varied resources than Lee found at hand in the years immediately following her death, and these later studies provide more definitive biographies of the queen for today's reader. But as C. H. Firth, in his memoir of Lee, says of the *DNB* article and the subsequent full biography, "Its production in 1901 was a remarkable feat."

After *Queen Victoria: A Biography,* Lee resumed the pursuit of his two primary interests – Shakespearean studies, and Elizabethan history and literature. He wrote a significant introductory essay for a volume he edited of facsimile reprints of *Shakespeare's Comedies, Histories, & Tragedies* (1902) for the Clarendon Press and published *Shakespeare in Oral Tradition* (1902) along with *A Census of Extant Copies of the First Folio* (1902). This last volume was supplemented several years later with the publication of *Notes & Additions to the Census of Copies of the Shakespeare First Folio* (1906).

Early in 1903 Lee began an eighteen-week lecture tour of the United States, a most unusual undertaking for one who had not been initially regarded as a good lecturer and who had never ventured beyond his native British soil. His tour included stops at numerous universities – among them Columbia, Harvard, Yale, Brown, Princeton, Cornell, Northwestern, the University of Chicago, the University of Wisconsin–Madison, Vassar, Wellesley, Bryn Mawr, Wells College, Johns Hopkins, and the University of North Carolina. Eight of these lectures given in Boston constituted the 1903 Lowell Institute Series and covered "Great Englishmen of the Sixteenth Century." These addresses were subsequently collected and published under that title in 1904 in both American and British editions, and a final British edition was republished in 1925. Four other lectures in Lee's repertoire were given, at Johns Hopkins, as the 1903 Donovan lectures on "Foreign Influences in Elizabethan Literature." In these Lee outlined ideas on French and Italian influences which he was to develop more fully in a lecture series at Oxford in 1909. These ideas were still later incorporated in *The French Renaissance in England* (1910) and *Shakespeare and the Italian Renaissance* (1915). Two other lectures, one on Shakespearean biography and another on the study of English as an academic discipline, comprised the total of fourteen addresses which Lee very successfully presented to various audiences. During the tour he met President Theodore Roosevelt, Mark Twain, and Andrew Carnegie as well as many influential American scholars and men of letters, including Shakespeareans Brander Matthews, W. J. Rolfe, and Horace Howard Furness.

While Lee had been lecturing in the United States, his *Dictionary of National Biography: Index and Epitome* (1903), more commonly known as the *Concise DNB,* was being published. This was followed by *The Dictionary of National Biography: Errata* (1904), three hundred small-print pages which reveal how meticulously Lee, as editor, undertook the task of trying to establish and maintain for the dictionary a reputation for accuracy. *The Supremacy of Petrarch* (1904) and two essays published as part of *The Cambridge Modern History* – "The Last Years of Elizabeth" and "The Elizabethan Age of English Literature" – both appeared in 1904. Lee also edited and wrote an introductory essay for one- and two-volume editions of *Elizabethan Sonnets* in that same year.

In 1905 he edited for the Clarendon Press another series of five facsimile Shakespearean texts: *Shakespeare's Lucrece, Shakespeare's Pericles, Shakespeare's Sonnets, Shakespeare's Venus and Adonis,* and *The Passionate Pilgrim.* A paper on Samuel Pepys and Shakespeare which Lee had presented to the Samuel Pepys Club late in 1905 was published as *Pepys and Shakespeare* (1906), and *Notes & Additions to the Census of Copies of the Shakespeare First Folio* (1906) also appeared as the publication of a twenty-volume American edition of *The Complete Works of William Shakespeare* (1906–1908) was beginning under Lee's gen-

eral editorship. For this elaborate edition Lee contributed annotations throughout and wrote a general introduction as well as prefaces to some of the individual plays. This was subsequently republished by another American firm in forty volumes before its British republication in twenty volumes as *The Caxton Edition of the Complete Works of William Shakespeare* (1910). Late in 1906 Lee collected and published a series of eleven essays in *Shakespeare and the Modern Stage,* the title essay offering a study of how differences between the staging of Shakespearean plays in Elizabethan times and in the early twentieth century significantly influenced the writing, production, and audience's appreciation of those works.

In 1907 Lee was awarded honorary degrees by both Oxford and Glasgow Universities, and he began a long term of service as registrar of the Royal Literary Fund, a society founded to aid writers and their dependents in distress. *Four Quarto Editions of Plays by Shakespeare* (1908) was reprinted at Stratford-upon-Avon under Lee's editorship for the Trustees and Guardians of Shakespeare's Birthplace: Lee wrote the preface for this edition, which included *The Merchant of Venice* (circa 1596), *A Midsummer Night's Dream* (circa 1596), *King Lear* (circa 1605), and *The Merry Wives of Windsor* (1602). In 1909 he edited a facsimile of *The Chronicle History of King Leir,* which intrigued Lee for the interesting study it provided of Shakespeare's artistry in adapting and transforming historical narratives as sources of his dramas. *The Impersonal Aspect of Shakespeare's Art* (1909) expounded once again Lee's position on the question of the relationship that existed between the artist's own life, character, and experiences – and those depicted in his artistic creations. Lee compiled a catalogue titled *A Shakespeare Reference Library* (1909), initially as a pamphlet for the English Association before he republished as a monograph that same year. He had in 1906 been among the founders of the association, which aimed to promote the teaching and study of both the English language and English literature. Lee became its president in 1917 and remained an active member throughout his life: he revised his Shakespearean pamphlet catalogue, with the assistance of Sir Edward Chambers, for the association in 1925, and served as the first editor of its journal, *The Year's Work in English Studies,* in 1921.

After some two decades of having advocated various measures to ensure the preservation of documents by institutions or agencies which would maintain their accessibility to the public as well as to scholars, Lee was appointed in 1910 to the

Royal Commission on Public Records. He was also elected a fellow of the British Academy and, late that same year, published *The French Renaissance in England,* a work which traced the role that sixteenth-century French writers had played in fostering and purveying the Renaissance spirit to British writers in Elizabethan times. Its preface's claim that "every great national literature is a fruit of much foreign sustenance and refreshment, however capable the national spirit may prove of mastering the foreign element," propounded one of the premises underlying a new type of literary study — that of comparative literature. Lee's pioneering efforts in such work, which he had begun as early as his 1903 lectures in America and his introductory essay to *Elizabethan Sonnets* (1904), distinguished him in the eyes of a 4 December 1910 *New York Times* reviewer as "the leading exponent in England to-day" of such comparative and historical literary studies.

In 1911 another of his studies, "The Elizabethan Sonnet," appeared in volume three of *The Cambridge History of English Literature,* and Lee was elected president — for the first of fifteen successive annual terms — of London's Sunday Shakespeare Society. Soon after delivering his Leslie Stephen Lecture on "Principles of Biography" at Cambridge in May, Lee was granted knighthood — in recognition of his service as editor of the *DNB* and as chairman of the executive committee for the Shakespeare's Birthday Trust at Stratford-upon-Avon. This recognition of his *DNB* work came shortly after he had begun preparing in October 1910 to edit the *Second Supplement* of the *DNB* (1912), three more volumes which Mrs. George Smith was determined to publish in order to fulfill her deceased husband's plan for his biographical dictionary. George Smith had always intended to continue adding new volumes at regular intervals, to maintain thereby the work's commemorative and reference values for its readers, by including biographies of those who were deemed worthy of such recognition and who had died since publication of its last volume.

Editing this *Second Supplement,* which was to include those who had died between January 1901 and December 1911, proved more arduous for Lee than editing the previous *Supplement* had been. Its standards for inclusion seemed more lenient than those for the first: the volumes of the *Second Supplement* included biographies on over six hundred additional figures and required over eight hundred pages more than the first *Supplement.* Furthermore, several of those who had comprised the staff of regular contributors to the original dictionary were no longer available: many had died and were themselves to be commemorated in the new *Supplement.* Lee therefore had to recruit and train many new contributors while the work was in progress, in addition to resuming his familiar editorial duties and writing, himself, many articles on some of his former *DNB* coworkers, such as Leslie Stephen, and on some of his former Shakespearean colleagues.

Among the articles Lee wrote for this *Second Supplement* was a long biography of King Edward VII, an article which, appearing in the first of the three volumes, attracted much attention. The London *Times* gave the article a separate review from that given the first volume upon its 6 June 1912 appearance, and the article's reviewer, while praising Lee's "careful preparation and judgment" in writing it, uneasily found some of what he had to say of King Edward "not altogether agreeable reading." Prince Albert, Edward's father, appeared to have been not as wise a father as many had believed before his death in 1861, for the reviewer found Lee's biography made the prince consort's great influence on the queen, even after his death, a serious handicap to young Edward's learning to assume responsibilities for the conduct of state affairs. A *New York Times* (7 June 1912) reviewer wryly noticed Lee's "use of constructive imagination" in characterizing King Edward as being "prone to intellectual dissipation, rather shallow, pleasure loving, and essentially indolent." But another popular London newspaper was quite upset with such "tactlessness" and "gaucherie" it found in Lee's essay, and yet another reported that King George V was "in a rage over the biography of his father" and intended to arrange for a more satisfactory royal biography to be commissioned.

Lee's immediate response to such attacks was to defend his essay as a biography worthy of the high standards for accuracy and credibility of the *DNB,* "a work of historical reference, which exists to furnish the historical student with carefully treated facts in as concise a form as is consistent with completeness." Nearly a decade later, Lee himself would begin researching and writing, at the request and with the assistance of King George V, a full-length biography of King Edward VII like that which critics of his *DNB* article were calling for.

Following publication of the *Second Supplement,* Lee edited an *Index and Epitome* (1913) for it, in addition to publishing *The Place of English Literature in the Modern University* in October 1913. This last work was initially presented as an address at East London College, where Lee had been appointed to a new professorship of English language and literature in

Drawing of Lee from a portrait by Professor William Rothenstein

the University of London. He remained as editor of the *DNB* until June 1917, after the death of Reginald Smith in December 1916 had marked the impending dissolution of the Smith, Elder publishing house. The heirs of founder George Smith had decided to award the copyright and stock of the *DNB* to Oxford University. So after 1913 and until his retirement in 1924, Lee's livelihood shifted primarily to teaching and academic administration.

In 1916, the year of Shakespeare tercentenary celebrations, Lee published *A Catalogue of the Shakespeare Exhibition Held in the Bodleian Library to Commemorate the Death of Shakespeare, April 23, 1616* and wrote a preface for *Stratford-upon-Avon: Shakespeare's Birthplace,* another exhibition catalogue compiled by Frederick C. Wellstood. He also edited *Shakespeare's England* (1916), a two-volume collection of historical essays describing the daily life and manners of the time. Lee had begun editing this collection — to which he was to contribute one coauthored essay —

in 1909, but he had had to suspend his work on it in 1911, and the volumes were finally completed under the editorship of Charles Talbot Onions.

Shakespeare and the Red Cross, a Shakespearean exhibition lecture given in January 1917, was published soon after its presentation, and another important address presented to the English Association was published in 1918: *The Perspective of Biography* was the last of Lee's three major statements of his views on the nature, aims, and methods of biography and biographical work. In 1918 Lee assumed administrative duties as dean of the Faculty of Arts at the University of London, and in October of that year he presented *Modern Language Research* (1919) as the inaugural address to the Modern Language Research Association.

In July 1920 the death of Elizabeth Lee, the older sister to whom Lee had always been very close, came as a great loss. She had shared his interests in literature, had assisted him in correcting proofs and compiling the index for his revised Shakespeare biography, and had contributed articles such as the biography of Ouida to the *DNB* under Lee's editorship. In late July 1921 Lee entered a London nursing home for treatment of a condition which required a "severe operation," according to brief notices in the London *Times*. In September Lee was able to leave London for Hove, where he was to complete his recovery from this surgery.

In 1923 Lee wrote a preface for the London Shakespeare League's *Tercentenary of the Publication of the First Folio*, and in the following year he was appointed trustee of the National Portrait Gallery. His health was continuing to decline, however: he had been compelled to resign his lectureship at East London College in late 1922, and in January 1924 Lee announced his intention to retire from the college at the close of that academic year. Lee had begun researching materials for his last full-length biography, that of King Edward VII, in 1921, when he had begun publishing in the London *Times* a series of articles on the former king's skill in handling international relations. King George V had specifically requested Lee to write such a biography of his father and had granted Lee free access to documents in the royal archives at Windsor Castle and Buckingham Palace.

In the years following World War I, when Lee began research for this biography, much interest prevailed in better understanding the international politics which had presaged that cataclysm. In presenting and assessing King Edward's life and character, therefore, Lee intended his study to contribute to just such an understanding, as his preface was to indicate. In this respect his biography differed in aim and method from what he had long insisted was appropriate for the biographer: to attend scrupulously to the historical facts of his subject's life, judiciously assess his subject's character only through those facts, and subordinate to his narrative background those broad social events which surround and infuse his subject's life. Although *King Edward VII: A Biography* (1925–1927) still presented, through the first volume's 803 pages, the same amassing of facts which Lee had lovingly incorporated in his earlier studies of Shakespeare and Queen Victoria, in this final biography Lee seemed more blatantly willing to offer the kind of "impressionist" assessments of character which he earlier had adamantly discouraged the biographer from attempting.

In discussing the shaping of Edward's character, for instance, Lee freely presented his opinion on the effects of his upbringing:

it was from his high-spirited, shrewd, and quickwitted mother in the early pride of Queen and wife, rather than from his grave and reserved father, that King Edward drew many traits as boy and man. In course of time, . . . her example taught him how to reconcile free play of personal will in the ways of political criticism and suggestion, with a full recognition of the constitutional principles of ministerial responsibility and the disqualification of the Crown for the personal exercise of political power. From his father he may have derived something of his organizing aptitude, of his philosophic activity, and his zest for foreign politics. . . . [But it] is plain that he inherited little of his father's austerity or cautious reticence and nothing at all of those studious and academic predilections which spoke eloquently of Prince Albert's German temperament.

Interpretive judgments are standard features of most exposition, and despite his caveats about their appearance in others' biographies, Lee had in fact always presented in his what he found to be justifiable inferences from his own research of his subjects' lives. To critics who remarked this inconsistency between his precepts and his practice as a biographer, Lee's only response, when he made any, was to reaffirm his assurances that his narratives were based on the most exhaustive examination of available resources and their conclusions judiciously formed from what those resources would permit. In *King Edward VII*, written more than a decade after the king's death and when far more information was available than Lee had possessed in writing his biographies of Shakespeare and Victoria, Lee provided what reviewer P. W. Wilson in *The New York Times* (30 October 1927) called "an admirable if opinionative" study of Edward's personality, as well as of the king's influence and skill in conducting international relations.

For such reasons, reviews of the first volume found Lee's biography at least as controversial as his *DNB* article on King Edward had been in 1911. Wilson noted in *The New York Times* that "As a painter of portraits Sir Sidney Lee . . . is not brilliant as an impressionist, but [he is] an encyclopedia for detail" whose work "gives the impression throughout . . . that his statements are backed by an overwhelming authority." Herbert W. Horwill, a *New York Times* reviewer stationed in London, later reported that the first volume of the biography was "so far . . . the book of the season," although reviewers were not unanimous in their pleasure with it. The *Times Literary Supplement*, he reported, regretted Lee's experience with the *DNB*, which it perceptively claimed had begotten in him "an undue preference for facts over ideas" and made what the *TLS* called the book's "breathless and unending procession of occurrences" something which Lee should have "occasionally suspended in favor of a chapter or two discussing the problems involved," as Horwill himself ventured. The *Spectator,* he also noted, found the work free of the too-familiar "intolerable obsequiousness" of royal biographies, but G. H. Mair of the *Evening Standard* objected to Lee's "sedulous courtiership," and A. G. Gardiner of the *Daily News* labeled the biography "an achievement of conventional politeness" in those interpretations which Lee offered.

Lee was gratified, nonetheless, with many congratulatory letters from readers in France, Sweden, Italy, Germany, and Austria following publication of this first volume of King Edward's biography, and he responded to such critics with his standard explanation for those interpretations as he continued to work on the second volume, despite his failing health. Late in 1925 he wrote a preface for *The Journalist in the Making,* a collection of sixty-two addresses that the University of London's School of Journalism published. This was to be his last major publication. Near the end of October, Lee wrote to his favorite organization, the Shakespeare Birthplace Trustees, to explain that his work on the second volume of Edward's biography required so much of his diminishing energy that he could no longer manage to continue serving as chairman of the executive committee, as he had for twenty-three consecutive years. Sympathetically refusing to grant his resignation request, the committee unanimously resolved to excuse him from actively pursuing further committee work until its next annual meeting in May 1926 — when, the members hoped, his completed biography and improved health would enable him to resume his duties as committee chairman.

But on 3 March 1926 Lee died at his home in Lexham Gardens, Kensington, leaving his secretary, F. S. Markham, to complete the final volume of *King Edward VII* in 1927. Lee was cremated and his remains interred in the cemetery at Stratford-on-Avon, as he had requested. Having remained a bachelor, he had directed that his personal possessions be distributed among the wide number of people, organizations, and institutions with which he had spent so many active years of his life. *Elizabethan and Other Essays* (1929), a final collection of Lee's addresses and essays, was posthumously edited and published as a tribute to him by his friend and colleague Frederick S. Boas.

Sir Sidney Lee's reputation as a biographer and as a scholar-historian has altered considerably from the early years of the twentieth century, when he was internationally renowned as editor of the *Dictionary of National Biography* and as an Elizabethan scholar whose biography of Shakespeare was the definitive study of England's greatest dramatist-poet. Even in the years soon after his death, in fact, such a new Shakespearean authority as G. B. Harrison expressed regret at how Lee's limitations as a biographer may inadvertently and ironically have contributed to undermining some serious Shakespearean scholarship. "In his imagination," Harrison wrote in 1930, "Shakespeare was 'a village youth' (Stratford, incidentally, was not a village), who became 'stagestruck and longed to act and write plays . . . he was singularly industrious, singularly levelheaded, and amply endowed with that practical common sense which enables a man to acquire and retain a modest competence.' Lee could not understand how incredible to sensitive people was this pallid bourgeois author of *A Midsummer Night's Dream* and *Lear;* and because his pronouncements on Shakespeare unluckily came to be regarded as oracle, some of his weaker brethren, instead of examining the evidence for themselves, rejected Lee's Shakespeare in favour of Bacon, or Derby, or Oxford, or some other creature of their own creating."

Samuel Schoenbaum, in a much more recent assessment of Lee's work as a biographer and Shakespearean scholar, mixes praise for Lee's *DNB* biographies with similar criticism for the consequences he finds such writing engendered when Lee turned to writing his full biography of Shakespeare. For such modern readers as Schoenbaum, Lee's "essential mediocrity of mind," which is adequate if not helpful in writing effectively the kind of biography required by the *DNB,* helps explain some peculiar deficiencies that mar Lee's *A Life of William Shakespeare* today: Lee's unreliability in matters of precise factual detail, his inconsistencies in interpretive positions he assumed at different points, and his adamant self-assurance in making and presenting judgments in the face of facts one would think conducive to hesitation.

But even critics writing at such different times as Schoenbaum and Harrison share some appreciation of Lee's contributions to the history of literary study and literary scholarship. Lee was an interested, early student of cross-cultural literary relations today institutionalized in the study of comparative literature, and his pioneering scholarship in this realm is worthy of remembering. Likewise, his efforts both as a member of many organizations and as an individual advocate committed to the establishing and sustaining of institutions or agencies responsible for preserving public records and cultural artifacts remains another worthy contribution to literary and historical studies. And despite reservations today's scholars may hold toward the particular findings Lee's studies uncovered, assimilated, and presented, his work as *DNB* editor and writer of many biographical sketches of the lives and accomplishments of literary figures and scholars represents a significant continuing contribution to the history of literary scholarship.

References:

Frederick S. Boas, "The Elizabethan Literary Society, 1884–1934," *Quarterly Review,* 262 (April 1934): 242–257;

Boas, ed., "Introduction," in his *Elizabethan and Other Essays* (Oxford: Clarendon Press, 1929), pp. xiii–xxii;

Boas, "Some Oxford Memories, 1881–1886," in English Association, *Essays and Studies,* new series, 9 (1956): 113–121;

C(harles) (H)arding Firth, "Memoir of Sir Sidney Lee," in H. W. C. Davis and J. R. H. Weaver, eds., *The Dictionary of National Biography, Founded in 1882 by George Smith, 1912–1921* (London: Oxford University Press, 1927), pp. xiii–xxvi;

Firth, *Sir Sidney Lee, 1859–1926* (London: H. Milford, [1931]);

William Dana Orcutt, "From a Publisher's Easy Chair," in his *Celebrities Off Parade* (Chicago and New York: Willett, Clark, 1935), pp. 192–202;

A[rthur] F. Pollard, "Sir Sidney Lee and the 'Dictionary of National Biography,'" *Bulletin of the Institute of Historical Research,* 4 (June 1926): 1–13;

Frederick Rogers, "Labour Movements" and "The Elizabethan Society," in his *Labour, Life and Literature,* edited by David Rubenstein (Brighton: Harvester Press, 1973), pp. 63–75, 157–177;

S[amuel] Schoenbaum, "Sidney Lee: *DNB*" and "Lee's *Shakespeare,*" in his *Shakespeare's Lives,* new edition (Oxford: Clarendon Press, 1991), pp. 367–382.

Papers:

The largest body of Sir Sidney Lee's papers lies in the Bodleian Library at Oxford University. These holdings include over seven thousand pages of personal letters between Lee and various people, as well as over 150 pages of letters sent by many prospective contributors to the editor of the *DNB,* and Lee's copy of his speech delivered at his presentation for an honorary degree at Oxford. The Houghton Library at Harvard University houses over forty letters from Lee to various figures, while the Folger Shakespeare Library in Washington, D.C., also holds over twenty letters from Lee to many authors. Most of these Folger letters and notes relate to Lee's 1904 *Elizabethan Sonnets* volume, his personal copy of which, with inscribed annotations, comprises part of the library's collection of Lee papers. Also included are his manuscripts used as printer's copies for the introductions to the Caxton edition of Shakespeare published in England in 1910 and his proof sheets for the 1915 revision of the Shakespeare biography. The Edinburgh University Library, National Library of Scotland, and British Museum each hold smaller collections of Lee's letters.

Percy Lubbock

(4 June 1879 – 2 August 1965)

D. W. Jefferson
University of Leeds

BOOKS: *Elizabeth Barrett Browning in her Letters* (London: Smith, Elder, 1906);

Samuel Pepys (London: Hodder & Stoughton, 1909; New York: Scribners, 1909);

George Calderon. A Sketch from Memory (London: Grant Richards, 1921);

The Craft of Fiction (London: Cape, 1921; New York: Scribners, 1921);

Earlham. Reminiscences of the Author's Early Life at Earlham Hall, Norfolk (London: Cape, 1922; New York: Scribners, 1922);

Roman Pictures (London: Cape, 1923; New York: Scribners, 1923);

The Region Cloud (London: Cape, 1925; New York: Scribners, 1925);

Mary Cholmondeley. A Sketch from Memory (London: Cape, 1928);

Shades of Eton (London: Cape, 1929; New York: Scribners, 1929);

Portrait of Edith Wharton (London: Cape, 1947; New York: Appleton, 1947).

OTHER: *A Book of English Prose*, 2 volumes, edited by Lubbock (Cambridge: Cambridge University Press, 1913);

Henry James, *The Ivory Tower*, preface by Lubbock (London: Collins, 1917; New York: Scribners, 1917);

James, *The Sense of the Past*, preface by Lubbock (London: Collins, 1917; New York: Scribners, 1917);

James, *The Middle Years*, editor's note by Lubbock (London: Collins, 1917; New York: Scribners, 1917);

The Letters of Henry James, selected and edited by Lubbock (London: Macmillan, 1920; New York: Scribners, 1920);

The Novels and Stories of Henry James, 35 volumes, edited by Lubbock (London: Macmillan, 1921–1923);

Percy Lubbock

The Diary of Arthur Christopher Benson, edited by Lubbock (London: Hutchinson, 1926; New York: Longmans, Green, 1926).

SELECTED PERIODICAL PUBLICATION – UNCOLLECTED: "Henry James," *The Quarterly Review,* 226 (July 1916): 60–74.

Percy Lubbock stands in a remarkably special relationship to literary biography. It is characteristic of him that two of his books, on George Calderon (1921) and Mary Cholmondeley (1928), have the subtitle *A Sketch from Memory.* Both of them are personal memoirs with the central emphasis on qualities of character as experienced by the author, nuances of personality carefully pondered and described. There is a certain amount of information about their lives but no systematic record such as a professional biographer would provide. There are brief comments on their literary works but no attempt to trace a literary career. In assessing the worth of the person he is concerned with such virtues as integrity and genuineness, moral and social qualities, not with the techniques and methods of an artist. In his last book, where his subject is a more important writer, Edith Wharton, the approach is similar. The preface, a letter to Gaillard Lapsley, provides an explicit statement of his attitude to the task Lapsley invited him to undertake after Wharton's death. Lubbock asks the question, what sort of book should it be? His answer is that it should not be a formal literary biography. He also rejects the idea of a collection of letters. He had done this for Henry James, providing biographical material in an introduction and short prefaces to the chronological sections of letters, but he decided that Wharton's letters would not reveal her personality sufficiently. So the book was to be a portrait, a "likeness of her as her friends knew her and as she lives in their memory." There would be no critical discussion of her works. He would not "take them from her and deal with them as ours, the possession of us all." Lubbock of course was an accomplished critic of novels, but the combination of the two functions, the appraisal in one book of an author as a person and also as an artist, was to him antipathetic. In his other writings about authors his method is more akin to that adopted in his edition of James's letters, except in the case of *Samuel Pepys* (1909).

Percy Lubbock was the fourth son of Frederick Lubbock and Catherine Gurney Lubbock of the celebrated family of Quakers whose home was Earlham Hall near Norwich. His paternal grandfather was Sir John W. Lubbock, a banker and a distinguished astronomer and mathematician, and he was the nephew of Sir John Lubbock, later Lord Avebury, also a banker and a notable scientist. Percy was to achieve a different kind of distinction. His best book is that in which he remembers his childhood: *Earlham. Reminiscences of the Author's Early Life at Earlham Hall, Norfolk* (1922). Though not a biography of a person, it won the James Black Tait Memorial Prize for biography in 1922. It is a sustained meditation on a much-loved place, every aspect and part of which, with its human associations, are cherished and preserved. He begins with a wonderful description of morning prayers: his grandfather seated at the round table with his large Bible while his grandmother "lifted up her singularly sweet and resonant voice" to lead the singing of the unaccompanied hymn. His grandfather then ex-

pounded the scriptural passage he had read: "Presently the arm that embraced the Bible began slowly, slowly to close it, and the exposition was at an end, and we knelt." Lubbock's touch is so sure that he can afford to refer to "a little rhythmical fidgeting" on the part of the children without spoiling the grace and dignity of the scene. Lengthy quotation, much too lengthy for the occasion, would be necessary to do justice to this remarkable work. Edmund Gosse, in a piece reprinted in *More Books on the Table* (1923), praised it in words that capture its tone: "This book . . . has but a single subject, namely, the solid mass of Earlham with the author's grandmother as the soul of it, described exclusively as they impressed a sensitive and observant child. The child wanders, in a restless ecstasy, up and down the staircases and through the congeries of rooms, haunted by the warm, fitful presence of the delicious, wayward chatelaine. But the house, in these memories, predominates even over the grandmother; she appears occasionally, but the house is present, like a dumb, huge guardian or an immense lidless eye of red brick, on every page. Mr. Lubbock has written a book which reminds me of no other, a book in which a beautiful old house is treated as though it were a benevolent personage, full of human life and movement, but in itself more interesting, because more consistently beautiful, than any of its inhabitants." There are echoes of an illustrious past and references to the great Joseph John Gurney, who opposed capital punishment and once walked with William Wilberforce, "plotting the holy war against the slave-driver," along a garden path since known as Wilberforce's Walk. "Aunt Fry," the prison reformer, was another of the figures in the family record.

The course of Lubbock's early life can be followed through his writings. He went to a private school and then to Eton, both of which are described in *Shades of Eton* (1929). This book lacks the classic perfection of *Earlham* but has some of its virtues, and it tells a good bit, though in a rather reticent, indirect way, about his time there. Much of it is in celebration of notable schoolmasters of whom the headmaster, Edmund Warre, is preeminent, his presence dominating the first three chapters. It was not in Lubbock's nature to reduce complexities to simple terms, but what emerges from this account of the magnificent and vigorous Warre is that Eton in the 1890s represented something new. The emphasis is on those who would "do greatly, honourably," in a tougher world. "The world is no longer a place that will submit to be awed and swayed by a tasteful young gentleman." Character and conduct (Matthew Arnold is invoked here) are to be the prevailing emphases. But Lubbock, with his unfailing tact, hints at survivals of the "elegant tradition": "belated signals," he calls them, but he will not "display their faintness." There were "Eton roofs under which the free spirit . . . was supreme." He refers to what was understood as "the right thing," "the real right thing," and the question was whether one conformed, but "entering certain doors, you suddenly find these categories reversed — or rather the category abolished." It is in such general terms that he prefers to indicate the shades of difference between a new outlook and that which it replaces. Later in the book he tells of how he made "the great refusal, not in revolt, but only in flight"; that is, how he avoided, not without subterfuge, the discipline of compulsory games to enjoy "shimmering meadows . . . bird-song in the woods." But the tone is not one of egoism; the personal note is very subdued: his subject is always Eton, and in his last sentence he writes that "Eton lives and will live to be loved." But he expresses doubts whether it gave one an education. Doubts about Eton were felt and later expressed by his housemaster, Arthur Christopher Benson, one of the abiding influences on Lubbock. Benson must clearly have seen some promise in Lubbock, and this is shown by Benson's bringing eminent men to meet him. Gosse was one of them. "I was shaking hands with Stevenson's friend." But there was another, more distinguished, encounter with a man who is described as "sturdy and large-headed with a close dark beard." Unfortunately, he did not catch the name, and the meeting was rather abortive. Later he discovered that he had met James, and this event, low-keyed though it was, brings the book to a kind of climax. James was to be the greatest presence in Lubbock's life.

One of Lubbock's idiosyncrasies was a tendency to be rather selective in his use of particular details, sometimes eschewing them altogether in a way that has its own rhetorical effect. In an early chapter of *Shades of Eton* he recalls Warre's "genial talk" with the boys about some items of behavior, but Lubbock confesses that he feels unable to say exactly what they were: "it is not memory that fails me, only the face to do so." A similar avoidance of details that might spoil the picture, often a humorous avoidance, has been noted in James, Lubbock's master in so many matters of style. Studied omission of certain elements of his subject are, as we have seen, characteristic of his policy in literary biography to such an extent as to raise questions about his relation to that genre. In presenting an imaginative portrait of an author he avoided the facts and documentary items that might obtrude and not harmonize with the delicate impression that he sought to convey. But sometimes he could quote the actual words said by his friends when they had an especially memorable quality.

After Eton, Lubbock went to King's College, Cambridge, where he read for the Classical Tripos, obtaining a first class in 1901. It was in that year that we have evidence of a visit to Lamb House, Rye, the home of James, and here begins his long association not only with James but with the circle of writers that included Howard Sturgis, author of the novel *Belchamber* (1935), whose home near Windsor, Queen's Acre (often referred to as Qu'Acre), was a center of hospitality; Lapsley, a young American who taught history at Cambridge; Benson; Wharton; and others who appeared later. It was Benson, a fellow of Magdalene College, Cambridge, who enabled Lubbock to become librarian of the Pepysian Library in that college in 1906, the year in which he published *Elizabeth Barrett Browning in her Letters*. But he resigned his librarian's post in 1908 to devote himself to literature. The fruit of his connection with the Pepysian Library was his biography of Pepys.

His early books differ in several ways from the later ones. In writing of Elizabeth Barrett Browning and of Pepys he was not producing personal memoirs as he was in his work on James, Calderon, Cholmondeley, Benson, and Wharton, and none of the questions arising from the personal connection were relevant here. The later works were exercises in the art of memory, and their style reflected his deep absorption in past impressions. But in some ways these early books show tendencies confirmed in the later works. There is nothing immature in these books published at the ages of twenty-seven and thirty respectively. In the book on Barrett Browning, the larger part consists of selections from the letters, the rest being biographical passages, some of a few pages, others of a mere sentence or two, linking these selections. The same pattern appears again in the edition of selections from Benson's diaries. It would seem that, from the outset, Lubbock was attracted to a form in which the central place was occupied by the personal writings of the subject. The alternative would have been to produce a literary biography with the entire narrative in his hands, the life and the literary career, with incidental quotations from the author and discussion of the works. The method he chose had two advantages. It allowed the reader to hear the author's voice more continuously and more di-

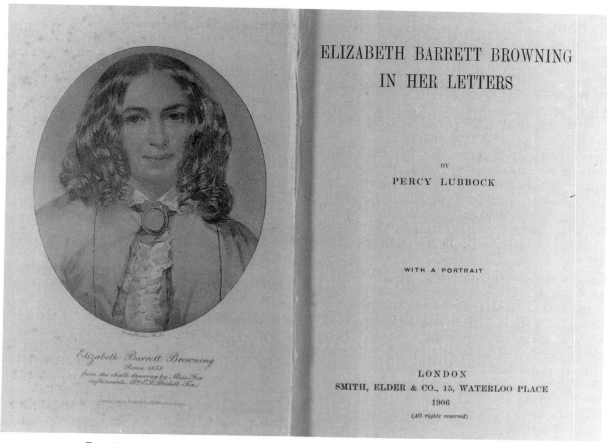

ELIZABETH BARRETT BROWNING
IN HER LETTERS

BY

PERCY LUBBOCK

WITH A PORTRAIT

LONDON
SMITH, ELDER & CO., 15, WATERLOO PLACE
1906
(All rights reserved)

Frontispiece and title page for the first edition of Lubbock's life in letters of the Victorian poet

rectly. And it avoided the mixture of kinds within what purports to be one literary genre, the history of a person combined with a history and description of what that person has given to the world, which is on a different plane of reality.

In the book on Barrett Browning he does not carry his principles so far as when his subject, for example, is Wharton. He writes, "How much of her work up to this time [1844] has kept its life after sixty years, is too large a question to fit the scope of a book which does not profess to deal critically with her poetry," but he does in fact make some interesting remarks on the sonnets and on *Aurora Leigh* (1856), and the main lines of her career as a poet are traced briefly. Lubbock had not at this stage developed the idiosyncrasies that make his later work so individual. His subject here is well chosen; the story is one of the best and happiest in literary history, and Lubbock tells it eloquently insofar as it is his to tell. His narrative supplies necessary facts relating, for example, to the maneuvers required to facilitate Robert Browning's visits to the Barrett home on Wimpole Street and to the state of affairs in her

family with the oppressive father whom she nevertheless loved; and this helps to give the letters a context altogether enhancing. He is alert to changes in the situation which are reflected in the form of his narrative and the conditions governing his task. At the point when the marriage has taken place and the flight to Italy has been achieved we are to have no more letters between the two: "Here, then, the curtain falls on this strange and exquisite story . . . here on the very verge of its fulfillment we are suddenly extruded." The reader will no longer see them looking at each other but will see them only as they turn to the outside world. Lubbock's sense almost of drama here is an indication of his sensitivity to the importance of structure in this kind of writing.

What remains of her story is crowded with incident, and the letters are full of descriptions of people whom the Brownings met. There is a vivid account of George Sand, as well as pleasant impressions of Walter Savage Landor, John Ruskin, and many other figures in literature and art. But Barrett Browning's enthusiastic admiration for Napoleon III is presented as excessive and uncritical, and Lubbock sees her emotional response to the cause of Italian liberty, in some respects, as a sign of weakness. The "freer, ampler life" of her years of marriage had perhaps been accompanied by some loss of the intellectual power that had characterized her earlier period.

Samuel Pepys may appear to be an exception to Lubbock's usual practice. It appears to be a straight literary biography, and so it is, but the author's life and his work are to a large extent contained within the *Diary* (published in 1819) so that to survey the one is to survey the other. The greater part of his life of course comes after the *Diary* was abandoned, but here Pepys virtually ceases to be a literary figure so that Lubbock does not have the problem of the literary biographer of combining two unlike things, the problem that he was aware of when he wrote to Lapsley. He was writing on Pepys before the major developments in Pepys scholarship associated with the work of J. R. Tanner and others and before the great Robert Latham and William Matthews's edition of the *Diary* (1970–1983). He admits that he is indebted to publications on Pepys by H. B. Wheatley. With all of these limitations Lubbock's volume can still be regarded as an admirable introduction to Pepys. He is much more readable than Wheatley.

The danger for some biographers would lie in the contradictions in Pepys's character which lend themselves too easily to facile exploitation, such as his jealousy concerning his wife and his easy acceptance of his own infidelities. Lubbock's feeling for balance and his sense of the mysteries of human personality (Pepys's motives for keeping the *Diary* were profoundly mysterious) give the right note of moderation combined with candor. His book is beautifully but simply written. One of his judgments on Pepys exemplifies his unassuming virtues: "Nothing is more readily to be illustrated from the Diary than his severe sense of the proper way for people of position to comport themselves. It was not precisely moral, this sense, it was rather artistic. He objected to effrontery and loose talk, not so much as being wrong in itself, as being unbecoming and out of place. It is, perhaps, a slender distinction, but it is enough to save his disapprobation from being pharisaical. His professions of respectability, placed side by side in the *Diary* with the loving record of his own lapses, are thus not entirely unreal." One of the best chapters, a good example of Lubbock's success in the organization of his book, begins with an account of the London of Pepys's time, the

"crowded, red-roofed, walled town, with its spires gleaming in clean air," and here Lubbock's sense of place is evident. Economical but alive with detail, the description moves on from taverns to theaters, including some facts about the plays Pepys saw. In the same chapter he writes most impressively about Pepys's considerable prowess as a musician with comments on the difference between his age and the later period dominated by the pianoforte: "The lute, the viol, and the harpsichord were severer trainers of taste." He quotes a well-known passage in the *Diary* where Pepys writes of the effect on him of the wind music in a performance of *The Virgin Martyr*, "which is so sweet that it ravished me and indeed, in a word, did wrap up my soul so that it made me really sick, just as I have formerly been when in love with my wife; that neither then, not all the evening going home, I was able to think of anything, but remained all night transported."

Lubbock notes the naturalness with which Pepys can include every kind of incident in the inexhaustible profusion of his narrative: "He buys a pair of lobsters for dinner, leaves them behind in the coach, and suddenly remembers them while he is in the middle of saying grace"; "A man had a great and dirty fall over a waterpipe," and so on. He chooses the best but with no air of self-indulgent gusto. His position as librarian of the Pepysian Library gave him the advantage of familiarity with its contents and structure, which he describes in the last chapter with details of Pepys's testamentary directions concerning the future. This book is the first case of what was to become the norm. Each of his later works in the biographical field has its origin in a personal relationship with his subject.

After the Pepys biography Lubbock published no books for over a decade except for the two volumes of *A Book of English Prose* (1913), selections of passages from eminent authors "Arranged for Preparatory and Elementary Schools." Then follows an important phase dominated by his work on James. His 1916 obituary on James in *The Quarterly Review* is a remarkable appreciation of his art as a novelist and establishes Lubbock as one of the most perceptive of his admirers, perhaps the critic who did most to create an atmosphere of recognition of James's special qualities. He saw James as the most original novelist of the age and also as a man of great sensitivity and magnanimity. In addition to editing the two unfinished novels and the unfinished third section of the autobiography, Lubbock later edited a selection of James's letters with a brief biographical introduction and short biographical prefaces to the eight sections of the letters themselves. These introductory passages reach a total of more than seventy pages. He also edited the complete or almost complete fictional works, adding several volumes to the selection made by James for the New York edition. James had rejected much that later readers have praised highly, so Lubbock rescued some fine novels and stories. In *The Craft of Fiction* (1921) James has a place of honor, the section on *The Ambassadors* (1903) being an eloquent exposition of his method. What Lubbock learned from James in his own work is seen at its best in *Earlham*. In the autobiographical writings James cultivated the art of memory, the art of living imaginatively in a much cherished past, and in all his later writings about people and places Lubbock was James's remarkably impressive disciple.

Some of his remarks in the introduction to the letters are highly relevant to literary biography. He begins by saying that to anyone who knew James it would be clear that it was impossible to write his life. James never ceased to create his own life in his imagination; everything that presented itself to his mind was subjected to a poetic refashioning, and this process was manifest in his conversation, his letters, and his relationships with others. Instead of attempting literary biography, a possible solution was to present such a person's life directly through letters with a modest biographical commentary providing a minimal framework of fact. This is what Lubbock does for James. He does something similar for Barrett Browning and Benson. The alternative was to write a sketch of the author as remembered by the biographer, but as a human being with little or no consideration of the works that represent that person's imaginative life. This approach is adopted in his treatment of Calderon, Cholmondeley, and Wharton.

His tribute to playwright Calderon is a curious example of this method. He begins by saying that as he tries to define the quality of "his rare nature . . . it is his own figure that continually appears, vivid as life, with a well-known look which checks and deflects any undertaking of that kind." Not that he was especially reserved or that he "held one off" but rather because he was always concerned with whatever was new, with things to be done, not with anything relating to himself. He "adopted no part, he held no theory of himself." He goes on to describe Calderon's capacity to fall in with whatever was afoot, his adaptability to all kinds of people, his strong sociable interest in the activities of others. It would

seem that Calderon was an outgoing person, not self-questioning, genial and amiable though capable of expressing differences of opinion to the point of creating discord: a man of great honesty and integrity, disinclined to compromise. The "critical part of him was so highly organised and elaborated, the instinctive so straight and simple": not a man easy to understand. It is entirely typical of Lubbock that he should dwell in this way on riddles of human personality without trying to resolve them. Some aspects of Calderon are perhaps rather disconcerting. We see him playing the role of strikebreaker in the coal strike of 1912, reasoning that he disliked despotic action of any kind on whatever side. He was just as capable of taking the part of the poor man against the rich when the occasion required it. One oddity in his outlook was his open opposition to woman suffrage, a subject on which he spoke in public and also wrote.

On the question of his literary works Lubbock makes the interesting comment that drama was a form that suited his temperament. It is inappropriate to write plays if one's nature demands "big, slow subjects" that need a great deal of development. A dramatist must reach his conclusion by the shortest route. Modern comedy requires "immediate clash of character" rather than "the natural history of its growth." He describes a production of Calderon's play *Revolt,* produced in Manchester in 1912, and also refers briefly to *The Fountain,* produced by the Stage Society in 1909, and to his blank verse historical drama *Cromwell Mall o' Monks,* published in Calderon's collected plays in 1921–1922.

Earlier in his life Calderon had studied in Saint Petersburg, Russia, and had developed an ambitious research project on Slavic elements in Greek religion. For a short time he was employed at the British Museum library with a special interest in Slavic subjects, but he resigned this post to devote himself to study. He fought in World War I and was killed at Gallipoli in 1915, leaving his scholarly work unfinished. Lubbock's book concludes with some extracts from his letters home. Lubbock's motives in writing a memorial of a friend are entirely in character, but it is difficult not to feel that Calderon was a more fascinating person to know than to read about. For all the versatility, openness, and vitality of spirit attributed to him he does not come to life as a figure of enduring interest, nor was he very important as a dramatist.

The Craft of Fiction for some readers is Lubbock's most important achievement, a pioneer work of its kind with some splendid passages describing and discussing the methods of various novelists. In

Lubbock (left), H. O. Sturgis (center), and A. C. Benson at Hinton Hall, Benson's home, in 1906

the present context it is necessary only to stress again that for Lubbock literary criticism was a separate activity not to be combined with a personal account of the author. Among his works this book is in a category by itself.

In the mid 1920s Lubbock made two excursions into fiction. *Roman Pictures* (1923), a social comedy with fewer actual pictures of Rome than one could wish, was praised by E. M. Forster in *Aspects of the Novel* (1927). *The Region Cloud* (1925) is the story of a young man who is adopted as a satellite by a grossly egotistical artist and eventually breaks with him. The theme is superficially similar to that of James's "The Author of Beltraffio," in which a novelist of provocative outlook confides in a young admirer. Lubbock's artist is too monstrous, and the outcome is quite different. In general Lubbock was not successful in fiction, and he did well to return to writing about authors.

The Diary of Arthur Christopher Benson (1926) is one of his characteristic products. Of the three hundred or so pages in this volume, from a fifth to a quarter are occupied by Lubbock's introduction and linking passages. In the introduction he attempts to come to terms with a human character, in this case a highly complex one with extraordinary contradictions. Benson began to keep a diary in 1897 when he was thirty-five, and he wrote in it voluminously and with great swiftness in the free moments of busy days. He was a man who lived fully

in his professional and social activities to which he added an immense amount of letter writing. He wrote many books and had a great facility as a writer, yet he had time and energy for an extremely lively social life. There were walks in the Cambridgeshire lanes with good conversation and provocative argument. Yet, as Lubbock notes, Benson talking to himself and Benson talking to another were two different people. He could give himself to others with lavish generosity but was virtually a slave to his courtesy and sense of duty, having a profound need for privacy and solitude; not for rest but for those labors that required total freedom from company. Lubbock dwells fully and most skillfully on these contrasts and paradoxes in his personality. Benson "preferred to meet people upon his own terms, not upon theirs." If a new acquaintance felt that a greater intimacy had been achieved than was actually the case, Benson would be distraught to find that "more was expected where he had given so much." He "lived and thought and worked too fast" and paid for this with years of depressive illness. He developed extremely regular habits of work about which he became obsessive.

In the linking passages Lubbock deals with the basic facts of his career: Eton; King's College, Cambridge; a first class in the classical tripos; and then immediately back to Eton as a master where he began to be a presence in Lubbock's life. Lubbock testifies to Benson's success there: the liberality of his rule, his freedom from narrowness, and his gift for discipline.

The year 1899 was marked by two events in Benson's life: his mother went to live in a beautiful house in Sussex, Tremans, for which he developed a great affection, and he met Howard Sturgis. Lubbock loved beautiful places and never neglected an opportunity to dwell upon their importance for his friends, and Sturgis was also to become one of his own closest associates. Benson's friendship with Henry James has also been noted. In 1900 he paid a visit to Lamb House, Rye, an event handsomely recounted in the diary.

The excerpts from the diary are rich in descriptions of meetings with eminent people. There was an extraordinary visit to Theodore Watts-Dunton and Algernon Charles Swinburne in 1903 and some entertaining episodes with Thomas Hardy, whom he met with James at the Athenaeum in 1904 and who many years later was installed as an honorary fellow at Magdalene College. In 1906 Benson went to live in the village of Haddenham, and it is here at Hinton Hall that Benson, Sturgis, and Lubbock are seen in an engaging photograph of 1906. Lubbock gives a brief account of leading events in Benson's life: the commission to edit the letters of Queen Victoria, his move to Cambridge, the first phase of illness in 1907, the gift of money from an American lady that enabled him to be generous to Magdalene College, and more illness in 1917 prolonged for some years but from which he recovered before the final stage. Benson died in 1925. As with other books this is a work of personal piety.

Lubbock's sketch of novelist Cholmondeley, not much more than twenty thousand words in length, is a small work of art. As in other personal memoirs he describes his central figure with a respect that imposes on him a degree of reticence. "Of such a woman," he writes, "truth must be thought and spoken with a peculiar vigilance." She was definitely a product of her tradition with its sense of honor: "her race was potent in her blood; and to her own veracity there was added a high tradition of faith and loyalty, sound as the soil from which her race had grown." In saying such things Lubbock has no sense of a need to provide illustrative examples: "Civilised as she was, with her gracious and scrupulous ways, and complicated as she seemed, mazily and mystically ruminating, she had a large aboriginal simplicity, in which her imagination slowly grew and flowered." She was utterly honest, she was a firm friend, and she was coura-

geous: these are the kind of things he had to say of her but in words that express his own high and delicate sense of human character. They reveal little in detail. Characteristically, Lubbock describes the place where he first met her, the Knightsbridge flat which became her father's home and hers after he was obliged for financial reasons to sell his ancestral home. It was an inappropriate setting for such people. Much better was The Cottage at Ufford in Suffolk to which Cholmondeley and her younger sister were later able to retreat for long summers, and this is lovingly portrayed. In a paragraph about the Knightsbridge phase Lubbock describes Cholmondeley's aged father, who greets the visitor with the greatest charm and says his farewell with equal kindness but for the rest of the time simply sleeps: "he slept as candidly, as courteously as he woke to say goodbye."

Lubbock's art is at its best in his amiable dramatization of Cholmondeley's social life among her fellow writers. "Our Rhoda," that is Rhoda Broughton, the redoubtable veteran novelist who had shocked people in her day, is shown with her "straight back, her sumptuous raiment" and the "cut of her talk, the cheerful slash of her phrase, and crackle of her wit." Then James appears, and there is a comic clash between them over the latter's comment on Shakespeare. And later, well heralded, enters Sturgis, with whom Cholmondeley is on easy terms so that they can play up to each other's idiosyncrasies and make an enjoyable game of their relationship. Lubbock refers to a "silent but appreciative youth" — himself of course — who had been introduced into this company.

Lubbock dwells briefly on literary influences, the importance for Cholmondeley of Ralph Waldo Emerson and George Eliot. He has a few words to say about her grasp of character, her weakness for melodrama, and her knowledge of the life of her day, but when the novels are named — *Red Pottage* (1899) was the most celebrated — it is largely as a matter for gossip among her acquaintances and mild public scandal. It is clear that Lubbock did not wish to come too near to the more painful areas of feeling in her work. He concludes with some extracts from her journals, mainly of her early years. She had expressed the desire to bequeath them to him, and he wrote the sketch in the belief that she would have wished him to do so.

The 1920s were an extremely productive period in Lubbock's life, but with *Shades of Eton* published when he was fifty it must have seemed that his literary career was over. It was after seven years that he received Lapsley's request to write the biography of Wharton, who had just died. His procedure in *Portrait of Edith Wharton* (1947) was similar to that which we have seen in the memoirs of Calderon and Cholmondeley but with one difference: he wrote to many friends and acquaintances of Wharton for material which could supplement his own memories. This may give the measure of the magnitude of his task as he saw it, and it may also point to a lack of confidence. More than ten years before her death there had been a breach in the friendship between Wharton and Lubbock caused by the latter's marriage in 1926 to Lady Sybil Scott after the breakup of her marriage to Geoffrey Scott. Lubbock had later sought a reconciliation with Wharton which was refused. R. W. B. Lewis, who tells this story in *Edith Wharton: A Biography* (1975), expresses surprise that Lubbock should have been asked to write her life. There were areas of her life that were unknown to him — her early years, for example — so other reasons can be found for his use of so many informants. Rather less than a quarter of the book consists of these contributions, which are spaced out in relation to the chronological plan. But inevitably certain general qualities are revealed only when a particular witness happens to be quoted so that the realization of what she was like does not proceed by orderly stages.

The book opens magnificently with a description of a typical occasion when Wharton would descend upon Lamb House so that James knew that he was "warned for duty," a privilege of course but calling for a drastic change in his arrangements, dedicated as he was to a life of seclusion and intense creative activity. Her demands were overwhelming, but his response was total. There were "large enfolding embraces"; however, James felt safe only when he had delivered her to another. Lubbock provides a splendid picture of Wharton at Sturgis's home at Windsor, Qu'Acre — so alive, so elegant, "expensive in her neatness" — and a wonderful description of James's orotund manner and her response, with Sturgis making his special contribution. Since James and Sturgis have been treated in Lubbock's earlier books, this is a kind of culmination, a marvelous tribute to friends long dead. Mention is made of a young man, a little awkward, very much in the shade. This is Lubbock himself, who would later have a larger share in her friendship.

After this opening chapter of Lubbock at his best, there is an account of Wharton's youth in an environment of which he has no detailed knowledge; the various informants come into play. Further chapters deal with her first beginnings as an author — she was relatively late but was from the outset entirely professional — and with her decision to settle in Europe. She was never, he notes, one of the "passionate pilgrims" of James. What she wanted was "the best society within view, the best talk within earshot," and it was Paris that she chose; "the right Paris," he adds. Here we have the testimony of friends who knew her at this phase and later. "Why must [she] be treated as royalty?" was one of the questions, and there is a piquant account of an encounter with Broughton in which that formidable lady failed to respond to her "proffer of graciousness." References are made to her shyness, a controversial issue. One early witness says that "nobody can rightly picture her as she was who does not see her as capable at times of marked — and often apparently quite uncalled-for — asperity." The strenuousness of her enjoyment of everything that others were doing and saying was seen by one friend as "extremely exhausting." Another comments that Wharton never refused an occasion for charity and that she gave generously not only money and time but personal interest and sympathy. Her ways with children varied from fear and dislike of them, according to some informants, to a remarkable capacity to treat some of them as "normal human beings." All this suggests that the truth was mixed and complex and that she was not an easy person to understand. Lubbock would not be expected to compose a wholly consistent, easily intelligible portrait. The fact that our information comes from such varying sources does not make her less elusive, but the effect is always alive. Millicent Bell in *Edith Wharton and Henry James* (1965) found this memoir "tantalizingly vague," and of course what is lacking, what is always lacking in Lubbock's memoir writing, is the systematic detailed treatment usual in biography. There is no adequate account of her complicated relationship with her husband or of her love affair with Morton Fullerton. On the subject of Walter Berry, whom Lubbock disliked, there is a marked reticence. We need to turn to Lewis's biography for information on these central facts of her life.

But the book is full of good stories and humorous touches. When Lubbock was about to pay his first visit to the rue de Varenne, Wharton's address in Paris, James warned him against the "succulent and corrupting meals," which were a feature of her hospitality. Referring to her reading habits, he notes that when she went to bed clasping a new book "Sometimes it was thought that the book had a scared look . . . as though it knew what it was in for."

The *Portrait of Edith Wharton* has raised many problems which would be difficult to resolve without the most exhaustive study of Wharton and her associates. Gordon S. Haight, who reviewed it in the *Yale Review* (December 1947), expressed the opinion that Wharton "did not share" certain intimate parts of her life with "the inner circle," that is Lubbock and others, and that they resented it. Lewis accuses Lubbock of subtle malice in his handling of her character. It may well be felt that his reticence about her novels and her concern for her art has a diminishing effect, but his reasons for concentrating on personal impressions are clear.

Awarded the CBE (Commander of the British Empire) in 1952, Lubbock spent the later years of his life in Italy, at first in the Villa Medici in Fiesole and then in Lerici on the Gulf of Spezia, where he died on 2 August 1965.

References:

Millicent Bell, *Edith Wharton and Henry James. The Story of Their Friendship* (New York: Braziller, 1965);

Edmund Gosse, *More Books on the Table* (London: Heinemann, 1923);

R. W. B. Lewis, *Edith Wharton. A Biography* (London: Constable, 1975; New York: Harper & Row, 1975).

E. V. Lucas

(11 June 1868 – 26 June 1938)

Glyn Pursglove
University College of Swansea

See also the Lucas entry in *DLB 98: Modern British Essayists, First Series.*

BOOKS: *Sparks from a Flint: Odd Rhymes for Odd Times,* as E. V. L. (London: Howe, 1891);

Songs of the Bat (London: W. P. Griffith, 1892);

Bernard Barton and His Friends: A Record of Quiet Lives (London: Edward Hicks, Jr., 1893);

The Flamp, The Ameliorator, and The Schoolboy's Apprentice (London: Richards, 1897);

All the World Over (London: Richards, 1898);

Willow and Leather: A Book of Praise (Bristol: Arrowsmith / London: Simpkin, Marshall, Hamilton, Kent, 1898);

Charles Lamb and the Lloyds (London: Smith, Elder, 1898; Philadelphia: Lippincott, 1899);

The Book of Shops (London: Richards, [1899]);

What Shall We Do Now? A Book of Suggestions for Children's Games and Enjoyment, by E. V. Lucas and Elizabeth Lucas (London: Richards, 1900; New York: Stokes, 1901);

Domesticities: A Little Book of Household Impressions (London: Smith, Elder, 1900);

Four and Twenty Toilers (London: Richards, 1900; New York: McDevitt-Wilson, 1931);

The Visit to London (London: Methuen, 1902);

England Day By Day, by Lucas and C. L. Graves (London: Methuen, 1903);

Wisdom on the Hire System, by Lucas and Graves (London: Isbister, 1903);

Highways and Byways in Sussex (London & New York: Macmillan, 1904; revised, London: Macmillan, 1935); published as *West Sussex, Mid-Sussex, East Sussex,* 3 volumes (London: Macmillan, 1937);

The Life of Charles Lamb, 2 volumes (London: Methuen, 1905; New York: Putnam, 1905; revised and corrected, 1 volume, London: Methuen, 1907; revised and corrected, 2 volumes, London: Methuen, 1921);

A Wanderer in Holland (London: Methuen, 1905; New York: Macmillan, 1905; revised, London: Methuen, 1923, New York: Macmillan, 1924; revised, London: Methuen, 1929);

Fireside and Sunshine (London: Methuen, 1906);

Listener's Lure: An Oblique Narration (London: Methuen, 1906); published as *Listener's Lure: A Kensington Comedy* (New York: Macmillan, 1906);

Change for a Halfpenny, by Lucas and Graves (London: Rivers, 1906);

Signs of the Times, by Lucas and Graves (London: Rivers, 1906);

A Wanderer in London (London: Methuen, 1906; New York: Macmillan, 1906; revised, London: Methuen, 1913; New York: Macmillan, 1918; revised, London: Methuen, 1923; New York: Macmillan, 1924; revised, London: Methuen, 1926; revised, London: Methuen, 1931);

Character and Comedy (London: Methuen, 1907; New York: Macmillan, 1907);

The Doll Doctor (London: G. Alleri, 1907);

A Swan and Her Friends (London: Methuen, 1907);

Over Bemerton's: An Easy-Going Chronicle (London: Methuen, 1907; New York: Macmillan, 1907);

Anne's Terrible Good Nature (London: Chatto & Windus, 1908; New York: Macmillan, 1908);

If: A Nightmare in the Conditional Mood, by Lucas and Graves (London: Pitman, 1908);

Hustled History, by Lucas and Graves (London: Pitman, 1908);

One Day and Another (London: Methuen, 1909; New York: Macmillan, 1909);

A Wanderer in Paris (London: Methuen, 1909; New York: Macmillan, 1909; revised, London: Methuen, 1911; revised, London: Methuen, 1922; New York: Macmillan, 1924; revised, London: Methuen, 1928; revised by Audrey Lucas, London: Methuen, 1952);

Farthest from the Truth, by Lucas and Graves (London: Pitman, 1909);

Mr. Ingleside (London: Methuen, 1910; New York: Macmillan, 1910);

E. V. Lucas

The Slowcoach (London: Wells Gardner, 1910; New York: Macmillan, 1910);

Harvest Home (London: Methuen, 1911; New York: Macmillan, 1913);

Old Lamps for New (London: Methuen, 1911; New York: Macmillan, 1911);

What a Life!, by Lucas and G. Morrow (London: Methuen, 1911);

A Little of Everything (London: Methuen, 1912; New York: Macmillan, 1912);

London Lavender (London: Methuen, 1912; New York: Macmillan, 1912);

A Wanderer in Florence (London: Methuen, 1912; New York: Macmillan, 1912; revised, London: Methuen, 1923; New York: Macmillan, 1924; revised, London: Methuen, 1928);

The British School: An Anecdotal Guide to the British Painters and Paintings in the National Gallery (London: Methuen, 1913; published as *British Pictures and Their Painters* (New York: Macmillan, 1913);

Harvest Home (London: Methuen, 1913; New York: Macmillan, 1913);

A Group of Londoners (Minneapolis: Privately printed for Edmund D. Brooks and his friends, 1913);

Loiterer's Harvest (London: Methuen, 1913; New York: Macmillan, 1913);

All the Papers, by Lucas and Graves (London & New York: Pitman, 1914);

Landmarks (London: Methuen, 1914; New York: Macmillan, 1914);

Swollen-headed William (London: Methuen, 1914; New York: Dutton, 1914);

A Wanderer in Venice (London: Methuen, 1914; New York: Macmillan, 1914; revised, London: Methuen, 1923; New York: Macmillan, 1924);

Guillaumism (London: Privately printed, 1915);

In Gentlest Germany (London & New York: John Lane, 1915);

Cloud and Silver (London: Methuen, 1916; New York: Doran, 1916);

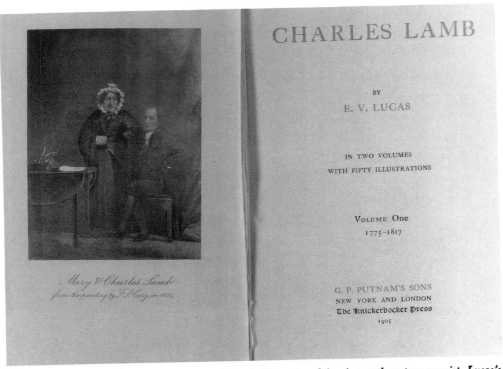

CHARLES LAMB

BY

E. V. LUCAS

IN TWO VOLUMES
WITH FIFTY ILLUSTRATIONS

VOLUME ONE
1775-1817

G. P. PUTNAM'S SONS
NEW YORK AND LONDON
The Knickerbocker Press
1905

*Mary & Charles Lamb
from the painting by F. S. Cary in 1834*

Frontispiece and title page for the American edition of Lucas's biography of the nineteenth-century essayist. Lucas's book is still considered unequaled.

London Revisited (London: Methuen, 1916); published as More Wanderings in London (New York: Doran, 1916; revised, London: Methuen, 1926);

Variety Lane (London: Methuen, 1916);

The Vermilion Box (London: Methuen, 1916; New York: Doran, 1916);

A Boswell of Baghdad with Diversions (London: Methuen, 1917; New York: Doran, 1917);

His Fatal Beauty: or, The Moore of Chelsea (London: Privately printed by Clement Shorter, 1917);

Outposts of Mercy: The Record of a Visit to Various Units of the Red Cross in Italy (London: Methuen, 1917);

'Twixt Eagle and Dove (London: Methuen, 1918);

Mixed Vintages (London: Methuen, 1919);

The Phantom Journal and Other Essays and Diversions (London: Methuen, 1919);

Quoth the Raven, by Lucas and Morrow (London: Methuen, 1919);

Traveller's Joy (London: Smith, 1919);

Adventures and Enthusiasms (New York: Doran, 1920);

David Williams: Founder of the Royal Literary Fund (London: John Murray, 1920);

Specially Selected (London: Methuen, 1920);

Verena in the Midst: A Kind of a Story (London: Methuen, 1920; New York: Doran, 1920);

Edwin Austen Abbey, 2 volumes (London: Methuen, 1921; New York: Scribners, 1921);

Rose and Rose (London: Methuen, 1921; New York: Doran, 1921);

Roving East and Roving West (London: Methuen, 1921; New York: Doran, 1921);

Urbanities (London: Methuen, 1921);

Genevra's Money (London: Methuen, 1922; New York: Doran, 1923);

Giving and Receiving (London: Methuen, 1922; New York: Doran, 1922);

Vermeer of Delft (London: Methuen, 1922);

You Know What People Are (London: Methuen, 1922);

Advisory Ben (London: Methuen, 1923; New York: Doran, 1924; revised and enlarged, London: Methuen, 1932);

Luck of the Year (London: Methuen, 1923; New York: Doran, 1923);

As the Twig is Straightened (London: Methuen, 1924);

Encounters and Diversions (London: Methuen, 1924);

John Constable the Painter (London: Halton & Truscott Smith, 1924; New York: Minton, Balch, 1924);

Little Books on Great Masters, 8 volumes (London: Methuen, 1924–1926; New York: Doran, 1924–1926);

The Same Star (London: Methuen, 1924);

A Wanderer among Pictures: A Companion to the Galleries of Europe (London: Methuen, 1924; New York: Doran, 1924);

Chardin and Vigée-Lebrun (London: Methuen, 1924; London: Methuen / New York: Doran, 1924);

Michael Angelo (London: Methuen, 1924; London: Methuen / New York: Doran, 1924);

Rembrandt (London: Methuen, 1924);

Introducing London (London: Methuen, 1925; New York: Doran, 1925);

Playtime & Company (London: Methuen, 1925; New York: Doran, 1925);

Zigzags in France and Various Essays (London: Methuen, 1925);

Frans Hals (London: Methuen, 1926; London: Methuen / New York: Doran, 1926);

Giorgione (London: Methuen, 1926; London: Methuen / New York: Doran, 1926);

Leonardo da Vinci (London: Methuen, 1926; London: Methuen / New York: Doran, 1926);

Van Dyck (London: Methuen, 1926; London: Methuen / New York: Doran, 1926);

Velasquez (London: Methuen, 1926; London: Methuen / New York: Doran, 1926);

E. V. Lucas's London: Being 'A Wanderer in London' and 'London Revisited' in One Volume, Rearranged with New Matter (London: Methuen, 1926);

Events and Embroideries (London: Methuen, 1926; New York: Doran, 1927);

Selected Essays, edited by E. A. Woodhouse (London: Methuen, 1926);

Three Hundred and Sixty-five Days and One More (London: Methuen, 1926);

A Wanderer in Rome (London: Methuen, 1926; New York: Doran, 1926; revised, London: Methuen, 1930; Philadelphia: Lippincott, 1932; revised, London: Methuen, 1951);

Wanderings and Diversions (New York & London: Putnam, 1926);

A Cat Book (New York & London: Harper, 1927);

A Fronded Isle and Other Essays (London: Methuen, 1927);

The More I See of Men: Stray Essays on Dogs (London: Methuen, 1927);

The Colvins and Their Friends (London: Methuen, 1928);

Introducing Paris (London: Methuen, 1928);

Mr. Punch's County Songs (London: Methuen, 1928);

Out of a Clear Sky: Essays and Fantasies about Birds (London: Methuen, 1928);

A Rover I Would Be (London: Methuen, 1928);

If Dogs Could Write: A Second Canine Miscellany (London: Methuen, 1929; Philadelphia: Lippincott, 1930);

Turning Things Over (London: Methuen, 1929; New York: Dutton, 1929);

Vermeer the Magical (London: Methuen, 1929);

Windfall's Eve: An Entertainment (London: Methuen, 1929; Philadelphia: Lippincott, 1930);

'. . . And Such Small Deer' (London: Methuen, 1930; Philadelphia: Lippincott, 1931);

Down the Sky: An Entertainment (London: Methuen, 1930; Philadelphia: Lippincott, 1930);

The Pekinese National Anthem (London: Methuen, 1930);

Traveller's Luck (London: Methuen, 1930);

The Barber's Clock: a Conversation Piece (London: Methuen, 1931; Philadelphia: Lippincott, 1932);

French Leaves (London: Methuen, 1931);

No-Nose at the Show (London: Methuen, 1931);

Visibility Good: Essays and Excursions (London: Methuen, 1931; Philadelphia: Lippincott, 1931);

At the Sign of the Dove (London: Methuen, 1932);

The Day of the Dog (London: Methuen, 1932);

Lemon Verbena and Other Essays (London: Methuen, 1932; Philadelphia: Lippincott, 1932);

Reading, Writing and Remembering: A Literary Record (London: Methuen, 1932; New York: Harper, 1932);

English Leaves (London: Methuen, 1933; Philadelphia: Lippincott, 1933);

Saunterer's Rewards (London: Methuen, 1933; Philadelphia: Lippincott, 1934);

Animals All: being 'And Such Small Deer' and 'Out of a Clear Sky' (London: Methuen, 1934);

At the Shrine of St. Charles: Stray Papers on Lamb brought together for the Centenary of his Death in 1834 (London: Methuen, 1934; New York: Dutton, 1934);

The Old Contemporaries (London: Methuen, 1935);

Pleasure Trove (London: Methuen, 1935; Philadelphia: Lippincott, 1935);

London Afresh (London: Methuen, 1936; Philadelphia: Lippincott, 1937);

Only the Other Day (London: Methuen, 1936);

All of a Piece (London: Methuen, 1937; New York: Lippincott, 1937);

As the Bee Sucks (London: Methuen, 1937);

Adventures and Misgivings (London: Methuen, 1938);

Cricket all his Life, edited by Rupert Hart-Davis (London: Hart-Davis, 1950);

Selected Essays of E. V. Lucas, edited by H. N. Wethered (London: Methuen, 1954).

OTHER: *A Book of Verses for Children,* edited by Lucas (London: Richards, 1898);

Charles Lamb and the Lloyds, edited by Lucas (London: Smith, Elder, 1898; Philadelphia: Lippincott, 1899);

The Open Road, edited by Lucas (London: Richards, 1899; New York: Holt, 1901; revised and enlarged, London: Methuen, 1905);

Charles Lamb, *The Essays of Elia,* introduction by Lucas (London: Methuen, 1902);

The Works of Charles and Mary Lamb, edited by Lucas, 7 volumes (London: Methuen, 1903–1905; republished, 6 volumes, London: Methuen, 1912);

The Friendly Town, edited by Lucas (London: Methuen, 1905);

Mr. Punch's Children's Book, edited by Lucas (London: Punch Office, 1905);

Forgotten Tales of Long Ago, edited by Lucas (London: Gardner, Darton, 1906; New York: Stokes, 1906);

Another Book of Verses for Children, edited by Lucas (London: Gardner, Darton 1907; New York: Macmillan, 1907);

The Gentlest Art, edited by Lucas (London: Methuen, 1907; New York: Macmillan, 1907);

The Hambledon Men, edited, with contributions, by Lucas (London: Frowde, 1907);

The Ladies' Pageant, edited by Lucas (New York: Macmillan, 1908);

Runaways and Castaways, edited by Lucas (London: Gardner, Darton, 1908);

William Cowper's Letters: A Selection, edited by Lucas (London & New York: Frowde, 1908);

Her Infinite Variety, edited by Lucas (London: Methuen, 1908);

Good Company, edited by Lucas (London: Methuen, 1909);

Some Friends of Mine, edited by Lucas (New York: Macmillan, 1909);

The Second Post, edited by Lucas (London: Methuen, 1910; New York: Macmillan, 1910);

Remember Louvain!, edited by Lucas (London: Methuen, 1914);

The Joy of Life, edited by Lucas (London: Methuen, 1927);

Postbag Diversions, edited by Lucas (London: Methuen, 1934; New York: Harper, 1934);

The Letters of Charles Lamb, edited by Lucas, 3 volumes (London: Dent/Methuen, 1935; New Haven: Yale University Press, 1935); revised and abridged by G. Pocock, 2 volumes (London: Dent, 1945; New York: Dutton, 1945).

Though he was an immensely prolific writer, the range of E. V. Lucas's sensibility was actually rather narrow. His work as an essayist and a novelist is charming but lightweight; his essays perhaps mark the end of the bellelettristic tradition in England. He achieves and sustains an attractive and effective lucidity of style but is prone to lapse into the sentimental. His work seems consciously to avoid any confrontation with the extremes of human experience and to cultivate a rather cozy optimism safely sheltered from real unpleasantness. His work is thoroughly gentlemanly, its "politeness" a matter of both idiom and matter. Such considerations impose severe limitations on his range and understanding as a literary critic and a literary biographer. His literary interests seem on the evidence of his published work to be confined almost totally to a small group of writers, of whom Charles Lamb (Lucas was to refer to him as Saint Charles, borrowing a phrase from William Makepeace Thackeray) was, without doubt, the figure with whom he felt most in sympathy. Lamb was of such centrality to Lucas that his autobiography, *Reading, Writing and Remembering: A Literary Record* (1932), contains a chapter "Concerning Lamb." Lucas made a major contribution to the study of Lamb. But it is a contribution limited by the constraints outlined above and one that, in the light of modern scholarly methods, now appears dated. Lucas was, above all, a great popularizer, a sharer of his enthusiasms. His literary biographies are the products of enthusiasm, and his delight in his subjects is evident; his powers of analysis and judgment are not always so certain. His two-volume *The Life of Charles Lamb* (1905), however, has retained readers ever since its initial publication and has yet to be superseded.

Edward Verrall Lucas was born on 11 June 1868 at Eltham in Kent; he was the second of the seven children of Alfred and Jane Drewitt Lucas, who were Quakers. Not long after his birth the family moved from Eltham to Brighton in Sussex. Alfred Lucas worked as an agent for insurance companies and building societies. He seems to have been an unsatisfactory father and husband. According to E. V. Lucas's daughter, Audrey, Alfred Lucas was "spoiled and lazy," and, being "blatantly selfish," he kept his family "short of money," an aspect of a larger irresponsibility and thoughtlessness. Lucas attended some eleven different schools, leaving most of them in turn because his father quarreled over the bill. Alfred Lucas had an intelligent love of

INTRODUCTION.

The present edition of the letters of Charles Lamb is the
first to bring all the known material into one book: a desirable
condition made possible by Messrs. Dent's acquisition of the
residuary legatee's rights, by the courtesy of collectors and &
the friendly cooperation of other publishers.   Thus not only
do these three volumes contain all the letters in the editions
of Talfourd, of Percy Fitzgerald, of Bohn's Library, of Ainger,
of W. Carew Hazlitt, of William Macdonald, of the Everyman Library,
of the Boston Bibliophile Society, 1905, and of my own in its
latest form, 1912, but it contains also whatever has come to light
since their day.

That Lamb wrote many more letters than we possess is made
evident by the leanness of certain years - say, for instance,
from 1809 to 1818, while there is nothing preceding those to
Coleridge beginning with May 27, 1796, when the writer was twenty,
marvellously preserved by their not too orderly recipient, We
know also, from references in certain letters, that others must
have been written From time to time new letters will, I feel
sure, emerge.   Meanwhile here is as complete a harvest as now
can be.

When, more than thirty years ago, I was first engaged in
this most agreeable of tasks, there was less concentration.   The

Typescript page, with corrections, for Lucas's introduction to his edition of Charles Lamb's letters (Dartmouth College Special Collections)

travel, a quality which Lucas was to inherit. He is said, too, to have had a gift for irony, as Lucas also did. Lucas was more closely attached to his mother, an unobtrusive woman of humor and intelligence. She was related to A. W. Verrall, the Cambridge classicist, and to Roger Fry.

At the age of sixteen Lucas was apprenticed to a Brighton bookseller; from 1889 to the early months of 1892 he was a reporter on the staff of the *Sussex Daily News*. These two early positions neatly stand as tokens of Lucas's bookishness and his journalistic flair, the hallmarks of most of his later work. The generosity of his uncle, Samuel Drewett, enabled Lucas to spend a period of eighteen months at University College, London, where, among other studies, he attended the lectures of critic and scholar W. P. Ker. An introduction to the novelist Richard Whiteing gave him an entry into literary and artistic circles. In April 1893 he began work at a London evening paper, the *Globe;* the work was not demanding, and Lucas was able to spend many hours in the library of the British Museum. His family connections were perhaps responsible in part for his being commissioned by the Society of Friends to produce a memoir of Bernard Barton (1784–1849), Quaker poet and correspondent of Lamb. In 1896 he was working for the *Academy* and writing for that and for other literary periodicals. In 1897 he married Elizabeth Griffin, daughter of an American father, James T. Griffin, and a Scottish mother. His work in the journals attracted the attention of London publishers; Grant Richards commissioned work from him and employed him as a reader. He began to make contributions to *Punch* and soon after the turn of the century was a valued adviser on the magazine. In 1900 he was commissioned by Methuen to undertake a work on Lamb. He worked as a reader for Methuen and rose, eventually, to become chairman of the house in 1924, on the death of Sir Algernon Methuen. From 1900 until his death Lucas was a central figure in the London publishing establishment. He seems to have had a considerable gift for friendship. His daughter's memoir recounts that Joseph Conrad and his wife frequently dined with the Lucases, and it mentions among other regular visitors Sidney Colvin, Charles Tennyson, William Archer, Maurice Hewlett, and A. E. W. Mason. In *Postbag Diversions* (1934) Lucas published a selection of letters from his various correspondents; they include Max Beerbohm, Hilaire Belloc and John Galsworthy; G. M. Trevelyan, Rudyard Kipling, M. R. James, Walter De La Mare, and a great many others.

Lucas's first literary biography was his account of Bernard Barton. The work's full title is in-

structive: *Bernard Barton and His Friends: A Record of Quiet Lives* (1893). Most of Lucas's biographical work was to be addressed to the presentation of "quiet lives," and he sees his subjects, most often, in terms of their circles of friends. In another respect, too, this early account of Barton anticipates Lucas's later biographical work in its method. Lucas's essential method as a biographer is one of quotation; wherever possible he quotes, often at great length, from his sources, rather than paraphrasing or retelling the contents of those sources. In this study of Barton he follows closely the model provided by Edward Fitzgerald's memoir of Barton, which was published as the preface to an 1849 selection of Barton's letters and poems. Lucas has, he tells us, "on every possible occasion used the words of the memoir rather than my own." The bulk of Lucas's additions are made in the form of quotation. So, to take an example, between pages 91 and 106 all but some eighty lines (enough perhaps to occupy two pages) are quotation. Lucas's conception of Barton, naturally enough, given his method, is essentially Fitzgerald's. Lucas's own pleasure in Barton's character is everywhere evident, however. He writes of Barton's "inveterate preference for the genial and unsullied side of life," a judgment which might just as readily be made of the mature Lucas himself. Lucas's main sources are the correspondence of Barton and his friends: Dr. Nathan Drake, Rev. John Mitford, Fitzgerald, John Linnell, and, of course, Lamb. Lucas orders and quotes the letters; he is little tempted to analyze what they might imply. He acknowledges, for example, the putative improbability of a friendship between Lamb and Barton but will only say that "It is a vile thing to stir among the roots of a friendship between two men to dig out the why and wherefore of their attachment, and it shall not be done here. The affinity of true friendship defies analysis." We could hardly be further from the psychological curiosity which is the defining characteristic of so much modern biography; even those who are not wholly convinced of the value of modern psychological biography will surely need little persuading that Lucas's method dooms him to a pleasant, but eventually frustrating, superficiality. Analysis is absent; we are offered, instead, a fancied visit paid by reader and Lucas to Barton at his home in Woodbridge. When he tells us that his biography of Barton will be free of "those extremes or eccentricities that so often make biographies hardly less piquant than romance," it is clear that Lucas is delighted that this should be the case. The account of Barton is largely unquestioning, ignorant of any possible complexity; his Barton

Lucas in his office, 1931 (photograph by Howard Coster)

is "a plain man ... whose every thought was kindly, whose every word was gentle, whose leisurely walk through life lay along sheltered lanes and over level meads."

Charles Lamb and the Lloyds (1898) is again heavily dependent upon correspondence; it is significant that Lucas should have been an anthologist of English correspondence, as in *The Gentlest Art* (1907) and *The Second Post* (1910). In his preface to *Charles Lamb and the Lloyds* Lucas explains that the book "grew from the discovery, in 1894, of two masses of correspondence relating to the family of Charles Lloyd, the Quaker philanthropist and banker of Birmingham." The letters concerned included twenty by Lamb, hitherto unknown, and others by Samuel Taylor Coleridge, William Wordsworth, Anna Seward, Priscilla Lloyd (who married Christopher Wordsworth), and others. Lucas writes sensitively and with some understanding of Charles Lloyd the poet, devoting chapters to "Coleridge and the Young Lloyd" and "Lamb and the Young Lloyd," and to Lloyd's novel *Edmund Oliver* (1798) and its ef-

fects. As in his earlier book Lucas quotes extensively, though not perhaps to quite such a striking degree as in the memoir of Barton. Of particular interest are some critical letters by Seward in which she discusses the general state of poetry and makes some perceptive (unexpectedly so, given her reputation), detailed comments on the translations of Homer made by Alexander Pope, William Cowper, and Charles Lloyd the elder. Lamb had been an important presence in both of Lucas's first ventures in literary biography. It was with Lamb himself that Lucas made his most substantial, and best-known, contribution to the genre.

Audrey Lucas begins her memoir of her father by quoting some of A. A. Milne's words about him: "One would save for him the little gleanings of the week; ridiculous things, odd things, damnable things: heard, read, discovered: thinking, 'I must tell E. V. that,' knowing that his comment would give just that extra flavour to one's own emotion." It is Lucas's relish for the odd and ridiculous, for the quirkily individual, that is both the strength and the limitation of his *The Life of Charles Lamb*. When it comes to writing about Lamb's minor eccentricities, the bizarre behavior of George Dyer, or the freaks of James White (of the *Original Letters of Sir John Falstaff*, 1796) — even the extraordinary career of Thomas Griffiths Wainewright (painter, man of letters, forger, and poisoner) — Lucas is at his best. His irony and sense of humor serve him well in such matters. In dealing with some areas of Lamb's life, however, Lucas's approach does little more than scratch the surface. His account, for example, of Mary Lamb's fatal stabbing of their mother and her subsequent madness is poignant, though the poignancy resides in the letters of Lamb which are quoted at great length, rather than in any words of Lucas's. Of the effects on Lamb, however, the account is underdeveloped and lacking in any real penetration. Lucas suggests that the disaster was, in effect, the very thing which matured Lamb:

> Before the tragedy he was a youth, mistrustful of his powers, fond of his melancholy, a little inclined to self-pity, and, although intellectually vigorous, not unwilling to be dependent and a hero-worshipper. With the tragedy came a rallying of his stronger qualities; the spirit of responsibility informed him; he became a man and the equal of any man, even Coleridge. Henceforward, although frailties beset him and occasionally conquered, he was never anything but himself and he saw nothing but his duty.

So positive an assessment does not very comfortably lie alongside such poems as "Written a year after the Events" ("Alas! how am I chang'd"), in which Lamb seeks redemption from the state of "spiritual death"; "Written Soon After the Preceding Poem"; and "Composed at Midnight," with its harrowing evocation of loneliness and desperation. At the end of 1795 and the beginning of the following year, Lamb himself had spent some six weeks in "a madhouse at Hoxton," to use Lamb's own phrase. He may have been able to treat the matter humorously in a letter to Coleridge ("I am got somewhat rational now, & dont [*sic*] bite any one"), but the episode surely suggests that Lucas draws too simple an antithesis in considering Lamb before and after the "disaster." This is surely a case of something rather more than a young man "fond of his melancholy." Other than quoting from Lamb's letter to Coleridge, Lucas makes only the slightest of references to the episode, which occupies no more than ten lines. Of the trauma of Mary's intermittent madness, and of her murder of Mrs. Lamb, Lucas's account will seem to most modern readers altogether inadequate and external. Where a later

biographer feels the need to examine those qualities in Lamb's mother which made her "the more or less typical parent of the manic depressive" or to understand Lamb's speech impediment in the context of modern psychoanalytic accounts of speech disorders, Lucas is content with the bare narrative of facts, presented, wherever possible, in Lamb's own subjective terms rather than with the objectivity of the biographer. Lucas would certainly have been profoundly out of sympathy with the kind of psychoanalytical readings which fuel such recent discussions of Lamb as those by Jane Aaron and Gerald Monsman. This same absence of psychological speculativeness ensures that Lucas's discussion of the *Essays of Elia* (1823) fails to explore their biographical implications save in the most literal manner. The games of identity acted out in those marvelous essays, their counterpointing of "truth" and "lie," and what they suggest of Lamb's psychological makeup go almost wholly undiscussed.

In *The Life of Charles Lamb* Lucas once again works chiefly by quotation. Indeed, in the preface to the edition of 1921 he writes that "It was my aim when I wrote the present biography sixteen years ago to collect and fuse into a single narrative the sum of [the] scattered information [about Lamb]. As in carrying out that task I tried as far as possible to keep the story of Lamb's life in his own and his sister's words and in those of his contemporaries, my part will be found to be less that of author than of stage-manager." Lucas's major source, of course, is in the letters of Lamb himself. At times, indeed, one feels that one is reading an anthology of Lamb's letters rather than a biography. Lamb's letters are so entertaining that this is no criticism of the resulting book's readability. Where letters are not numerous, the interest of Lucas's account often slackens. There are, naturally, other sources to be drawn on, too. For the years from 1811 onward Lucas makes extensive use of the diaries of Henry Crabb Robinson. Nor is he sparing in his quotation from other memorialists of Lamb, from Payne Collier's *Old Man's Diary* (1871–1872), for example, or from Mary Balmanno's recollections of Lamb or Sir Thomas Noon Talfourd's *Final Memorials* (1848). His material is not, however, drawn only from the expected literary sources. Chapter 29 closes (with no particular appositeness) with the following paragraph, which has about it an air that is thoroughly typical of Lucas:

> A curious item of information concerning Lamb's "immaterial" physique has just come (1920) to my notice. The ancient firm of wine merchants in St. James's Street, Messrs. Berry Brothers & Co., have been for a hundred

and fifty years in the habit of weighing distinguished customers and keeping a record of the result. Charles Lamb mounted the scales on June 14th, 1814, and the entry in the book runs: "in boots, 9 stone 3 1/2 lbs."

It is equally characteristic of Lucas that one of the things he should value about Lamb is his capacity for friendship. Chapter 17 records, with evident admiration, that though he was "only twenty-six" . . . "Lamb had already as interesting and varied a band of friends as perhaps any man in England. Coleridge and [Thomas] Manning, [William] Wordsworth and Dorothy Wordsworth, [Robert] Southey and Captain Jackson, George Dyer and John Rickman, Burnett and James White, Fenwick and Charles Lloyd, [William] Godwin and Fell — these are diverse enough." One of the abiding interests of Lucas's biography, indeed, is the wide sympathy and knowledge with which its author discusses Lamb's circle; it would probably not be unreasonable to say that in many respects the book is more valuable, now, from this point of view than in terms of its insight into Lamb's own character. Previous writers on Lamb (such as Thomas De Quincey, George Henry Lewes, and J. R. Rees) had already written on Lamb and his friends; but Lucas's biography was a major encouragement to such later works as Orlo Williams's *Lamb's Friend the Census Taker: Life and Letters of John Rickman* (1912) and Dudley Wright's "Charles Lamb and George Dyer," published in *English Review* (1924).

For the modern student of Lamb, Lucas's biography remains indispensable. It is still the most comprehensive account of the man and his circle. Yet its deficiencies are readily apparent; allusions to some of these have been made above. Naturally enough, information not available to Lucas has come to light since the last revision of *The Life of Charles Lamb* in 1921 (some was incorporated in Lucas's notes to his 1935 edition of Lamb's letters). It has to be said that Lucas's handling of his materials does, in any case, leave something to be desired by modern standards. His extensive quotations are not always identified with anything like scholarly thoroughness or precision, and his transcriptions of letters have been shown, in articles by George L. Barnett and others, to be careless and inaccurate on occasion and sometimes "edited." In *The Life of Charles Lamb* he was too often dependent on inadequate editions of the letters derived from Talfourd's unreliable text. Yet Barnett has no hesitation in judging that Lucas "is outstanding among those who have written on Lamb" and in concluding that "In the dual capacity of biographer and editor of the

works and letters, Lucas performed an immense service." With Lamb, Lucas had a great sympathy; his admiration for the man and the works was, indeed, only just "this side idolatry."

In *A Swan and Her Friends* (1907) his approach was more one of mockery than of admiration. In Anna Seward and her circle of friends Lucas found one of those "phases of human incompetence that really are worth examination." Lucas always admired and valued humor; Seward he judged to be "the last and greatest of the unhumourous women." Lucas is ready at every turn to laugh at the "pontifical confidence . . . floridity . . . and sentimentalism" of his subject. The laughs are perhaps rather too easy to find, and it is disappointing that Lucas makes little attempt to address the serious questions that Seward's manner and matter, let alone her considerable contemporary reputation, might seem to provoke. Once again, Lucas's work is firmly based on the letters of his subject; his chief source this time is the 1811 edition of the *Letters of Anna Seward written between the years 1784 and 1807.* Unsurprisingly, Lucas proves highly adept in the evocation of the literary atmosphere of both the period and Anna Seward's environment, as well as in the creation — in large part by intelligently selective quotation — of vigorous character sketches, that of Major André, fiancé of Seward's friend Honora Sneyd, being particularly striking. Lucas writes well of Samuel Johnson and his Lichfield connections — Johnson's schoolmaster, Rev. John Hunter, being none other than the maternal grandfather of Seward. There is much, too, to enjoy in the book's treatment of "The Ladies of Llangollen," Lady Eleanor Butler and Sarah Ponsonby. It remains, however, a slight and rather gossipy book, too ready to settle for easy laughter at the expense of its central subject who has more of substance to her than Lucas's selective treatment allows.

David Williams: Founder of the Royal Literary Fund (1920) is a short account of an interesting and little-known figure done with good humor and sympathy. The narrative of Williams's life and career in fact occupies only the first half of this eighty-page booklet; the second half is an account of the speeches given at the Anniversary Dinners of the Royal Literary Fund. While this second part has its occasional felicities and amusements, it is largely for the discussion of Williams that the booklet retains its interest. An inveterate organizer of clubs and a perennially well-intentioned campaigner with a capacity for gaining and losing friends, Williams brings out the best of Lucas's ironic manner. Williams's friends, at various times, included Benjamin Franklin, Josiah Wedgewood, and John Nichols. Lucas relates rather fetchingly Williams's attempts (eventually successful, of course) to win support for a fund which might extend financial support to impoverished authors and their dependents. An approach to Edmund Burke is recounted quite splendidly in Williams's autobiographical narrative, from which Lucas several times quotes (without, characteristically enough, ever giving proper scholarly references to his source). The delicious humor of the narrative certainly justifies the length of the quotation:

> At the appointed hour, he entered his drawing-room, into which I had been shown, like a maniac, uttering execrations on authors and scribblers. He approached me with such gesticulations as my Welsh constitution interpreted into hostile signals and I prepared for battle; but the gesticulations were oratorical. He looked fiercely in my face and said, "Authors, writers, scribblers, are the pests of the country, and I will not be bothered with them!"
>
> His fury infected me: "Who, and what, are you, to use such language? If you hadn't been a man of letters, you would have been a bog-trotter. You are not a gentleman and I will quit your house."
>
> He rolled at once like an intoxicated person receiving a blow and made an apology that he had mistaken me for another person of my name, but I was rolling downstairs like a true Welshman, and thus terminated my interview with Mr. Burke.

Lucas is ever alert for an anecdote of this kind, and his narrative of Williams's career is a brief, but genuine, pleasure because of such alertness.

In *The Colvins and Their Friends* (1928) Lucas's gently mocking humor necessarily has less freedom to operate. Production of the book had, effectively, been entrusted to Lucas by Sir Sidney Colvin himself, and the book was published only a year after Colvin's death. In the preface Lucas explains that the book is the result of Colvin's wish that "a record of his own and Lady Colvin's friendships should be published." Like so much else in Lucas's work as a biographer, this book is essentially a redaction of relevant correspondence. Colvin had, we are told,

preserved letters from many friends with just such a purpose in mind, and Lucas explains that "the principal part" of the book is made up of his choice from among those letters, supplemented by autobiographical passages from Colvin's *Memories and Notes* (1921). The field is a rich one; Colvin's friendships ranged in time from Edward Burne-Jones and George Eliot to Henry James and Joseph Conrad. He corresponded with Robert Browning and George Meredith. His letters from Robert Louis Stevenson are an important source of information about that author. Lucas's book is made up of extensive quotations with brief linking passages, a pattern apparent in his previous works. Equally familiar and characteristic are the unspoken premise that it is through the nature and quality of a man's friends and friendships that modern readers are best able to know him and the assumption that it is through his correspondence, through letters written and received, that readers are able to gain surest knowledge of those friends. Lucas is far from being a conscious theorist of literary biography; the consistency of his practice, however, is such that these essential tenets of his work as a biographer are not hard to trace.

As a popularizer and an enthusiast Lucas did much valuable work; all those interested in Charles Lamb will surely hold him in the greatest respect, even if they are aware of the shortcomings of some of his work. Lucas made a major contribution to the knowledge of Lamb and his work. *The Life of Charles Lamb* remains a foundation stone for all later study of the essayist and his circle of friends.

References:

Arthur St. John Adcock, *The Glory that was Grub Street* (London: Sampson Low, 1923);

George Leonard Barnett, "A Critical Analysis of the Lucas Edition of Lamb's Letters," *Modern Language Quarterly*, 9 (1948): 303–314;

Audrey Lucas, *E. V. Lucas: A Portrait* (London: Methuen, 1939);

Claude A. Prance, *E. V. Lucas and his books* (West Corwall, Conn.: Locust Hill Press, 1988).

John Middleton Murry

(6 August 1889 – 12 March 1957)

Robert L. Ross
University of Texas at Austin

BOOKS: *Fyodor Dostoevsky: A Critical Study* (London: Secker, 1916; New York: Dodd, Mead, 1916);

Still Life (London: Constable, 1916; New York: Dutton, 1922);

Poems: 1917–1918 (Hampstead: Heron Press, 1918);

The Critic in Judgement; or, Belshazzar of Baron's Court (Richmond: Hogarth Press, 1919);

Cinnamon and Angelica: A Play (London: Cobden-Sanderson, 1920; New York: Saunders, 1941);

Aspects of Literature (London: Collins, 1920; New York: Knopf, 1921);

The Evolution of an Intellectual (London: Cobden-Sanderson, 1920; Freeport, N.Y.: Books for Libraries Press, 1967);

Poems: 1916–20 (London: Cobden-Sanderson, 1920);

The Problem of Style (London: Humphrey Milford/Oxford University Press, 1922; New York: Oxford University Press, 1922);

The Things We Are (London: Constable, 1922; New York: Dutton, 1922);

Countries of the Mind: Essays in Literary Criticism (London: Collins, 1922; New York: Dutton, 1922; revised and enlarged edition, London: Oxford University Press, 1931); republished with *Countries of the Mind: Essays in Literary Criticism, Second Series* (London: Oxford University Press, 1937; Freeport, N.Y.: Books for Libraries Press, 1968);

Pencillings: Little Essays on Literature (London: Collins, 1923; New York: Seltzer, 1925);

The Voyage (London: Constable, 1924);

Discoveries: Essays in Literary Criticism (London: Collins, 1924; revised edition, London: Cape, 1930);

To the Unknown God: Essays Towards a Religion (London: Cape, 1924; New York: Peter Smith, 1930);

Wrap Me Up in my Aubusoon Carpet (New York: Greenberg, 1924);

Keats and Shakespeare: A Study of Keats' Poetic Life from 1816 to 1820 (London: Humphrey Milford/Oxford University Press, 1925; New York: Oxford University Press, 1925);

The Life of Jesus (London: Cape, 1926); published as *Jesus, Man of Genius* (New York: Harper, 1926);

Things to Come: Essays (London: Cape, 1928; New York: Macmillan, 1928);

God: Being an Introduction to the Science of Metabiology (London: Cape, 1929; New York: Harper, 1929);

Studies in Keats (London: Humphrey Milford/Oxford University Press, 1930; New York: Oxford University Press, 1930); enlarged edition published as *Studies in Keats, New and Old* (London: Oxford University Press, 1939); third edition, revised, published as *The Mystery of Keats* (London: Peter Nevill, 1949); fourth edition published as *Keats* (London: Cape, 1955; New York: Noonday Press, 1955);

D. H. Lawrence: Two Essays (Cambridge: Gordon Fraser, 1930);

Countries of the Mind: Essays in Literary Criticism: Second Series (London: Humphrey Milford/Oxford University Press, 1931); republished with *Countries of the Mind* (1922) as *Countries of the Mind, First and Second Series* (London: Oxford University Press, 1937; Freeport, N.Y.: Books for Libraries Press, 1968);

Son of Woman: The Story of D. H. Lawrence (London: Cape, 1931; New York: Cape & Smith, 1931); republished, with a new introduction, as *D. H. Lawrence: Son of Woman* (London: Cape, 1954);

The Fallacy of Economics (London: Faber & Faber, 1932);

The Necessity of Communism (London: Cape, 1932; New York: Peter Smith, 1932); republished with a new introduction (New York: Seltzer, 1933);

Reminiscences of D. H. Lawrence (London: Cape, 1933; New York: Holt, 1933);

William Blake (London: Cape, 1933; New York: McGraw-Hill, 1964);

John Middleton Murry

Between Two Worlds: An Autobiography (London: Cape, 1935); published as *The Autobiography of John Middleton Murry: Between Two Worlds* (New York: Messner, 1936);

Shakespeare (London: Cape, 1936; New York: Harcourt, Brace, 1936);

The Necessity of Pacifism (London: Cape, 1937);

God or the Nation? (London: Peace Pledge Union, 1937);

Heaven — and Earth (London: Cape, 1938); published as *Heroes of Thought* (New York: Messner, 1938);

The Pledge of Peace (London: Herbert Joseph, 1938);

Peace at Christmas (Birmingham: School of Printing, 1938);

The Price of Leadership (London: Student Christian Movement Press, 1939; New York: Harper, 1939);

The Defence of Democracy (London: Cape, 1939);

Democracy and War (London: Nisbet, 1940);

Europe in Travail (London: Sheldon Press, 1940; New York: Macmillan, 1940);

The Brotherhood of Peace (London: Peace Pledge Union, 1940);

The Betrayal of Christ by the Churches (London: Andrew Dakers, 1940);

The Dilemma of Christianity (London: James Clarke, 1941);

Our Long Term Faith (London: Peace Pledge Union, 1942);

Christocracy (London: Andrew Dakers, 1942);

Adam and Eve: An Essay Towards a New and Better Society (London: Andrew Dakers, 1944);

The Free Society (London: Andrew Dakers, 1948);

Looking Before and After: A Collection of Essays (London: Sheppard Press, 1948);

The Challenge of Schweitzer (London: Jason Press, 1948; Folcroft, Pa.: Folcroft Press, 1970);

Katherine Mansfield and Other Literary Portraits (London: Peter Nevill, 1949);

John Clare, and Other Studies (London: Peter Nevill, 1950; New York: Krause, 1968);

The Conquest of Death (London & New York: Peter Nevill, 1951);

Community Farm (London: Peter Nevill, 1952);

Jonathan Swift: A Critical Biography (London: Cape, 1954; New York: Noonday Press, 1955);

Swift (London: Longmans, Green, 1955);

Unprofessional Essays (London: Cape, 1956);

Love, Freedom and Society (London: Cape, 1957);

Katherine Mansfield and Other Literary Studies, with a forward by T. S. Eliot (London: Constable, 1959);

Not as the Scribes: Lay Sermons, edited, with an introduction, by Alec R. Vidler (London: SCM Press, 1959; New York: Horizon, 1960);

Selected Criticism 1916–1957, chosen and introduced by Richard Rees (London: Oxford University Press, 1960);

Poets, Critics, Mystics: A Selection of Criticisms Written between 1919 and 1955 by John Middleton Murry, edited by Richard Rees (London: Feffer & Simons, 1970; Carbondale: Southern Illinois University Press, 1970);

Defending Romanticism: Selected Essays of John Middleton Murry, introduced and edited by Malcolm Woodfield (Bristol: Bristol Press, 1989).

OTHER: Katherine Mansfield, *The Doves' Nest, and Other Stories,* with an unsigned introductory note attributed to Murry (London: Constable, 1923; New York: Knopf, 1923);

Mansfield, *Poems,* with an introductory note by Murry (London: Constable, 1923; New York: Knopf, 1924);

Mansfield, *Something Childish, and Other Stories,* with an unsigned introductory note attributed to Murry (London: Constable, 1924); published as *The Little Girl, and Other Stories* (New York: Knopf, 1924);

Mansfield, *In a German Pension,* with an introductory note by Murry (New York: Knopf, 1926);

Journal of Katherine Mansfield, edited, with an introduction, by Murry (London: Constable, 1927; New York: Knopf, 1927);

The Letters of Katherine Mansfield, edited by Murry, with his narrative annotations preceding some letters (London: Constable, 1927; New York: Knopf, 1929);

Mansfield, *The Aloe,* with an introduction by Murry (London: Constable, 1930; New York: Knopf, 1930);

Mansfield, *Novels and Novelists,* edited by Murry (London: Constable, 1930; New York: Knopf, 1930);

Stories by Katherine Mansfield, selected by Murry (New York: Knopf, 1930);

The Short Stories of Katherine Mansfield, with an introduction by Murry (New York: Knopf, 1937);

The Scrapbook of Katherine Mansfield, edited by Murry (London: Constable, 1939; New York: Knopf, 1940);

Stories of Katherine Mansfield, selected by Murry (Cleveland: World, 1946);

Katherine Mansfield's Letters to John Middleton Murry, 1913–1922, edited by Murry (London: Constable, 1951; New York: Knopf, 1951);

Journal of Katherine Mansfield, edited by Murry (London: Constable, 1954).

John Middleton Murry remains an intriguing and enigmatic literary figure. His forty or so books range in subject matter from literary theory to politics and religion to engaging discussions of such writers as William Blake, Fyodor Dostoyevsky, and John Keats. As a reviewer for British periodicals, he wrote scores of discerning reviews and in many of them recognized works that were to become twentieth-century classics. As an editor of influential journals, he served for a time as an important spokesman for the modernist movement. His approach to literature has been described both as a precursor to the New Criticism and an embodiment of moral vision. During his lifetime his writing was read throughout the English-speaking world, and some of it was translated into various languages. On the other hand, Murry and his work — the two being inseparable according to his detractors — have been denigrated. He has been called an opportunist, a shallow critic who too often relied on intuition and personal revelation for judgments, a sloppy, often bombastic, self-indulgent writer, a political dabbler. Ironically, the two matters that led to the accusation of opportunism have also helped to assure his lasting reputation. First, he became the tireless promoter of the work of his wife, Katherine Mansfield, after her death in 1923. Second, his friendship with D. H. Lawrence, who died in 1930, either inspired or resulted in Murry's subsequent critical and autobiographical work on the novelist. Today Murry is undoubtedly best known as the great short-story writer's husband and the great novelist's friend.

Born in Peckham, London, on 6 August 1889 to poor but hardworking parents, Murry early on proved himself precocious; according to family mythology, for instance, he read the newspaper aloud when he was two years old. His father, John Murry, a civil servant, had through sheer determination and ambition escaped the squalor of the working-class life into which he had been born; on his own

Murry, right, with D. H. Lawrence, left, Katherine Mansfield, and Frieda Lawrence, at the Lawrences' home, 9 Selwood Terrace, 1914

he taught himself to read and write, which gave him entry into the civil service as a clerk. Murry's mother, Emily Wheeler Murry, also understood the necessity of sacrifice for those struggling to move into the lower middle class, not an easy situation at that time in England; accepting without question the long hours her husband worked in two jobs, she added to their scant income by taking in lodgers. The elder Murry, firmly believing in his son's potential, harbored great ambition for him and was determined to see the young John Murry one day rise to the upper levels of the civil service. He placed the boy in school at age two and a half and took great pains in the years that followed to oversee his son's education, even though his own extended workdays prevented much companionship between the two. Balancing these stern paternal demands were the tenderness and sensitivity of his mother. Murry's biographer, F. A. Lea, proposed in *The Life of John Middleton Murry* (1959) that the intimidating strictness and dourness of Murry's father and the warmth of his mother — along with that of his aunt and grandmother — helped to formulate Murry's sometimes contradictory traits of combativeness

and sensibility. That these two sides of his character did not always coexist peacefully, Lea suggests, led to the insecurity that haunted Murry throughout his life: "The sense of being a stranger in a strange land dates back further than I can remember," Murry wrote in a 1931 letter to a friend. In 1901 Murry won a scholarship to Christ's Hospital — a school for the sons of the gentry, thus realizing the first stage of his father's dream. While he fulfilled all expectations from an academic standpoint, Murry discovered literary interests far afield from those that would prepare him for a distinguished civil service career. Further, the school's rich environment alienated him from his family, and he attempted to hide his humble origins — a combined shame and guilt that continued to haunt him once he reached Brasenose College, Oxford, on scholarship. There he studied Classics and in 1912 earned a first in Greats.

For someone of Murry's class who had received a gentleman's education, an academic career or one in the church might well have been the next step, but Murry was determined to earn his living by writing. He had initiated his literary career as an undergraduate by establishing with Michael Sadleir in 1911 the quarterly *Rhythm* (later called the *Blue Review*), which was intended as an organ of modernism. A failure financially and ceasing publication in 1913, the journal attracted brilliant contributors and helped to establish Murry's reputation. In 1912 he started his journalistic career as a reviewer for the *Westminster Gazette* and other London newspapers; before long he began his lifelong association with the *Times Literary Supplement* (*TLS*). A year earlier he had met Katherine Mansfield, who was still married to George Bowden, and they began living together; in 1918 they married. He met D. H. Lawrence in 1913. These two writers were to influence his life in countless and significant ways.

Murry at this point was definitely a man on the way up in British literary circles. In 1916 his first two books appeared: *Fyodor Dostoevsky: A Critical Study* and a novel, *Still Life*. Commissioned by the publisher Secker to pay off a thirty-pound debt from the bankrupt *Rhythm,* the book on Dostoyevsky offers a provocative examination of the Russian writer's spiritual longing. The study does not focus on Dostoyevsky as an artist but views him instead as a seeker of truth who uses the novel simply as an instrument to carry out his metaphysical explorations and to answer the overriding question: "What must he *do* to be saved?" Murry goes on to say that "The posing of that terrible problem and the attempt to answer it with something more than barren silence, forms the deep argument of his [Dostoyevsky's] greatest books." The novel, *Still Life*, was less successful. A thinly disguised rendition of the author's personal quest for identity, the narrative shifts from London to the English countryside, then to Paris, as it follows the struggles and misfortunes of lost souls who take themselves all too seriously. Though discouraged by Mansfield, who was often brutally honest about his wooden writing, and advised by Lawrence to stay with criticism, Murry published two more novels, poetry, and a play in verse. None was successful, and it has surprised some observers that a critic so discerning of talent in others could be altogether blind to his own lack of creativity. The second work of fiction, *The Things We Are* (1922), appeared six years later and is generally considered his best literary work, even though it turns all too static as its characters search their souls endlessly and employ their intellects more vigorously than their emotions.

Two volumes of lyric poetry and a philosophical poem, *The Critic in Judgement; or, Belshazzar of Baron's Court* (1919), also appeared during this time.

The lyrics tend to be imitative and often burdened with inappropriate diction. The discursive nature of *The Critic in Judgement,* on the other hand, was better suited to Murry's ability and, in spite of its poetic limitations, effectively voices what were to become the principles of his critical credo: that literature must incorporate a moral vision and universalize experience; that it must be judged by how well it accomplishes those tasks; that literature and life cannot be separated.

Undaunted by his previous failures, Murry turned next to the theater and wrote a verse drama, *Cinnamon and Angelica* (1920), which expressed in cliché-ridden poetry both his pacifist views and his obsession with romantic love. In 1924, when his third novel, *The Voyage,* attracted even less attention — be it damning or mildly favorable — than that accorded his earlier work, Murry forsook the exercise of his own creative spirit and devoted himself to the examination of that indefinable quality in others.

Even while Murry unsuccessfully sought recognition as a novelist, poet, and playwright, he continued working as an editor and critic. From 1919 to 1921 he edited the *Athenaeum,* the content of which he changed from current affairs to the arts, literature in particular; contributors to this magazine included Mansfield, Aldous Huxley, Lytton Strachey, E. M. Forster, and T. S. Eliot. He left his editorial post when the *Athenaeum* merged with the *Nation* but continued to contribute major signed reviews regularly until 1923. Although his tenure on the *Athenaeum* was brief and the publication lost money, his editorship had helped to establish him as a major literary critic. A collection of Murry's critical essays appeared in 1920 as *Aspects of Literature;* most of the work had been published in the *Athenaeum* and took up such writers as Jean-Jacques Rousseau, William Butler Yeats, Gerard Manley Hopkins, John Keats, Anton Chekhov, Thomas Hardy, and Samuel Taylor Coleridge, along with a discussion of American poetry, comments on "the present condition of English poetry," and Shakespearean criticism. During the same year *The Evolution of an Intellectual* appeared, which collected essays originally published in the *TLS,* the *Nation,* and the *Athenaeum;* while discussions of Siegfried Sassoon's war verses and realism are included, many of the essays focus on more general topics, such as "The Problem of the Intelligentsia," "The Defeat of Imagination," "The Nature of Civilisation," and "Democracy and Patriotism." Another of Murry's significant critical books appeared in 1922, *Countries of the Mind,* again a collection of work published earlier in various periodicals; in addition to discussions of Shakespeare and

Notes, in Murry's handwriting, for Jonathan Swift: A Critical Biography *(1954)*

the poetry of William Collins, John Clare, and Walter De La Mare, Murry examines three French authors, Charles Baudelaire, Gustave Flaubert, and Stendhal. The final essay in this book is called "A Critical Credo," in which Murry states — much as he did in his poem — that literature is primarily a moral project and must be judged hierarchically on how well it fulfills this high purpose stylistically and thematically. In 1921 he was invited to present a series of lectures at Oxford. Published the following year as *The Problem of Style,* the six lectures covered the "meaning" of style, its "psychology" and its "central problem," the "testing" of poetry and prose, "the process of creative style," and "the grand style" in relation to the English Bible. Murry's definition of style, as given in the first lecture, remains an apt one: "Style consists in adding to a given thought all the circumstances calculated to produce the whole effect that the thought ought to produce. Much is concealed beneath that little word 'ought.'"

Several additional collections of Murry's essays from periodicals appeared over the next few years, but more often than not they focus on philosophy and religion rather than on literature. Both Murry's admirers and detractors agree that his major literary criticism was written from about

1916 to 1922. It was a short-lived heyday for the promising young man who had taken London by storm a few years earlier and for whom, it seemed, every door had opened. Yet this change in fortunes was in large part self-determined. After the death of Katherine Mansfield in 1923, Murry underwent a mystical experience that, he said, brought about a spiritual rebirth. According to Sharron Greer Cassavant in her study of Murry (1982), "Murry did not so much become a different man in 1923 as begin to follow his personal inclinations more freely." Cassavant surmises that Mansfield had discouraged Murry's tendency toward subjectivity and encouraged intellectual sophistication. Once she was gone, he could exercise his essentially emotional approach and rely on his intuition, for, as Cassavant points out, "Murry's ultimate stand was that the poet's imaginative world is invulnerable to intellectual analysis."

No longer a professional literary critic, most certainly a failed creative writer, Murry was still determined to make his living by writing, and did so until his death. At one point he was offered an academic post at Oxford but refused on the grounds that it would be both too safe and too confining. In 1923 he founded another magazine, the *Adelphi,* which was intended as a reaction against the very

Murry in 1950 (Radio Times Hulton Picture Library)

literary and intellectual establishment of which Murry had once been a part. Over the years the *Adelphi,* later to become the *New Adelphi,* carried poems by writers such as Hardy, Lawrence, Robert Graves, and Edwin Muir, along with previously unpublished stories and poems by Mansfield. While much of Murry's writing for *Adelphi* dealt with literary topics, William Shakespeare in particular, he also explored his religious beliefs through numerous essays; in them Murry argued that church membership hindered an individual's recognition of the Christ idea because ritual and doctrine had paralyzed the traditional denominations. Murry's voicing of this Romantic individualistic philosophy gave rise to a famous exchange of articles in the *Criterion* with T. S. Eliot, who adhered to the hierarchy embodied in Catholicism. Several of the books Murry published during this period also reflect his dramatic shift from literature to religious philosophy: *To the Unknown God: Essays Towards a Religion* (1924); *The Life of Jesus* (1926); and *God: Being an Introduction to the Science of Metabiology* (1929). Murry remarried

in 1924, to Violet le Maistre; they had two children, a girl named Katherine and a boy named John Middleton Murry, Jr. Suffering from tuberculosis like her predecessor, Violet died on 30 March 1931. Much to his friends' dismay, less than two months later Murry married Betty Cockbayne, the nurse who had been employed to assist with Violet and the children.

Not only was 1931 a significant year in Murry's personal life, but it marked as well a change in his philosophical stance: he announced his conversion to Marxism. A year later he published a pamphlet, *The Fallacy of Economics,* and a book, *The Necessity of Communism,* to propagate his newfound views. This political shift affected as well the study of William Blake on which he was working at the time. Published in 1933, *William Blake* depicts the poet as "a great communist" whose work expresses an apocalyptic vision of a new world order. Although Murry does elucidate Blake's work, his emphasis on the political, religious, and sexual elements in the poetry obscures its lyricism and artistry. Moving away from Marxism in 1936, Murry joined the Peace Pledge Union, a pacifist society. Several of the books and pamphlets he published over the next few years, as in the past, reflected his altered political philosophy: *The Necessity of Pacifism* (1937); *God or the Nation?* (1937); *The Pledge of Peace* (1938); and *The Defence of Democracy* (1939). Probably the most significant work coming out of Murry's pacifist period was *Heaven – and Earth* (1938), published the same year in the United States as *Heroes of Thought*. Most Murry admirers consider this his best book outside of the critical writing. Through studying twelve key figures who represent different eras of Western thought, Murry formulates and presents with lucidity his view of modern civilization. The figures include Geoffrey Chaucer, Michel Eyquem de Montaigne, Shakespeare, Oliver Cromwell, John Milton, Rousseau, Johann Wolfgang von Goethe, William Godwin, William Wordsworth, Percy Bysshe Shelley, Karl Marx, and William Morris. In 1940 Murry took over the editorship of *Peace News,* and he remained in that post for the next six years, writing articles, editorials, and a regular column called "Pacifist Commentary." He left the pacifist publication a year after he had concluded that nonviolence would not work in totalitarian states.

The 1930s were productive years in other ways in spite of his unhappy marriage to Betty, whom he finally left in 1941 in order to live with Mary Gamble; following Betty's death in 1954, Gamble and Murry were married. One of the most significant books from this period was Murry's autobiography, *Between Two Worlds* (1935). The title comes from the poem "Between Two Worlds" (1867) by Matthew Arnold, and two lines are quoted in the autobiography as an inscription: "Wandering between two worlds, one dead, the other powerless to be born." Murry's acute feeling of isolation and incertitude literally dominates the book – from the beginning chapters that recall his childhood and education to the final chapter that records the end of World War I and the faltering health of Katherine Mansfield. Murry reveals first how his father's ambition for him constricted his early years, even though he understood that the elder Murry wanted his son to escape once and for all the drabness of poverty. Still, Murry considered that his childhood had been stolen, and in one of those rare flashes that occur in the book he captures the frustration perfectly: "I crept down from my peep-hole awe struck, and smitten with a wild and impossible desire to get a scholarship and have

an air-gun. One day I got a scholarship: but an air-gun I never had."

Murry then gives full attention to the years at Christ's Hospital and at Oxford, all the while placing too great an emphasis on his own inadequacy, which he seems to blame on his humble background: "I had been uprooted and unrooted in my early boyhood. I had no organic connection either with the class from which I had been taken, nor with the class into which I had been thrust. . . . I had no people; I belonged nowhere." Recorded, too, are the first ventures abroad, early romances, the heady days in London when he started to publish, and the first meeting with Katherine Mansfield. Thereafter the autobiography focuses in large part on their relationship. Murry does admit that Mansfield was not always well liked in the society the couple kept: "Yet there is no doubt that she was regarded by many of her acquaintance as a rather icily perfect, remote and forbidding figure." According to Mansfield biographers, some of the remarks contemporaries made about her efforts to be a "forbidding figure" were certainly harsher than Murry suggests. He saw her as "a woman simple and lovely in all her ways. . . . a totally exquisite being." Wondering why she should have chosen him, Murry goes on to say: "Everything she did or said had its own manifest validity. I do not think it ever entered my head, at any time, to criticize her in any way." In addition to the revealing portrait of Mansfield – even if it is romanticized, Murry talks about numerous other literary figures whom he met, and these passages, especially those concerned with Lawrence, offer a look into an exciting literary period. The book ends with the end of World War I and the decline of Mansfield's health. "Peace, and there was no peace," Murry writes as he concludes this strange, sometimes painful, at other points self-indulgent and overwrought account of his life from 1889 to 1917. In a final note, Murry mentions his "desire and hope" to write the second part of his life story, but he never did.

Long an admirer of Keats, whom he considered a spiritual model, Murry published in 1930 his first work devoted entirely to the poet, *Studies in Keats*. Possibly one reason for his enthusiasm was that both he and Mansfield saw her own condition as a young, dying genius similar to that of Keats. Five years earlier Murry, in *Keats and Shakespeare,* linked Keats with the great playwright whose poetic genius, Murry argues, the Romantic figure had inherited. Cassavant proposes that when Murry set out to write his 1930 study of Keats, he had so immersed himself in the poetry and letters that he became the poet's alter ego. This poet of poets, according to Murry, resolved the questions of good and evil, of life and death, by discovering the principle that beauty dwelt in all things. Murry's passion for Keats's work continued throughout his life; revised and enlarged versions of the original study appeared in 1939, 1949, and 1955. A book titled simply *Shakespeare* was published in 1936. While Murry approached Shakespeare with the same awe he brought to Keats, the sheer immensity of the playwright's work did not allow him to exercise quite so fully his intuitive theory of literary criticism; thus his Shakespearean analyses tend to be more traditional and intellectual in nature. In addition to the book devoted to Shakespeare, Murry wrote over the years numerous essays on the writer in whom, he believed, coalesced all of the qualities the true poet must possess.

After giving up the editorship of *Peace News* in 1946, Murry turned most of his efforts to the development of Lodge Farm at Thelnetham in Norfolk. In this final decade of his life he found the greatest contentment he had ever known, for with Mary Gamble he had at last formed the kind of relationship with a woman he had always exalted but never experienced. He continued to publish, and in addition to his ongoing studies of Keats he issued several collections of earlier essays and wrote some literary portraits, including some new work on Mansfield. One book that stands out during this period is *Jonathan Swift: A Critical Biography*, which appeared in 1954. In the preface Murry states that his "aim has been to write a book which should be at once a life of Swift and a critical study of his works . . . to hold them apart is, very often, to refuse illumination." Both a psychological study, especially in regard to Swift's attitude toward women, and a keen analysis of Swift's writing, the book was well received, and many critics considered it the most complete account of Swift's life and work that had been published so far.

Yet, in spite of Murry's impressive and varied critical writings, to say nothing of those on religion, culture, and politics, he is undoubtedly still best known among the general readership as Katherine Mansfield's husband and D. H. Lawrence's friend — and not always favorably. The perpetuation of this negative view results in part from Mansfield and Lawrence biographers, who often depict Murry as a kind of foolish third party who outlived his more talented wife and friend, then set out to exploit them. True enough, beginning in 1923, the year of Mansfield's death, Murry initiated what became a lifelong practice: the posthumous publication of

Mansfield's stories, letters, journals, scrapbooks, and poems, often with an introduction by himself. Supposedly, Mansfield wanted these incomplete and private papers destroyed, and her friends were often appalled when the materials appeared in print, sometimes first in the *Athenaeum,* then in book form. Murry also wrote several essays about Mansfield, such as the extensive one in the book titled *Katherine Mansfield and Other Literary Portraits,* published in 1949. Here he finds it "curious how little good criticism" on her stories has been written and praises V. S. Pritchett's analysis of her work, even though he does not agree with it for the most part. In particular, he bristles when Mansfield is accused of imitating Virginia Woolf, whose writing, Murry insists, left Mansfield cold. The essay then goes on to defend Mansfield against Pritchett's charge that she lacked a spiritual home, arguing that she did not recreate New Zealand but "a universal country, the land of innocence, to which the soul aspires. . . . Home, for her, was the security of love — of 'being in some perfectly blissful way at peace.' "

While Murry's publication of Mansfield's private papers, his recurring defense of her sometimes unseemly life, and praise of her work annoyed her admirers and offended her detractors, later generations of Mansfield readers owe him a debt of gratitude. That there is no lack today of "good criticism of Katherine Mansfield's stories" must certainly depend in large part on what some called — and still do — Murry's exploitation of his dead wife. Similarly, Murry wrote extensively on Lawrence, beginning long before the novelist's death. A year after Lawrence died, Murry published *Son of Woman: The Story of D. H. Lawrence.* It is neither a biographical nor a critical study but more accurately an effort to trace the formation of Lawrence's thinking, in particular about sex and love, and to explain the role that thought played in the creative process. Characteristically downgrading himself, Murry warns in a note to readers that "If, at the end of the story, they feel that this great and frail and lovely man, this man of sorrows, this lonely hero, has been judged by one who was once his friend, then not Lawrence has been judged, but the friend." Like Mansfield, Lawrence needed a champion after his death. And, like Mansfield's work, that of Lawrence has since been the object of wiser criticism, certainly of approaches more detached and objective. Readers of Lawrence, though, can still learn from Murry.

The last book to appear in Murry's lifetime, *Love, Freedom and Society*, was published early in March 1957. His previous book, *Unprofessional Essays,* which came out a year earlier, had been well received, and the *London Magazine* had asked him to contribute an essay. It seemed that his reputation was on the rise again, which must have pleased Murry; but the strength that had enabled him to write even under the most difficult circumstances was at last ebbing. On 12 March 1957 John Middleton Murry died of a heart attack after a brief illness. He was buried in the Thelnetham churchyard, where the stone marking his grave describes him simply as an "Author and Farmer" and carries the inscription, "Ripeness is All."

A year later Philip Mairet published a pamphlet on Murry in Longman's Writers and Their Work series. At the outset he states that Murry's work with "the most literary value and . . . most likely to appeal to posterity is his literary criticism"; then Mairet goes on to say that "In his output and in the public reaction to it there was much that tended to divert attention" from the critical writing that "will have the most enduring claim upon students of English letters." Unfortunately, this claim has never been fully staked, for Murry's reputation has continued to suffer from those matters that "tended to divert attention" away from his work. In recent years, however, there have been attempts to realize this "enduring claim." Cassavant's study, *John Middleton Murry, The Critic as Moralist,* for example, focuses on the kind of criticism Murry wrote rather than criticizing him for what he did not do. While admitting Murry's shortcomings, this critic forthrightly defends him against his detractors and discovers in his work a desire to bring "literature out of the academy, . . . to make art a life force, not a subject of esoteric study." Cassavant concludes that "When we are tempted to deride Murry's enthusiastic rhetoric, his offenses against the decorum of intellectual exploration, it is wise to recall that he became, as he intended, an influential middle-brow writer whose books sold well even during periods of official unpopularity, whom people stopped on the street to talk about Shakespeare." In another recent book, *Defending Romanticism: Selected Criticism of John Middleton Murry* (1989), the editor Malcolm Woodfield also places Murry and his approach to literature in a more favorable light. In his lengthy introduction Woodfield traces the genesis and development of Murry's career and concludes that "Murry

was in his own time, and might be again in our time, 'influential,' largely as an example of the organic intellectual life: he does not ask you to adopt his view of life and literature, but he does ask you to consider what it means to have one, or to claim not to have one."

Letters:

The Letters of John Middleton Murry and Katherine Mansfield, selected and edited by C. A. Hankin (New York: Franklin Watts, 1983);

The Letters between Katherine Mansfield & John Middleton Murry, selected and edited by Cherry A. Hankin (London: Virago, 1988).

Bibliography:

George P. Lilley, *A Bibliography of John Middleton Murry* (Toronto: University of Toronto Press, 1974).

Biography:

F. A. Lea, *The Life of John Middleton Murry* (London: Methuen, 1959).

References:

Sharron Greer Cassavant, *John Middleton Murry, The Critic as Moralist* (Tuscaloosa: University of Alabama Press, 1982);

Ernest G. Griffin, *John Middleton Murry* (New York: Twayne, 1969);

Rayner Heppenstall, *Middleton Murry: A Study in Excellent Normality* (London: Cape, 1934);

Philip Mairet, *John Middleton Murry,* Writers and Their Work, 102 (London: Longmans, Green, 1958);

Malcolm Woodfield, "Introduction," in *Defending Romanticism: Selected Criticism of John Middleton Murry,* edited by Woodfield (Bristol: Bristol Press, 1989), pp. 1–52.

Papers:

Although Murry's papers are scattered throughout major research libraries in Great Britain and the United States, the most concentrated collections are at the University of Reading, United Kingdom, and the British Library.

Harold Nicolson

(21 November 1886 – 1 May 1968)

Sondra Miley Cooney
Kent State University

See also the Nicolson entry in *DLB 100: Modern British Essayists,* Second Series.

BOOKS: *Paul Verlaine* (London: Constable / Boston & New York: Houghton Mifflin, 1921);

Sweet Waters: A Novel (London: Constable, 1921; Boston & New York: Houghton Mifflin, 1922);

Tennyson: Aspects of His Life, Character and Poetry (London: Constable, 1923; Boston & New York: Houghton Mifflin, 1923);

Byron: The Last Journey, April 1823–April 1824 (London: Constable, 1924; Boston: Houghton Mifflin, 1924; enlarged edition, London: Constable, 1940; New York: Archon, 1969);

Swinburne (London & New York: Macmillan, 1926);

Some People (London: Constable, 1927; Boston & New York: Houghton Mifflin, 1927);

The Development of English Biography (London: Hogarth Press, 1927; New York: Harcourt, Brace, 1928);

Sir Arthur Nicolson, Bart., First Lord Carnock: A Study in the Old Diplomacy (London: Constable, 1930); republished as *Portrait of a Diplomatist: Being the Life of Sir Arthur Nicolson, First Lord Carnock, and A Study of the Origins of the Great War* (Boston & New York: Houghton Mifflin, 1930);

Swinburne and Baudelaire (Oxford: Clarendon Press, 1930; Folcroft, Pa.: Folcroft Press, 1969);

People and Things: Wireless Talks (London: Constable, 1931);

Public Faces: A Novel (London: Constable, 1932; Boston & New York: Houghton Mifflin, 1933);

Peacemaking, 1919 (London: Constable, 1933; Boston & New York: Houghton Mifflin, 1933);

Curzon: The Last Phase, 1919–1925. A Study in Post-War Diplomacy (London: Constable, 1934; Boston & New York: Houghton Mifflin, 1934);

Dwight Morrow (London: Constable, 1935; New York: Harcourt, Brace, 1935);

Politics in the Train (London: Constable, 1936);

Helen's Tower (London: Constable, 1937; New York: Harcourt, Brace, 1938);

The Meaning of Prestige: The Rede Lecture Delivered before the University of Cambridge on 23 April 1937 (Cambridge: Cambridge University Press, 1937);

Small Talk (London: Constable, 1937; New York: Harcourt, Brace, 1937);

National Character and National Policy (Nottingham: University College, 1938);

Diplomacy (London: Butterworth, 1939; New York: Harcourt, Brace, 1939);

Marginal Comment, January 6–August 4, 1939 (London: Constable, 1939);

Why Britain is at War (Harmondsworth: Penguin, 1939);

Germany's Real War Aims (London, 1940);

The Desire to Please: A Story of Hamilton Rowan and the United Irishmen (London: Constable, 1943; New York: Harcourt, Brace, 1943);

The Poetry of Byron (London: Oxford University Press, 1943; Folcroft, Pa.: Folcroft Press, 1969);

Friday Mornings, 1941–1944 (London: Constable, 1944);

The Congress of Vienna, a Study in Allied Unity: 1812–1822 (London: Constable, 1946; New York: Harcourt, Brace, 1946);

The English Sense of Humour (London: Dropmore Press, 1946);

Harold Nicolson (photograph by Howard Coster)

Tennyson's Two Brothers (Cambridge: Cambridge University Press, 1947; Folcroft, Pa.: Folcroft Library Editions, 1973);

Comments, 1944–1948 (London: Constable, 1948);

Benjamin Constant (London: Constable, 1949; Garden City, N.Y.: Doubleday, 1949);

The Future of the English-Speaking World (Glasgow: Jackson, 1949);

King George the Fifth: His Life and Reign (London: Constable, 1952; Garden City, N.Y.: Doubleday, 1953);

The Evolution of Diplomatic Method: Being the Chichele Lectures Delivered at the University of Oxford in November 1953 (London: Constable, 1954; New York: Macmillan, 1954);

Good Behaviour: Being a Study of Certain Types of Civility (London: Constable, 1955; Garden City, N.Y.: Doubleday, 1956);

The English Sense of Humour, and Other Essays (London: Constable, 1956; New York: Funk & Wagnalls, 1968);

Sainte-Beuve (London: Constable, 1957; Garden City, N.Y.: Doubleday, 1957);

Journey to Java (London: Constable, 1957; Garden City, N.Y.: Doubleday, 1958);

The Age of Reason: 1700–1789 (London: Constable, 1960); republished as *The Age of Reason: The Eighteenth Century* (Garden City, N.Y.: Doubleday, 1961);

The Old Diplomacy and the New (London: David Davies Memorial Institute of International Studies, 1961);

Monarchy (London: Weidenfeld & Nicolson, 1962); republished as *Kings, Courts and Monarchy* (New York: Simon & Schuster, 1962);

Diaries and Letters, 3 volumes, edited by Nigel Nicolson (London: Collins, 1966–1968; New York: Atheneum, 1966–1968).

OTHER: Sir Horace G. M. Rumbold, *The War Crisis in Berlin, July–August 1914,* introduction by Nicolson (London: Constable, 1944);

Another World than This: An Anthology, edited by Nicolson and Victoria Sackville-West (London: Joseph, 1945);

Christopher B. Hobhouse, *Fox,* introduction by Nicolson (London: Constable/Murray, 1947);

John R. Strick, *Poems,* memoir by Nicolson (London: Marshall, 1948);

Henri Benjamin Constant de Rebecque, *Adolphe; and, The Red Note-Book,* introduction by Nicolson (London: Hamilton, 1948);

Peter Coats, *Great Gardens,* introduction by Nicolson (London: Weidenfeld & Nicolson, 1963).

Harold Nicolson was one of the major biographers of the modern period and a leading theorist of the biographical art as well. By training he was a diplomat, and he became, because of his intellectual and temperamental gifts, an unequaled communicator. Born in the Victorian period, Nicolson was a perceptive interpreter of the unfamiliar and hostile twentieth-century world for his English readers.

Harold George Nicolson was born in Tehran, Iran (then Persia). His father, Arthur Nicolson, who was Scottish by birth and became eleventh Baron and first Lord Carnock, was then chargé d'affaires at the British embassy. His mother, Catherine Rowan Hamilton, was of Anglo-Irish descent; in the eighteenth century her great-grandfather, Hamilton Rowan, rebelled against English rule in Ireland and eventually settled in America before being pardoned and returning to Ireland. Nicolson's early childhood was spent wherever his father was posted – Budapest, Constantinople, and Morocco. In 1895, when Nicolson was nine years old, his family sent him to an English boarding school, The Grange in Folkeston, where his brothers were already enrolled. When it was not possible for him to join his family during school holidays, he spent them in Ireland with his mother's family.

After having lived in foreign places, Nicolson found school not very exciting. Indeed, recalling it in retrospect, he categorized his dominant emotion during these years as fear. The strict regime of the school was not congenial, and he was bad at games; and he felt that the separation of boys into small groups so that the bad could not influence the good retarded him mentally and socially. To escape his uncongenial surroundings he retreated into books, reading in his youth Charles Dickens; Sir Walter Scott; Alfred, Lord Tennyson; and Algernon Charles Swinburne, among others. Five years later, at age fourteen, he joined his brothers at Wellington School in Berkshire. His experience was most memorable for his study of the classics with the master, the Reverend Bertram Pollock. The standard assignment was one hundred lines of Latin or Greek a day. By 1903 he had passed the exams for Balliol (and was accepted to study there). But because he was too young to enter, his parents sent him to Weimar, Germany, to study for six months. He studied in the home of the Reverend S. F. Freese, British chaplain in Weimar, and continued *Iliad* and *Aeneid* studies. While there he became saturated in Johann Wolfgang von Goethe – but considered him quite dull.

By the autumn of 1904 Nicolson entered Balliol. Although not a particularly serious student, he had already decided on entering diplomatic service. The greatest value of his university years to him were the acquaintances he made, relationships established not only among other students but also with the junior dean, F. F. ("Sligger") Urquhart – who became Nicolson's mentor for life. He recognized Nicolson's qualities, particularly his taste for literature. Vacation periods he spent in travel and study abroad – in Paris or wherever his father was stationed, in Spain and Russia, and with family relatives in England. He admittedly did not work hard enough and finished with only a Third in Greats. Looking back upon these years when he was made an honorary fellow of Balliol in 1953, he said that it was "dearer to [me] than any institution on this earth."

After graduation he began studying for the Diplomatic Examination, primarily in Paris under the tutelage of the crammer Mlle. Jeanne de Henaut. He continued not only to polish his French, but during times away from Paris he continued his German studies and Italian during study trips to Italy. During vacations he traveled all over Europe in addition to visiting his family in Saint Petersburg, where his father was ambassador. Despite his family's doubts about his capabilities, he passed the diplomatic exams in September 1909, one of two who received higher marks than had ever been won. Only twenty-three years old, he had a cosmopolitan background, being well traveled and a master of French and German, with some command of Italian and Spanish – and, of course, Latin and Greek.

At the beginning of 1910 Nicolson was appointed a junior clerk at the Foreign Office. The work was essentially clerical and low-paying in those years of peace. It made so few demands on the clerks that Nicolson's chief concern was becoming involved in the London social whirl. His first over-

Sissinghurst, the Nicolson family home

seas appointment came in January 1911 when he was made attaché to the British embassy at Madrid. Briefly returning to London, in January 1912 he was sent as third secretary to Constantinople. At the time the Balkan states were on the verge of declaring war. Turkey had already gone to war with Italy in September 1911, but they had reached a peace agreement by October 1912. Threats of more major warfare were at hand. The year 1913 began with a coup d'état in Turkey and the outbreak of the first Balkan War. A second Balkan War erupted in June of the same year, a war which brought an end to the Ottoman Empire.

In the meantime, Nicolson's personal life was transformed. During the summer of 1910, his first at the Foreign Office, Nicolson had become acquainted with Vita Sackville-West. After a courtship of two years, they were married on 1 October 1912. Following a honeymoon through the Mediterranean and Egypt, they settled in Constantinople, remaining there until the outbreak of World War I. It was the last time they would carry out the traditional duties expected of a British diplomat and diplomat's wife. Much of the story of their unconventional marriage has been recounted in *Portrait of a Marriage* (1973) by their son Nigel Nicolson. Based on Vita's secret diary discovered after their deaths, it reveals the extent to which she, as well as he, had been romantically involved, before and during their marriage, with members of the same sex. According to Nicolson's biographer, James Lees-Milne, they would not have discussed their sexual proclivities before their marriage. Such topics were not readily discussed in those times, and they may well have supposed at the time of their marriage — he was twenty-five and she twenty — that in the course of their marriage they would grow out of their homosexual inclinations. Instead their pattern of behavior continued throughout their marriage. He engaged in numerous, but casual, relationships with men; her affairs with women, especially with Virginia Woolf, were fewer and more intense. After the first few years, theirs was not a marriage in the sexual sense; however, it continued on a cerebral and emotional level to the benefit of both. This fact is attested to in their extensive correspondence; when they were separated he wrote daily. Their diaries substantiate the importance of their mutual interests — their children, each other's writing, and their homes and gardens at Long Barn, Knole, and Sissinghurst.

Returning to London from Tehran, Nicolson was formally transferred from the Diplomatic Service to the Foreign Office in June 1914. He spent the whole four years of World War I in the Foreign Office. Although he wanted to enlist in the armed service, his department would not release him. He consoled himself somewhat with the thought that he was nonetheless doing work important to the country's defense. Because of his diplomatic experience, he served as an important Eastern European adviser to government leaders. Significant activity during wartime was his work on Pope Benedict XV's peace proposals. He wrote the official summary of it, preparing the government reply in concert with President Woodrow Wilson. In addition, he spent much of this period drafting and redrafting the Balfour Declaration.

As the war drew to a close, he was no less busy at the Foreign Office. He provided advice on Persia, writing a series of memorandums on the political and diplomatic future of the area and on the oil question. In 1919 Nicolson was named to be a junior adviser on the staff of the British delegation to the peace conference in France because, according to Lees-Milne, of his "reputation for brilliant diagnosis and sound judgment." One of the first tasks the Council of Ten — representatives of the European Allies and Japan — addressed was setting up the League of Nations Commission. Nicolson was invited to help organize the Secretariat of the League of Nations. In August 1919 the league formally requested that he be released from the Foreign Office to work for it; he was officially assigned to the league until 31 May 1920. In January of that year he was awarded the C.M.G. (Companion of Saint Michael and Saint George) for his services to the state during the peace conference. He was named a first secretary of the foreign service on 3 March 1920. Nicolson had become so used to being

overworked during the peace conference and during his service to the league that he wondered what to do with his time once he returned to his more routine government work. His friend Michael Sadleir, a partner in the Constable publishing firm, suggested that he write a book. Nicolson agreed, deciding to write a biography of Paul Verlaine. Thus began his long and distinguished writing career. He wrote six major literary biographies, four in the 1920s and the remaining two in the 1940s and 1950s. All shared similar characteristics. First he chose as his subjects writers either unfamiliar to or unpopular with his English reading audience. Almost as if he were at a treaty-negotiating table, he would summarize the status of the writer's reputation, present the evidence of that writer's life and work, and include an account of times and places in the writer's life. Although he visited places associated with the individual, most of his sources for background information were secondhand. If the person had spent some influential period of life in England, Nicolson emphasized this point. In identifying the individual's characteristic behavior, he typically saw each subject as being torn between two opposing aspects of his personality. The tone of his writing was fairly informal; he referred to himself in the first person and directly addressed his readers as "you."

Nicolson had been interested in Verlaine at least as early as 1910 when he read Edmond Lepelletier's *Life of Verlaine* (1906; translated, 1910) in its new English translation. While in Paris for the peace conference, Nicolson had taken the opportunity to visit many Paris sites associated with Verlaine. By 15 May 1920 he had completed sixteen-thousand words of the life. By 20 July Constable had accepted the manuscript. Other than the English translation of Lepelletier's *Life,* there was no biography of Verlaine specifically intended for the English reading audience. Nicolson cites among his reasons for writing the monograph Verlaine's unique place in French literature, his "un-French" temperament which might be accepted by "less conventional Anglo-Saxons," and his relationship with Arthur Rimbaud. The book is arranged in sections according to the phases of life. Nicolson presents Verlaine as a docile creature who liked discipline, whether of the prison, the hospital, or the church. But he lacked self-discipline, a characteristic aggravated by his alcohol problem. His marriage to Mathilde Mouté, by whom he was at first inspired, was shattered by the onset of the Franco-Prussian War. He became acquainted with Arthur

Nicolson and Vita Sackville-West in his sitting room at Sissinghurst

Rimbaud and visited England with him. After Verlaine was sentenced to a term in prison for shooting Rimbaud, he worked on *Romances sans paroles* (1874) and *Sagesse* (1881) and was reconciled to Catholicism. He returned to England as a teacher. He then returned to France; he maintained discipline for a few years but again lost control of himself. Periods of control and loss of control characterized the remainder of Verlaine's life. In Nicolson's estimation, "Verlaine, unlike most Frenchmen, who are too intelligent for so auto-erotic a process, had, in addition to 'la gaite francaise' in addition also to 'l'esprit Gaulois,' a quite Anglo-Saxon sense of humor. It led in his case to the complete annihilation of all will-power." By 21 November 1920 Nicolson finished *Verlaine;* it was published on 10 March 1921. The *Morning Post* declared that it contained the best summary of French poetry of the last half of the nineteenth century. The *Observer* attacked it for Nicolson's superior tone toward Verlaine and thought he disliked Verlaine. A much later criticism came from Edmund Wilson, writing in 1944 a review of Nicolson's *The Desire to Please* (1943). Wilson was especially harsh on him for having not been forthright about the homosexual nature of Verlaine's relationship with Rimbaud. But in Nicolson's defense, Lees-Milne contends, the morals and manners of Verlaine would have struck the average reader of the time as "highly ambiguous."

His next writing project was *Sweet Waters* (1921), a semi-autobiographical novel. When he finished it Nicolson decided in December 1921 that a biography of Tennyson would be his next book. He took as many books on Tennyson as he could from the London library and started to work; by Good Friday 1922 he had begun writing. By the end of April he set out to visit Cambridge, where he looked at Tennyson manuscripts, as well as other sites having Tennyson associations — White Hart Inn in Lincoln and Somersby Rectory. He followed Tennyson's wanderings and Alford to Markethorpe to follow along the beach. He wrote steadily and quickly during May and June, finishing the entire book by 28 August. After he read the proofs in November 1922, he was off to his next Foreign Office assignment, the Lausanne Conference in Switzerland.

Although Tennyson was by no means an unfamiliar figure to English readers, he was not especially popular. Only thirty years had elapsed since his death, and the twentieth-century reaction against the "exaggerated workshop" of "our grandfathers" had set in. Nicolson's intention was "to induce some people to approach Tennyson with an unbiased mind — to read him for their pleasure, profit and even their amusement, as a poet who flourished prodigiously between the years 1832 and 1892." In introducing Tennyson, Nicolson says he sees two Tennysons — the lyric poet and the civic prophet or communal bard. The lyric poet was the good poet; the instructional bard was second-rate. After opening chapters in which he establishes the twentieth-century response to the poet and his early years, Nicolson analyzes Tennyson's career, identifying four periods of his productive life. The first, from 1827 to 1832, was a luxuriant period when he wrote under the influence of John Keats; the second — 1833 to 1855, and covering the years from the death of Arthur Hallam to *Maude* (1855) — was the most important of the four; the third, 1857 to 1872, he considers the "unfortunate mid-Victorian phase" which can have no appeal whatever to the modern mind; after Tennyson's playwriting came the fourth stage, 1880 to 1892, which Nicolson describes as the "splendid Aldworth period."

Especially strong in describing the places associated with Tennyson and with Tennyson himself, the principal value of the life is its reappraisal, not in a highly technical or scholarly sense, of the poet, his life, and his poetry. His analysis of poetry is weakened because he habitually uses it as biographical evidence. When Tennyson's biography was published on 15 March 1923, general response was positive. Sir Edmund Gosse, reviewing it in the London *Sunday Times,* thought nothing contradicted it; the *Spectator* congratulated its "beautiful workmanship." Nicolson was delighted with the reception. He could not have known that at the time Lytton Strachey called it disgusting and stupid or that Virginia Woolf "threw it onto the floor in disgust."

While Nicolson was working on the Tennyson biography, a coup d'état in Greece occurred, tensions increased in the Balkans, and British troops were confronting the Turkish at the Dardanelles. Although the crisis was temporarily over when the Turks signed the Mudania Armistice, it was not completely resolved until a conference of all parties involved was held in Lausanne. Nicolson was to attend. Before it could begin in November 1922, coup d'états took place in both Turkey and Italy. After the Lausanne Conference ended in February 1923, Nicolson returned to London and worked in the Foreign Office except for brief trips abroad.

In the meantime, Nicolson was working on his third literary biography. After delivering the Tennyson manuscript in August 1922, Nicolson notes in his diary that he had begun thinking about a book on George Gordon, Lord Byron. Nicolson had always been infatuated with Byron, having read his works as early as 1908. Reading and taking notes in late 1922, he began to work in earnest by January 1923, reading works by and about Byron, visiting Lady Lovelace, widow of Byron's grandson, and visiting Newstead Abbey. Working at his usual speed, Nicolson began writing the book on 29 June 1923 and had finished the first draft by 26 July. Concentrating on the last year of Byron's life, Nicolson was less concerned with the poet's work than with his revolutionary activities. Acknowledging the importance of Richard Edgecumbe's scholarship, Nicolson suggests that Byron's story could be told again because Byron material had become available and he was telling the story from the viewpoint of a younger man, and also because "the living fascination of Byron arises from the perpetual conflict between his intelligence and his character." Byron's importance for the contemporary reader lay in the fact that through a "single act of heroism he secured the liberation of Greece. Had Byron, as he was urged, deserted the Hellenic cause in February 1824, there would . . . have been no Navarino; the whole history of South-eastern Europe would have developed differently."

Nicolson's account of the last year of Byron's life opens with a dramatic description of Genoa, Lady Blessington's arrival there, and her diary entry anticipating a meeting with Byron. After two chapters of biographical material, pictorial setting, and dramatic events, Nicolson moves on to chapters analyzing the Greek War of Independence and England's response to the Greek War. The account of Byron's departure for Greece, his arrival there and settling at Missolonghi, and his illness and last days is vividly described, drawing upon Edward John Trelawney's and Byron's letters and the diaries and letters of friends.

When the book was published on 3 March 1924, it received positive press. The review in the

Nicolson and Sackville-West with their sons, Ben and Nigel, in 1929, just before Nicolson resigned from the diplomatic service

New Statesman went so far as to call it the "best and most entertaining piece of biographical narrative . . . since Lytton Strachey's *Eminent Victorians* [1918] and his *Queen Victoria* [1921]." In Edmund Gosse's London *Sunday Times* review, he observed that it would "enhance [Nicolson's] reputation." Indeed, according to Lees-Milne it made him a leading authority on Byron.

In July 1924 Nicolson was asked to write a volume on Algernon Charles Swinburne for the English Men of Letters series. After several months of preparation, he began writing the book in November 1924, but Foreign Office work intervened and he was not able to do serious work on it until 1925. He did have time in the early part of 1925 to interview people who had known Swinburne, particularly Sir Edmund Gosse. Nicolson benefited as much from Gosse's research for his own biography of Swinburne as from his recollections. Nicolson's treatment of Swinburne offered little that was new. In fact, he acknowledged the superiority of Gosse's work: "Sir Edmund Gosse has once and for all set the key or tone for all future study of the poet. . . ."

Hence Nicolson thought his own work had a "guide-book character." Considering it a monograph, he regularly excluded material. He gives a detailed treatment of 1838–1857 but only a cursory treatment of the years that follow. Once again, Nicolson sees a fundamental conflict within Swinburne — his impulse toward revolt and his impulse toward submission. He says that psychologists would call these his "instinct of self-assertion" and the "instinct of self-abasement." In Swinburne's best works these conflicting elements were balanced — in *Atlanta in Calydon* (1865), "Hertha" from the *Songs before Sunrise* (1871), and the *Poems and Ballads, Second Series* (1876). But often there was a lack of sympathy between Swinburne and his readers because of faulty communication, the result of interposition or overemphasis of his technique. Moreover there was "no sufficient basis of common interest" between poet and reader because of Swinburne's eccentricity.

Nicolson concludes with a discussion of Swinburne's prose, observing that it is beyond the scope of the monograph to examine in detail everything the poet wrote after 1879. He contends that the critical prose is marred by Swinburne's ill temper, "idolatries and hatreds," and his "appalling prose." Few of the features which distinguished Nicolson's other biographies are evident in this one. There are none of the descriptions of settings or of the poet himself, little effort to enliven the times and their relationship to the poet. Although there was some favorable response to the book – Gosse thought it succeeded all its predecessors in originality – Nicolson later admitted that it was a "half dress book" and that he would never write another.

By the time Swinburne appeared, Nicolson had already left for Tehran. Although he was reluctant to leave England for a foreign post, he knew that doing so was important if he hoped to advance in the diplomatic service. Despite the fact that this was a particularly critical period in Persian-British relations, Nicolson was not happy in his assignment. He did not like to be separated from Vita, even though she came for a winter visit while he was there; he missed his friends in England as well. Moreover he began to dislike the nature of his diplomatic responsibilities and the social duties which were attendant upon this position. He did not earn much. Finally he discovered that he was happiest when he was writing and in the company of writers and intellectuals. Returning to England in the spring of 1927, he notified the Diplomatic Service that he would not go back to Persia; he preferred to be in the Foreign Office. He finally agreed to stay in the Diplomatic Service and to accept an appointment to Berlin.

Before leaving for Berlin in October 1927, Nicolson finished *The Development of English Biography*. It was the fourth volume in the Hogarth Press series Lectures on Literature edited by George Rylands and Leonard Woolf. According to Nicolson's biographer, the book is indebted to some degree to Gosse's article on biography in the *Encyclopaedia Britannica*, especially Gosse's warning against theoretical writing, treating the history of the times with the subject's life, and sanctifying the subject. Nicolson defines biography as "the history of the lives of individual men as a branch of literature." He distinguishes between "pure" and "impure" biography, on the other hand, which has as its objective the "desire to celebrate the dead," "uses the life as an illustration of some extraneous theory or conception," and reveals "undue subjectivity in the writer."

He then surveys the history of biography in England. Biography began with celebrations of dead and legendary warriors in runic inscriptions and the old sagas and epics. From then until the thirteenth century, biography was actually hagiography. By the fourteenth century "all educated interest in facts suffered an elapse," and biography waned. Interest in history revived in the sixteenth century with the Tudor chronicles. Two biographies of particular interest in this period were William Roper's of Thomas More (1626) and George Cavendish's of Cardinal Thomas Wolsey (1641). Because of these two, "English biography was first differentiated as a species of literary composition distinct from history and romance." Biography again declined in the seventeenth century because of the political situation and the moral conflict in the country. Although Horace Walpole's lives are of this period, they are not pure biography; they are not "complete or even probably portraits," and Walpole allows his own feelings to intrude. Nonetheless he was a pioneer, the first "deliberate biographer."

By the eighteenth century, Nicolson proposes, biography became more artificial, in large part because the drama, essayists such as Joseph Addison and Richard Steele, and the novel had become sources of enjoyment for people of the time. But it was also the age of the great biographers, Samuel Johnson and James Boswell. Johnson's success lay in his great emphasis on truth, his good sense, and his interest in the character of individuals. "Johnson, with his mistrust of history and his dislike of fiction, found in biography a satisfaction such as no other brand of literature could provide." Boswell possessed that talent essential for a biographer – an independent intellect and passionate interest in life united with courage and originality. "[H]e discovered and perfected a biographical formula in which the narrative could be fused with the pictorial, in which the pictorial in its turn could be rendered in a series of photographs, so vividly, and above all so rapidly projected as to convey an impression of continuity, of progression – in a word, of life."

The Romantic biographers of the early nineteenth century, in Nicolson's estimation, were good biographers; in fact, Lockhart's *Life of Sir Walter Scott* (1837–1838), after Boswell's *Life of Samuel Johnson, LL.D.* (1791, 1793), is the "most convincing biography we possess." This is due to Lockhart's use of the inductive method, his highly conscious artistry, and his ability to work up the subject's portrait through the impressionistic method. Victorian moral earnestness, however, nearly destroyed pure biography in the latter part of the century. Nicolson believed that "a deep be-

Nicolson in 1967 (photograph by Ian Graham; courtesy of Nigel Nicolson)

lief in a personal deity destroys all deep belief in the unconquerable personality of man."

As for the twentieth century, Nicolson felt that until then no effort had been made to isolate biography as a separate form. Although it could be distinguished from history and fiction by applying the tests of individuality and truth, its relationship to science and literature still needed to be established. To satisfy the scientific interests of the times, the biographer would have to accumulate a great amount of authentic material, while at the same time producing that in a "synthetic form" to meet the demands of literature. Nicolson cites Gosse and Strachey as the preeminent biographers of the age. He praises Strachey's *Queen Victoria* (1921) for artistically shaping so much material. On the other hand, Strachey's principal shortcoming is that he wrote from a "thesis," and "any personal thesis on the part of the biographer is destructive of 'pure' biography." As for the future of biography, Nicolson felt that the scientific interest in biography would destroy the literary interest because "the

former will insist not only on the facts, but on all the facts; the latter demands a partial or artificial representation of facts." Reviews of the book were generally complimentary. It was especially well received in the United States.

In October 1927 Nicolson unhappily set off for his last Diplomatic Service assignment in Berlin; it was not a city which he particularly liked, and he was struggling with his plans for the future. He finally decided to leave diplomatic life altogether because he so disliked being separated from home, Vita, and his sons.

While in Berlin, he continued work on the projected biography of his father, Lord Carnock. In the middle of July 1929 the question of his future employment seemed answered; he received a letter from Bruce Lockhart announcing that newspaper magnate Lord Beaverbrook was looking for someone like Nicolson to edit a column for the *Evening Standard* like the "Londoner's Diary" in the *Express*. To be written with Lockhart, it would be fifteen paragraphs a day of social, political, and literary gossip. Beaverbrook would allow him to retain his political views, and the pay was good. Thus, he joined the *Evening Standard* on 1 January 1930. Leaving the profession of diplomacy and turning to journalism marked the "great divide" in Nicolson's life.

Although from the first Nicolson disliked writing for the *Evening Standard,* he engaged in other kinds of writing as well. He wrote articles for the *Express* and *Standard;* he was a reviewer for the *Express;* he reviewed five books a week, three weeks each month for the *Daily Telegraph;* and he had a weekly broadcast on BBC called *People and Things.* And in April 1930 *Sir Arthur Nicolson, Bart. First Lord Carnock: A Study in the Old Diplomacy* was published. Still interested in the larger questions affecting the country, he became involved at this time in a disastrous political byroad. He became allied with Oswald Moseley's Fascist New Party. Moseley, finding himself more and more dissatisfied with the apathy of the government, resigned his government position. He told Nicolson he wanted to start a new party. Although Nicolson had some doubts about Moseley's doctrines, he joined the New Party in January 1931. Upon his joining, he was publicly declared by others to be a Fascist, but he was always ambivalent about the party's stands. However, he became editor of its official publication, *Action,* and he contested the Combined English Universities seat for the party and was defeated. In his estimation, "everything has gone wrong [in 1931]. I have lost not only my fortune but much of my reputation."

Much of the 1930s was an unsettled time for Nicolson. He continued writing reviews and other articles and his own books. *Public Faces* was published in 1932, and he began working on *Peacemaking, 1919* (1933). In December 1932 he and Vita left for their first visit to the United States. Although America was in the depths of the Depression, they were both extremely well received, having well-established reputations on this side of the Atlantic. When they arrived back home, he began the third book in his diplomatic trilogy: *Curzon: The Last Phase, 1919–1925* (1934). A product of his American visit was a request from the Morrow family to write a biography of Dwight Morrow. When it was published in 1935, he said he had never taken more pains with a book which was less appreciated by his English audience. He felt it was the worst book he had written because it was a command performance.

But at forty-eight years of age, he found that journalism, his own writing, and domestic pursuits alone did not satisfy him. He needed to be back in public life. He got that chance in 1935. He was asked by the National Government Party to stand for a seat at West Leicester. After going through the distasteful process of campaigning, he won the seat by thirty-seven votes and joined the House of Commons. He loved the House of Commons – its setting and its history. He loved being in the thick of things. And he felt he could make a contribution in matters of foreign affairs. Unfortunately, he did not enjoy party politics, the canvasing, the public speaking. All the while he continued writing. By the end of the decade he had written thirteen books; in December 1938 he agreed to write a weekly article for the *Spectator* – "People and Things" – which became "Marginal Comment" and continued until 1952. And he was lecturing and speaking around the country, trying to explain to the people of England what Munich really meant – no easy task since Neville Chamberlain was still prime minister.

Throughout the course of World War II he continued serving in Parliament. As the war became more intense, he became more active, speaking out more often. Drawing upon his years of foreign service, he fought against the Conservative Party under the leadership of Chamberlain. He served in other ways as well as continuing his own writing, his BBC work, and his reviews. In May 1943 his *The Desire to Please,* the story of the Irish Nationalist Hamilton Rowan, his maternal great-great-grandfather, was published. By the end of 1943 he joined the Historic Buildings Committee of the National Trust. He also served as parliamentary secretary to the Ministry of Information. But when Winston Churchill became prime minister, he asked Nicolson to step down and join the BBC Board of Governors. When the postwar elections were held, Nicolson ran for reelection but lost.

By 1946 England and Europe were dealing with postwar issues. In July the BBC asked Nicolson to go to Paris for the opening of the peace conference. They asked him to give two talks a week on home service, plus one in French and one in English for the overseas service, the latter to treat international affairs from a diplomatic perspective. He had been to see the opening of the Nuremberg trials earlier that year. It was difficult not only because of the exhibits of Nazi atrocities but also because he had known some of the men from his years in Germany. He used his time in Paris to visit places associated with French novelist and thinker Benjamin Constant, about whom he would write his next biography.

But before he could begin work on it, he had to campaign for election. Having joined the Labour

Party, he was asked to stand for a by-election in North Croydon. He did not enjoy one minute of the three months of campaigning. He did not like the electorate and made remarks in his columns which suggested he was not taking the entire process seriously. The Conservative candidate won by twelve thousand votes.

He began writing Benjamin Constant's biography in June 1948. It went slowly, but he finished the text, introductory note, and bibliography by the end of August. It was not published, however, until midsummer 1949. Like the Byron biography, *Benjamin Constant* is more a political biography than a literary one. Even Constant's years of association with Madame de Staël heavily involved him in politics. Nicolson notes at the outset that it is "not a work of original research." Anyone writing about Constant is too indebted to his French biographers. Instead he intended it as a "cautionary tale" for "English readers." Constant was a "classic example of the conflict between intellect and character." This duality "arose from the circumstance that his compelling intelligence was not accompanied by an equally decisive will." His character did not become integrated because his mother had died when he was born, he never had any sense of home or country, and his father possessed an "impetuous eccentricity." Nicolson attributes the eighteen months Constant spent in Edinburgh with teaching him about liberty, "not merely as a political formula, but as the only ethical purpose in which he unwaveringly believed." It was as a politician and publicist that he made his greatest impact in France. He constituted himself as the "school-master of Liberty."

As in all his other biographies, Nicolson gives great attention to places — the village of Colombier, the home of the de Charrières, the Château de Mézéry. Descriptions of people and scenes with them — Madame de Charrière in the bath, Constant with his dogs — are sharply presented. In researching the book, Nicolson even studied Constant's letters carefully because he believed that the handwriting revealed something of an individual's character. Reviewers responded to it with what Lees-Milne calls "reverential respect." The *Times Literary Supplement* astutely observed that there was a noticeable parallel between Constant and his biographer. As predominantly literary men in politics, neither understood that the most intellectual person does not necessarily make the most effective politician.

Although Nicolson's political career was over with the defeat at North Croydon, his writing continued apace. In that year he severed his relations with the *Daily Telegraph* and *Figaro*. He agreed to write for the *Observer* weekly eight-hundred-word articles on books of his choice; he did so for the next fourteen years. In the summer of 1948 a request came which would occupy most of his time for three years. He was asked to write a biography of King George V. Nicolson's biographer calls it his magnum opus. It was his longest book, the most important, and the most widely read.

Nicolson returned to literary biography in 1955, despite his declining health. He had suffered two strokes. But he hated not having a book to write, and he thought Vita would feel better to see him writing. So he undertook a biography of the French poet and critic Charles-Augustin Sainte-Beuve. As in the Constant book, he "makes no claim to original research." His only aim is to introduce Sainte-Beuve "in biographical form to English readers." Saint-Beuve presented Nicolson a twofold challenge — he was not well known to English readers, and the French disliked him intensely. In fact, French literary people were surprised that Nicolson wanted to bother writing about Sainte-Beuve. Despite his health problems, Nicolson made his customary visits to locations in France associated with Sainte-Beuve — his homes in Paris and Port Royal, the center of Jansenist learning. The book was finished by September 1956 and published in June 1957. The main interest for Nicolson in Sainte-Beuve's story is the "unceasing conflict between an unusually lucid intelligence, an unusually active curiosity, and a character that was confused and weak." Sainte-Beuve, too, had made a short visit to England in 1828 which had left him with a literary impression of England. Nicolson did not particularly appreciate Sainte-Beuve's poetry; he found the prose inspiring. Sainte-Beuve's critical stance was intellectually appealing to Nicolson. Sainte-Beuve reconciled novelty with tradition, replaced the old deductive method with the inductive method, and taught his generation to rely less on rules and principles and more on individual psychology. But the only warm feeling Sainte-Beuve engendered in Nicolson was pity. He found him most unattractive personally. In fact, the reviewers were surprised that he could have written so sympathetically about Sainte-Beuve. Lees-Milne suggests that Nicolson could do so because his biographies are in some degree autobiographical, that he saw something of himself in the French critic.

Although Nicolson wrote two more books after the Sainte-Beuve, his health made it impossible for him to work at his usual standard of quality. He gave up his *Observer* reviewing with the result that he had a limited income. His son Nigel sold the serialization rights for Nicolson's diaries to the *Observer*, the book rights to Collins. He thought that his father might enjoy editing them. Unfortunately, he was not physically or mentally up to the task.

Nicolson probably best described his secret as a biographer in his 1954 *Cornhill Magazine* essay, "The Practice of Biography." Writing of his contemporary – and rival – Lytton Strachey, he criticizes Strachey's ironic tone in his biographies. "The drudgery of collecting and checking material, the mechanical labour of completing a long book, require an effort more continuous than can be sustained by glimpses of self-satisfaction. The biographer must be constantly fortified by a fundamental respect, or affection, for the person whom he is describing; if all that he experiences is superficial contempt, his work will turn to ashes and his energy wilt and fail. No writer can persist for five hundred pages in being funny at the expense of someone who is dead." Harold Nicolson died on 1 May 1968; his ashes were buried in Sissinghurst churchyard.

References:

Ralph Arnold, *Orange Street and Brickhold Lane* (London: Rupert Hart-Davis, 1963);

Victoria Glendinning, *Vita: The Life of V. Sackville-West* (New York: Knopf, 1983);

James Lees-Milne, *Harold Nicolson: A Biography*, 2 volumes (London: Chatto & Windus, 1980–1981);

Nigel Nicolson, *Portrait of a Marriage* (New York: Atheneum, 1973);

Edmund Wilson, "Through the Embassy Window: Harold Nicolson," *The New Yorker*, 20 (1 January 1944): 63–67.

Papers:

Harold Nicolson's correspondence with Michael Sadleir is at Temple University, Philadelphia, Pennsylvania. His other papers are in the possession of his son Nigel Nicolson.

George Paston
(Emily Morse Symonds)
(1860 – 12 September 1936)

Rebecca Brittenham
Rutgers University

BOOKS: *Little Memoirs of the Nineteenth Century* (London: Privately printed, 1893);

A Modern Amazon (London: Osgood & McIlvaine, 1894);

A Bread and Butter Miss; a Sketch in Outline (New York: Harper, 1895; London: Osgood & McIlvaine, 1895);

A Study in Prejudices (New York: Appleton, 1895; London: Hutchinson, 1895);

The Career of Candida (London: Chapman & Hall, 1896; New York: Appleton, 1897);

A Fair Deceiver (London & New York: Harper, 1898);

A Writer of Books (London: Chapman & Hall, 1898; New York: Appleton, 1899);

Mrs. Delany (Mary Granville) a Memoir, 1700–1788 (London: Richards, 1900);

Little Memoirs of the Eighteenth Century (New York: Dutton, 1901; London: Richards, 1901);

Sidelights on the Georgian Period (London: Methuen, 1902; New York: Dutton, 1903);

George Romney (London: Methuen, 1903);

Old Coloured Books (London: Methuen, 1905);

Social Caricature in the Eighteenth Century (London: Methuen, 1905; New York: Blom, 1968 [facsimile]);

B. R. Haydon and His Friends (London: Nisbet, 1905);

Lady Mary Wortley Montagu and Her Times (London: Methuen, 1907; London & New York: Putnam, 1907);

Mr. Pope, His Life and Times, 2 volumes (London: Hutchinson, 1909);

Feed the Brute (New York: French, 1909; London: Lacy's Acting Edition, 1909);

Tilda's New Hat (London: Lacy's Acting Edition, 1909; New York & London: French, 1909);

The Parents' Progress (New York: French, 1910; London: Lacy's Acting Edition, 1910);

The Naked Truth; a Farcical Comedy in Three Acts, by Paston and William Babington Maxwell (New York: French, 1910; London: French, 1921);

Stuffing (London: Lacy's Acting Edition, 1912; London: French, 1912);

Double or Quits. A Comedy in One Act (London: French, 1919);

Clothes and the Woman. A Comedy in Three Acts (New York & London: French, 1922);

Nobody's Daughter. A Play in Four Acts (London: "The Stage" Play Publishing Bureau, 1924);

Stars; a Comedy (New York & London: French, 1925);

At John Murray's; Records of a Literary Circle, 1843–1892 (London: John Murray, 1932);

"To Lord Byron": Feminine Profiles Based Upon Unpublished Letters, by Paston and Peter Quennell (New York: Scribners, 1939; London: John Murray, 1939).

SELECTED PERIODICAL PUBLICATIONS – UNCOLLECTED: "Lady Journalist," *The English Illustrated Magazine,* 12 (January 1895): 65–73;

"A Censor of Modern Womanhood," review of *Mrs Lynn Linton* by George Somes Layard, *Fortnightly Review,* 76 (1902): 505–519;

"An Apostle of Melodrama," *Fortnightly Review,* 100 (November 1913): 962–975.

Emily Morse Symonds wrote literary biography at a time when the field was dominated by – though by no means limited to – male writers. Following in the tradition of "the many women writers who have succumbed to the mysterious attraction of the name 'George,'" as one reviewer put it, she used the male pseudonym "George Paston," partly in order to gain an unqualified entrance into the profession (*The Academy,* 24 December 1898). However, like George Eliot, Symonds consistently retained the pseudonym for all her published work

LADY MARY
WORTLEY MONTAGU
AND HER TIMES

BY

GEORGE PASTON

WITH TWENTY-FOUR ILLUSTRATIONS

METHUEN & CO.
36 ESSEX STREET W.C.
LONDON

LADY MARY WORTLEY MONTAGU
FROM THE PORTRAIT BY JONATHAN RICHARDSON

Frontispiece and title page for Paston's biography of the seventeenth-century poet that utilized many newly discovered letters

long after the fact of her gender was publicly known and acknowledged. As a determined lobbyist for women's rights, she used her biographical and novelistic work to add to the contemporary understanding of the position of women by tracing idealized models of behavior, educational practices, and the marital institutions that had shaped the experiences of women in previous centuries. In addition, her passion for archival work and her broad-ranging exploration of various kinds of documents — periodicals, newspapers, letters, diaries, and memoirs, as well as literary sources — frames that feminist agenda within a larger cultural understanding of the characters, the fashions, the controversies, and the friendships of the eighteenth and nineteenth centuries.

Symonds was born in 1860 in the city of Norwich, where her father, the Reverend Henry Symonds, was the precentor of the Norwich Cathedral. When her father died (approximately 1896), she and her mother, Emily Evans Morse Symonds,

moved to South Kensington, where they lived on an income comfortable enough to allow them to travel, entertain, and support the initial years of her writing career. The novelist Arnold Bennett enjoyed several evenings at their house in Thurloe Square and offers a description of them in his journal for 11 October 1897:

> As I listened to this mother and daughter recounting their deeds and wanderings since I last saw them, I was struck by their faculty for extracting from life pleasure and amusement. They read everything that appears, travel during several months in the year, gamble soberly when gambling is to be had, and generally make it a duty to go through life with as much pleasantness and change as will not fatigue them. Both are witty, and neither is afraid of criticizing her friends, or of getting fun out of idols. The daughter writes clever novels, and exhibits a good-humoured, railing tolerance for all "missions" including her own.

> They live alone, and love to throw a dart at "men." They are cultured and latitudinarian. They are never

shocked, or very seldom, and then instead of showing it, they faintly sneer at the objectionable thing. Backed by a certain income, they know they can hold their own in any way against anybody, and the thought gives them a fine sense of security. No struggle for them! They are among the conquerors, for they have brains and wit, as well as money, and they are philosophers enough to know how to live, calmly, reticently, yet gaily, and sometimes with abandon. They have attained wisdom, in that they accept the world as it is, endeavour to improve it according to their talents, eschew impossible ideals and look after themselves.

Whether or not this "certain income" made the Symondses "conquerors" it did allow for the private publication of Emily Morse Symonds's first collection of biographical essays, *Little Memoirs of the Nineteenth Century,* in 1893. These essay-portraits of nineteenth-century characters, based largely on each subject's memoirs and letters, also include engravings or illustrations gleaned from family collections or archives — a feature Symonds would always include in later work. The characters in this collection include Lady Morgan, governess, novelist, and travel writer who "in spite of her egoism and her many absurdities" achieved a following that included many of the literary and social celebrities of the day, as well as figures who are well known today such as Lady Hester Stanhope. An essay on the painter Benjamin Robert Haydon in this volume paved the way for Symonds's 1905 full-length study of him. It was not until the later success of *Mrs. Delany (Mary Granville) a Memoir, 1700–1788* (1900) and the *Little Memoirs of the Eighteenth Century* (1901) that this early collection was reprinted in 1902, received a wider circulation, and was reviewed. One review in the *Atheneum* (10 May 1902) called it an "intelligent condensation . . . which will serve agreeably to those who have not the leisure for the originals" but accused the author of bald summarizing, obvious commentary, and several "blunders." The *Bookman* praised its "commendable sense of proportion and scale" (May 1902).

For the next few years (1894–1899) Symonds directed her energies toward novel writing. Many of the novels from this early period depict physically or intellectually strong and individualistic women who break from proscribed roles in order to pursue independence through their careers. In *The Career of Candida* (1896) the young Candida is given a boy's education by her unusual father and, when offered her choice of the careers available to women, trains to become a gymnastics instructor. Since Symonds lists her recreations in the *Who's Who* of 1908 as "reading, bicycling, gymnastics," this fictional ca-

reer woman who is stronger and healthier than most men may reflect Symonds's own determination to cultivate physical strength and a career over marriage. Thus, when Candida's unhappy marriage to an unfaithful alcoholic becomes unbearable, she is able to leave her husband and support herself and her child by returning to her career, and when the ailing husband reappears, the narrator offers a clear indictment of Candida's acceptance of marital self-sacrifice: "And Candida walked home through the darkening streets, her eyes shining because the future lay dim before her, her step buoyant because the yoke was upon her neck again, her mind at ease because she had just assumed a grave responsibility, and her heart satisfied because she had flung all hopes of happiness away." The disjunction implied here between happiness and marriage is reinforced in most of Symonds's novels, and — since Symonds herself never married — was presumably a belief that affected her life. Although the institution of marriage was under attack in much of the "New Woman" literature and some of the suffrage material of the period, Symonds's views on marriage were by no means widely accepted. Reviews of *Candida* and of *A Writer of Books* (1898), in which the protagonist is able to write a great novel only after leaving her husband, objected to the novel being used for didactic purposes. The *Spectator* (15 October 1898), for instance, reviewed the novel favorably but criticized Symonds's views on marriage: "The Pictures of the Feminine side of New Grub Street are admirably done, and the ease and excellence of the style are so remarkable as to make one regret that this brilliant writer cannot find it in her heart or her conscience to take a happier view of the possibilities of married life."

Although the protagonist of *A Writer of Books,* Cosima Chudleigh, begins to write articles using eighteenth-century manuscripts only when she has run out of creative steam for her next novel, George Paston was an established literary figure in 1900 when Symonds resumed her work in literary biography with a series of eighteenth-century portrait essays — and she never returned to the novel. Her first full-length study, *Mrs. Delany (Mary Granville) a Memoir, 1700–1788,* was actually an abridged edition of an eighteenth-century autobiography by Mary Granville, interspersed with correspondence that Symonds had collected and some additional commentary. This technique was to become the basis for all of her biographical studies including her longer work on Haydon, Alexander Pope, and others; in each case she relies heavily on the subject's letters and the letters of their contemporaries, as well as diary entries, memoirs, newspaper and periodical accounts. When she collates these archival materials, adding her own commentary and general information about the period, the effect is to historicize the subject not only in the context of contemporary mores and estimations but also within the ironic gaze of the biographer, which effectively highlights the subjects' rhetorical masks and deflates their pretensions.

Symonds's fascination with the eighteenth century is documented by Arnold Bennett as early as 1896, when, having rushed to Thurloe Square by bicycle and bus, he arrived "at South Kensington, literature, quietude, the restraint of an eighteenth-century demeanor — and sincere artistic purpose too. Miss Symonds is a frank worshipper of the eighteenth century. Her mother, an ample little lady, with a quick cheerful laugh and a most pleasant manner, is ready to enjoy anything." He adds the additional comment that "Miss Symonds, on the whole the most advanced and intellectually fearless woman I have met, stuck to the old formula that a woman should marry a man 10 years her senior" because "a woman matures earlier than a man." Since Symonds would have been about seven years Bennett's senior (he twenty-nine to her thirty-six), their discussion of this point may have had personal applications.

Little Memoirs of the Eighteenth Century offers some choice examples both of Symonds's passion for this period and of her biographical technique. For instance, in her account of Richard Cumberland, a "playwright, novelist, poet, essayist, editor, civil servant, and amateur diplomatist" of the mid eighteenth century, Symonds relies heavily on his memoirs, which provide remarkable commentary on contemporaries such as Samuel Johnson, James Boswell, Oliver Goldsmith, Thomas Gray, and Horace Walpole. However, she also supplies the opinions those contemporaries held of Cumberland, the nicknames bequeathed to him by Garrick ("the Man without a Skin") and Sheridan ("Sir Fretful Plagiary"), as well as Fanny Burney's summing up of his literary jealousies. In addition, she intersperses these accounts with her own canny assessment of his rhetorical strategies, pointing for instance to a letter in which "he covers his wounded vanity with a mask of stately severity."

This collection of essays included, in Symonds's words, "two *grande dames* of the second George's Court, a poet playwright who dabbled in diplomacy, an aristocratic *déclassé* who died in the odour of royalty, an ex-shoemaker turned bookseller, a Highland lady with literary proclivities,

and a distinguished scholar who was chiefly remarkable for his misfortunes." Symonds's qualifications for including characters in this remarkable group are their "sociable garrulity," their notoriety in their own day, and their subsequent obscurity. Her instinct about the interest these characters would provide seems to have been accurate since the collection, published in March 1901, sold out almost immediately and was reprinted in May of the same year. An approving review in the *Bookman* (May 1901) was joined by a review in the *Atheneum* (4 May 1901) which thanks "her" for "the interesting collection of portraits she has brought together" but rates some of her choices of characters low on the scale of historical importance or interest and corrects two or three inaccuracies.

The next year Symonds consolidated the success of the eighteenth-century *Memoirs* by coming out with a new collection of essays spanning the late eighteenth and early nineteenth centuries, *Sidelights on the Georgian Period* (1902). E. P. Dutton and R. Richards reprinted *Little Memoirs of the Nineteenth Century* in New York and London, respectively, in order to capitalize on the attention that the earlier work had received. In many of the reviews of both the eighteenth- and the nineteenth-century *Memoirs,* the reviewers assume that the purpose of Symonds's work is in part to save the reader the work of wading through the reminiscences and correspondence of the characters themselves. As if to combat that author-effacing impression, Symonds's *Sidelights on the Georgian Period* broadens out into topical essays on various aspects of the Georgian period in addition to several character portraits (most of which had been previously published in *Longman's Magazine* or in the *Monthly Review*). Of the broader essays, "The Felon," "The Illustrated Magazine," and "The Ideal Woman" are particularly interesting because of the comparisons they draw between past social and political phenomena and those of Symonds's own time period. In "The Felon" this takes the more predictable form of contrasting the judiciary and penal chaos of the past with the more effective methods of the present; however, in "The Illustrated Magazine" she historicizes the "tidal wave" of periodical publications in the late nineteenth century by establishing its roots in the illustrated publications produced from 1765 to 1800. Symonds both points out the contrasts in latter-day systems of production and distribution and finds remarkable similarities in content between the *Idler* of 1892 and the *Maccaroni* of a century before. "There is a wonderful similarity in the contents of these eighteenth-century magazines, in their lack of 'topical' interest, their failure to reflect the spirit of the times."

"The Ideal Woman" is a precursor to Virginia Woolf's *A Room of One's Own* (1929) in its polemic and cautionary account of the educational practices and social pressures that constructed eighteenth-century women as "an interesting compound of moral perfection and intellectual deficiency." Unlike Woolf, however, Symonds seems acutely aware of the strata of class distinctions that are excluded or obscured in this construction of an ideal femininity: "It is probably needless to explain that the word 'woman' is here used to indicate the female of the upper class, since it is with the conditions of her life alone that the masculine idealist ever troubles himself." Symonds attempts to remedy this deficiency in her own work by including the letters of Elizabeth Girling, the "daughter of a yeoman farmer" in this collection, just as she included James Lackington, "bootmaker and bookseller," as a representative of the "trading or labouring classes of the period" in *Little Memoirs of the Eighteenth Century.* This attempt was not appreciated by the *Bookman* (December 1902) reviewer, G. Forrester Scott, who argued that this inclusion "quite fail[s] to improve our acquaintance with the order just below Miss Austen's upper middle class subjects," although he approved of the collection in general. The collection also received a favorable response from the *Atheneum* (December 1902), this time with the exception of the "Ideal Woman" essay, which the reviewer saw as unnecessarily didactic: "it can hardly, we should think, be necessary in these days to point the moral in addition to adorning the tale."

Symonds's biography of the painter George Romney, which was published in 1903, refines the techniques used in these earlier essays — and refers back to the essay on Richard Cumberland in *Little Memoirs of the Eighteenth Century.* In the earlier essay Cumberland gives an account of visiting Romney's studio and offering him patronage. One of the highlights of Symonds's biographical work as a whole is this attention to the social and generational interactions of her characters' lives. Beginning with *Little Memoirs of the Eighteenth Century,* her biographical work is indexed, a feature that provides a revealing sense of both the extent to which these studies overlapped and the interwoven texture that she has created with their correspondence. Within the longer format of a full-length study, she is able to make effective use of Romney's reminiscences and correspondence; however, like the earlier collections of essays, this becomes much more a study of the

times and of the artistic and literary circle that Romney inhabited than it does an analysis of character.

Even in this longer study, Symonds's own commentary is limited and seems primarily aimed at linking documents together into a meaningful and generally chronological account. Her real strength in this and in her succeeding full-length studies, *B. R. Haydon and His Friends* (1905), *Lady Mary Wortley Montagu and Her Times* (1907), and *Mr. Pope, His Life and Times* (1909), inheres in her ability to present the reader with a network of personal and contemporary accounts that not only contextualize each artist's or writer's work within contemporary debates but also highlight both the distorted nature of accounts and the political maneuvers involved in patronage, publication, and artistic success. In this sense, Symonds's biographical studies become useful because of the eighteenth-century manifestations she records, but also as artifacts of the early-twentieth-century conception and use of those primary documents.

Her full-length studies were well received for the most part; although *The Academy* (October 1905) complained that "Miss Symonds is rather too cold a biographer," the *Spectator* (November 1905) claimed that "his [Paston's] 'Life' of Haydon does not contain a page that is not alive with a grim comedy or poignant with a yet grimmer tragedy." *B. R. Haydon and His Friends* remains a gripping study of the "Historical Painter," as he called himself, who was firmly convinced of his own genius but was unable to convince his patrons of it. The combined interest of his friends, who included William Hazlitt, Charles Lamb, Robert and Elizabeth Barrett Browning, and William Wordsworth, could not prevent him from being imprisoned for debt at least four times. He eventually committed suicide in 1846, leaving behind letters and debts for his family and friends, commodious journals, and several vast paintings, one of which — a reviewer in the *Bookman* (November 1905) tells us — "adorns the billiard-room of a popular restaurant."

In addition to their own merits, however, Symonds's choices of subject reveal her astuteness about the receptiveness of the marketplace to the popular genre of period studies. The Edwardian absorption with the eighteenth century in all its manifestation becomes the focus of Symonds's *Old Coloured Books* and her *Social Caricature in the Eighteenth Century,* both published in 1905. The latter traces the rise of caricature as an art form in England from the work of illustrators like William Hogarth to that of James Gillray and Thomas Rowlandson. After an initial historical survey, the illustrations are arranged thematically under headings such as "The Beau Monde" and "Popular Delusions and Impostures" and are accompanied by Symonds's explanations of each caricature, its context, and its implications. In *Old Coloured Books,* a much smaller study with fewer illustrations, she gives an account of eighteenth- and nineteenth-century illustrated manuscripts produced by – among others – the team of Rudolph Ackermann, art publisher, and illustrator Rowlandson. The book focuses on the details of the engraving and production process used by this team, as well as that of Robert and George Cruikshank, the illustrators of the Grimm brothers' "Popular Stories" and many of Charles Dickens's novels.

Symonds's next project, a biographical study entitled *Lady Mary Wortley Montagu and Her Times,* capitalized on popular interest in this lively character. When Symonds took up this subject – a witty and prolific writer, poet, and correspondent with Pope and Walpole among others, famous in part for introducing smallpox inoculations into England – several collections of letters and manuscripts had already been published. As with Haydon, whose autobiography, letters, and "table talk" had been previously collected and published, various collections of Lady Mary's letters had been compiled, from eighteenth-century editions up to a collection published in 1892. Symonds thus prefaces her account by pointing to hitherto-unpublished correspondence which she discovered in the manuscript collection at Sandon Hall: "I had little hope that any considerable gleanings, in the shape of unpublished letters, would have been left by former workers in the same field . . . [but] I found four or five hundred unpublished letters, many of great interest, relating to the first half of the eighteenth century." She includes along with these letters an interesting and balanced account of this controversial character and an overview chapter called "England in 1709." In this remarkable chapter, she sketches out the political, social, and literary scene in which Lady Mary participated, from the position of women writers like Mary Astell and Mrs. Manley to the censorship struggle of the Theatre Royal in Drury Lane. Symonds's collection was followed by many others, including Lewis Melville's (pseudonym of Lewis Benjamin) edition in 1925, in which he refers to "that sound authority on the eighteenth century, 'George Paston,' who was so fortunate as to discover many scores of letters hitherto unpublished." Even when Robert Halsband produced a biography of Lady Montagu in 1956, he mentioned Symonds's work as a "thorough biography," with the qualifica-

tion that she had relied on "superficial printed sources and the Wortley Manuscripts."

Symonds's two-volume biographical study of Pope, *Mr. Pope, His Life and Times,* was perhaps her most ambitious project. Like Lady Mary, Pope had been the subject of previous biographies – although he had suffered a loss of prestige in Symonds's day – so that, rather than focusing on readings of his poetry or analyses of the creative process, Symonds presents an ample account of his indulgences, hypocrisies, and feuds, as well as a gossipy portrait of the milieu in which he produced his work. She is neither censorious nor fawning, but her summing up of his literary contribution reveals an ironic distance:

> But for the true lover of Pope, the exquisite [*sic*] "filigree work: of the "Rape of the Lock," the force and brilliance of the "Epistles," and the biting wit of the "Imitations of Horace," can never lose the potency of their charm. . . .

> There are signs that the day of a wider popularity for Pope may dawn again. That his work, with all its limitations, is typical of English thought and English character, is proved by the fact that, next to Shakespeare, he has provided us with the largest number of those words and phrases which are the common coin of literature and conversation.

The reviewer for the *Bookman* (November 1909), Walter Jerrold, unfavorably compared *Mr. Pope, His Life and Times* to Symonds's earlier work on Lady Mary: "In Pope, however, she has . . . the added disadvantage of writing about one with whom she evidently has, to use Lamb's euphemistic phrase, an imperfect sympathy." He accused her of being yet another representative of a "self-righteous age" that was too ready to "accentuate the errors of an earlier generation." Relenting toward the end of the review, however, he commented that "we may welcome her work as a clearly told story of Pope's life, a thoughtful exposition of his writings and as a possible aid towards a revival of interest in the work of a man who, however we label him, stands as one of the dominating literary figures of the eighteenth century."

As early as 1904 Symonds had tried her hand at her first stage production, *The Pharisee's Wife,* which was produced in London that year. After the publication of *Mr. Pope, His Life and Times* in 1909, she focused exclusively on drama until 1932; the next fifteen years show the publication of eight plays, most of which are comedies or farces. *Nobody's Daughter,* a feminist drama which was first officially published in 1924 – although it was performed as early as 1910 – lasted 185 performances.

Her other plays were moderately successful as well, although she is still listed in the *Who's Who* of the period as a novelist. In 1923 she moved to 7 Pelham Place, where she lived alone until her death on 12 September 1936.

Symonds's last completed work, *At John Murray's; Records of a Literary Circle, 1843–1892* (1932), returns to the nineteenth century to give an account of the literary circle of friends and debtors associated with the John Murray publishing house at 50 Albemarle Street from 1843 to 1892. Focusing on the life of John Murray III, Symonds recounts the traditions he carried on from his father and grandfather: a passion for the works of George Gordon, Lord Byron; a canny sense of the market and the tastes of the time; and the habit of launching short-lived literary magazines. She also gives an account of the traditions he broke, such as the day in 1882 when he decided to publish fiction for the first time – *Hurrish* by Miss Emily Lawless. The friends and correspondents that Symonds drew on for the study include William Makepeace Thackeray, Herman Melville, Dickens, Charles Darwin, Sir Walter Scott, and William Gladstone, thus "holding up a mirror" – in the words of a reviewer in the *Christian Science Monitor* (31 December 1932) – to the "busy center of the intellectual life of England. The men and women who were representative of the thought of that apparently rather solemn age move in and out across its pages. We have here in miniature a complete picture of Victorian England."

In the process of collecting material for this study, Symonds became "inevitably infected with the Byronism which may be said to be endemic in 50 Albemarle Street since 1812." In particular, she found hundreds of letters in the archives at Albemarle Street which were written to Byron by various women throughout his life. The letters, along with some mementos, had been recently willed to the publishing house by their last surviving holder, Lady Dorchester, and thus had never been published – offering too tempting an opportunity for Symonds to pass up. In the preface to the collection that followed, *"To Lord Byron": Feminine Profiles Based Upon Unpublished Letters* (1939), Symonds describes opening the box and finding "a mass of yellowing parchment," various ringlets of human hair preserved by Byron, along with other relics that "bear witness, if not to the constancy of Byron's attachments, at least to the odd strain of retrospective sentimentality that made him an inveterate hoarder of tokens and trifles." The book roughly traces Byron's romantic career through the challenging, lustful, and beseeching letters of Elizabeth Pigot, Mary Chaworth, Mrs. Spencer Smith, Lady Caroline Lamb, Lady Oxford, Augusta Leigh, Lady Melbourne, Annabella Milbanke, Susan Boyce, and Claire Clairmont, among others. Halfway through the project, however, Symonds fell ill, and the work was completed after her death by Peter Quennell.

Like many of the eighteenth- and nineteenth-century characters whom Symonds resurrected for her early essays, she was once well known and prolific and has now "fallen, whether deservedly or not, into neglect, if not oblivion." There is no biography of her life and no bibliography or contemporary criticism of her work. As Robert Halsband's response to *Lady Mary Wortley Montagu and Her Times* in 1956 shows, her longer biographical studies were consulted well into this century; they probably outlasted other contemporary biographies as useful resources because of the wealth of primary materials that Symonds collected. Her biographical work as well as her period studies become doubly interesting now, both as fascinating historical accounts and as testimony of Symonds's richly varied perspective on those accounts.

Hesketh Pearson
(20 February 1887 – 9 April 1964)

Charles Calder
University of Aberdeen

BOOKS: *Modern Men and Mummers* (London: Allen & Unwin, 1921);

A Persian Critic (London: Chapman & Dodd, 1923);

The Whispering Gallery: Being Leaves from a Diplomat's Diary (London: John Lane, 1926); published as *The Whispering Gallery: Being Leaves from the Diary of an Ex-Diplomat* (New York: Boni & Livewright, 1926);

Iron Rations (London?: Cecil Palmer, 1928);

Ventilations: Being Biographical Asides (Philadelphia & London: Lippincott, 1930);

Doctor Darwin (London & Toronto: Dent, 1930; New York: Walker, 1964);

The Fool of Love: A Life of William Hazlitt (London: Hamish Hamilton, 1934; New York: Harper, 1934);

The Smith of Smiths: Being the Life, Wit and Humour of Sidney Smith (London: Hamish Hamilton, 1934; New York: Harper, 1934);

Gilbert and Sullivan: A Biography (London: Hamish Hamilton, 1935; New York: Harper, 1935);

Labby: The Life and Character of Henry Labouchere (London: Hamish Hamilton, 1936);

Tom Paine, Friend of Mankind (London: Hamish Hamilton, 1937; New York: Harper, 1937);

Skye High: The Record of a Tour Through Scotland in the Wake of Samuel Johnson and James Boswell, by Pearson and Hugh Kingsmill (London: Hamish Hamilton, 1937; New York: Oxford University Press, 1938);

Thinking It Over: The Reminiscences of Hesketh Pearson (London: Hamish Hamilton, 1938; New York: Harper, 1938);

The Hero of Delhi: A Life of John Nicholson (London: Collins, 1939; West Drayton, N.Y.: Penguin, 1948);

A Life of Shakespeare (Harmondsworth: Penguin, 1942); enlarged as *A Life of Shakespeare, with an Anthology of Shakespeare's Poetry* (London: Carroll & Nicholson, 1949; New York: Walker, 1961);

Bernard Shaw: His Life and Personality (London: Collins, 1942); published as *G. B. S: A Full Length Portrait* (New York: Harper, 1942); enlarged as *G. B. S.: A Full Length Portrait, And A Postscript* (New York: Harper, 1952) – includes *G. B. S.: A Postscript* (New York: Harper, 1950; London: Collins, 1951); complete British edition, *Bernard Shaw: His Life and Personality* (London: Methuen, 1961);

This Blessed Plot, by Pearson and Kingsmill (London: Methuen, 1942);

Conan Doyle: His Life and Art (London: Methuen, 1943);

The Life of Oscar Wilde (London: Methuen, 1946); published as *Oscar Wilde: His Life and Wit* (New York: Harper, 1946); revised edition (London: Methuen, 1954);

Talking of Dick Whittington, by Pearson and Kingsmill (London: Eyre & Spottiswoode, 1947);

Dickens: His Character, Comedy and Career (London: Methuen, 1949; New York: Harper, 1949);

The Last Actor-Managers (London: Methuen, 1950);

Dizzy: The Life and Personality of Benjamin Disraeli, Earl of Beaconsfield (London: Methuen, 1951; New York: Harper, 1951);

About Kingsmill, by Pearson and Malcolm Muggeridge (London: Methuen, 1951);

The Man Whistler (London: Methuen, 1952);

Walter Scott: His Life and Personality (London: Methuen, 1954; New York: Harper, 1954);

Beerbohm Tree: His Life and Laughter (London: Methuen, 1956; New York: Harper, 1956);

Gilbert: His Life and Strife (London: Methuen, 1957; New York: Harper, 1957);

Johnson and Boswell: The Story of Their Lives (London: Heinemann, 1958; New York: 1959);

Charles II: His Life and Likeness (London: Heinemann, 1960); published as *Merry Monarch: The Life and Likeness of Charles II* (New York: Harper, 1960);

Hesketh Pearson

The Pilgrim Daughters (London: Heinemann, 1961); published as *The Marrying Americans* (New York: Coward-McCann, 1961);

Lives of the Wits (London: Heinemann, 1962; New York: Harper & Row, 1962);

Henry of Navarre: His Life (London: Heinemann, 1963); published as *Henry of Navarre: The King Who Dared* (New York: Harper & Row, 1963);

Extraordinary People (London: Heinemann, 1965; New York: Harper & Row, 1965);

Hesketh Pearson By Himself (London: Heinemann, 1965; New York: Harper & Row, 1965).

OTHER: *Common Misquotations,* collected by Pearson (London: Hamish Hamilton, 1934; Folcroft, Pa.: Folcroft Library Editions, 1973);

The Swan of Lichfield: Being a Selection from the Correspondence of Anna Seward, edited, with a biography and preface, by Pearson (London: Hamish Hamilton, 1936);

Essays by Oscar Wilde, edited, with an introduction, by Pearson (London: Methuen, 1950);

Oscar Wilde, *Selected Essays and Poems,* edited by Pearson (Harmondsworth: Penguin, 1954); revised as *De Profundis and Other Writings* (Harmondsworth: Penguin English Library, 1973);

W. S. Gilbert, *Selected Bab Ballads,* edited, with an introduction, by Pearson (Oxford: Printed at the University Press for Sir Allen Lane, 1955).

SELECTED PERIODICAL PUBLICATION – UNCOLLECTED: "About Biography," *Transactions of the Royal Society of Literature of the United Kingdom,* third series, 29 (1958): 55–72.

Hesketh Pearson was an accomplished and prolific biographer whose work is distinguished by enthusiasm, wit, and geniality. He was at his best when writing on the major literary and theatrical figures of the nineteenth century. *The Life of Oscar*

Wilde (1946) and *Gilbert: His Life and Strife* (1957) bring the reader irresistibly under the spell of their subjects. It is safe to predict that Pearson's best biographies will continue to give pleasure and instruction to fresh generations of readers.

Edward Hesketh Collins Pearson was born on 20 February 1887 at Hawford in Worcestershire to Thomas Henry Collins Pearson and Constance Biggs Pearson. His father was a gentleman-farmer; his paternal grandfather, John Pearson, was in Anglican orders. On completing his schooling at Bedford Grammar School, Pearson, by his own admission, "wasted two years in a City shipping office." He joined the theatrical company of Sir Herbert Beerbohm Tree in 1911 and later worked in the companies led by Harley Granville-Barker and Sir George Alexander; Pearson was thus able to observe firsthand the last of the actor-managers. Pearson married Gladys Gardner, an actress, on 6 June 1912.

Pearson enlisted at the outbreak of World War I in August 1914 and was invalided out the following year. After helping to organize the celebrations for the Shakespeare Tercentenary of 1916, he reenlisted in the Army Service Corps. He saw service in Mesopotamia and Persia and earned the rank of captain. Pearson received the Military Cross; but, as his biographer, Ian Hunter, observes, "he characteristically omits to allude to this in his memoirs. Basil Harvey claimed that he would have forfeited Pearson's friendship ever to mention the MC." Indeed, the whole period of his war service induced in Pearson not pride but detestation; he was appalled by the dirt, decay, and cruelty that he discovered all around him. "Pearson hated the East in general and Persia in particular . . . he had been sending dispatches and features [*sic*] articles back to the *Star* and the *Manchester Guardian*. These articles . . . have one consistent theme running through them – a deep, passionate loathing of the region and its inhabitants."

On his discharge Pearson returned to the stage. The great consolation of these postwar years was his friendship with Hugh Kingsmill – a friendship which continued until Kingsmill's death in 1949. Through the 1920s Pearson combined acting and writing. *The Whispering Gallery* (1926), a collection of unflattering sketches of the great which Pearson rashly attributed to Sir Rennell Rodd, created a cause célèbre. Pearson left the stage in 1932 and thereafter concentrated on writing biographies. One could argue that the profession of actor gave Pearson an invaluable preparation for the trade of biographer. Owen Dudley Edwards writes of the enjoy-

ment which he derived from "debating" with Pearson's *Conan Doyle: His Life and Art* (1943), and he continues: "from boyhood I have been delighted by the verve and wit of Pearson's biographies in which, as a former actor, he sought to play the parts of his subjects." Edwards sums up succinctly the appeal which is exerted by the best of Pearson's biographies.

Doctor Darwin, a life of Pearson's ancestor Erasmus Darwin, appeared in 1930, followed in 1934 by *The Fool of Love: A Life of William Hazlitt* and his life of Sydney Smith, *The Smith of Smiths: Being the Life, Wit and Humour of Sidney Smith*. Of the early biographies, the most impressive is *Gilbert and Sullivan: A Biography* (1935). Pearson loved the Savoy Operas; an infectious enthusiasm runs throughout the book. It is a concise and tightly organized work, containing chapters on Gilbert; Sullivan; Gilbert and Sullivan; Sullivan; Gilbert. Pearson emphasizes the extent of the theatrical revolution brought about by the collaborators and pays particular tribute to Gilbert's thoroughness as a producer. As usual, anecdotes and aphorisms are woven easily into the narrative. This is not self-advertising technique, but there is solid constructional skill at work. Pearson also shows his ability to vary tone, allowing the narrative to flow easily and urbanely and to accommodate the heightening of effect.

The 1930s were a decade of literary success and achievement for Pearson. His close friendships with Kingsmill and from 1932 with Malcolm Muggeridge were a source of much joy and satisfaction. Muggeridge has left us his own vivid evocation of those days in his *Chronicles of Wasted Time* (1972, 1973); and Richard Ingrams has produced an affectionate memoir of the trio in *God's Apology* (1977). But the 1930s also brought great sadness to Pearson and his wife through the loss of their son Henry. Henry Pearson had become estranged from his father as a result of his commitment to communism. He went to Spain to fight for the Republican cause, and the news of his death in action reached his parents in January 1939. This was the greatest grief of Pearson's life.

The 1940s show Pearson in his most commanding form as a biographer. It was perhaps inevitable that he would find himself writing a life of Bernard Shaw. Under the beneficent influence of Kingsmill, Pearson had freed himself from his early Shaw worship, but he remained an admirer of the man and his work. *Bernard Shaw: His Life and Personality* (1942) brought Pearson acclaim and financial success; it was a best-seller which ranks as the most entertaining of Shaw biographies. It is also a curios-

Pearson, right, with Bernard Shaw in 1945

ity of literature, being the product of an unacknowl-edged collaboration between biographer and sub-ject. Michael Holroyd summarizes the unusual tex-tual history in the third volume of his study of Shaw, *Bernard Shaw: The Lure of Fantasy* (1991). Shaw's rewriting of Pearson's text involved both emendation of phrasing and wholesale substitu-tion; particularly heavy revision occurred in the sections on Shaw's politics, especially his attitudes to Soviet communism. Pearson wanted to acknowledge the collaboration openly, suggest-ing "that his contributions should be shown in the text between square brackets or by indentation. But Shaw was horrified at the thought of his col-laboration being exposed . . . 'Not on your life, Hesketh,' he wrote." Shaw advised Pearson to burn the typescript once the book was safely in print. Not for the first (or last) time, Pearson ig-nored Shavian advice; the typescript is held by the Harry Ransom Humanities Research Center at the University of Texas at Austin. Holroyd de-scribes the complex literary processes that are at work in *Bernard Shaw: His Life and Personality*. "Pearson had derived his technique as a biogra-pher from his earlier career on the stage. To some degree he acted his characters on the page. Shaw's

method of ghostwriting his [*Life*] involved borrow-ing something of the character of his biographer. As Pearson's 'uninvited collaborator,' he was faced with an intriguing linguistic exercise of im-personating someone who was Pearsonifying him." The method is unorthodox, but the result is highly entertaining and appealing. One can see why *Bernard Shaw: His Life and Personality* has held its place of interest since its publication.

Conan Doyle: His Life and Art is on a much more modest scale. This biography has been, in the words of Edwards, "unjustly traduced"; its im-perfections, he notes, are well below its merits. In his introduction to a 1987 reprint, Graham Greene wrote that "Mr. Pearson . . . has some of the quali-ties of Dr. Johnson – a plainness, an honesty, a sense of ordinary life going on all the time. A dull biographer would never have got behind that poker-face; an excited biographer would have made us disbelieve the story, which wanders from whal-ing in the Arctic to fever on the West Coast of Af-rica, a practice in Portsea to ghost-hunting in Sus-sex. But from Mr. Pearson we are able to accept it." Greene makes the further point that "Conan Doyle has too often been compared with Dr. Watson: in this biography it is Mr. Pearson who plays Watson to the odd enigmatic product of a Jesuit education, the Sherlock-hearted Doyle."

The Life of Oscar Wilde (1946) is Pearson's most satisfying work – no ordinary biography but a memorably sympathetic evocation of Wilde's life and personality. The prime achievement was the lifting of Wilde "out of the fog of pathology into the light of comedy." As Pearson notes, the trial and its aftermath occupied five years out of forty-six; the final phase, he argued, should not be allowed to dominate the rest of the story. Shaw had given a succinct opinion when Pearson mentioned he was intending to write on Wilde ("Don't"); modern readers can be grateful Shavian counsel was resisted. In Wilde, Pearson found the ideal subject. From the age of nineteen he had been attracted to Wilde; he recalls in the prologue that "Just after leaving school I came across *The Soul of Man Under Socialism* [1912], and it performed the vital operation of making me think for myself . . . I dare say I should have been emancipated in time from the beliefs of my class without the help of Wilde's *Soul of Man,* but I doubt if any other work could have shaken me up so quickly and successfully. . . . For ridiculing all the beliefs in which I had been brought up, for laughing my mind out of its rut and so enabling me to think freely with the aid of what inner light God had given me, I have always been grateful to Oscar Wilde." In *The Life of Oscar Wilde,* Pearson repaid that debt of gratitude handsomely.

In re-creating Wilde as a "genial wit and humorist," Pearson made full use of the reminiscences he had gathered during his acting days from Beerbohm Tree and George Alexander. Pearson knew and corresponded with such friends of Wilde as Alfred Douglas, Robert Ross, and Adela Schuster. He also had access to the published recollections of Richard Le Gallienne, Vincent O'Sullivan, Charles Ricketts, and Graham Robertson. Pearson harmonized all this information to present a splendidly vivid and authentic portrait of Wilde and his times. For Harold Nicolson, writing in the London *Observer, The Life of Oscar Wilde* was "the most true, the most sensible and the fairest book which has yet been written about Oscar Wilde." Hunter (following Kingsmill) has complained that "one could read all but a dozen of Pearson's four hundred pages without realizing that Wilde was a notorious, practising homosexual." For Pearson a dozen pages was sufficient for the purpose, and he noted: "passion is interesting; evacuation is not."

Gladys Pearson died in 1951; "forty years of a deeply affectionate relationship closed with her last breath." Shortly afterward, Pearson married Joyce Ryder. In Hunter's words: "Pearson was sixty-four, twenty years Joyce's senior, but she told him that, since he habitually acted more like six than sixty, it scarcely mattered." Certainly the verve and high spirits of the biographer were undiminished. He found an excellent subject in *The Man Whistler* (1952). If James Abbott McNeill Whistler lacked the breadth and geniality of Wilde, he nevertheless appealed to Pearson's curiosity and interest in human variety. Whistler was a wit ("though a cruel one"); and there was the desire to reconcile the conflicting qualities of "the poet who could paint the tender portrait of Carlyle or the lovely dream-picture of Cremorne Lights and the man whose bitter tongue suggested hate as his primary emotion." The resulting book provides entertaining likenesses of Whistler, his friends, and his enemies. Benny Green has praised "the skill and perception with which Pearson has sketched in the supporting cast." Pearson was too modest a man to make claims for the literary merit of his biographies; but Green's comment suggests that among Pearson's virtues is a sense of dramatic construction. The biographies are built on firm foundations, the author maintaining a pleasing balance and proportion. His subjects preserve a correctly judged relationship to the supporting characters. In the Whistler circle Pearson found abundant talent and eccentricity, but Whistler remains the principal actor. The book is laid out in fourteen chapters bearing such titles as "Adolescent," "Bohemian," "Bourgeois," "Personal," "Artistic," and "Social"; chapter 14 is entitled "Mortal." This organization does not, in the event, cramp the narrative but supplies a satisfying support or frame. A good example of Pearson's economy is provided by chapter 5 ("Personal"). In ten pages he portrays the oddity, exuberance, and vitality of his subject. Ellen Terry recorded that the most remarkable men she had known were Wilde and Whistler; "there was something about both of them more instantaneously individual and audacious than it is possible to describe." In Pearson's pages the individuality and audacity shine out.

There is no lessening of literary power in *Gilbert: His Life and Strife.* This is a full-scale study which draws upon (and quotes extensively from) the private papers of W. S. Gilbert. The Gilbert papers had been placed at Pearson's disposal by F. B. Cockburn, the executor of Nancy McIntosh's estate. The incorporation of so many unpublished letters shed new light on the tensions and difficulties within Gilbert's family and on the relationship between Gilbert and Arthur Sullivan. Pearson be-

Pearson, right, and Malcolm Muggeridge, 1950 (photograph by Margaret Ryder)

lieved that "Life is a mystery; and however we may probe into the conduct of human beings and satisfy ourselves that we have found a reason for this or that, the preponderant residue of personality remains inexplicable. . . . It is safer for a biographer to exhibit his subject than attempt to explain him." In accordance with this dictum, Pearson exhibits Gilbert without attempting to explain him. Pearson supplies no psychological "reading" of his subject; he lets the documentary evidence speak for itself. This approach is eminently sane and sensible; the reader can hardly avoid establishing a link between the "unhappy and unstable conditions" of Gilbert's upbringing and the qualities of touchiness, insecurity, and irritability that he displayed as an adult. But the author does not claim to possess any psychological "key" to Gilbert's character; he is content to act as biographer rather than analyst. The story of Gilbert – dramatist, librettist, producer, theater reformer – is sufficiently rich and full of incident that it requires no garnishing or speculation. Pearson is thoroughly at home when writing about the

nineteenth-century theater, and this familiarity stands him in good stead when he recounts Gilbert's irruption into the mid-Victorian theatrical scene. It is refreshing to read a study which gives recognition to Gilbert's various talents – so often one is accustomed to superficial accounts of "Gilbert-and-Sullivan" that fail to mention the individual genius of the collaborators. As usual, Pearson conveys a great deal of information and insight with the minimum of fuss; chapter 4 ("Mainly Blank Verse") exemplifies Pearson's ability to write entertainingly and instructively. In this chapter Pearson illuminates the London theater of the 1870s and indicates Gilbert's contribution to the drama of the time. Pearson reminds us that, with the exception of Wilde, Gilbert "was the leading figure in the chronicle of the British drama between the production of Robertson's *School* in 1869 and that of Arthur Pinero's *The Second Mrs. Tanqueray* in 1893." He convinces us that "for sheer versatility of production . . . no playwright has equalled Gilbert, who even adapted . . . *Great Expectations,* which was done at the

Court Theatre in the spring of 1871." Pearson links the achievement of Gilbert with that of Tom Robertson; "what Robertson invented Gilbert perfected." We can understand, from reading the early chapters of the book, that the rigorous methods which Gilbert the producer was to apply when rehearsing the Savoy Operas were already second nature to the Gilbert of the 1870s. Pearson suggests that the thoroughness with which Gilbert supervised every aspect of presentation entitles him to be called "the father of modern play-production." In illuminating this part of Gilbert's legacy, Pearson brings to light a significant aspect of stage history. It is only recently that students of English theater have begun to build on Pearson's pioneering work.

Pearson's last biographies show a distinct decline. His *Charles II: His Life and Likeness* (1960) is a rather pedestrian retelling; in spite of the biographer's liking for Charles, one feels that he is not at his happiest when dealing with the world of seventeenth-century politics. Pearson's preferred subjects were literary and theatrical; he is entirely at his ease when writing of Samuel Johnson, Sydney Smith, and the great figures of the 1890s. His touch is less sure when he tackles the political intricacies and religious fervors which distinguish the reign of Charles II. In writing about Gilbert or Wilde, Pearson is fresh, original, and a master of his material; *Charles II: His Life and Likeness* suffers by comparison with Sir Arthur Bryant's classic 1931 *King Charles II*. Pearson's final biographical effort was *Henry of Navarre: His Life* (1963).

Pearson was not solely a biographer; he wrote engaging reminiscences, *Extraordinary People* (1965) and *Hesketh Pearson By Himself* (1965). He collaborated with Hugh Kingsmill in three books of "talk and travel": *Skye High: The Record of a Tour Through Scotland in the Wake of Samuel Johnson and James Boswell* (1937), *This Blessed Plot* (1942), and *Talking of Dick Whittington* (1947). Shared memories of Kingsmill led Pearson and Muggeridge to produce *About Kingsmill* (1951). In Kingsmill, Pearson found his ideal literary counterpart; the exchanges between the two are marked by humor, vivacity, "good sense and good nonsense." Both men loved English literature, the English countryside, and the English past; we are fortunate that the travel books commemorate, in such an intimate and pleasant way, the warmth of their companionship.

Green has recorded an anecdote which illustrates the character of this delightful and unpretentious man. "I can remember seeing Pearson towards the end of his life finding himself washed up on the unlikely shore of the [BBC] Brains Trust,

and modestly declining to set the world right between Sunday lunch and Sunday tea. Eventually, on being pressed by a despairing chairman, he calmly shattered the sepulchral quietude of the proceedings by announcing that, with regard to the subject under discussion – some piffling geopolitical frivolity – he knew nothing about it and cared even less, and therefore declined to say anything, with which he cheerfully resumed cleaning out his pipe-bowl with the wrong end of a pencil." This incident, as Green indicates, confirms the impression which a reader would gather from the books; here was a man who stuck to his last, made no claims to omniscience, and had a healthy distrust of orthodoxies and abstractions. How refreshing to encounter such modesty; the literary celebrities of our own age are less self-denying. A period of Pearsonian abstinence would indeed be welcome.

Green has summarized Pearson's virtues: humor; compassion; the assimilation of complex evidence into a harmonious record; the ability of the biographer to "place himself inside the skin of the subject"; and a natural gift for narrative. But there is, says Green, something more – a compound of tact, wit, style, and urbanity. A passionate interest in human variety is unencumbered by moralizing and censoriousness. This characterization seems to capture Pearson's literary qualities perfectly. He can be recommended as a witty, knowledgeable, and appreciative guide whom we happily follow.

Pearson died of cancer on 9 April 1964. He left behind a distinguished literary legacy. It is encouraging to find that a new generation of readers is discovering Pearson's work as books that have been out of print for some years are being republished. Pearson chose subjects who appealed to him because they exemplified the qualities he held to be of supreme value: "wit, humour, good nature, and invincible gaiety of spirit." Johnsonians may choose *Johnson and Boswell: The Story of Their Lives* (1958) as his best book; Wildeans *The Life of Oscar Wilde*; Gilbertians prize *Gilbert: His Life and Strife*. In tackling such subjects as *Labby: The Life and Character of Henry Labouchere* (1936) and *Beerbohm Tree: His Life and Laughter* (1956) Pearson helped to illuminate the richly fascinating social and artistic world of the Victorians. Hunter has suggested that Pearson's achievement is synoptic; that he provides "a panorama of eccentricity, wit and genius unique in British literature. . . . By reading through his biographies one may obtain, with remarkably few gaps, an accurate and lively cultural and literary history of England." That is a fine and apposite tribute; the achievement extends beyond individual books and does indeed embrace the literature and identity of a country.

Biography:

Ian Hunter, *Nothing to Repent: The Life of Hesketh Pearson* (London: Hamilton, 1987).

References:

Benny Green, Introduction to Pearson's *The Man Whistler* (London: Macdonald & Jane's, 1978);

Michael Holroyd, *Bernard Shaw: The Lure of Fantasy* (London: Chatto & Windus, 1991);

Holroyd, *Hugh Kingsmill, A Critical Biography* (London: Unicorn Press, 1964);

Richard Ingrams, *God's Apology: A Chronicle of Three Friends* (London: Deutsch, 1977);

Paul Murray Kendall (New York: Norton, 1965);

Malcolm Muggeridge, *Chronicles of Wasted Time,* 2 volumes (London: Collins, 1972–1973; New York: Morrow, 1973–1974);

Muggeridge, *Like It Was: The Diaries of Malcolm Muggeridge* (New York: Morrow, 1982).

Papers:

Pearson's papers are located at the University College Library, London. The typescript for *Bernard Shaw: His Life and Personality* is held at the Harry Ramson Humanities Research Center, University of Texas at Austin.

Herbert Read

(4 December 1893 – 12 June 1968)

Dennis Paoli
Hunter College of the City University of New York

See also the Read entry in *DLB 20: British Poets, 1914–1945*.

BOOKS: *Songs of Chaos* (London: Elkin Mathews, 1915);

Eclogues: A Book of Poems (London: Beaumont, 1919);

Naked Warriors (London: Art & Letters, 1919);

Mutations of the Phoenix (Richmond: Leonard & Virginia Woolf, 1923);

In Retreat (London: Leonard and Virginia Woolf, 1925);

Reason and Romanticism (London: Faber & Gwyer, 1926; New York: Russell & Russell, 1963);

Collected Poems, 1913–25 (London: Faber & Gwyer, 1926);

English Stained Glass (London & New York: Putnam, 1926);

English Prose Style (London: Bell, 1928; New York: Holt, 1928; revised edition, London: Bell, 1942; revised again, 1952);

Phases of English Poetry (London: Leonard & Virginia Woolf, 1928; New York: Harcourt, Brace, 1929; revised edition, London: Faber & Faber, 1950; Norfolk, Conn.: New Directions, 1950);

The Sense of Glory: Essays in Criticism (Cambridge: Cambridge University Press, 1929; Freeport, N.Y.: Books for Libraries Press, 1967);

Staffordshire Pottery Figures (London: Duckworth, 1929);

Ambush (London: Faber & Faber, 1930);

Julien Benda and the New Humanism (Seattle: University of Washington Press, 1930);

Wordsworth (London: Cape, 1930; New York: Cape & Smith, 1931);

The Place of Art in a University (Edinburgh & London: Oliver & Boyd, 1931);

The Meaning of Art (London: Faber & Faber, 1931); republished as *The Anatomy of Art* (New York: Dodd, Mead, 1932); revised and enlarged as *The Meaning of Art* (London: Faber & Faber, 1936; revised again, 1951);

Form in Modern Poetry (London: Sheed & Ward, 1932; revised edition, London: Vision, 1948);

The Innocent Eye (London: Faber & Faber, 1933);

Art Now: An Introduction to the Theory of Modern Painting and Sculpture (London: Faber & Faber, 1933; New York: Harcourt, Brace, 1937);

The End of a War (London: Faber & Faber, 1933);

Art and Industry: The Principles of Industrial Design (London: Faber & Faber, 1934; revised, 1944; revised again, 1953; New York: Horizon, 1954; revised again, London: Faber & Faber, 1956; revised again, 1966);

Essential Communism (London: Nott, 1935);

The Green Child: A Romance (London: Heinemann, 1935; New York: New Directions, 1948);

Poems, 1914–1934 (London: Faber & Faber, 1935; New York: Harcourt, Brace, 1935);

In Defense of Shelley and Other Essays (London: Heinemann, 1936);

Art and Society (London: Heinemann, 1937; New York: Macmillan, 1937; revised edition, London: Faber & Faber, 1945; revised again, 1956; revised again, 1967);

Collected Essays in Literary Criticism (London: Faber & Faber, 1938); republished as *The Nature of Literature* (New York: Horizon, 1956);

Poetry and Anarchism (London: Faber & Faber, 1938);

Annals of Innocence and Experience (London: Faber & Faber, 1940; revised and enlarged, 1946); republished as *The Innocent Eye* (New York: Holt, 1947);

Thirty-Five Poems (London: Faber & Faber, 1940);

The Philosophy of Anarchism (London: Freedom Press, 1940);

To Hell with Culture (London: Kegan Paul, 1941);

Education Through Art (London: Faber & Faber, 1943; revised, 1958);

The Politics of the Unpolitical (London: Routledge, 1943);

A World Within a War: Poems (London: Faber & Faber, 1944; New York: Harcourt, Brace, 1945);

Herbert Read

The Education of Free Men (London: Freedom Press, 1944);

A Coat of Many Colours: Occasional Essays (London: Routledge, 1945; revised, 1956; New York: Horizon, 1966);

Collected Poems (London: Faber & Faber, 1946; revised, 1953; Norfolk, Conn.: New Directions, 1953; revised again, London: Faber & Faber, 1966; New York: Horizon, 1966);

The Grass Roots of Art (New York: Wittenborn, 1947; London: Drummond, 1947; revised edition, London: Faber & Faber, 1955);

Culture and Education in World Order (New York: Museum of Modern Art, 1948);

Coleridge as Critic (London: Faber & Faber, 1949);

Education for Peace (New York: Scribners, 1949; London: Routledge & Kegan Paul, 1950);

Byron (London & New York: Longmans, Green, 1951);

Contemporary British Art (Harmondsworth: Penguin, 1951; revised, 1954; revised again, 1961);

The Philosophy of Modern Art: Collected Essays (London: Faber & Faber, 1952; New York: Horizon, 1953);

The True Voice of Feeling: Studies in English Romantic Poetry (London: Faber & Faber, 1953; New York: Pantheon, 1953);

Anarchy and Order: Essays in Politics (London: Faber & Faber, 1954);

Icon and Idea: The Function of Art in the Development of Human Consciousness (London: Faber & Faber, 1955; Cambridge, Mass.: Harvard University Press, 1955);

Moon's Farm and Poems Mostly Elegiac (London: Faber & Faber, 1955; New York: Horizon, 1956);

The Art of Sculpture (London: Faber & Faber, 1956; New York: Pantheon, 1956);

The Tenth Muse: Essays in Criticism (London: Routledge & Kegan Paul, 1957; New York: Horizon, 1958);

A Concise History of Modern Painting (London: Thames & Hudson, 1959; New York: Praeger, 1959);

The Forms of Things Unknown: Essays towards an Aesthetic Philosophy (London: Faber & Faber, 1960; New York: Horizon, 1960);

Truth Is More Sacred, by Read and Edward Dahlberg (New York: Horizon, 1961; London: Routledge & Kegan Paul, 1961);

Vocal Avowals (Saint Gallen, Switzerland: Tschudy-Verlag, 1962);

A Letter to a Young Painter (London: Thames & Hudson, 1962; New York: Horizon, 1962);

To Hell with Culture, and Other Essays in Art and Society (London: Routledge & Kegan Paul, 1963; New York: Schocken, 1963);

The Contrary Experience: Autobiographies (London: Faber & Faber, 1963; New York: Horizon, 1963);

Lord Byron at the Opera: A Play for Broadcasting (North Harrow: Ward, 1963);

Selected Writings: Poetry and Criticism (London: Faber & Faber, 1963);

A Concise History of Modern Sculpture (London: Thames & Hudson, 1964; New York: Praeger, 1964);

Henry Moore: A Study of His Life and Work (London: Thames & Hudson, 1964; New York: Praeger, 1966);

The Origins of Form in Art (London: Thames & Hudson, 1965; New York: Horizon, 1965);

The Redemption of the Robot: My Encounter with Education through Art (New York: Trident, 1966; London: Faber & Faber, 1970);

Art and Alienation: The Role of the Artist in Society (London: Thames & Hudson, 1967; New York: Horizon, 1967);

Poetry and Experience (London: Vision, 1967);

The Cult of Sincerity (London: Faber & Faber, 1968);

Collected Poems of Herbert Read (London: Sinclair-Stevenson, 1992).

The career of Herbert Read spanned vast and varied times and types of literature — Edwardian to postmodern — and art — art nouveau to pop art. His bibliography is a spill of creative and critical literature, in standard forms and genres and their modern mutations — such as radio lectures — with isolated anomalies — like his philosophical, and sole, novel, *The Green Child: A Romance* (1935) — and patchwork collections of revised periodical pieces and academic addresses. James King's biography of Read, *The Last Modern* (1990), is full of Read's indecision, false starts, wrong turns, conflicting desires, and divided loyalties. He had little intellectual pedigree but definitive intellectual strengths: the impulse and satisfaction of appreciation and what he

would have characterized as his Yorkshire stock but which can be found in poor-school poets and working-class hacks across cultures and centuries, a genius for labor. He was knighted as England's home-grown hero of twentieth-century sensibility, but he was always, despite his title, a yeoman of modernity.

Read was born on 4 December 1893 to Herbert Edward and Eliza Strickland Read. One of the three most important facts of Read's life was that he was born on a farm. Muscoates Grange was situated on the margin of modern England, between the Yorkshire moors and the last reaches of the industrial revolution; his father was the tenant farmer there. *The Innocent Eye* (1933), for most critics one of Read's finest works, recounts in vividly impressionistic recollection his childhood experiences of farm life. The aesthetic economy of the imagist prose gives an edge to the otherwise sensual idylls. The style is not unlike James Joyce's in *A Portrait of the Artist as a Young Man* (1916), but there is no ironic detachment; there is conceptual control of diction and structural constraint, but the memories shimmer with presence, and the chapters, thematically topographical, shiver with life. "All life is an echo of our first sensation," he wrote, "the only real experiences in life being those lived with a virgin sensibility."

While there is longing in the remembrance, there is little sentiment in the rendition. His rhetoric is authenticity, as illustrated in his description of "the first kill at which I was present" and the culminating rites of the hunt:

> I had to be "blooded." The severed head of the fox was wiped across my face till it was completely smeared in blood, and I was told what a fine huntsman I should make. I do not remember the blood, nor the joking huntsmen; only the plumed breath of the horses, the jingle of their harness, the beads of dew and the white gossamer on the tangled hedge beside us.

If this is self-consciously imagistic, the self is an honest one. The hunt is a leveling ritual of English country society, tenants riding with landlords; the sensory perception of the innocent sensibility is the leveling ground of human experience; the image is the ground of meaningful expression. The quality of Read's achievement in *The Innocent Eye* demonstrates the significance of his childhood experience in his life, his social awareness and his aesthetic.

At age nine Read lost his father, the family gave up the farm, and he was sent with his younger brother William to an orphanage in industrial Hali-

Read, left, with his brothers, Charles and William, and his mother Eliza (Read family)

fax. This end of innocence is almost too precipitous, too unambiguous, but the bold relief is less the product of dramatic catastrophe than it is of the anachronistic nature of his early youth. Read had one of the last English childhoods of its kind; his passage to experience is Coleridgean, Dickensian, a product of the previous century. It realizes the Romantic/Victorian roots of modernity: "From fields and hedges and the wide open spaces of the moors; from the natural companionship of animals and all the mutations of farm life, I had passed into a confined world of stone walls, smoky skies, and two hundred unknown and apparently unsympathetic strangers."

Though Read discovered as a child at Muscoates the pleasures of reading, his attachment to literature may be seen as a response to the rigors, roughhouse, and empty regimen of the orphan home. Pulp romances freed his imagination, fed his increasingly private sense of self, and reestablished the immanent experience of his rural boyhood in an intellectual context: "never have I known," he later confessed, "such absorption and excitement as gripped me when I first read *King Solomon's Mines* [1885]." Each new novel was just that — novel, a fresh field welcoming "a virgin sensibility."

At the end of 1908 Read left the orphanage and went to live with his mother in Leeds. At the beginning of 1909 he took a position as a bank clerk. Read's progress through his teenage years was predictable: he found his job boring, and his plans to adopt various professions defined his alienation from his labor; his widowed mother was overprotective of her children, which he took for meddling at best and stifling in the extreme, exaggerating his alienation from his family and his sense of his own intellectual isolation. He became a Tory, following his father's conservative bent, but the influence of literature — after he got through the works of Benjamin Disraeli — and the evidence of daily life in working-class Leeds led him to socialism. He became a devout Anglican, but dogma doused his ecstatic fervor and he lost faith. He adopted a father figure, a bookish tailor (William Prior Read — no relation, though Read met him through his brother William, who coincidentally worked for him) whose library he consumed and who introduced him to the works of William Blake. Read started to write poetry.

Read entered the University of Leeds in 1912. He was torn between broadening his mind or his prospects and by his second year was attempting both, reading logic and social economy. Often, though, he found his nose in a volume of Continental European literature or philosophy, especially Friedrich Nietzsche. He entered the limited but blooming cultural life of Leeds and took his first looks at modern painting and his first measure of contemporary writers. He tasted from mysticism, postimpressionism, vorticism, futurism, imagism, cubism, and abstraction; he made vorticist drawings and imagist poems, but more than any individual movement Read was attracted by the intellectual-aesthetic whirl of opinions and art-world figures. In 1914 he met a fellow student, Evelyn Roff, who shared some of his nonconformist views, but not others (like sexual rebellion), and with whom he began a relationship that offered an intimate arena for impassioned argument. At the university Read became a student of himself, of his tastes and desires, of his difference.

Read never earned his degree. In 1912, his first year of study, his mother was diagnosed with incurable cancer. She died in 1914, after two years of suffering, and he had grief-stricken dreams of her. During her last months war was declared with Germany. Read, in his intellectual adventuring, had surveyed and engaged socialism, syndicalism, collectivism, anarchism, pacifism, and a Nietzschean superrace but had always indulged a practical patriotism, joining the Royal Army Medical Corps when he thought he wanted to become a doctor, then moving on to the Officers' Training Corps. After his mother's death he pressed for a commission and was eventually posted to the front.

The second radical fact of Read's life was World War I, which served to solidify his intellectual stance, substantiate his political inclinations, and further his self-study. During the war he read voraciously and wrote serious letters, periodical pieces for literary journals back home, and trench poetry. He found most of his fellow officers to be fatuous or mean-spirited elitists and preferred the company of enlisted men. Though they were in the majority grossly materialistic, their shared travails prompted a shared spirit and respect that, more than any theory or postwar observation, were the foundation of Read's future politics. The war, like the hunt, was a bloody, leveling experience, the empirical ground of his humanist-anarchist principles.

And he discovered that he was courageous. He was decorated with the Military Cross and the Distinguished Service Order for heroism and dedication to both duty and his men in actions that were later described in *In Retreat* (1925) and "The Raid"

(1927). His bravery in the face of hissing bullets and exploding comrades gave his ego an existential authority that never appealed to religious consolations or rationalizations and a residual stability that allowed the relatively unobstructed, unsubverted reign and play of his appreciative gifts. He had seen the worst that men could do; he was neither intimidated by nor jealous of the best.

On the way to the war Read saw London for the first time (indeed, left Yorkshire for the first time) and saw into publication a vanity edition of his first volume of poetry, the Blakean titled *Songs of Chaos* (1915). He was back on leave in 1917 when he met T. S. Eliot at a literary lunch, beginning a lifelong friendship. On his return the next year, less than three weeks from the armistice (and three weeks after his youngest brother, Charles, was killed in action), he met, in a single day at separate hours, Ezra Pound, Wyndham Lewis, and the Sitwell brothers, Osbert and Sacheverell. Read soon was dining at Bloomsbury tables and became friends with Ford Madox Ford. He was the new man on the London literary scene; yet when he married Roff and they moved to the suburbs, he dubbed their home Muscoates. He was ready to write and did, producing several of imagism's most anthologized poems and publishing essays and verse in the most forward magazines of the day, including Eliot's *Criterion*. His day job, however, as a civil servant at the treasury, stole his time and sapped his energy, instituting a structure in his experience and a theme in his letters and autobiographical writings of frustration and forced labor within sight of the promised land of literary creation.

Throughout his literary life Read identified himself as a poet. Though his output was meager relative to that of his contemporaries and to the volume of his critical prose, he considered poetry his best work and its creation his most private and satisfying activity. He fully invested his self in his poetry; his use of personae and imagist economy of expression keep the verse from taking a confessional tone, but the masks and discipline are objective correlatives, to use Eliot's critical conceit current at the time, of his personal reserve, allowing him to broach his inner arguments — between agnostic doubt and spiritual values, existential choice and essential symbols, Romantic enthusiasm and classical cool. Whatever question or conflict beat in his blood drove his poems. His fears and lust and daily life are in them, his philosophy and failure. Richard Aldington's assessment of Read's *Mutations of the Phoenix* (1923) — that the approach is cerebral and

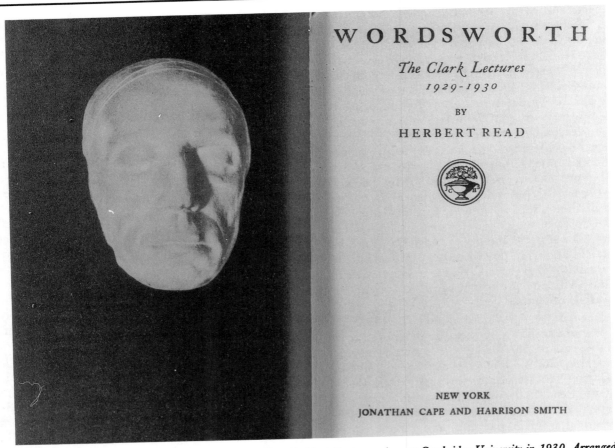

Frontispiece and title page for the American edition of Read's Clark Lectures, given at Cambridge University in 1930. Arranged by T. S. Eliot, the lectures helped Read attain a professorship in fine arts at the University of Edinburgh.

analytical – describes the tone of the verse less than the tenor of the poet's personality and the chilling effect of writing in Eliot's shadow.

In 1922 Read took a critical step. He left the civil service and a possible political career for a lower-paying position in the ceramics department of the Victoria and Albert Museum. The work still interfered with his poetic aspirations, but the move proclaimed Read's awareness of his talents and the evolution of his principles. From this point he dedicated the larger part of his labor and owed most of his fame to the visual arts. His writer's romance and grappling with language focused on the demands of representing visual experience and elaborating interpretation in modest histories of crafts (pottery and stained glass) and grand histories of art, in biographies of friends and exhibition catalogues, in critical theory and comment. From this point his political views oriented to a cultural pole, and their rationalizations stood on cultural grounds. His aesthetic nationalism led him to flirt with Fascist ideology, and his art-historical notions always betrayed the racial-geographical theories of Wilhelm Worringer, but ultimately his anarchist/internationalist politics renounced the artist-as-superman for the acknowledgment of everyman-as-artist, and his staunchest partisanship was reserved for the revolutionary potential of art. Taking the job at the museum was the third structurally significant fact of Read's life.

Though Eliot was only five years older than Read, his influence was fatherly. The gravity of his character and the mass of his literary accomplishment demanded for the expatriate American a centrality among the English-speaking poets of his generation. The museum job nudged Read into a further, more eccentric orbit, for while he still socialized with Eliot and contributed regularly to the *Criterion,* he now had an expertise, a platform, and an audience that his famous friend did not. Read's growing awareness of the plastic operation of his own critical instincts across media, across cultures, across politics and aesthetics; his recognition of the synthetic nature of his opinions; and his intuition of a common symbology of language and nonverbal, visual artistic expression all led him to critical rebellion against Eliot's authority, his classicism and elitism. Read came to admire what Eliot abhorred, Romantic sensibility, not simply in its appeal to the emotions or its engagement with nature but in its quest for the wellsprings of experience, its exploration of organic form and the descriptive-meditative process model, and its dedication to visionary art and revolutionary politics. If his poetry continued for the extent of his career as Aldington found it, cerebral and analytical, virtues Read recognized as classical, Read would argue that all poetry, in its profoundest nature, in its creation and communication, even the experimental, "abstract" poetry of *Vocal Avowals* (1962), was Romantic. Eliot and Read remained personal friends, but as critics they made a quarreling couple.

Their relationship proved deeper and more lasting than his marriage to Evelyn, which suffered from depressing clichés of authorship: Read, on the lofty perch of poetic inspiration or in the literary mines of hackwork, smoking cigarettes and composing every evening, abandoning his wife for his muse. He was in isolation, having the time of his life, cranking out work, indulging passions, achieving regard, if not reward. But it became obvious that he had realized a worse cliché: when the romance passed, he was trapped in a loveless marriage. It did not help when, in 1923, they had a son, John, or when Evelyn miscarried, then developed a thyroid condition, losing her health and gaining weight. She openly resented, not without wit, her husband's cold shoulder, which drove him further into his poetry and poet's pose.

Eliot brokered several academic opportunities for Read, proposing that he deliver the Clark Lectures at Trinity College, Cambridge, which he did in 1930, and feeling him out for the only full-time professorial post in the fine arts in Britain, the Gordon Chair at the University of Edinburgh, which he took in 1931. If the objects of seeking employment in academia were higher pay, "infinitely more liberty" to write, and the dissemination and legitimization of his opinions, his success at attaining them was limited to negligible. He may also have been, perhaps without awareness, seeking romance, for that is what he found. Edinburgh had more cultural history than currency, and Read thought it disappointingly provincial, but he had not been long in town when, at a lunch on the city's limited salon circuit, he was seated beside a young violinist, Margaret Ludwig.

"Ludo," as she was known to everyone, was thirteen years younger than the thirty-eight-year-old lecturer, who found her vivacious, artistic, insecure, and rebellious. Even her adopted Catholicism was a rebellion against her Episcopalian father, who was himself an apostate Catholic. She and Read began a barely concealed liaison, to Evelyn's dismay and young John's distress. By all accounts the affair was only intellectually and spiritually adulterous during this period, but Read could be blithely hurtful. When, though an unmusical man, he wanted a piano moved into the house, Evelyn recognized the influence of her rival, as she recognized in her husband's complaints about her wardrobe a lack of sympathy for her illness, which left her swollen and unattractive.

Evelyn's bitterness waxed with the progressive stages of Read's withdrawal, through separation and divorce, until her mental health deteriorated with her physical condition. Read made analogies to Eliot's marriage, but Vivienne Haighwood's psychological problems were of a different order, clinically and chronologically. Read meant to make the case, at least by implication, that Evelyn's behavioral imbalance drove him away, while the converse is more probably true, that his distancing himself drove her into obsession and oddity. Evelyn, unlike Vivienne, was not institutionalized until long after her husband left her (over thirteen years later, after World War II), and Read left his son with her, so it is unlikely, during their breakup, that she was as depressive or ill-adapted as Mrs. Eliot. The analogy holds only in a sense ironic relative to Read's, that both husbands are culpable in the psychological decline of intelligent, capable women unfortunate enough to marry intellectually aloof, emotionally chilly poets.

Read enjoyed cohabiting with Ludo while getting his divorce; it reestablished his bohemian credentials and appealed to the sense of mischief that occasionally spiked his principled defense of the avant-garde, especially since Ludo's sincere Catholicism authenticated their "living in sin." Their romance and marriage reestablished passionate argument in Read's private life, since his principles almost always conflicted with his wife's faith. (Evelyn would remain a rationalist leftist, like her former husband, through breakdowns and shock treatments.) They would eventually have three children (including the author Piers Paul Read), and she would ultimately endure the overt attentions of rivals (like the patron Peggy Guggenheim) for Read's affection, and his overt attentions to other women (like the artist Ruth Francken).

Read's first wife, Evelyn, and their son John (John Read)

Read wrote the Clark Lectures, then, at a pivotal point in his life, when he was turning away from Eliot and his first marriage, toward independence and maturity, or at least toward his own ideas and rationalizations. The shift appears dramatic, but in influence and effect it is tidal, reaching back to Muscoates Grange and forward for the rest of his life. Read called the time between the world wars "no man's years," when brilliance was ineffectual, and peace and personal freedom and art, for all its efforts, were marginalized. The march-step approach of another world war is captured in the grim and anxiety-ridden imagery of one of Read's finest poems of the period, "A Northern Legion." Yet it was over this difficult temporal terrain that Read hit his stride, if a halting one. As he rediscovered romance in another relationship, he found his taste in the neglected art of the avant-garde and the maligned poetry of two generations of English genius, and in their defense, his voice. In the text of the Clark Lectures, collected soon after delivery as a critical biography, and their choice of subject, William Wordsworth, Read was speaking, as he was finding, his mind. As an art critic, Read wrote several manifestos; this biography was his manifesto of poetry, of self.

Wordsworth (1930) rehearsed Read's critical method as he would practice it the rest of his life. He was a pioneer among literary critics in applying psychoanalysis to the lives and works of authors, particularly poets, further defining his difference from Eliot, who objected to psychoanalytic criticism. Read puts Wordsworth on the couch, exploring the etiology of the poet's neurotic personality for the effect on his poetry, or its cause. The repression of Wordsworth's guilt over his affair with Annette Vallon and the child she bore him out of wedlock, sublimated in his poetry, created "the emotional complex from which all his subsequent career flows in its intricacy and uncertainty," including "the highest reach of his poetic powers" and the five fallow decades that followed. *Wordsworth* is less a biography than a case study; it focuses on "this key to his emotional development" and denies the biographical imperative to present the life as lived: "The plan of this book does not allow any detailed record of this period" — the last forty-eight years of his life. Later, in a review of Virginia Woolf's *Roger Fry: A Biography* (1940), he referred to the biographical "inscape," a metaphor meaningful to Read in its yoking of landscape and emotional experience, the locus of value and intention in biography, as it provides the ground for psychological insight.

That insight is most meaningful in the service of criticism, of understanding the poetic process, and hence, the poetry. The "first task" he takes up in his biographical-critical tract *Byron* (1951) is "an attempt at a diagnosis of his state of mind, for out of it proceeded not only the almost daemonic energy with which he lived and wrote, but also the substance and . . . the quality of what he wrote." Conversely, the poetry and poetics reveal the mind and are evidence of the personality of the poet, if read analytically. With a subject such as Wordsworth, "biography becomes an analysis," as Read writes in his introduction to *Wordsworth,* and he goes on to use Sigmund Freud's terms and techniques to illuminate and disassemble Wordsworth's texts and the text of his character, as compiled from the verse, correspondence, and criticism of the poet, his contemporaries (especially his sister Dorothy and his great friend Samuel Taylor Coleridge), and the biographer's contemporaries (primarily the venerable Wordsworth scholar Ernest de Selincourt). Freudian analysis, of dreams and literature and in the "talking cure," is a verbal model, a critical language, structurally analogous to literary criticism. An even closer analogy can be made to literary biography, in which the subject, usually a dead writer, is an entirely verbal construct. Criticism of *Wordsworth* as a work of criticism argues from a premise different from Read's own. If, for a major portion of the text, poetry is the subject, the poet is still present, still central, for Read makes the same claims for his study of Wordsworth that he makes for his study of his friend Henry Moore (*Henry Moore: A Study of His Life and Work,* 1964), that "the story of (his) life . . . after his childhood and early education, is mainly the story of his art."

Of Wordsworth's childhood and early education, we learn little from Read, certainly less than the poet himself tells us in his *Prelude* (1840). However, while that epic of intellectual development is crucial evidence for understanding the poet's mind and method at the height of his powers, "the difficulty of accepting the *Prelude* (1840) as simple evidence for the events of Wordsworth's life" outweighs the expediency. The first chapter of Read's biography focuses mostly on this problem, "that all autobiography is disguised fiction," and on his subject's heritage of character, his northern taciturnity. Few facts are assembled, but impressions are left of a moody youth, implying "abnormal sensibility," a life "blessed with early liberty" attaining a young manhood "in passion and in pride unchecked." Though nonclinical applications of psychoanalytic method, especially in literary analysis, tend naturally to be less rigorous and more speculative than those involving the welfare of patients, Read's lack of attention to his subject's formative childhood experiences, especially in a subject whose signature dictum — "the child is father of the man" — prefigures Freud's central, founding idea,

is difficult to excuse, even in an "amateur interpretation of Wordsworth's psychological development." Read argues aggressively, and reasonably persuasively, for his "hypothesis" explaining how "the treasury of (Wordsworth's) unconscious mind, so richly stored in childhood, was opened and given forth in the poetry of one wonderful decade," then petered out in uninspired, conventional versifying and careerism, and why "the events of 1791–1792, and the mental crisis that endured for the following five or six years, tend to render insignificant all the events that precede this period." Read devoted most of the preface to a later edition (written in 1948) to further promotion and proof of his "theory." Since, however, like fiction, biography is also "disguised autobiography," the author's focus on the crisis in his subject's poetic career is at least as telling evidence of an obsession with his own.

In the 1802 preface to *Lyrical Ballads,* Wordsworth describes "good poetry" as "the spontaneous overflow of powerful feelings." Read, contemplating poetry at a source, pouring forth and then failing, was moved to the spontaneous overflow of powerful passion — into analysis. Perhaps this is one reason he was not the poet he wished to be, as often as he wished to be. Throughout his professional life, Read feared and complained that he used up his literary reserves writing criticism, but he may not have been conscious of the full extent of self he gave to his prose works. Read's interest in Wordsworth was personal, and the similarities between them, besides establishing the biographer's authority to comment from knowledge on aspects of his subject's life, establishes for the author a biographical analogue to his own. As northerners they shared a generic character, a racial "capacity for masking their emotions," both were essentially orphaned at roughly the same age, and both became poets with a special interest in diction. Daffodils, prominent in the verse of both, are emblematic of the power of nature, especially landscape, in their works and lives, especially their youths. More particularly, both had fallen out of love with their first loves. The resultant crisis in Wordsworth's poetic career did not, of course, necessarily prefigure one in Read's, but Read's career was in something like a continual crisis, especially at the time: he was stepping away, in taste and philosophy, from Eliot; and if he was not stepping away professionally from poetry toward the visual arts, he was uneasily astride the two. But it was the effect of the former – love, and the waning of it – on the latter – inspiration, and the loss of it – that attracted Read's attention and prompted his identification.

Read and Carl Jung at Küssnacht, Switzerland, circa 1930

There were lessons for Read in Wordsworth's life. Unhappy in his marriage, Read was considering leaving Evelyn and John, as Wordsworth had abandoned Annette and their daughter Caroline. The parallel is tenuously broad, for the two men were different ages at their breakup points, *of* different ages, a century apart, and under dissimilar pressures; but if the analogy is even tenuously accepted, Read's method of applying a found psychoanalytic dynamic to the work and life of an author to explain behavior and rhetoric could be regarded as predictive as well. So, if Wordsworth's remorse was indeed suffered, sublimated, and displaced in his philosophy and the best of his poetry, Read's thought could be nourished and his poetry enriched by the same dynamic. Even the suffering might appeal to Read, who "thought his own existence had been too outer directed," too concerned with character as opposed to personality. Any projections the biographer might have been able to make from his subject's failed responsibilities toward his mistress, though, were purely speculative; on the other hand, Read's recognition of the failure of Wordsworth's

1802 marriage to Mary Hutchinson was all too realistic, all too real. It was wedlock with a vengeance, the public reformation of the republican rake, the defiant denial of a poet "jealous of his own past," an embrace of convention rather than of flesh, if judged from the poetry his wife inspired, which shows not "any trace of sensuous ecstasy." The poet now had a reputation, social and professional, attained at the sacrifice of inspiration. The bourgeois swallowed the poet whole, in Read's account, and his best verse was soon behind him; what lay ahead was a "dreadful deadness . . . domestic tyranny and provincial narrowness . . . decaying sensibility and the slow growth of a thick shell of convention." The specter for Read, again, was his own marriage.

As a model, Wordsworth's life let Read have it both ways: a poet must abandon a moribund relationship, "extinction of passion" being a stage in the psychological process culminating in "recollection in tranquility," the emotional medium of Wordsworth's great poetry; and a poet must not make "merely a placid convention of marriage" or risk

Read in 1963 (photograph by Jonathan Williams)

"killing his feelings at the root." No matter that Wordsworth lived these events in an opposite order to that contemplated by Read (marriage, then abandonment). Wordsworth's impulse, even in the first case, was toward convention, whereas Read categorically rejected all "obsessions, fixed ideas, inhibitions, and repressed psychological factors" institutionalized as norms – for, as Read knew and felt, "a poet may be regarded as a very sensitive instrument which only records under certain conditions," and he was naturally, dramatically drawn to those instances in which Wordsworth qua instrument yielded readings consonant with his own. He examines the strain and estrangement in the friendship of Wordsworth and Coleridge at some length, identifying in that case with Coleridge – a more likely identification in any case, considering their mutual philosophical bent and their difficulties in composition – responding from his sense of his similar situation with Eliot. And when *Wordsworth* sounds less like a biography or a case study than a romance –

"There speaks a lover, and a man never loves twice in exactly the same way" – the author is sympathizing with himself, telling his own story.

Read's most important claim in the biography, and some of his best work as a critic, results from his appreciation of Wordsworth's practical poetics and his method. Ultimately Read's deepest sympathy is not with Wordsworth in love or in denial, but with Wordsworth at work. Read's crucial effort in the rescue of Wordsworth from the quasi-religious, faddist awe of the Victorians and the reactionary modernist backlash, and his almost single-handed rehabilitation of Romanticism, derided and dismissed by most of his contemporaries as a digression from English poetic tradition into embarrassing backwaters of emotionalism, irrelevant pantheism, and youthful politics, stem from his discovery of empiricism at the source of Wordsworth's poetry. Read recognized in the images and diction that "everything followed from the primary physical sensations." Wordsworth "belongs to the empirical and objective school," and his philosophy "is based on a psychological theory" — David Hartley's theory of the association of ideas, a precursor of Freud's pleasure principle — "the most empirical of its day." In this recognition is Read's most authentic identification with Wordsworth, for he was an empiricist, too, in his poetic practice and aesthetic theorizing. From his earliest imagist verse, to the keystone concept of his later criticism of art — that the image is prior to the idea — to the dialectical foundations of his politics, Read's thinking was empirical. He, too, looked for a science on which to base his poetics, and remained a devotee of psychoanalysis, especially as developed by Carl Jung, whose archetypes and focus on the artistic temperament eventually appealed to his sensibility more than Freud's biological musings and marginalizing of the artist as neurotic. Read's own biography is full of dialectical oppositions — from Romanticism and classicism, abstraction and surrealism, capitalism and anarchism, to pottery and porcelain, Yorkshire and London, and Wordsworth, "Man and Mask"; when he collected and expanded his autobiographical writings, he called the volume *The Contrary Experience* (1963). "Respectable Bohemia," the oxymoron Woolf used to describe Read's lifestyle, symbolized by his habitual bow ties and berets, follows the dialectical pattern beyond his philosophy to his taste, and in his memoir *The Innocent Eye,* written several years after *Wordsworth* and likened often by critics to the *Prelude,* it is revealed in his seminal experiences. As a boy at Muscoates he and his brothers made "gleaming silver bullets" for their slingshots, melting scrap lead and pouring it into a rudimentary mold, a recollection vivid with recapturing: "The joy was in the making of them, and in the sight of their shining beauty . . . fire was real, and so was the skill with which we shaped hard metals to our design and desire." This "first sensation" of the creative act from the crucible of his youth, of the dialectic of materials and desire, and the anal stage satisfaction with its empirical products is at the core of all Read's writing, of his endless efforts to resolve intellectual conflicts and synthesize in a concept or an image, of his sympathetic understanding of Wordsworth and the Romantics. When he generalizes in *Wordsworth* that "a poet is a man for whom the visible world exists *in disjunction,*" he speaks from his own authority, no less than he does when considering his subject in particular: "The world was so visible and real to him because he had to build it up from brute sensation, element by element." When, in his essay "The Romantic Revolution" from *The Tenth Muse: Essays in Criticism* (1957), he identifies "the essential no-

tion" of that revolution as the identity of form with substance, he uses a telling metaphor to define form: "it is the crystallization of . . . substance as it cools in the mind of the poet," like the lead shot he made in the saddle room at Muscoates, which "rolled away to cool on the stone floor."

Biography would remain an important component of Read's critical method, in all its applications, including the autobiographical. His *In Defense of Shelley and Other Essays* (1936), written during his divorce in 1935 and his remarriage to Ludo in 1936, is deft in its analysis of Shelley's poetics and its psychoanalysis of Shelley, but it is abject in its service to its subject and its self-service. The same dynamics Read discovered in *Wordsworth* seem willfully, even cynically applied in the *Defense:* he reacts to Eliot, who demeans Shelley's thought and work as immature, with analytical parry and ideological thrust; he amasses evidence from the life and verse of the subject to support a psychoanalytical paradigm that in turn explicates and accounts for the quality of the poetry; he focuses on the subject's love life, particularly the abandonment of a lover and child, in Shelley's case a wife and children. His case for the writing and his case study of the writer are, as with Wordsworth, founding exegeses of modern hermeneutics with respect to Romantic sensibility; his justification of Shelley's forsaking his family is shameless. Read's reading of the major poetry is as responsible as any for Shelley being in the contemporary canon; his theory of the poet as a repressed homosexual can still be argued; his bullying, name-calling attack on the Westbrook sisters and his tone-deaf reading of Shelley's "lost letters" to Harriet, published in 1930, are transparently prejudiced. When Read writes in his editorial voice of "our nearer and more sympathetic point of view," his sympathy does not extend to the poet's teenage wife — his first teenage wife — but it does embrace himself as he, like his subject, changed partners.

It was for Ludo that he wrote *The Innocent Eye,* to acquaint her with his self's source, his farmboy's youth. In 1949 he acquired Stonegrave, a farmhouse with land in Yorkshire, two and a half miles from Muscoates Grange. For the rest of his life he would commute between London and Yorkshire, when he was not peddling opinions on various lecture tours, in conference appearances and judgings around the world. The northern landscape appears in some of his best later poetry, like *Moon's Farm,* a radio play in verse, broadcast in 1951. But the city/country opposition, like most of the others in Read's conflicted existence, was never satisfactorily resolved except as an arena for his striving intellect. He pined for a "one-job life" but lived one of "petty fights and meaningless travel"; his hope for a revolution of politics and sensibility devolved into a less ambitious but no less strenuous life of humbler "attempts to make the world slightly better." When, in 1952, he was offered a knighthood "for services to literature," Read the anarchist joked about the absurdity of the situation, but Read the practical patriot, the endless encourager of English art, the editor who recommended Samuel Beckett's *Murphy* (1938) for publication, the critic who rehabilitated the Romantics, the poet proud to have served literature, accepted. He spent his life in the avant-garde and must have understood when a new generation of artists in the 1950s attacked him because he was "all there was" to rebel against. On 12 June 1968 he died of head and neck cancer, the same cancer that killed Freud. Read was still, at his death, an agnostic, an anarchist, and, as Stephen Spender called him, a "Recognizer." Spender meant it as a slight, though a friendly one, but it was Read's great gift. In essays on Jung and the *Prelude,* he uses the same phrase to characterize the psychologist and the poet, "the spectator *ab extra,*" that is, "the merciless, objective analyst," "the scientist," and it is the empiricist in the poet that lends substance and strength to his biographies and his use of biography in his lifetime of literature.

Biography:

James King, *The Last Modern: A Life of Herbert Read* (New York: St. Martin's Press, 1990).

References:

Paul Fussell, *The Great War and Modern Memory* (New York & London: Oxford University Press, 1975);

Robin Skelton, ed., *Herbert Read: A Memorial Symposium* (London: Methuen, 1970);

Henry Treece, ed., *Herbert Read: An Introduction to his Work by Various Hands* (London: Faber & Faber, 1944);

George Woodcock, *Herbert Read: The Stream and the Source* (London: Faber & Faber, 1972).

Papers:

Read's manuscripts are held in various collections in the United Kingdom, the United States, and Canada, including the Read Archive in the McPherson Library of the University of Victoria, British Columbia; the Houghton Library, Harvard University; the Brotherton Library, the University of Leeds; the Firestone Library, Princeton University; the Harry Ransom Humanities Research Center, University of Texas at Austin; and the Victoria and Albert Museum.

George Saintsbury

(23 October 1845–28 January 1933)

P. E. Hewison
University of Aberdeen

See also the Saintsbury entry in *DLB 57: Victorian Prose Writers After 1867.*

BOOKS: *Primer of French Literature* (Oxford: Clarendon Press, 1880; New York: Harper, 1881; revised and enlarged, Oxford: Clarendon Press, 1884, 1888, 1896, 1912);

Dryden (London: Macmillan, 1881; New York: Harper, 1881);

A Short History of French Literature (Oxford: Clarendon Press, 1882; revised and enlarged, 1897);

Marlborough (London: Longmans, Green, 1885; New York: Appleton, 1886);

A History of Elizabethan Literature (London & New York: Macmillan, 1887);

Manchester (London: Longmans, Green, 1887);

Essays in English Literature: 1780–1860 (London: Percival, 1890; New York: Scribners, 1891);

Essays on French Novelists (London: Percival, 1891; New York: Scribners, 1891);

The Earl of Derby (London: Low, Marston, 1892; New York: Harper, 1892);

Miscellaneous Essays (London: Percival, 1892; New York: Scribners, 1892);

Inaugural Address Delivered at Edinburgh on the 15th October, 1895 (Edinburgh & London: Blackwood, 1895);

Essays in English Literature: 1780–1860, Second Series (London: Dent, 1895; New York: Scribners, 1895);

Corrected Impressions (London: Heinemann, 1895; New York: Dodd, Mead, 1895);

A History of Nineteenth Century Literature: 1780–1895 (New York & London: Macmillan, 1895);

The Flourishing of Romance and the Rise of Allegory (Edinburgh & London: Blackwood, 1897; New York: Scribners, 1897);

Sir Walter Scott (Edinburgh & London: Oliphant, Anderson & Ferrier, 1897; New York: Scribners, 1897);

A Short History of English Literature (New York & London: Macmillan, 1898);

Matthew Arnold (Edinburgh: Blackwood, 1899; New York: Dodd, Mead, 1899);

A History of Criticism and Literary Taste in Europe from the Earliest Texts to the Present Day, 3 volumes (Edinburgh & London: Blackwood, 1900–1904; New York: Dodd, Mead, 1900–1904); parts revised and enlarged as *A History of English Criticism; Being the English Chapters of A History of Criticism and Literary Taste in Europe, Revised, Adapted, and Supplemented* (Edinburgh & London: Blackwood, 1911; New York: Dodd, Mead, 1911);

The Earlier Renaissance (Edinburgh & London: Blackwood, 1901; New York: Scribners, 1901);

A History of English Prosody from the Twelfth Century to the Present Day, 3 volumes (London & New York: Macmillan, 1906–1910);

The Later Nineteenth Century (Edinburgh & London: Blackwood, 1907; New York: Scribners, 1907);

Historical Manual of English Prosody (London: Macmillan, 1910);

A History of English Prose Rhythm (London: Macmillan, 1912);

The English Novel (London: Dent / New York: Dutton, 1913);

A First Book of English Literature (London: Macmillan, 1914);

The Peace of the Augustans: A Survey of Eighteenth Century Literature as a Place of Rest and Refreshment (London: Bell, 1916);

A History of the French Novel (to the Close of the 19th Century), 2 volumes (London: Macmillan, 1917–1919);

Notes on a Cellar-Book (London: Macmillan, 1920; New York: Macmillan, 1933);

A Scrap Book (London: Macmillan, 1922);

A Second Scrap Book (London: Macmillan, 1923);

A Last Scrap Book (London: Macmillan, 1924);

George Saintsbury

A Consideration of Thackeray (London: Oxford University Press, 1931);

Prefaces and Essays, edited by Oliver Elton (London: Macmillan, 1933);

George Saintsbury: The Memorial Volume: A New Collection of His Essays and Papers, edited by John W. Oliver and Augustus Muir (London: Methuen, 1945); republished as *A Saintsbury Miscellany: Selections from His Essays and Scrap Books* (New York: Oxford University Press, 1947);

French Literature and Its Masters, edited by Huntington Cairns (New York: Knopf, 1946);

A Last Vintage, edited by Oliver, Muir, and Arthur Melville Clark (London: Methuen, 1950).

Collection: *The Collected Essays and Papers of George Saintsbury,* 4 volumes (London & Toronto: Dent / New York: Dutton, 1923–1924).

OTHER: *Specimens of French Literature from Villon to Hugo,* selected and edited by Saintsbury (Oxford: Clarendon Press, 1833; revised, 1892);

John Dryden, *The Works of John Dryden,* 18 volumes, edited by Sir Walter Scott; revised, corrected, and enlarged by Saintsbury (London: Paterson, 1882–1893);

Specimens of English Prose Style from Malory to Macaulay, selected and annotated by Saintsbury (London: Kegan Paul / Chicago: Jansen, McClurg, 1886);

Henry Fielding, *The Works of Henry Fielding,* 12 volumes, edited by Saintsbury (London: Dent, 1893–1899);

English Prose, 5 volumes, edited by Sir Henry Craik; contains 37 introductions by Saintsbury (London: Macmillan, 1893–1896);

Honoré de Balzac, *Comédie humaine,* 40 volumes, edited by Saintsbury (London: Dent, 1895–1900);

Minor Poets of the Caroline Period, 3 volumes, edited by Saintsbury (Oxford: Clarendon Press, 1905–1921);

The Cambridge History of English Literature, 14 volumes, edited by Sir A. W. Ward and A. R.

Waller; contains 20 chapters by Saintsbury (Cambridge: Cambridge University Press, 1907–1921);

William Makepeace Thackeray, *The Oxford Thackeray,* 20 volumes, edited by Saintsbury (London: Oxford University Press, 1908).

George Saintsbury's literary output was massive. He wrote nearly fifty books and over eight hundred essays, introductions, and reviews. The actual total remains unknown. Among all these there are only five works that can be classified as biographies as such. They are important as studies of their subjects and for the light they throw on their author; but Saintsbury's greatest importance for biography is probably his general influence on other biographers. For in his time Saintsbury's stature was as colossal as his output. He simply could not be ignored. The descriptions by his contemporaries are indicative: to Irving Babbitt he was "the official English critic"; Helen Waddell commented that "There'll never be another Saintsbury"; to Christopher Morley he was simply "King of Critics."

George Edward Bateman Saintsbury was born on 23 October 1845 in Southampton, where his father was superintendent of the docks owned by the London and South Western Railway. Southampton always had a hold on him: he returned to live there briefly after his retirement, he married a Southampton girl, and he is buried there. Saintsbury's father died when George was fourteen: from him he derived a love of the sea, of books, and of wine and a somewhat-Tory outlook. He was then left under the influence of his mother, born Elizabeth Wright, about whom virtually nothing is known, and his two elder sisters, governesses who instilled in him a love of languages. By now the family was living in Notting Hill in London, where Saintsbury attended a small dame school and then a preparatory school for King's College School, where he eventually entered at just under age thirteen in 1858. Saintsbury always paid tribute to this school, especially for its firm and wide-ranging teaching of the classics; but equally important was his own reading. His tastes at this stage tended strongly toward the romantic, both in the sense of the medieval romance and of such authors as Alfred Tennyson and George Gordon, Lord Byron. Combining these, his favorite literature was Arthurian — again, as it always would be.

A Tory, a great reader, something of a dreamer, with "King Charles the Martyr" alongside the Arthurian knights on his private list of "Things and Persons to be Adored," Saintsbury was obviously heading for Oxford, and probably Christ Church. In 1862, however, he failed the Christ Church scholarship examination, apparently through "weakness of scholarship." There is perhaps something prophetic about this. Nevertheless, in 1863 he was awarded a postmastership at Merton College, the news reaching him on the same day as he nearly drowned after capsizing his boat on the Thames. Oxford basically confirmed and deepened the central aspects of Saintsbury's character, his High Church and Tory beliefs and his voracious reading, as well as other traits — the love of wine, walking, cards, and horse racing. What it did not bring him was a First Class degree. The shock of his Second in Greats marked him for life. "The sting of a Second is all almost incurable," he wrote later.

In 1868 Saintsbury left Oxford, accepted a teaching post at Manchester Grammar School, stayed six months, proceeded to a similar post at Elizabeth College in Guernsey, and married Emily Fern King, a Southampton friend of his sisters. Saintsbury admitted that "I never *liked* schoolmastering," but he seems to have been reasonably happy in the Channel Islands. His friendship with Paul Stapfer, the French master at Elizabeth College, himself a friend of Victor Hugo, who was then living on Guernsey, in the meantime encouraged his already-considerable interest in French literature. His next post, however, as headmaster of the newly founded Elgin Educational Institute, was a complete disaster. He resigned in 1876 after only two years and headed for London and eighteen years as a literary journalist. There he wrote principally for the *St. James Gazette* under Frederick Greenwood, the *London* under W. E. Henley, and the *Saturday Review* under Philip Harwood and later Walter Pollock, with a brief return to Manchester for the *Manchester Guardian* under C. P. Scott. The Saintsbury displayed in these journals is essentially the Saintsbury who wrote the five biographies. The political articles for Henley show the High Tory, especially in his hatred (there is no other word) for William Gladstone and Irish Home Rule. The literary articles show equally combative and controversial attitudes: his defense of French literature; his insistence on the primacy of form in literature, as opposed to subject, theme, or (some said) moral; and his extraordinary prose style. Much of the journalistic writing was of course expository, informative, and instructive; but when Saintsbury wanted to be rough, he could be extremely rough indeed.

Saintsbury's earliest nonjournalistic writing reflects one of his enthusiasms, with thirty-six articles on French literature for the *Encyclopaedia*

Britannica (ninth edition) in 1879, and his first book, *A Primer of French Literature,* in 1880. His second book, and first biography, *Dryden,* was published in 1881. In many ways *Dryden* is his best biography. It contains most of the usual Saintsbury virtues (and vices) but is helped by a superbly clear style much unlike that of the later Saintsbury and by his admirable balance and fairness toward the subject. Over a century later this is still probably the best basic introduction to John Dryden, although this may have as much to do with Dryden, a notoriously tricky man to talk about, as with Saintsbury. From the beginning there is a virtuoso touch to the book: the opening chapter places Dryden in a series of contexts – geographical, political, and literary – revealing a deep understanding of the seventeenth century, and also a fine wit.

There are, however, some problems: the next chapter's first sentence states "the chief difficulty of writing a life of Dryden – the almost entire absence of materials." There is some truth in this, but not much. Saintsbury's goal is to justify his general approach to the writing of biography, especially of literary men, that it is the works, not the life, which should be stressed. Saintsbury later makes this explicit: "a biography of him, let it be repeated at the close as it was asserted at the beginning, must consist of little but a discussion and running comment on those works." This is in fact part and parcel of his overall idea of criticism: as he says in his *A Short History of English Literature* (1898): "The thing is important in literature, not the man." This statement may make Saintsbury look rather worryingly like a biographer not interested in biography; but the Romantic side of Saintsbury does not allow him to adhere too closely to these strictures. In this chapter Saintsbury justifies the approach with detailed and acute discussion of Dryden's early poetry; but the following chapter, on Dryden's plays, is much less successful. Saintsbury's lament over the "licence of language" which prevents quotation is part of a larger refusal to engage with a whole aspect of Restoration literature, producing for example a hopelessly inadequate account of John Wilmot, Earl of Rochester, "the worst of all the courtiers of the time . . . radically unamiable." All is well with the ensuing discussion of the great satires, a notable combination of background and close reading; and with a genuinely biographical section on the "Life from 1680 to 1688," including a fine put-down for those who question the motives behind Dryden's conversion to Roman Catholicism: "Is Dryden's critic nowadays prepared to question the sincerity of Cardinal Newman?" As Saintsbury moves into the last

decade of Dryden's life, the approach becomes even more sympathetic, with a fine discussion of the "tour de force" nature of Dryden's later plays and a brilliant analysis of Dryden's contribution to the development of seventeenth-century prose style and his relationship here with John Tillotson. The final chapter gives an excellent general picture of Dryden and his achievement, concluding with the verdict that he is "the greatest craftsman in English letters." This is immediately linked to Saintsbury's central emphasis on form or "method of treatment" as opposed to content, with a dismissal of the uselessness of "a definition of poetry which regards it wholly or chiefly from the point of view of its subject-matter." This virtually forces Saintsbury to produce his own definition of poetry, which of course he duly does: "the power of making the common uncommon by the use of articulate language in metrical arrangement so as to excite indefinite suggestions of beauty."

The next two biographies are much different affairs. To start with, the subject of *Marlborough* (1885), an archetypal Whig, and a corrupt and treacherous one by any standards, is going to pose problems for a High Tory like Saintsbury. Furthermore, he increases these problems in two ways. First, the book is to be "a portrait of John Churchill, first Duke of Marlborough's life and character, taking knowledge of the historical surroundings mostly for granted." This means not only that there is little narrative as such; but that the reader has to be already extremely well informed: anyone coming to this subject for the first time will find large sections of the book simply incomprehensible. Second, the book "excludes minute description of military operations" since these are available elsewhere "at a length, perhaps, greater than is agreeable or profitable." In other words, Saintsbury is not interested in military history. This is obviously a terrible handicap in discussing any great commander, but particularly so with Marlborough, where the best, probably the only, way to defend him is to stress his military achievements. In fact, right at the very end, this is exactly what Saintsbury finds himself doing.

Altogether then, *Marlborough* is a muddle of a book. As with Dryden, there is little on the early life. There is less than a page on the military details of the Sedgemoor campaign, then page after page to show that Marlborough was not involved in its bloody aftermath (which in fact he was). The attitudes to James II and the Glorious Revolution are pretty confused but ultimately seem to be pro-Whig. The account of the battle of Blenheim is short, difficult to follow, and shows more interest in

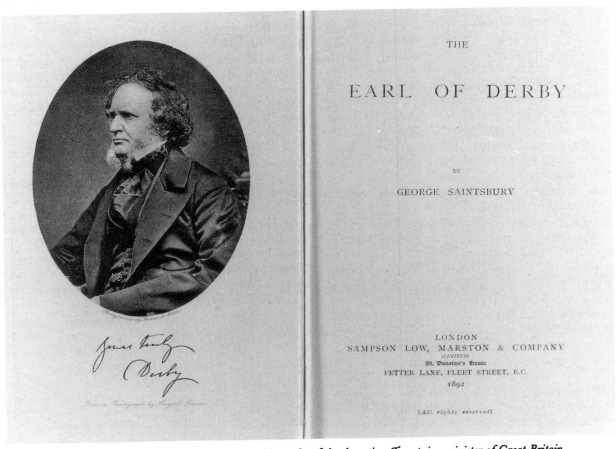

Frontispiece and title page for Saintsbury's biography of the three-time Tory prime minister of Great Britain

Prince Eugène than Marlborough. Fortunately the book improves through its second half. Some interest is actually shown in the battles of Oudenarde and Malplaquet. There is a clear account of the later stages of the War of the Spanish Succession and the Treaty of Utrecht. Saintsbury's sense of humor makes a belated appearance, notably in the treatment of Charles XII of Sweden. His Toryism also at last asserts itself in his treatment of Robert Harley and Henry St. John and in his dismissal of the Whig government as "a set of Ministers who were much more intriguers than statesmen." Marlborough's fall from power is traced clearly and sympathetically. The last chapter produces some interesting anecdotes and an attempt at a general defense of Marlborough's career. Some of the latter is not terribly convincing, notably the comparison to the Duke of Wellington or the assertion of Marlborough's softheartedness. The final point, however, is unanswerable: Marlborough beat the French. And no English army had done that for three hundred years. Saintsbury admits that to some this point might

seem a bit vulgar; but not to him. It is after all the basic reason readers "ought to reverence the memory, stained as it is . . . of Jack of Marlborough."

The next biography, *The Earl of Derby* (1892), that is of the fourteenth earl of Derby, the Victorian prime minister, resembles its predecessor in its faults, the reasons for them, and the way in which it improves toward the end. It is probably more successful in that Saintsbury's Tory approach is clearer and indeed at times rampant. The first page of the preface leaves the reader in no doubt: "this little book is written from the point of view of a Tory. And as I have heard several persons say, that they do not exactly know what a Tory means, I may add that I define a Tory as a person who would, at the respective times and in the respective circumstances, have opposed Catholic Emancipation, Reform, the Repeal of the Corn Laws, and the whole Irish Legislation of Mr. Gladstone." Nevertheless, familiar weaknesses appear. The first twenty-one years of Derby's life are covered in less than two pages. Too much knowledge is assumed, so that the narrative is compressed; and the brevity tends to increase a suspicion that Saintsbury is fudging some issues about Derby, his reliability and loyalty, or as Saintsbury puts it, "logical consistency of general creed was by no means Lord Derby's strong point." It was probably a mistake to raise, and then attempt to dismiss, the point that switching sides was a tradition in the Stanley family, most notably at the Battle of Bosworth. Things improve at the end of chapter 3, with an excellent summary of the political situation in the mid nineteenth century, and in chapters 4 and 5, where Derby's character and weaknesses are at last properly examined. It is still typical that the most interesting pages in these chapters are those dealing with Derby's time as chancellor of Oxford University. A further problem is caused by Saintsbury's self-imposed "rule of not giving quotations, necessitated by the limits of this book." This deprives the reader of Derby's rhetorical eloquence and humor, which consequently makes him less and less attractive, especially as Saintsbury becomes more honest about his shortcomings, culminating in the refusal to form a government in 1855, "the great mistake of Lord Derby's life." As ever, though, the book then begins to get better. This is partly because great issues are now at stake: the Crimean War, the Reform Bill, the Indian mutiny, Schleswig-Holstein in 1864, "the one occasion in the last half-century when England ought to have plunged into war." Also Saintsbury starts to introduce more personal details, especially in chapter 9, where he discusses Derby's success in horses and his literary work. Saintsbury is of course in his element here, as much with the horses as the translations. It all culminates in a brilliant tour de force in which he compares the translations of the same passage from Homer by Thomas Hobbes, Dryden, Alexander Pope, William Cowper, William Sotheby, and Derby to prove that Derby's is the best. He at last starts quoting from Derby to illustrate Edward Bulwer-Lytton's description of him as "the Rupert of Debate" and reminds readers that it was indeed Derby who "dished the Whigs." The last chapter, as might be expected, puts up a general defense of its subject. Saintsbury has of course never admitted it, but it is quite possible to regard the fourteenth earl of Derby as a political failure. Here Saintsbury explains any weaknesses in terms of the transitional nature of the Tory Party at this time, between the ages of John Scott, first Earl of Eldon, and Benjamin Disraeli; and in terms of his personality, "not that he did not take politics seriously enough, but that he took everything with equal seriousness." Readers are finally invited to see Derby as an archetypal aristocratic statesman, that is, one possessing "absolute personal independence, and a sincere and undaunted patriotism."

During the 1880s Saintsbury had become increasingly dissatisfied as a literary journalist and had been looking toward the academic world. His lack of a First and his journalistic background could be balanced by an increasing reputation as literary critic and historian. Failures at universities of Aberdeen, Glasgow, and (inevitably) Oxford in the 1880s ended in 1895 in his appointment as regius professor of rhetoric and English literature at Edinburgh University. He succeeded David Masson, his chief rivals were W. E. Henley and Walter Raleigh, and he was the first non-Scot to hold the chair. The appointment was made by Lord Balfour, Tory secretary of state for Scotland, and was considered by many to be a political choice. Saintsbury had to overcome problems of national prejudice, his own unimpressive lecturing style, and the rowdyism traditional in nineteenth-century Scottish universities; but his formidable character and opinions eventually made him both successful and popular in the post he held for twenty years. In terms of writing, it freed him from things like political biographies, which were not really his forte, to concentrate on the academic and the literary.

His next biography, *Sir Walter Scott* (1897), nevertheless possesses by now familiar characteristics. Saintsbury assumes a great deal of prior knowledge; in particular he assumes the reader possesses and more or less knows backward John Gibson Lockhart's biography. There is little material on Scott's early years. The emphasis is definitely on the works as opposed to the life. Personal details do come in later, and in consequence the book improves in its second half. There is a fair amount of whitewashing over financial activities, in this case notably the Ballantyne and Company debacle. Fortunately the Saintsbury virtues are here as well. He is able to make crucial and central points clearly and memorably. Thus he compares Scott's verse romances with their eighteenth-century predecessors: with Scott, " 'The hunt is up' in earnest; and we are chasing the tall deer in the open hills, not coursing rabbits with toy terriers on a bowling green." More comment on the verse applies equally to the novels: "Scott could tell a story as few other men . . . Construction, of course was not his forte; it never was." He is especially acute on Scott the inventor of the historical novel, Scott the Scottish patriot, and the complex interrelationship between the two. One notable insight is that Scott "seems to have possessed

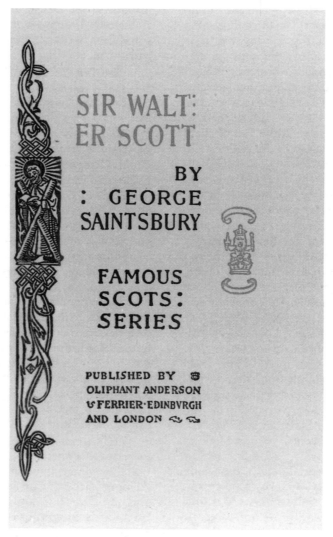

Title page for Saintsbury's biography of the Scottish novelist; the book gives little biographical detail, emphasizing instead the novels and assuming the reader's familiarity with John Gibson Lockhart's Life of Scott *(1838).*

by instinct (for there was nobody to teach him) the paramount secret of the historical novelist, the secret of making his central and prominent characters fictitious, and the real ones mostly subsidiary." The ensuing survey of all the novels is, as one might expect, thorough in terms of characters, story, and descriptions, but to a modern critic lacking in symbolism and theme. In the last chapter Saintsbury arouses sympathy for the pitiableness of Scott's last years, for his Toryism (of course), for his humor, for his depth of feeling. Readers are finally invited to see in Scott "Spenser and Fielding blended" and a "medley of tragic and comic" comparable to Shakespeare. This is perhaps going a little too far. The best definition of Scott's achievement is actually reached here by a daring comparison between him and the Elizabethan writer John Lyly. Saintsbury knew about Elizabethan writers. What is significant here is not just what we learn about Scott, but what we learn in a brilliant one-page analysis about Lyly. The suspicion arises, as it often has ever since *Dryden,* that Saintsbury is not writing about the right people.

That suspicion is more than confirmed in the next and last biography, *Matthew Arnold* (1899). The abiding impression of this book is of Saintsbury's total contempt for Arnold and just about everything he represents. It all begins in a familiar way, with the emphasis on works rather than life, a mere two pages on the first twenty years but a poem-by-poem analysis of the first three volumes of poetry. This thoroughness and the tone of cool appreciation may well be a ploy by Saintsbury to persuade the reader that this book is actually going to be fair. The trouble eventually starts as Saintsbury confronts "Mr. Arnold's own unlucky and maimed definition of poetry as 'a criticism of life.'" Saintsbury does admire some of Arnold's poetry, for example *Sohrab and Rustum* and *The Scholar Gypsy* (both 1853), but he simply detests the man, his theories, and his values. A parallel might be found in Dr. Samuel Johnson's attitude to Milton. The book becomes more and more hostile as it proceeds. The techniques deployed against Arnold include the dismissal of the whole 1885 volume of poems in a page; elsewhere the devotion of five pages to wiping out one single poem, *Merope* (1858); the summing-up of his criticism as "unfair, out of place, out of taste"; the clinching general comment: "what we go to Mr. Matthew Arnold for is not fact, it is not argument, it is not even learning. It is phrase, attitude, style." The most powerful attacks are in chapter 4, on Arnold's political and social, rather than specifically literary, ideas. The major target is *Literature and Dogma* (1873), it being Arnold's "worst" book, "in hopelessly bad taste," where "There is not only begging of the question but ignoring of the issue." Saintsbury concludes: "I do not remember that any one smashed it"; he has clearly put that right. Chapter 5 returns to literary matters, where Arnold's two central ideas on poetry as "a criticism of life" and "high seriousness" are quite simply annihilated in three pages. The final chapter, as usual, introduces some personal details and becomes friendlier: the comparison between Arnold and Thomas Gray, for example, is particularly interesting. The last sentence of the book, Saintsbury's last sentence as a biographer, significantly is as much about himself as about Arnold: "Whenever I think of Mr. Arnold it is in those own words of his . . . which I quoted to myself on the hill by Hinksey as I began this little book in the time of fritillaries

'Still nursing the unconquerable hope,
Still clutching the inviolable shade.' "

From this point on, Saintsbury dedicated himself mainly to a series of massive productions on criticism, prosody, and prose rhythm, which are a tribute to both his breadth and his precision of reading: of their kind, they will probably never be surpassed. He retired from Edinburgh in 1915 to spend a year in Southampton, and then the rest of his life at 1a, Royal Crescent, Bath. His idiosyncratic *The*

Peace of the Augustans (1916) contains some biographical material, with both an unusual approach to its period and also Saintsbury's highly individual style at its best (or worst). This style consists of extremely long sentences, highly involved in syntax and full of parentheses, quotations, references, foreign words and phrases, unusual and actually invented words, and even slang. It seems to have resembled his actual manner of speaking: on the printed page it can be extremely enjoyable or extremely irritating, sometimes both at once. Another intensely individual book is the marvelous *Notes on a Cellar-Book* of 1920, reflecting Saintsbury's enormous knowledge and enjoyment of wine. Finally in this area are the three "Scrap Books" (1922–1924), a combination of thoughts, memories, and opinions, which are at once autobiographically fascinating and highly entertaining, except of course to faint-hearted liberals.

In 1923–1924 Saintsbury produced the four volumes of his *The Collected Essays and Papers of George Saintsbury:* included in these is one on "Some Great Biographies." What is remarkable about this essay is that the excellent principles expounded in it were largely ignored by Saintsbury in practice as a biographer himself. He tells us that the "secret consists in fixing the attention of the reader . . . at once on the character of the subject"; that "the main and principal thing . . . [is] to let the subject speak for himself"; and that the best type of biography, Lockhart's *Scott* being "the capital example," is "more than the presentation of mere materials . . . The whole ought to be passed through the mind of a competent and intelligent artist . . . in such a way that we see a finished picture, a real composition." Admittedly, Saintsbury did at least attempt the last of these, although not at all the first two. He fully succeeded only with Dryden, partially with Derby and Scott, and barely with Marlborough, where he is unconvincing, or Arnold, where he is too hostile. Perhaps Saintsbury was not a natural writer of biography; perhaps, as has been suggested, he chose (or was assigned) the wrong subjects. One wonders what a Saintsbury biography of John Donne would have been like.

George Saintsbury died peacefully in Bath on 28 January 1933. He was buried in the family plot in Southampton. There were six mourners: one academic, five family. Despite a small but enthusiastic band of supporters his reputation plummeted rapidly and permanently. Only one of his books was in print in 1993: *Notes on a Cellar-Book.* The irony of this would have amused him: what is not so amusing is what it says about the present state of literary criticism. For Saintsbury was more than an entertaining High Tory literary raconteur (although he was that, too): he was a master of many literatures and hence a pioneer and master of comparative literature; a colossus in terms of his understanding of the history of literature, of the history of criticism, of prosody and prose rhythm; and a supreme exponent of the most important gift of all, the ability to communicate the enthusiastic interpretation of literature. The basis of all this was of course his vast reading. In the end, the best way to see him is as Helen Waddell saw him: "the solitary scholar who was his own best company, 'Lord not only of Joyous Gard but also of Garde Douleureuse,' reading, reading, reading through the small hours in the familiar chair with the two tall candlesticks behind it. And the light falls, not on his face, but on the open book."

Bibliographies:

W. M. Parker, "A Saintsbury Bibliography," in Saintsbury's *A Last Vintage,* edited by John W. Oliver, Augustus Muir, and Arthur Melville Clark (London: Methuen, 1950), pp. 244–255;

"George Saintsbury," in Christopher C. Brown and William B. Thesing, *English Prose and Criticism, 1900–1950: A Guide to Information Sources* (Detroit: Gale, 1983), pp. 387–397.

Biography:

Dorothy Richardson Jones, *"King of Critics:" George Saintsbury 1845–1933* (Ann Arbor: University of Michigan Press, 1992).

References:

Oliver Elton, "George Edward Bateman Saintsbury: 1845–1933," *Proceedings of the British Academy,* 19 (1933): 325–344;

John Gross, *The Rise and Fall of the Man of Letters* (London: Weidenfeld & Nicolson, 1969), pp. 139–149;

Walter Leuba, *George Saintsbury* (New York: Twayne, 1967);

Harold Orel, *Victorian Literary Critics* (London: Macmillan / New York: St. Martin's Press, 1984), pp. 151–176;

Stephen Potter, "King Saintsbury," in his *The Muse in Chains: A Study in Education* (London: Cape, 1937), pp. 126–139;

J. B. Priestley, "Mr. George Saintsbury," in his *Figures in Modern Literature* (London: Lane, 1928), pp. 170–195;

Dorothy Richardson, "Saintsbury and Art for Art's Sake in England," *PMLA,* 59 (March 1944): 243–260;

A. Blyth Webster, "A Biographical Memoir," in *A Saintsbury Miscellany,* edited by John W. Oliver and Augustus Muir (New York: Oxford University Press, 1947), pp. 27–73;

René Wellek, *The Later Nineteenth Century,* volume 4 of *A History of Modern Criticism* (New Haven & London: Yale University Press, 1965), pp. 416–428;

Edmund Wilson, "George Saintsbury's Centenary," in his *Classics and Commercials* (New York: Farrar, Straus, 1950), pp. 306–310;

Wilson, "George Saintsbury: Gourmet and Glutton," in his *Classics and Commercials* (New York: Farrar, Straus, 1950), pp. 366–371.

Papers:

Saintsbury's letters to Edmund Gosse are in the Brotherton Library, University of Leeds. Other collections of his correspondence are at Merton College, Oxford; the National Library of Scotland; and Queen's College, Belfast.

Geoffrey Scott
(11 June 1884 – 14 August 1929)

Pat Rogers
University of South Florida

BOOKS: *The Death of Shelley: The Newdigate Poem* (Oxford: Blackwell, 1906);

The National Character of English Architecture: The Chancellor's Essay (Oxford: Blackwell, 1908);

The Architecture of Humanism: A Study in the History of Taste (London: Constable, 1914; Boston: Houghton Mifflin, 1915; revised edition, London: Constable, 1924);

A Box of Paints (London: Bookman's Journal, 1924);

The Portrait of Zélide (London: Constable, 1925; New York: Scribners, 1925);

Poems (London: Oxford University Press, 1931).

OTHER: [Isabel de Charrière], *Four Tales by Zélide,* introduction by Scott (London: Constable, 1925; New York: Scribners, 1925);

Private Papers of James Boswell from Malahide Castle, 18 volumes, volumes 1–6 edited by Scott (Mount Vernon, N.Y.: Privately published, 1928–1934).

Geoffrey Scott wrote one full-scale biography, as well as composing one work of architectural history and laying the foundations for the major edition of the private papers of James Boswell, the crucial biographical source for one of the greatest of all literary biographers. Scott's first substantial work, *The Architecture of Humanism* (1914), has been among the most influential books on architectural history in the twentieth century and remains a classic in the field. Finally, his *The Portrait of Zélide* (1925), a life of the Dutch *bas-bleu* (bluestocking) Isabel de Charrière, is regarded by some as the most exquisitely crafted life of a literary figure to be written in the immediate aftermath of Lytton Strachey's *Eminent Victorians* (1918). Scott was prevented by his death from embarking on a planned biography of Boswell, but he produced enough in his lifetime to warrant a lasting reputation.

Geoffrey Scott, born in Hampstead, London, on 11 June 1884, was the youngest of seven children born to Russell Scott and Jessie Thurburn

Scott. His father was a prosperous Unitarian businessman and brother of the celebrated journalist Charles Prestwich Scott (1846–1932), editor of the *Manchester Guardian* for over fifty years and arguably the greatest of all British newspaper editors. The family background was one of material comfort and serious moral purpose. Geoffrey attended Rugby School from 1898 to 1902, and having won a scholarship in classics at New College, Oxford, he entered the university in 1903. He graduated in 1907 with second-class honors in *literae humaniores,* a degree involving the study of ancient history, philosophy, and politics as well as literature. In 1906 he was awarded the main undergraduate poetry prize, the Newdigate, for verses on the death of Shelley: this made a fourteen-page pamphlet. In 1908, by which time he had left Oxford, came the award of the chancellor's prize for an English essay for a short study titled "The National Character of English Architecture," published in the same year as a pamphlet running to less than fifty pages.

Up to this time his ambitions seem to have been mainly literary. He was to publish two small collections of poetry (one posthumous), and an extract from one of his later works found its way into *The Oxford Book of Modern Verse,* edited by W. B. Yeats in 1936. However, one of two major landmarks in Scott's life occurred when he was summoned by the great collector and critic Bernard Berenson to his villa outside Florence. Scott represented the rising promise of Oxford, and also invited as the bloom of Cambridge youth was John Maynard Keynes. The two young men in some respects had not dissimilar minds, though their later avocations took them in far different directions. It should be added that, although both were largely, if not exclusively, homosexual at this stage of their lives, Scott and Keynes managed to maintain a cordial friendship without any known sexual element. At the end of his university career Scott returned to Berenson's villa, I Tatti, and acted as librarian and secretary to the noted connoisseur for the next two years. In time he moved to an apartment in the city

Geoffrey Scott (Berenson Archives)

of Florence, shared with an architect named Cecil Pinsent, and together the two men started a small practice. Their most notable commission was that of remodeling I Tatti, a job Scott is supposed to have won through his romantic attachment to Mary Berenson, his patron's wife. In 1914 the firm was also invited to redesign the Villa Medici at Fiesole by owner Lady Sybil Cutting. Scott never became a practicing architect on a wide scale, and this may owe less to his predominantly historical interests than to a lack of careerism, if not of professionalism. He was tall, impressive looking, and attractive to women; he enjoyed the pleasures of high society. But the main factor may have been the publication and success of his polemical study, *The Architecture of Humanism;* this confirmed him in the role of author and controversialist and indicated where his real talents lay.

Outwardly Scott continued to prosper, seemingly rather little affected by World War I (he be-

came an honorary official in the British embassy at Rome in 1915). At the end of the war he married Lady Sybil Cutting, the widow of an American diplomat. She was the daughter of an Irish peer, the fifth and last earl of Desart, and had been married to William Bayard Cutting (a child of this marriage was the distinguished author Iris Origo). Lady Sybil was a noted hostess, and it is generally believed that the Villa Medici is the basis of the imaginary Villa Malaspina in Aldous Huxley's *Those Barren Leaves* (1925), a novel of intellectual comedy. The marriage seems to have been unsuccessful almost from the start. Scott was something of a philanderer, and his most prominent — some might say unlikely — affair, conducted in the mid 1920s, was with Vita Sackville-West, the wife of Harold Nicolson, famous for her own writings, her passionate relations with Virginia Woolf, and her influential gardening style at Sissinghurst. Scott and Lady Sybil were divorced in 1926; there were no children. She subsequently married Percy Lubbock, the biographer, critic, and author of *The Craft of Fiction* (1921).

Scott's major incursion into formal biography, *The Portrait of Zélide*, was dedicated "To Sybil." Possibly at some level this study of an eighteenth-century precursor (an intellectually liberated woman from an ancient and distinguished Dutch family) was an act of propitiation toward his wife. The subject of the book was then little known. Born Isabella van Serooskerken van Tuyll van Zuylen, she is more familiar to history by her married name, Isabel de Charrière. Recently her works have been edited, and she has reclaimed some of her reputation as a novelist. But almost the only facts known to the educated public in 1925 were that she had had an affair with James Boswell when the young man was studying at Utrecht in 1763–1764 (she had already adopted the sobriquet of "Zélide") and later, between 1786 and 1796, with the Swiss novelist and politician Benjamin Constant. Scott indeed concentrates on these relationships, but he does give some sense of his subject's wider aspirations and frustrations in the confined role of a bluestocking. The concluding note to the book is signed from Villa Medici on 23 October 1924; this marks the culmination of Scott's early career.

The second great turning point in his life came when he met the American collector Col. Ralph Isham in 1927 and was invited to edit the great haul of papers relating to Boswell which Isham had started to acquire from Malahide Castle, near Dublin. When Scott died two years later, Isham wrote a brief obituary notice for the *Saturday Review of Literature* (24 August 1929). In this he describes the circumstances of their first meeting. Isham was in London, seeking an editor for his trove of materials, and he consulted the distinguished collector A. Edward Newton, who happened also to be in London. So, fortunately, was Scott himself, though he was thought to have settled in Italy. In fact Scott had received a commission to write a life of Boswell, whom he had treated with some condescension in *The Portrait of Zélide*. But the project was delayed because Scott knew of the well-publicized Malahide find. His marriage at an end, and entering his mid-forties, he appears to have been casting about for a fresh world to conquer. The deal with Isham was soon sealed, and he moved to the collector's home on Long Island in October 1927 to begin work on the project. Within less than two years he had prepared a text for all the materials then known to be extant and had completed the editorial apparatus for the first six volumes of the series, out of eigh-

teen which were eventually to form *Private Papers of James Boswell from Malahide Castle* (1928–1934). The subsequent portions were edited by the Boswellian scholar Frederick A. Pottle. With good reason Isham refers in his obituary to Scott's great powers of application and concentration: he worked all day and even after dinner retreated with his host to the library, "from which Boswell seldom let us emerge before morning hours."

Sadly, at what should have been Scott's moment of triumph, he died. *The Architecture of Humanism* had been a brilliant and lastingly influential polemic; *The Portrait of Zélide*, an intriguing, sensitive, and individual study of a fascinating life; but with the Boswell papers Scott was poised to carve for himself a substantial niche in scholarship and letters. His death and early departure from the Boswell project limited, if not effaced, his reputation. He had returned to England for a holiday in the summer of 1929. He arrived back in New York on 4 August; three days later a chill which he had caught on the boat turned into pneumonia, and a week later he was dead. His ashes were laid to rest in the cloisters of his old Oxford college, with a commemorative plaque paying tribute to his career as "Humanist & Boswellian Scholar." A second volume of his poems was published posthumously, but his great work was left unfinished. New editions have appeared of *The Architecture of Humanism*, and *The Portrait of Zélide* still finds readers. But Scott's death at forty-five undoubtedly robbed the world of much that was in prospect, including perhaps the postponed life of Boswell.

The Portrait of Zélide followed a decade of silence after *The Architecture of Humanism*, disregarding a small volume of poems. It is an altogether different book on the surface at least. Scott's impressive debut had been made with a pungent, direct, and yet somewhat cerebral work. The biography was much more oblique, gentler in tone, apparently immersed in a relatively quiet period, one which had been favored by pre-Stracheyan belletrists such as Edmund Gosse and Austin Dobson. But, though the differences are real, there are also important common threads with his earlier work. Scott's gift for trenchant epigram is again in evidence when he turns to biography, along with his liking for paradox. The opening sentence is revelatory: "La Tour has painted Madame de Charrière: a face too florid for beauty, a portrait of wit and wilfulness where the mind and sense are disconcertingly alert; a temperament impulsive, vital, alarming; an arrowy spirit, quick, amusing, amused." The manner is sustained throughout the narrative, and events are rap-

Scott, late 1920s

idly summarized: "For, all this time, there had been another gentleman in the background; a very quiet, correct, gentlemanly gentleman with a stammer; a gentleman who understood conic sections and had, in fact, come to Zuylen long ago as the tutor of Belle's brothers." Details are singled out to stand for a whole collection of unmentioned facts. As in Strachey's work, key traits, physical and psychological, are used to suggest an entire personality. There is no long-winded Victorian rehearsal of genealogy, friendships, or historical setting. The book sticks to Zélide and her immediate circle and explores her sensibility rather than her intellectual interests (though it admits to these).

Isabel de Charrière led an outwardly uneventful life, despite her fiery spirit. Almost the only major biographical data concerned her marriage to Charles-Emmanuel de Charrière (the gentlemanly

tutor) in 1771, together with the fiction she published in the 1780s. Scott uses the latter for their undoubtedly autobiographical content but makes little by way of direct assessment. He treats the marriage as a sad necessity for this high-spirited woman and reserves most of his attention for the more passionate episodes, with Boswell and, especially, with Constant. The narrative is secondary to the revelation of character, and Scott treats all the principal personages with a certain amusement.

By the standards of modern literary biography, even the less scholarly kind, the book is radically defective. Scott mentions scarcely any dates: the year of his heroine's birth, the date of Boswell's departure for Holland, the date of Constant's birth, and little beyond that. One can only just tease out that Isabel died in 1810: the narrative fades off in a sentence without so much as a main verb: "The mind has drawn its pattern. The Portrait of Zélide: a frond of flame; a frond of frost." This is a style closer to that of present-day novelists such as Fay Weldon than to the professional biographical manner now routinely employed. Moreover, the book has no index and only the briefest of bibliographic notes at the end. Here Scott reveals his chief and practically his only source: "in 1906, M. Philippe Godet published at Geneva his opus magnum, 'Mme de Charrière et ses Amis....' He spent twenty years in collecting the records; nor is it the least likely that further sources of information will be added to those he methodically explored. The figure in my book is built from his materials." No contemporary biographer of repute would be fool-hardy enough to make such confident pronouncements about future discoveries. In fact, Scott's rash assumption was to be falsified almost immediately, and in time the great Boswell archive – though not the original trove which Scott edited – would fill out the picture of the affair between Boswell and Isabel de Charrière. Other sources have also been utilized by recent scholars.

But Scott was not a research scholar; at least he had shown no interest in such activity before Isham hired him. Facts play a remarkably small part in assembling the portrait of Zélide, and as Scott candidly acknowledges, they were secondhand. Scott knew a good deal about the period, but as an old-style liberally educated Oxford humanist; there is no sign that he undertook any special reading for his task outside Godet's book and the subject's own works. He may also have refreshed his acquaintance with the published books of Boswell and Constant. Such a procedure is unthinkable today. The nearest equivalent to the book in the last forty years may be Nancy Mitford's *Voltaire in Love* (1957), which likewise centers on a liberated intellectual woman with strong interests in science and philosophy – in this case Madame du Châtelet. Mitford was best known as a popular novelist and had no academic pretensions. Nevertheless, she embarked on a wide program of reading and distilled the findings of many scholars. Scott, as we have seen, makes no pretense of doing anything of the kind. "All I have here done," he writes, "is to catch an image of her in a single light, and to make from a single angle the best drawing I can of Zélide, as I believe her to have been." This naked subjectivity limits the value of the study as a work of reference, but it supplies the essential basis of its literary power and fascination.

In the most interesting general assessment of Scott yet written, an essay titled "Promise and Achievement," included in *A Small Part of Time* (1957), Michael Swan makes a shrewd assessment of the book's tone: "The *Architecture* is written in excellent, witty prose, but Scott has now become a stylist – a dandy perhaps.... An irony, delicate and sympathetic, now finds a place in his writing. He has, in fact, joined the new school of biographers, careful of his own individuality, aware of the faults of his subject but – unlike other members of the school – refusing to make moral judgements on their account. He can make fun of Zélide's preoccupation with conic sections because he would not for the world have her without her conic sections." Swan even goes so far as to contend that Strachey "never wrote so perfect and controlled a work as *The Portrait of Zélide*." This is a defensible view, and the overall description is just, except that Swan may underrate the judgmental effect of Scott's habitual irony, which does at times belittle his heroine, despite his obvious affection for her. On the other hand, there is a certain evenhandedness about the irony. And Scott is at his best in describing the meeting of two *femmes fortes,* Isabel and Madame de Staël, when the air was "electric with antipathy": "Madame de Charrière eyed the Ambassadress narrowly, scanning the thick too powerful figure, and meeting the dark penetrating gaze that redeemed the coarse-bred features. And reluctantly she admitted – for she was always just – that the impression was one of beauty."

For most English-speaking readers today, it is likely that the section on the affair with Boswell will be the most absorbing segment. This occupies only one chapter near the start, and it was written before Boswell's journal surfaced, yielding his own full account of the episode. Despite these limitations, Scott provides a neat cameo treatment, concluding with a mixture of sadness and relief (much as his heroine might have done), "Destiny reserved for Mademoiselle de Tuyll a much duller, much better man than James Boswell." Boswell is not spared any of the habitual Scott diminution by detail. Instead of saying, "Boswell was officially in Utrecht to study law, but actually intended to have a good time," he renders Boswell comic, as Strachey would do, in a single reference: "His ostensible motive in visiting that city was to perfect himself in the study of law, and in particular to attend the prelections of Professor Trotz upon the Theodosian Code." Three words in succession, the dull *prelections,* the slightly ridiculous *Trotz,* and the egregious *Theodosian Code,* form a masterly sequence of rebarbative constraints to be thrown off by any spirited youngster. Scott goes on to say that "[Boswell] did not realize that his chief weapon was his absurdity," but this is not the sheer silliness of Thomas Babington Macaulay's portrait. It is rather a kind of heroic unrealism, a naiveté carried to the lengths of unconquerable self-belief. Even with the added materials we now possess, Scott's reading of the episode is still worth pondering for its human insights.

At the end of the first edition there was announced, as uniform with the biography, *Four Tales by Zélide* (1925), translated by Lady Sybil Scott, with an introduction by Geoffrey Scott. This duly appeared, with the translation ascribed to S. M. S. (Sybil Marjorie Scott), but within months of the book's appearance the couple had divorced and Sybil had married Percy Lubbock, who came to live at the Villa Medici.

As already indicated, Scott would not seem to have been a natural choice for the editor of the massive Boswell haul, in view of the resolutely antifactual and largely unresearched nature of the book on Zélide. But both Isham and Newton were evidently satisfied, and their judgment was fully vindicated. The first six volumes of the *Private Papers of James Boswell from Malahide Castle* were all that Scott had time to complete, and it is remarkable that he should have been able to do so much in less than two years. It is not just that the individual volumes are competently edited; more noteworthy is the overall grasp of Boswell's working methods which allowed Scott to compose for the sixth volume a survey of the making of the *Life of Johnson*. An extract from this was reprinted in 1970 by the Johnsonian scholar James L. Clifford; and despite the major advances in our knowledge of Boswell, pioneered above all by Frederick A. Pottle (who succeeded Scott as editor), his outline of Boswell's compositional habits remains a significant appraisal of the subject. The two authors who have told the story of the Boswell discoveries and the Isham saga, Pottle and David Buchanan, have both paid tribute to Scott's work. He could not know that a vast amount of material was still to be uncovered at Malahide — some of it, no doubt, strategically held back by the family — and that another immense cache was to turn up at Fettercairn in Scotland. He could not have guessed that the later finds would include a large part of the manuscript of *The Life of Samuel Johnson, LL.D.* (1791), although this has still to be presented to the public, as well as fuller documentation of Boswell's experiences on the Grand Tour. It can only be speculated whether Scott would have stuck at his task, as Pottle was to do, in the face of this growing accumulation of materials. There was in him a certain restless streak, and maybe the projected biography of Boswell would have been jettisoned for some fresh exploration in a different area of cultural history. All that can be said for certain is that Scott's three main contributions to literature have left him an enduring place in history, and *The Portrait of Zélide* stands as a monument to a revolutionary form of early-twentieth-century biography. We may never return to writing lives in that way, but that same consideration does not stop us from enjoying Boswell — the books of the past are often most readable precisely because we order these things differently nowadays.

References:

Ralph H. Isham, "Geoffrey Scott," *Saturday Review of Literature,* 24 August 1929, p. 74;

Michael Swan, "Promise and Achievement: Geoffrey Scott," in his *A Small Part of Time* (London: Cape, 1957), pp. 233–242;

David Watkin, *The Rise of Architectural History* (London: Architectural Press, 1980).

Lytton Strachey
(1 March 1880 – 21 January 1932)

Paul H. Schmidt
Georgia State University

See also the Strachey entry in *DS 10: The Bloomsbury Group.*

BOOKS: *Euphrosyne: A Collection of Verse* (Cambridge: Elijah Johnson, 1905);

Landmarks in French Literature (London: Williams & Norgate / New York: Henry Holt, 1912);

Eminent Victorians (London: Chatto & Windus, 1918; Garden City, N.Y.: Garden City Publishing, 1918);

Queen Victoria (London: Chatto & Windus, 1921; New York: Harcourt, Brace & Howe, 1922);

Books and Characters: French & English (London: Chatto & Windus, 1922; New York: Harcourt, Brace, 1922);

Pope (Cambridge: Cambridge University Press, 1925);

Elizabeth and Essex: A Tragic History (London: Chatto & Windus / New York: Harcourt, Brace & Howe, 1928);

Portraits in Miniature and Other Essays (London: Chatto & Windus, 1931; New York: Harcourt, Brace, 1931);

Characters and Commentaries (London: Chatto & Windus, 1933; New York: Harcourt, Brace, 1933);

The Greville Memoirs, edited with Roger Fulford, 8 volumes (London: Macmillan, 1937–1938);

The Collected Works: Landmarks in French Literature, Eminent Victorians, Queen Victoria, Elizabeth and Essex, Biographical Essays, Literary Essays, 6 volumes (London: Chatto & Windus, 1948);

Spectatorial Essays (London: Chatto & Windus, 1964);

Ermyntrude and Esmerelda: An Entertainment, edited by Michael Holroyd (London: Anthony Blond, 1969);

Lytton Strachey By Himself: A Self Portrait, edited by Holroyd (London: Heinemann, 1971);

The Really Interesting Question and Other Papers, edited by Paul Levy (London: Weidenfeld & Nicolson, 1972);

The Shorter Strachey, edited by Michael and Paul Levy (London: Oxford University Press, 1980).

PLAY PRODUCTION: *Son of Heaven,* London, Scala Theatre, July 1925.

OTHER: "Ely: An Ode," in *Proclusionae Academicae* (Cambridge: Cambridge University Press, 1902).

Lytton Strachey, critic and biographer, created a new kind of biography. His studies of Queen Elizabeth and Queen Victoria, powerful and dramatic, though relatively conventional, are excellent biographies, but his *Eminent Victorians,* published in 1918, established his reputation as a revisionist of the Victorian public figures he loved to loathe and of the idea of biography itself. Though Strachey never wrote a full-length biography of a literary figure, his biographies represent a major influence on the writing of biography in general and literary biography in particular. Because Strachey's methods and approach, especially in *Eminent Victorians,* often rely on psychological insights that are finally unverifiable, few modern biographers adopt his method completely. His influence does, however, have the effect of liberating the biographer from the enslavement of data, of making more room for the flashes of insight that illuminate without relying on strict proof. Equipped with psychological acuity, and bearing a sharp cynicism deepened by his disillusionment over World War I, Strachey, in writing *Eminent Victorians,* invented a novel method of short biography that, rather than insisting on careful documentation and scrupulous source hunting, thrives on its author's subjective response to his subject. This method produced a livelier, though less responsible, form of biography than had previously been seen before.

Giles Lytton Strachey was born in Stowey House, Clapham Common, London, on 1 March

Lytton Strachey (portrait by Vanessa Bell, Anthony d'Offray Gallery)

1880. The fourth son of Lt. Gen. Sir Richard Strachey and Lady Jane Maria Strachey, ten of whose thirteen children survived childhood, his family traced its ancestry back to William Shakespeare's day. Sir Richard Strachey, a member of the Royal Society, spent his career in India, where he became director of public works. An energetic administrator during his career in India, in his later years Sir Richard became a distant figure, studying maps and reading novels in his study, leaving domestic duties and the rearing of the children to his determined wife. As a younger child, Lytton was cared for largely by his mother, though a French governess assisted in monitoring his study of French literature. He played with his sisters almost exclusively, and his mother often dressed him as a girl. After a brief stay at a boarding school in Poole, Dorset, Strachey was sent on a five-month cruise to the Cape of Good Hope.

In September 1893 Strachey began a brief but catastrophic stay at Abbotsholm School in Derbyshire, whose director, Dr. Cecil Reddie, stressed physical as well as intellectual labor. The former shortly proved far too strenuous for the thin, sickly thirteen-year-old boy, so his mother removed him, placing him in Leamington College, where the bullying of other boys, who nicknamed him "Scraggs" because of his emaciated physical appearance, made him miserable. It is likely that at Leamington the feeble, nearsighted boy first fell in love with older, stronger, more physically able boys.

In 1897 the seventeen-year-old Strachey entered Liverpool University College, where he spent the next two years under the kindly tutelage of family friend Sir Walter Raleigh. At Liverpool the boy's chronic misery became at times acute, as revealed in the following passage from his diary: "My self conscious vanity is really most painful. As I walk through the streets I am agonized by the thoughts of my appearance, of course it is hideous, but what *does* it matter? I only make it worse by peering into people's faces to see what they are thinking. And the worst of it is that I hate myself for doing it. The truth is I want companionship. . . . I wonder if I shall ever 'fall in love.' I can't help smiling at the question – if they only knew – if they only knew! But it is a tragedy also."

This passage, when placed near several earlier passages where he seeks to justify his "sinning" by explaining that the ancient Greeks and Shakespeare committed the same sin, has suggested to some scholars that Strachey's homosexuality was already a central concern for him. Except for brief periods following literary success and during a rare successful love affair, Strachey's inner torture stayed with him until his death.

After being rejected by Christ Church, Oxford, for inadequate Greek, Strachey was admitted to Trinity College, Cambridge, in October 1899. At Cambridge he met Thoby Stephen, Clive Bell, and Leonard Woolf, the latter two of which were to marry Vanessa and Virginia Stephen. Cambridge provided Strachey with a period of relative activity and happiness, though his personal discomforts never completely ceased. He helped form the Midnight Society, received a scholarship, and was elected to the Cambridge Conversazione Society, better known as the Apostles, through which he probably met G. E. Moore, Bertrand Russell, and John Maynard Keynes. Throughout his life Strachey preserved a special ability for writing verse. He received the Chancellor's Medal for English Verse, the high point of his Cambridge career. In April 1902 Strachey became a scholar at Trinity, and in June 1903 he finished his undergraduate career with a disappointing second-class honors in history.

In an effort to win a fellowship to Trinity, Strachey began working on a long thesis on Warren Hastings, a project which twice failed to win him the fellowship. Meanwhile, he had fallen in love with his cousin, Duncan Grant, who reduced Strachey to illness in 1907 by rejecting him for Keynes, who had previously jilted Strachey to have an affair with Arthur Hobhouse. In 1909, perhaps in rebound from another disappointing homosexual affair, Strachey successfully proposed to Virginia Stephen, a proposal even at the moment of making he found repulsive and which he soon retracted without damaging his deepening friendly love for the woman who eventually became one of the twentieth century's greatest novelists.

In 1911 he grew his trademark long, red beard about which he wrote to his mother on 9 May, "Its color is very much admired, and it is generally considered very effective, though some ill-bred persons have been observed to laugh." The self-mockery here distinctly presages the kind of ridicule he later turns against his biographical subjects in *Eminent Victorians*. Its method, the use of the passive voice to mention the derisive reaction of unknown, and usually untraceable, persons to his subject, while harmless here, becomes a potent and sometimes irresponsible weapon when, for example, he records the undocumented reactions of anonymous undergraduates to Dr. Thomas Arnold in *Eminent Victorians*. By this time Strachey's inner character and outward appearance were taking on the form that later generations would recall. Max Beerbohm describes him thus: "an emaciated face of ivory whiteness, above a long square-cut auburn beard, and below a head of very long sleek dark brown hair. The nose was nothing if not aquiline. The eyes, behind a pair of gold-rimmed spectacles, eyes of an inquirer and a cogitator, were large and brown and luminous." Beerbohm goes on to remark on Strachey's lankiness and writes that the author of *Eminent Victorians* "looked rather like one of the Twelve Apostles . . . especially the doubting one." Strachey's two voices also caught the attention of many listeners. When talking in confidence he had a low, rich, baritone voice that communicated his deepest feelings, but his public voice, high and piping, produced a comic effect and is the voice recalled by most people who heard him speak but did not know him well.

By now the Trinity fellowship was a lost cause, and Strachey began writing reviews and working on his *Landmarks in French Literature* (1912). In 1910 he fell in love with the painter Henry Lamb. At this time the pattern of his life involved writing, illness, rest cures abroad, and more reading and writing. The success of *Landmarks in French Literature* gave him the inspiration he needed to devote his life to writing. But while the book sold some twelve thousand copies in two years and received lavish praise from the critics, it did not bring him fame and did not earn him enough money to retire from writing reviews. But with help from his mother and friends and the money he earned from the reviews, he was able to live in comfort and still write his books.

By 1915 Strachey had begun work on the portraits that were eventually to become, if not his masterpiece, then certainly his most distinctive and characteristic work, *Eminent Victorians*. Strachey felt Victorian hypocrisy had led England into the hor-

107

Preface.

The history of the Victorian Age will never be written: we know too much about it. For ignorance is the first requisite of the historian — ignorance, which simplifies and clarifies ~~which selects and omits~~ which selects and omits, with a placid perfection unattainable by the highest art. Concerning the Age which has just passed, our fathers and our grandfathers have poured forth and ~~never~~ accumulated so vast a quantity of information that the industry of a Ranke would ~~have~~ be submerged by it, and the perspicacity of a Gibbon would quail before it. It is not by the direct method of a scrupulous narration that the explorer of the past can hope to depict that singular epoch. If he is wise, he will adopt a subtler strategy. He will attack his subject in unexpected places; he will fall upon the flank, or the rear; he will shoot a sudden, revealing searchlight into obscure recesses, hitherto undivined unexplored. He will row out over into that great ocean of material, and lower down into it, here and there, a little bucket, which will bring up to the light of day some characteristic specimen, from those far depths, to be examined with a careful curiosity. Guided by these considerations, ~~with~~ I have written the ensuing studies. I have attempted, through the medium of biography, to present some Victorian visions to the modern eye. They are, in one sense, haphazard visions — that is to say, my choice of subjects has been determined by no desire to construct a coherent picture ~~than~~ by simple motives of convenience and of art. It has been my purpose to illustrate rather than to explain. It would have been futile I hope to tell even a précis of the truth about the Victorian Age; for the shortest précis must fill innumerable volumes. But, in the lives of an ecclesiastic,

First page from the manuscript for Strachey's preface to Eminent Victorians *(British Library, MS 54219f107)*

228

ror of World War I, and writing portraits of certain Victorians who he felt exemplified such contradictions and hypocrisy allowed him to hit the exact tone to mock them lightly without appearing to attack them. To use Beerbohm's assessment, "The vein of mockery was very strong in him. . . . A satirist he was not. Mockery is a light and lambent, rather irresponsible thing. . . . Strachey was always ready to mock what he loved. In mockery there is no malice." While Strachey does often seem to mock without the serious intent of satire, it would be hard to prove that he bore his subjects in *Eminent Victorians* no malice. In 1912 he wrote to Virginia Woolf, "Is it prejudice, do you think, that makes us hate the Victorians, or is it the truth of the case? They seem to me a set of mouthing bungling hypocrites."

In 1916 Strachey, along with his brother James, joined Russell in actively opposing the war. In March he appeared before the draft board and declared himself a conscientious objector: "I have a conscious objection to assisting," he wrote, "by any action of mine, in carrying on the war. This objection is not based on religious belief, but upon moral considerations at which I arrived after long and careful thought, I do not wish to assert the extremely general proposition that I should never in any circumstances, be justified in taking part in any conceivable war; to dogmatise so absolutely on a point so abstract would appear to me to be unreasonable." When asked by the tribunal, "what would you do if you saw a German soldier trying to rape your sister," he made his famous mocking reply: "I would attempt to come — between them." Strachey's objection rested on principle only, since he must have known that the medical examiner would find him unfit to serve. He later received full medical exemption from military service.

By late 1917 Strachey had moved into the Mill House, Tidmarsh, in Berkshire with Dora Carrington. Shortly before taking up residence there, he sent the manuscript of *Eminent Victorians* to Chatto and Windus; before the end of the year the firm had accepted it for publication. *Eminent Victorians* contains four short biographies and a preface. The chief feature of the book, aside from its frankly subjective nature and its total lack of documentation, is its aloof style and its adroit irony. Strachey presents his detached portraits by artfully pairing incongruous or contradicting observations that make seemingly laudatory propositions but which in fact reflect discredit on his subject. His description of high church Christianity is a case in point. Even those with whom he had some sympathy, like John Henry Newman, are not exempt from his mockery. Chris-

tians like John Keble and Newman, he writes, "saw a transcendent manifestation of Divine power, flowing down elaborate and immense through the ages; a consecrated priesthood, stretching back, to the very Godhead; a whole universe of spiritual beings brought into communion with the Eternal by means of wafers." The bathetic reference to wafers at the end of this grave passage represents one of Strachey's keenest ironic reversals, undercutting the tone of all that precedes it. In writing this essay Strachey knew he was doing something that had never before been done in biography. Using his awareness of psychology, on which subject his brother James, the editor and translator of Sigmund Freud, was becoming a respected authority, and employing the principle of selection that he learned from his literary hero, Jean Racine, he sought to discredit his apparently self-sacrificing subjects by suggesting in his subtle way that their true motives were self-serving. Tired of the top-heavy two-volume Victorian biography, Strachey sought to shorten it, putting the emphasis on his own conception of his subject's character, which Strachey felt often seemed to get lost in the heavy documentation of the traditional form.

Of course Strachey found some examples of English biography that he could admire. If one plans to write a long biography, one could do no better, he felt, than to follow the model of James Boswell. For short biographies he liked John Aubrey. He found much to admire in James Froude's two-volume biography of Thomas Carlyle and in the writings of Edmund Gosse, about whom he was otherwise less than enthusiastic, as Gosse and Strachey became engaged in controversy later over Strachey's depiction of Lord Cromer in the biography of Gen. Charles Gordon. That which he admired he usually tried to put to work in his own writing. As he states in the preface to *Eminent Victorians,* "It is not by the direct method of a scrupulous narration that the explorer of the past can hope to depict [the Victorian Age]. . . . He will attack his subject in unexpected places; he will fall upon the flank, or the rear; he will shoot a sudden revealing searchlight into obscure recesses, hitherto undivined." He will try in this way to overcome the problems of traditional English biography. The two-volume biography, with few exceptions, lacks the keys to Strachey's method — selection, detachment, design. He desires to do what most previous biographers have been unable to do, to be brief, and to "maintain . . . a freedom of spirit." In a strange conclusion to the preface, Strachey describes his aims in the book as being far different from those of

Strachey and Virginia Woolf in 1923

earlier panegyric biographers: "to lay bare the facts of some cases, as I understand them, dispassionately, impartially, and without ulterior intentions." No reader of *Eminent Victorians* can read the essay on Henry Edward Cardinal Manning, for example, without finding it full of partiality and ulterior intentions. The difference is that where the biographers Strachey meant to discredit tended toward hagiography, his impartiality and ulterior motives tended toward mockery and derision, his dispassion toward impish irony. In writing *Eminent Victorians* Strachey establishes himself as a leader of the reaction against the Victorians that followed World War I.

In Strachey's depiction of Cardinal Manning, the English priest appears as a hypocrite whose piety masked excessive worldly ambition. If Strachey's tone reaches beyond lambent mockery into bitter irony in *Eminent Victorians,* Manning's portrait is one place where it does so. While there is some disagreement about Manning's character among scholars, Strachey's version is an extremely unfavorable one. Manning became the archbishop of Chichester in 1840. He joined the Roman Catholic church in 1851, became archbishop of Westminster in 1865, and cardinal in 1875. He has generally been considered a great preacher and a subtle controversialist.

In the first paragraph Strachey announces his plan and establishes the irreverent tone: "Henry Edward Manning was born in 1807 and died in 1892. His life was extraordinary in many ways, but its interest for the modern inquirer depends upon two considerations — the light which his career throws upon the spirit of his age and the psychological problems suggested by his inner history. He belonged to that class of eminent ecclesiastics — and it is by no means a small class — who have been distinguished less by saintliness and learning than for practical ability." The emphasis on the "modern inquirer" suggests the frankly ahistorical attitude of Strachey: Manning will be judged by the values and assumptions of a later age.

The tension between Strachey's expectations of how unworldly a priest should be and his laying bare of Manning's worldly motives becomes the structure of the essay. "Manning succeeds," he argues, "less through merit than through a superior facility for gliding adroitly to the front rank." Manning becomes a leader in a secular world because he has at the deepest levels compromised his spiritual beliefs. As a strategy to insinuate the essential worldliness of Manning and to demonstrate that he recognizes true religiosity when he sees it, Strachey employs the contrast of the career of Newman. For Strachey, Newman's fame arose from his natural abundant merit — talent, intelligence, and true commitment to his spiritual ideals. As such, he stood in the way of Manning's retention of power among Catholics in England. Upon becoming an archbishop, Manning, who had "scented a peculiar peril" in Newman's plans for setting up an oratory at Oxford, "privately determined that the author of the *Apologia* should never be allowed to return to his old university." For the author of *Eminent Victorians* Manning was an eagle, Newman a dove: "there was a hovering, a swoop, and then the quick beak and the relentless talons did their work." With the aid of Monsignor Talbot, Manning succeeded: Strachey writes, "Dr. Newman's spirit had been crushed."

As for Manning's conversion to Catholicism, Strachey again describes it as a calculated political gamble: Strachey is sure that Manning coveted the blandishments of Rome but worried about falling into Catholic obscurity, as Newman had. Was the satisfaction of spiritual well-being enough for Manning? Strachey suggests no, that Manning would not have gone to Rome without a strong assurance of success and the sure promise of an illustrious future. It appeared that Manning had taken a big chance and been fortunate, but Strachey will have none of it: "[It] is difficult to feel quite sure that Manning's plunge was as hazardous as it appeared. Certainly he was not a man who was likely to forget to look before he leaped, nor one who, if he hap-

pened to know that there was a mattress spread to receive him, would leap with less conviction." Strachey goes on to speculate that in Manning's interview with the pope three years earlier, Pio Nono may have said something like "Ah dear Signor Manning, why don't you come over to us? Do you suppose that we would not look after you?" This passage illustrates Strachey's frequent resort to conjectures and innuendo when no facts avail or where existing facts may fail to support the conclusion he wishes his readers to infer. Manning's biographers dispute Strachey's claims, but Strachey aims not to document and prove anything factual but instead to register his impressions. He notices that by 1915 Manning's fame had already faded, that the cardinal's "impression was more acute than lasting" and that his "memory is a dim thing today." It is one of the stranger ironies of this portrait that if Manning's fame is firmer now than in Strachey's day, it owes much of its endurance to Strachey's infamous portrait.

The readers of "Florence Nightingale" will not find the same degree of bitterness in her portrait that they found in Cardinal Manning's. While Strachey found Florence Nightingale troublesome, horrible, tyrannical, unintelligent, and disagreeable, he also knew that she was efficient and capable; the problem for Strachey is that he considered the latter usually admirable qualities just as annoying as the former. Strachey could never quite forgive the fact that she possessed energy, efficiency, and zeal to such an extreme degree; but that she used these traits to accomplish important and good things he grudgingly had to admit and admire.

Strachey uses the same mode for revealing his discomfort with Nightingale that he uses to discredit Manning — the subtle juxtaposing of contradictory observations which seem to cast doubt on that which looks almost like praise. The popular conception of the "saintly, self-sacrificing . . . Lady with the Lamp" is at conflict with the truth, he suggests in his opening paragraph. Nightingale was in fact possessed by a demon. But her driven nature never turns him completely against her. The fact of his ambivalence made it difficult for him to write the portrait. He claims in a letter to Virginia Woolf that he finds Nightingale "indigestible."

The most problematic part of her behavior involves her treatment of two men who spent important parts of their late careers trying to help her — Arthur Hugh Clough and Sidney Herbert. Strachey tends to blame Nightingale because men like Herbert and Clough seemed to give up their lives to assist her. She exhausted the people she worked with, he suggests, sublimating her sexuality in her devotion to work and thereby using up good men in almost inhuman ways. Such is the case with her treatment of the poet Clough: "Ever since he had lost his faith at the time of the Oxford Movement, Clough had passed his life in considerable uneasiness. . . . [Eventually in London he] fell under the influence of Miss Nightingale." With her he felt he could make himself useful. "There were a great number of miscellaneous little jobs which there was nobody handy to do. For instance when Miss Nightingale was travelling, there were the railway tickets to be taken; and there were proof sheets to be corrected; and then there were parcels to be done up in brown paper and carried to the post. Certainly he could be useful. And so, upon such occupations as these, Arthur Clough was set to work. 'This that I see is not all,' he comforted himself by reflecting, 'and this that I do is but little; nevertheless it is good, though there is better than it.'" Clearly Strachey feels it is a waste of time for a poet like Clough to devote himself to these menial tasks. And while the mockery in the passage does reflect onto Clough, the real target of the passage; is Nightingale for using her devotee in this way.

Strachey finds even more offensive her treatment of Herbert, the extraordinarily gifted politician. He cannot forgive Nightingale for being stronger than this man who devoted himself to her: "She took hold of him, taught him, shaped him, absorbed him, dominated him through and through. . . . only that terrific personality swept him forward at her own fierce pace and with her own relentless stride. Swept him – Where to? . . . one has the image of those wide eyes fascinated by something feline, something strong; there is a pause; and then the tigress has her claws in the quivering haunches [of the "stag," Herbert]; and then – !" The word *fascinated* here suggests the possibility of some sort of infatuation on the part of Herbert for Nightingale, an infatuation which she used to exploit the man even more fully. Here, as in the eagle and dove passage from the Manning essay, Strachey demonstrates the distinguishing mark of his work in *Eminent Victorians,* a mark that is both his strength and his weakness as a biographer. His strength is the gift for sharp, incisive expression of character. His weakness is the lack of real evidence to support the characterization he so artfully suggests. As in the Clough passage, Strachey wants us to resent Nightingale for having so much power over great men. Thus despite his own experimentation with gender and the feminine side of his own character, Strachey

is not ready to accept a woman who participates so fully in the masculine.

Still, the author's ambivalence shows itself in direct and largely unmocking descriptions of her accomplishments during the Crimean War. Upon arriving at Scutari her position was difficult because of the hostile suspicion of the majority of the surgeons. "But gradually she gained ground. . . . with consummate tact, and with all the gentleness of extreme strength, she managed at last to impose her personality upon the susceptible, overwrought, discouraged, and helpless group of men in authority who surrounded her." She also proved adept at overcoming the stultifying wartime bureaucracy: "She alone, it seemed, whatever the contingency, knew where to lay her hands on what was wanted; she alone could dispense her stores with readiness; above all she alone possessed the art of circumventing the pernicious influences of official etiquette." Thus Strachey shows that Nightingale accomplished great things in Crimea and actually revolutionized the profession of nursing, accomplishments for which he has almost pure admiration.

But by the end of the portrait he returns to the more mocking tone. In noting that Herbert and Clough died "almost at the same moment," Strachey claims that he does not hold her responsible, but the tone of the passage makes his judgment against her unmistakable: "If Miss Nightingale had been less ruthless, Sidney Herbert would not have perished; but then she would not have been Miss Nightingale." The description of Clough's death is more ironic but with a similar sting: "Arthur Clough, worn out by labours very different from those of Sidney Herbert, died too: never more would he tie up her parcels." If one is not convinced of the irony and mockery here, the passage that follows increases the tone of accusation of Nightingale's self-centered ruthlessness. "And yet a third disaster followed. The faithful Aunt Mai did not, to be sure, die; no, she did something almost worse: she left Miss Nightingale. She was growing old, and she felt that she had closer and more imperative duties with her own family. Her niece could hardly forgive her. She poured out, in one of her enormous letters, a passionate diatribe upon the faithlessness, the lack of sympathy, the stupidity, the ineptitude of women." In saying that what Aunt Mai did was "almost worse," Strachey implies that Nightingale placed the deaths of Clough and Herbert almost in the same category as Aunt Mai's departure, as though the importance of their deaths lay only in the effect which they had on her. Of course Strachey offers no real evidence to support such a

Photographs chosen by Strachey to illustrate the four figures included in Eminent Victorians: *clockwise from top left, Cardinal Manning, Florence Nightingale, Thomas Arnold, General Gordon*

claim, so he makes it by innuendo rather than statement. Once again the power of Strachey's method of sharp criticism of his subject is disabled somewhat by the irresponsibility of it.

One Strachey scholar has accurately described the portrait of Dr. Thomas Arnold, the third short biography in *Eminent Victorians,* as "the briefest, most biased, and perfunctory" in the book. Where the Manning representation contains mockery, it never lapses into pure caricature; while the Nightingale portrait records its author's ambivalence, it avoids blatant oversimplification; "Dr. Arnold" contains both. In other words, Strachey's tendency to ridicule his subjects receives little check in his limning of Arnold. One explanation for the imbalance here lies in the circumstances of this essay's production. While World War I raged during the composition of all four of the essays in *Eminent Victorians,* Strachey composed "Dr. Arnold" during the height of his preoccupation with the conscription issue. The shortest essay in the book took him twice as long (ten months) to write as the Nightingale biography, which is double the length of "Dr. Arnold." Strachey refers to Arnold in a letter as a "self-righteous blockhead," and it is this conception that dominates the essay. A passage from his short portrait called "A Victorian Critic" demonstrates that Strachey's distaste for Arnold did not exclude his subject's offspring: Matthew Arnold, he writes at the end of the short, sardonic essay, "might, no doubt, if he had chosen, have done some excellent and lasting work upon the movements of glaciers or the fertilization of plants, or have been quite a satisfactory collector in an up-country district in India. But no; he *would* be a critic."

Strachey finds little to recommend in any aspect of Matthew Arnold's father's career. One almost suspects that Strachey distinguishes Arnold from his other subjects by the degree of domestic comfort he attained. Whereas the other three, suspect as their motives might have been, all forewent domestic harmony in favor of their work, Arnold lived the life of a comfortable married man with ten children. Strachey could assuage his contempt for people as long as they experimented with lives marginalized from the Victorian heterosexual mainstream, but he could not overcome his discomfort, either because of envy or disdain or both, at domestic felicity unplagued by any gender-role ambivalence.

Strachey's scorn begins with Arnold's adolescence. While granting that Arnold's early industry and intelligence gave him a place of prominence in school, he also notes that "a certain pompousness in the style of his letters home suggested to the more clear-sighted among his relatives the possibility that young Thomas might grow up into a prig." No footnote identifies these prescient kinsmen. For Strachey an even greater affront than Arnold's early potential for priggishness was the ease with which he put away his religious doubt. Arnold disposed of his religious skepticism, Strachey points out, much more easily than he did "his dislike of rising early." With this juxtaposition of the grave and the frivolous worthy of Alexander Pope, whom he greatly admired, Strachey achieves a withering criticism of his subject's shallowness without ever really making the accusation.

Strachey makes Arnold's physical appearance part of his criticism, noting that he had legs "perhaps . . . shorter than they should have been." And he claims in a famous description that while Arnold's face was honest, it had another quality that did not recommend him as an intellectual leader: "And yet — why was it? — was it in the lines of the mouth or the frown on the forehead? — it was hard to say, but it was unmistakable — there was a slightly puzzled look upon the face of Dr. Arnold."

But Strachey reserves his sharpest contempt for his subject's work as headmaster of Rugby School. Arnold, hired to reform the school that Strachey agrees was much in need of reforming, determines to makes his changes in the wrong area, deciding to reform the moral rather than the intellectual side of the problem. "Doubtless it was important to teach boys something more than the bleak rigidities of the ancient tongues; but how much more important to instill into them the elements of character and the principles of conduct." Strachey also ridicules Arnold's decision to exclude physical science from the Rugby curriculum. And he does so by citing Arnold's words, allowing them to act as their own parody: "Rather than have Physical Science the principal thing in my son's mind [he exclaimed in a letter to a friend], I would gladly have him think that the sun went round the earth, and that the stars were so many spangles set in the bright blue firmament. Surely the one thing needful for a Christian and an Englishman to study is Christian moral and political philosophy."

To achieve this moral education Arnold installed the praeposter system wherein the older boys ruled the younger, a system that Strachey, with his history of having been brutalized by stronger boys, would have found suspect. Arnold himself, he contends, "ruled remotely, through his chosen instruments, from an inaccessible heaven." The younger boys lived in "extreme fear" of their

The Lacket, in Lockeridge (near Marlborough), where Strachey lived from October 1913 through mid-September 1915 and wrote two of the four portraits in Eminent Victorians

headmaster, "and it would often happen that a boy would leave Rugby without having had any personal communication with him at all." The effect of this system, Strachey admits, was remarkable, producing an awe among most of the Rugby boys. But Strachey's deep reservations come through when he observes how Arnold would stop immediately, "with startling earnestness . . . the slightest approach to levity," and how he used the method of "personal correction" (flogging) for improvement of the boys, and how he encouraged, Strachey informs us, the older boys to flog the younger: "The younger children, scourged both by Dr. Arnold and by the elder children, were given every opportunity of acquiring the simplicity, sobriety, and humbleness of mind which are the best ornaments of youth."

One of the things most remembered about Arnold's tenure at Rugby were his sermons. In a long paragraph which mostly lists seemingly straightforward statements about these sermons and their edifying effects on his congregation, Strachey inserts short comments that tend to undermine the overall effect of the passage: for example, "His con-

gregation sat in fixed attention (with the exception of the younger boys, whose thoughts occasionally wandered)." To suggest that to some of the boys Dr. Arnold's sermons were a bit of a joke, in the same paragraph Strachey makes this observation: "It was noticed that even the most careless would sometimes, during the course of the week, refer almost involuntarily to the sermon of the past Sunday, as a condemnation of what they were doing. Others were heard to wonder how it was that the Doctor's preaching, to which they had attended at the time so assiduously, seemed, after all, to have such a small effect on what they did."

Strachey also notes with implicit disdain Arnold's intolerance: "He believed in toleration, too, within limits; that is to say, in the toleration of those with whom he agreed. 'I would give James Mill as much opportunity for advocating his opinion,' he said, 'as is consistent with a voyage to Botany Bay.'" And while Arnold claimed to have sympathy for the poor, Strachey mocks his division of the lower orders into the "good poor" and the "others" and notes that Arnold protested the admission of Jews into

Parliament and the failure to make Scripture an obligatory subject at London University.

He generally derides his subject's continual moral worrying. The sight of the Lake of Como makes him think of "moral evil" so that he is moved to pray that he will always maintain a "deep sense of moral evil." As Strachey says, "His prayer was answered: Dr. Arnold was never in any danger of losing his sense of moral evil." The headmaster of Rugby is pained by the fact that so many of the youths he met seemed to be in the grip of evil without knowing it. Strachey's version of this sentiment: "The naughtiest boys positively seemed to enjoy themselves the most."

Not even Arnold's death escapes the reach of his biographer's derisive pen: "Dr. Arnold had passed from his perplexities for ever." In Strachey's estimate, Arnold's life resulted in nothing salutary for his own day or for the time to follow. He was partly responsible, Strachey suggests, for keeping alive Christian hypocrisy. Given the chance to bring education into the modern world, Arnold "threw the whole weight of his influence into the opposite scale," plunging Rugby even more deeply into the outmoded "ancient system." Strachey even identifies the headmaster of Rugby, in an implied *post hoc ergo propter hoc* argument, as the "founder of the worship of athletics and the worship of good form," the two poles, Strachey writes, on which the English public schools have turned for a long time. "Yet it was not so before Dr. Arnold; will it always be so after him? We shall see."

The final essay of *Eminent Victorians*, "The End of General Gordon," differs from the other three in some important ways. First of all, while, like the other portraits, this one concentrates on a single subject, "The End of General Gordon" aims its mockery at a more general target. Whereas Gordon receives some rough treatment, primarily through innuendos of alcoholism and homosexuality and suggestions of irrational Christian beliefs, Strachey has more sympathy for him than he does for any other main figure in the book. The objects of Strachey's scorn in this essay are those who he feels are responsible for Gordon's violent and unnecessary demise: William Gladstone, Evelyn Baring, Lord Hartington, and the imperialist minority in the government. The Gordon that Strachey describes is in basic outline, except perhaps for the noted innuendos, the Gordon that Strachey's audience expected to see. The essay departs from the expected in its rendering of the home events leading to Gordon's end.

"The End of General Gordon" begins with Gordon in the Holy Land late in his career but soon regresses briefly through his youth, to his service in the Crimea and his work in China, where his work earned him the nickname China Gordon. It also explores his career at Gravesend and his time as governor general of the Sudan. But clearly the main interest of the essay lies in its latter half, exploring Gordon's final days in the Sudan during the rebellion of the Mahdi, and in these pages the focus of the essay shifts from the establishment of Gordon's character, which is complexly rendered but never satisfactorily developed, to the machinations of the men who, in Strachey's version, sealed his fate.

In exploring the complex events leading up to Gordon's death in 1884, Strachey starts with the War Office's reaction to the Mahdi rebellion and the slaughter of the army of Col. William Hicks, who had been ordered to put down the rebellion. The Egyptian pashas favored simply amassing another army and trying again, but the English government, despite the opposition of the powerful imperialist faction who favored reconquest, saw the dangers of that policy and began making plans for a slow withdrawal from the Sudan. Meanwhile, the situation in Khartoum was growing desperate, the Madhi closing in by the hour on the outnumbered Egyptian troops. Something had to be done. When the War Office finally decided to withdraw from the Sudan, it realized that the task would require the talents of a special emissary. The selection of Gordon for this job, Strachey contends, arose mysteriously, especially since, with his background of aggressive heroism, he was precisely the wrong man to engineer a retreat. Baring, the English representative in Egypt and the intermediator between the Egyptian government and England during the crisis, opposed Gordon's appointment, as his policy advocated immediate withdrawal, but Lord Granville, asking for the third time, finally got Baring to agree on the grounds that the policy be one of "withdrawal from the Sudan as quickly as possible."

Why, Strachey asks, was this man of war sent to conduct a peaceful operation? "The precise motives of those responsible for these transactions are less easy to discern. It is difficult to understand what the reasons could have been which induced the government, not only to override the hesitations of Sir Evelyn Baring, but to overlook the grave and obvious dangers of sending such a man as General Gordon to the Sudan. The whole history of his life, the whole bent of his character, seemed to disqualify him from the task for which he had been chosen." In fact, Gordon publicly declared himself opposed to the intentions of the government. He favored overpowering the Mahdi and reconquering

Portrait of Strachey, painted by Carrington in 1916 (collection of Mrs. Frances Partridge)

the Sudan. But, Strachey concedes, it appears that Gordon did agree to carry out the policy that directly violated his own stated beliefs, and Strachey notes that "it is possible for a subordinate to suppress his private convictions and to carry out loyally, in spite of them, the orders of his superiors." But, he reasoned, "how rare are the qualities of self-control and wisdom which such a subordinate must possess! And how little reason there was to think that General Gordon possessed them!" Therefore, Strachey contends, so singular is the thinking of the government on this occasion that one is tempted "to account for it by some ulterior explanation."

In searching for this explanation, Strachey resorts to Baring's official explanation, which he says grants some credence to the claim that in appointing Gordon the government was bowing to the popular pressure of the press, which favored sending China Gordon, a proven war hero, into the Sudan, but he soon dismisses this as contradicting the actual facts of the case. Perhaps the government was carried away, along with the public, "by a sudden conviction that they had found their saviour." Maybe so, he answers, but continues to look for darker, "more definite" influences. Strachey speculates that more

likely the imperialist section of the government managed to persuade the rest to send Gordon because they knew he would disobey, involving the English government in a necessary military action leading to the reconquest and subsequent occupation of the Sudan by British troops, an eventuality that would solidify Britain's currently ambiguous position in Egypt as a whole. Next comes Strachey's strategic qualification: "With our present information, it would be rash to affirm that all, or any of these considerations were present to the minds of the imperialist section of the Government. Yet it is difficult to believe that a man such as Lord Wolseley [a close friend of Gordon's and the person who first asked him about going to Khartoum], for instance, could have altogether overlooked them." Even the intellectually dilatory Lord Hartington must have seen the possibility. "Lord Hartington, indeed, may well have failed to realize at once the implications of General Gordon's appointment — for it took Lord Hartington some time to recognize the implications of anything." Perhaps he only recognized it, Strachey proposes, "instinctively, perhaps unconsciously." But however and for whatever reasons, it became clear almost immediately after Gordon's appointment that his mission to report on the situation "had already swollen into a Governor Generalship," with Gordon exercising powers far exceeding those of mere retreat.

Of course upon his arrival in Khartoum, "The man who had left London a month before to 'report upon the best means of effecting the evacuation of the Sudan,' was now openly talking of 'smashing up the Mahdi.'" Within a month things had taken a turn for the worse, and the situation in Khartoum became desperate, but the very government men who seemed so heartily to support Gordon before now seemed to abandon him. Even Queen Victoria now realized that Gordon was in peril. But the government did not act. Gladstone, Strachey suggests, in an almost inscrutable display of stubbornness, because he had originally agreed to send Gordon on the condition that he be allowed to report only, now refused to act to save him, because he believed Gordon was in no real danger from the Mahdi, who, Gladstone argued, only sought freedom for his people. Baring, as far as Gordon himself was concerned, bore the blame for the government inaction. And Strachey's portrait of him sustains his subject's interpretation of events. In fact, during the height of the crisis and at the time of Gordon's death, Baring was not at his post in Egypt but in London attending a financial conference.

The slow-acting Hartington finally overcame governmental inertia, and especially the reluctance of Gladstone, and sent help to Khartoum, but it arrived too late: Gordon's head had already been presented to the Mahdi. Clearly Strachey identified more fully with Gordon than with any of the other three of his subjects. While he saw Gordon as a fanatic, not all that different from the Mahdi himself, he sympathized with Gordon's feelings of betrayal at the hands of a hypocritical, slow-footed, self-serving government. And while the portrait that emerges is a striking one, the truly memorable parts of the essay are those in which he attacks the government. In *Eminent Victorians* Strachey's greatest art thrives on tension and opposition. He is less memorable when he is sympathetic. His truest gift is for sardonic unmasking of pretension, but he was learning the art of sympathetic rendering of his subject which he would develop more fully in *Queen Victoria* (1921).

Virginia Woolf loved *Eminent Victorians*, remarking about the Manning portrait, "It is quite superb – It is far the best thing you have ever written . . . how divinely amusing and exciting and alive you make it." While her reaction was the reaction of many of her contemporaries, it was not the feeling of all. Those who shared Strachey's feelings that the Victorian age was one of hypocrisy tended to read the book with pleasure. But understandably, some surviving Victorians were offended by the book. Gosse attacked the portrait of Baring (later Lord Cromer) that emerged from the Gordon essay in "The Character of Lord Cromer," a *Times Literary Supplement* article, on 27 June 1918. But in general the book was a smashing success, both financially and with the majority of critics. It is said that Bertrand Russell laughed out loud while reading *Eminent Victorians* during his stay in prison for anti-war activities. Even Prime Minister Herbert Asquith recommended "Strachey's subtle and suggestive art" in a lecture at Oxford.

While *Eminent Victorians* was being prepared for press, Strachey was at Tidmarsh with Dora Carrington and already reading the letters of Queen Victoria in preparation for writing his next book. Fearing a reaction against a satiric portrait of the queen, Strachey's mother tried to lead him away from Victoria as a subject, but her personal knowledge actually helped him a great deal in writing the book. With the publication of *Eminent Victorians*, Strachey acquired wealth and celebrity, but he retained close contact with his closest friends from Cambridge – John Maynard Keynes, Desmond McCarthy, Clive Bell, and Leonard Woolf. Vanessa and Virginia Stephen, both now married, remained close to Strachey. This group, known as Bloomsbury (named after the bohemian section of London in which many of them resided), which had been meeting since 1906, continued to influence one another in important ways. Strachey's relationship with Carrington developed mainly out of a mutual respect, though there was probably a sexual component, despite Strachey's general distaste for heterosexuality. The relationship became more complex when Ralph Partridge, the writer and intellectual, joined the two at Tidmarsh. The dynamics of this bisexual ménage à trois were as follows: Strachey was attracted to Partridge, Partridge to Carrington (whom he eventually married), and Carrington to Strachey. Carrington and Strachey were to remain deeply devoted to one another. Shortly after Strachey's death in 1932 she committed suicide. During the years of writing and researching Queen Victoria, Strachey lived with Carrington and Partridge in relative happiness, each day reading to them what he had written and getting helpful responses from his listeners. Their lives together took on definite domestic patterns. Carrington did the cooking. Strachey bought a car with his earnings from *Eminent Victorians*, but Partridge did all the driving. When the group traveled by train, Strachey went first class, while his two friends traveled third class. In 1919 Carrington and Partridge entered into a trial marriage, but the bisexual ménage à trois continued.

In 1921 Chatto and Windus published *Queen Victoria,* a book that departs in important ways from the methods and the tone of *Eminent Victorians,* though, as noted, develops the technique of softened irony that Strachey had already begun to use in the Gordon biography. One might have expected from the author of *Eminent Victorians* a rendering of the queen that attempted to see her as the flagship representative of the very pretense and hypocrisy he exposed in Arnold, under whose educational system the queen was schooled. But the bitterness of *Eminent Victorians* had receded into a mellow humor and pleasant amusement. Strachey himself seems to have been somewhat bothered by the altered tone, calling *Queen Victoria* "a slightly pointless book, on a depressing subject." Virginia Woolf, to whom Strachey dedicated the book, while stating that she thought it better than *Eminent Victorians,* noticed the change as well. "I think one is a little conscious of being entertained. It's a little too luxurious reading – I mean one is willing perhaps to take more pains than you allow." She even suggests that the jokes do not run as deeply as before. With World War I over, Strachey's domestic life had achieved relative stability and happiness, and he simply found less to be sardonic about in the life of the queen whose name gave him part of the title of his earlier, angrier book.

In reading the ten chapters of *Queen Victoria,* one first notices that in contrast with *Eminent Victorians* the book is carefully documented. Whereas the sections of the earlier book contained brief bibliographies (that of "Dr. Arnold" comprising a meager seven entries) and no footnotes, the later biography contains a solid bibliography of over seventy-five works and adequate, if not ample, documentation. Strachey makes a serious effort at scholarly biography. One also notices early on that the tone has changed. Readers looking for the sarcastic turns found in the portraits of Manning and Arnold look in vain in *Queen Victoria.* He approaches the subject with gentle humor, but the malice is missing.

In chapter 1, "Antecedents," Strachey compiles a straightforward genealogical essay, establishing the line that led to the "not very impressive circumstances" of his subject's birth. The style retains its liveliness, but some of the tension created by his earlier ironic point of view has noticeably vanished. Strachey's training as a historian seems to dominate his depiction of the queen, whereas earlier his desire

to expose pretense seemed to overcome his training. Chapter 2, "Childhood," takes the princess Alexandrina Victoria from her birth to her accession to the throne. In this chapter Strachey details her upbringing at the domineering hands of the duchess of Kent and the latter's wrangling arguments with King William and King Leopold, Victoria's uncle and eventual mentor. He also establishes the powerful influence of the Baroness Lehzen, Victoria's German governess, and depicts Victoria's early meetings with her cousin Albert, the eventual prince consort.

Chapter 3, "Lord Melbourne," begins a pattern in which the chapters of the book describe the queen's relationship with one of the important men to influence her life. Lord Melbourne proves to be the great formative influence in the early years of Victoria's reign. At the point of reaching her majority, Victoria removes her bed from her mother's bedroom and symbolically releases herself from the control of the duchess of Kent, who did not accept this state of affairs but was powerless to stop it. Strachey sympathizes with the young queen's desire to escape from the stultifying influence of her mother. Throwing off the maternal influence left Victoria with four major authority figures – that of her governess; her uncle, King Leopold, who counseled her through letters; Baron Stockmar; and the gentle, competent guidance of the great Whig, Lord Melbourne.

Lord Melbourne, as Strachey sees him, acted as the perfect early influence for the queen, who loved him: "She found him perfect; and perfect in her sight he remained. Her absolute and unconcealed adoration was very natural." Melbourne in turn found her delightful. He taught her many things about governing, helping her, for example, to avoid the occasionally too intrusive advice of King Leopold. In one fascinating passage Strachey explains how Victoria almost single-handedly kept the government from changing hands at a time when the dreaded Robert Peel was ready to form a new government based on the failure of the Whigs to maintain a solid majority. One of the rights of the new prime minister is to appoint new ladies to attend the queen's bedchamber. Victoria staunchly refused to give up her present ladies, even at the urging of the duke of Wellington. Eventually, both Wellington and Peel gave in; the Whigs stayed in power, and Melbourne remained with the queen. As Strachey puts it, "the venerable conqueror of Napoleon was outfaced by the relentless equanimity of a girl in her teens."

The central figure of chapter 4, "Marriage," is of course Prince Albert, and Strachey describes in this chapter with great delicacy the early period of

*Title page for the American edition of Strachey's Leslie Stephen
Lecture, which caused a great outcry among defenders of the
eighteenth-century poet*

the married life of the two as they struggled to find their relationship. He is especially keen on Victoria's possible hesitancies shortly before the wedding: "For two years she had been her own mistress. . . . And now it was all to end! She was to come under alien domination – she would have to promise that she would honor and obey . . . someone who might, after all, thwart her, oppose her – and how dreadful that would be. . . . Why had she not been contented with Lord M.? No doubt, she loved Albert; but she loved power too. At any rate, one thing was certain: she might be Albert's wife, but she would always be Queen of England." Here the Strachey of old might have dropped into his savage mockery, but he never goes beyond amusement.

Strachey clearly describes the prince's gradual accommodation to his role as husband of the queen. Despite his imputations of Albert's misogyny, he never allows them to interfere with his evenhanded presentation of the prince's life. He shows how the prince's strong intelligence overcame his reluctance to learn about the affairs of state and how he gradually gained more and more power to influence the queen and thus the policies of England itself. By 1846, Strachey remarks, all who knew the inner workings of English government knew that "Albert had become, in effect, the King of England." Again Strachey never dips into irony, even when describing that most Victorian event, the Great Exhibition, the brainchild of the prince consort himself. The queen, referring to the Great Exhibition and especially of her husband's role in it, said in a letter to her uncle, "The triumph is immense." Strachey could only agree: "It was. The enthusiasm was universal; even the bitterest scoffers were converted, and joined in the chorus of praise." Strachey himself, firmly established as one of the Victorian period's "bitterest scoffers," certainly appears to have been converted here. He concludes the chapter by noting, through a citation of the queen's correspondence, that the closing of the exhibition took place on the twelfth anniversary of her betrothal to the prince, bringing together here the good fortune of the queen in her happy, successful marriage and the success of her kingdom, for which 1851 was one of its greatest years.

A misunderstanding regarding the prince becomes the focus of chapter 5, "Lord Palmerston." Despite Strachey's suggestions that Albert is controlled by Baron Stockmar, he continues to develop in this chapter the growth of Prince Albert's power and prestige. Lord Palmerston, impatient of having to gain the royal perspective in conducting his diplomacy, began to move in a direction that would eventually contribute to the relegation of the monarch to a mere figurehead. He began to send dispatches to heads of foreign states without so much as consulting either Albert or the queen. This proved exasperating, embarrassing, and downright dangerous. Victoria, attempting to gain some form of control over the maverick statesman, sought to set some rules for him to follow about consulting her. In the midst of such negotiations "the nation found itself under the shadow of imminent war." During this foreign-policy crisis Albert's views differed from those of Lord Palmerston, a highly popular man who resigned much to the disenchantment of the public. The people then turned against the foreign-born Albert as the cause of the problem: "The moment that Palmerston's resignation was known, there was a universal outcry and an extraordinary tempest of anger and hatred burst, with unparalleled violence, upon the head of the Prince." The people called Albert a traitor, a "tool of the Russian court." It was even whispered that both Albert and the queen herself had been arrested, and crowds gathered at the Tower of London to catch a glimpse of the "royal miscreants." And while, as Strachey notes, such rumors were "fantastic hallucinations," "there were underlying elements [particularly Albert's foreignness and English suspicions about foreigners] in the situation which explained, if they did not justify, the popular state of mind." But in the end, of course, Albert is fully vindicated: "leaders of both the parties in both the Houses made speeches in support of the Prince, asserting his unimpeachable loyalty" and recognizing his right to "advise the sovereign in all matters of state."

Chapters 6 and 7, "Last Years of the Prince Consort" and "Widowhood," deal with the gradual weakening of the prince and the story of Victoria's changes after the death of her beloved husband. Whereas early in the biography Strachey had portrayed the prince as a "weak-willed youth who took no interest in politics and never read a newspaper," he sees him late in his career as "a man of unbending determination whose tireless energies were incessantly concentrated upon the laborious business of government and the highest questions of state." He was also devoted to the education of his children, and here he has trouble with Bertie, the Prince of Wales, who possessed a "deep-seated repugnance to every form of mental exertion." Strachey almost appears to sympathize with young Bertie, and though he admires the prince's hard work, he portrays it as verging on the morbid. The Crimean War occupies most of his time, and his helpful suggestions began to prove more and more valuable. Even Albert and Palmerston could find plenty to agree about where it concerned their Russian enemy. But despite all his accomplishment and excellent work, Strachey's portrait indicates an unhappy prince. "There was something that he wanted and that he could never get. What was it? Some absolute, some ineffable sympathy? Some extraordinary, some sublime success?" Strachey contends that England was forever a land of exile for Albert and that the prince felt that his life's work had accomplished little: "he believed he was a failure and he began to despair."

In March 1861 the duchess of Kent died after an illness. In November of the same year Albert became ill. He had once told Victoria that he did "not cling to life." He also said that "if I had a severe illness, I should give up at once, I should not struggle for life. I have no tenacity of life." By 14 December he was dead. At his death, Strachey tells us, "she shrieked one long wild shriek that rang through the terror-stricken castle — and understood that she had lost him forever."

Strachey writes that with the death of the prince consort, a veil descended over the events of Victoria's life. He tries to evoke sympathy by detailing the degree of her devastation: "'The poor fatherless baby of eight months,' she wrote to the King of the Belgians, 'is now the utterly heart-broken and crushed widow of forty-two! My life as a happy one is ended.'" She determined to keep a vigilant mourning "for the rest of her life." She lived, Strachey informs us, in almost complete seclusion, barely seeing even her ministers. Strachey also observes the degree to which the queen's seclusion hurt her popularity with the public. Despite her near disappearance, the exigencies of governing eventually forced Victoria to carry on Albert's work, but she also determined "to impress the true nature of his genius and character upon the minds of her subjects," first through commissioning a long biography, then through work on several memorials to Albert's memory, culminating in the ten-ton bronze gilt statue that graced the Albert Memorial and Hall. Strachey concludes the chapter with the following observation on the statue: "It was rightly supposed that the simple word 'Albert,' cast on the base, would be a sufficient means of identification."

Strachey explores Victoria's later career in chapter 8, "Mr. Gladstone and Lord Beaconsfield." In a delightful portrait Strachey shows Benjamin Disraeli helping the queen from her sadness through a combination of flattery, "we authors Ma'am," and sincere regard. Disraeli gave Victoria the nickname The Faery, short for the Faery Queen. And as scholars have pointed out, Strachey uses the elements of romance and theater to depict the relationship of Disraeli and the queen. Disraeli seemed to revive the queen's confidence. His methods were the opposite of Gladstone's, who tended to harangue the queen's increasingly unsympathetic ear: "It was not his [Disraeli's] habit to harangue and exhort and expatiate in official conscientiousness; he liked to scatter flowers along the path of business, to compress a weighty argument into a happy phrase, to insinuate what was in his mind with an air of friendship and confidential courtesy." His genius, Strachey contends, was one of "skillfully confusing the woman and the queen," so as to please both. He helped her to gain the title "Empress of India," and on the day of proclamation of that title Beaconsfield went to Windsor to dine: "That night the Faery, usually so homely in her attire, appeared in a glittering panoply of enormous uncut jewels, which had been presented to her by the reigning Princes of her *Raj*. At the end of the meal the Prime Minister, breaking through the rules of etiquette, arose, and in a flowery oration proposed the health of the Queen-Empress. His audacity was well received, and his speech was rewarded by a smiling curtsey."

The Beaconsfield portrait is of course a complete contrast with Strachey's depiction of Gladstone, for whom both the queen and her biographer have little sympathy. When the prime minister invoked the Lord as sanction for his reforming plans, the queen was unmoved: "The Queen . . . did not share her new Minister's view of the almighty's intentions. She could not believe that there was any divine purpose to be detected in the programme of sweeping changes which Gladstone was determined to carry out." Gladstone's

awe of the royal personage did not please her majesty. "But unfortunately the lady did not appreciate the compliment. The well-known complaint – 'He speaks to me as if I were a public meeting' – whether authentic or no . . . undoubtedly expresses the essential element of her antipathy."

In chapter 9, "Old Age," Strachey describes how with the loss of Albert and finally of Disraeli, the queen comes to depend on John Brown, who had been the prince's gillie and now became Victoria's attendant. His rough manner and rough speech became a positive pleasure to the queen. But two years after the loss of Disraeli, John Brown died as well. Strachey handles these late years of the queen with tenderness: "The busy years hastened away; the traces of Time's unimaginable touch grew manifest; and old age, approaching, laid a gentle hand upon Victoria. The grey hair whitened; the mature features mellowed; the short firm figure amplified and moved more slowly, supported by a stick." In contrast to his burlesque of Arnold and his short legs, this looks like the kindest of descriptions. After the last of six assassination attempts failed in 1882, it became clear that Victoria had regained the national sympathy. After Gladstone's failed ministry, the country agreed with its queen that the liberals had failed. The disaster in the Sudan with Gordon solidified this opinion. In 1887, the Golden Jubilee year of Victoria's reign, the country celebrated in "solemn pomp." Strachey writes, "In that triumphant hour the last remaining traces of past antipathies and past disagreements were altogether swept away. The Queen was hailed at once as the mother of her people and as the embodied symbol of their imperial greatness."

For the final pages of this chapter Strachey explores the quiet solemnity of the queen's final years, including her special attentions to the memory of Albert and daily work. Her children married and produced children who in turn produced more children, and still the queen lived on. She opposed women's suffrage: "The Queen is most anxious" she wrote, "to enlist everyone who can speak or write to join in checking this mad, wicked folly of 'Women's rights.'" In estimating the reasons for her success as a queen, Strachey points out that she successfully combined the morality of the middle class with some inherent qualities of aristocracy: "The middle classes, firm in the triple brass of their respectability, rejoiced with a special joy over the most respectable of Queens." In manners, on the other hand, she was utterly aristocratic. It was her sincerity of personality that Strachey identifies as her supreme characteristic: "Her truthfulness, her singlemindedness, the vividness of her emotions and her unrestrained expression of them, were the varied forms that his central characteristic assumed." In the concluding paragraphs Strachey grows nostalgic about the last years of Victoria's reign, and the final moving paragraph and description of the death scene, almost Dickensian in its style and sentiment, is one of the most famous Strachey ever wrote: "When two days previously [to her death on 22 January 1901] the news of the approaching end had been made public, astonished grief had swept over the country. It appeared as if some monstrous reversal of the course of nature was about to take place. The vast majority of her subjects had never known a time when Queen Victoria had not been reigning over them. She had become a part of their whole scheme of things, and that they were about to lose her appeared a scarcely possible thought. She herself, as she lay blind and silent, seemed to those who watched her to be divested of all thinking — to have glided already, unawares, into oblivion. Yet, perhaps, in the secret chambers of consciousness, she had her thoughts, too. Perhaps her fading mind called up once more the shadows of the past to float before it, and retraced, for the last time, the vanished visions of that long history — passing back and back, through the cloud of years, to older and ever older memories — to the spring woods at Osborne, so full of primroses for Lord Beaconsfield — to Lord Palmerston's queer clothes and high demeanor, and Albert's face under the green lamp, and Albert's first stag at Balmoral, and Albert in his blue and silver uniform, and the Baron coming in at Windsor with the rooks cawing in the elm-trees, and the Archbishop of Canterbury on his knees in the dawn, and the old King's turkey-cock ejaculations, and Uncle Leopold's soft voice at Claremont, and Lehzen with the globes, and her mother's feathers sweeping down towards her, and a great old repeater-watch of her father's in its tortoise-shell case, and a yellow rug, and some friendly flounces of sprigged muslin, and the trees and the grass at Kensington."

When he had finished *Queen Victoria,* Strachey left Tidmarsh to visit his family in their new Bloomsbury home. By this time he was an established author, living off the money he had earned as a writer. Meanwhile, Carrington and Partridge had married and spent part of their honeymoon with Strachey. After much traveling he returned to Tidmarsh in October to continue living with the now-married Partridges. In 1922 Strachey collected his best critical and biographical essays and pub-

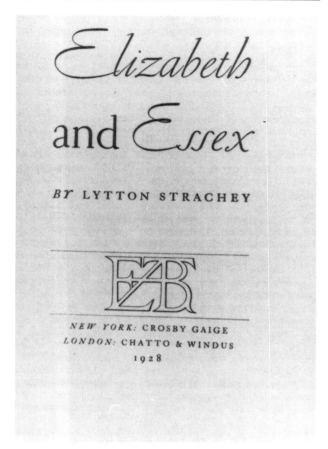

Title page for the American edition of Strachey's last major biographical work, which was attacked by many critics for its lurid portrayal of the monarch's sexuality

lished *Books and Characters: French & English.* The fact that he had attained the stature at which his collected essays could command an audience marks the degree of importance which he had reached.

Among the essays in this collection appears his essay on Jean Racine, perhaps his most famous short work of criticism, in which he refutes John Bailey's claim that Racine belongs among the second class of writers. In a work of straightforward appreciation, Strachey attempts to show that Racine's psychological acuity and gift for a deep understanding of the human mind place him among the greatest of all poets. His essay on Thomas Browne seeks to overturn Gosse's dismissal of Browne's importance and to clarify the significance of Browne's influence on the prose of the eighteenth century. These essays, like those in this volume on Shakespeare, William Blake, Thomas Lovell Beddoes, and Stendhal are almost strictly critical, not biographical. Some of the other essays combine the critical and the biographical. The three essays on

Voltaire, for example, combine biographical information with critical assessment. "Madame du Deffand" also supplies biographical information and an analysis of her importance to the study of eighteenth-century literature. "The Rousseau Affair" provides historical analysis of Frederika Macdonald's exculpatory book on Jean-Jacques Rousseau and attempts to show that despite new information produced by Macdonald, the bulk of the evidence still manages to work against Rousseau. Other essays on such figures as Lady Hester Stanhope and Thomas Creevey are more exclusively biographical studies of these relatively minor figures.

Late in 1923 Partridge had an affair that marked the start of the demise of his marriage to Carrington. Early in 1924, after one of his many trips to France, Strachey bought Ham Spray house in Berkshire, where he spent most of the remainder of his life. Despite the strains created by Partridge's relationship with Frances Marshall, he continued to live with and care for both Strachey and Carrington. In mid 1924 Strachey sadly left Tidmarsh. He felt the years spent there had been the happiest of his life, and he regretted their end. In 1925 Strachey delivered the prestigious Leslie Stephen Lecture at Cambridge. His subject was Alexander Pope, and Strachey's portrait of the great poet has angered Pope's defenders. But Strachey identified strongly with "the little monster of Twit'nam," not only because of his physical deformities and his love of beauty but also because of his willingness to attack and "ridicule the polite world." This essay marks an example of a form in which Strachey excelled, the short critical and biographical essay. Also in this year Strachey's play *The Son of Heaven* was performed at the Scala Theater but was unsuccessful, though it ran posthumously for three weeks at a revival in London in 1949. In 1925 Partridge moved to London to live with Marshall, causing pain to both Carrington and Strachey, who turned even more deeply to one another for comfort. Carrington felt that Strachey was the only person in whom she could confide without the slightest fear of betrayal.

Late in 1925 Strachey began working on *Elizabeth and Essex: A Tragic History* (1928), his last major biographical work. In this book Strachey capitalizes on his ability to write with scholarly care but does not shy from using his reading of Sigmund Freud to experiment with novel interpretations of his subject. Not surprisingly, some critics have found the book lurid and showing a prurient interest in sexuality. There is more of Strachey's own personal dramatization in this

biography than in any of his earlier writings, though this tendency could always be identified.

That Strachey emphasizes the secular interests of his characters is apparent from the first line of the book: "The English Reformation was not merely a religious event; it was a social one too." And it is the interest of this world that Strachey focuses on throughout the biography. Strachey emphasizes the sexual energy between Elizabeth and Essex from the very beginning: "It was plain to all — the handsome, charming youth, with his open manner, his boyish spirits, his words and looks of adoration, and his tall figure, and his exquisite hands, and the auburn hair on his head, had fascinated Elizabeth." But Strachey is not satisfied with the physical side of his characters or of the age he studies. His reading of Freud had led him to deeper interests: "More valuable than descriptions, but what is more unattainable, would be some means by which the modern mind might reach to an imaginative comprehension of those beings of three centuries ago — might move with ease among their familiar essential feelings — might touch, or dream that it touches (for such dreams are the stuff of history) 'the very pulse of the machine.'" But even with the help of Freud, Strachey is skeptical about our chances: "the contradictions of the age . . . baffle our imaginations and perplex our intelligence."

Still Strachey seems confident in his depiction of his characters. His sketch of Elizabeth shows no sign of its author's doubts. It was, he tells us, Elizabeth's ability to float that made her a successful queen: "Her femininity saved her. Only a woman could have shuffled so shamelessly, only a woman could have abandoned with such unscrupulous completeness the last shreds not only of consistency, but of dignity, honor and common decency, in order to escape the appalling necessity of having, really and truly, to make up her mind." She passed her life, he tells us, "in a passion of postponement." In explanation of her legendary virginity, Strachey uses Freud, identifying hers as a "neurotic condition." "Her sexual organization was seriously warped." Perhaps, he suggests, she remembered her father leading her to mass in great pomp; "But it is also possible that her very earliest memory was of a different kind: when she was two years and eight months old, her father cut off her mother's head. Whether remembered or no, the reactions of such an event upon her infant spirit must have been profound." Or perhaps her sexual problems arose because of the strange attentions paid her by Lord Admiral Seymour, the husband of her stepmother. When later the death of his wife freed him, he proposed to Elizabeth. His brother the protector, taking his title seriously, had the admiral beheaded. Such a childhood may have given her "a deeply seated repugnance to the crucial act of intercourse" which may bring about, Strachey theorizes, "a condition of hysterical convulsion, accompanied, in certain cases, by intense pain." This problem was accompanied by an "amorousness so irrepressible as to be always obvious and sometimes scandalous." Into this complicated and paradoxical world came the young earl of Essex.

The early history of the earl's relationship with Elizabeth is one of small triumphs marred by major failures. While descriptions and psychological interpretations play an important role in the book, Strachey is equally adept at denoting character through action. Strachey details the court intrigues as Essex tries twice to place his nephew Francis Bacon in high office. Both times he failed painfully: "Essex had failed – failed doubly – failed where he could hardly have believed that failure was possible. The loss to his own prestige was serious; but he was a gallant nobleman, and his first thought was for the friend whom he had fed with hope, and whom, perhaps, he had served ill through over-confidence or lack of judgement. As soon as the appointment was made, he paid a visit to Francis Bacon. 'Master Bacon,' he said, 'the Queen hath denied me yon place for you, and hath placed another.'" Essex blamed himself for the failure and offered Bacon some land, which, after some demurring, he finally accepted. Such a story tells much about Essex's straightforward character.

Less flattering are the characterizations of Elizabeth, Essex, and the other high courtiers that emerge from Strachey's rendering of the affair of the aged Ruy Lopez, a Portuguese-Jewish doctor accused of plotting against England on behalf of Spain. In what Strachey plays as a clear miscarriage of justice, including prejudice, perjured incriminating testimonies, and confessions acquired through torture, the man is found guilty, hanged, and mutilated. In later chapters Strachey, continuing throughout his association of Essex with stars and fire, shows him successful on the first battle with Spain and then returning home ignominiously, defeated by a storm in the second attempt. It is this failure that begins to suggest, along with the tragic description of Lopez's fate, that Essex's end may not be a happy one, that the tale may well be, as Strachey has suggested, a tragic one. One of the most striking portraits to emerge is that of Bacon, who saw more clearly than anyone the potential dangers of his patron's position. Essex seemed, be-

fore the second Spanish expedition, almost to be on his way to "becoming before long the real Ruler of England." "Yet there was one pair of eyes – and one only – that viewed the gorgeous spectacle without blinking. The cold viper-gaze of Francis Bacon, heedless of the magnificence of the exterior, pierced through to the inner quiddity of his patron's situation and saw there nothing but doubt and anger." But Bacon's advice to Essex was bound to fail because Bacon had not the psychological insight to present his views in a way that his patron could accept. Profound in everything except psychology, the actual steps which he urged Essex to take in order to preserve the queen's favor were totally unfitted to the temperament of the earl. He advised the straightforward, honest earl to behave with "Machiavellian calculation" and "to enter into an elaborate course of flattery, dissimulation, and reserve." Clearly, Strachey shows, "the frank impetuosity of Essex" could never "bend itself to these crooked ways." Bacon's advice had been to avoid at all cost getting caught up in military problems. Of course Essex's manner forced the issue in the wrong direction, and Elizabeth made him head of the fleet for the second, ill-fated Spanish expedition, which did so much to harm the earl's prestige. Yet the ultimate disruption of their relationship still waited far off.

Ireland proved to be the final undoing of Essex, and the villain of his demise is not Tyrone, the Irish rebel whom the queen sent him to Ireland to destroy, but his old friend Bacon, whom Strachey argues betrayed Essex out of a superior sense of where power lay and a desperate need to solve his serious financial problems. Essex failed to subdue Tyrone, instead submitting to a rather ignominious truce. Upon his unannounced return he was placed under house arrest, and when he eventually attempted to save himself by actually overthrowing the crown, he was abandoned by many of his followers. The queen apprehended him, imprisoned him, and finally, Strachey argues, following up the psychological suggestion from much earlier in the biography, "she condemned her lover to her mother's death." Essex becomes the betrayed lover; Bacon, a Judas figure, sells his patron for twelve hundred pounds; and Elizabeth finally emerges as the romantic heroine who retains her kingdom but loses her love. "It was all too clear," Strachey writes, "her inordinate triumph had only brought her to solitude and ruin."

While critics recognized the originality and brilliance of *Elizabeth and Essex,* they saw in it something less than the classic they saw in *Queen Victoria* and nothing like the tour de force represented by

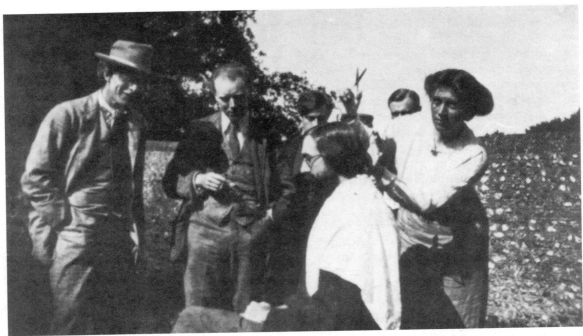

Vanessa Bell cutting Strachey's hair as Roger Fry, Clive Bell, Duncan Grant, and an unidentified guest look on, Asheham, 1913

Eminent Victorians. Some critics objected to the conjecture on which much of the book's ideas were based and refused to accept the lurid depiction of Elizabeth's sexuality as historically sound. Edmund Wilson found the book "slightly disgusting." Professional historians have largely ignored the book, though some literary critics found it to be a remarkable success. Freud himself wrote to congratulate Strachey. Freud is known to have read all of Strachey's books and had this to say about *Elizabeth and Essex:* "you have known how to trace back [Elizabeth's] character to the impressions of her childhood, you have touched upon her hidden motives with equal boldness and discretion, and it is very possible that you have succeeded in making a correct reconstruction of what occurred."

The writing of *Elizabeth and Essex* proved exhausting and agonizing for Strachey, and during its entire composition he was conducting his painful affair with Roger Senhouse. He made slow progress on the book, alternating hard work and holidays with Senhouse and at times with his brother James and Carrington. Finally in April of 1928 he completed the work. Keynes has suggested that in his last biography Strachey most clearly dramatizes himself in the characters of both Elizabeth and Essex. Thus in some ways the book is a kind of autobiography as well as a kind of Freudian fiction.

His work on *Queen Victoria* had led him to the discovery of the disgraceful expurgations of the Greville memoirs, and in September he was at the British Museum working on his edition of them. He was working on the Greville papers when he discovered that Senhouse had left for France with a friend, leaving him with yet another failed love affair.

In 1931 Strachey published *Portraits in Miniature and Other Essays,* a collection of about half of the essays he wrote during the decade of the 1920s. It contains some of Strachey's most important critical essays, such as "John Aubrey," in which he theorizes his preference for the shorter biographies of Aubrey over the longer ones he criticizes in his preface to *Eminent Victorians.* In another essay he describes, in a "shattering refutation of the lessons of cheap morality," the paradox of the great literary success of James Boswell, "an idler, a lecher, a drunkard, and a snob." The section of the book called "Six English Historians" includes essays on David Hume, Edward Gibbon, Thomas Carlyle, Thomas Macaulay, James Froude, and Mandell Creighton; presents some of Strachey's important observations on history as an art; and announces once again his clear preference for the eighteenth century over the nineteenth. While the essays focus on these authors as historians, the reader can see the developing biographer at work. But more than anything these essays demonstrate Strachey's literary critical method, never really developed in a book-length literary study. For example, consider this comment on Hume's "ironic malice," especially in the way it seems to describe Strachey's own method in *Eminent Victorians:* "Hume's writing [is] at its best," he suggests, when "the pungency of sense varies in direct proportion with the mildness of the expression." He finds new ways of directing his legendary venom at the Victorians in his study of Carlyle: While one is at first overwhelmed by Carlyle's achievement, he argues, "one recovers – very quickly. That is the drawback. The Northern lights after all, seem to give out no heat, and the great guns were only loaded with powder." Carlyle, he writes, lived in an "age in which everything was discovered and nothing known." He offers more sympathy for Froude as Carlyle's biographer: Strachey claims that for his contemporaries, it is "very difficult to believe that real red-hot lava ever flowed from that dry, neglected crater [Carlyle]" but that because Froude had the advantage of having heard Carlyle speak, his worship of the Chelsea sage could be excused if not really understood. *Portraits in Miniature and Other Essays* offers a sample of Strachey's short prose written after the publication of *Eminent Victorians* that shows the transition from his most venomous moods to the more mellow, scholarly attitude he adopts later. The book contains many brief but interesting essays on such minor figures as John North, Lodowick Muggleton, Madame de Lieven, and others.

By March 1931 Strachey had begun to have premonitions of death. He left in September for a final journey to Paris, but by October he had fallen ill and did not respond to treatments. His friends came to be by his side during his illness, and his sisters took care of him, but he seemed to be unafraid of death: "If this is death," he remarked, "I don't think much of it." At 1:30 P.M. on 21 January 1932 Strachey died. An autopsy revealed that he had been suffering from cancer of the stomach. His doctors had diagnosed him with colitis. That night Carrington tried to commit suicide by shooting herself and died soon after. Strachey's body was cremated and his ashes placed in the Strachey Chapel at Chew Magna Church, Somerset. In *Downhill all the Way* (1967), Leonard Woolf includes this moving passage, which well sums up Strachey's importance for his own generation: Strachey's death marked "the beginning of the end of what we used to call Old Bloomsbury. Lytton was perhaps the most individual person whom I have ever known. . . . He had an extremely subtle and supple mind, with a tremendously quick flicker of wit and humor continu-

ally playing through his thought. . . . His conversation was entrancing, for his talk was profounder, wittier, more interesting, and original than his writing . . . [His death] was the beginning of the end, for it meant that the spring had gone out of our lives."

By the time of his death Strachey's fame had already been in eclipse for some time. *Eminent Victorians* had made him famous, and *Queen Victoria* was felt by many to be his masterpiece, but his essay on Pope had earned him some enemies, and *Elizabeth and Essex* was widely felt to be brilliant but abortive. His reputation has waned even more since his death. The 1948 edition of his works did not have great sales figures, though since that time a great deal of critical and scholarly work has been done, though much remains to be done. Despite his many short essays and his work on Elizabeth and Victoria, it seems that what is true today about his reputation will remain true for some time: Strachey is known as a minor writer whose fame depends on his ironic portraits of the Victorian age in *Eminent Victorians.* It is in that book that Strachey located his best vein – that of mockery and the ironic undercutting of seemingly straightforward praise, a vein that he returned to infrequently after *Eminent Victorians.* He will also be remembered as having revived biography at a time when it desperately needed reviving, rejecting the moribund two-volume format for the short, subjective biography that relied on lively and incisive writing rather than careful scholarship. In this way he anticipated postmodern adventures into the relationship between fiction and nonfiction.

Letters:

Virginia Woolf and Lytton Strachey: Letters, edited by Leonard Woolf and James Strachey (London: Hogarth Press / Chatto & Windus, 1956).

Bibliography:

Michael Edmonds, *Lytton Strachey: A Bibliography* (New York & London: Garland, 1981).

References:

Max Beerbohm, *Lytton Strachey* (Cambridge: Cambridge University Press, 1943);

Guy Boas, *Lytton Strachey* (English Association Pamphlet, no. 93, November 1935);

Clifford Brower-Shore, *Lytton Strachey: An Essay* (London: Fenland, 1933);

C. Clemens, *Lytton Strachey: A Critical Study* (London: Chatto & Windus, 1939);

Leon Edel, "Biographer and Subject: Lytton Strachey and Van Wyck Brooks," *Prose Studies*, 5 (December 1982): 281–293;

William H. Epstein, *Recognizing Biography* (Philadelphia: University of Pennsylvania Press, 1987);

John Ferns, *Lytton Strachey* (Boston: Twayne, 1988);

Harold Fromm, "Holroyd/Strachey/Shaw: Art and Archives in Literary Biography," *Hudson Review*, 42 (Summer 1989): 201–221;

Michael Holroyd, *Lytton Strachey* (London: Chatto & Windus, 1994);

Holroyd, *Lytton Strachey: A Critical Biography, Volume I: The Unknown Years 1880–1910* (London: Heinemann, 1967);

Holroyd, *Lytton Strachey: A Critical Biography, Volume II: The Years of Achievement 1910–1932* (London: Heinemann, 1968);

Richard A. Hutch, "Strategic Irony and Lytton Strachey's Contribution to Biography," *Biography*, 11 (Winter 1988): 1–15;

Aldous Huxley, "The Author of *Eminent Victorians*," in *On the Margin* (London: Chatto & Windus, 1923), pp. 141–157;

K. R. Iyengar, *Lytton Strachey: A Critical Study* (London: Chatto & Windus, 1939);

Martin Kallich, *The Psychological Milieu of Lytton Strachey* (New Haven: Yale University Press, 1961);

John Maynard Keynes, *Two Memoirs* (London: Hart-Davis, 1949);

U. C. Knoepflmacher, "The Subject of Biography: The Victorianism of *Eminent Victorians*," *Victorians Institute Journal*, 18 (1990): 1–15;

Ira B. Nadel, "The Smallest Genius and 'The Wittiest Mind': Max Beerbohm and Lytton Strachey," *English Literature in Transition*, 27 (1984): 289–295;

Nadel, "Strachey's 'Subtler Strategy': Metaphor in *Eminent Victorians*," *Prose Studies*, 4 (September 1981): 146–152;

Eileen Overend, "Attitude, Drama, and Role in Strachey's *Elizabeth and Essex*," *Biography*, 7 (Spring 1984): 158–168;

Bruce B. Redford, "The Shaping of the Biographer: Lytton Strachey's *Warren Hastings*," *Princeton University Library Chronicle*, 43 (Autumn 1981): 38–52;

C. R. Sanders, *Lytton Strachey: His Mind and Art* (New Haven: Yale University Press, 1957);

Barry Spurr, "Camp Mandarin: The Prose Style of Lytton Strachey," *English Literature in Transition*, 33 (1990): 31–45;

Barbara Strachey, *The Strachey Line* (London: Gollancz, 1985).

Papers:

Strachey's papers are widely scattered. His correspondence with Vanessa Bell and B. W. Swithinbank, along with some other letters, can be found in the library at King's College, Cambridge. Most of his other papers and letters are either in the possession of Mrs. Alix Strachey or of the families of the recipients of the letters. The manuscript of *Elizabeth and Essex* is in the Duke University library; that of *Queen Victoria* is at the Humanities Research Center, University of Texas at Austin; and that of *Eminent Victorians* is in the British Library.

A. J. A. Symons
(16 August 1900 – 26 August 1941)

Edmund Miller
C. W. Post Campus, Long Island University

BOOKS: *A Bibliography of the First Editions of Books by William Butler Yeats* (London: First Edition Club, 1924);

Frederick Baron Corvo (London: privately printed, 1927);

Emin, the Governor of Equitoria (London: Fleuron, 1928);

An Episode in the Life of the Queen of Sheba (London: privately printed, 1929);

H. M. Stanley (London: Duckworth, 1933);

The Quest for Corvo: An Experiment in Biography (London: Cassell, 1934);

Inaugural Address of His Oddshippe Bro. A. J. A. Symons (Speculator); Delivered to the Sette of Odd Volumes at Its 525th Meeting Held at the Savoy Hotel on October 18, 1938 (London: privately printed, 1938);

The Unration Book (London: Wine & Food Society, 1939);

Essays and Biographies, edited by Julian Symons (London: Cassell, 1969);

A. J. A. Symons to Wyndham Lewis: Twenty-Four Letters, with comments by Julian Symons (London: Tragara, 1982).

OTHER: Ambrose Bierce, *Ten Tales,* introduction by Symons (London: First Edition Club, 1925);

An Anthology of "Nineties" Verse, edited by Symons (London: Elkin Mathews & Marrot, 1928);

"Tradition in Biography," in *Tradition and Experiment in Present-Day Literature* (Oxford: Oxford University Press, 1929);

"An Essay of the Epicure and the Epicurean," in *The Epicure's Anthology,* compiled by Nancy Quennell (London: Golden Cockerel, [1934]);

"Appraisal," in *The Nonesuch Century: An Appraisal, a Personal Note, and a Bibliography of the First Hundred Books Issued by the Press, 1923–34,* by Symons, Desmond Flower, and Francis Meynell (London: Nonesuch, 1936), pp. 1–30;

"Theodore Hook," in *English Wits,* edited by Leonard Russell (London: Hutchinson, 1939).

SELECTED PERIODICAL PUBLICATIONS – UNCOLLECTED: "Edgar Allan Poe," *Life and Letters,* 2 (1929): 163–178;

"A Book-Collector's Apology," *Book-Collector's Quarterly,* 1 (1930): 45–56;

"The Anatomy of Bibliomania," *Book-Collector's Quarterly,* 1 (1930): 93–96;

"Point Counter-Point," *Book-Collector's Quarterly,* 3 (1931): 82–87;

"Edition and Impression," *Book-Collector's Quarterly,* 5 (1932): 1–8;

"Mise en Page," *Book-Collector's Quarterly,* 6 (1932): 45;

" 'Issue' and 'State,' " *Book-Collector's Quarterly,* 6 (1932): 79–82;

"Two Reformers," *Book-Collector's Quarterly,* 8 (1932): 56–59;

"Old Title-Page Borders," *Book-Collector's Quarterly,* 11 (1933): 87–88;

"Charles Ricketts," *Book-Collector's Quarterly,* 12 (1933): 41–42;

"An Unacknowledged Movement in Fine Printing," *Fleuron: A Journal of Typography,* 7 (1933);

"Post-War English Bookbinding," *Book-Collector's Quarterly,* 13 (1934): 1–6;

"Modern English Bindings at the First Edition Club Reviewed," *Book-Collector's Quarterly,* 13 (1934): 81–86;

"Nineteenth-Century Forgeries," *Book-Collector's Quarterly,* 15 (1934): 1–16;

"Notes on the Fifty Books of the Year," *Book-Collector's Quarterly,* 15 (1934): 59–67;

"Shelley Fragments," *Book-Collector's Quarterly,* 15 (1934): 89–90;

"Alexandre Dumas père," *Book-Collector's Quarterly,* 16 (1934): 86–87;

"Two Unusual Books," *Book-Collector's Quarterly,* 16 (1934): 87–88;

A. J. A. Symons (photograph by Howard Coster)

"Wilde at Oxford," *Horizon: A Review of Literature
    and Art,* 3 (1941): 235–236, 336–348;

"The Diner-Out [i.e. Oscar Wilde]," *Horizon: A Re-
    view of Literature and Art,* 4 (1941): 251–258.

A. J. A. Symons is remembered chiefly for his
biography of Fr[ederick] Rolfe (or Baron Corvo).
He did, however, publish two other substantial biographies and a range of miscellaneous works in his
short life, and his younger brother, the prolific mystery writer Julian Symons, has salvaged additional
short biographical studies. But *The Quest for Corvo:
An Experiment in Biography* (1934) broke new ground
in its format, and while perhaps not the lineal ancestor of modern biographical writing, it is yet the precursor of an attitude and a methodology now commonplace. Symons showed both readers and writers
how empathy and character study rather than fact
gathering and chronology could be made the focus
of biography.

Alphonse James Albert Symons (he later
claimed the initials stood for Albert James Alroy)
was born 16 August 1900, the son of an émigré Russian Jew who had adopted the name Maurice Albert
Symons and of his English wife Minnie Louise Bull
Symons. Raised in a London suburb but leaving
school at the age of fourteen, as was usual at the
time for those unable to afford further education, he
nevertheless hoped to attain a position in society,
perhaps as a writer. In his search for recognition, he
was attracted to many cultural fads but not always
with the social consequences he envisioned. His
study of calligraphy, for example, led him to dabble
in forgery. His epicurean tastes led to dandyism.
The collection of books and music boxes thrust him
into debt.

In 1924 he married Victoria Emily Gladys
Weeks after a soul search which culminated in his
confessing to her his embarrassment about the period of his childhood when he was taken out of
school and sent to work, apprenticed to a furrier.
Like the novelist Charles Dickens, with whose situation he compared his own, he had been profoundly
marked by this episode.

Symons's primary employment during the 1920s was as secretary of the First Edition Club. The object of the club was the publication of limited-run fine editions of "books worthy of the cultured community." Beginning with almost no specialized knowledge of the book trade, he had in a few years acquired the expertise to present to the world his own compilation of a bibliography of the poet William Butler Yeats among the club's early publications.

Symons's first major biographical work was *Emin, the Governor of Equitoria,* published in 1928 by Fleuron in a limited edition using the new typeface Lutetia. He was attracted to the romantic story of the impoverished doctor Eduard Schnitzer (1840–1892), who taught African tribes government by conciliation as Emin Bey or Emin Pasha. In addition to the colorful story, the book also has a special interest because of the epigrammatic language, witty even when not quite true; for example, "There are but two methods of government: conciliation and coercion; though there are as many methods of misgovernment as there are active political parties." Symons had arrived as an author.

Pursuing his interest in more literary material, Symons next published *An Anthology of "Nineties" Verse* (1928), the only fruit of a projected comprehensive annotated bibliography of the authors of the 1890s viewed as a literary movement. The anthology did not attract much enthusiasm among reviewers when first published, although it has in more recent years acquired historical, documentary significance. The most curious thing about this work from the point of view of Symons's career as a biographer is the argument in the introduction that the accumulation of facts is, apart from any analysis, itself a useful activity. In a way this argument is a justification of publication of the volume in place of the projected bibliography. But even such a completed bibliographical project would have, in essence, contradicted Symons's mature biographical theory, which was expressed for the first time in its full form in a talk he made the following year.

In 1929 Symons delivered this watershed talk on "Tradition in Biography" at the City Literary Institute in London. In it he laid out entirely new principles for biography as a literary genre. Pointing out that very few biographies retain their readership over time, he suggested that writers had lost sight of the main purpose of such works, which is to reveal, not simply record, the facts of a life. He identified the goal of biography as establishing sympathetic understanding of the subject and additionally noted the need for biographers to aspire to the same high standards of prose style as essayists and novelists. He criticized the traditional chronological biography as essentially undramatic because chronology forestalls the telling juxtaposition of pertinent facts and incidents. "Completeness," he argued, "is not merely impossible; it is undesirable."

In 1929 Symons also published a satiric jeu d'esprit, *An Episode in the Life of the Queen of Sheba.* This pamphlet re-creates the biblical visit of the Queen of Sheba to King Solomon as a begging call of a client in arrears asking extension on a loan payment from a Jewish moneylender. In this anachronistic fantasy the queen's love is sought by many great figures of history but won in the end by the Marchese Guglielmo Marconi with his gift of a radio to sate her weariness. Perhaps Symons exorcised some of his ambivalence about his Jewish ancestry with this work.

In 1930 Symons assumed the main editorial duties of the defunct *Bibliophile's Almanack,* revived as the *Book-Collector's Quarterly.* The first issue for which he was responsible included his article called "The Book-Collector's Apology." In this he described the joys of book collecting in general and celebrated the special aura of first editions. Ironically, later in the same year, financial reverses, in particular some involving the First Edition Club, forced him to sell at auction his collection of 1890s materials, including two Corvine manuscripts still unpublished at that time. Unfortunately, the offering, coming as it did at the beginning of the Great Depression, realized less ready cash than he needed.

His hand perhaps forced by simple need, he produced his first full-length biography, *H. M. Stanley,* in 1933. He chose not to focus the story of Sir Henry Morton Stanley on the celebrated discovery of Dr. David Livingstone in Africa, although this is highlighted in the first chapter. Rather, he was attracted to Stanley's life of disguise because of the parallels to his own subterfuges in hiding his Jewish parentage and his invented family name. Stanley, it seems, was not the American he claimed to be, but a runaway workhouse boy, self-educated like Symons. The book provided a major opportunity for illustrating the new theory of biography. And on this account it is still pleasantly readable, like everything of Symons's. The biographer's compassion for his subject is evident on every page, although the mysteries of Africa no longer work quite the magic they once did.

Symons next became fascinated by a minor writer of the 1890s who called himself variously Fr. Rolfe and Baron Corvo. A major stylist of decadence, Rolfe fueled his career by a paranoia that not

Title page for Symons's innovative biography of the minor decadent writer of the 1890s

only drove away anyone who tried to befriend him but also provided the subject matter and perhaps generated the distinctive stylistic excesses of his works, including *Stories Toto Told Me* (1898), *Chronicles of the House of Borgia* (1901), *The Desire and Pursuit of the Whole* (1934), *Nicholas Crabbe* (1958), and his masterpiece, *Hadrian the Seventh* (1904). *The Quest for Corvo* (1934) is, as its subtitle announces, *An Experiment in Biography*. While this subtitle suggests a more radical approach than Symons had until that time attempted, the result is more than simply a justification of the new theory of biography. As in *H. M. Stanley,* the traditional chronological sequence of the subject's life was abandoned. Symons substituted the sequence of his own search for biographical information. Indeed, the book is not really about

Rolfe or Corvo at all but instead about the biographer's developing understanding of his subject as he uncovered more and more byways of life records and unpublished books. The strangely similar tastes and careers of biographer and subject undoubtedly enabled Symons to bring unusual empathy to this work.

This masterpiece continues to reward and stimulate readers because of its disarming technique. Symons manages to keep his subject in a sympathetic light even when Rolfe is at his most bizarre and most paranoid. But it is with its self-reflective attention to the perceptions of the biographer that *The Quest for Corvo* is a peculiarly modern book, pioneering a technique in biographical writing that has grown into the wretched excesses of

Oil portrait of Symons by Natalie Sieveking

contemporary scandal sheets. But the focus of *The Quest for Corvo* is unlike that of contemporary supermarket tabloids insatiable for scandal at the expense of anyone famous. While Symons, for example, reports the fact of Rolfe's homosexuality, he does so without sensationalism and with worldly understanding of human nature, as when he comments disingenuously on Rolfe's lifelong aspiration to the priesthood: "Set among those who had voluntarily embraced celibacy, his abnormality became, not a possible vice, but a sign of Vocation. Hence it came about that the young student, whose unsuitability for holy orders was recognized by his fellows almost without exception, aspired to ordination." And even when Symons is most Victorian in his censoriousness, he sounds a modern note well ahead of his time and yet far removed from sensationalism in his acknowledgment of the ways of the world and in his unwillingness to be shocked by them:

> [If Rolfe's] dark letters are to be believed, he had embarked in Venice on a course of life which not even

well-founded wrongs, even by his own standard, could justify. It was not only that he stood self-revealed as a patron of that homosexual underworld which exists in every city. He had become a habitual corrupter of youth, a seducer of innocence, and he asked his wealthy accomplice for money, first that he might use it as a temptation, to buy bait for the boys whom he misled, and secondly that he might efficiently act as pander when his friend revisited Venice. Neither scruple nor remorse was expressed or implied in these long accounts of his sexual exploits and enjoyments, which were so definite in their descriptions that he was forced, in sending them by post, so to fold them that only blank paper showed through the thin foreign envelopes.

The reference to the envelopes is the significant stylistic touch here, humanizing at the very moment of exposé. The work as a whole is distinguished by the fullness of its presentation of documentary evidence through which the various characters speak for themselves, thus revealing the contradictory character of Rolfe without resolving it. Giving the book an added dimension of interest is the fact that some contradictions in Symons's own character also emerge, as in his elaborate narration of his dealings with the eccentric millionaire spy A[rthur] J[ohn] Maundy Gregory to recover lost Rolfe books. Symons maintains a charming ingenuousness both while recounting his obsequious awe of Maundy Gregory's style and resources and while describing himself as overcharging the man for miscellaneous manuscripts.

Unfortunately, after his ascent to literary greatness with *The Quest for Corvo,* Symons failed to complete a biography of the playwright and wit Oscar Wilde or any other major work in the following five years, the last years of his active career. In "An Essay of the Epicure and the Epicurean," which he wrote for a collection called *The Epicure's Anthology* (1934), Symons distinguished the Epicurean, who believes pleasure is the highest good, from the epicure, merely a person who appreciates the pleasures of life. For a sumptuous book with many tipped-in plates celebrating the first hundred books published by the Nonesuch Press, Symons contributed an introductory essay describing two pivotal developments in modern quality bookbinding. Symons credited the designer and poet William Morris with establishing the idea of a press with craftsmanlike standards as something apart from the mere jobbery of a printer. Symons pointed out, however, that it was not until the careful work of John Lane and Charles Elkin Mathews showed the possibility of attractive layout and binding in editions for the general public that the real renaissance in the book trade began. The Nonesuch Press is credited with pioneering the combination of these two forces by using fresh typefaces and finer materials in their editions of classic works at reasonable prices.

In 1936 Symons's wife discovered he was having an affair and divorced him. In 1939 he suffered partial paralysis which eventually brought about his death on 26 August 1941, when he was scarcely into his forties. Doctors were unable to identify the origin of his malady, although the autopsy determined that the cause was a hemangioma of the brain stem.

In 1969 his brother and biographer Julian Symons printed a collection of *Essays and Biographies* by A. J. A. Symons. This volume reprints the essay "Tradition in Biography," the whole of the biography of *Emin, the Governor of Equitoria,* early short biographies of Rolfe and Edgar Allan Poe originally published in *Life and Letters,* and the biography of the novelist Theodore Hook from Leonard Russell's collection *English Wits* (1939). It constitutes the first publication of a biographical study of the religious reformer Edward Irving and of chapters of never-completed books on Wilde and on the family of Tennant of Glenconner.

Biography:

Julian Symons, *A. J. A. Symons: His Life and Speculations* (London: Eyre & Spottiswoode, 1950).

References:

Percy Muir, obituary of A. J. A. Symons, *Times Literary Supplement,* 30 August 1941, p. 422;

Julian Symons and Vyvyan Holland, "A. J. A. Symons, 1900–1941: Two Personal Notes," *Horizon: A Review of Literature and Art,* 4 (1941): 258–264.

Papers:

While the manuscript of *The Quest for Corvo* seems to have been sold by him to an unidentified collector, some of Symons's miscellaneous papers, including letters written and received, corrected galley sheets for the unfinished bibliographies, and corrected manuscripts of shorter published works, are at the Harry Ransom Humanities Research Center, University of Texas at Austin. The New York Public Library, Berg Collection, has some proof sheets for unfinished bibliographies of Oscar Wilde and of the poet Arthur Symons (no relation). The music boxes form the Symons Collection at the Pitt-Rivers Museum, Oxford.

Arthur Symons
(28 February 1865 – 22 January 1945)

Elizabeth Haddrell
Hunter College of the City University of New York

See also the Symons entries in *DLB 19, British Poets, 1880–1914* and *DLB 57, Victorian Writers After 1867.*

BOOKS: *An Introduction to the Study of Browning* (London & New York: Cassell, 1886; revised and enlarged, 1887);

Days and Nights (London & New York: Macmillan, 1889);

Silhouettes (London: Elkin & Mathews & John Lane, 1892; revised and enlarged, London: Smithers, 1896; Portland, Maine: Mosher, 1909);

London Nights (London: Smithers, 1895; London: Smithers / New York: Richmond, 1896; revised, London: Smithers, 1897);

Amoris Victima (London: Smithers, 1897; London: Smithers / New York: Richmond, 1897);

Studies in Two Literatures (London: Smithers, 1897);

Aubrey Beardsley (London: Unicorn Press, 1898; revised and enlarged, London: Dent, 1905);

The Symbolist Movement in Literature (London: Heinemann, 1900; revised, London: Constable, 1908; New York: Dutton, 1908; revised again and enlarged, New York: Dutton, 1919);

Images of Good and Evil (London: Heinemann, 1900);

Poems, two volumes (London: Heinemann, 1901; New York: John Lane, 1902);

Cities (London: Dent / New York: Pott, 1903);

Plays, Acting and Music (London: Duckworth, 1903; revised and enlarged, London: Constable, 1909; New York: Dutton, 1909);

Studies in Prose and Verse (London: Dent, 1904; London: Dent / New York: Dutton, 1904);

Spiritual Adventures (London: Constable, 1905; New York: Dutton, 1905);

A Book of Twenty Songs (London: Dent, 1905);

The Fool of the World & Other Poems (London: Heinemann, 1906; New York: John Lane, 1907);

Studies in Seven Arts (London: Constable, 1906; New York: Dutton, 1906);

Cities of Italy (London: Dent, 1907; New York: Dutton, 1907);

William Blake (London: Constable, 1907; New York: Dutton, 1907);

The Romantic Movement in English Poetry (London: Constable, 1909; New York: Dutton, 1909);

Knave of Hearts, 1894–1908 (London: Heinemann, 1913; New York: John Lane / London: Heinemann, 1913);

Figures of Several Centuries (London: Constable, 1916; New York: Dutton, 1916);

Tragedies (London: Heinemann, 1916; New York: John Lane, 1916);

Tristan and Iseult: A Play in Four Acts (London: Heinemann, 1917; New York: Brentano, 1917);

Cities and Sea-Coasts and Islands (London: Collins, 1918; New York: Brentano, 1919);

Colour Studies in Paris (London: Chapman & Hall, 1918; New York: Dutton, 1918);

The Toy Cart: A Play in Five Acts (Dublin & London: Maunsel, 1919);

Studies in the Elizabethan Drama (New York: Dutton, 1919; London: Heinemann, 1920);

Cesare Borgia, Iseult of Brittany, The Toy Cart (New York: Brentano, 1920);

Charles Baudelaire (London: Elkin Mathews, 1920; New York: Dutton, 1920);

Lesbia and Other Poems (New York: Dutton, 1920);

Love's Cruelty (London: Secker, 1923; New York: Boni, 1924);

Dramatis Personae (Indianapolis: Bobbs-Merrill, 1923; London: Faber & Gwyer, 1925);

The Café Royal and Other Essays (London: Beaumont Press, 1923);

Studies on Modern Painters (New York: Rudge, 1925);

Parisian Nights: A Book of Essays (London: Beaumont Press, 1926);

Notes on Joseph Conrad, With Some Unpublished Letters (London: Myers, 1926);

Arthur Symons (courtesy of Princeton University Press)

Eleonora Duse (London: Elkin Mathews, 1926; New York: Duffield / London: Elkin Mathews & Marrot, 1927);

A Study of Thomas Hardy (London: Sawyer, 1928);

Studies in Strange Souls (London: Sawyer, 1929);

Mes Souvenirs (Chapelle-Réanville, France: Hours Press, 1929);

From Toulouse-Lautrec to Rodin. With Some Personal Recollections (London: John Lane, 1929; New York: King, 1930);

Confessions: A Study in Pathology (New York: Cape & Smith, 1930);

A Study of Oscar Wilde (London: Sawyer, 1930);

Wanderings (London & Toronto: Dent, 1931);

Jezebel Mort and Other Poems (London: Heinemann, 1931);

A Study of Walter Pater (London: Sawyer, 1932);

Amoris Victimia [*sic*] (London: Privately printed, 1940);

The Memoirs of Arthur Symons: Life and Art in the 1890s, edited by Karl Beckson (University Park & London: Pennsylvania State University Press, 1977).

Collection: *The Collected Works of Arthur Symons,* nine volumes (London: Secker, 1924).

OTHER: *Essays by Leigh Hunt,* edited by Symons (London: Walter Scott, 1887);

Philip Massinger, edited by Symons, two volumes (London: Vizetelly, 1887–1889);

The Works of William Shakespeare, edited by Henry Irving and Frank A. Marshall (London: Blackie & Son, 1888–1890) — volumes 4–8 include introductions by Symons;

The Book of the Rhymers' Club (London: Elkin, Mathews, 1892) — includes poems by Symons;

The Second Book of the Rhymers' Club (London: Mathews & John Lane / New York: Dodd, Mead, 1894) — includes poems by Symons;

Charles Baudelaire, *Les Fleurs du mal, Petits Poèmes en prose, Les Paradis artificiels,* translated by Symons (London: Casanova Society, 1925); republished as *Baudelaire: Prose and Poetry* (New York: Boni, 1926).

In a letter dated 24 October 1885 to the author James Dykes Campbell, Arthur Symons wrote, "I like always to trace the course of a man's work in the circumstances of his life – to see, when it is possible to do so, how such a result came from such a cause." Symons is known for his work in the late nineteenth and early twentieth centuries as a translator, playwright, editor, short-story writer, and, most particularly, as a poet. But it was his work as a critic and biographer, tracing the "course of a man's work in the circumstances of his life," that has provided our greatest understanding of fin de siècle literature, particularly in the case of the French symbolists such as Arthur Rimbaud and Paul Verlaine. Though Symons suffered a severe mental breakdown in 1908 which greatly affected the coherence of his future literary output, his body of work remains important in creating a necessary bridge between the Romantic movement and modernism.

Surprisingly, Symons, who in some measure came to exemplify the avant-garde man of letters, came from relatively conservative beginnings. Arthur William Symons was born in Milford Haven, Wales, on 28 February 1865 to the Rev. Mark Symons, a Wesleyan minister, and Lydia Pascoe Symons, the daughter of a prosperous farmer. Reverend Symons's ministerial duties required moves from parish to parish every three years or so. This produced a strong feeling of rootlessness in Symons which led him to write later that he "had never known what it was to have a home, as most children know it." His memories of his father were of a distant man whom he respected but who never truly interested him. Yet the Nonconformist minister did support young Symons in his literary pursuits and even accepted, though not happily, his decision to stop attending church while he was still a teenager. Symons's mother was always discussed in glowing terms by her son. Her spiritual faith was intense, but her "joy of life" was equally strong, and Symons wrote that she was "never indifferent to any moment that ever passed her by." This "joy of life" that his mother possessed fascinated him but at the same time created within him a fear of that other, spiritual world. For it seemed to Symons that embracing the latter would be a "giving up of all that I cared for."

Symons's interest in literature blossomed at an early age. Although he could not read until the age of nine because he "absolutely refused to learn," he had passionate responses to those works which were read to him, despite holding a belief that "a boy must never show any emotion." Once entered into school and forced to take account of the fact that other people existed in the world against whom he would be judged, his literary skills developed with amazing rapidity. He wrote his first poem, "The Lord is Good," at age nine and soon discovered a host of poets including George Gordon, Lord Byron; Henry Wadsworth Longfellow; Algernon Swinburne; Alfred Lord Tennyson; and particularly Robert Browning, all of whose works would serve as models for his earliest poetic endeavors.

After the family moved to Bideford in the West Country in 1879, Symons was enrolled in the High Street Classical and Mathematical School, where he was to meet a young schoolmaster named Charles Churchill Osborne. Only six years older than Symons, he served as a mentor for the young man. Osborne's tenure as a teacher was short-lived, but after he left to pursue a career as a newspaper editor and critic, he and Symons corresponded for the next nine years, and he was instrumental in providing Symons with books, music, and magazine articles not available in the small town of Bideford, which were to help shape his development as a writer.

When Symons's school term ended in June 1882, he wrote to Osborne, telling him that he had decided not to return in the autumn. One of the factors influencing this decision, beyond a desire for a more contemporary course of literary study than the school offered, was undoubtedly Symons's membership in the newly formed Browning Society, which allowed him to "feel a part of the London literary world." He began a correspondence with the society's cofounder, Frederich J. Furnivall, who took an interest in the young man. Furnivall's acceptance in 1884 of a paper Symons submitted to the Browning Society titled "Is Browning Dramatic?" came as most welcome news to Symons, who had spent the past two years "pestering editors with prose & verse, long & short, good & bad . . . and so far had [only] some dozen pieces printed."

Furnivall was suitably impressed with this article and asked Symons (who was engaged at that time in translating French and Italian poetry) to write introductions to "Venus & Adonis" and other works in the edition of Shakespeare Quartos Facsimiles that Furnivall was editing. As noted Symons biographer Karl Beckson writes, these "introductions revealed a talent on the part of this nineteen year old for combining biography, history and criticism in a pleasing striking style."

Symons's first love was poetry, and he was working diligently during these early years to develop his craft, but it was his criticism that was establishing his literary reputation. At the request of Furnivall, Symons wrote a primer on Browning, which was published in 1886 as "An Introduction to the Study of Browning," and this piece garnered favorable reviews. Due in part to the relative fame which the Browning study had brought him, in 1887 Symons was asked to write a biography of his own choosing for the Great Writers series by its editor, Frank Marzials. Symons decided to undertake a study of Nathaniel Hawthorne despite knowing comparatively little about his work or about that period of American literature. When he discovered in August that a biography on Hawthorne was already forthcoming, he dropped the project and decided to write about Edgar Allan Poe instead. This project, too, however, was abandoned the following year when a Poe biography was issued by Lowell and Company.

Symons, still only twenty-one when the Browning primer appeared, expressed concern that he would be viewed thereafter as a critic playing at being a poet. As he wrote to Campbell in 1887, "I do not at all despise prose criticism in general or my own prose criticism in particular, but I wish my life's work to be as far as possible, poetry." This desire began to be realized in 1889 when Symons's first volume of poetry appeared. He dedicated this work, *Days and Nights,* to Walter Pater, whose Renaissance studies had so impressed Symons when he was doing research for the Shakespearean introductions. The critical response was moderately favorable, and Pater himself wrote a glowing review for the *Pall Mall Gazette* (23 March 1889) which concluded "in this new poet the rich poetic vintage of our time has run clear at last." Yet John M. Munro suggests in his 1969 Symons study that "this rich poetic vintage" was really a "rather flavorless watered-down Browning." Despite Symons's desire to be seen as a poet first and foremost, it appears that much of his poetry would be no more than rather pale imitations of those whom he blatantly hero-worshiped; most of his contemporaries agreed that Symons's most vivid writing came through his biographical sketches and critical reviews.

The years following the publication of *Days and Nights* were to be active ones for Symons. Still at work on his critical pieces, he began to travel extensively for the first time in his life. He paid a three-

month visit to Paris with Havelock Ellis, whom Symons had met the previous year. The friendship between the two men was to continue throughout the remainder of their lives, for their seemingly disparate personalities were complementary. During their trip to Paris, Ellis's more practical nature placed him in charge of the day-to-day minutiae, while Symons's letters of introduction provided them with entrée to those figures whom Ellis would have been unable to meet on his own. Symons renewed his acquaintance with Remy de Gourmant, whom he had met the previous year. Among the other literary figures Symons met were Stephane Mallarmé, Leconte de Lisle, Joris-Karl Huysmans, and Verlaine, whose decadent verse and image attracted the young poet in many ways. Verlaine's poetry and life provided Symons with a vision of a "final harmony" which Symons longed for yet was unable to find in his own life.

Upon returning to England in 1890, Symons received a request from James Sutherland Cotton, the editor of the *Academy,* asking him to edit the newspaper while Cotton took a three-week vacation in August. Symons agreed, though with some trepidation, and took rooms in Hampstead with Ernest Rhys so as to be near the offices of the paper. Symons and Rhys moved in the autumn to another house and remained there until Rhys married, leaving Symons "desolate at Hampstead" and determined to move to a more central spot in London.

Through his relationship with Rhys, Symons was introduced to the newly formed Rhymers' Club (also known as the Rhymsters' Club). The membership was comprised primarily of young literary figures with Celtic ties, and Symons, ever conscious of his Welsh birthplace and Cornish forebears, was particularly attracted to this aspect of the club. Although Symons would contribute poetry to the Rhymers' Club anthologies in 1892 and 1894, he was most interested in the personalities involved, and in late 1890 Symons became acquainted with the youthful Celtic literary community, particularly William Butler Yeats, with whom he would have a long friendship.

Following Rhys's marriage in 1891, Symons took rooms in Fountain Court, The Temple, where Havelock Ellis was also to take rooms, and would remain there until his own marriage in 1901. The Temple was in the heart of London, yet Symons termed it an "oasis . . . the quietest spot in all the great city" and a perfect place in which to do the book and music reviews that, along with translations of Rimbaud, Charles Baudelaire, Verlaine,

Portrait of Rhoda Bowser Symons by J.-E. Blanche. Symons married the aspiring actress in January 1901.

and Mallarmé, were taking up the majority of his days. However, his intense desire to be an active participant in life can be discovered in this letter he wrote to his friend Katherine Willard on 20 May 1891, saying "I really like [your brother] very much. What a lot he has gone through – how rich he is in the one thing I for one care to be rich in, manifold experiences. . . . more and more do I care about life, about experiences, less and less about books." This was perhaps a wistful proclamation for one to whom books were, of necessity, the focus of his life.

By 1892 Symons had become the chief reviewer of drama and music-hall programs for the *Star*. His interest in all the arts, and the ballet in particular, made him an especially avid visitor to London entertainments, and his style, which was both literary and scholarly, gave the reviews a flair which had not often been associated with these arts.

The nom de plume which he used for these reviews, Silhouette, lent itself to the title of his second volume of poetry. When *Silhouettes* appeared in 1892, Symons's poetry no longer had a Browningesque air but now showed the influence of the leading French poets of the day, especially Baudelaire and Verlaine, both in the brevity of the poems and in their impressionistic moods.

Symons's attempts to introduce the French currents of decadence and symbolism to the English literary world continued in 1893. He hosted Verlaine when the poet arrived for a series of lectures in England. Symons was to remain a passionate supporter of Verlaine, calling him "the greatest French poet since Baudelaire." As with so many of the literary figures he admired throughout his life, Symons's identification was made manifest in his memoir of the poet, within which was a recollection of Verlaine saying that he dated "all his misfortunes from a woman he met coming out of [the Alhambra]." Perhaps Symons felt that his own later misfortunes could be traced in part to a similar combination of theater and women, for it was at the Empire Theatre in 1893 that Symons made the acquaintance of a ballet dancer named Lydia. Though no last name is known, Symons's relationship with this woman lasted for several years, and perhaps in his writings about her he showed more of his true self than in his writings on any other subject. The sense of sin and sexual perversity which he perceived in their tempestuous relationship both attracted and repelled him, and his third volume of poetry, which, as with all his writings, reflected the influences present in his life, included a series of poems about a woman named Lydia. This volume, titled *London Nights,* was published in 1895 and firmly established his position as one of the leading new poets in London's literary circle.

Poetry could not wholly provide for Symons's economic needs, however, and he continued to pursue other, more lucrative, avenues of expression. In 1896 he was asked to become editor of a newly conceived magazine, which was to be known as the *Savoy.* Symons determined, with backing from his "cynical publisher," Leonard Smithers, to create a literary publication, which far from being sensationalist would instead offer to its readers "good work" from all points of view. As Symons would write in his editorial note, "all art is good which is good art." The *Savoy* proved to be the only truly avant-garde publication of the late nineteenth century. To produce the illustrations for the quarterly magazine, Symons engaged the young artist Aubrey Beardsley, who had recently been fired as art director by the *Yellow Book* due to his professional association with Oscar Wilde. Beardsley had provided the illustrations for Wilde's *Salome* (1894), and Wilde's sensational trial and subsequent imprisonment, which stemmed from his relationship with Lord Alfred Douglas, compromised Beardsley's reputation as well. During its brief existence, the *Savoy* included the works of Joseph Conrad, Ernest Dowson, Ellis, Bernard Shaw, Verlaine, Yeats, and Symons himself. The response to the first issue was generally favorable, although parts were found to be offensive by some critics, particularly Beardsley's prose work, "Under the Hill." But the decision to publish the magazine on a monthly basis instead of quarterly, though made for sound financial reasons, was in part responsible for its eventual downfall.

In August 1896 Symons and Yeats took a vacation in Ireland and the Aran Islands. There Symons caught hold of the mystical pull of the Celtic heritage which he believed to be his birthright. Since a childhood discovery of George Borrows's *Lavengro* (1851), a semi-autobiographical portrait of the author's time with the gypsies, Symons had felt himself drawn to living a presumably free and somewhat magical existence. The time spent in Ireland with Yeats reinforced this feeling in Symons, and Yeats himself was, in this sense, a kindred spirit who reportedly spent some of his time there invoking visions to visit Symons and their hosts in the dead of night. Yeats wrote in a letter to William Sharp in August that, with the invocation of the second spirit, Symons "locked his door to try to keep it out."

Upon Symons's return to England, he completed his latest volume of poetry, *Amoris Victima* (1897), which was fundamentally a response to his estrangement from Lydia. Shortly before she broke with him, Symons's mother had died, and the loss of these two female influences, coming at the same time, intensified his feelings of abandonment and rejection. Aside from his poetry, Symons also brought out in 1897 *Studies in Two Literatures,* which was comprised primarily of essays on some of the leading French and English writers, including William Morris, Christina Rosetti, and Guy de Maupassant, and paid close attention to the decadent and Symbolist movements. Though concentrating on the literature itself, Symons never separated the work from the writer. In his discussion of the poet William Watson, Symons wrote that "in his study of the great writers [he] seems never to have realized that what matters chiefly . . . is not the great phrase but the personality behind the phrase." Symons went on to say of Watson that "[h]e has never put any vital part of himself into his work; he has told us nothing of what he is when he is not a writer."

In 1898 Oscar Wilde was released from prison, and his *The Ballad of Reading Gaol* was reviewed by Symons who offered his belief that the ballad showed an acquaintance with "real things [which] was precisely what was required to bring into relation both with life and art, an extraordinary talent." Coincidentally, given their previous connection, in this same year the always-fragile Beardsley died at the age of twenty-six. Symons wrote an essay which served as an obituary and which was hailed as a masterpiece by Yeats. Symons wrote about Beardsley's life and art, recognizing that he had been one who would "rather have been a great writer than a great artist . . . [and noted] his insistence on describing himself as a man of letters." The manner in which Symons latched on

Symons in 1915 (photograph by Elliott & Fry)

to both Wilde's presumed final understanding of "real things" as well as Beardsley's dissatisfaction with the art he was best known for again points to Symons's need to associate his own thoughts and sentiments with those of the subjects of his critical works.

The next few years were significant for Symons. He began preparation of what was to become perhaps his most important work, *The Symbolist Movement in Literature*. This book, released in 1900 (though 1899 appears on the title page), was Symons's attempt to present a unified theory of the meaning of symbolism and how it was distinct from the earlier strains of decadence. He put this book together, relying primarily on revised articles written earlier for the *Saturday Review* which discussed the life and work of those writers Symons felt deserving of the name symbolists. The changes his mental processes were to undergo subsequent to his breakdown in 1908 can be seen in a later edition of this work, which includes essays about many of those whom Symons had categorically denied were symbolists when the work was first released.

The poets, dramatists, and novelists originally selected by Symons as representative of the Symbolist movement included Mallarmé, Verlaine, Rimbaud, Maurice Maeterlinck, and Huysmans, and the word *symbolism* appears to have had slightly different meaning when applied to each of the men. However, taken as a unifying theory, symbolism could be understood as a movement in which those associated with it were passionately interested in all the arts, fought against the materialistic tradition, and were particularly adept at using evocative, musical language to draw out the submerged emotional understanding of their readers. In these essays Symons seemed especially concerned with including biographical details along with critical analysis. In the case of Rimbaud, whose entire literary career spanned only from his fifteenth to his twenty-first year, his world travels, his varied occupations, and his relationship with Verlaine defined the essence of his artistic being for Symons more than did his poetry. Symons wrote that "[Rimbaud's] influence upon Verlaine was above all the influence of a man of action upon the man of sensation"; here it was the man of action upon whom Symons focused.

It was also during this time that Symons was introduced to Rhoda Bowser, the daughter of a wealthy Newcastle shipbuilder. A friend of Ernest Rhys's sister, she met Symons when he was thirty-four (some nine years older than she). Up until this point, most of his female companionship had come from the ranks of various corps de ballets and the demimonde. Despite their regard for each other, difficulties were apparent in their relationship. Rhoda in particular was concerned about their financial prospects and often warned him about her extravagance. In a letter to Rhoda written shortly before their marriage, Symons begged, "I hope you won't get into debt before you come up: it will really be rather nice if we can both start clear."

On 19 January 1901 Symons and Bowser were married. He left his rooms at Fountain Court, and the couple took up residence in Maida Vale. Almost immediately the money troubles which Rhoda had been expecting began to appear. Rhoda had brought a great deal of money into the marriage, specifically the portion of the family estate that she had inherited when her father passed away soon after her marriage. But the couple had agreed to live on his earnings alone, and Symons was forced to spend much of his time writing reviews and criticism to maintain the lifestyle his wife required.

However, new volumes of Symons's poetry were also appearing with some regularity in the early years of the twentieth century, and Symons was instrumental in bringing other poets' work to the light of day, specifically James Joyce's early collection *Chamber Music* (1907). At the same time, Symons was working on a comprehensive study of the Romantic poets, which was completed in 1908 and published in 1909 as *The Romantic Movement in English Poetry.* Symons's belief in the all-but-unbreakable ties between an artist's life and work can be glimpsed in his preface to this work, where he wrote, "I have tried to get at one thing only: the poet in his poetry, the poetry in the poet; it is the same thing." This work was uneven, with one or two lines being judged sufficient for those whom he characterized as minor, and the format, which had entries placed in chronological order, was unsatisfactory. But Symons's longer biographical studies, including essays on William Blake, Byron, Samuel Taylor Coleridge, John Keats, Percy Bysshe Shelley, William Wordsworth, and Sir Walter Scott, revealed the artists behind the art. Drawing on letters, conversations, and verses, Symons often allowed the poets to speak for themselves, yet never without

his own response to those words. Noting that Byron was convinced that "the great object of life is sensation — to feel that we exist, even though in pain," Symons commented that "Byron was constantly satisfying himself of the latter part of his conviction."

These years were to see the greatest outpouring of Symons's works. In 1903 two volumes appeared: *Cities,* a collection of previously published travel essays; and *Plays, Acting and Music,* put together in large part from reviews written when he served as the drama and music critic for the *Academy.* These were followed in November 1904 by *Studies in Prose and Verse,* which similarly used previously published works. In this volume was included a short study of Hawthorne, which allowed Symons to express some of the opinions which would have been part of the long-abandoned biography. He wrote that "to Hawthorne what we call real life was never very real, and he has given . . . a picture of life as a dream in which the dreamers themselves are, at intervals, conscious that they are dreaming."

Symons's attempts to come to grips with the ambiguity between dreams and reality came in October 1905 when *Spiritual Adventures,* a collection of short fiction, was published. The stories speak primarily to a sense of isolation often resulting in madness, which had been a common theme in much of his earlier writing. Symons wrote in this volume, "I wanted to write books for the sake of writing books; it was food for my ambition, and it gave me something to do when I was alone, apart from other people. It helped to raise another barrier between me and other people." Symons appears to have had another reason for writing these stories apart from raising the barriers he saw between himself and the rest of the world. As he would say in his introduction to the *The Romantic Movement in English Poetry,* "It is . . . in prose that men confess themselves, with minute fidelity. . . . All the best fiction, narrative or dramatic, is a form of confession, personal or vicarious; and, in a sense, it is all personal."

Symons was highly prolific throughout 1907; almost forty reviews and articles were published. He was also hard at work completing what would become a major study of William Blake, an important piece of research that revealed, as Beckson has noted, "Symons's Paterian belief that scholarship was as important to the impressionistic critic as a cultivated sensibility." In Symons's preface he noted that the second part of the biography included "every personal account of Blake which was printed during his lifetime, and between the time of his death and the publication of [Alexander]

Gilchrist's *Life* in 1863 . . . not correcting their errors, for even errors have their value as evidence." This critical biography went further than Yeats and Edwin Ellis's 1893 two-volume discussion of Blake's mythology and symbolism (*The Works of William Blake: Poetic, Symbolic and Critical*), and followed the French symbolists' belief in the transcendence of art over poetic technique. Much of Blake's artistry lay in what Symons believed was an abnormal sanity. That Blake saw visions and that he believed his poetry was often dictation, "under the direction of messengers from heaven," was part of his desire "to question that imagination which he knew to be more real than the reality of nature."

Despite this productivity, Symons's personal life was showing strains. In December the Symons's dog, Api, died at the age of one year. To the childless couple, Api had been something of a surrogate child who connected Symons to humanity by "at least one link of friendship," and his death caused both Symons and his wife a considerable amount of grief. Added to this loss, money worries were building. The couple had purchased a new home, Island Cottage, in Wittersham, in 1906, and repairs to this seventeenth-century timbered cottage brought a great deal of financial hardship. Indeed, at one point Rhoda sent a letter to Julia Marlowe in which she noted that they had only eighteen pounds in the bank and nothing coming in.

The year 1908 began in much the same way, but despite their lack of ready cash, the Symonses borrowed money in order to take a trip to Italy and France in the middle of the year. The work that Symons did during this time showed the increasing incoherence of his thoughts, and the last piece written before his breakdown was to show a strangely prescient notion of the ordeals that were soon to come. This article, a travel essay on Venice which would be published in the *Saturday Review* on 17 October 1908, contained a passage about the dungeons under the Bridge of Sighs and evoked the plight of doomed men imprisoned in those dungeons, who were destined to eke out the remainder of their days in chains, water lapping at their feet, suffering agonies with no hope of reprieve.

On 26 September 1908 Symons left Rhoda alone in Venice and went off to Bologna, but after some frantic searching, Rhoda appeared at his hotel the next day. In a rambling and all but illegible letter to his friend, the novelist Edward Hutton, Symons wrote that he and Rhoda had spent the week in Bologna quarreling and that she was, happily, on her way back to England, but that he was lonely. Symons went alone to Ferrara and wandered aim-

lessly. He soon began to exhibit signs of madness and was taken by the local magistrates, imprisoned, and placed in manacles in what he termed a dungeon. Symons was not released until Rhoda had located him with help from the Italian ambassador in London and arranged for her husband to be brought home. On 2 November he was certified insane and committed to Brooke House in East London.

The earliest medical reports offered no hope of recovery, and the doctors informed Rhoda that at best she could hope for an eighteen-month life expectancy for her husband. In 1909 Symons developed a severe case of pneumonia, but he recovered from this and, against all expectations, began to show some signs of mental recovery as well and was moved out of the hospital to a residence in Hampstead, though he was to remain under a doctor's care. In 1910 Rhoda arranged for his return to Island Cottage and enlisted Edmund Gosse's aid in obtaining a grant from the Royal Literary Fund and the Civil List Pension of 120 pounds. This was accepted, though, with some resentfulness since Yeats had already been awarded a grant that was thirty pounds a year higher.

Back at Island Cottage, Symons, whose mental faculties were showing a marked improvement, made the acquaintance of Joseph Conrad, who had recently moved to Kent, not far from Symons's home. Before the ill-fated trip to Venice, Symons had written a study of Conrad's works, seeing in his writing a mysterious sensibility. This pleased Conrad for the most part, although Symons's evaluation of a dark side in Conrad's work which delighted in evil and blood was disturbing; when this study was reprinted, Symons would remove the offending sections. Symons and Conrad were to become friends, but never particularly close, and the trend toward isolation would become increasingly clear in the years to follow. Even Yeats, who as Rhoda later would bitterly note had "begged for a winter's home with him in the Temple . . . when he was homeless – & who often enough came in the early days of our marriage, to ask A[rthur] if a certain line scanned" began to "studiously avoid meeting him." Yeats did visit Symons occasionally after 1908 but believed that Rhoda was the major cause of Symons's breakdown and neither wanted to spend time with her nor with his erstwhile friend, whose altered mental state saddened him. Symons himself sought other causes for the breakdown, attributing it in large part to the sudden death of Api.

Feeling the strain of day-to-day existence with Symons, Rhoda embarked upon a long-dreamed-of

Symons at his home, Island Cottage, Wittersham, Kent

acting career, while Symons attempted to return to his earlier level of writing. Several major essay collections were published at this time, *Figures of Several Centuries* (1916), *Cities and Sea-Coasts and Islands* (1918), and *Colour Studies in Paris* (1918). All three works consisted of material which had appeared earlier in papers and periodicals, but their publication did serve to keep Symons's name in the public eye in addition to bringing in some much needed money. With the backing of John Quinn, an American lawyer and noted patron of the arts, Symons was successful in seeing some new poetry published in *Vanity Fair,* but as early as 1917 Quinn was beginning to express dissatisfaction with the amount of money he was sending to Symons.

In January 1920 Symons wrote to Quinn, saying that Rhoda had determined to sell Island Cottage. He expressed some fears that in the "unlikely" recurrence of madness "there would be nowhere for [him] to go," and noted that his life had been "absolutely saved" by returning to the cottage after "those unutterable horrors he had undergone."

In May 1919 Symons published *Studies in the Elizabethan Drama,* a collection of new essays along with the Shakespearean introductions which had first appeared in the 1880s. This volume, thanks in part to a glowing two-part review by T. S. Eliot, was a great success. With money from Quinn, Symons and his wife followed this with a visit to Paris to renew old acquaintanceships, and here Symons began work on *Confessions: A Study in Pathology* (1930), which charted the course of his breakdown and the events of the years which followed. *Confessions* included biographical sketches of many of those whom Symons called friends. A short article on Quinn appears, but it was tinged with some hostility as Quinn had by this time had enough with Symons's requests for money.

While his wife continued to pursue her theatrical career, Symons went on a visit to Cornwall, staying first with Ellis. Symons's mental state was noticeably improved by the publication of the first nine volumes of a proposed sixteen-volume edition of his collected works. But Symons remained in what was in effect both physical and literary seclusion, and it was soon apparent that his new works would never contain the insight or reach the standards of his old writings. When a biographical study of Eleonora Duse was published in 1926, it showed clearly the level to which his writing ability had sunk. The book was a mismatched pastiche, combining old and new writing on Duse, as well as many irrelevant sections. This would be typical of all of his new works, both poetry and prose, throughout the remainder of his life.

By this time, Rhoda's brief theatrical career had ended, due in part to her worsening health. She finally succumbed to leukemia on 3 November 1936. Symons was left in the care of the couple's housekeeper, Bessie Seymour, who had also seen to Rhoda during the final stages of her illness. When World War II began, Seymour took Symons to stay with her in London to keep him safe from the threat of coastal invasion. He returned alone to Island Cottage in 1944, where he died on 22 January 1945.

When the Symons obituary was printed in the *New Statesman and Nation* (17 February 1945), it noted that he had died "physically, officially, notifiably," and the implication was that the true Arthur Symons had "passed away" long ago. The contributions of those writers associated with the aesthetic movement had long been ignored, and Symons was grouped with those whose works were considered to have little bearing on the concerns of the day. Yet in Ruth Z. Temple's study *The Critic's Alchemy* (1953), Frank Kermode's *Romantic Image* (1957), and John M. Munro's critical study *Arthur Symons* (1969) there are suggestions that modernism could not have come into existence without the literary forces of the late nineteenth century that Symons was a part of and helped to bring to public attention.

Karl Beckson wrote that "above all, [Symons] cherished the mystery of human personality and art, and he professed that the creative process could never be explained." But it was his lifelong attempt to explain this process through his writing, particularly in his biographical work and in his criticism, that earns Symons his place in literary history.

Letters:

Karl Beckson and John M. Munro, "Letters from Arthur Symons to James Joyce, 1904–1932," *James Joyce Quarterly,* 4 (Winter 1967): 91–101;

Bruce Morris, "Arthur Symons's Letters to W. B. Yeats," in *Yeats Annual No. 5,* edited by Warwick Gould (London: Macmillan, 1987), pp. 46–61.

Beckson and Munro, *Arthur Symons: Selected Letters, 1880–1885* (Iowa City: University of Iowa Press, 1989);

Bibliographies:

Carol Simpson Stern, "Arthur Symons: An Annotated Bibliography of Writings about Him," *English Literature in Transition,* 17, no. 2 (1974): 77–133;

Karl Beckson, Ian Fletcher, Lawrence W. Markert, and John Stokes, *Arthur Symons: A Bibliography* (Greensboro, N.C.: ELT Press, 1990).

Biographies:

Roger Lhombreaud, *Arthur Symons: A Critical Biography* (London: Unicorn Press, 1963);

Karl Beckson, *Arthur Symons: A Life* (Oxford: Clarendon Press / New York: Oxford University Press, 1987).

References:

Anna Balakian, *The Symbolist Movement* (New York: Random House, 1967);

Karl Beckson, "The Critic and the Actress: The Troubled Lives of Arthur and Rhoda Symons," *Columbia Library Columns,* 33 (November 1983): 3–10;

Beckson, "Symons' 'A Prelude to Life,' Joyce's *A Portrait,* and the Religion of Art," *James Joyce Quarterly,* 15 (Spring 1978): 222–228;

Beckson and John M. Munro, "Symons, Browning, and the Development of the Modern Aesthetic," *Studies in English Literature,* 10 (Autumn 1970): 687–699;

Barbara Charlesworth, *Dark Passages: The Decadent Consciousness in Victorian Literature* (Madison: University of Wisconsin Press, 1965);

Patricia Clements, "Symons: The Great Problem," in her *Baudelaire and the English Tradition* (Princeton: Princeton University Press, 1985), pp. 184–217;

Richard Ellmann, "Discovering Symbolism," in his *Golden Codgers: Biographical Speculations* (New York & London: Oxford University Press, 1973);

Ellmann, "Introduction" to Symons's *The Symbolist Movement in Literature* (New York: Dutton, 1958);

Ian Fletcher, "Explorations and Recoveries – II: Symons, Yeats and the Demonic Dance," *London Magazine,* 7 (June 1960): 46–60;

Frank Kermode, "Poet and Dancer Before Diaghilev," *Partisan Review,* 28 (January–February 1961): 48–75;

Kermode, *Romantic Image* (London: Routledge & Kegan Paul, 1957);

Bruce Morris, "Elaborate Form: Symons, Yeats, and Mallarmé," in *Yeats: An Annual of Critical and Textual Studies,* edited by Richard Finneran (Ann Arbor: UMI Research Press, 1986), pp. 99–119;

John M. Munro, *Arthur Symons* (New York: Twayne, 1969);

Munro, "Arthur Symons and W. B. Yeats: The Quest for Compromise," *Dalhousie Review,* 45 (Summer 1965): 137–152;

Ruth Z. Temple, *The Critic's Alchemy: A Study of the Introduction of French Symbolism into England* (New York: Twayne, 1953);

R. K. R. Thornton, *The Decadent Dilemma* (London: Arnold, 1983);

T. Earle Welby, *Arthur Symons: A Critical Study* (New York: Adelphi, 1925);

Katherine Worth, *The Irish Drama of Europe from Yeats to Beckett* (Atlantic Highlands, N. J.: Humanities Press, 1978);

W. B. Yeats, *The Letters of W. B. Yeats* (New York: Macmillan, 1955);

Yeats, "The Tragic Generation," in *The Autobiography of William Butler Yeats* (New York: Macmillan, 1938).

Papers:

The largest collection of Symons's letters and literary manuscripts is at Princeton University. Columbia University has more than two thousand letters, consisting of Arthur and Rhoda Symons's exchanges. Less extensive holdings are at the British Library, the Bodleian Library (Oxford), the New York Public Library, and the libraries of Harvard University, Queen's University (Kingston, Ontario), University of Iowa, University of Arizona, Northwestern University, Yale University, and the University of Texas at Austin.

Mona Wilson
(1872 – 26 October 1954)

Margaret Carter
Bradley University

BOOKS: *The Story of Rosalind, Retold from Her Diary*,
as Monica Moore (London: Sidgwick & Jackson, 1910);

These Were Muses (London: Sidgwick & Jackson, 1924);

The Life of William Blake (London: Nonesuch Press, 1927; revised and enlarged edition, London: Hart-Davis, 1948);

Sir Philip Sidney (London: Duckworth, 1931);

Queen Elizabeth (London: Davies, 1932);

Queen Victoria (London: Davies, 1933);

Jane Austen and Some Contemporaries (London: Cresset, 1938; Port Washington, N.Y.: Kennikat, 1966).

OTHER: *Our Industrial Laws: Working Women in Factories, Workshops, Shops, and Laundries, and How to Help Them,* edited by Wilson (London: Duckworth, 1899);

Sir Philip Sidney, *Astrophel and Stella,* edited by Wilson (London: Duckworth, 1931);

"Travel and Holidays in Early Victorian England," in *Victorian England 1830–1865,* 2 volumes, edited by G. M. Young (London: Oxford University Press, 1934), pp. 282–313;

Samuel Johnson, *Johnson, Prose and Poetry,* edited by Wilson (London: Hart-Davis, 1950).

Mona Wilson began her twenty-six-year career as a literary biographer after retiring from a distinguished career in government service. Her choice of subjects, ranging in time from the sixteenth century to the early nineteenth century, reflects the breadth and depth of her literary and scholarly interests. Her purpose was to bring new evidence and appreciation to bear upon the lives and works of English writers who were misunderstood, neglected, or even unknown. Wilson's major biographies of William Blake and Sir Philip Sidney are notable for their emendations of earlier studies; and her biographical studies of little-known eighteenth-century women writers brought them to the attention of both general readers and literary scholars.

Born in 1872 in Clifton, just south of Nottingham, England, Mona Wilson was the eldest daughter of the Reverend James Maurice Wilson, D.D., headmaster of Clifton and later canon of Worcester. She attended Clifton High School and Saint Leonard's School in Saint Andrews. In 1892 she entered Newnham College, Cambridge. After completing her studies, she moved to Manchester, where her father had recently been appointed archdeacon. Her investigations into labor and social conditions in the industrial north soon attracted the attention of women prominent in the fight for better conditions for working women.

In recognition of her efforts to reform working conditions, Wilson was appointed secretary of the Women's Trade Union League. She was also appointed, under the Trade Board Act, to the chain-making and paper-box-making trade boards. In 1904, as a member of the Home Office Departmental Committee on industrial accidents, she undertook exhaustive studies of social and industrial conditions in West Ham and Dundee.

From 1912 to 1917 Wilson was the sole woman member of the National Health Insurance Commissioners, earning the highest salary then paid to any woman in state employment. At the end of her seven-year term, Wilson retired from her career in public administration and settled in Marlborough. She served as a member of the Industrial Fatigue Research Board from 1917 to 1929 and as a justice of the peace for many years; however, for the remainder of her life she devoted the greater part of her energies to literary scholarship and publication.

When Wilson retired, she was already a practiced writer with several publications, including a short novel written under the pseudonym of Monica Moore which had been published in 1910. Titled *The Story of Rosalind, Retold from Her Diary,* the novel reflects Wilson's interest in biography and narrative techniques, particularly point of view and plot manipulation. Rosalind's story is narrated by her uncle, to whom she had given her diary shortly before her fatal riding accident. Quoting extensively from her diary, the narrator gives a touching account of the young woman's struggle to pursue a career in social work, her broken love affair and emotional breakdown, and her marriage to a Sussex farmer. She remains a restless and haunted woman, whose fall from her galloping horse may have been her means of joining her recently deceased young son.

The Story of Rosalind was Wilson's only published novel, but her interest in narrative led to her first literary biography, published in 1924. *These Were Muses* is a brief introduction to the works of nine eighteenth-century women writers whose renown, according to Wilson's preface, "has faded or in the case of Sara Coleridge, remained unfulfilled." Wilson explains that her book is intended for the "curious general reader," and its contents reflect her enthusiastic efforts to introduce her readers to women's writing. She gives brief biographical sketches of her subjects, including Susannah Centlivre, a playwright; Charlotte Lennox, author of *The Female Quixote* (1752) and editor of a women's magazine; Frances Chamberlaine Sheridan, writer of plays and novels and the mother of the playwright Richard Brinsley Sheridan; Hester Mulso Chapone, author of *Letters on the Improvement of the Mind* (1773); Sydney Morgan, famous for *The Wild Irish Girl* (1806); Frances Trollope, referred to as the "now forgotten" author of over a hundred volumes of fiction and travel; and Sara Coleridge, daughter of Samuel Taylor Coleridge and author of *Phantasmion* (1837), a verse fairy tale based on her life. To encourage reader interest, Wilson quotes extensively from each woman's works.

Wilson's first major biography, *The Life of William Blake,* was published in 1927, the centenary of the poet's death. The work was hailed as a valuable supplement to Alexander Gilchrist's biography of Blake, written in 1863 and revised in 1880. In her extensive research into newly available diaries and correspondence, Wilson uncovered evidence that either questioned or effectively disproved inaccuracies in the Gilchrist biography. One of her primary objectives was to disprove Blake's insanity, which she believed many readers used to discredit his prophetic books. Proof of his essential sanity is presented in extensive quotations from his personal correspondence and in documents discrediting the myth of his confinement in Bedlam.

Wilson's biography is an ambitious attempt to interrelate Blake's activities as lyric poet, mystic, and artist. Its epigram, "Because he kept the Divine Vision in time of trouble," reflects her sympathetic view of Blake as a "true mystic" who remained committed to the restoration of the visionary imagination in life and art. Although she finds that Blake's

powerful visionary faculty caused his symbolic works to be at times impenetrable, she disagrees with those critics who argue that Blake's mysticism slowly stifled his poetic genius. She contends that Blake instinctively made the wisest use of this power, dividing it among his poetry and painting, his designing and engraving. Furthermore, she believes that if Blake had repressed his visionary imagination, his mind might have become unbalanced.

In tracing Blake's development as a poet and artist, Wilson uses the stages of the Mystic Way described in J. Foster Damon's *William Blake, His Philosophy and Symbols* (1924). She connects Blake's early visionary experiences with what Damon calls the conversion stage, in which occurs a visionary intuition of the Eternal. She traces possible sources for his early visions, including his long hours sketching the Gothic sculpture in Westminster Abbey and other London churches. Wilson places Blake's early poetry in the conversion stage, assessing his *Poetical Sketches* (1783) and *Songs of Innocence* (1789) as the work of a young man whose visionary powers enabled him to live for brief moments in an ideal world. Describing his poetic images as mental pictures seen "in a flash," she cautions readers not to base their interpretations of his lyric poetry upon his later symbolic works. Yet she allows that some of the early poems become clear only in the light of later symbolic references.

Wilson relates Blake's personal and artistic life during his middle years to Damon's second and third stages of the Mystic Way. She believes that his mental suffering while writing the symbolic poems from approximately 1790 to 1800 can be connected with the purgation stage, a period of guilt over not sustaining the original visionary state. During these years, known as his Lambeth Period, Blake began to develop symbolic structures to portray the division between reason and inspiration that he was struggling to transcend in his art, his poetry, and his personal life. Although these were the years of Blake's greatest prosperity and productivity, he suffered from mental fatigue and self-isolation.

Yet during the Lambeth years and even more during the following three years in Felpham, Blake experienced occasions of true harmony. Wilson identifies these as the illumination stage, in which a renewal of the visionary faculties occurs. She shows that Blake's illumination came in the form of rebellion against established religion, morality, and art. Wilson connects Blake's regenerated visionary life with his sense of victory over two perceived enemies of his freedom. The first victory was his rejec-

THE LIFE OF WILLIAM
BLAKE
BY MONA WILSON

*"Because he kept the Divine Vision
in time of trouble"*

THE NONESUCH PRESS
16 GREAT JAMES STREET LONDON

MCMXXVII

WILLIAM BLAKE AT HAMPSTEAD

*Frontispiece and title page for Wilson's biography of the visionary British Romantic poet and artist. Wilson used newly available diaries
and correspondence to correct inaccuracies in Alexander Gilchrist's* Life of William Blake *(1863; enlarged 1880).*

tion of his possessive Felpham mentor, William Hayley, from whose employ he returned to London. The second victory was his acquittal from charges of sedition resulting from his altercation with an English soldier. Wilson concludes that during the divisive Lambeth and Felpham years, Blake was eliminating the ideas and forms that were foreign to his genius.

According to Wilson, Blake's final twenty years can be described as the unitive life, the last stage of the Mystic Way. With his intellectual and visionary powers harmoniously integrated, he completed the prophetic books and produced his finest drawings and engravings. Wilson calls *Milton* (1804 [i.e., 1808?]) the most personal of Blake's prophetic books, in which his own struggle to achieve visionary knowledge is symbolized in Milton's quest for spiritual knowledge. Praising Blake's last symbolic poem, *Jerusalem* (1804 [i.e., 1820?]), as an uncompromising rejection of conventional standards, she speculates that its defects resulted from the poet's advanced age and lack of sympathetic readers.

Wilson gives a particularly sensitive account of Blake's last fifteen years, during which he was surrounded by young artists who admired his drawings and engravings but did not know his poetry. They included him in their club, the Ancients, and sought his advice on their work. She shows that, although he was aware that they had not read his prophetic books, he was happy in their company and absorbed in illustrating Dante's *Divine Comedy*. He continued to work on his drawings until his final brief illness. He died on 12 August 1827. As a final note on Blake's death, Wilson quotes his friend Samuel Palmer's observation, "If asked whether I ever knew, among the intellectual a happy man, Blake would be the only one who would immediately occur to me."

Throughout her account of Blake's life, Wilson's objective is to provide a sympathetic, but accurate, assessment of his poetry and art. To encourage reading of the symbolic works, she provides extensive paraphrases of significant passages. She warns that Blake must be read with one's specter and emanation united (Blake's terms for reason and imagination), or one will reproduce Blake's doctrines in a distorted form. To acquaint readers with Blake's drawing and engraving, she provides detailed accounts of his works. Calling him a great imaginative painter of figures in watercolor, she cites the originality of his inventions and the brilliance, subtlety, and opalescence of the coloring.

Wilson concludes that, although Blake's artwork is blemished by haste and crowded vision, his genius is easier to recognize in his art than in his writings. She praises him for guarding his inspiration until the end of his life, pointing to his sketches for the Book of Job as proof. Agreeing with others who have found a sympathy of thought between Percy Bysshe Shelley and Blake, Wilson speculates that Shelley was the young poet of a new poetic age for whom Blake had looked in vain. If they had known each other, Shelley might have inspired the older poet to continue writing poetry. Yet in her final analysis Wilson finds that Blake's genius "of its very nature stands aloof and solitary."

Wilson's biography received praise for its sound scholarship and its sympathetic, but rational, approach to Blake's life, beliefs, and artistic productions. B. R. Redman of the *Saturday Review of Literature* (8 July 1950) found that Wilson was "more interested in getting at the truth about Blake and in elucidating his ideas and intentions than in spinning ingenious dubious theories of her own." The *Manchester Guardian* (21 January 1949) commended Wilson's sensitive treatment of the poet's works: "[She] neither distorts his doctrines nor involves herself unduly in the symbolic complexities of his Prophetic Books." All of the reviews welcomed Wilson's valuable contributions to Blakean scholarship. Although the *Chicago Sunday Tribune* (16 July 1950) reviewer Edward Barry did not feel that Wilson had succeeded in "bringing the poet to life," he noted the enormous amount of minute information that she had packed into the text and appendixes. Kathleen Raine in the *New Statesman and Nation* (5 February 1949) wrote that Wilson had done "great service to scholarship by her thorough winnowing of some of the damaging legends that have grown up around the great visionary."

Wilson published her next biography, *Sir Philip Sidney*, in 1931. Again her objective was to interest readers in her subject's neglected literary works, particularly the sonnet cycle *Astrophel and Stella*, written circa 1582 and published in 1591. Spurred by the 1926 publication of the first complete edition of Sidney's works and personal letters, Wilson undertook a historically accurate account of Sidney's brief life and contributions to the development of Elizabethan literature. Also among her valuable primary sources were Sir Fulke Greville's

1652 account of Sidney and the 1926 release of the Penshurst archives, which shed light on the Sidney family's finances.

Wilson's succinct narrative of Sidney's life emphasizes the contrast between his unrealized political aspirations and his successful literary accomplishments. Wilson contends that a secret antagonism existed between Sidney and Queen Elizabeth I, caused by the queen's resentment of his intellectual and moral rigor. She recounts how Sidney prepared for the position of courtier and statesman by attending Oxford and completing a three-year Continental tour, during which he made several important friends, including the French scholar-diplomat Hubert Languet. Yet upon his return to England, the twenty-three-year-old Sidney was disappointed in his efforts to win an important appointment at court. Elizabeth made him her ambassador to the funeral of Emperor Maximilian but then refused to pursue Sidney's carefully made diplomatic connections with Protestant German princes. Wilson speculates that the queen was suspicious of Sidney's foreign friendships and political projects.

Wilson contends that Sidney's brief, but significant, literary career flourished because his political aspirations were dashed. Frustrated by lack of money and the queen's political intrigues, he spent considerable time away from court with leading young poets of the day, most notably Edmund Spenser and Edward Dyer. They respected his assimilation of Italian Renaissance culture and were eager to follow his leadership in modernizing English poetry, which had seen little development in the last fifty years. Wilson credits Sidney with realizing that the time was right for poetic experiment. She contends that the considerable volume of work in his ten-year literary career should be measured less by its stature than by its development.

Wilson gives a balanced assessment of Sidney's first work, the pastoral romance *Arcadia*, completed in 1581. She calls the poems significant for showing how Italian prosody could be reproduced in English but considers the highly ornamented prose style regrettable. She contends that if Sidney had followed his natural bent for terse, lucid prose, he might have set the same standard for English prose as his poems set for English poetry. Wilson shows the breadth of her literary scholarship in her evaluation of Sidney's final two major works, *Defence of Poesie,* written in 1579–1580, and *Astrophel and Stella*. She compares the *Defence* with similar works by Blake and Shelley, finding that, like theirs, Sidney's defense of poetry is essentially a defense of the imaginative life. Wilson says that the originality of Sidney's work lies in his enthusiastic belief in poetic inspiration and his appeal for imaginative expression. Wilson uses historical evidence to argue that the *Astrophel and Stella* sonnet sequence is the record of Sidney's love for Penelope Devereux. She contends that to think otherwise is to credit Sidney with a dramatic art beyond his years. Tracing parallels between events in Sidney's life and the experiences of Astrophel, Wilson reasons that Devereux's engagement to Lord Rich caused the poet's emotional crisis and that the sequence concluded when Sidney married Frances Walsingham in 1582. Wilson believes that the sonnets reveal the voice of a sustained poetic genius, but she concedes that they contain an unreconciled duality of ornamental excess and dignified spontaneity.

Wilson concludes her account of Sidney's life with brief accounts of his service in the House of Commons, his failed negotiations with Sir Francis Drake to establish an English naval base in Spanish America, and his final ill-fated political and military campaign in the Netherlands. She explains Queen Elizabeth's complicated strategy for using the Low Countries as bargaining chips in her war of nerves against the Spanish monarchy and for appointing Sidney governor of one of the coastal towns. Wilson describes the frustrating conditions under which Sidney tried to carry out his leadership of a small force of underpaid, poorly fed, and ill-trained men. He was under orders to the vacillating Robert Dudley, first Earl of Leicester, who refused to initiate an offensive; and he was forbidden permission to return to England when his father, and then later his mother, died. He eventually succeeded in capturing a strategic coastal town, but in the siege of Zutphen he was wounded. Despite the doctors' early optimism, Sidney grew steadily worse and died several days later at age thirty-two.

Wilson follows up the account of Sidney's death with details about the financial problems that caused a three-month delay of his burial. She gives a moving description of the funeral — "memorable for its solemn splendour even in an age when every funeral was a pageant" — and the deep mourning of the English and Dutch, who felt that his life had been uselessly sacrificed. The biography concludes with an eloquent eulogy for Sidney as the epitome of the golden age of young English manhood.

The reviewers praised Wilson's straightforward yet sensitive handling of Sidney's biography. The *Christian Science Monitor* (18 June 1932) said that she had "fashioned a convincing and life-like portrait not by the addition of picturesque details from her imaginative conception of the man but by let-

ting the facts speak for themselves." Herbert Gorman, in the *New York Times* (1 May 1932), called the book "charming," remarking that Wilson's account of Sidney's last year and his death was told "simply and movingly." J. D. Wilson, in the *Spectator* (23 May 1931), observed that "the documents are allowed to speak for themselves, with never a trace of sentimentality. . . . The artist's hand, however, is revealed in the planning and the presentment of facts." The *Times Literary Supplement* (7 May 1931) found that "something more than knowledge went to the making of the last paragraph of this excellent book."

In 1932 Wilson was made an associate of Newnham College, Cambridge. In 1932–1933 she wrote two biographies for the Short Biographies series published by Peter Davies and intended for the general reader. The first, *Queen Elizabeth* (1932), is an accurate outline of the main events in the monarch's life. In the preface Wilson explains that she makes no claim to originality, but only to "a truthful and discriminating use of my material." The reviewer for the *Times Literary Supplement* (21 July 1932) praised the biography as a "bright and well-planned narrative" and concluded that Wilson had succeeded in recalling "the high purpose and vivid personality of the great Queen."

In the preface to the second biography, *Queen Victoria* (1933), Wilson refers to the "alluring challenge" of comparing Victoria and Elizabeth. Her method is again highly selective with emphasis placed upon those events which, according to Wilson, seem "to throw the most light on [Victoria's] character, methods and influence as a constitutional monarch." The work provides an illuminating contrast between Queen Victoria's early reign with her consort Prince Albert and her reign after his death. In the former Victoria leaned upon her husband to oversee the country. Wilson quotes extensively from the queen's letters to show that as a wife and mother of seven children she found the monarchy a difficult and, at times, distasteful burden. After her husband's death, according to Wilson, the queen was in many ways hard and unsympathetic, but she was committed to the punctual discharge of her duties as she understood them. Wilson concludes that during the forty years of Victoria's widowhood, the English people developed for her a reverence and affection that transformed the English monarchy "from a political institution to a habit of feeling."

The *Times Literary Supplement* (12 October 1933) did not find Wilson's biography of Queen Victoria as satisfactory as her biography of Queen Elizabeth. Although the review acknowledged Wilson's reputation for shrewd judgment and thorough scholarship, it argued that she had failed to give the queen sufficient credit for native intelligence and political common sense. The reviewer did, however, commend the biography's unsentimental style.

In 1938 Wilson returned to her favorite literary period with *Jane Austen and Some Contemporaries*. In this collection of essays, Wilson's focus is upon the childhood and education of eight late-eighteenth-century women based upon their own accounts. In the preface Wilson explains that her purpose is to present these women as models of intellectual achievement for the enlightenment of contemporary feminists. She advises the latter to exchange their militant espousal of women's rights for rational acceptance of their sexual differences but right to equality. The women selected by Wilson, including Austen, Eliza Fletcher, and Harriet Grote, possessed intelligent and independent minds and achieved public notice for their intellectual accomplishments. Wilson shows that these women refused to conform to social expectations; rather, they followed the bent of their particular genius, believing in a woman's right to the full development of her personality.

Wilson provides a provocative analysis of the causes for these women's successes. She says that they were able to acquire the freedom for self-development and intellectual accomplishments either due to an iron will, an indomitable personality, or the "sheer, quiet impulsion of genius." She describes the crucial elements of their education: in-

stead of being sent to finishing schools to be trained as "young ladies," they were allowed to associate with well-educated adults and to "run wild," that is, to pursue their own interests. The reviewer for the *Times Literary Supplement* (9 July 1938) called *Jane Austen and Some Contemporaries* a "fascinating study," commenting that Wilson had been "particularly successful in welding together a book about diverse personalities into a comprehensive whole."

In 1950 Wilson returned to her interest in eighteenth-century literature by producing an anthology of Samuel Johnson's work, *Johnson, Prose and Poetry*. The *Times Literary Supplement* (6 April 1951) called it a book "for which the lover of Johnson may be grateful; one, moreover, likely to make more lovers of Johnson." The Johnson anthology was Wilson's last publication. She died on 26 October 1954 at her home in Oare, Wiltshire. Her obituary in the London *Times* (30 October 1954) noted with what would surely have struck her as ironic praise that she "combined to a degree unusual in men and rare in women a talent for practical administration and for literature." In her dual careers Wilson was dedicated to improving women's working conditions and to rediscovering women writers. Through her revision and reassessment of the literary careers of misunderstood or neglected male and female writers she has enlightened both the general reader and the literary scholar. Her works are noteworthy for their sound historical and literary scholarship, their clear and graceful style, and their pleasant sense of humor.

Appendix

Sir Sidney Lee, "Principles of Biography," in his *Elizabethan and Other Essays* (Oxford: Clarendon Press, 1929): pp. 31–57;

Lytton Strachey, Preface to *Eminent Victorians* (London: Chatto & Windus, 1918);

Harold Nicolson, "The Practice of Biography," in his *The English Sense of Humour* (London: Constable, 1968): pp. 145–159;

Virginia Woolf, "The New Biography," in her *Granite and Rainbow* (New York: Harcourt, Brace, 1958): pp.149–155.

Sir Sidney Lee, "Principles of Biography," in *Elizabethan and Other Essays*

I

I appreciate very highly the honour which the electors have done me in conferring on me the office of Leslie Stephen Lecturer in this University. A word of respectful admiration seems due to the liberality of the electors in bestowing this dignity for the second time in succession on a graduate of the sister University.

I propose to deal broadly with a very familiar ambition – the ambition to record in written words, on the printed page, the career of a man or woman. My design is to consider in the first place the essential quality of the theme which justly merits biographic effort, and in the second place to discuss the methods of presentment which are likely to serve the true purpose of biography to best effect. Some paths which the biographer should avoid will also call for notice. I hope to suggest causes of success or failure in the practice of biography.

II

It is outside my scope to deal in any detail with the biography of particular persons. But I think I may without impropriety venture at the outset on a few words about the man in whose memory this lectureship has been founded, and whose name it bears. I am conscious that I lack many of the qualifications which my two predecessors in this honourable office [Professors A. C. Bradley and W. P. Ker] enjoyed. But I believe I may without immodesty claim one advantage in this post, which neither of them shared with me. Leslie Stephen was the master under whom I served my literary apprenticeship, and it was as his pupil that I grew to be his colleague and friend. He gave me my earliest lessons in the writing of biography, and in speaking of its principles I am guided by his teaching. I am expressing views coloured by the experience for which he trained me.

There still happily survive members of this University and literary friends in London who knew Leslie Stephen in days far earlier than those of my first acquaintance with him. Compared with the companions of his youth or early middle age I have small right to speak of him. My association with him only concerned the last twenty-one years of his life. Yet I may plead that outside the ranks of his family I owe him debts of knowledge and encouragement which have not, I think, been excelled.

Stephen belonged to a notable generation, a generation the heroes of which seem to have been cast in a larger mould than those of my own. Stephen was the affectionate disciple of Darwin, the admiring acquaintance of Tennyson, the frequent but rather critical companion of Froude, the close friend of Henry Sidgwick, of George Meredith, of James Russell Lowell. He was personally known to Browning, Ruskin, Fitzgerald, and Carlyle. With such men as these he would be the first to disclaim equality, but he belonged to their orbit.

It was Stephen's habit to depreciate himself, and to underestimate the regard in which others held him. His qualities did not make for wide popularity. He did not seek what Tennyson calls 'the blare and blaze of fame.' Yet he established a reputation which his greatest coevals acknowledged – a reputation which came of the virility and perspicuity of his work in ethics, in literary criticism, and, above all, in biography.

Justly may the University claim some share in his fame. To Cambridge Stephen owed mainly the greatest blessing of life – health, as well as a large stock of his intellectual equipment. In Stephen's case Cambridge made of a weakly boy an athletic man. His training as an undergraduate turned him into an athlete in body no less than in mind. Not that his physical health was ever obtrusively robust, but the physical exercise of his undergraduate days, in which he engaged with a wholly spontaneous zeal, clearly helped him to measure a span of life exceeding the psalmist's three score years and ten. Even more notable is the influence which this place exerted on his intellectual temper. The ideal of dry common sense, which dominated thought here in his youthful days, was his guiding star through life. He was always impatient of rhetoric, of sentimentality, of floridity in life or literature. His virtues as man and writer were somewhat of the Spartan kind. It was his life here in youth and early middle age that chiefly bred the terseness, the frankness, the dialectical adroitness which gave his literary work its savour. Although he severed his connexion with his University before he was forty, and though to some extent his sympathies with Cambridge afterwards decayed, its beneficent influences were never obliterated in him.

To the world at large as years advanced he seemed reserved and melancholy. I have heard him groan for hours together over the verbosity and blindness of biographers. But his seasons of depression, save in sickness, were passing moods. No man found richer solace than he in the early friendships which he formed in his University. His enthusiasm for his college while undergraduate, fellow, and tutor, always kept alive happy memories, which helped to assuage sorrow, as I can testify from some evenings spent with him, when heavy domestic grief bowed down his spirit. 'I love the sleepy river,' he said in his last days, 'not even the Alpine scenery is dearer to me.'

Often a gladiator wielding unsparingly the sword of plain speech against orthodox beliefs, he dealt his strokes fairly and squarely, and few of his adversaries cherished lasting resentment. Wary of enthusiasm and impatient of insincerity or incompetence, he admired without reserve all greatness in deed or thought. Every honest endeavour won his sympathy. His tenderness of heart was without any uncharitable leaven. There was always abundance of affectionate interest in those with whom he worked. Notably in his case is the style of the author the character of the man. 'I think,' wrote Robert Louis Stevenson, 'it is always wholesome to read Leslie Stephen.' The dictum is in too minor a key to sound the whole truth, but it is the unpretending sort of language which Stephen would have appreciated about himself, especially from such a quarter.

III

Biography exists to satisfy a natural instinct in man — the commemorative instinct — the universal desire to keep alive the memories of those who by character and exploits have distinguished themselves from the mass of mankind. Art, pictoral, plastic, monumental art, competes with biography in preserving memories of buried humanity. But Jacques Amyot, the great prose writer of the French Renaissance — Amyot who, by his French translation of the works of Plutarch, first made the Greek master of biography an influence on modern thought and conduct — wrote these wise words on the relative values of biography and art as means of commemorating men's characters and achievements: 'There is neither picture, nor image of marble, nor arch of triumph, nor pillar, nor sumptuous sepulchre, can match the durableness of an eloquent biography, furnished with the qualities which it ought to have.' 'Furnished with the qualities which it ought to have' — there is the problem which we are met to face. Biography is not so imposing to the general eye as pyramids and mausoleums, statues and columns, portraits and memorial foundations, but it is the *safest* way, as Thomas Fuller wrote, to protect a memory from oblivion. Plutarch, Tacitus, and Suetonius' biographical memorials of distinguished men have worn better than the more substantial tributes of art to their heroes' fame.

The aim of biography is, in general terms, to hand down to a future age the history of individual men or women, to transmit enduringly their character and exploits. Character and exploits are for biographical purposes inseparable. Character which does not translate itself into exploit is for the biographer a mere phantasm. The exploit may range from mere talk, as in the case of Johnson, to empire-building and military conquest, as in the case of Julius Caesar of Napoleon. But character and exploit jointly constitute biographic personality. Biography aims at satisfying the commemorative instinct by exercise of its power to transmit personality.

The biographic aim implies two constant and obvious conditions. Firstly, the subject-matter, the character and achievement out of which the biography is to be woven, must be capable of moving the interest of posterity. Secondly, the manner or style of the record should be of a texture which is calculated to endure, to outlive the fashion or taste of the hour. In other words, biography depends for its successful accomplishment on the two elements of fit matter and fit manner, of fit theme and fit treatment.

Good treatment will not compensate for a bad theme, nor will a good theme compensate for bad treatment. Theme and treatment must both answer equally a call of permanent distinction. There are cases in which a good subject is found in combination with a bad form. That indeed is no uncommon experience. In the result, the commemorative instinct remains unsatisfied and biography fails to perform its function. The converse association of a bad theme with good treatment, of bad matter with good manner, is rarer, and may kindle some literary interest, although not an interest of biographic concern. For the life of a nonentity or a mediocrity, however skilfully [sic] contrived, conflicts with primary biographic principles. Unless subject-matter and style be both of a commensurate sufficiency, biography lacks 'the qualities which it ought to have,' the qualities which ensure permanence, the qualities which satisfy the commemorative instinct.

What constitutes fitness in a biographic theme? The question raises puzzling issues. The commemorative instinct which biography has to satisfy scarcely seems to obey in its habitual working any one clear immutable law. The Italian poet Ariosto imagined, with some allegorical vagueness, that at the end of every man's thread of life there hung a medal stamped with his name, and that, as Death severed life's thread with its fatal shears, Time seized the medal and dropped it into the river of Lethe. Yet a few, a very few, of the stamped medals were caught as they fell towards the waters of oblivion by swans, who carried off the medals and deposited them in a temple or museum of immortality. Ariosto's swans are biographers: by what motive are they impelled to rescue any medals of pesonality from the flood of forgetfulness into which they let the mass sink?

Perhaps the old Greek definition of the fit theme of tragedy may be usefully adapted to the fit theme of biography. A fit biographic theme is, in the Aristotelian phrase, a career which is 'serious, complete, and of a certain magnitude.' An unfit biographic theme is a career of trivial aim, incomplete, without magnitude, of or below mediocrity. The second clause in this definition, which prescribes the need of completeness, offers no ambiguity. It excludes from the scope of biography careers of living men, careers which are incomplete, because death witholds the finishing touch. Death is a part of life, and no man is fit subject for biography till he is dead. Living men have been made themes of biography. But the choice defies the cardinal condition of completeness. There is usually abroad an idle curiosity about prominent persons during their lifetime. It is not the business of biography to appease mere inquisitiveness. Its primary business is to be complete. The living theme can at best be a torso, a fragment. There clings to it, too, a savour either of the scandal or of the unbalanced laudation which living men rarely escape. Politicians, while they are yet active on the political stage, are often panegyrized or vilified by biographical partisans. The efficient commemorative instinct, which sets little store by such panegyric or vilifica-

tion, craves, before all things, the completeness which death alone assures. No man's memory can be accounted great until it has outlived his life.

At the same time there is danger in postponing indefinitely biographic commemoration in cases where it is rightly due. There are insuperable obstacles to writing the lives of men long after their relatives and associates have passed away. Even the life of Shakespeare has suffered through the long interval which separates the date of his death from the first efforts of his biographers, and there are some of Shakespeare's literary contemporaries, whose biographic commemoration has been postponed to so distant a date after their career has closed that the attempt to satisfy the just call of the commemorative instinct has altogether failed.

But the theme of biography must be far more than 'complete.' It must be, in addition, both 'serious' and 'of a certain magnitude.' By seriousness we may understand the quality which stirs and firmly holds the attention of the earnest-minded.

What constitutes the needful 'magnitude' in a biographic theme? It is difficult to set up a fixed standard whereby to measure the dimensions of a human action. But by way of tentative suggestion or hypothesis, the volume of a human action may be said to vary, from the biographer's point of view, with the number of times that it has been accomplished or is capable of accomplishment.

The magnitude of human action is necessarily of many degrees; the scale ascends and descends. The production by Shakespeare of his thirty-seven plays is an action of the first magnitude, because the achievement is unique. The victory of Wellington at Waterloo is an action of great but of lesser magnitude, because deeds of like calibre have been achieved by other military commanders, and are doubtless capable, if the need arise, of accomplishment again. As we descend the scale of achievement, we reach by slow gradations the level of action which forms the terminal limit of the biographic province. Actions, however beneficent or honourable, which are accomplished or are capable of accomplishment by many thousands of persons are actions of mediocrity, and lack the dimension which justifies the biographer's notice.

The fact that a man is a devoted husband and father, an efficient schoolmaster, an exemplary parish priest, gives him in itself no claim to biographic commemoration, because his actions, although meritorious, are practically indistinguishable from those of thousands of his fellows. It follows further that official dignities, except of the rarest and most dignified kind, give *in themselves* no claim to biographic commemoration. That a man should become a peer, a member of parliament, a lord mayor, even a professor, and attend to his duties, are actions or experiences that have been accomplished or are capable of accomplishment by too large a number of persons to render them in themselves of appreciable magnitude. At the same time office may well give a man an opportunity of distinction which he might otherwise be without; official responsibility may well lift his career to the requisite level of eminence.

In appraising the magnitude – the biographic capacity or content – of a career, one must needs guard against certain false notions – ειδωλα or idols in Baconian terminology – which prevail widely and tend to distort the judgement. Domestic partiality, social contiguity, fortuitous clamour of the crowd – such things frequently cause mediocrity to masquerade as magnitude. The biographer has to forswear the measuring rods of the family hearth, of the hospitable board, of journalistic advertisement. A kinsman or a kinswoman, an intimate companion, is easily moved by private affection to credit undiscriminatingly a man or woman's activity with the dimensions that justify biographic commemoration. A newspaper records day by day the activities of some seeker after notoriety, until his name grows more familiar to his generation than that of Shakespeare or Nelson. Evanescent repute may very easily, through journalistic iteration, be mistaken for that which will excite the commemorative instinct hereafter.

In estimating the magnitude of human action, there is need of some workable measure or gauge which shall operate independently of mere contemporary opinion. Contemporary fame is often withheld as arbitrarily as it is bestowed. Posthumous fame at times comes into being with strange suddenness, without any contemporary heralding at all. How suggestive to the student of biography is the fact that the name and work of Gregor Mendel, the Austrian monk and biological inquirer, who died nearly thirty years ago 'unwept, unhonoured, and unsung,' should fill ten volumes of the new edition of the *Encyclopaedia Britannica,* a space in excess of that devoted to any one of the numerous heroes of science who enjoyed repute in their own lifetime. Current fame is no sure evidence of biographic fitness. The tumult and the shouting die and they may leave nothing behind which satisfies the biographic tests of completeness, seriousness, and magnitude.

IV

The biographer having found his fit theme is faced with the problem of its treatment. His aim is to transmit personality, to satisfy the commemorative instinct. He may learn something of the lawful processes from a preliminary study of the processes which are unlawful. The main path which he should follow may gain in clear definition if he be warned at the outset against certain neighbouring paths which are easily capable of leading him astray. Biography must resolutely preserve its independence of three imposing themes of study, which are often seen to compete for its control. True biography is no handmaid of ethical instruction. Its purpose is not that of history. It does not exist to serve biological or anthropological science. Any assistance that biography renders these three great interests – ethical, historical, and scientific – should be accidental; such aid is neither essential nor obligatory. Biography rules a domain of its own; it is autonomous – an attribute with which it is not always credited.

It was an amiable tenet in the orthodox creed of an ancient biographic school, that the career destined for biographic treatment should directly teach morality, should be conspicuously virtuous. The biography should, before all else, 'show virtue her own feature,' or at any rate hymn her worth. Gentle Izaak Walton, like many biographers who wrote before and after him, regarded biography as 'an honour due to the virtuous dead, and a lesson in magnanimity to those who shall succeed them.' In Walton's demure judgement, dead men who are morally unworthy lie outside the scope of biography. It speaks well for the goodness of the world that good men have occupied more biographic pens than bad men, and that biographers have always cherished a charitable preference for benefactors over malefactors. But therein lies no proof that the merits of biography depend on its powers of edification.

It is with very large qualifications that Walton's ethical presumption can pass current. Sinners excite the commemorative instinct as well as saints. The careers of both Napoleon I and Napoleon III satisfy all conditions of the biographic theme, in spite of their spacious infringements of moral law. Suetonius defied no biographic principle when he treated of Roman emperors, many of whom were monsters of infamy. Biography is a truthful picture of life, of life's tangle skein, good and ill together. Biography prejudices its chances of success when it is consciously designed as an ethical guide of life.

Candour, which shall be innocent of ethical fervour or even of ethical intention, is a cardinal principle of right biographic method. It is often the biographer's anxious duty to present great achievements in near alliance with moral failings. Coleridge was a great poet and an illuminating thinker. But he was deficient in the moral sense, and justified himself for his offences by 'amazing wrigglings and self-reproaches and astonishing pouring forth of unctuous twaddling.' Byron, Porson, Nelson, Parnell, and many more for whom the commemorative instinct assuredly demands biographic commemoration combined great exploits with notorious defiance of virtue.

The ethical fallacy of biography has sanctioned two evasive methods of handling such perplexing phases of life – a method of suppression and a method of extenuation. The method of suppression has found distinguished advocates. Tennyson asked 'what business has the public to want to know about Byron's wildnesses? He has given them fine work and they ought to be satisfied.' Here indeed we are advised, either to dispense with all biography of Byron, or only to accept a biography of him from which his 'wildnesses' are excluded. The cravings of the commemorative instinct which Byron's career has already excited render both these counsels futile.

The alternative method of extenuation has been adopted by an eminent man of letters of our own day in treating of an illustrious poetic contemporary of Byron – of Shelley. Writing Shelley's life under the admiring eyes of surviving relatives, the biographer has made other people responsible for most of Shelley's flagrant errors of conduct and has credited the poet's personality with an unfailing beneficence. In view of the biographer's true goal it is difficult to speak of the whitewashing method more indulgently than of the method of suppression. The biographer is a narrator, not a moralist, and candour is the salt of his narrative. He accepts alike what clearly tells in a man's favour and what clearly tells against him. Neither omission nor partisan vindication will satisfy the primary needs of the art.

At the same time the biographer is likely to miss his aim of transmitting personality truthfully if he give more space or emphasis to a man's lapses from virtue than is proportioned to their effects on his achievement. Although he may not fill the preacher's pulpit, a touch of sympathy with human frailty, of charity for wrongdoing, will the better fit him for his task.

There is a French proverb: *Tôt ou tard, tout se sait* – 'Sooner or later everything comes to light.' There is another French proverb: *Tout comprendre, c'est tout pardonner* – 'To understand all is to pardon all.'

Both apophthegms make appeal to the biographer, and the second is quite as relevant to his work as the first. Lives written in a hostile spirit may not be wholly untruthful. But they tend to emphasize unpleasing features and thereby give a wrongful impression. Scurrility is not candour. To pander to a love of scandal is a greater sin in a biographer than in anybody else. Lord Campbell wrote lives of lawyers, which satisfy many of the conditions of biography. But their depreciatory tone, which prompted the epigram that biography lends a new sting to death, suggests malignity and distorts the true perspective. The competent biographer may fail from want of sympathy even when his skill is not in question. Like the portrait painter who is fascinated by forbidding aspects in a sitter's countenance, he may, even without conscious intention, produce a caricature instead of a portrait.

All gradations of moral infirmity, from serious crime to mere deviation from accepted codes of good manners, will from time to time claim the biographer's notice and call for presentation in due perspective. Downright offences are not his only sources of embarrassment. Perhaps more often is he confronted with inconsistencies of conduct or opinion, with sudden changes of beliefs, religious or political, which are currently suspected of dishonesty. Defective sympathy or partisan hostility is here as harmful as any resolve to point a moral. 'That conversion,' says the moralist, 'will always be suspected which concurs with interest.' The suspicion is inevitable, but is conversion invariably dishonest? May not increase of knowledge or a greater concentration of thought on the questions at issue induce a natural and an honest process of development? Was Wordsworth a lost leader who left the revolutionary companions of his early years for the orthodox Tories just to receive a handful of silver and a bit of ribbon to stick in his coat? Was Disraeli's early abandonment of a radical programme the act of a self-seeking adventurer? Was Gladstone's unexpected adoption of the policy of Irish Home Rule prompted by impulses of reckless ambition, by the hope of stealing meanly a march on political rivals? The biographer must hold the scales even. He must look before and after, and close his ears to party resentments of the hour. He must abide by the just and generous principles which move a critical friend's judgement. Wherever he honestly can, a friend allows the benefit of the doubt; he extenuates nothing, nor sets down aught in malice. Brutus claimed that the record of Caesar's life in the Capitol presented the dictator's 'glories wherein he was worthy' by the side of the dictator's 'offences wherein he was unworthy.' Neither were the merits under-estimated nor were the defects over-emphasized. Brutus's simple words suggest the nicely adjusted scales in which the moral blemishes of great men should be weighed by the biographer. The aim of biography is not the moral edification which may flow from the survey of either vice or virtue; it is the truthful transmission of personality.

V

The pursuit by the biographer of the historian's aims may prove as disastrous as any competition with the austere aims of the moralist. The historical method is as harmful to biography as the method of moral edification. History encroaches on the biographer's province to the prejudice of his art. Bacon, in his survey of learning, carefully distinguished the 'history of times' (that is, annals or chronicles) or the 'history of action' (that is, histories in the accepted sense) from 'lives.' Bacon warns us that history sets forth the pomp of public business; while biography reveals the true and inward sources of action, tells of private no less than of public conduct, and pays as much attention to the slender wires as to the great weights that hang from them.

The distinction between history and biography lies so much on the surface that a confusion between them is barely justifiable. History may be compared to mechanics, the science which determines the power of bodies in the mass. Biography may be compared to chemistry, the science which analyses substances and resolves them into their constituent elements. The historian has to describe the aggregate movement of men and the manner in which that aggregate movement fashions political or social events and institutions. The historian has only to take into account those aspects of men's lives which affect the movements of the crowd that co-operates with them. The biographer's concern with the crowd is quite subsidiary and secondary. From the mass of mankind he draws apart those units who are in a decisive degree distinguishable from their neighbours. He submits them to minute examination, and his record of observation becomes a mirror of their exploits and character from the cradle to the grave. The historian looks at mankind through a field-glass. The biographer puts individual men under a magnifying glass.

It goes without saying that the biographer must frequently appeal for aid to the historian. An intelligent knowledge of the historical environment – of the contemporary trend of the aggregate movement of men – is indispensable to the biographer, if he would portray in fitting perspective all the operations of his unit. One cannot detach a sovereign or a statesman from the political world in which he has his being. The circumstance of politics is the scenery of the statesman's biography. But it is the art of the biographer sternly to subordinate his scenery to his actors. He must never crowd his stage with upholstery and scenic apparatus that can only distract the spectators' attention from the proper interest of the piece. If you attempt the life of Mary Queen of Scots, you miss your aim when you obscure the human interest and personal adventure, in which her career abounds, by grafting upon it an exhaustive exposition of the intricate relations of Scottish Presbyterians with Roman Catholics, or of Queen Elizabeth's tortuous foreign policy. These things are the bricks and mortar of history. Fragments of them may be needed as props in outlying portions of the biographical edifice, but even then they must be kept largely out of sight.

On these grounds I am afraid that that mass of laborious works which bears the title of 'the life and times' of this or that celebrated person, calls for censure. These weighty volumes can be classed neither with right history nor with right biography. Most of them must be reckoned fruit of a misdirected zeal. One would not wish to speak disrespectfully of the self-denying toil which has raised a mountain of stones on however sprawling a plan to a great man's memory. But when one surveys that swollen cairn *The Life of John Milton narrated in connexion with the political, ecclesiastical and literary history of his time* which occupied a great part of David Masson's long and distinguished career, I accept in spite of the varied uses of the majestic volumes that plaintive judgement of Carlyle: 'Masson has hung on his Milton peg all the politics, which Milton, poor fellow, had never much to do with except to print a pamphlet or two.' Masson has hung on 'his Milton peg' not only 'all the politics which Milton, poor fellow, had never much to do with' but also all the ecclesiastical and literary history with which Milton had even less concern. Biography is not a peg for anything save the character and exploits of a man whose career answers the tests of biographic fitness.

I should hardly be bold enough to speak of the relations of biography and science, and of the peril to biographic method of bringing the two studies into too close a conjunction, had not the late Sir Francis Galton and several living correspondents urged on me, in my capacity of editor of *The Dictionary of National Biography,* the general advantage of adapting the biographic method of the *Dictionary* to the needs of the scientific investigation of heredity and eugenics.

Biography, it has been argued, should serve as handmaid to this new and absorbing department of biology and anthropology. The biographer should collect, after due scrutiny, those details of genealogy, habit, and physiological characteristics which may help the student of genetics to determine human types, to diagnose 'variations from type,' to distinguish acquired from inherited characteristics, and to arrive by such roads at a finite conception of human individuality. If biography, without deviating from its true purpose or method, can aid the scientific inquiry into the origin and development of ability or genius, all is well. But, if biographic effort is to be swayed by conditions of genetical study, if it is to inquire minutely and statistically into the distant ramifications of every great man's pedigree, with the result that undistinguished grandfathers, grandmothers, fathers, mothers, even second cousins, shall receive almost as close attention as the great man himself, then dangers may be apprehended. Whether the secret of genius will ever be solved is for the future to determine. The biographer has no call to pursue speculation on the fascinating theme.

VI

Like all branches of modern literature, biography was efficiently practised by Greece and Rome, and it is to classical tuition that the modern art is deeply indebted. It was Amyot's great French translation of Plutarch which introduced the biography of disciplined purpose to the modern world, with lasting benefit to life and literature.

Plutarch's method is in one respect peculiar to himself. He endeavours to emphasize points of character and conduct in one man by instituting a formal comparison of them with traits of similar type in another man. He writes what he calls 'parallel lives' of some twenty great Greeks and Romans. Having written of Alexander the Great, he gives an account of Caesar; having written of Demosthenes, he gives an account of Cicero. In every instance he adds to his pair of lives a chapter of comparisons and contrasts. The parallel method enhances the vividness of the portraiture, but it is not the feature of his work which gives it its permanent influence. His individual themes, and his detached treatment of them, deserve chief scrutiny.

Plutarch's subjects are all leaders in politics or war. Heroes of literature and art lie outside his sphere. From the modern point of view the range is arbitrarily limited. But his limitation of theme does not prejudice the value of his example. His guiding principles of treatment are of universal application. He collects authorities in ample store. His materials included not only written books and documents, but also experience and knowledge gathered in converse with well-informed persons. He bases his narrative on contemporary evidence wherever it is accessible, but he is watchful of the lies and fables of hearsay accretions. Where two conflicting versions of one incident are at hand, he selects the one which is in closer harmony with his hero's manners and nature.

But wide as is Plutarch's field of research, he is discriminating in his choice of detail. He knows the value of perspective. He did not, he tells us, declare all things at large. At times he wrote briefly of the noblest and most notorious achievements. He preferred to concentrate his attention upon what to the unseeing eye looked insignificant — upon 'a light occasion, a word or some sport.' 'Therein,' he adds, 'men's nature, dispositions, and manners appear more plainly than the famous battles won, wherein are slain 10,000 men.'

Personality was Plutarch's quarry. It was therefore needful for him to bring into due prominence the singularity of each human theme. His studies inevitably acquainted him with many unhappy or ungracious features in great men's lives, which asked admission to his canvas. The frailties were neither suppressed nor extenuated. Yet a sense of what he called 'reverent shame' deterred him from enlarging on men's frailties beyond the needs of his art. He was a just biographer who was not distracted from his proper aim by ethical fervour or by partisanship. Nor were the purposes of history or science within his scope.

None of Plutarch's biographic principles can be ignored with impunity. Very efficiently does his example warn the biographer against two faults to which biography of more modern date has shown itself peculiarly prone — the fault of misty sentimentality or vague rhapsodizing and the fault of tediousness. The value of rhapsodical or sentimental biography is commonly over-estimated when it is credited with any method at all. In a few instances an eloquent piece of literature is the outcome. But it is literature which belongs to another category than that of biography. Boccaccio's rhapsodical account of Dante is a favourable specimen of its class. We learn there much of the effect of love on youthful hearts. There is a fiery denunciation of the city of Florence for her guilt in banishing her greatest citizen. But Boccaccio's impassioned rhetoric leaves the story of Dante's life untold.

The rhapsodical or sentimental mode of biography will always have its votaries. It often makes a powerful appeal to the hearts of the ingenuous kindred of a departed relative. But the vapour of sentimentality is usually fatal to biographic light. I have already suggested how liable domestic partiality is to err in the choice of the biographic theme. It is no less harmful in ordinary conditions to biographic treatment or method. Very rarely will domestic sentiment recognize the limitations of the biographic art, or obey the cry for candour and perspective. Whether the theme be fit or no, the pen which is guided by domestic enthusiasm will, as a rule, flow to satiety with sentimental vagueness and inaccuracy. The advantage of intimate knowledge which might seem to come of a kinsman's personal propinquity to the biographic hero counts, save in a few notable instances for very little or for nothing. The domestic pen is too often innocent of literary experience. The faculty of selection and arrangement is wanting, or is at any rate lost in the stream of cloudy panegyric. There are tendencies to emphasize the immaterial and to ignore the material. The sentimental image has to be protected at all hazards. How often has one found in biographies of distinguished men, which are compiled under the domestic eye or by the domestic hand, that youthful struggles with sordid poverty or suffering, that irregular experiences of budding manhood are ignored or half told from a misguided fear of disturbing sentimental bias. I may not reveal the secrets of my own prison-house. But I could recall many a surprising example of domestic anxiety to gloss over or misrepresent truthful and pertinent details in careers of immediate ancestors, because domestic illusion, which is often bred of the blindest conventions of propriety, scents an unedifying savour in facts which are quite harmless but quite necessary.

Domestic sentimentality has been known to exert pressure on the biographer who stands outside the domestic circle. He at times lacks the nerve to resist all its assaults. The peril is indeed ubiquitous. It is perhaps some consolation that Shakespeare's life was written after all his descendants were dead; for who knows, had they been alive, that such a detail as that his father was a village shopkeeper and went bankrupt would have been dismissed to oblivion by an invertebrate and conciliatory biographer, at the call of an ill-balanced domestic pride.

VII

Leslie Stephen said of a recent biography — which enjoyed some vogue — that it was 'too long and too idolatrous.' Those epithets 'too long and too idolatrous' indicate the two worst faults in biographic method, which Plutarch's teaching condemns. Of the biographic vice of idolatry, which springs largely from domestic partiality, I have already spoken enough. The vice of undue length is equally widespread and its prevalence stands in little need of illustration. It is a failing against which Plutarch's example warns us even more loudly than against idolatry. Yet it flourishes luxuriantly in spite of the master's warning. The lineal measurement of biography has no single, fixed scale. There is a threefold graduation answering in the first place to the importance of the career, in the second place to the gross amount of available material, and in the third place to the intrinsic value or biographic pertinence of the surviving records. The correspondence or the journals or the reports of conversation out of which the biographic web is to be woven vary immensely in biographic service. Lack of the raw material would make it impossible to write a life of Shakespeare of the same length as Lord Morley's *Life of Gladstone*. But brevity may be enjoined, in the case of men of the first eminence, not solely on the ground that the raw material is scanty. Even where the raw material be abundant, it may be deficient in the quality which illumines personality and may prove useless for biographic purposes. Among men of action especially, the faculty of self-expression in letters and papers is often crude and ill-developed. Diaries are filled with formalities of daily experience, with excerpts from travellers' guidebooks, or with commonplace reflections. The intrinsic interest for the biographer amounts to little more than proof of the writer's inability to transmit his individuality through his pen. Here drastic summarizing is alone permissible. In citing diaries the half or much less than half is very frequently more valuable than the whole. Rigid selection and lavish rejection of available records are processes which the biographer has often to practise in the sternest temper.

It may be needful for the biographer to examine mountainous masses of manuscript, but he must sift their contents in the light of true biographic principles. The balance has to be kept even between what precedes and what follows. No digression is permissible from the straight path of the hero's personality. The mode of work, which was adopted by one of the most skilful[*sic*] artists in black and white of our time, Phil May, may well offer the biographer suggestion here. Phil May in his drawings presented character with admirable fidelity. In the finished result the fewest possible lines were present. But the preliminary draft was, I understand, crowded with lines, the majority of which were erased by the artist before his work left his hand. Let the biographer note down every detail in fulness[*sic*] and at length. But before offering his labour to the world, let him excise every detail that does not make for graphic portrayal of character and exploit. No mere impressionist sketch satisfies the conditions of adequate biography. But personality is not transmitted on the biographic canvas through overcrowded detail. More than ever at the present day is there imperative need of winnowing biographic information, of dismissing the voluminous chaff while conserving the grain. The growing habit of ephemeral publicity, the methods of reporting the minutiae of prominent people's daily life, not merely by aid of the printing-press, but by the new mechanical inventions of photograph, phonograph, and even cinematograph, all accumulate raw biographic material in giant heaps at an unprecedented rate. The biographer's labours will hereafter be immensely increased; but they will be labours lost, unless principles of discrimination be rigorously applied.

VIII

A discriminating brevity is a law of the right biographic method — a brevity graduated by considerations on the one hand of the genuine importance of the theme or career, and on the other of the genuine value and interest of the available material. Instances of biographic failure, owing to infringements of this law of brevity, are legion, and one or other recent examples will leap to the minds of every one who subscribes to a circulating library. But every law is liable in uncovenanted conditions to a temporary suspense. To every rule there are exceptions, which prove its normal justness. The longest biography in the English language is also the best. Boswell's *Life of Johnson* is indeed reckoned the best specimen of biography that has yet been written in any tongue. Critics agree that life on a desert island would be tolerable with Boswell's biographic work for companion. That verdict may be a metaphorical flight. But it has not been risked in comment on any other biography, and only in comment on two other books in English, the English Bible and Shakespeare.

To what is attributable Boswell's unique triumph, in spite of its challenge of the law of bio-

graphic brevity? The triumph is primarily due to an unexampled confluence of two very unusual phenomena. A biographic theme of unprecedented breadth and energy found biographic treatment of an abnormally microscopic intensity. The outcome is what men of science might well call a 'sport.'

There is no precise parallel to the episode of which Boswell's biography was bred. Dr. Johnson, a being of rare intellectual and moral manliness, draws to himself, when well advanced in years, the loyal and unquestioning adoration of a rarely inquisitive young man, whose chief virtues are those of the faithful hound. Boswell's personality, save in his aspect of biographer, deserves small respect. Self-indulgent, libidinous, drunken, vain, he develops in relation to Johnson a parasitical temper which makes him glorious. Boswell pursues Johnson for twenty years like his shadow, and takes note of all that fell from the great man's lips, the tones of his voice, the expressions of his countenance. It is fortunate for us that he should have done much which self-respecting persons would scorn to do. The salt of Boswell's biography is his literal reports of Johnson's conversation, reports in the spirit of the interviewer, which run to enormous length and account for the colossal dimensions of the book.

No other biographer has sought or obtained the like opportunity of interviewing his hero and reporting his conversation. It is doubtful if any hero save Johnson could have come through the ordeal satisfactorily. It is fallacious to suggest that a mediocrity would, if submitted to the pertinacious scrutiny of a Boswell, give occasion for a biographic *tour de force* comparable with Johnson's life. There was a singular union of two exceptional human forces which, despite dissimilarity, proved to be mutually complementary. That miracle is responsible for the supreme effect. Until such a conjunction be repeated, Boswell's work will stand alone, quite out of the sphere of normal biography.

Boswell's book defies all traditional biographic scale; its flood of reported talk is biographic license, not law. Yet it is the paradoxical truth that Boswell's work illustrates to perfection many features of first importance to right biographic method. In spite of its unconscionable length and diffuseness, Boswell's biography always keeps with admirable tenacity to the fundamental purpose of transmitting personality. Every page makes its contribution to this single end. There are no digressions, no superfluities, no distracting issues. All the meticulous detail makes for a unity on which Plutarch could hardly improve.

In the second place, Boswell is the supreme champion of the great principle of biographic frankness; his native candour robs his tendency to idolatry of its familiar mischiefs. He declines to suppress anything that helps his reader to realize Johnson's personality. He bluntly refused Miss Hannah More's request 'to mitigate some of the asperities of our most revered and departed friend.' He would 'not cut off the doctor's claws nor make his tiger a cat to please anybody.' He was so faithful to the biographic law of candour that the frequent snubs which the doctor administered to the writer himself find a due place in the record.

Boswell's presentation of himself in the biography offers a third piece of valuable instruction to the biographer. It was not in Boswell's nature to efface himself. Yet it cannot be said of him, as of some other biographers, that he brings himself on the stage at the expense of his subject. There are biographies which fail helplessly because the writer is always thinking as much, or perhaps more, of himself than of his theme. He is seeking to share in the honours of publicity. Boswell does not efface himself, but he envelops himself in the spirit of his theme; he stands in its shadow and never in its light.

Lastly, Boswell was an industrious collector of information. It may be objected that for the fifty-four years of Johnson's life which preceded Boswell's introduction to him, something more than Boswell knew has come to light since he wrote. It may be admitted that Boswell neglected a few sources of information from petty personal grudges against those who controlled them. The cry has indeed been lately raised, that some pigmy contemporary biographers of Johnson reveal a few phases of the doctor's character which Boswell either wilfully[sic] or unwittingly overlooked or minimized. Spots have been detected in the sun, but the sun's rays are undimmed. Boswell's achievement glows with a steadier and more expansive radiance than any other star in the biographic firmament.

There is yet another biography in the English language which transgresses the law of brevity without marring its effect, nay, with enhancement of its effect. There is a second exception to the principle of brevity which fails to impugn the normal rule, if on grounds quite different from those which Boswell pleads with security. Lockhart's *Life of Scott* is the second best biography in the language, Boswell's biography being the first. But Lockhart's merit is mainly due to the excellence and the abundance of the raw material provided for him in Scott's ample journals and correspondence. He was

spared Boswell's toil of reporter and collector of information; almost all was ready to his hands, and he had merely to apply to his vast store those faculties of selection and arrangement which came of his literary efficiency and experience. It is very rare for a man of Sir Walter Scott's supreme genius, whose career and character, too, are free of dark places or mysteries prompting suppression or extenuation, to leave to a competent biographer an immense mass of fit biographic records penned by his own hand. So happy an event seems as unlikely to recur as a second meeting of a Johnson with a Boswell. Lockhart's challenge of the law of brevity is justified, and the justification barely touches normal experience.

IX

Encyclopaedic or collective biography is a special branch of biography which has not been infrequently practised, both in classical and modern times. To collective biography, in the form of national biography, Leslie Stephen dedicated immense energy, and to it I, in succession to him, have devoted almost all my adult life. The methods of collective or national biography clearly differ from those of individual biography in literary design and in the opportunity which is offered of literary embellishment. But there are points at which the method of the two biographic kinds converge. Collective or national biography, which brings a long series of lives within the confines of a single literary scheme, presses the obligations of brevity and conciseness to limits which individual or independent biography is not required to respect. Facts and dates loom larger in collective or national biography than in other biographic forms. The object of national as of all collective biography is Priestley's object in scientific exposition – 'to comprise as much knowledge as possible in the smallest compass.' Indulgence in rhetoric, voluble enthusiasm, emotion, loquacious sentiment, is for the national biographer the deadliest of sins. Yet his method will be of small avail if he be unable to arrange his bare facts and dates so as to indicate graphically the precise character of the personality and of the achievement with which he is dealing – if he fail to suggest the peculiar interest of the personality and the achievement by some happy epithet or brief touch of criticism. There are instances in which a miniature memoir thus graced has given a reader a sense of satisfaction almost as great as any that a largely planned biography can give – the feeling, namely, that to him is imparted all the information for which his commemorative instinct craves.

The methods of national biography are Spartan methods heartlessly enforced by an editor's vigilance. It might perhaps be doubted if any of the Spartan methods of collective biography could be adopted with advantage by independent biographers who are free of the collective biographer's shackles.

Yet the virtue of liberty may be overvalued. The collective biographer submits from the outset to a strict discipline. Without underrating the dissimilarity of the conditions in which the independent biographer works, one may often impute to him without injustice a lack of any such training as is required of his humbler brother-craftsmen. In the absence of disciplinary control, an untrained biographer has been known to fling before his readers a confused mass of irrelevant and inaccurate information, to load his page with unimpressive sentiment, with the result that the hero's really eminent achievements and distinctive characteristics are buried under the dust and ashes of special pleading, commonplace gossip, and helpless eulogy. Occasionally, at any rate, nothing would be lost by an exchange of a shapeless and woolly effigy from the unchartered workshop of a free and independent biographer, for a skeleton of facts and dates from the collective biographer's law-ridden factory.

X

None the less, from the purely literary point of view, a contribution to collective biography however useful and efficient cannot rank with a thoroughly workmanlike effort in individual biography. It is individual biography which gives unrestricted opportunities of literary skill. Where the theme is fit, the independent biographer has scope for the exercise of almost every literary gift.

Varied qualities are demanded of the successful biographer. He must have the patience to sift dust heaps of written or printed papers. He must have the insight to interpret what he has sifted, and the capacity to give form to the essence of his findings. A Frenchman has said that the features of Alexander ought only to be preserved by the chisel of Apelles. The admonition implies that magnitude in a career demands corresponding eminence in the biographer. No doubt the ideal partnership is there indicated. But like all counsels of perfection, this ideal union shrinks from realization. Did the precept prevail, the field of biography would be very circumscribed and few biographers would find employment. It is more workaday counsel to bid the biographer avoid unfit themes and to treat fit themes with scrupulous accuracy, with perfect frankness, with discriminating sympathy, and with resolute brevity. Not otherwise is one of ordinary clay likely to minister worthily to the commemorative instinct of his fellow men and to transmit to an afterage a memorable personality.

Lytton Strachey, Preface to *Eminent Victorians*

The history of the Victorian Age will never be written: we know too much about it. For ignorance is the first requisite of the historian – ignorance, which simplifies and clarifies, which selects and omits, with a placid perfection unattainable by the highest art. Concerning the Age which has just passed, our fathers and our grandfathers have poured forth and accumulated so vast a quantity of information that the industry of a Ranke would be submerged by it, and the perspicacity of a Gibbon would quail before it. It is not by the direct method of a scrupulous narration that the explorer of the past can hope to depict that singular epoch. If he is wise, he will adopt a subtler strategy. He will attack his subject in unexpected places; he will fall upon the flank, or the rear; he will shoot a sudden, revealing searchlight into obscure recesses, hitherto undivined. He will row out over that great ocean of material, and lower down into it, here and there, a little bucket, which will bring up to the light of day some characteristic specimen, from those far depths, to be examined with a careful curiosity. Guided by these considerations, I have written the ensuing studies. I have attempted, through the medium of biography, to present some Victorian visions to the modern eye. They are, in one sense, haphazard visions – that is to say, my choice of subjects has been determined by no desire to construct a system or to prove a theory, but by simple motives of convenience and of art. It has been my purpose to illustrate rather than to explain. It would have been futile to hope to tell even a *précis* of the truth about the Victorian age, for the shortest *précis* must fill innumerable volumes. But, in the lives of an ecclesiastic, an educational authority, a woman of action, and a man of adventure, I have sought to examine and elucidate certain fragments of the truth which took my fancy and lay to my hand.

I hope, however, that the following pages may prove to be of interest from the strictly biographical no less than from the historical point of view. Human beings are too important to be treated as mere symptoms of the past. They have a value which is independent of any temporal processes – which is eternal, and must be felt for its own sake. The art of biography seems to have fallen on evil times in England. We have had, it is true, a few masterpieces, but we have never had, like the French, a great biographical tradition; we have had no Fontenelles and Condorcets, with their incomparable *éloges,* compressing into a few shining pages the manifold existences of men. With us, the most delicate and humane of all the branches of the art of writing has been relegated to the journeymen of letters; we do not reflect that it is perhaps as difficult to write a good life as to live one. Those two fat volumes, with which it is our custom to commemorate the dead – who does not know them, with their ill-digested masses of material, their slipshod style, their tone of tedious panegyric, their lamentable lack of selection, of detachment, of design? They are as familiar as the *cortège* of the undertaker, and wear the same air of slow, funereal barbarism. One is tempted to suppose, of some of them, that they were composed by that functionary, as the final item of his job. The studies in this book are indebted, in more ways than one, to such works – works which certainly deserve the name of Standard Biographies. For they have provided me not only with much indispensable information, but with something even more precious – an example. How many lessons are to be learnt from them! But it is hardly necessary to particularise. To preserve, for instance, a becoming brevity – a brevity which excludes everything that is redundant and nothing that is significant – that, surely, is the first duty of the biographer. The second, no less surely, is to maintain his own freedom of spirit. It is not his business to be complimentary; it is his business to lay bare the facts of the case, as he understands them. That is what I have aimed at in this book – to lay bare the facts of some cases, as I understand them, dispassionately, impartially, and without ulterior intentions. To quote the words of a Master – "Je n'impose rien; je ne propose rien: j'expose."

– *L. S.*

Harold Nicolson, "The Practice of Biography," in *The English Sense of Humour and Other Essays*

1

In an age when, within a few hours, men can be transported from Croydon to Khartoum; when children, seated in their own small chairs, can watch Presidents being inaugurated, atomic bombs exploding, or fish with round eyes and muslin fins circling in an aquarium; when experience has transcended imagination and reality has proved more terrible than any phantom; — in such an age it is inevitable that the sense of wonder should become atrophied, that the fictional should lose its stimulus, and that people should prefer to read about what happened in the unfrightening past rather than about what may happen in our awful present or future.

The modern propensity to write and read biographies is not, however, due solely to a desire to escape from anxiety. The young men and maidens who, without possessing any compulsive creative gift, think that it would be nice to write a book, are attracted to this form of composition, since it provides them with a ready-made plot, need entail no tremendous energy of research, and enables them to relieve their sensibility without placing too taut a strain upon their imagination. The common reader, for his part, feels that in learning about the adventures, passions and misfortunes of real heroes and heroines he is indulging in no idle relaxation, but is acquiring knowledge, is 'teaching himself history.' That, when all is said and done, is a commendable thing to feel. For him modern fiction has become so intricate, so self-centred and so cruel that it leaves behind it an after-tone of bewilderment and distress: it is both more comforting and more instructive to read about the past. In this manner biographies accumulate and prosper.

It is noticeable also that in ages of faith, when the minds of men are fixed upon the eternal verities and the life after death, the practice of biography tends to decline; whereas in the succeeding periods of doubt, speculation and scepticism, the interest in human behaviour increases. Thus in the fourteenth century in England we had all the elements of good biography, whereas in the succeeding century the interest waned: in the sixteenth century again the impulse of curiosity became active and productive, only to recede with the advent of puritanism in the age that followed. Then came the eighteenth century and the phase of enlightened humanism which produced our greatest biographies, whereas with the revival of theological preoccupations in the Victorian epoch both the demand and the supply declined. The twentieth century should have coincided with a powerful revival of pure biography, but although many books are published, it does not appear that any modern formula has as yet become established.

The ease with which biographies are written and sold to-day entails a danger that an art so perfectly attuned to the Anglo-Saxon temperament may become inflated. Moreover, the tendency manifested by many elderly ladies and gentlemen to publish autobiographies — hoping thereby to recapture the security of their childhood and to demonstrate the triumph of character over environment — will still further debase this currency. It may therefore be opportune to reconsider whether there do in fact exist any fundamental biographical principles; and to examine what are the perils and illnesses to which the art of biography is by its very nature exposed.

The Oxford English Dictionary defines Biography as 'the history of the lives of individual men, as a branch of literature.' This excellent definition contains within itself the three principles that any serious biographer should observe. A biography must be 'history,' in the sense that it must be accurate and depict a person in relation to his times. It must describe an 'individual,' with all the gradations of human character, and not merely present a type of virtue or of vice. And it must be composed as 'a branch of literature,' in that it must be written in grammatical English and with an adequate feeling for style.

A biography combining all these three principles can be classed as a 'pure' biography: a biogra-

287

phy that violates any one of these principles, or combines them in incorrect proportions, must be classed as an 'impure' biography. A pure biography is written with no purpose other than that of conveying to the reader an authentic portrait of the individual whose life is being narrated. A biography is rendered impure when some extraneous purpose intrudes to distort the accuracy of presentation.

Thus Voltaire's *Histoire de Charles XII,* although written and composed with consummate mastery, is not a 'pure' biography, in that it does not depict an individual character in relation to the background of the times. Carlyle's *Life of John Sterling,* although from the literary point of view his most attractive work, is 'impure' biography, since it is not very precise, not a true portrait, and written with a purpose other than that of the direct delineation of an individual. Walton's *Lives* are without question masterpieces of English prose; but they sin against the principles of biography, since Walton is not describing human beings, but types of the particular form of quietism that he himself regards as desirable. Many biographies, on the other hand, are perfectly historical, really do paint, even if with clumsy strokes, the portrait of an individual, but are so badly written that they cannot for one instant qualify as literature. A biography therefore which does not combine all three of these fundamental principles must be defined as impure.

The development of the art throughout the ages shows us how ancient and how recurrent are these 'extraneous purposes' by which the purity of biography is infected. There is no better method of isolating the principles of pure biography than to trace the sources of these infections.

2

The original cause of all biography was the desire to commemorate the illustrious dead. A leader dies: his tribe or family feel that some strength has passed from them: they seek to perpetuate his magic by a monument. Cairns and monoliths arise; we have the regal sites of mighty pyramids; men scale the precipices and engrave a cenotaph upon the rocks of Bisitun; epics and sagas sing the legends of tribal heroes; the wrath of Achilles is rendered immortal and to this day men read with elation of the endurance and resource of Ithacan Odysseus; Balder and Beowulf come to swell the paean; the whole world echoes with the praise of famous men. With this epic strain there mingle elegies and laments. Widow-biographies are an early phenomenon; to the *Complaint of Deor* we add *The Wife's Complaint.*

This commemorative instinct is bad for pure biography, since it leads the commemorator to concentrate solely upon the strength and virtue of his hero and to omit all weakness or shadow. Endemic, and sometimes epidemic, is this passion for commemoration; it has infected biography throughout the centuries.

The impulse is not primitive only; it operates to this day. It is but natural that when a great man dies his family should desire that his life should be written in such a manner as to emphasise his nobility and to hide his faults. Even the most enlightened survivors are inclined to entrust the biography of their dead chief, not to an outsider who may take too objective a view of his subject, but to some inexpert, but loyal, member of the family, who can be trusted to suppress all unfavourable truth. Occasionally the widow herself undertakes the task, sometimes with results as fantastic as those of Lady Burton's biography of her erratic but gifted husband. Even when an honest outsider is commissioned, he may be precluded from outspokenness by a laudable desire not to wound the susceptibilities of those to whom he is obliged. An even more curious and subtle effect of such family-inspired biographies is that the author may become influenced by the petty grievances or animosities cherished by the hero or his widow in their later years; instead of creating an impression of greatness he creates an impression of smallness. A classic instance of this unintentional diminution of a hero's character is provided by General Sir C. Callwell's *Life and Letters of Sir Henry Wilson*: there have been others since. The commemorative instinct assuredly operated in devious ways; but it is always perilous to pure biography.

A second extraneous purpose is the didactic purpose. People have always been tempted to take the lives of individual men as examples of virtue, or as cautionary tales indicative of the ill-effects of self-indulgence or ambition. Plutarch himself, the father of biography, admitted that he chose his characters as types of certain virtues and vices and as examples for emulation or avoidance by the young. Yet Plutarch happened to be a natural biographer, in that he was passionately interested in the way that individuals behaved; thus, although his lives of Anthony or Alcibiades, for instance, were intended to be cautionary tales, he soon forgot his didactic purpose in the fascination exercised upon his mind by the splendour of Anthony or the gaiety of Alcibiades. Flashes of admiration and delight illumine his pages, until both he and his readers forget entirely that an extraneous purpose of moral precept ever existed.

It is not so with other hagiographers. The lives of the saints and martyrs were not, it can be admitted, always intended to be historical accounts of individuals. Yet in more disguised form the didactic purpose continues to intrude upon biography; the desire to teach or preach, the desire to establish examples, the desire to illustrate some moral, theological, political, economic or social theory — all these irrelevant intentions infect biography with strong, and sometimes subtle, doses of impurity. The nineteenth-century biographers were most susceptible to the didactic temptation. 'The history of mankind,' wrote Carlyle, 'is the history of its great men.' 'To find out these, clean the dirt from them, and to place them on their proper pedestal' appeared to him and his contemporaries a proper function of biography. This doctrine led to such impurities as *The Saintly Lives Series* in which, among other worthies, Lord Tennyson was portrayed, not as he was, but as the sort of Laureate that the author felt he ought to be. The reaction against the hagiography of the Victorians led to a development, valuable as a corrective, but, in its baser derivatives, damaging to the pure biographic stream. I refer to the introduction, by Froude and his successors and imitators, of the element of irony.

The satirical attitude of the biographer towards his subject may have come as a relief from the hagiography of the Victorians, but it can easily degenerate into false history and false psychology. Froude certainly provided a true picture of Mr. and Mrs. Carlyle; his portraits were condemned by his contemporaries as cynical, disloyal and in shocking bad taste. The influence of Samuel Butler came to transform Froude's attitude of negative scepticism into positive derision of conventional legends. Lytton Strachey, with his ironical titters, emerged as the deftest of iconoclasts; yet Strachey, who enjoyed paradox more than he respected precision, and who had little sense of history, exaggerated the lights and shadows of his portraits. His sketches were certainly vivid, personal and well written; but they were not 'history' in the sense that pure biography demands. In the hands of his imitators the manner of Strachey deteriorated so rapidly that it became an irritating habit of superciliousness. Philip Guedalla, with his trick of dramatic contrast, diminished the very real value of his writings by too great insistence on antithesis; his pictures became distorted and out of focus.

Irony is, in any case, a dangerous tincture and one that should be applied only with a sable brush; when daubed by vigorous arms it becomes wearisome and even offensive. It is not merely that the reader is irritated by a biographer who implies in chapter after chapter that he is himself more enlightened, sensitive, or sincere than the hero whom he is describing. It is also that biography, if taken seriously, is an exacting task and not one that can be carried through with a sneer. The drudgery of collecting and checking material, the mechanical labour of completing a long book, require an effort more continuous that can be sustained by glimpses of self-satisfaction. The biographer must be constantly fortified by a fundamental respect, or affection, for the person whom he is describing; if all that he experiences is superficial contempt, his work will turn to ashes and his energy wilt and fail. No writer can persist for five hundred pages in being funny at the expense of someone who is dead.

There are other poisons, other temptations, to which this difficult art is liable. Biography is always a collaboration between the author and his subject; always there must be the reflection of one temperament in the mirror of another. The biographer should thus be careful not to permit his own personality to intrude too markedly upon the personality that he is describing; he should be wary of assigning his own opinions, prejudices or affections to the man or woman whose life he writes; he should take special pains to deal fairly with views which he does not share, or interests that bore him; his egoism should be muzzled and kept on a chain. He should constantly remind himself that it is not an autobiography that he is composing, but the life of someone else; the statue of Modesty should dominate his study, a finger on her lips.

A further temptation that may afflict the affable biographer is that of adding to his narrative the colours of fiction or romance. He may seek to convey reality by introducing imaginary conversations, or to brighten his pages by inserting really beautiful passages of scenic description:

> 'As their little cavalcade breasted the hill and emerged from the grove of umbrella pines (*pineus pinea*) that crowned its summit, the fair city lay before them, basking all amethyst in the fading light. The Palazzo Pubblico had already melted into the pink and azure shadows of the Piazza del Campo, but the Torre del Mangia soared upwards, straight as a tulip against the sunset sky. Galeazzo turned to his venerable companion. "Messir," he said . . .' "

Such passages fail to convince the attentive reader, who is aware that umbrella pines are but few at Sienna and that the company at the moment were travelling west to east. The imagination, as well as the self-assertiveness, of the author must be held in check.

Such then are the instincts, poisons and temptations that render biography impure. An undue desire to commemorate, a too earnest endeavour to teach or preach, a tendency to portray types rather than individuals, the temptation to enhance self-esteem by indulging in irony, the inability to describe selflessly, and the urge to slide into fiction or to indulge in fine writing; — all these are the pests and parasites that gnaw the leaves of purity. Yet these are negative precepts, indicating the faults that should be eschewed. Are there any positive principles that can be recommended to the intending biographer?

3

It is self-evident that he should not select a subject outside the range of his sympathy or the area of his general knowledge. It would thus be a mistake for a man to embark upon a life of Pope if he were ill-attuned to the heroic couplet and disliked small stratagems. It would be a mistake to start writing a life of Anselm without some knowledge of Plato's doctrine of ideas, or to embark upon Erasmus when ignorant of the humanities. It would be foolish for an Englishman to venture on a biography of Calvin Coolidge, without having spent at least a year at Amherst and absorbed the indelible quality of that academy.

The ideal subject is one of which the author has direct personal experience and with which he can enter into sympathetic relationship. This raises the question whether it is in fact possible for any author — however skilled, courageous, or sincere — to write a 'pure' biography of a contemporary. It is clear that it will be of great advantage to him to have been personally acquainted with his hero and to have seen him, not only in his moments of public triumph or efficiency, but also in those interludes of lassitude, dyspepsia, or elation that reveal the character of a man. Important it is also to be able to visualise a person, not in the set postures of official busts or portraits, but in the more illuminating attitudes of ordinary life. It is valuable to be able to recall the manner in which he coughed or grunted, the exact shape of his smile or frown, the sound of his laughter, and above all the tone of his voice. We are all conscious that the personality of our acquaintances is conveyed to us, not merely by their physical appearance and expression, but also by their accent and intonation. It is illuminating to be told that Bismarck spoke with the piping notes of a schoolboy, that Napoleon, when angry, relapsed into the Corsican manner of speech, or that Tenny-

son when reciting his poems used the broad vowels of the Lincolnshire wold. It is valuable also for a biographer to be personally acquainted with the men and women who exercised an influence upon the life of his subject and to be able, by his own judgement, to assess their relative value. 'How strange,' he will reflect, 'that my hero could ever for one moment have been taken in by such a charlatan as I know X to have been! How curious that he was never able to appreciate the shy wisdom, the fundamental integrity, of my dear friend Y!' This wider knowledge provides a system of triangulation, enabling the author to fix the position of his hero with greater accuracy than would ever be possible were he writing about people whom he had never personally known.

Such are the advantages — and they are immense — which the biographer enjoys when writing the life of a contemporary. The disadvantages are also apparent. He will be inhibited by his disinclination to offend the susceptibilities of survivors. It is not only that he will hesitate to wound the feelings of relations and friends; it is also that the enemies of his hero may still be living and will protest violently against any criticisms that may be made. To some extent he can evade this difficulty by refraining from expressing any personal opinion and relying solely upon the documents in the case. But the necessity of maintaining a certain level of taste, consideration, caution and kindliness, will certainly prevent him from revealing the truth in its most naked form.

Does this mean, I repeat, that it is impossible for an author to write a 'pure' biography of a contemporary? I do not think so. He will realise of course that, human nature being what it is, the reader of his book will pay more attention to those passages which reveal defects hitherto concealed, than to those which eulogise merits already familiar. The essential truth of any portrait depends upon the proper statement of relative values. A biographer should be aware that the 'startling revelation' is certain to startle, and will thus assume in the reader's mind and memory an importance out of proportion to the portrait as a whole. His revelations therefore should not be picked out in scarlet or orange but introduced in neutral tints. His aim should be, not to conceal defects or lamentable episodes, but to refer to them in such a manner as will indicate to the attentive reader that these shadows existed, without disconcerting the inattentive reader or wounding the legitimate feelings of surviving relations and friends. It is a question of tact and skill.

It has always interested me, when reading the biography of a person with whom I had been personally acquainted, to observe how the author deals with his faults. A device frequently adopted is to reveal the fault by denying its opposite. An extreme example of this method can be found in Sir Sidney Lee's biography of King Edward VII. Sir Sidney was an honest biographer, who desired to paint his portrait warts and all. I had often heard that King Edward was a voracious eater and that he was apt to pounce and gobble at the dishes placed before him. I wondered whether Sir Sidney would mention this genial characteristic and was impressed by the delicacy of his device. 'He had,' wrote Sir Sidney, 'a splendid appetite at all times, and never toyed with his food.' It is by such ingenuity that the biographer is able to omit no detail and yet to cause no offence.

I should cite as an excellent example of the way in which an intelligent biographer can indicate defects without wounding feelings, Mr. Rupert Hart-Davis's biography of Sir Hugh Walpole. The attentive reader is made aware of all the lights and shadows in the character portrayed, whereas the inattentive reader is not for one moment startled or shocked. Every weakness of Walpole's character is abundantly illustrated, yet the resultant impression is that of a gifted and charming man. I recommend this work to all those who question whether it is possible to write a 'pure' biography of a contemporary figure. The artist has produced an authentic portrait owing to his sense of values; without such a sense, any biography is bound to be unconvincing.

4

It is here that a natural gift of selection is so valuable. The aim is to convey the personality of some interesting individual to people or generations who never knew him when alive. It is not possible for a biographer, even if he take twenty years and volumes, to present the whole man to posterity. He can hope only, by intelligent and honest selection, to convey the impression of the aggregate of his

hero's merits and defects. If he allows himself to deck his portrait with striking little snippets and tags, the unity of impression will be destroyed. His curiosity therefore must be moderated by selection and taste; he must preserve throughout a uniform tone; and he must try, — he must try very hard, — to arrange his facts in the right order.

'The value of every story,' remarked Dr. Johnson, 'depends on its being true. A story is a picture, either of an individual, or of life in general. If it be false, it is a picture of nothing.' This precept should, I feel, be inscribed in lapidary letters on the fly-leaf of every biographer's note-book. A pure biography should furnish its readers with information, encouragement and comfort. It should provide, if I may again quote Dr. Johnson, 'the parallel circumstances and kindred images to which we readily conform our minds.' It should remind the reader that great men and women also have passed through phases of doubt, discouragement and self-abasement; that — perhaps on the very eve of their noblest achievements — they have been assailed with diffidence, or have resigned themselves to the fact that their vitality is ebbing, their zest has gone, their memory has become unreliable, and their will-power decayed. Without seeking for one moment to preach a lesson, a good biography encourages people to believe that man's mind is in truth unconquerable and that character can triumph over the most hostile circumstances, provided only that it remains true to itself. Amusing books can be written about ridiculous people; fiction and romance can be twined as honeysuckle around the silliest head; but I am convinced that a pure biography, if its effect is to be more than momentary, can only be written about a person whom the writer and the reader can fundamentally respect.

Does this imply a return to hagiography? No, it implies only that the intending biographer should be as cautious in his choice of subject as in the method he pursues.

Virginia Woolf, "The New Biography," *New York Herald Tribune*, 30 October 1927

'The aim of biography,' said Sir Sydney Lee, who had perhaps read and written more lives than any man of his time, 'is the truthful transmission of personality,' and no single sentence could more neatly split up into two parts the whole problem of biography as it presents itself to us to-day. On the one hand there is truth; on the other there is personality. And if we think of truth as something of granite-like solidity and of personality as something of rainbow-like intangibility and reflect that the aim of biography is to weld these two into one seamless whole, we shall admit that the problem is a stiff one and that we need not wonder if biographers have for the most part failed to solve it.

For the truth of which Sir Sidney speaks, the truth which biography demands, is truth in its hardest, most obdurate form; it is truth as truth is to be found in the British Museum; it is truth out of which all vapour of falsehood has been pressed by the weight of research. Only when truth had been thus established did Sir Sidney Lee use it in the building of his monument; and no one can be so foolish as to deny that the piles be raised of such hard facts, whether one is called Shakespeare or King Edward the Seventh, are worthy of all our respect. For there is a virtue in truth; it has an almost mystic power. Like radium, it seems able to give off forever and ever grains of energy, atoms of light. It stimulates the mind, which is endowed with a curious susceptibility in this direction as no fiction, however artful or highly coloured, can stimulate it. Truth being thus efficacious and supreme, we can only explain the fact that Sir Sidney's life of Shakespeare is dull, and that his life of Edward the Seventh is unreadable, by supposing that though both are stuffed with truth, he failed to choose those truths which transmit personality. For in order that the light of personality may shine through, facts must be manipulated; some must be brightened; others shaded; yet, in the process, they must never lose their integrity. And it is obvious that it is easier to obey these precepts by considering that the true life of your subject shows itself in action which is evi-dent rather than in that inner life of thought and emotion which meanders darkly and obscurely through the hidden channels of the soul. Hence, in the old days, the biographer chose the easier path. A life, even when it was lived by a divine, was a series of exploits. The biographer, whether he was Izaak Walton or Mrs. Hutchinson or that unknown writer who is often so surprisingly eloquent on tombstones and memorial tablets, told a tale of battle and victory. With their stately phrasing and their deliberate artistic purpose, such records transmit personality with a formal sincerity which is perfectly satisfactory of its kind. And so, perhaps, biography might have pursued its way, draping the robes decorously over the recumbent figures of the dead, had there not arisen toward the end of the eighteenth century one of those curious men of genius who seem able to break up the stiffness into which the company has fallen by speaking in his natural voice. So Boswell spoke. So we hear booming out from Boswell's page the voice of Samuel Johnson. 'No, sir; stark insensibility,' we hear him say. Once we have heard those words we are aware that there is an incalculable presence among us which will go on ringing and reverberating in widening circles however times may change and ourselves. All the draperies and decencies of biography fall to the ground. We can no longer maintain that life consists in actions only or in works. It consists in personality. Something has been liberated beside which all else seems cold and colourless. We are freed from a servitude which is now seen to be intolerable. No longer need we pass solemnly and stiffly from camp to council chamber. We may sit, even with the great and good, over the table and talk.

Through the influence of Boswell, presumably, biography all through the nineteenth century concerned itself as much with the lives of the sedentary as with the lives of the active. It sought painstakingly and devotedly to express not only the outer life of work and activity but the inner life of emotion and thought. The uneventful lives of poets and painters were written out as lengthily as the lives of soldiers and statesmen. But the Victorian biography was a parti-coloured, hybrid, monstrous birth. For though truth of fact was observed as scrupulously as Boswell observed it, the personality which Boswell's genius set free was hampered and distorted. The convention which Boswell had destroyed settled again, only in a different form, upon biographers who lacked his art. Where the Mrs. Hutchinsons and the Izaak Waltons had wished to prove that their heroes were prodigies of courage and learning the Victorian biographer was dominated by the idea of goodness. Noble, upright, chaste, severe; it is thus that the Victorian worthies are presented to us. the figure is almost always above life size in top-hat and frock-coat, and the manner of presentation becomes increasingly clumsy and laborious. For lives which no longer express themselves in action take shape in innumerable words. The conscientious biographer may not tell a fine tale with a flourish, but must toil through endless labyrinths and embarrass himself with countless documents. In the end he produces an amorphous mass, a life of Tennyson, or of Gladstone, in which we go seeking disconsolately for voice or laughter, for curse or anger, for any trace that this fossil was once a living man. Often, indeed, we bring back some invaluable trophy, for Victorian biographies are laden with truth; but always we rummage among them with a sense of the prodigious waste, of the artistic wrongheadedness of such a method.

With the twentieth century, however, a change came over biography, as it came over fiction and poetry. The first and most visible sign of it was in the difference in size. In the first twenty years of the new century biographies must have lost half their weight. Mr. Strachey compressed four stout Victorians into one slim volume; M. Maurois boiled the usual two volumes of a Shelley life into one little book the size of a novel. But the diminution of size was only the outward token of an inward change. The point of view had completely altered. If we open one of the new school of biographies in its bareness, its emptiness makes us at once aware that the author's relation to his subject is different. He is no longer the serious and sympathetic companion, toiling even slavishly in the footsteps of his hero. Whether friend or enemy, admiring or critical, he is an equal. In any case, he preserves his freedom and his right to independent judgment. Moreover, he does not think himself constrained to follow every step of the way. Raised upon a little eminence which his independence has made for him, he sees his subject spread about him. He chooses; he synthesizes; in short, he has ceased to be the chronicler; he has become an artist.

Few books illustrate the new attitude to biography better than *Some People,* by Harold Nicolson. In his biographies of Tennyson and of Byron Mr. Nicolson followed the path which had been already trodden by Mr. Strachey and others. Here he has taken a step on his own initiative. For here he has devised a method of writing about people and about himself as though they were at once real and imaginary. He has succeeded remarkably, if not entirely, in making the best of both worlds. *Some People* is not fiction because it has the substance, the reality of truth. It is not biography because it has the freedom, the artistry of fiction. And if we try to discover how he has won the liberty which enables him to present us with these extremely amusing pages we must in the first place credit him with having had the courage to rid himself of a mountain of illusion. An English diplomat is offered all the bribes which usually induce people to swallow humbug in large doses with composure. If Mr. Nicolson wrote about Lord Curzon it should have been solemnly. If he mentioned the Foreign Office it should have been respectfully. His tone toward the world of Bognors and Whitehall should have been friendly but devout. But thanks to a number of influences and people, among whom one might mention Max Beerbohm and Voltaire, the attitude of the bribed and docile official has been blown to atoms. Mr. Nicolson laughs. He laughs at Lord Curzon; he laughs at the Foreign Office; he laughs at himself. And since his laughter is the laughter of the intelligence it has the effect of making us take the people he laughs at seriously. The figure of Lord Curzon concealed behind the figure of a drunken valet is touched off with merriment and irreverence; yet of all the studies of Lord Curzon which have been written since his death none makes us think more kindly of that preposterous but, it appears, extremely human man.

So it would seem as if one of the great advantages of the new school to which Mr. Nicolson belongs is the lack of pose, humbug, solemnity. They approach their bigwigs fearlessly. They have no fixed scheme of the universe, no standard of courage or morality to which they insist that he shall conform. The man himself is the supreme object of their curiosity. Further, and it is this chiefly which has so reduced the bulk of biography, they maintain that the man himself, the pith and essence of his character, shows itself to the observant eye in the tone of a voice, the turn of a head, some little phrase or anecdote picked up in passing. Thus in two subtle phrases, in one passage of brilliant description, whole chapters of the Victorian volume are synthesized and summed up. *Some People* is full of examples of this new phase of the biographer's art. Mr. Nicolson wants to describe a governess and he tells us that she had a drop at the end of her nose and made him salute the quarterdeck. He wants to describe Lord Curzon and he makes him lose his trousers and recite 'Tears, Idle Tears.' He does not cumber himself with a single fact about them. He waits till they have said or done something characteristic, and then he pounces on it with glee. But, though he waits with an intention of pouncing which might well make his victims uneasy if they guessed it, he lays suspicion by appearing himself in his own proper person in no flattering light. He has a scrubby dinner-jacket, he tells us; a pink bumptious face, curly hair, and a curly nose. He is as much the subject of his own irony and observation as they are. He lies in wait for his own absurdities as artfully as for theirs. Indeed, by the end of the book we realize that the figure which has been most completely and most subtly displayed is that of the author. Each of the supposed subjects holds up in his or her small bright diminishing mirror a different reflection of Harold Nicolson. And though the figure thus revealed is not noble or impressive or shown in a very heroic attitude, it is for these very reasons extremely like a real human being. It is thus, he would seem to say, in the mirrors of our friends, that we chiefly live.

To have contrived this effect is a triumph not of skill only, but of those positive qualities which we are likely to treat as if they were negative — freedom from pose, from sentimentality, from illusion. And the victory is definite enough to leave us asking what territory it has won for the art of biography. Mr. Nicolson has proved that one can use many of the devices of fiction in dealing with real life. He has shown that a little fiction mixed with fact can be made to transmit personality very effectively. But some objections or qualifications suggest themselves. Undoubtedly the figures in *Some People* are all rather below life size. The irony with which they are treated, though it has its tenderness, stunts their growth. It dreads nothing more than that one of these little beings should grow up and becomes serious or perhaps tragic. And, again, they never occupy the stage for more than a few brief moments. They do not want to be looked at very closely. They have not a great deal to show us. Mr. Nicolson makes us feel, in short, that he is playing with very dangerous elements. An incautious movement and the book will be blown sky high. He is trying to mix the truth of real life and the truth of fiction. He can only do it by using no more than a pinch of ei-

ther. For though both truths are genuine, they are antagonistic; let them meet and they destroy each other. Even here, where the imagination is not deeply engaged, when we find people whom we know to be real like Lord Oxford or Lady Colefax, mingling with Miss Plimsoll and Marstock, whose reality we doubt, the one casts suspicion upon the other. Let it be fact, one feels, or let it be fiction; the imagination will not serve under two masters simultaneously.

And here we again approach the difficulty which, for all his ingenuity, the biographer still has to face. Truth of fact and truth of fiction are incompatible; yet he is now more than ever urged to combine them. For it would seem that the life which is increasingly real to us is the fictitious life; it dwells in the personality rather than in the act. Each of us is more Hamlet, Prince of Denmark, than he is John Smith of the Corn Exchange. Thus, the biographer's imagination is always being stimulated to use the novelist's art of arrangement, suggestion, dramatic effect to expound the private life. Yet if he carries the use of fiction too far, so that he disregards the truth, or can only introduce it with incongruity, he loses both worlds; he has neither the freedom of fiction nor the substance of fact. Boswell's astonishing power over us is based largely upon his obstinate veracity, so that we have implicit belief in what he tells us. When Johnson says 'No, sir; stark insensibility,' the voice has a ring in it because we have been told, soberly and prosaically, a few pages earlier, that Johnson 'was entered a Commoner of Pembroke, on the 31st of October, 1728, being then in his nineteenth year.' We are in the world of brick and pavement; of birth, marriage, and death; of Acts of Parliament; of Pitt and Burke and Sir Joshua Reynolds. Whether this is a more real world than the world of Bohemia and Hamlet and Macbeth we doubt; but the mixture of the two is abhorrent.

Be that as it may we can assure ourselves by a very simple experiment that the days of Victorian biography are over. Consider one's own life; pass under review a few years that one has actually lived. Conceive how Lord Morley would have expounded them; how Sir Sidney Lee would have documented them; how strangely all that has been most real in them would have slipped through their fingers. Nor can we name the biographer whose art is subtle and bold enough to present that queer amalgamation of dream and reality, that perpetual marriage of granite and rainbow. His method still remains to be discovered. But Mr. Nicolson with his mixture of biography and autobiography, of fact and fiction, of Lord Curzon's trousers and Miss Plimsoll's nose, waves his hand airily in a possible direction.

Checklist of Further Readings

Aaron, Daniel, ed. *Studies in Biography*. Cambridge, Mass.: Harvard University Press, 1978.

Alter, Robert. *Motives for Fiction*. Cambridge, Mass.: Harvard University Press, 1984.

Altick, Richard Daniel. *The Art of Literary Research*. New York: Norton, 1963.

Altick. *Lives and Letters: A History of Literary Biography in England and America*. New York: Knopf, 1965.

Altick. *The Scholar Adventurers*. New York: Macmillan, 1950.

Anderson, James William. "The Methodology of Psychological Biography," *Journal of Interdisciplinary History*, 11 (Winter 1981): 455–475.

Atlas, James. "Literary Biography," *American Scholar*, 45 (Summer 1976): 448–460.

Barzun, Jacques. "Biography and Criticism – a Misalliance Disputed," *Critical Inquiry*, 1 (March 1975): 479–496.

Bell, Susan Groag, and Marilyn Yalom, eds. *Revealing Lives: Autobiography, Biography, and Gender*. Albany: State University of New York Press, 1990.

Berry, Thomas Elliott, ed. *The Biographer's Craft*. New York: Odyssey Press, 1967.

Birkets, Sven. *An Artificial Wilderness: Essays on 20th-Century Literature*. New York: Morrow, 1987.

Bloom, Harold, ed. *Dr. Samuel Johnson and James Boswell*. New York: Chelsea House, 1986.

Bloom, ed. *James Boswell's Life of Johnson*. New York: Chelsea House, 1986.

Bowen, Catherine Drinker. *Adventures of a Biographer*. Boston: Little, Brown, 1959.

Bowen. *Biography: The Craft and the Calling*. Boston: Little, Brown, 1969.

Brady, Frank, John Palmer, and Martin Price, eds. *Literary Theory and Structure: Essays in Honor of William K. Wimsatt*. New Haven: Yale University Press, 1973.

Britt, Albert. *The Great Biographers*. New York: McGraw-Hill, 1936; London: Whittlesey House, 1936.

Bromwich, David. *Choice of Inheritance: Self and Community from Edmund Burke to Robert Frost*. Cambridge, Mass.: Harvard University Press, 1989.

Browning, J. D., ed. *Biography in the 18th Century*. New York & London: Garland, 1980.

Cafarelli, Annette. *Prose in the Age of Poets: Romanticism and Biographical Narrative from Johnson to De Quincey*. Philadelphia: University of Pennsylvania Press, 1990.

Clifford, James Lowry. *From Puzzles to Portraits: Problems of a Literary Biographer.* Chapel Hill: University of North Carolina Press, 1970.

Clifford, ed. *Biography as an Art: Selected Criticism, 1560–1960.* New York: Oxford University Press, 1962.

Clingham, Greg. *James Boswell: The Life of Johnson.* New York & Cambridge: Cambridge University Press, 1992.

Clingham, ed. *New Light on Boswell: Critical and Historical Essays on the Occasion of the Bicentenary of* The Life of Johnson. New York & Cambridge: Cambridge University Press, 1991.

Cockshut, A. O. J. *Truth to Life: The Art of Biography in the Nineteenth Century.* London: Collins, 1974; New York: Harcourt Brace Jovanovich, 1974.

Connely, Willard. *Adventures in Biography: A Chronicle of Encounters and Findings.* London: W. Laurie, 1956; New York: Horizon, 1960.

Daghlian, Philip B., ed. *Essays in Eighteenth-Century Biography.* Bloomington: Indiana University Press, 1968.

Daiches, David. *Critical Approaches to Literature.* Englewood Cliffs, N.J.: Prentice-Hall, 1956.

Davenport, William H., and Ben Siegel, eds. *Biography Past and Present.* New York: Scribners, 1965.

Denzin, Norman K. *Interpretive Biography.* Newbury Park, Cal.: Sage, 1989.

Dowling, William C. *Language and Logos in Boswell's Life of Johnson.* Princeton: Princeton University Press, 1981.

Dunn, Waldo H. *English Biography.* London: Dent, 1916; New York: Dutton, 1916.

Durling, Dwight, and William Watt, eds. *Biography: Varieties and Parallels.* New York: Dryden, 1941.

Edel, Leon. *Literary Biography.* Toronto: University of Toronto Press, 1957; London: Hart-Davis, 1957; revised edition, Garden City, N.Y.: Doubleday, 1959; revised again, Bloomington: Indiana University Press, 1973; revised and enlarged as *Writing Lives: Principia Biographica.* New York & London: Norton, 1984.

Edel. *Stuff of Sleep and Dreams: Experiments in Literary Psychology.* New York: Harper & Row, 1982.

Ellmann, Richard. *Golden Codgers: Biographical Speculations.* New York & London: Oxford University Press, 1973.

Ellmann. *Literary Biography: An Inaugural Lecture Delivered Before the University of Oxford on 4 May 1971.* Oxford: Clarendon Press, 1971.

Epstein, William H. *Recognizing Biography.* Philadelphia: University of Pennsylvania Press, 1987.

Epstein, ed. *Contesting the Subject: Essays in the Postmodern Theory and Practice of Biography and Biographical Criticism.* West Lafayette, Ind.: Purdue University Press, 1991.

Flanagan, Thomas. "Problems of Psychobiography," *Queen's Quarterly,* 89 (Autumn 1982): 596–610.

Folkenflik, Robert. *Samuel Johnson, Biographer.* Ithaca, N.Y.: Cornell University Press, 1978.

Fowler, Alastair. *Kinds of Literature: An Introduction to the Theory of Genres and Modes.* Cambridge, Mass.: Harvard University Press, 1982.

Frank, Katherine. "Writing Lives: Theory and Practice of Literary Biography," *Genre,* 13 (Winter 1980): 499–516.

Friedson, Anthony M., ed. *New Directions in Biography: Essays.* Honolulu: Published for the Biographical Research Center by the University of Hawaii Press, 1981.

Fromm, Gloria G., ed. *Essaying Biography: A Celebration for Leon Edel.* Honolulu: Published for the Biographical Research Center by the University of Hawaii Press, 1986.

Frye, Northrop. *Anatomy of Criticism: Four Essays.* Princeton: Princeton University Press, 1957.

Frye. *The Well-Tempered Critic.* Bloomington: Indiana University Press, 1963.

Gardner, Helen Louise, Dame. *In Defence of the Imagination.* Cambridge, Mass.: Harvard University Press, 1982.

Garraty, John Arthur. *The Nature of Biography.* New York: Knopf, 1957.

Gittings, Robert. *The Nature of Biography.* London: Heinemann, 1978; Seattle: University of Washington Press, 1978.

Greene, Donald. " 'Tis a Pretty Book, Mr. Boswell, But — , " *Georgia Review,* 32 (Spring 1978): 17–43.

Hamilton, Ian. *Keepers of the Flame: The Making and Unmaking of Literary Reputations from John Donne to Sylvia Plath.* New York: Paragon House, 1993.

Hampshire, Stuart N. *Modern Writers and Other Essays.* London: Chatto & Windus, 1969; New York: Knopf, 1970.

Havlice, Patricia Pate. *Index to Literary Biography,* 2 volumes. Metuchen, N.J.: Scarecrow Press, 1975.

Heilbrun, Carolyn G. *Hamlet's Mother and Other Women.* New York: Columbia University Press, 1990.

Heilbrun. *Writing a Woman's Life.* New York: Norton, 1988.

Hoberman, Ruth. *Modernizing Lives: Experiments in English Biography, 1918–1939.* Carbondale: Southern Illinois University Press, 1987.

Holland, Norman Norwood. *The Dynamics of Literary Response.* New York: Oxford University Press, 1968.

Holland. *Poems in Persons: An Introduction to the Psychoanalysis of Literature.* New York: Norton, 1973.

Holmes, Richard. *Footsteps: Adventures of a Romantic Biographer.* New York: Viking, 1985.

Homberger, Eric, and John Charmley, eds. *The Troubled Face of Biography.* New York: St. Martin's Press, 1988.

Honan, Park. *Authors' Lives: On Literary Biography and the Arts of Language.* New York: St. Martin's Press, 1990.

Honan. "The Theory of Biography," *Novel,* 13 (Fall 1979): 109–120.

Horden, Peregrine, ed. *Freud and the Humanities*. New York: St. Martin's Press, 1985; London: Duckworth, 1985.

Hough, Graham. *Style and Stylistics*. London: Routledge & Kegan Paul, 1969; New York: Humanities, 1969.

Hyde, Marietta Adelaide, ed. *Modern Biography*. New York: Harcourt, Brace, 1926.

Johnson, Edgar. *One Mighty Torrent: The Drama of Biography*. New York: Stackpole, 1937.

Johnson, ed. *A Treasury of Biography*. New York: Howell, Soskin, 1941.

Kaplan, Justin. "In Pursuit of the Ultimate Fiction," *New York Times Book Review*. 19 April 1987, pp. 1, 24–25.

Kazin, Alfred. *The Inmost Leaf: A Selection of Essays*. New York: Harcourt, Brace, 1955.

Kendall, Paul Murray. *The Art of Biography*. New York: Norton, 1965.

Kenner, Hugh. *Historical Fictions: Essays*. San Francisco: North Point, 1990.

Kermode, Frank. *The Art of Telling: Essays on Fiction*. Cambridge, Mass.: Harvard University Press, 1983.

Kermode. *The Genesis of Secrecy. On the Interpretation of Narrative*. Cambridge, Mass.: Harvard University Press, 1979.

Kermode. *The Sense of an Ending: Studies in the Theory of Fiction*. New York: Oxford University Press, 1967.

Krupnick, Mark L. "The Sanctuary of Imagination," *Nation*, 209 (14 July 1969): 55–56.

Levin, David. *In Defense of Historical Literature: Essays on American History, Autobiography, Drama, and Fiction*. New York: Hill & Wang, 1967.

Levin, Harry. *Contexts of Criticism*. Cambridge, Mass.: Harvard University Press, 1957.

Lomask, Milton. *The Biographer's Craft*. New York: Harper & Row, 1986.

Longaker, Mark. *English Biography in the Eighteenth Century*. Philadelphia: University of Pennsylvania Press, 1931.

Mandell, Gail Porter. *Life into Art: Conversations with Seven Contemporary Biographers*. Fayetteville: University of Arkansas Press, 1991.

Maner, Martin. *The Philosophical Biographer: Doubt and Dialectic in Johnson's Lives of the Poets*. Athens: University of Georgia Press, 1988.

Mariani, Paul L. *A Usable Past: Essays on Modern and Contemporary Poetry*. Amherst: University of Massachusetts Press, 1984.

Marquess, William Henry. *Lives of the Poet: The First Century of Keats Biography*. University Park: Pennsylvania State University Press, 1985.

Maurois, Andre. *Aspects of Biography*. New York: Appleton, 1929.

Meyers, Jeffrey. *The Spirit of Biography*. Ann Arbor, Mich.: UMI Research Press, 1989.

Meyers, ed. *The Biographer's Art: New Essays*. New York: New Amsterdam, 1989.

Meyers, ed. *The Craft of Literary Biography*. New York: Schocken, 1985.

Mintz, Samuel T., Alica Chandler, and Christopher Mulvey, eds. *From Smollett to James: Studies in the Novel and Other Essays Presented to Edgar Johnson*. Charlottesville: University Press of Virginia, 1981.

Nadel, Ira Bruce. *Biography: Fiction, Fact and Form*. New York: St. Martin's Press, 1984.

Nagourney, Peter. "The Basic Assumptions of Literary Biography," *Biography*, 1 (Spring 1978): 86–104.

Nicolson, Harold George, Sir. *The Development of English Biography*. London: Hogarth, 1928; New York: Harcourt, Brace, 1928.

Noland, Richard. "Psychohistory, Theory and Practice," *Massachusetts Review*, 18 (Summer 1977): 295–322.

Novarr, David. *The Lines of Life: Theories of Biography, 1880–1970*. West Lafayette, Ind.: Purdue University Press, 1986.

Oates, Stephen B., ed. *Biography as High Adventure: Life-Writers Speak on Their Art*. Amherst: University of Massachusetts Press, 1986.

Pachter, Marc, ed. *Telling Lives, The Biographer's Art*. Washington, D.C.: New Republic Books, 1979.

Pascal, Roy. *Design and Truth in Autobiography*. Cambridge, Mass.: Harvard University Press, 1960.

Passler, David L. *Time, Form, and Style in Boswell's Life of Johnson*. New Haven: Yale University Press, 1971.

Pearson, Hesketh. *Ventilations: Being Biographical Asides*. Philadelphia & London: Lippincott, 1930.

Plagens, Peter. "Biography," *Art in America*, 68 (October 1980): 13–15.

Powers, Lyall H., ed. *Leon Edel and Literary Art*. Ann Arbor, Mich.: UMI Research Press, 1987.

Quilligan, Maureen. "Rewriting History: The Difference of Feminist Biography," *Yale Review*, 77 (Winter 1988): 259–286.

Reed, Joseph W. *English Biography in the Early Nineteenth Century, 1801–1838*. New Haven: Yale University Press, 1966.

Reid, B. L. *Necessary Lives: Biographical Reflections*. Columbia: University of Missouri Press, 1990.

Rose, Phyllis. *Writing of Women: Essays in a Renaissance*. Middletown, Conn.: Wesleyan University Press, 1985.

Runyan, William McKinley. *Life Histories and Psychobiography: Explorations in Theory and Method*. New York: Oxford University Press, 1982.

Said, Edward W. *Beginnings: Intention and Method*. New York: Basic Books, 1975.

Schaber, Ina. "Fictional Biography, Factual Biography and Their Contaminations," *Biography*, 5 (Winter 1982): 1–16.

Scholes, Robert E. *Structuralism in Literature: An Introduction*. New Haven: Yale University Press, 1974.

Shelston, Alan. *Biography*. London: Methuen, 1977.

Siebenschuh, William R. *Fictional Techniques and Factual Works*. Athens: University of Georgia Press, 1983.

Smith, Barbara Herrnstein. *On the Margins of Discourses: The Relation of Literature to Language*. Chicago: University of Chicago Press, 1978.

Sontag, Susan. "On Style," *Partisan Review,* 32 (Fall 1965): 543–560.

Spence, Donald Pond. *Narrative Truth and Historical Truth: Meaning and Interpretation in Psychoanalysis*. New York: Norton, 1982.

Stauffer, Donald A. *The Art of Biography in Eighteenth-Century England*. Princeton: Princeton University Press, 1941; London: H. Milford, Oxford University Press, 1941.

Stauffer. *English Biography before 1700*. Cambridge, Mass.: Harvard University Press, 1930.

Thayer, William Roscoe. *The Art of Biography*. New York: Scribners, 1920.

Vance, John A., ed. *Boswell's Life of Johnson: New Questions, New Answers*. Athens: University of Georgia Press, 1985.

Veninga, James F., ed. *The Biographer's Gift: Life Histories and Humanism*. College Station: Published for the Texas Committee for the Humanities by Texas A&M University Press, 1983.

Vernoff, Edward, and Rima Shore. *The International Dictionary of 20th Century Biography*. London: Sidgwick & Jackson, 1987; New York: New American Library, 1987.

Weintraub, Stanley, ed. *Biography and Truth*. Indianapolis: Bobbs-Merrill, 1967.

Wendorf, Richard. *The Elements of Life: Biography and Portrait-Painting in Stuart and Georgian England*. Oxford: Clarendon Press, 1990; New York: Oxford University Press, 1990.

Wheeler, David, ed. *Domestick Privacies: Samuel Johnson and the Art of Biography*. Lexington: University Press of Kentucky, 1987.

Whittemore, Reed. *Pure Lives: The Early Biographers*. Baltimore: Johns Hopkins University Press, 1988.

Whittemore. *Whole Lives: Shapers of Modern Biography*. Baltimore: Johns Hopkins University Press, 1989.

Winslow, Donald J. *Life-Writing: A Glossary of Terms in Biography, Autobiography, and Related Forms*. Honolulu: Published for the Biographical Research Center by the University of Hawaii Press, 1980.

Woolf, Virginia. *Collected Essays*. London: Hogarth, 1967; New York: Harcourt, Brace & World, 1967.

Contributors

Rebecca Brittenham .... *Rutgers University*
Charles Calder .... *University of Aberdeen*
Margaret Carter .... *Bradley University*
Sondra Miley Cooney .... *Kent State University*
Steven H. Gale .... *Kentucky State University*
Elizabeth Haddrell .... *Hunter College of the City University of New York*
P. E. Hewison .... *University of Aberdeen*
D. W. Jefferson .... *University of Leeds*
A. R. Jones .... *University of Wales*
W. P. Kenney .... *Manhattan College*
Carolyn Lengel .... *Graduate Center of the City University of New York*
Phillip Mallett .... *University of Saint Andrews*
Michael Mandelkern .... *Graduate Center of the City University of New York*
Edmund Miller .... *C. W. Post Campus, Long Island University*
William Over .... *Saint John's University*
Dennis Paoli .... *Hunter College of the City University of New York*
Glyn Pursglove .... *University College of Swansea*
Pat Rogers .... *University of South Florida*
Robert L. Ross .... *University of Texas at Austin*
Paul H. Schmidt .... *Georgia State University*
Marcy L. Tanter .... *University of Massachusetts — Amherst*
D. Mori Thomas .... *Bilkent University*
R. S. White .... *University of Western Australia*

301

Cumulative Index

Dictionary of Literary Biography, Volumes 1-149
Dictionary of Literary Biography Yearbook, 1980-1993
Dictionary of Literary Biography Documentary Series, Volumes 1-12

Cumulative Index

DLB before number: *Dictionary of Literary Biography*, Volumes 1-149
Y before number: *Dictionary of Literary Biography Yearbook*, 1980-1993
DS before number: *Dictionary of Literary Biography Documentary Series*, Volumes 1-12

A

D

G

Cumulative Index

W

ISBN 0-8103-5710-0